American Anthropology
1971–1995

Papers from the *American Anthropologist*

EDITED AND WITH AN INTRODUCTION
BY REGNA DARNELL

AMERICAN ANTHROPOLOGICAL ASSOCIATION
ARLINGTON VA
UNIVERSITY OF NEBRASKA PRESS
LINCOLN AND LONDON

♾

Library of Congress Cataloging-in-Publication Data
American anthropology, 1971–1995 : papers from the American
anthropologist / edited and with an introduction by Regna Darnell.
p. cm.
Includes bibliographical references.
ISBN 0-8032-6635-9 (pbk. : alk. paper)
1. Anthropology. I. Darnell, Regna. II. American anthropologist.
GN29 .A43   2002
01 — dc13   2002017978

Contents

AMERICAN ANTHROPOLOGY, 1971–1995

Editor's Introduction

Regna Darnell

The American Anthropological Association has been known to celebrate its ongoing maturation process by periodically culling and reprinting the best that has been thought and written in the pages of its flagship journal, the *American Anthropologist* (*AA*). This is the fourth such volume, issued alongside the reprintings of the first three collections (of the years 1888–1920, edited by Frederica de Laguna in 1960; of 1921–45, edited by George W. Stocking Jr.; and of 1946–70, edited by Robert Murphy in 1976). Each of the first three volumes established a synergy between the moment of its assemblage and the ongoing retrospective reflexivity of disciplinary history.

Volume four, representing the years 1971 through 1995, simultaneously establishes historiographic continuity and its own unique perspective. Arbitrary though the attainment of a century may be, centennials hold their magic nonetheless. Like the millennium that coincides with this volume's preparation for the hundredth birthday of the AAA in 2002, centennials are times to take stock. This compilation is the product not solely of a single editor but of feedback received from members of the Centennial Executive Commission appointed by AAA president Jane Hill in 1999. As chair of the commission I acknowledge particularly the contributions of Frederic W. Gleach, Stephen O. Murray, and Susan Trencher.[1] The intense debate of this collaborative ethos has sharpened the agonizing urge to justify selecting only 30, or 4.6 percent, of the 648 papers that appeared during those years (compared to 1,006 papers from 1946–70 [Murphy 1976]).

The *AA* is no longer the sole mediator of professional identity for the anthropological discipline as it functions in North America. Most of the AAA's 34 sections produce publications reflecting disciplinary specialization that developed after the end of World War II.[2] The *AA* has faced an ongoing challenge to retain its centripetal, holistic role in anthropology's professional identity formation and maintenance. Already during the prior quarter century each subdiscipline developed its own organizational network and publication outlets.[3] The *American Ethnologist* was established in 1973 as a specialized outlet for the sociocultural majority of American anthropologists. Thereafter, the flagship journal could no longer envision itself as the sole voice of the AAA. Rather, its role became one of crossover, hybridization, and cross-pollination of the traditional four-square discipline. The increasingly strident claims of practicing anthropologists combined with the 1970s job crunch were normalized as a fifth subdiscipline outside of and ambivalently related to the academy.

The year 1971 reflects a real turning point in the affairs of the AAA and its relationship to the larger society. The Thai controversy of 1970 "marked the receding [of] the activist tide" (Trencher 2000:134). The earlier anthropological rhetoric of complicity with U.S. foreign policy and counterinsurgency initiatives turned inward, away from public policy, and resulted in the creation of the "Principles of Professional Responsibility" in 1971. Anthropologists shunned the role of collaborator at the price of the elimination of a public forum for cross-cultural insight. Increasingly, global politics were writ small in the personal experiences of fieldworking anthropologists whose primary loyalties lay with the local. Activism, to the extent that it continued, moved to domestic arenas (Trencher 2000:138).

AA editorial policy increasingly engendered a polarization that threatened the inclusiveness of what some saw as a floundering flagship publication. In short, many American anthropologists felt themselves left out and found little in the journal to address their specialized interests. Others concluded that the discipline itself lacked sufficient integrity to sustain an abiding loyalty to any one publication. The personal proclivities of the several editors who served during the period had less to do with the journal's contents than expectations from oral tradition might suggest.[4] I was unable to identify editorial transitions on content grounds alone.[5] Yet over the period the journal's editors were increasingly supported by specialized associate editors for materials from various subdisciplines, films, book reviews, and museum exhibits.

No quantitative index can convey either the adequacy or the inadequacy of disciplinary representation or cross-fertilization within the AA's pages. Nevertheless, a rough yardstick suggests certain trends and documents a consistent editorial commitment to diversity. Sociocultural topics have always dominated (440 articles, or 68 percent), with submissions from biological anthropology (93 articles, or 14.3 percent) and archaeology (90 articles, or 12.5 percent) fairly evenly balanced. Linguistics has always been the smallest of the subfields (37 articles, or 5.7 percent). (Topical review articles and short essays were not tabulated.)

Self-conscious gender equity has long been of interest to anthropologists. For the previous 25 years Murphy (1976:5) counted 1,219 authors of whom 10 to 13 percent were women (with a spike of 22 percent in the immediate postwar period). The 648 papers appearing between 1971 and 1995 had 834 authors (including co-authorships). Of these, 224 or 26.8 percent were women. Women constituted 32 percent of Ph.D.'s in 1972 and 59 percent of them in 1995 (Givens and Jablonski 1995:3).

Each editor during the period acceded to the range of subdisciplines that expected a voice in the AA. Every volume included a majority of sociocultural papers. Biological papers were absent in only one year's issues, archaeological were absent in three, and linguistic in five. Six issues appeared annually (half of them devoted to book reviews) until 1974, when the journal returned to a quarterly format and book reviews began dominating each issue for several years. Film reviews appeared in issues throughout those years. Book reviews followed the pattern found in the subdisciplinary proportions of articles mentioned above. Forum contributions in the early 1990s reduced the number of articles substantially.

Each editor of AA selected papers has attempted to echo this same proportion of papers submitted and published. Of the quarter century's issues represented here, many papers cross subdiscipline boundaries and seek an audience across specializations (making tabulation by subdiscipline somewhat arbitrary). About a third of the articles reprinted are on topics outside the boundaries of what is commonly known as sociocultural anthropology.

The largest number of articles with an easily identifiable ethnographic emphasis (slightly over half) were on Africa (72) and Latin America (combining the Caribbean, Central America, and South America) (71), both of which contained considerable biological anthropology and archaeology, respectively. There were 58 articles on Native American topics (many archaeological in nature), 37 that focused on the contemporary United States, 35 on the Pacific islands, 33 on Asia, 21 on Europe, and 13 on the Near East. Stephen O. Murray (1999:58) has argued that Americanist (that is, American Indian) work was not eclipsed in the immediate postwar period as accepted oral tradition in anthropology would have it, but rather that overseas fieldwork increased gradually alongside it. By the 1970s attention had moved away from Africa (with independence established and fieldwork access increasingly problematic) toward the Pacific Rim and Latin America where American imperial interests were focused. More anthropologists did fieldwork at home as well. The Near East emerged as a significant area.[6] Murphy's contention (1976:19) that "the common enterprise" of fieldwork is the glue, and that this "praxis of anthropology" uniting American anthropologists persists into this quarter century (although a growing inter- and subdisciplinary ethos provides an additional kind of glue).

Length has largely precluded the inclusion of ethnographic papers, site reports, and detailed experimental results, and potentially produced an overrepresentation of state-of-the-art syntheses, usually in the distinguished lecture format. Papers over 30 pages have been excluded arbitrarily, as have linked papers covering single topics. No author is represented more than once. Only four authors — Clifford Geertz, Ward Goodenough, Marshall Sahlins, and Eric Wolf — also appeared in the 1946–70 volume.

After suffering an initial reaction of panic, I wondered whether it is possible to think historically about such a recent period. The quarter century spans most of my own career. I began to study anthropology in 1961, joined the AAA a few years later, and specialized in disciplinary history from the mid-sixties on. By 1971 the AA formed only a background presence for me. I read its book reviews avidly and, despite the fact that I published only reviews during the period, I was a participant, a consumer, with personal axes to grind. To summarize and contextualize required standing outside.

As I became reacquainted with it I quickly discovered that the journal was not like I remembered it. I read most articles as they appeared but recall feeling no conviction that this single journal would, or could, or even should reflect the complexity of the discipline. The inclusion of diverse specializations and subdisciplines outstripped my recollections. I was gratified to observe that many articles defied subdisciplinary categorization. In retrospect and en masse, most of anthropology's major debates are reflected in the AA's pages, although primary elaboration often occurred elsewhere. Change over the period was sufficiently gradual to elude the participant-observer who read from the standpoint of proximate personal preoccupations. Despite substantial continuities within the journal, however, American anthropology in 1995 was a far cry from that of 1971.

Let us turn to a review of the selections themselves and an overview of the larger set of papers from which they were selected. The process of choosing was a fluid, ultimately personal and interpersonal act that reflects a surprising consensus among the Centennial Executive Commission members. Nonetheless, as primary editor I take full responsibility for the final choices presented here. Many of the papers that were omitted for reasons of space but that are mentioned below help to contextualize those that were selected.

Biological Anthropology

Although biological anthropology has become increasingly interdisciplinary and technical in nature, particularly in relation to the natural sciences, biological anthropology papers found in the AA reflect an overlapping with other areas of anthropology and seek audience rapprochement to the discipline as a whole. Cross-ties to archaeology and linguistics are more commonly found than are ties to sociocultural anthropology. Biological anthropologists have not entered the sociocultural nature versus nurture debate (see Derek Freeman's critique of Margaret Mead in Samoa, this volume). Human evolution is the most common focus of biological anthropology papers in the AA.

The "Contemporary Issues Forum," which focuses on current controversies in the theories of human evolution (edited by Robert W. Sussman 1993:9–96), captures for nonspecialists the intellectual energy of a subfield in foment. Cladistics—the analysis of mitochondrial DNA, which presents its greatest diversity in Africa—and the "molecular clock" of immunological differences in blood proteins have revised the commonly accepted ideas of the origin of anatomically modern humans. Only a recent perusal and summary of the literature can do justice to the rapid development of this field. Fossil evidence is supplemented by genetic studies of living populations and of related primate species. Leslie C. Aiello (1993, 95:73–96) reviews conflicting models favoring diverse lines of evidence that have yet to converge, rendering the idea of having a choice among models at present "rather subjective" (59). Alan R. Templeton's critique of the so-called Eve hypothesis (1993, 95:12–72) also stresses the complexity of reconciling evidence obtained using different methods. Sussman's introduction (1993, 95:9–11), however, asserts that the present chaos "will be resolved" through the gathering of additional data and making advances in dating technologies (11).

David Pilbeam's distinguished lecture, "Hominid Evolution and Hominid Origins" (1986, 88:295–312; this volume), reflects an earlier state of the field and proposes that prehominoid and Miocene fossil "speculations will become more realistic." Hominoid evolution emerges from the pages of the AA as a field in which increasingly sophisticated methods and data produce better but certainly not final models for the biology of humanness.

To the extent that biological anthropologists have wrestled with problems of culture versus nature or the biological causes that underlie cultural patterns, four-field training perhaps enhances the sophistication of sociobiological models. Cynthia M. Beall and Melvyn C. Goldstein (1981, 83:5–12; this volume) test sociobiological theory in terms of Tibetan fraternal polyandry, which decreases reproductive success for the individual male. Social, political, and economic factors seem to outweigh biological imperatives. Local explanation as a force for control of material resources fits with the correlation of polyandry to wealth as well as the unmarried status of nearly a third of Tibetan adult women. Another instance of this line of research, Alice Kehoe and Dody H. Giletti's "Women's Preponderance in Possession Cults: The Calcium Deficiency Hypothesis Extended" (1981, 83:549–561), shows that women, who normally do not consume much protein, improve their nutritional status through prestige acquired from participation in spirit possession cults. These cults provide a culturally acceptable way for women to supplement their nutritional intake without threatening the access that powerful men have to preferred food.

Crossing subdisciplinary boundaries in a matter-of-fact way, Ward H. Goodenough's "Evolution of the Human Capacity for Belief" (1990, 92:597–612; this volume) deploys evidence from primatology to explore the foundations of contemporary social structure, seeing language "as a tool for implementing intentionality in social interaction" (597). Human agency is deeply embedded in evolutionary content. A similar cross-field logic underlies Jane Hill's speculations on the evolutionary foundations of language (1972, 74:308–317). Both emphasize the symbolic or cognitive consequences of complex neurological systems.

A reconstruction of cultural history also may draw in biological anthropology. Harold K. Schneider's "Prehistoric Transpacific Contact and the Theory of Culture Change" (1977, 79:9–25) adopts a genetic mutation analogy as a nonlinear model to explain cumulative old world and new world cultural parallels. In a critique of Schneider, Laurie R. Godfrey and John R. Cole's "Biological Analogy, Diffusionism, and Archaeology" (1979, 81:37–45) cleaves the subdisciplines alternatively, arguing that diffusion carries the burden of proof; a case-by-case assessment will not sort out the complexities of divergent, parallel, or even convergent evolution.

Archaeology

Both substantive and theoretical archaeology papers abound in the pages of the *AA*, although a relative lacuna appears between 1974 and 1989. Oppositions recur between the material and the symbolic, and between applied and theoretical approaches that are parallel to debates within sociocultural anthropology. Many papers seek links to ethnographic evidence or audiences.

Kent V. Flannery's distinguished lecture, "The Golden Marshalltown: A Parable for the Archaeologist in the 1980s" (1982, 84:265–278; this volume), caricatures the succession of archaeological generations to remind colleagues that the much-maligned old-timer, with his golden trowel earned at Kidder's first Marshalltown dig, continues to believe in culture; the culture concept provides data to test theory and supplies a base for archaeology as a profession.

Patty Jo Watson's distinguished lecture to the archaeology division, "Archaeology, Anthropology, and the Culture Concept" (1995, 97:683–694; this volume), describes archaeology's increasing "markedly asymmetric . . . separatist themes" (684). Mental culture versus subsistence economy and reflexivity versus ethnoarchaeology both correlate with the primary dichotomy of theory versus practice. Watson agrees with Flannery that the culture concept is still thriving, that anthropology still defies rumors of its disintegration, and that anthropologists continue to ask broader questions than practitioners from any other discipline. Comparable polarization of method and theory appears in Patty Jo Watson and Michael Fotiadis's "The Razor's Edge: Symbolic-Structuralist Archaeology and the Explanation of Archaeological Inference" (1990, 92:613–629). The razor's edge is a skeptical, post-processualist, empirically based research tool that acknowledges the underdeterminism of archaeological explanation.

Robert McC. Adams's distinguished lecture, "World Picture, Anthropological Frame" (1977, 79:265–279; this volume), laments the subversion of boundary crossings at the annual AAA meetings and the loss of "older identifying symbols like cultural holism or participant observation" (265). Long before most of us were talking about globalization or hyperurbanization, Adams called on anthropologists to develop critical revisionist strategies that could transcend traditionally studied closed-bounded communities. World system thinking has been around for a long time (cf. Wolf, this volume). History will be more useful than "misdirected" scientism (274). Fragmentation has been lessened by recent convergence at the intersection of archaeology and ethnology.

Other papers convey the range of substantive research. Archaeology provides one line of evidence for distant human history, such as George H. Odell's "Addressing Prehistoric Hunting Practices through Stone Tool Analysis" (1988, 90:335–356). In "Scavenging or Hunting in Early Hominids: Theoretical Framework and Tests" (1986, 88:27–43) Pat Shipman establishes the minor role of hunting by long bone use patterns and analogizes that role to modern hunter-gatherers.

Archaeological data is applied more easily to questions of social complexity. David S. Friedel and Linda Schele's "Kingship in the Later Preclassic Maya Lowlands: The Instruments and Places of Ritual Power" (1988, 90:547–567) uses inscriptions and public symbols of ruling status to explore the ideologies of trade elitism that conflict with an egalitarian ethos. Gary Graffam's "Beyond State Collapse: Rural History, Raised Fields, and Pastoralism in the South Andes" (1992, 94:882–904) postulates a bottom-up continuity of rural rhythms through voluntary collective action; the technology of local high-yield raised fields survived a massive restructuring of the temporarily imposed state-level society. Elizabeth M. Brumfiel's "Aztec State-Making: Ecology, Structure, and the Origin of the State" (1983, 85:261–284) identifies administrative complexity as the key to state formation. Brumfiel proposes that as social and environmental variables interact, the state arises differently according to local conditions. The Aztec state grew rapidly from the convergence of small autonomous polities each of which controlled a limited geographical area.

Stuart Struever and Kent D. Vickery's "The Beginnings of Cultivation in the Midwest-Riverine Area of the United States" (1973, 75:1197–1220) distinguishes the tropical (that is, maize) complex after 800 A.D. from an apparent earlier indigenous agricultural complex that was based on sunflowers, marsh elders, and strawberries. Social complexity evolves from local roots.

Archaeology overlaps with cognitive anthropology in Gary Paul Nabhan and Amadeo Rea's "Plant Domestication and Folk-Biological Change: The Upper Piman/Devil's Claw Example" (1987, 89:57–73). Contemporary ethnological evidence of the changing taxonomy of a basketry fiber plant clarifies the cognitive dynamics of plant domestication. Wild and domestic strains intergrade, overgrazing changes the lexical domain, and Coyote intervenes in old ladies' stories of cognitive decisions that are not necessarily consciously made.

Michael A. Joachim's "Archaeology as Long-Term Ethnography" (1991, 93:308–321) applies ethnographic reasoning to ecological determinants of behavioral variation, stressing the risk and environmental variability of hunter-gatherer adaptations. Richard A. Gould's "The Anthropology of Human Residues" (1978, 80:815–835) uses a materialist ethnoarchaeology to posit universal patterns of "discard behavior and residue formation" (815). Gould rues what he considers the dominance of contemporary archaeology with nonmaterial studies of symbol, cognition, values, beliefs, and social organization. He argues that western Australian Aboriginal lithics are better interpreted from circumstantial evidence of human behavior than from nonverbalized raw material preferences. Following the archaeology-ethnology link, Michael B. Schiffer's "Archaeology as Behavioral Science" (1975, 77:836M–848) foregrounds nomothetic archaeology that is based on "behavioral-material correlates" (841), and laments contemporary trends in ethnographic writing that make ethnographies less useful for archaeological inference.

Thomas C. Patterson encapsulates "The Last Sixty Years: Toward a Social History of Americanist Archaeology in the United States" (1986, 88:7–26) by identifying the conflicting ideological discourses of the eastern elite and the core culture of the West and Midwest (with a more recent Midwestern alternative) and by documenting the field's transformation in the 1970s to a non-university-based profession. Bruce Trigger's "Constraint and Freedom: A New Synthesis for Archaeological Explanation" (1991, 93:551–569) rejects positivism for a Boasian postprocessual tack between particularism and neo-evolution, between idealism and materialism. General constraints can tell us little about cultural traditions, although prehistory is rarely able to transcend external constraints.

Culture historic reconstruction from archaeology and ethnology has long been associated with the Boasian historical particularist mode in ethnology. Jeffrey L. Hantman's "Between Powhatan and Quirank: Reconstructing Monocan Culture and History in the Context of Jamestown" (1990, 92:676–690) documents the invisibility in the historical record of Powhatan's major enemy and generic "other," the Monocan. Because Europeans had access to a Powhatan interpretive history, the cultural continuity and shared ideology of the coastal area must be reconstructed through trade patterns and burial mounds. Madonna L. Moss's "Shellfish, Gender, and Status on the Northwest Coast: Reconciling Archaeological, Ethnographic, and Ethnohistorical Records of the Tlingit" (1993, 95: 631–652) reveals that actual food resources were devalued, due to "the ritual impurity of an apparently optimal food" (646) that was eaten more often by women and lower-class persons, and are still spoken about reluctantly by contemporary Tlingit.

Linguistics

Of the four traditional subdisciplines, linguistics is the least represented in the pages of the *AA*. Its importance as part of the thinking of anthropologists in other subdisciplines is demonstrated, however, by research in cognitive anthropology and by a continuing fascination with the relation of language to human biology and prehistory. The small number of linguistic articles does not reflect its significance. Interestingly, within the articles there is virtually no direct reflection of the so-called Chomskian Revolution in linguistics. Linguistic anthropologists are, if anything, critical of the theory's trivialization of ethnographic particularity in the facile proclamation of universals (see the biological anthropology section in this volume).

Richard Bauman's "Verbal Art as Performance" (1975, 77:290–311; this volume) moves folklore from text to performance and communicative function, calling for ethnographic specificity such as audience participation in emergent displays of communicative competence. An "etic list of communicative means" alternates with specific exemplary cultural conventions of meaning construction (295). Joel Sherzer's "A Discourse-Centered Approach to Language and Culture" (1987, 89: 295–309; this volume) presents a reconceptualization of the language and culture problem in its Boas-Sapir-Whorf formulation, with discourse as the key to social interaction. Grammatical categories are not static determinants of thought-worlds but rather are resources for communicative competence, a view that requires the broadening of linguistic theory to include its instantiation in social behavior. Sherzer's long-term Kuna fieldwork provides his primary exemplars. He notes postmodernist correspondences of communicative convention, such as about temporal sequencing in narrative, warning that Kuna language and culture is avant garde to the external, Western observer only. The Kuna arrive at these conventions from within their own traditions.

Judith T. Irvine's "Formality and Informality in Communicative Events" (1979, 81:773–790) distinguishes conflated aspects of formality and informality that fail to correlate descriptively in cross-cultural examples. The question as to whether some features of code structuring, code consistency, positional identities, and situational foci are universals must be established empirically. Formality proves real but not analytically useful. David D. Laitin and Guadalupe Rodriguez Gomez's "Language, Ideology, and the Press in Catalonia" (1992, 94:9–30) compares the post-Franco editorials of two Catalonian and two Castilian newspapers; leftist and rightist politics are subordinated to positioning in the centralized state. Catalonian passion for autonomy refracts in "understatement or precision" (27), while Europe rather than Spain is presented as the "supra-political entity" (19).

In "Linguistic Knowledge and Cultural Knowledge: Some Doubts and Speculations" (1979, 81:14–36; this volume), Roger M. Keesing employs linguistic methods to uncover the "semantic systems and pragmatic rules" presupposed in cultural assumptions (14). Formal grammatical theory must be expanded to incorporate cross-cultural variability, which debunks the assumption that language is self-contained. Kwaio assumptions about ancestor spirits, sacredness and pollution, and the human ability to manipulate causal connections are integral to interpreting Kwaio utterances. Pragmatics is culture-specific, that is, situationally and contextually determined.

Ellen B. Basso's "Kalapalo Biography: Psychology and Language in a South American Oral History" (1989, 91:551–569; this volume) moves from structure and history to personal narrative. In a blatant contrast to Napoleon Chagnon's "fierce people," the Kalapalo have replaced the blood feud of the warrior-hunter with an agricultural extension of their moral sphere beyond the local settlement, where interpersonal conflict is resolved through witchcraft accusations. The warrior or bow-master undergoes ascetic leadership training to achieve an arrogant detachment from social relations. The personal narrative of Tapoge the Bow-Master never resolves the ambiguous identification of hostile enemies who are also his own distant relatives. The lifestory of the memorable person must be told, because the telling articulates its lack of closure concerning contested ideologies. A rhetoric of conflict alternates with one of conventional ideology.

J. R. Rayfield's "What Is a Story?" (1972, 74:1085–1106) seeks cross-culturally valid criteria for categorizing oral narrative as story, as "a natural psychological unit" (1085) which it is "assumed that everybody knows" (1089). The structure of the narrative is parallel to that of language itself. M. A. K. Halliday's "Anti-Languages" (1976, 78:570–584) examines the social construction of reality through conversation and classifies variable social dialect as part of normal sociolinguistic order.

Floyd Lounsbury's distinguished lecture, "Recent Work in the Decipherment of Palenque's Hieroglyphic Inscriptions" (1991, 93:809–825), chronicles the "history of opinion change" about Mayan hieroglyphics (811), which increasingly over time have been seen as phonetic. Inscriptions reveal the world of elite politics, cosmology, and religion; official histories are "politically motivated and in part fictitious" (819). Linguistics must operate as the handmaiden of archaeology to be able to approach and study the "structures of whole societies and their economic underpinnings" (822).

Linguists have long contributed to the search for universals of culture as well as of language (see Goodenough, mentioned above). Anna Wierzbicka's "Human Emotions: Universal or Culture-Specific?" (1986, 88:584–594) insists that universals cannot be approached solely through English, or, indeed, through the "ready-made" categories of any single language. Decomposition into semantic primitives, or simpler paraphrases, empirically clarifies universals. Terms denoting emotions are particularly elusive because their contexts are cultural and historical, such as *toska* or the sadness caused by separation, a term commonly used after the 1830 Polish Great Emigration which tore apart countless families. Wierzbicka's "Soul and Mind: Linguistic Evidence for Ethnopsychology and Cultural History" (1989, 91:41–58) explores the noncorrespondence of English and Russian folk terms for the word "soul," and seeks a meta-language of semantic primitives that are capable of transcending ethnocentric European Cartesian dualism. English treatment of emotion, morality, and spirituality, moreover, has changed over time. Wierzbicka recognizes cautious clues to lingering Whorfian questions of "different cultural universes associated with different languages" (55).

Another approach taken in the cultural-linguistic-biological relations of humans to one another and their environment is presented in Elliott D. Chapple's "The Science of Humanics: Multi-Disciplinary Renaissance of General Anthropology" (1978, 80:42–52) and "The Unbounded Reaches of Anthropology as a Research Science, and Some Working Hypotheses" (1980, 82:741–758). Humanics intends to preserve the scientific character of anthropology, even in the study of emotions.

Charles Hockett's distinguished lecture "F" (1985, 87:263–281) links linguistics with biological anthropology. Over the last few thousand years the relatively rare "f" sounds have been distributed alongside the expansion of Indo-European agricultural practices and horse domestication. In a "blend of genetic and evolutionary factors" (275), diet changed dental wear patterns which in turn modified the vocal tract as it was being reshaped by the needs of communication.

Practicing Anthropology

Practicing anthropology, initially understood as applied anthropology at work outside the academy, emerged as a fifth subdiscipline and focus of attention during the 1970s for academic and nonacademic anthropologists alike (although major projects in practicing anthropology can be dated much earlier). The discipline's soul-searching was enjoined by the inverse relationship of rapidly expanding professional growth and a contracting job market. Simultaneously, postcolonial states challenged the scientific authority of anthropologists and began to restrict anthropologists' access to the peoples they had traditionally studied. Papers in the AA devoted to the subject are more concerned with the changing structure of the profession than with the areas in which anthropologists practice.

Lawrence Rosen is the only author to make contributions twice in this debate. He was sufficiently pessimistic to suggest in the AAA newsletter that zero growth in size of the profession was appropriate and that anthropological interventions in the real world were ineffective (Trencher 2000:151). In "The Anthropologist as Expert Witness" (1977, 79:555–578; this volume) Rosen deploys legal research standards alongside anthropological ethics to confirm long-held and accepted precedents of expert testimony (citing Robert Redfield on "separate but equal" education in 1949, and John Hostetler on the destruction of Amish value systems through enforced public education in 1972). Rosen urges the AAA to restructure court testimony toward narrative formats that reveal "the Native point of view." Strategies developed for the Indian Claims

Commission should prove adaptable for anthropologists, even those working outside the United States. The facts of Rosen's "The Excavation of American Burial Sites: A Problem of Law and Professional Responsibility" (1980, 82:5–27) are thoroughly outdated by NAGPRA in 1990; what archaeologists failed to do voluntarily was legislated. The legislation has been normalized within a single professional generation. Rosen urged certification of anthropologists and AAA sanctions of unethical behavior. The concerns he identified persist, though the particular issues have changed.

Susan W. Almy writes about "Anthropologists and Development Agencies" (1977, 79:280–292) from her position within the Rockefeller Foundation, emphasizing the ill-preparedness of patronizing and academically trained anthropologists for agency-sponsored participant research. Anthropologists share the general "public distaste" for allowing specialists to design social systems (because presumably they run roughshod over the agency of subjects). Academic individualists work poorly on teams and are frustrated by short-term projects; academic freedom too easily becomes academic imperialism. Indictment is at war with optimism in this paper. Despite its impressionistic overgeneralizations, the stereotypes Almy presents illustrate how the field stays polarized, as practicing anthropologists feel like fish out of water in development contexts.

Dorothy Willner's "For Whom the Bell Tolls: Anthropologists Advising on Public Policy" (1980, 82:79–94) matter-of-factly enjoins anthropologists to face employment realities and seek research funding and jobs outside the academy. She questions the ethics of doing so, however. Anthropologists are not specialists equipped to make decisions about the distribution of misery and prosperity because they do not share the lives of their research subjects. We no longer work with dependent peoples; indeed, the grounds of collaboration have changed quite dramatically.

Questions of anthropological praxis are less salient in the issues of the 1980s but are revived in new forms within the so-called postmodernism of the 1990s. John Terrell's "Disneyland and the Future of Museum Anthropology" (1991, 93:149–153) approaches the uses of anthropology from the standpoint of public education and the challenges to museum-based scholarship that are posed by contemporary exhibition procedures. Terrell pleads for a sensible balance, in a debate which escalated in the subsequent decade. In Gary Lee Downey and Juan D. Rogers's "On the Politics of Theorizing in the Postmodern Academy"

(1995, 97:269–281) the authors acknowledge recent delegitimation of scientific knowledge, the association of science with elite domination, and a crisis of representation; they call for the popularization of the far-from-nihilistic methods of critical knowledge development.

Anthropologists, particularly our elders speaking to the AAA, have approached the crisis of the social reproduction of the discipline in both theoretical and pragmatic ways. Walter Goldschmidt's presidential address, "Anthropology and the Coming Crisis: An Autoethnographic Appraisal" (1977, 79:293–308) urges his colleagues to use their knowledge in the service of creating social order, despite the relative unimportance of anthropology in the power structures of world affairs. Professional survival requires a "return to pragmatism," despite the prevalent nostalgia for a more cohesive discipline (in Helm, ed. 1984:171). Goldschmidt celebrates anthropologists' egalitarian identification with the usually powerless subjects of their study and the goal of interweaving their lives with our own, while acknowledging the researcher's frequent alienation from his or her own culture, a distrust of power and success, a self-defeating self-deprecation, and a romantic escapism. The 1970s recapitulated the intellectual foment and job crisis of the Great Depression. Goldschmidt laments our failure, in the guilty disillusion we experienced following the Viet Nam War, to build on precedents of community, national, and broader ethnic culture studies. To transcend cultural breakdown and malaise is the "peculiarly anthropological problem" of seeking common welfare.

In a guest editorial submitted the previous year titled "Anthropology as Context" (1976, 78:519–520), Goldschmidt argues that the AAA must strike a balance between the need for specialized networks and the danger of losing its holistic context. He argued for the structural enshrinement of biological anthropology and archaeology in the national association, insisting that "intellectual attitudes" underlaid "organization defection," and he challenged colleagues to meet "the hubris of [our] eponym" (520). Richard Newbold Adams's guest editorial, "The Problem of Unity and Diversity in Anthropology" (1977, 79:263–264), called on anthropology to expand into the public sector, as it did during the Great Depression; subdisciplines "shift their most profound assumptions" over time (264).

Elizabeth Colson's distinguished lecture, "Culture and Progress" (1976, 78:261–271), blames problems being confronted in social anthropology and ethnography on the larger world beyond the discipline.

Our subject matter persists although so-called primitives are increasingly rarely found. Within the context of short funds and few jobs she recommends studying "large-scale organizations" in the West (264) rather than searching for holistic cultures and bounded societies resembling those of the past. Scientific humanism, with its goal of expanding the options for our ethnographic subjects, is the characteristic ideology of anthropology. We advance by "spiralism" (269), whereas peoples and cultures cope with change.

R. G. D'Andrade, E. A. Hammel, D. L. Adkins, and C. K. McDaniel's "Academic Opportunity in Anthropology, 1974–90" (1975, 77:753–773) predicted a serious decline in employment of persons holding doctorates granted after 1982, when they predicted that two-thirds of all new jobs in anthropology would be nonacademic. Combining the exponential growth in universities with anthropology's even more rapid expansion placed the discipline already "close to the saturation point" (766). The academic orientation of existing anthropologists must change to meet these challenges.

Regardless of the mechanisms of regulation that came into operation, these dire predictions have not come to pass. The AAA survey of anthropological doctorates (Givens and Jablonski 1995:1) reports a "remarkably stable" Ph.D. production: 400 per year since 1974, when that figure was first reached. Over the same period half were awarded in sociocultural anthropology, 30 percent in archaeology, 10 percent in biological anthropology, 3 percent in linguistics, and 7 percent in applied (practicing) anthropology. The latter was "a growth industry" in the 1990s, as it was in the 1970s (2). Since the mid-seventies academic positions for new Ph.D.'s have declined from 74 percent to 38 percent; salaries were higher for less-prestigious nonacademic positions (5–6). Givens and Jablonski recommend focusing on statistics, analytical methods, field research, subdiscipline breadth, teaching experience, interdisciplinarity, and budget management (7), all of which definitely can be placed on the pragmatic, scientific side of the discipline.

Beverly McElligott Hurlbert's "Status and Exchange in the Profession of Anthropology" (1976, 78:272–284) documents the domination of academic anthropology by a small number of elite departments that exchange graduates to preserve their high status. Expansion until 1965 partially masked the ingrown character of these elite departments and consequently the unlikelihood of individual anthropologists moving to more prestigious employment.

A. E. Rogge's "A Look at Academic Anthropology: Through A Graph Darkly" (1976, 78:829–843) documents an exponential expansion of the number of practicing anthropologists within the academy, showing that the discipline doubled in 15+/−5 years (depending on the index used), and called for feedback mechanisms to slow the growth "without conscious effort" (834). The built-in oligarchy of the present discipline limits productivity to an elite few, many working within "invisible colleges," although the days are long gone when everyone in anthropology knew everyone else. "Doing science is basically a social phenomenon" (especially in archaeology), and it confers productive advantage on these elites. We are just beginning to study our "own life's work from a sociological perspective" (838). Most anthropologists want a more egalitarian structure of production, access to publication, and employment, yet the elite hegemony seems self-reinforcing.

Roger Sanjek's "The Position of Women in Major Departments of Anthropology, 1967–76" (1978, 80:894–904), which followed the 1972 AAA resolution on "Fair Practices in the Employment of Women," examines the records of 22 major Ph.D.-producing departments. Women were less successful at holding jobs and gaining tenure; those who left were more likely to disappear altogether from the profession than men (who usually gained employment elsewhere). Women, often hired more recently, tended to hold lower-ranking positions. More surprising, the core departments varied considerably in their equity records, though 15 out of the 22 made progress over the reporting period.

Linda Marie Fedigan's "Science and the Successful Female: Why There Are So Many Woman Primatologists" (1994, 96:529–540) documents the proportions of women in anthropology and related disciplines. Primates are not cute and cuddly, and primatology is not a mothering type of activity. Women primatologists are recruited by the coincidence of the women's movement with the growth of primatology, the smaller size of primatology's professional societies, the presence of female role models and mentoring men within it, and the marginality of this area of science. In fact, the prestige of primatology may decrease as women's influence in it is perceived to increase.

Sociocultural Anthropology

In addition to its quantitative domination of the overall discipline, sociocultural anthropology is far more diverse internally than the other subdisciplines. If one set of tensions within the AAA revolves around the conflict of methods and subject matters between subdisciplines, another set resides within sociocultural anthropology itself. Centripetal forces lead toward other disciplines in the humanities and other social sciences. American, British, and French national traditions often seem incommensurable in their priorities and procedures. The characteristic anthropology of broad culture areas is not always transferable to the larger discipline (see Fardon, ed. 1990). No single paradigm is shared, and acrimony often reigns within debates directly engaging such differences. Indeed, our discipline is known within the academy for its internal contentiousness, for our inability to speak for our discipline as a whole, and for the nature of its claims to knowledge.

Subdivisions within sociocultural anthropology are necessarily somewhat arbitrary, but display an overall turn toward interpretation. We can begin our examination with an assessment of the continuity from the previous quarter century, then turn to ethnographic analysis of data from the humanities, to sociocultural models of racism, ethnicity, and gender, and to contemporary hunter and gatherer adaptations. Questions of the status of knowledge in sociocultural anthropology are discussed under the rubric of problematizing ethnographic authority, invention of tradition, positivism versus postmodernism, political engagement versus dispassionate science, and ethnography versus theory. The contentiousness of these latter topics has not abated in the years since 1995; juxtaposing them in our discussion, however, may reveal common space in our debates as well as document where we have been.

Continuing Paradigms

Symbolic anthropology, cultural ecology, and structuralism were the reigning paradigms of the 1960s according to Sherry Ortner (1984), with variations on Marxism coming into favor during the 1970s. At the beginning of our quarter century she argued that the counterculture, antiwar, and women's movements originated in the academy as anthropology obsessed over its relationship to colonialism; in the 1980s varieties of practice theory ranged from ethnography of communication to symbolic interaction to Marxist symbolic domination (focusing on the interactions of structure and agency). The 1990s, to extrapolate her trajectories, perhaps returned to a more polarized struggle between the scientific-Marxist and humanist-postmodernist camps.

Culture and personality had largely run its course by 1971, when it was subsumed by ethnoscience and cognitive anthropology. Early issues contain a number of papers on the subject, however, as represented here by Melford E. Spiro's "Whatever Happened to the Id?" (1979, 81:5–13; this volume). Spiro objects adamantly to the Lévi-Straussian denial of aggression in myth through a reduction to nature versus culture: "the code converts all acts of violence into metaphors for non-violent social structural relationships" (7). Spiro prefers to retain psychological assumptions about sex and aggression in human nature and the norms devised to control them.

Thomas H. Hay's "The Windigo Psychosis: Psychodynamic, Cultural, and Social Factors in Aberrant Behavior" (1971: 1–22) explains the Northern Algonquian phenomenon as an "ethno-specific mental disorder" (1). Lack of alternatives forced unritualized cannibalism with a trajectory from melancholy to dreams to violent action based on the dreams. Cannibals, rarely lone individuals, were often killed but also were seen as curable if someone took responsibility for them. The famine interpretation was an ethnocentric white fantasy. Joel S. Savishinsky's "Mobility as an Aspect of Stress in an Arctic Community" (1971, 73:604–618) shows how the alternation between bush and town represses stress for the Colville Lake Hare. Tensions are exacerbated by juggling contact with two very different cultural traditions. Morris E. Opler's "Cause and Effect in Apachean Agriculture, Division of Labor, Residence Patterns, and Girls' Puberty Rites" (1972, 74:1133–1151) uses the integration of traits (with the "feeling tone" of women's importance in Apachean society) to pose an alternative to the Pueblo practice of borrowing of matrilocal residence alongside the adoption of agriculture.

Structuralism intersected with culture and personality and interpretivism in various ways, with American anthropologists generally not adopting the full Lévi-Straussian paradigm. Abraham Rosman and Paula G. Rubel's "The Potlatch: A Structural Analysis" (1972, 74:658–671; this volume) uses classic Boasian examples of variable areal patterning of rank to examine rules for actual marriage strategies, particularly in defining who is an affine in various Northwest Coast tribes.

Interpretivism is represented by Sherry B. Ortner's "On Key Symbols" (1973, 75:1338–1346; this volume). Rituals alternate with cultural performances to clarify usually unarticulated strategic metaphors. Meaning is sought in objects of cultural interest, in an intriguing foreshadowing of Ortner's later practice theory. In her "Sherpa Purity" (1973, 75:49–63) Ortner contrasts explicit symbols and underlying cultural orientations without relying on assumptions about cultural universals. Pollution affects individuals, gods, and communities, while symbols provide strategies for action.

Cognitive anthropology, which remains robust, originated in 1960s interpretivism and depends heavily on models and techniques borrowed from linguistics (Murray 1994:391–418). A. Kimball Romney, Susan C. Weller, and William H. Batchelder's "Culture as Consensus: A Theory of Culture and Informant Accuracy" (1986, 88:313–338; this volume) proposes the adoption of systematic criteria to gain confidence in the inference of correct answers to cultural questions. Culture is defined as an unequally distributed, learned and shared information pool within which reliable answers are widely shared. If specialists are queried, a smaller sample is needed.

Much of the cognitive anthropology literature explores particular semantic domains in unfamiliar languages. Roger Sanjek's "Brazilian Racial Terms: Some Aspects of Meaning and Learning" (1971, 73:1126–1143; this volume) berates the absence of quantitative methods in the "new ethnography." Sanjek proposes various measures to use in sampling racial terms in contemporary Brazil to reveal systematic variability among subjects. Salience is of more interest than gross frequency; variables of skin color and hair forms appear in the use and recognition of terms.

Joseph Bastien's "Qollahuaya-Andean Body Concepts: A Topographical-Hydraulic Model of Physiology" (87:595–611) explores the semantic domain as a precondition to integration of modern medicine with traditional healing. Peggy R. Sanday's "Analysis of the Psychological Reality of American English Kin Terms in an Urban Poverty Environment" (1971, 73:555–570) employs a formal approach to understanding expert knowledge and attempts to move from componential analysis to prediction. Information processing and memory variables reveal semantic and cognitive variability as well as a ladder structure of Black kin terms and a cluster structure of White ones.

Roy A. Rappaport's "Ritual, Sanctity, and Cybernetics" (1971, 73:59–76; this volume) approaches an examination of Tsembaga rituals through interacting variables in local and regional systems, both social and ecological. Ritual control draws ancestors into a homeostatic cycle of peace, pork distribution, feasting, and realignment of hostilities, with sufficient cryptic maneuvering room to allow for change. In J. Stephen Lansing and James N. Kremer's "Emergent Properties of Balinese Water Temple

Networks: G-Adaptation on a Rugged Fitness Landscape" (1987, 89: 321–341), human intention modifies natural-biological models. The co-operative behavior of Balinese farmers demonstrates the co-adaptive fitness value of rice terraces that emerges even without conscious planning. Spontaneous self-adaptation of complex systems was predicted by Rappaport "a generation ago" with regard to ritual (112). (The focus of Rappaport's later work shifted from reductive ecological models to more symbolic ones founded on global systems theory.)

Humanistic Excursions

Some anthropologists have turned from the humanities to unconventional subject matters. On the one hand these papers claim an analytic applicability of ethnographic method beyond conventional face-to-face fieldwork; on the other they suggest a critique of anthropological praxis from the standpoint of the humanities.

Jennifer Brown's "Plato's *Republic* as an Early Study of Media Bias and a Charter for Prosaic Education" (1972, 74:672–675) situates Plato as the transition point from oral poetic to literate prose. Karin R. Andriolo's "A Structural Analysis of Genealogy and Worldview in the Old Testament" (1973, 75:1657–1669) identifies genealogy as the basis for resolving conflicting worldviews in ancient Israel. First-born sons are listed by name and hereditary status, while heroes are younger brothers. Only in the generation of Jacob is the twelve-way segmentation of brothers into tribes held coordinate. The homology of descent and worldview created a self-perception of unification in the pre-monarchy tribal confederacy. William Harmon's "T. S. Eliot: Anthropologist and Primitive" (1976, 78:797–811) explores the "socially and historically ancient" poetic function of Eliot's synthetic use of totemism and animism in his poetry (806). Erve Chambers's "Thalia's Revenge: Ethnography and the Theory of Comedy" (1989, 91:589–598) identifies characters in 18th-century English satire as representing groups and classes with a comic expression too rarely found in ethnography, despite "common moral, descriptive and philosophical problems" across these genres (596).

Racism, Ethnicity, and Gender

Most of the papers on race are actually about racism, that is, they stress the cultural rather than the biological construction of categories such as race, ethnicity, and gender. Francis L. K. Hsu's "Prejudice and Its Intel-

lectual Effect in American Anthropology: An Ethnographic Report"
(1973, 75:1–19; this volume) speaks firsthand of "deep prejudice" stem-
ming from the tradition of Western individualism, as documented from
his own experience as well as sociological analysis. Theorizing remains
the prerogative of white male anthropologists. Hsu calls on mainstream
anthropologists to confront their own irrational assumptions and work
through them both ethnographically and professionally.

Hsu's presidential address, "The Cultural Problem of the Cultural
Anthropologist" (1979, 81:517–532), explores the ethnocentrism of
Malinowski's diaries, with their racial and cultural superiority, hypo-
chondria, and preoccupation with sex. Hsu reveals the multiple racisms
of Malinowski's Trobriand interactions, and lambastes Malinowski's failure of affect and his resorting to merely providing instrumental interactions. Anthropologists should ask themselves if they have friends in the
field in the same way that they do at home. Only a systematic study of the
ethnographer's own culture can mitigate against such ethnocentrisms.

Little appears in the *AA*'s pages on feminist theory, although gender
continues to be a category for sociological and ethnographic investigation. Many papers take a statistical approach, testing generalizations
against a cross-cultural sample. William Tulio Divale and Marvin Harris's "Population, Warfare and the Male Supremist Complex" (1976,
78:521–538) explores warfare as a regulation of population growth. Matrilineal and patrilineal descent rules are not mirror images. The pair
concludes, contra-Freud, that aggression is not a directly biological
phenomenon.

Gender is sometimes considered biologically. For example, Seymour
and Hilda Parker's "The Myth of Male Superiority" (1979, 81:289–309)
emphasizes a social-exchange model to define the elastic nature of male
and female division of labor, distinguishing role adaptation from male
superiority: the (nearly) universal is not necessarily biologically determined, although it must have emerged early in human evolution. Male
superiority results from a widely institutionalized cultural reward system
that compensates men for the risks inherent in their optimal labor contributions. Increased contemporary overlap of labor roles renders the
male superiority complex increasingly dysfunctional.

Karen Sacks's "State Bias and Women's Status" (1976, 78:565–569)
suggests that nonstate systems can obtain sexual equality by means other
than androgyny, which is its capitalist form. Difference in roles does not
entail male dominance; both women and men are needed for social

order. W. Penn Handwerker and Paul V. Crosbie's "Sex and Dominance" (1982, 84:97–104) postulates the existence of initially unstratified groups and concludes that authority and chauvinism are rooted in relative size, although their biological basis cannot be generalized. In Peggy Sanday's "Toward a Theory of the Status of Women" (1973, 75:1682–1700), an extensive cross-cultural sample correlates gendered economic and political status with contribution to subsistence. Belief systems intervene even when women are critical to achieving subsistence, although women have more status if they also control the production of valued goods.

James R. Gregory's "The Myth of the Male Ethnographer and the Woman's World" (1984, 86:313–327) reports his own efforts to rectify "lopsidedly male-centered" ethnography (316) and suggests that male dominance of public affairs is overstated and men have used it to evade a dual gender role in the field. It is a myth that women are inaccessible to male ethnographers (although he cites no examples of men attempting to study women's institutions). Roger M. Keesing's "Kwaio Women Speak: The Micropolitics of Autobiography in a Solomon Island Society" (1985, 87:27–39) explores "how and why women open their lives to view" (27). Kwaio women acceded to recording their experience of *kastom* in order to legitimate it, despite women's taboos and male ideological control of childbirth. Keesing and his female collaborator obtained 15 life histories that show a stronger public role for women than previously recorded. "Reflective autobiography" required a conviction by women that their lives were worth recording when a context was available to do so.

Hunters and Gatherers

The ethnography of contemporary hunters and gatherers has educed considerable cross-fertilization of sociocultural anthropology and archaeology, particularly in the discussion of human evolution and neo-evolutionary theories of culture. Richard Lee's "Art, Science, or Politics? The Crisis in Hunter-Gatherer Studies" (1992, 94:31–54; this volume) distinguishes humanistic, scientific, and political economy approaches, with poststructuralist radical skepticism perhaps even claiming that anthropologists invented the hunter-gatherers. Lee opts for the political economy model grounded in history, which reveals foraging patterns that are adapted to particular circumstances, symbiotic with other local cultures, and participants in world systems.

Fiona Marshall's "Origins of Specialized Pastoral Production in East Africa" (1990, 92:873–894) explores the archaeological origins of specialized pastoralism about 2,000 B.P., postulating an earlier generalist phase in which pastoral, agricultural, and hunter-gatherer economies were "interconnected and complementary" (888). Carbohydrate honey might be the critical contribution to the hunter-gatherer diet. Marshall warns against direct analogies between ethnology and archaeology because contemporary pastoralists vary immensely.

Robin Ridington's "Knowledge, Power, and the Individual in Subarctic Hunting Communities" (1988, 90:98–110; this volume) developed interpretive language to show how nomadic hunters deploy a religious phenomenology of contextualized knowing that is accessed through dreaming. Such individual experience takes context for granted and entails interpersonal interdependence. The hunter depends on knowledge and technique rather than on artifacts in a co-evolution of individual and cultural systems of information.

Problematizing Ethnographic Authority

Anthropologists seem particularly prone to disparaging their discipline's culture heroes. This volume goes to press as anthropology deals with another guerrilla attack — Patrick Tierney's *Darkness in El Dorado* (2000) — which is a purported debunking of the research work among the Yanomami by anthropological entrepreneur Napoleon Chagnon, biologist James Neal, and visual anthropologist Timothy Asch. Neal and Asch are recently deceased. The controversy manifests a déjà vu quality of public debate lacking professional civility and a backlash defense of our own by anthropologists who want to reveal a more complex story of Amazon research. Between 1971 and 1995 two comparable scandals divided anthropologists and placed their lack of consensus in the public eye.

In an effort to sort out the final lessons of dissension, Ivan Brady edited a special section, "Speaking in the Name of the Real: Freeman and Mead on Samoa" (1983, 85:908–947), which criticizes Derek Freeman's attack on Americanist anthropology icon Margaret Mead as bad science which had nonetheless engendered salutary critical self-reflection for "anthropologist-citizens of the wider world" (908). In the same section Annette Weiner emphasized Freeman's unprofessional conduct and his dangerous misrepresentation of eugenics as ordinary science. Such attacks "alter what people think about the value of anthropology" (918).

Freeman's "ethnographic determinism" (910) ignored the interpretation inherent in all ethnography, taking Samoan direct testimony at face value as if Western positivism were the only legitimate method. Theodore Schwartz, a Mead research collaborator, insisted that Mead's scholarship was not "sacrosanct" (919). The real issue to be considered is the clash between conflicting views of human nature. Lowell Holmes, who re-studied Mead's primary Samoan village in 1954, emphasized the personal animus motivating Freeman's "blatant misuse of the anthropological literature" (933). Brad Shore reminds colleagues that we have apologized for Mead's errors but have forgotten her insights. He locates conflicting evidence and epistemological differences at the core of the Samoan so-cialization process. Martin G. Silverman recasts the debate as a Victorian melodrama in "Our Great Deception, or, Anthropology Defiled" (941).

Another controversial figure of the period was Carlos Castaneda, whose New Age bestsellers earned him a doctorate from UCLA and a minor body of literature of deconstructive criticism of his purported fieldwork and its Yaqui roots (e.g., DeMille 1980). In "Sonoran Fantasy or Coming of Age?" Ralph L. Beals (1978, 80:355–362) records his "per-sonal reaction" to Castaneda's purported discovery of Don Juan, the eth-nographic inconsistencies of Castaneda's fieldwork as reported, and Beals's own exclusion, despite his ethnographic expertise in the area, from Castaneda's further work and publication. Beals implicitly dismisses the work as creative imagination, which he did not "confuse" with an-thropology (356). In a follow-up comment UCLA colleague Jacques Ma-quet defends the department on trial because of Castaneda, blaming the "silence and uneasiness" of the profession (362) on jealousy, psychotro-pics, and disciplinary ethnocentrism. Maquet declines to address issues of bad faith, either in Castaneda or in Castaneda's academic supervisors.

Invention of Tradition

The mere phrase "invention of tradition" has been enough to polar-ize responses of sociocultural anthropologists to the interpretive turn, which dominated the 25 years. Allan Hanson's "The Making of the Maori: Cultural Invention and Its Logic" (1989, 91:890–902; this vol-ume) valorizes contemporary invention over stable heritage, calling into question our own methods of knowledge production. Maori uses of history, partly anthropologically constructed, moved from assimilation at the turn of the century to contemporary Maori distinctiveness. Heroic migrations no longer make sense, which reflects outdated diffusionist theory. Authenticity is acquired through interpersonal communication, talk, and practice.

The invented tradition debate was scarcely confined to the pages of the AA, but a commentary forum on Hanson's paper (1991, 93:440–450) clarifies the range of positions. Robert Langdon postulates that Caucasian Maoris resulted from the shipwrecking of a 16th-century Spanish vessel that was ignored by conventional scholarship. (To Langdon's way of thinking, this historically inaccurate invention served to create a single European culture into which Maoris could be assimilated.) H. B. Levine argues that Hanson conflates invention with inevitable political ideology and thus exaggerates its importance; Hanson also overstates the influence of anthropologists and the grounding of the invention arguments in Maori-Pakeha (white) relations. Contemporary land claims make these matters more than moot. Ownership is subordinated to the "property" or "valuable" nature of land in a powerful "rhetoric of ethnic politics" (445) to which "invention" provides limited analytic utility. The argument is more spiritual than rational or material. Jocelyn Linnekin focuses on anthropological ethics. Nonspecialists equate invention with falsehood, justifying indigenous peoples' anger, the "unintended consequences" (446) of the paradigm. The challenge to ethnographic authority is a theoretical problem internal to anthropology; continuity with the past is part of the contemporary identity struggle. Anthropologists can take control of this discourse by not implying inauthenticity of contemporary cultures and by applying the same theory to Western discourse and colonial contact as it applies to indigenous traditions (see Bruner and Dietler in this volume).

Historical anthropology has pursued many of these structures, attempting to reconstruct the point of view of Native actors in contact situations. Marshall Sahlins's distinguished lecture "Other Times, Other Customs: The Anthropology of History" (1983, 85:517–544; this volume), eschews an elite history of the life of communities in favor of their own modes of historical practice. A structural historical anthropology revitalizes the received historiography by posing obscure and remote histories alongside Europe's ethnocentric history, revealing the "myth of everyday life" (525). Habitus replaces the mythopoetic objectification of heroic history.

Edward M. Bruner's "Abraham Lincoln as Authentic Reproduction: A Critique of Postmodernism" (1994, 96:397–415) explores the hyperreality in which Lincoln's New Salem Museum in central Illinois may be an "authentic reproduction" that exceeds the original. The museum's inaccuracies render it more effective in sorting out competing voices around which history is institutionalized. The "Honest Abe" image arose after Lincoln left the region, during his first presidential campaign; he wasn't an important personage in Springfield while there. The invention of tradition paradigm is a revisionist constructivism in which the copy changes our perception of the original (in this case, the 1830s).

Michael Dietler's "Our Ancestors the Gauls: Archaeology, Ethnic Nationalism, and the Manipulation of Celtic Identity in Modern Europe" (1994, 96:584–605; this volume) eliminates the disrespect of applying "invention" to other traditions by examining our own traditions. Dietler begins from Iron Age archaeology and follows the Celts (the Greek term) or the Gauls (the Roman term) through imagined communities and nation-states over time and space. Archaeology ties ethnicity to local sites and events; thus, the politics of archaeology become an issue in many nation-states. Brittany used the Celts to resist French hegemony and claim European community, while France itself valorized Celtic roots after the French Revolution. Archaeology has a duty, Dietler believes, to expose manipulation of the past.

Positivism versus Postmodernism

Despite the concurrent humanistic heritage of anthropology, at least as it is found in North America, the *American Anthropologist* has a long tradition of claiming scientific status on both theoretical and methodological grounds. Philosopher of science I. C. Jarvie's "Epistle to the Anthropologists" (1975, 77:253–266) identifies a crisis of theoretical stagnation as profound as the one in which anthropology reinvented itself around fieldwork. This second revolution revolves around the mutual entanglement of language and social reality and the subject position of the ethnographer. Jarvie returns to the anthropological past, presumably of British social anthropology, and produces a critique beyond the actor's contemporary language or situated position. A critical history of anthropology for him must employ a rhetoric of continuity.

J. Tim O'Meara's "Anthropology as Empirical Science" (1989, 91: 354–369) rues the trend of denying the possibility of an empirical human science as overreaction to excesses of logical positivism. Science and humanism should be complementary, using the limited objectivity of human affairs to infer meanings.

Alison Dundes Rentein's "Relativism and the Search for Human Rights" (1988, 90:56–72) grounds the characteristic Americanist cultural relativism as a value theory in her critique of racist evolutionary stages. The position enables a critique of one's own embedded ethnocentrisms. Universal consensus on some human values provides a test case for ethical relativism and rehabilitates the possibility of judgements of right and wrong according to cultural ideals. Anthropologists, lamentably, have turned to philosophy rather than empirical investigation and have worried overly much about the dangers of imposing liberal values on others, such as through the United Nations Statement on Human Rights. (This position is no longer in fashion, but it helps make sense of the persistence of relativist debates within and beyond anthropology.)

Despite the dissatisfaction of many anthropologists, particularly those longing for an exclusively scientific anthropology, the trend toward what is loosely defined as postmodernism was underway in anthropology before the publishing of the first issue edited by Barbara and Dennis Tedlock in mid-1994. Though there is certainly an acceleration of interpretivist work, more traditional articles continued to appear. The final judgement on the alienation of many readers from the AA under the Tedlocks' editorship, the increased subscription rates during the same period based on enthusiasm generated from previously nonparticipating camps, and the backlash that followed the next change of editorial control are stories to be told in another quarter century, when the dust has settled.

Interpretive anthropology evinces numerous continuities to later work labeled by many as postmodernist. George E. Marcus's review article, "Repatriating an Interpretive Anthropology: The American Studies–Cultural Criticism Connection" (1983, 85:859–865), examines the permeable boundaries of academic disciplines. American Studies has attempted to devise an anthropological emphasis without having a cross-cultural focus, while anthropologists remain trapped by representing "unmediated small group worlds" (862). We need to figure out how to talk about larger cultural entities.

Karl G. Heider's "The Rashomon Effect: When Ethnographers Disagree" (1988, 90:73–81) focuses on what can be learned from apparently contradictory truths and suggests the systematic study of standpoints producing multiple but not random interpretations. (Rashomon is a Japanese story made into a film telling the "same" story from four incommensurable points of view.) Multiplicity is inevitable but not necessarily disabling. Paul B. Roscoe's "The Perils of Positivism in Cultural Anthropology" (1995, 97:491–504) argues that the human sciences cannot employ natural science methods simplistically. Positivism is a scapegoat constructed by its critics and used since the early 1970s to debunk science. Roscoe argues Heider's Rashomon effect is normal science and that interpretivists must go beyond a single culture. Humanistic anthropology can be scientific within its own subject matter without the authorial monopoly of the ethnographer. We must target bad science.

Margaret Rodman's "Empowering Place: Multilocality and Multivocality" (1992, 94:640–656; this volume) emphasizes the localization of meaning, in which reflexive relationships to place form a metaphorical parallel to voice. Polysemic landscape and decentered place are approached from multiple views and amplify silenced conversations, ensuring authority to speak in public about names and places.

Kirin Narayan's "How Native is a 'Native' Anthropologist?" (1993, 95:671–686; this volume) problematizes the essentialism of insider-versus-outsider access and knowledge. She envisions individual anthropologists "in terms of shifting identifications amid a field of interpenetrating communities and power relations" (671). Her own "Nativeness" is not a simple matter, and nation-state labels no longer locate people unambiguously. What we ought to mean by a "Native" anthropology is one that is constructed from other premises and which therefore reframes what our own society already knows. Narrative ethnography has its legitimate place alongside theory in depicting and translating such hybrids, among both anthropologists and their subjects. It follows that ethnographic writing must change as well.

Renato Rosaldo's "Whose Cultural Studies?" (1994, 96:524–529) reflects on the loss of anthropology's monopoly over the culture concept. Young anthropologists (that is, younger than himself) are democratizing American institutions, including universities, as cultural studies demand diversity and respect. Anthropologists whine that literary critics ignore them but at the same time they fail to respond to challenges posed by cultural studies, feminism, and postcolonial studies, to name just a few. Paul Stoller's "Embodying Colonial Memories" (1994, 96:634–648) interprets the Hauka spirit possession movement among the Songhay as the sentient embodiment of cultural memory inadequately encompassed in textuality.

Alma Gottlieb's "Beyond the Lonely Anthropologist: Collaboration in Research and Writing" (1995, 97:21–26) calls attention to the continued silence about private lives and personal collaborations. Western male authors are consistently named in the singular while their women spouses are rarely credited adequately. Elizabeth Lapovsky Kennedy's "In Pursuit of Connection: Reflections on Collaborative Work" (1995, 97:26–32) catalogues her three successive collaborations grounded in feminism, anticolonialism, and interpretivism, each with characteristic strengths and frustrations.

Political Engagement versus Dispassionate Science

David Kaplan's review article, "The Anthropology of Authenticity: Everyman His Own Anthropologist" (1974, 76:824–839) calls on anthropology to avoid reinventing itself as politically and morally partisan. Radical scholarship, as envisioned by contributors to Dell Hymes's edited collection *Reinventing Anthropology* (1969), requires no special method or logic. The core anthropological notion of common humanity arose only in the West and transcends the "narcissistic preoccupation with the [anthropological] self" that invalidates the scientific authority of anthropology in public debates (825).

"Human Rights and the Rights of Anthropologists," Johnnetta B. Cole's opening plenary address at the Atlanta AAA meeting in 1994 (1995, 97:445–456), is the AA's most articulate post–Viet Nam call to activist arms. She celebrates both her city (without denying its poverty and angst) and the AAA meetings as an institution, which lead to "the sheer joy of seeing folks we care about but only manage to see at such gatherings of far-flung clans of anthropology" (445). Cole grounds the anthropological search for human rights in the discipline's Boasian history. According to Ruth Benedict, "At 84, Franz [Boas] had not sold out, or stultified himself, or locked himself in a dogmatic cage" (445). Anthropologists, regardless of subdiscipline, are situated ideally to observe violations of human rights. Atrocities accumulate, including the contemporary "denial of the full rights of citizenship to America's people of color" (446). We must balance credibility of intellectual objectivity with responsibility to apply our knowledge to change the world. Our history confirms consensus if not unanimity, with the acceptance of four AAA resolutions against racism between 1968 and 1972; the 1994 resolution addressed the resurgence of scientific racism. The debate, however acrimonious, has been more about whether we speak as citizens or as anthropologists than about whether the tolerance inherent in our habitual cultural relativism masks a more insidious indifference to pain not our own.

Ethnography and Theory

Many papers are ethnographic gems, not divorced from theory. Most purely theoretical papers are overviews, that is, distinguished lectures that summarize the larger state of an art to which the speaker-author has contributed. The give-and-take between particular data and theory in the AA is persistent across approaches and subdisciplines. Many ethnographic papers explore social cohesion and social conflict, the latter linked to revising the culture concept to account for change and personal agency.

Gary Witherspoon's "Sheep in Navajo Culture and Social Organization" (1973, 75:1441–1446; this volume) explores the centrality of sheep in a value system inseparable from the operation of the herd. Despite only partial economic dependence on them, sheep represent personal identity, security, motherhood, and reproduction, with an attending moral responsibility for their care. The sheep economy is noncompetitive and communally organized.

Gail Lansman's "Ganienkeh: Symbol and Politics in an Indian-White Conflict" (1985, 87:826–839) laments the vagueness of symbolic anthropology and illustrates a public mobilization of symbols in the 1974 takeover (or repossession, depending on your point of view) of Mohawk land at Moss Lake. The standoff polarized rural upstate versus urban downstate New Yorkers. State minorities were assumed to be urban and all Mohawks were assumed to be traditionalists. Calvin Morrill's "The Customs of Conflict Management among Corporate Executives" (1991, 93:871–893) uses an ethnographic method to explore how bureaucratic elites at two American corporations (one national in scope, the other regional) handle conflict without confrontation. Studying up, as Laura Nader long ago suggested, deploys anthropological skills in our own society.

Elliott P. Skinner's "Political Conflict and Revolution in an African Town" (1972, 74:1208–1217) shows how colonial administration prevented the overt conflict of rural and modern urban social structures. Widespread acceptance of the fiction that chiefs no longer held power allowed both municipal and rural governments to use chiefly authority without challenging emergent urban power structures. Artificial stability now yields to flux until new forms develop.

Michael Verdon's "Where Have All the Lineages Gone? Cattle and Descent among the Nuer" (1982, 84:566–579) deconstructs the category of segmentary lineage on the grounds that its political consequences for the Nuer and Tallensi in the Sudan are quite different, with the latter producing a corporate entity in perpetuity. Nuer equilibrium depends more on demography than on descent groups, with flexible group membership enabling mobility.

Turning to the other side of the coin, theory backs off slightly from ethnographic particulars. Eric R. Wolf's distinguished lecture, "Facing Power — Old Insights, New Questions" (1990, 92:586–596; this volume), differentiates structural from tactical or organizational power and targets interpretive anthropology for avoiding questions of power in its political commitments. Only a political economy perspective can transcend a fragmented cultural analysis.

Clifford Geertz's distinguished lecture, "Anti Anti-Relativism" (1984, 86:263–278; this volume), laments the ill-defined concept of anthropological relativism, our discipline's greatest contribution to a larger public discourse. The real issue is "how to live with" cultural differences (265). Whatever the difficulties of applying the idea, it is indefensible in a cosmopolitan world to be against relativism in its sense of tolerance.

Roy A. Rappaport's distinguished lecture, "The Anthropology of Trouble" (1993, 95:295–303), relocates the core of anthropology to domestic research in order to "anthropologize . . . public discourse" (295) rather than politicize anthropology. We should make explicit our inevitable lack of value neutrality and force ourselves to function as subjects, not just as anthropologists. Biological and ecological maladaptations generate trouble.

Marvin Harris's distinguished lecture, "Anthropology and the Theoretical and Paradigmatic Significance of the Collapse of Soviet and Eastern European Communism" (1992, 94:295–305), identifies internal ethnic politics as the cause of downfall. There has been no test case for Marxism itself; although much of historical Marxism has proved inadequate, cultural Marxism or the primacy of infrastructure remains viable for anthropology. The Soviet system disintegrated because its own materialism selected against a political economy that impeded infrastructure performance.

Annette Weiner's distinguished lecture, "Culture and Our Discontents" (1995, 97:14–40), examines postmodernist poaching of the anthropological culture concept. Postmodernism is, for her, a useful term for taking stock in a time of transition. She laments the rivalry of AAA sections, rejects four-subfield unity, and proposes applying the "same subjectivity" to our disciplinary institutions as we do to the "worlds we research" (16). Boas long ago demonstrated the potential coexistence of politics within the academy. The new world disorder exposes and demystifies the "deepest discontents" of the anthropological concept of culture.

Paul Bohannan's distinguished lecture, "You Can't Do Nothing" (1980, 92:508–524), argues that the history of anthropology has only recently reached its appropriate historical context in worldwide colonialism. American internal colonialism persists and ethnology is more static than other fields in the escalating absence of tribal peoples. Anthropology is forced to navigate between sociobiology and the policy sciences.

Raymond Firth's distinguished lecture, "Spiritual Aroma: Religion and Politics" (1981, 83:282–301), brings British social anthropology into the AA, depicting a skeptical humanism fascinated by religion, which is about power. The Marxist metaphor of "spiritual aroma" inverts the priorities of capitalism.

Leonard B. Glick's "Types Distinct from Our Own: Franz Boas on Jewish Identity and Assimilation" (1982, 84:545–565; this volume) explores how Boas's rejection of Jewish cultural identity (what Boas calls merely the "shackles" of religious tradition) paralleled his insistence on biological plasticity and the falsity of group classification. Boas considered himself an assimilated German-American who could speak as an outsider about southern and eastern European immigration. Until the Nazi rise to power he defended his German homeland rather than defending the Jews.

Elvin Hatch's "Theories of Social Honor" (1989, 91:341–353; this volume) explodes the materialist idea that wealth and power matter everywhere in the same way. The rule-ruled dichotomy rapidly disintegrates into a continuous rank distribution, with status proving less real or functional than domination. Motivation is the critical factor, with a self-identity model most useful because it gives persons of low rank a stake in the system. Milhaly Csikszentmilhalyi and Stith Bennett's "An Exploratory Model of Play" (1971, 73:802–815) contrasts games of chance, strategy, and physical skills with play, holding social reality in abeyance and facilitating a self-actualizing paradox. Play is an important feature of evolution, one that distinguishes Homo sapiens.

Conclusion

The interpretivist trend that has dominated the final quarter of the century, both in anthropology and across the social sciences and humanities, has yet to reach closure. We have witnessed an evolution over the period nevertheless, from early 1970s flirtations with interpretation to 1980s denials of science by some and insistence on its importance by others. By the early 1990s anthropology was widely perceived (both within the discipline and outside it) to have rejected its own claims to expertise, the "being there" of fieldwork. Anthropologists could not seem to agree on the nature of their discipline or on the infallibility of their results. Ethics and epistemology seemed to lead many away from meaningful generalization (which to the discipline's detractors is synonymous with science). An agreed-upon middle ground between literary studies and the social sciences has remained an elusive goal. Boasian emphasis on "the Native point of view" and the observer effect that is inherent in social science research has predisposed many American anthropologists to experiment with the humanistic poles of their disciplinary heritage. Much has been said about babies and thrown-out bathwater. And yet, if the pages of the *AA* during this period are any indication, most anthropologists have continued doing anthropology, have continued to respond to new trends, and have continued to adapt them to particular research projects and abiding theoretical concerns. Interestingly, there are scientists and interpretivists in all subdisciplines just as there are papers and scholars crossing these traditional boundaries in the audience and in their framing of theoretical questions (if not in their detailed methods). Rumors of anthropology's demise, or even its fragmentation, appear to this observer to be considerably exaggerated.

Notes

1. The members of the Centennial Commission are: Regna Darnell (University of Western Ontario), chair; Lee D. Baker (Duke University); Jennifer Brown (University of Winnipeg); Raymond deMallie (Indiana University); Frederic W. Gleach (Cornell University); Jonathan Marks (University of North Carolina, Charlotte), and Stephen O. Murray (Instituto Obregón, San Francisco). Richard Handler (University of Virginia) served in the committee's early stages. Jane Hill, Louise Lamphere, Don Brenneis, and Carole Crumley have served ex officio as officers of the AAA. Susan Skomal, publications director, and Bill Davis, executive director, have facilitated for the AAA. Gary Dunham of the University of Nebraska Press has enabled the reissue of the volumes of earlier selected papers in the *Critical Studies in History of Anthropology* series edited by Stephen O. Murray and me.

2. Section publications include: *American Ethnologist*, *AES Monograph Series*;

Archaeological Papers of the AAA; *Transforming Anthropology* (Association of Black Anthropologists); *Voices* (Association for Feminist Anthropology); POLAR (Association for Political and Legal Anthropology); CSAS *Bulletin* (Central States Anthropological Society); *Anthropology and Education Quarterly*; *Museum Anthropology*; *Nutritional Anthropology*; *Culture and Agriculture*; *General Anthropology*; NAPA *Bulletin* (National Association of Student Anthropologists); *Teaching Anthropology: SACC Notes* (Society for Anthropology in Community Colleges); *Anthropology of Consciousness*; SAE *Bulletin* (Society for the Anthropology of Europe); *Anthropology of Work Review*; *Cultural Anthropology*; *Anthropology and Humanism* (Society for Humanistic Anthropology); *Journal of Latin American Anthropology*; SOLGAN (Society of Lesbian and Gay Anthropologists); *Journal of Linguistic Anthropology*; *Medical Anthropology Quarterly*; *Ethos* (Society for Psychological Anthropology); *City and Society* (Society for Urban, National, and Transnational Anthropology); and *Visual Anthropology Review*.

3. The Linguistic Society of America and its journal, *Language*, were established in 1925. The *American Journal of Physical Anthropology* became the organ of the American Association of Physical Anthropology in 1918 (n.s. 1943). Archaeology now resides primarily within the Society for American Archaeology, which split off from the AAA. *American Antiquity* was first published in 1935.

4. Laura Bohannan (1971–73); Robert A. Manners (1974–75); Richard B. Woodbury (1976–78); David L. Olmstead (1979–81); H. Russell Bernard (1982–85, 1986–89); Thomas C. Greaves (1985–86); Janet Dixon Keller (1990–93); Barbara and Dennis Tedlock (1993–97).

5. Stephen O. Murray (2001) documents that journal editors do not dramatically influence volume content toward their specializations.

6. Latin America, Europe, and the Near East each have their own sections of the AAA. Several sections concentrate on North American society. Asianists, Africanists, and Pacific specialists have societies that meet independently of the AAA.

References Cited

DeMille, Richard, ed.
1980 The Don Juan Papers. Santa Barbara CA: Ross-Erikson.

Fardon, Richard, ed.
1990 Localizing Strategies. Edinburgh: Scottish Academic Press.

Givens, David, and Timothy Jablonski.
1995 Survey of Anthropology PhDs. http://www/aaanet.org/surveys/95SURVEY.HTM

Goldschmidt, Walter.
1984 The Cultural Paradigm in the Post-War World. *In* June Helm, ed., Social Contexts of American Ethnology 1840–1984. Washington DC: American Anthropological Association, 164–174.

Hymes, Dell, ed.
1969 Reinventing Anthropology. New York: Random House.

Murray, Stephen O.

1994 Theory Groups and the Study of Language in North America. Amsterdam and Philadelphia: John Benjamins.

2001 Anthropology News.

Murphy, Robert F., ed.

1976 Introduction: 1–22. Selected Papers from the American Anthropologist 1946–70. Washington DC: American Anthropological Association.

Ortner, Sherry B.

1984 Theory in Anthropology since the Sixties. Comparative Studies in Society and History 26: 126–166.

Tierney, Patrick.

2000 Darkness in El Dorado: How Scientists and Journalists Devastated the Amazon. New York: Norton.

Trencher, Susan R.

2000 Mirrored Images: American Anthropology and American Culture 1960–1980. Westport CT: Bergin and Garvey.

Ritual, Sanctity, and Cybernetics

Roy A. Rappaport

VOL. 73, 1971, 59–76

I

The roles that ritual and sanctity play in communication, and in the regulation of the systems in which they participate are examined in this essay in an attempt to gain some additional understanding of the nature of religion.[1]

This essay differs from an earlier study I made of Tsembaga ritual (Rappaport 1967, 1968) in important ways. Whereas the earlier analysis focused upon the functions of ritual in a complex ecological system, the present attempts to elucidate those formal characteristics of Tsembaga ritual and belief—and through them, if possible, ritual and belief in general—which make them suitable to fulfill the functions the earlier analysis ascribed to them. Thus, although the arguments that I advance may have some generality, I shall have to allude to Tsembaga ethnography, and incorporate some of the earlier analysis. I ask the forbearance of those familiar with the earlier work, but promise to carry the discussion further. Moreover, coherence demands that some of the analysis published in the last chapter of *Pigs for the Ancestors* be incorporated into the present study.

It will be well, before proceeding, to make clear my use of such terms as "system," "regulate," and "control." I shall then review briefly some salient features of Maring ethnology and then discuss the formal characteristics of ritual that suit them for communication and regulatory functions. The discussion of ritual will lead to suggestions concerning the nature of sanctity and its role in communication and control.

II

I do not use the term "system" to designate collections of entities which share some ontological characteristic, as might be implied by such phrases as "belief system," or "kinship terminological system." The term "system" is meant merely to designate a collection of specified variables in which a change in the value or state of any one will result in a change in the value or state of at least one of the others. The ontological characteristics of the components of the physical world from which the variables are derived are irrelevant; we may include in the compass of a single system or subsystem variables abstracted from cultural, biological, and inorganic phenomena.

I use the terms "regulate" and "control" in a systemic, indeed a cybernetic, sense. A regulating mechanism, control mechanism or homeostat is one that maintains the values of one or more of the variables included in a system within a range or ranges that defines the continued existence of the system. Such ranges of viability may often be established empirically. Population size serves as a familiar example. We may be able to demonstrate, or at least have good reason for believing, that below a certain size a particular population will be too small to reproduce or defend itself, above a particular size it will destroy its subsistence base. The viable range, i.e., the set of possible states between these limits, is sometimes called the "goal range." Regulation is the process which maintains the value of the variable within the goal range, usually through negative feed-back. A familiar example from the universe of machines is the operation of the thermostat.

The terms "regulation" and "control" refer to operations which are central to "adaptation." Adaptation here refers to the processes by which organisms or groups of organisms, through responsive changes in their own states, structures, or compositions, maintain homeostasis in and among themselves in the face of both short term environment fluctuations and long term changes in the composition or structure of their environments.

III

We may now turn to the Tsembaga, one of about twenty politically autonomous local territorial groups of Maring speaking people living on the northern fall of the Bismarck Range in the Australian Trust Territory of New Guinea. They number about 200 people and their territory encompasses about three square miles of mountainside.

The Tsembaga participate in two distinct systems. First, they are a population in the ecological sense, that is, one of the components in a system of inter-species trophic (or feeding) exchanges occurring within a bounded area, Tsembaga territory. Conversely, Tsembaga territory and the biota inhabiting it (including the Tsembaga) constitute an ecosystem.

The Tsembaga participate in exchanges of women, valuables, and trade goods with other similar local groups occupying areas external to their territory. Another characteristic of relations between adjacent territorial groups is warfare, one of the processes by which land is redistributed among local groups and people redispersed over land. Thus, as the Tsembaga are participants in an ecosystem, a system of *localized inter-species* exchanges, so are they participants in a regional system, a system of *non-localized intra-species* exchanges.

Of course events in the local system affect events in the regional system and vice versa. Therefore these two systems are not separate systems but subsystems of a larger system which they together comprise. I have argued elsewhere (1967, 1968) that rituals, arranged in protracted cycles (up to twenty years), articulate the local and regional systems, and, furthermore, regulate relations within each of the subsystems and in the larger systems as a whole. To be more specific, I have interpreted the ritual cycles of the Tsembaga and other Maring as regulating mechanisms and have argued that their operation helps to maintain an undegraded biotic environment, limits fighting to frequencies which do not endanger the survival of the regional population, adjusts man/land ratios, facilitates trade, distributes local surpluses of pig throughout the regional population in the form of pork and assures to members of the local group rations of high quality protein.

We may begin an outline of the operation of the ritual cycle with the termination of warfare. Principal antagonists invariably are local groups, such as Tsembaga. Unless it has been driven off its land, when hostilities have ceased a local group ritually plants a shrub called *rumbim* at a traditional place. This act, symbolizing the connection of the group to its territory, is accompanied by a massive slaughter of pigs. Only juveniles survive; the rest are offered to the ancestors in reciprocation for their assistance in the fighting. But this sacrifice is not believed by the actors to discharge their debt to their deceased forebears, and the latter are told that when there are sufficient pigs a larger offering will be made to them. While they remain in debt to their ancestors the living cannot initiate new hostilities, for it is believed that martial success is impossible without the assistance of ancestors and that the assistance of the ancestors will not be forthcoming until they are repaid in pigs for their help in the last fight. A "truce of God" thus prevails until there are sufficient pigs to absolve the living of their debt to the dead. Thus, the number of pigs regarded as sufficient to repay the ancestors and the length of time it takes to acquire them are crucial factors in regulating the frequency of warfare.

Outside of the rituals associated with warfare and festivals, the slaughter and consumption of pigs is largely limited to the rituals associated with illness and injury. There are occasions in which it is likely that the affected organisms are experiencing psychological stress, and I have argued (Rappaport 1965:84ff) that reserving the limited amount of domestic pork available for consumption during stressful periods is highly functional for the Maring. Be this as it may, the amount of time required to accumulate sufficient pigs is obviously related to the success and well-being of the pigs' masters, since the slaughter of the beasts is associated with human misfortune. But, rapidly or slowly, the pig population does expand and sooner or later the pigs' ration of substandard sweet potatoes incidentally obtained in the course of harvesting for humans becomes insufficient, and additional acreage needs to be put into production especially for the pigs. The increment may be substantial. When the Tsembaga herd was at maximum in 1963, 36 percent of the acreage in production was devoted to the support of 170 pigs. The burden of the increased gardening falls upon women, and their complaints of overwork become increasingly strident as the number of animals in their charge increases. At the same time, garden invasions by pigs become more frequent and often lead to serious disputes. When the complaints of the women and the garden invasions become intolerable to a sufficient number of men to dominate the consensus there are sufficient pigs to repay the ancestors. To put this in ecological terms, there are sufficient pigs to repay the ancestors when the relationship of pigs to humans changes from one of mutualism to one of parasitism or competition. Empirical investigations indicate that this point lies below the carrying capacity of the territory for pigs (Rappaport 1968:93ff, 162ff, 295ff). When the herd reaches such a size (170 in 1962–1963), the *rumbim* is ritually uprooted and a year-long festival is staged, during which friendly groups are entertained from time to time and during which there are massive pig sacrifices which reduce the herd to tolerable size. This pork is then distributed to former allies. At the termination of its festival, a local group has fulfilled its obligations to ancestors (and allies) and is again free to open hostilities. The initiation of warfare is thus limited to once per ritual cycle.

The ritual cycle thus operates as a homeostat in the local subsystem by keeping such variables as the size of the pig population, women's labor, lengths of fallow periods, and other variables within viable ranges; it operates as a homeostat in the regional subsystem by regulating the frequency of warfare, while periodically allowing the expansion of more ecologically competent groups at the expense of those less competent. It further operates as a transducer — a device which transmits energy or information from one subsystem into another — for it articulates the local system to the regional system.

Our argument concerning sanctity demands that we examine more closely one aspect of the year-long festival, the entertainment of visiting groups. The Tsembaga entertained visiting groups on thirteen different occasions during their festival in 1962–1963. These occasions resemble in important ways events which seem to occur among a wide range of non-human animals.

First, they include massed epigamic, or courtship, displays (Wynne-Edwards 1962:17). Men dance in formations before the young women who are thereby acquainted with eligible males of local groups otherwise unfamiliar to them. The context also permits the young women to discriminate among this sample in terms of both endurance (signaled by how vigorously and how long a man dances) and wealth (signaled by the richness of a man's shell and feather finery).

More importantly, such massed dancing communicates information to the participants concerning the size of the groups. In many species of birds and insects such displays take place as a prelude to actions which adjust size or density (Wynne-Edwards 1962:16). Such is also the case among the Maring. The massed dancing of the visitors at a *kaiko* entertainment communicates to the hosts, while the *rumbim* truce is still in effect, information concerning the amount of support they may expect from the visitors in the aggression that they may embark upon following the termination of the pig festival.

There are no chiefs or other political authorities capable of commanding the support of a body of followers among the Maring, and whether or not to assist another group in warfare is a decision resting with each individual male. Allies are not recruited by appealing for help to other local groups as such. When a group is in need of military assistance, each of its members appeals to his cognatic and affinal kinsmen in other local groups. These kinsmen, in turn, urge other of their co-residents and kinsmen to "help them fight." The channels through which invitations to dance are extended are precisely those through which appeals for military support are issued. Dance invitations are not extended by one group to another, but from one kinsman to another. Those invited then urge their co-residents to "help them dance." Dancing and fighting are regarded as in some sense equivalent. This equivalence is expressed in the similarity of some pre-fight and pre-dance rituals, and the Maring say that those who come to dance come to fight. The size of a visiting dancing contingent is consequently taken to indicate the number and strength of warriors whose assistance may be expected in the next round of warfare.

IV

We may now examine those aspects of rituals which suit them to function as homeostats and communication devices. I shall take up communications first, because it is the more inclusive category and the more fundamental to ritual.

Let us note first that the term "ritual" is not confined to religious practices. Freud (1907) applied the closely related or even synonymous term "ceremony" to the behavior of some neurotics as well as to religious rituals, in an attempt to elucidate their putative similarities, and the latest Webster International Dictionary widens the perspective further when it informs us that the term "ritual" in its broadest sense refers to "any practice . . . regularly repeated in a set precise manner so as to satisfy one's sense of fitness . . ." (1965, 1961).

This definition, which easily subsumes the rites of the faithful, the performances of headwaiters and the obsessional behavior of some neurotics, explicitly identifies three aspects of rituals: namely, that they are composed of conventional, even stereotyped movements or postures, that they are performed "regularly" (at times fixed by clock, calendar or specified circumstance), and that they have affective or emotional value. There is, in addition, an implication that at least some of the components of rituals, in some instances even entire rituals, are non-instrumental in the sense that they do not contribute directly to the biological or economic well-being of the performer.

A rather wide range of human behavior may thus be labeled ritual but the term has even more general application. Ethologists have also used the term ritual to refer to animal displays, some of which bear close formal resemblance to human rituals. Animal rituals are likely to involve stereotyped, apparently non-instrumental postures and movements, and, as apparently useless paraphernalia are often manipulated in human rituals, so apparently useless biological structures are often waved, vibrated, suffused with color, or expanded in animal rituals. Like human rituals, animal rituals seem to occur under specified circumstances or at fixed times, and some animal rituals, like some human rituals, occur only in special places. As the faithful of a certain persuasion congregate on Sunday mornings only in a certain church, so the starlings congregate at dusk only in certain trees.

Ethologists have generally interpreted animal rituals as communication events. In light of such an interpretation even the very quality of the grotesque characteristic of some stereotyped ritual posturing becomes understandable. For a signal to be effective it must be distinguishable from ordinary instrumental activity. The more bizarre the ritual movement of structures the more easily may they be recognized as ritual.

Ritual to the ethologist, then, is a mode of communication distinguished from other modes of communication by its distinctive codes, namely conventionalized display. Now we have just seen that there is a close formal resemblance between human and animals rituals, and when we recall that Tsembaga rituals could easily be accommodated in categories developed for classifying animal displays we note that there is also a functional resemblance. As animal rituals are communication events, so are human rituals. It goes without saying that two examples drawn from the ritual of a single human group do not provide a sufficient sample for propositions of such a general nature, but no space is available to marshal further evidence. We can only assert that although in some human rituals aesthetic, ethical, or affective elements are emphasized there is in *all* human ritual (as well as in all animal rituals) a communication component. Accordingly, for our present purposes I define ritual, both animal and human, as conventional acts of display through which one or more participants transmit information concerning their physiological, psychological, or sociological states either to themselves[2] or to one or more other participants. Such a definition is hardly radical; similar ones have been adopted by Wallace (1966:236), Leach (1954:14), and Goffman (1956).

Both the content and the occurrence of rituals are important in communication. As far as content is concerned, many writers have dealt with ways in which information concerning social arrangements are represented (communicated) in the course of public rituals, and we need not discuss the matter here. But "pattern" or "structural" information is not all that is transmitted by the contents of rituals. So is quantitative information.[3]

We may note first that despite the stereotypic nature of rituals there is considerable room for variation in performance. Different numbers of organisms may participate, for instance, and in some displays this is the whole point of the exercise (Wynne-Edwards, 1962:16ff, passim). Nor is quantitative variation in performance limited to numbers of participants. In the potlatches of the Northwest Coast and in the pig feasts of some Melanesians rather precise information concerning social status and political influence is communicated by variations in the number of valuables distributed. Indeed, it might be suggested that these rituals are public counting devices operating by principles similar to those employed in analogue computers. In these machines numbers are represented by directly metrical quantities, such as voltages or rotations of wheels. In epideictic displays populations are represented by samples of themselves. In the potlatch representation is also directly metrical if less intrinsic. Here political influence is represented by numbers of commodities such as blankets and copper plaques. We may note here an additional possible function of these rituals. They not only count, they translate aspects of phenomena which are not themselves directly metrical into directly metrical and therefore comparable terms. It becomes easy to compare the political influence of two Melanesian big men when they are engaged in competitive feasting. One simply counts the valuables thrown into the struggle (see Oliver 1955).

If it is obvious that quantitative information can be transmitted through the content of ritual, it is perhaps less obvious that qualitative information may be transmitted by ritual occurrence. The mere occurrence of a non-calendrical ritual may be a signal. Since any ritual included in the repertoire of a people can, at a particular time, only be occurring or not occurring, ritual occurrence can be regarded as a binary mechanism or variable (a mechanism or variable having only two possible states). As such, occurrence can transmit binary information, which is qualitative information, information of a "yes-no" rather than a "more-less" sort. Of considerable interest and importance here, however, is that although the occurrence of a non-calendrical ritual may transmit a *"yes-no" signal*, it may have been triggered by the achievement or violation of a particular state or range of states of a *"more-less" variable* (i.e., one whose value can proceed through a continuous range of states), or even by the achievement or violation of a complex state or range of complex states involving the relationship among a number of such variables. Thus, the occurrence of the ritual may be a simple qualitative representation of complex quantitative information.

The importance of this aspect of ritual communication may be illustrated by reference to the ritual uprooting of the *rumbim* plant. The occurrence of this ritual, which commences the festival culminating the cycle, indicates or signals that a local ecosystem has achieved a certain complex quantitative state. The quantitative information that the qualitative or yes-no ritual statement (uprooting the *rumbim*) summarizes is not available to populations other than the one performing the ritual, and even if it were it would be subject to perhaps erroneous interpretation. Being summarized are not merely the constantly fluctuating values of a number of separate variables such as numbers of pigs, acreage in production, garden yields, settlement pattern, number of women, and clinical status of the human population, but the continually changing relationships among them. It would be difficult indeed to translate quantitative information concerning the constantly fluctuating state of the local subsystem directly into terms that would be unambiguously meaningful to other populations in the regional subsystem. This difficulty is overcome if a mechanism is available to summarize the quantitative information and translate it into a qualitative signal.

Uprooting the *rumbim* is such a mechanism, for its occurrence signals *unambiguously* that the local subsystem has achieved a certain state and that, therefore, the local population may now undertake previously proscribed actions likely to affect the regional subsystem. The absence of ambiguity from this message derives from the binary character of the ritual transduction device, which reduces a great complex mass of more-less information to a simple yes-no statement. In the ordinary course of things such a statement is free of ambiguity.

We may further note by way of clarification that the more-less information with which our illustration is concerned — information about labor, pigs, gardens, soils — is not directly meaningful in the regional system which is concerned with warfare. By "not directly meaningful" I mean that it cannot effect non-random proportional changes in the regional system. But the ritual, as transducer, summarizes and translates this quantitative information into a simple non-ambiguous and meaningful statement: "the non-belligerent is becoming a potential belligerent." Control transduction in physiological systems also seems to rely heavily upon binary mechanisms and information precisely because of the difficulties inherent in translating quantitative information directly from one subsystem to another (Goldman 1960).

In sum, both ritual content and ritual occurrence are involved in communication. While content is particularly important in the transmission of quantitative or more-less information and is of significance mainly *within* single systems or subsystems, occurrence is particularly important in the transmission of qualitative or yes-no information, and is important in the transmission of information *across the borders* of separate and unlike systems or subsystems.[4]

Let us now turn briefly to the regulatory functions of Maring rituals. Simple regulatory mechanisms typically perform three operations. First is the detection of changes in the state of the regulated variable. In a thermostat this operation is accomplished by a column of mercury or a bimetallic bar. Second, the value of the regulated variable is compared with a reference, or ideal, value. In the thermostat this value is fed in through a dial. Third, if there is a discrepancy between the reference and the detected value an error signal is transmitted to an effector, which initiates a corrective program. In the thermostat, the effector is a switch which turns the corrective program — heat from a furnace — on and off.

The Maring ritual cycle is more complicated than the thermostat not because more fundamental types of control operation are involved but because more variables are regulated. Whereas the thermostat regulates only temperature, the Maring ritual cycle regulates directly the frequency of warfare, the size of pig populations and population density, and through these variables yet others, such as acreage in production, women's labor, and lengths of fallow.

The picture is further complicated by a kind of economy of form. In some instances one ritual performs several control operations. For instance, the uprooting of the *rumbim*, insofar as it involves the entertainment of visiting dancers, operates as a detector with respect to military support. Insofar as it opens the way for animal sacrifices throughout the festival, it affects pig herd size; insofar as the slaughter of pigs accompanies it, this ritual incorporates a portion of the corrective program, i.e., the set of actions undertaken to correct deviations in herd size from a "reference" or "ideal" value. But the aim here is not to expand an analysis presented in detail elsewhere and sketched briefly earlier in this essay of the part that rituals play in the regulation of the ecological and regional relations of the Tsembaga. It is rather to discuss the formal characteristics of rituals which make them suitable to fulfill such functions.

Both ritual content and ritual occurrence are important in regulatory operation, and their importance rests upon the same formal characteristics that make them important in communication. This is hardly surprising since regulation is often a function of communication.

As far as contents are concerned, it is perhaps sufficient to recall that display, which may be the distinguishing characteristic of ritual, often offers opportunities for representing the states of important variables, such as population size, numbers of available marriage partners, the numbers of men who may provide military support, the political importance of different men. Thus, ritual contents are likely to be of particular importance in the operation of detection, the operation of assessing the states of critical variables. Insofar as the values of variables as detected in displays are compared during the ritual with reference or ideal values presumably derived from elsewhere (for instance, men's expectations or notions about how many men *should* be in a particular visiting dance contingent, or how many are necessary if aggression is to be undertaken), ritual contents are also important in the comparator operation.

As in the case of communication, the place of ritual occurrence in regulation is less obvious than the place of ritual contents. It may be observed first that in mechanical, electronic and physiological systems in which the states of other components may vary through a continuous range the output states of the regulator, that is, the state of its effector, is limited to two. As noted, the thermostat effector is a switch which, in response to a violation of an acceptable temperature range, goes on or off. The operation of a binary regulating device is remarkably simple. Indeed, its response to fluctuations in the state of a regulated component is the simplest conceivable: if change exceeds certain limits the regulator simply switches from one to the other of its two possible states.

Perhaps the very simplicity of the binary regulator minimizes the likelihood of its malfunction, but a more subtle aspect of binary operation is, I believe, of greater interest and importance. As I have argued elsewhere (1968:234), "Binary control eliminates the possibility of error from one phase of system operation: i.e., with binary operation an inappropriate response to a system-endangering change in the value of a variable can not be selected from a set of possible responses because the set of possible responses has only one member. To put it in anthropomorphic terms, the binary regulating mechanism, once it receives a signal that a variable has transgressed its tolerable range, does not have to decide what to do. It can do only one thing or nothing at all."

This statement seems to be as applicable to Tsembaga ritual as to mechanical regulators. Despite the complexity of the system its regulatory operations are simple, for the programs undertaken to correct deviations of variables from their acceptable or "goal" ranges are fixed. All that the actors need decide is whether in fact such a deviation has occurred. The Tsembaga reach such decisions through discussions, through which a consensus eventually forms.

While Maring ritual regulation benefits from its very simplicity it must be recognized that it also suffers from simplicity's limitations. Consensus concerning deviations from acceptable conditions form slowly, and corrective programs are both inflexible and unlikely to be proportional to deviations. While such sluggish and imprecise regulation has been sufficient to maintain the Tsembaga and other Maring in a relatively stable environment it is likely that the novel challenges presented frequently in rapidly changing environments might require more rapid and more flexible regulatory mechanisms, such as discrete human authorities occupying recognized offices. Polynesian chiefs, for instance, are more expensive to keep than ritual cycles and can make more mistakes. But they can respond to system-endangering changes in the environment with more sensitivity, speed, precision, and flexibility than ritual cycles.

V

Rituals, then, because of certain formal characteristics, are suitable for both communication and regulatory functions. But no *religious* notion inheres in our definition of ritual, nor does any religious belief seem to be vital to the functions which we have ascribed to ritual. Why, then, is it that religious beliefs should so often be associated with rituals and what indeed do we mean by religious beliefs? A comparison of religious rituals with the secular rituals of men and animals proves helpful here.

Earlier I underlined formal characteristics common to all rituals. Here I emphasize an important difference between religious and secular rituals: in the secular case the semantic content of the ritual is exhausted by the social information transmitted in the ritual. For example, when a baboon presents his rump, he transmits a statement of submission to a dominant animal. There are no meanings to be discovered in the content of this ritual other than that of submission. To put this a little differently, the semantic content of the ritual and the semantic content of the messages transmitted between those participating in the ritual are coextensive. This is also true of such human rituals as bowing and saluting.

Religious rituals seem to be different. For example, the culturally avowed purpose of rituals in which the Maring transmit messages about military support is to honor deceased ancestors. The messages transmitted in the ritual and the purposes of the ritual are thus distinct from each other. Since the ostensible purpose of the ritual is recognized in its contents, we may obviously say that the semantic content of the ritual and the semantic content of the social messages transmitted between participants in the ritual are *not* coextensive. Such lack of coextensiveness is characteristic, perhaps definitive, of religious rituals. In addition to messages concerning the physiological, psychological, and sociological states of the participants, a religious ritual *always* includes an additional term, such as a statement about or to spirits, who are usually, if not always, associated with the culturally avowed purpose of the ritual.

That there is semantic differentiation between messages and statements of purpose does not mean that the two are unrelated. They are related in an important way. Attention to the purpose of the ritual sanctifies the messages which are transmitted within it.

It may seem that this is a roundabout way to come to a shopworn definition of the religious as the sacred. But the procedure has not been an attempt merely to show that religious rituals are sacred while others are not, but to show that the sanctity of religious rituals stands in a certain relation to the communication which occurs in the rituals. Before returning to this point, I want to suggest that since the essence of ritual is communication, and since religious ritual is presumably found only among humans, there is likely to be a connection between sanctity and the special characteristics of human communication.

Linguists and ethologists, I think, generally agree that the most important distinction between human and animal signaling lies in the relationship of signals to their referents. I believe that this aspect of communication events distinguishes human from animal ritual as nicely as it does language from mere affective vocalization. This becomes clear in comparisons of formally similar rituals among men and beasts, for instance, the epigamic displays of peacocks or European ruffs on the one hand and New Guinea Highlanders on the other. In both, special feather paraphernalia adorning males is moved in stereotyped ways in the presence of females as a prelude to mating. But inasmuch as the peacock grew his fan himself, it is plausible to assume that the rustling of the fan is as much a part of his sexual arousal as his tumescence. His display, that is, is related to his arousal as a distant nimbus is to forthcoming rain. It is a perceptible aspect of an event indicating the presence of other imperceptible aspects of the same event. It is, in other words, a "sign."

Obviously, the relationship of the signal to the event in the human ritual is different. The waving of bird plumes and dancing are not intrinsic to the interest of the Maring dancer in women. They are merely arbitrary indications of that interest. As such the signal is not related to the referent as the nimbus is to rain, but as the word "rain" is to actual precipitation. In other words, it is a "symbol."

The advantages of symbolic over non-symbolic communication are so enormous that some anthropologists have claimed that the emergence of the symbol can be compared in novelty and importance to the emergence of life. With symbolic communication an unlimited variety of messages may be transmitted through the combination of a very small number of basic units, and discourse upon past, future, distant, and imaginary events becomes possible. These advantages have been thoroughly discussed by many authors and need not be belabored here. The point I want to make is that considering the fundamental importance of symbolic communication surprisingly little attention has been paid to a problem which is a concomitant of its very virtues, a problem which is central to our present concerns.

When communication is limited to signs, that is, when the signal is intrinsic to its referent, it is impossible for the signal to occur in the absence of its referent or for it not to occur in the presence of its referent. The implication is that it is impossible for lies to be transmitted by signs. Misinterpretation, misreading of received information, is of course possible, but the willful transmission of false information is not.

Lying seems possible if and only if a signal is not intrinsic to its referent. A Maring, for instance, can indicate an interest in women when he has no such interest. If this seems trivial, note that he can also indicate a willingness to help in warfare when he has no such intention, and similarly a group can plant *rumbim* when it does not plan to leave off warfare. Lies are the natural offspring of symbols. They are transmitted by symbolic communication and symbolic communication only. Although there seems to be some very limited use of symbols by infrahuman animals and some instances of possible lying among them have been observed[5] we can assert with considerable confidence that although man is not, perhaps, the world's only liar he is surely the world's foremost liar. Certainly his reliance upon symbolic communication exceeds that of other animals to such an extent that it is probably for man alone that the transmission of false information becomes a serious problem.

His very survival may be involved. It is plausible to argue that the survival of any population depends upon social interactions characterized by some minimum degree of orderliness[6] and that orderliness depends upon communication. But communication is effective only if the recipients of messages are willing to accept, as being in at least some minimum degree reliable, the messages which they receive. If they are unwilling or unable to give credence to received information, it is plausible to assume that their responses to particular stimuli will approach randomness. To the extent that actions are random they are unpredictable and are thus likely to elicit further apparently random responses on the parts of other actors. Randomness begets greater randomness, reducing orderliness more and more, perhaps eventually to such a degree that the population could not fulfill its biological needs. Credibility gaps are extremely dangerous, and societies which rely upon symbolic communication are faced with the problem of assuring some minimum degree of both credibility and credence in the face of the ever-present possibility of falsehood.[7]

Concerning some messages there may be little problem. It is possible, for instance, to transmit the proposition $1 + 1 = 3$, but the recipient of such a message has at his disposal a set of logical operations for verifying or falsifying such a statement. Given the meaning assigned to the terms, $1 + 1$ *always* equals two; to deny it, as does the statement $1 + 1 = 3$, is to be self-contradictory and therefore false. Similarly, we might have little difficulty with a statement such as the application of heat to liquid water causes it to solidify as ice. Such a statement, while not internally illogical, as is $1 + 1 = 3$, could again be invalidated empirically. But much socially important information is concerned not with the laws pertaining to variables, but with their contemporary states, and their contemporary states usually can not be ascertained by extrapolation from earlier experience, even when the earlier experience can be framed in terms of empirical law (for example, to know from experience that ice melts if sufficient heat is applied to it says nothing about the temperature of a particular body of H_2O at the present time). In sum, the recipients of messages concerning the states of variables are not always in a position to perform the operations necessary to verify or falsify either empirically or logically the information upon which they must act. In some instances, indeed, there may be no known operations of verification. This is particularly true and particularly important with respect to social commitments. For example, how do the hosts at a Maring festival know that those who have come to dance will come to fight? There seems to be no procedure by which their statements of commitment can be verified. How, then, can they be depended upon?

Let us be reminded that this message is transmitted in the course of a religious ritual, a ritual that has a purpose to honor dead ancestors, distinct from its message concerning military support. It is thus plausible to assume a belief on the part of at least some of the participants in the existence of deceased ancestors; to assume otherwise would make nonsense of the proceedings. We can thus say that fundamental to Maring religious rituals are such propositions as "Deceased ancestors persist as sentient beings."

Now statements such as the ancestors are alive and well in the other world are neither logically necessary truths nor are they subject to empirical confirmation or disconfirmation. Yet they are taken to be *unquestionably* true. Indeed, to paraphrase some theologians and philosophers (Bochenski 1965; Hick 1963), it is this characteristic rather than substantive content that is the criterion of religious discourse; since religious discourse is sacred discourse I take this characteristic to be the criterion of sanctity as well. *Sanctity*, I am asserting, *is the quality of unquestionable truthfulness imputed by the faithful to unverifiable propositions.* Sanctity thus is not ultimately a property of physical or metaphysical objects, but of discourse about such objects. It is not, for instance, the divinity of Christ, but the assertion of his divinity, which is sacred.

Following this line I suggest that it is not its substance which distinguishes religion from other aspects of human life, but rather the sacred nature of its assertions. The term religion, in my view, refers to public discourse which includes at least one sacred statement and the conventional social actions undertaken with respect to this discourse.

While sanctity inheres ultimately in such non-material propositions as "The Godhead is a trinity," setting them above any doubt, it penetrates to (sanctifies) sentences concerning material objects and activities.

Tight theological discourse may serve as the vehicle for transporting sanctity from an ultimate sacred proposition such as "The lord our God the lord is one" to sentences such as "Eating pork is evil," or "Pork may not be eaten," but the connection may be merely an association in time or space; that is, the connection may be ritualistic rather than linguistic. Messages such as "we will lend you military support," or "we have renounced warfare," when they are transmitted in a religious ritual, and are thus sanctified, are taken to be true, or at least sufficiently reliable to serve as the basis of important social action. Sanctity, although it inheres ultimately in unverifiable non-material propositions, is socially important as meta-statement about assertions of a material nature, such as "we will support you in warfare" or of a partly material nature such as "giving is blessed." Statements, all of whose terms are material, may be amenable to verification, but the receivers of messages containing such statements may be in no position to verify them. However, *to sanctify statements is to certify them.*

It would be naive to assert that sanctification insures the truth of messages. We all know, for instance, that people lie under oath. But it is also unnecessary to claim that sanctity eliminates falsehood, although it may help. Experience does inform us that most people are loath to sanctify information they know to be false. However, more weight should be given to the complimentary point: people are more likely to accept sanctified than unsanctified messages as true. Insofar as they do, their responses to these messages will tend to be non-random, and therefore predictable. It is not necessary that the messages be at all times in fact true. What is necessary for the survival of populations is that the social interactions of its members be in some minimum degree orderly. The acceptance of messages as true, whether or not they are, contributes to this orderliness. Indeed, I have been arguing that it makes this orderliness possible and, following a lead of Bateson's (1951:212ff), it may be claimed that belief, insofar as it results in non-random actions which lead to predictable responses, creates orderliness. To put this in other terms, the acceptance of messages as true has a result on social responses similar to that of self-fulfilling prophecy. Whereas in the case of the self-fulfilling prophecy an event is the function of its prediction, the validity of certain messages is a function of belief in them (Bateson 1951). Belief in them in the absence of evidence may be a function of their sanctification; as far as informing behavior is concerned, sanctity forms an additional[8] member of the set which also includes the necessary truth of logic and empirical truth of experience.

VI

Inasmuch as regulation depends upon communication, questions concerning the relationship between sanctity and communication are questions concerning the relationship between sanctity and regulation. But a large body of questions remains concerning the sanctification of particular regulatory mechanisms.

It may be observed first that religious discourse can include sentences concerning almost anything, including regulatory mechanisms. Indeed, it may be that sentences concerning regulation form the class of sentences most commonly sanctified. But this raises an important question. Although it may be that the operation of some regulatory mechanisms — even entire control hierarchies[9] — are dependent upon their sanctification and that their sanctity derives from their association with ultimate sacred propositions, upon what does the unquestionable status of these unverifiable propositions rest, and how is this status maintained?

In some societies, force is employed. But where coercion is relied upon to support propositions for which sanctity is claimed, it is coercion rather than sanctity upon which the operation of the control hierarchy depends. I wish to confine discussion at this point to systems distinguished by the absence or virtual absence of institutionalized differences in coercive ability between individuals or social segments, a state of affairs not uncommon among horticultural and hunting and gathering peoples. It is in such egalitarian societies that the importance of religious experience is clearest.

Although secular information of direct social import is transmitted within many religious rituals, religious rituals are undertaken implicitly or explicitly with respect to sacred propositions. While participants do not always experience strong emotion in the course of a ritual, ritual participation probably does affect the emotional states of the faithful at least some of the time. While some religions emphasize ecstasy, others cultivate serenity, and yet others involve "feelings of awe." All that seems to be common to religious experience generally is that it is ineffable, that is to say, non-discursive.

The importance of the non-discursive aspect of religious experience cannot be exaggerated. Inasmuch as the experience is non-discursive it

cannot be falsified. The truth of such an experience is sufficiently demonstrated by its mere occurrence; it cannot be discredited by the discourse of the conscious mind. It happens, it is felt, and it therefore
carries with it a subjective quality of truth (James 1902). Since the experience is a response to the enunciation of a sacred proposition or occurs
in a place or in a ritual associated with such a proposition, that proposition partakes of the same sense of truth. In other words, ultimate sacred
propositions are taken to be unquestionably true because their enunciation in ritual or in the symbols kept in holy places elicits from the faithful
a non-discursive, and therefore unfalsifiable, affirmation. Moreover, when
this affirmation is given by participation in a public ritual, it is thereby
transformed into a discursive statement (which might be rendered "I or
we affirm the sacred proposition") transmissible to other participants. As
already argued, the latter are likely to accept such messages as true
because of the sacred context in which they are transmitted. The cir-
cularity of this operation need not trouble us because it does not trouble
the faithful; indeed, they are unlikely to be aware of it. Ritual, thus, not
only invokes in the participants private religious experiences, it provides
a mechanism for translating these private experiences into messages of
social import; it also provides a means for certifying these messages.

The outlines of an encompassing cybernetic loop may now be suggested. Inasmuch as religious experience is an intrinsic part of the more
inclusive emotional dynamics of the organism, and inasmuch as the
emotional dynamics of an organism must be closely related to its material state, it is plausible to assume that religious experiences are affected
by material conditions. But the latter are, particularly in primitive societies, in some degree a function of the operation of the control hierarchy which the religious experience itself supports. Thus the willingness, indeed the ability, of the members of a congregation to affirm
through religious experience the ultimate sacred propositions which
sanctify the control hierarchy may be in considerable measure a function
of the effectiveness of the hierarchy in maintaining equilibria in and
among those variables which define their material well-being in the long
run, and thus adaptation. That is, if malfunctions in the control hierarchy adversely affect for protracted periods the states of social and
ecological variables bearing directing upon the material well-being of
the congregation, its members are likely to become, first, unable to
affirm through private religious experience the ultimate sacred propositions supporting the control hierarchy and, second, perhaps later, un-

willing even to participate in the rituals relating to them. Sooner or later, regulatory mechanisms themselves must be adjusted if men are not to seek new gods. It seems that ultimate sacred propositions and the control hierarchies which they support must be compatible with the affective processes of the communicants. This in itself could have corrective implications.

But if regulatory mechanisms or entire control hierarchies are sanctified, and that which is sanctified is taken to be unquestionably true, how is change possible?

Three aspects of religious discourse are significant with respect to change. The first is that the ultimate sacred sentences are propositions; the second is that they usually contain no material terms. That they are propositions prevents them from containing specific directives; if they contain no material terms they are prevented from becoming irrevocably bound to any particular social form. This means that the association of specific directives and social forms with ultimate sacred statements is not intrinsic, but is rather the product of interpretive acts. Any product of interpretation allows reinterpretation, but reinterpretation does not challenge ultimate sacred statements; it merely disputes previous interpretations.

The third characteristic of religious discourse of importance here is that it is often, if not usually, cryptic. In some cases the ultimate sacred statements are themselves cryptic; in others they may seem clear, but they are abstracted from cryptic contexts such as myths or the reports of revelations, and an apocryphal quality is often characteristic of the discourse which sanctifies sentences concerning particular social forms or containing specific directives by connecting them to ultimate sacred propositions. The importance of reducing ambiguity and vagueness in messages of social import was earlier noted. In contrast, it is perhaps necessary that considerable ambiguity and vagueness cloak the discourse from which sanctification flows. If a proposition is going to be taken to be unquestionably true, it is important that no one understand it. Lack of understanding insures frequent reinterpretation.

An important implication of such change through reinterpretation is that ultimate sacred propositions must remain non-specific with respect to particular regulatory mechanisms or processes. A possible malfunction of sanctification may be noted in this connection. It sometimes happens that sentences directly involved in regulation (thus including material terms and sometimes cast in the form of explicit directives) are taken not merely as sanctified by ultimate sacred propositions but as themselves ultimate sacred propositions. When this occurs, the control hierarchy becomes highly resistant to adjustment through reinterpretation with perhaps disastrous results. Possible modern instances of such confusion in the level of sanctity to which sentences are to be assigned are to be found in the resistance of the Vatican to the use of mechanical and chemical birth control devices, and perhaps also in its insistence upon clerical celibacy. To an outsider, it seems that both birth control devices and clerical marriage could be made acceptable through reinterpretation without challenge to dogma.

Although sanctification is subject to malfunctions, it may be asserted that sanctity contributes to the maintenance of systemic integrity even through changes in systemic structure and composition. Indeed, it may make this maintenance possible. Thus if the term "adaptation" is given the meaning earlier suggested, then the concept of the sacred is surely an important component of human adaptation.

VII

The sacred, we have argued, has played an important role in the adaptation of technologically simple communities to their social, biotic, and physical environments. But the role of the sacred changes with changing political circumstances, and these changes in turn seem in considerable degree to be a function of technological development.

It has already been noted that sentences concerning a wide variety of regulatory mechanisms may be sanctified. Among the Maring, for instance, most sentences are instructions for corrective programs, for example, sentences such as "the ancestors demand the slaughter of all adult and adolescent pigs during the festival." In other societies sanctification seems to invest sentences concerning authorities or regulatory agencies rather than specific programs, sentences such as "the chief has great mana," or "Henry is by grace of God King."

Although we, and perhaps the faithful, cast such sentences in the declarative, they imply that the directives of the regulatory agencies or authorities to which they allude should or must be obeyed. If political power is taken to be the product (in an arithmetic sense, much as force is the product of mass times acceleration) of [men] $\times$ [resources] $\times$ [organization] (Bierstadt 1950), it would seem that as far as securing compliance with directives is concerned, sanctity operates as a functional alternative to political power among some of the world's peoples. Indeed, if authorities are taken to be loci in communications networks from which directives emanate we may be able to discern in history and ethnography a continuum from societies, such as the Maring, that are regulated by sacred conventions in the absence or near absence of human authorities through societies in which highly sanctified authorities have little actual power (such as Polynesian chiefs), to societies in which authorities have great power but less sanctity. It would be plausible to expect this continuum to correlate roughly with technological development, for advanced technology places in the hands of authorities coercive instruments that are not only effective but also likely to be unavailable to those subject to them.

Our argument implies that the development of technology disrupts the cybernetics of adaptation. In the technologically undeveloped society, authority is maintained by sanctification, but sanctity itself is maintained by religious experience which is responsive to the effectiveness of the control hierarchy in maintaining variables defining adaptation in viable ranges. In the technologically developed society authority is freed, to the extent that technology has provided it with coercive instruments, from the constraints imposed by the need to maintain its sanctity and therefore from the corrective operations that the maintenance of sanctity implies.

This is not to say that authorities even in technologically advanced societies dispense entirely with sanctity. It is to say that the relationship between sanctity and authority changes. Previously a characteristic of the discourse associated with the regulation of the entire system, sanctity comes more and more to be concentrated in the discourse of a subsystem, "the church." When it is so confined, sacred discourse is likely to continue to ratify authority, but it tends also to become decreasingly concerned with the environment of the here and now and increasingly concerned with ethics and with the environment of the hereafter, the promise of which stirs the meek to religious experience. Religious experience, however, and the rituals in which it occurs, previously part of an encompassing corrective loop, are eventually left with little more than certain functions long recognized by students of society: they reduce anxieties produced by stressors over which the faithful have little or no control, and they contribute to the discipline of social organization (see, for example, Homans 1941:172). To the extent that the discourse of religion, religious ritual and religious experience contribute to the maintenance of orderliness and the reduction of anxiety without contributing to the correction of the factors producing the anxiety and disorder they are not adaptive but pathological. Indeed, their operation seems to resemble that of neuroses (see, for example, Freud 1907).

Whereas in the technologically undeveloped system authority is contingent upon sanctification, in technologically more developed societies sanctity becomes an instrument of authority. Compliance and docility are cultivated more efficiently and less expensively by religious experiences inspired by hopes of post-mortem salvation than by the coercion of police and inquisitions. Yet, although force may remain hidden, and although religious experience may be encouraged, in some systems the unquestionable status of the discourse for which sanctity is claimed rests ultimately upon force. In such societies authority is no longer contingent upon sanctity; the sacred, or discourse for which sanctity is claimed, has become contingent upon authority. It is interesting to recall here a distinction de Rougemont (1944) made some years ago between ordinary lies, the transmission of messages known by the sender to be untrue, and those lies which tamper with the very canons of truth. To these, in consideration of the devil's putative proclivity for appearing to be what he is not, de Rougemont applied the picturesque label "diabolical lies." It may not be inappropriate to place in this category assertions of sanctity for discourse the unquestionable status of which rests ultimately upon force while appearing to rest upon non-discursive affirmation, and which forms part of a pathology while appearing to confer advantages upon those who give it credence.

But although sanctity may become degraded in the churches of technologically developed societies, "true sanctity," that uniting the organism through its affective life to processes which may correct social and ecological malfunctions, remains a continuing possibility. Throughout history revitalistic movements have emerged in streets, in universities, in fields among men sensing, and perhaps suffering from, the malfunction of control hierarchies that cannot reform themselves. In the early stages of such movements, at least, the unquestionable status of ultimate propositions rests upon affirmation through the religious experiences of the participants who believe that they are participating in corrective action. Sometimes they are mistaken. Although such movements have not infrequently been more disruptive than that to which they are a response, they may nevertheless be regarded as one of the processes through which cybernetic systems including men, and sometimes other living things as well, rid themselves of the pathology of unresponsiveness.

VIII

This discussion has assumed the existence of a full-blown concept of sanctity. Another set of questions might be asked concerning the origin of the sacred, for it does not seem to be logically entailed by symbolic communication, as does falsehood.

Waddington (1961) has argued that before a man or animal can function as a unit in a proto-cultural or cultural system he must be prepared for the role of receiver or acceptor of socially transmitted information. A recent lead provided by Erikson (1968:713ff) suggests that we examine very closely in this regard the phylogeny of rituals of ontogeny, paying particular attention to their affective component. Experimental and clinical evidence suggests that among the higher vertebrates if the infant does not learn certain things at certain times ("sensitive periods," Hinde 1966:395ff) he has difficulty learning them at all and his later learning of other material is also likely to be impaired (Scott 1964:234ff). This early leaning is social in that it requires other organisms, and communication in some sense is always involved. In discussing human infants Erikson notes that this early communication takes place in "daily rituals of greeting and nurturance."

It is reasonable to refer to these interactions of mother and child as rituals, for although there is variation from one mother to the next, each handles her child in a more or less stereotyped way and vocalizes her own repetitive, stereotyped variety of baby talk at times fixed by the clock or particular circumstances. Although some of her behavior is concerned with the fulfillment of the child's bodily needs some of her actions, such as her conventional coos and caresses, are non-instrumental.

Perhaps this early interaction *must* be ritualized, for what the mother must communicate to the child is her dependability, and what better way to communicate dependability than through the performance of stereotyped, repetitive acts at fixed times? What the child is learning specifically in these earliest ritual experiences is that he will not be abandoned by her upon whom he depends utterly (Erikson 1968:716); that is, the infant is learning to trust, and it is interesting to note Erikson's suggestion that the mother whom he is learning to trust is experienced as a "hallowed presence" (1968:714). It may be suggested that the trust vested in this "hallowed presence" is a necessary precondition for the acceptance of symbolic messages, first from the mother herself and then from others, as true or at least sufficiently reliable to be acted upon. It seems that failure in these early ritual contacts has severe effects upon the later development of communicative ability in humans (Erikson 1968:714; Frank 1966).

Erikson's lead suggests that perhaps gradually, as symbolic communication became increasingly complex, the concept of sanctity arose out of the trust which, learned earliest of all things in the mother-offspring dependency relationship, is a necessary pre-condition for the acceptance of messages which the recipient cannot verify. There may be opportunities here for profitable dialogue among the members of several disciplines or even for interdisciplinary research in the evolution of the socialization of the young, focusing particularly upon the rituals of ontogeny. It is likely that we shall never know whether this suggestion is more than possible. Nevertheless, we may conclude by asserting that the concept of the sacred is not only made possible by man's symbolic communication. It makes symbolic communication and the social and ecological orders depending upon symbolic communication possible.

Notes

1. This paper was written while I was a fellow of the John Simon Guggenheim Foundation and of the East-West Center. I am grateful to both of these institutions for their support. I also wish to acknowledge the valuable suggestions I have received from Gregory Bateson, Herbert Long, Robert Levy, Mervyn Meggitt, Henry Orenstein, Eric Wolf, and Milton Yinger.

2. Wallace (1966:235) argues that private prayer and other stereotyped acts performed in solitude may be regarded as auto-communication, communication with the self. I agree. I do not believe that the admission of messages which are sent and received by components of a single organism or psyche to the category "communication events" should strain our notion of communication. We do regard as communication messages sent and received by components of a single system when that system is a social group or a machine. In any case we are dealing here only with rituals in which two or more organisms of the same species participate.

3. Here and throughout this essay the term "information" is generally used in its popular sense.

4. Occurrence is also, of course, important within systems or subsystems, for it can signal unambiguously to the participants a change of systemic state.

5. The late Warren McCullough told me that he had once seen a male baboon, in captivity, present his rump to another male, whom he bit as he mounted.

This might constitute an example of lying in a non-human species. I do not regard "playing possum" and similar ruses noted among other animals as true lying (if such a phrase is possible) because the deceived animal is a member of another species. That is, the senders and receivers of information in such cases do not share communication conventions. The carnivore, taking the marsupial for dead, is simply misinterpreting alarm behavior, and thus deceiving himself.

6. Orderliness is not synonymous with "order," as the latter term is used in such phrases as "law and order." By orderliness I mean here the opposite of randomness. Orderliness is a theoretically metrical aspect of all systems (see Wallace 1958).

7. This is not to say that the ability to lie is maladaptive, or that lying itself is in all cases destructive.

8. Yet another member of this set are propositions the validity of which depends upon belief in them, but in which the belief depends not on sanctification but upon what Bateson (1951:215f) has called "deutero-learning."

9. The concept of control hierarchies is related to the cybernetic concept of adaptation expressed earlier, which suggests that any living system, whether it be an organism or an aggregate of organisms, adapts to specific stresses through a large number of specific homeostatic mechanisms. But adaptation for any living system as a whole is much more than a bundle of more or less distinct feedback loops. When we refer to the adaptation of any living system in a general sense we imply much more than the sum of its special adaptations, for its special adaptations may be in part contradictory and must be adapted to each other. Thus, the total adaptation of an organism or group of organisms must take the form of enormously complex sets of interlocking feedback loops arranged, in part, hierarchically. That is, not only will mechanisms regulating material variables be present, but regulators regulating these regulators, and yet others regulating some of these are also likely to be included. The term "control hierarchy" designates such organization. In human societies they are likely to be in part embodied in governmental organizations and the like, and such familiar structures approximate what is designated by the term in this paper. The apparent familiarity of the structure of some control hierarchies should not lead us to believe that we are sufficiently familiar with their manner of operation, with the extent to which they are in fact cybernetic, with the conditions under which their operation remains cybernetic, with their enormous complexity. It may also be well to note that the structure of rational bureaucracies and business organizations may be to some extent misleading as a paradigm for control hierarchies in general. Whereas such organizations are likely to reflect at least to some extent the elegance of reasoned design, control hierarchies that have emerged through natural evolutionary processes are likely to reflect the opportunism and "messiness" characteristic of evolution (Kalmus 1966).

References Cited

Bateson, Gregory
1951 Conventions of communications: where validity depends upon belief. *In* Ruesch, Jurgen, and Gregory Bateson, Communication, the social matrix of society, pp. 212–227. New York: W. W. Norton.

Bierstadt, Richard
1950 An analysis of social power. American Sociological Review 15:730–738.

Bochenski, Joseph M.
1965 The logic of religion. New York: New York University Press.

Erikson, Eric H.
1968 The development of ritualization. *In* The religious situation, pp. 711–733. Donald Cutler, ed. Boston: Beacon Press.

Frank, Lawrence K.
1966 Tactile communication. *In* Communication and culture. Alfred G. Smith, ed. New York: Holt, Rinehart and Winston. [Reprinted from Genetic Psychology Monographs.]

Freud, Sigmund
1907 Obsessive acts and religious practices. *In* Reader in comparative religion, 2nd edition, pp. 197–202. William A. Lessa and Evon Z. Vogt, eds. and trans. [Also in Zeitschrift fur Religionpsychologie 1:4–12.] New York: Harper and Row.

Goffman, Erving
1956 The nature of deference and demeanor. American Anthropologist 58:473–503.

Goldman, Stanford
1960 Further consideration of cybernetic aspects of homeostasis. *In* Self-organizing systems. M. C. Yevits and Scott Cameron, eds. New York: Pergamon Press.

Hick, John
1963 Philosophy of religion. Englewood Cliffs, N.J.: Prentice-Hall.

Hinde, Robert A.
1966 Animal behavior. A synthesis of ethology and comparative psychology. New York: McGraw-Hill.

James, William
1902 The varieties of religious experience. New York: Longmans Green.

Kalmus, H.
1966 Control hierarchies. *In* Regulation and control of living systems. H. Kalmus, ed.

Leach, Edmund R.
1954 Political systems of Highland Burma. Boston: Beacon Press.

Oliver, Douglas
1955 A Soloman Islands society: kinship and leadership among the Sinuai of Bougainville. Cambridge: Harvard University Press.

Rappaport, Roy A.
1967 Ritual regulation of environmental relations among a New Guinea people. Ethnology 6:17–30.
1968 Pigs for the ancestors: ritual in the ecology of a New Guinea people. New Haven: Yale University Press.

De Rougemont, Denis
1944 La part du Diable, Nouvelle Version. New York: Brentano's.

Scott, J. P.
1964 The effects of early experience on social behavior and organization. *In* Social behavior and organization among the vertebrates, pp. 231–255. William Etkin, ed. Chicago: University of Chicago Press.

Waddington, C. H.
1961 The ethical animal. New York: Atheneum.

Wallace, Anthony F. C.
1958 Study of processes of organization and revitalization of psychological and socio-cultural systems, based on a comparative study of nativistic religious revivals, pp. 310–311. The American Philosophical Society year book 1957.
1966 Religion: an anthropological view. New York: Random House.

Wynne-Edwards, V. C.
1962 Animal dispersion in relation to social behavior. Edinburgh and London: Oliver and Boyd.

Brazilian Racial Terms:

Some Aspects of Meaning and Learning

Roger Sanjek

VOL. 73, 1971, 1126–1143

The new ethnography is by now a standard branch of American academic anthropology. Following the seminal papers by Goodenough (1956) and Lounsbury (1956), a series of programmatic papers (Wallace and Atkins 1960; Wallace 1962; Conklin 1962; Frake 1962), symposia (Romney and D'Andrade 1964a; Hammel 1965) and review articles (Sturtevant 1964; Colby 1966) have been published. So have a growing number of empirical studies, mostly of kinship terminologies. A critical literature has also been accumulating (Burling 1964; Berreman 1966; Harris 1964a, 1968).

But serious disagreements exist among the New Ethnographers. The most important of these I believe to be the division between what might be called the formalists, who evaluate contributions on the bases of elegance, economy and prediction (Hammel 1964; Hymes 1965; Lounsbury 1968) and those who argue for psychological validity as the basis upon which to accept or reject a given analysis (Wallace and Atkins 1960; Wallace 1965; Romney and D'Andrade 1964b; Goodenough 1965): a problem posed by Burling as the difference between "hocus-pocus" and "God's Truth" (1964). In an analysis of Brazilian racial vocabulary I attempt to extend some of the procedures of the latter on the basis of certain of the critiques which have been leveled against componential analysis.

I

The basic idea behind componential analysis is that each unit, or lexeme, within a semantic domain is composed of two or more sememes, or bits of meaning. These discriminative bits differentiate the lexemes within the domain. The more sememes shared by two lexemes, the closer they are in terms of meaning. Componential analysis is a procedure which isolates the sememes within a corpus of lexemes (Romney and D'Andrade 1964b:154, 168).

An example would be the hypothesized component of meaning (sememe) which distinguishes *book* from *magazine* for English speakers — periodicity of publication (Hymes 1964a:118). I could validate this analysis even though I would not have been able to articulate such a distinction. However, whether other representatives of my culture also find this solution satisfying is an empirical problem, and Hymes offers no statistical data on how, or whether, this analysis was confirmed by culture bearers.[1]

This brings me to a major criticism of the New Ethnography: the lack of quantitative methods. This lack affects several elements of New Ethnographic procedures: (a) the collection of the corpus of terms, (b) the specification of the population to which the analysis is to apply and (c) the verification of the analysis by the culture bearers.[2]

(a) In the componential analysis of a semantic domain, the collection of the terms contained within the boundaries of the domain is understood to be crucial (Sturtevant 1964:103–104, 110). In many analyses, however, the assemblage of the corpus has depended not upon the use of ethnographic discovery procedures within a fieldwork situation, but upon old ethnography performed for a different purpose (Lounsbury 1968; cf. Sturtevant 1964:111), a single informant (Goodenough 1965) or an unspecified procedure (Wallace and Atkins 1960). Romney and D'Andrade (1964b), on the other hand, have offered an operational method for the assemblage of the semantic corpus; it is replicable and indicates statistically to which population segment it applies.

(b) The indeterminacy of the population sample presents interpretative problems for the reader when Frake couches his generalizations with phrases such as "the Subanun themselves," "a Subanun ... he can tell us" and "they rarely disagree in the verbal definitions of the concepts themselves" (1961:124–125). Similar problems arise when Faris speaks of "people in Cat Harbour," "the common response" and "the way Cat Harbour folk classify 'occasions' " (1968:115–116). It is a legitimate question to ask how many informants told the ethnographer something and how thoroughly responses were cross-checked among different informants.[3]

(c) The use of a single informant to verify the psychological reality of a componential analysis (Goodenough 1965; Wallace 1965) opens the results to the kind of attack against which statistical data provides a defense.

These criticisms boil down to the point made by Harris (1968:419–421, 582–589) that the linguistic model cannot be applied to any and all domains of culture in an *a priori* fashion. Wallace has termed this fallacious assumption of the universality of the linguistic model as the "replication of uniformity" view of society: that "the society may be regarded as culturally homogeneous and that the individuals will be expected to share a uniform nuclear character" (Wallace 1961:26). Wallace contrasts this position with the "organization of diversity" model, and demonstrates logically that shared cognitive patterns are not a functional prerequisite of society.

But it is a mistake to see these two models as opposing views. In any population, all information (emic phenomena) is distributed in some way. Uniform distribution is a special case of this. And in any population, information is learned in some way, cumulatively or in a lump. The description of any semantic domain must take account of these two properties: distribution and learning. Domains of ambiguity (Harris 1968:582–589) should offer no problem if the New Ethnographers used appropriate sampling procedures and charted the distribution of information for the semantic domain under study. We could then proceed to such questions as "under what conditions do types of distributions of information occur within varieties of semantic domains?" and "what are the functions of ambiguity and of common knowledge?"

II

The domain of Brazilian racial vocabulary offers a test case for some of the assumptions of the New Ethnography. It also offers an arena for the testing of quantitative procedures in cognitive anthropology.

The present analysis is based on two months of fieldwork in Sitio, a coastal fishing village some eighty kilometers north of Salvador, Bahia, in northeast Brazil.[4] I collected 116 different terms which informants used to indicate racial types. This is the largest corpus of terms collected in a single locale (cf. Kottak 1963) but is considerably less than the 492 terms collected by Harris in several locations throughout Brazil (Harris 1970).

The terms were elicited in the following manner. A deck of thirty-six black and white drawings of male faces which included the possible combination of three hair forms (straight, wavy, kinky), three skin shades (light, medium, dark), two nose forms (thick, thin) and two lip forms (thick, thin) [$3 \times 3 \times 2 \times 2 = 36$] was shown to informants in a standardized random order; the responses for each card were recorded in the view of the informant. This test was given to sixty adults (29 male, 31 female) and produced eighty-six terms. A similar set of drawings of females was given to fifteen of the sixty informants, yielding sixteen more terms. Fourteen additional terms were elicited through conversations, informant self-identification or in the responses to the male set given by the 111 children who took the test.

A questionnaire was also administered to forty informants. They were asked to describe the skin color, the hair form, the hair color, the nose form and the lip form for each of thirty-one terms selected from the larger corpus. The terms had been ranked intuitively by me in order of darkest to lightest in hopes that informant responses would indicate contrasting features in adjacent terms.

My procedures accord more closely with what Romney and D'Andrade (1964c) term the "psychological approach" to cognitive studies than with the ethnographic approach of Frake (1964). I was not immediately concerned with the actual usage of terms by actors in "natural" situations, but rather with working in the opposite direction, attempting through "experimental" methods to control the environmental factors which intervene upon cognitive structure in natural behavior. Thus the theoretical basis for my study was quite different from an "ethnography of speaking" about racial types (Hymes 1964b). I view the two foci of interest as complementary. Nonetheless, I would argue for the logical priority of the kind of analysis I am about to present insofar as it provides controls for an examination of the situational and sociological variables involved in "natural" verbal usage of the racial lexicon.

I do not wish to represent these samples as true random samples of a community of 2500 people. The samples, however, are representative in at least five ways. Individuals from the most European-looking to the most African-looking are included, as are the various intermediate types. Individuals of all ages, from sixteen to seventy-two in the adult sample, are included. People from all parts of the village, from one end to the other, are included. About equal numbers from both sexes are included. And, judging from a division of households into three strata based upon the quality and construction of houses and upon occupation, the sample reflects the range of incomes within the village, from relatively rich to poor.

What I intend to do in this paper is to construct a model which maximizes the degree of underlying order contained in the data. I do not want to deny or gloss over the areas of disagreement and ambiguity which my statistics prove to be an unimpeachable property of the corpus (cf. Harris 1970). In presenting a cognitive map which I claim is shared in a modal sense (by at least five-sixths of my informants), I want to be clear that such competence does not have a one-to-one correspondence with verbal behavior. I believe rather that the expression of the cognitive classification is altered by environmental (situational, sociological) variables which are essential for an understanding of why any term is actually uttered. Such variables would include at least the economic class, the dress, personality, education and relation of the referrant to the speaker; the presence of other actors and their relations to the speaker and referrant; and contexts of speech, such as gossip, insult, joking, showing affection, maintenance of equality or of differential social status, or pointing out the referrant in a group.[5]

I doubt that the "meaning" of the full number of terms, and the possibilities for producing more terms, can be understood aside from such variables. The size, complexity and individual variation of the racial vocabulary can be explained only when it is understood that the underlying structure I attempt to isolate cannot be translated into behavior aside from the "intervening variables" I have just mentioned.

III

I decided to use the concept of salience to uncover the degree of order contained within the full corpus of terms. The salience concept arose from the study by Romney and D'Andrade of cognitive aspects of American kin terms (1964b). They were faced with the problem of more than one logically possible componential analysis of American kin terms. They realized that componential analysis was not "an automatic method of uncovering individual cognitive structures. . . . We feel that the solution to this problem lies in further behavioral measures of individual cognitive operations" (1964b:154). They used three "further measures," the first of which, a listing of kin terms in free recall by 105 high school students, led to the concept of salience.

> We were interested in the types of inferences we could draw concerning the cognitive structure of kin terms from the order, frequency of recall, and productiveness of modifiers. . . .

The 'saliency' of kin terms is not considered explicitly in most formal analyses but is of interest from a psychological point of view. There are two indices of saliency available in the listing data. The first is the position of a term in the list. . . . The second index of saliency is the percent of subjects who remember the term. We assume that the more salient terms will be recalled more frequently [1964b:155].

My measure of salience is not quite the same as that of Romney and D'Andrade. Although my informants did not list terms freely, in the male drawing test they each provided a list of terms. My measure of the salience of each term will be the number of informants who used that term. This approaches more closely Romney and D'Andrade's second index.

I took the sixty lists of responses to the set of male drawings and counted to see how many of the informants mentioned each of the eighty-six terms at least once. The ten most salient terms are given below.

Term	Responses (n=60)	Gross Usage (n=2160)	Percent
moreno	54	342	15.8
branco	52	425	19.7
sarara	46	276	12.8
preto	41	159	7.3
cabo verde	37	176	8.3
caboclo	32	98	4.5
negro	22	63	2.9
mulato	22	113	5.2
alvo	21	101	4.7
moreno claro	21	78	3.6
		1831	84.8

These ten terms account for 1831 or 84.8% of all responses [60×36=2160] to the set of male drawings. Any explanation of the structure of this semantic domain must involve an analysis of the meaning of these terms.

I think the ordering according to salience is more useful than the slightly different ordering according to gross usage. My reason is that the more people who offer a term, the closer that term approaches the status of a shared, or "cultural" trait. The fewer people who offer it, the more a term approaches the status of a subcultural, or possibly idiosyncratic element. A logical property of the salience concept reinforces my contention: a term could be highly specific (be applied to only one drawing) and be universally known. Therefore a salience of sixty and a gross usage of sixty (of 2160) is possible. Similarly, a low salience and a high gross usage is possible.

Before proceeding in the analysis of the most salient terms, let me present the salience data on the other seventy-six terms which together account for the remaining 15.2% of the gross usage:

Term	Responses (n=60)
escuro	14
moreno escuro	13
araçuabo (saruabo)	12
roxo	11
escurinho	8
claro	7
louro	6
sarará miolo	6
mulato claro	4
moreno de cabelo bom	4

Rroxinho, amarelo, mestico, branco de cabelo ruim, criolo and *moreninho* were used by three informants per term; *nega, bem alvo, branco legitimo, indio, moreno cor de canela* and *sararazado* were used by two informants per term. Fifty-four other terms were used by one informant per term (cf. Appendix).

Following another lead from Romney and D'Andrade, an examination of the corpus in terms of primitive terms and modified terms reveals roughly that the more salient a term is, the larger the number of modified terms which derive from it (*moreno escuro, moreno de cabelo bom, moreninho*, and so on, I am calling modified terms derived from the primitive term *moreno*).

Here the eleven most frequently modified terms from the corpus of 116 are listed in order:

Term	Term + Modified Forms
moreno	23
branco	12

Term	Term + Modified Forms
negro	7
sarará	7
caboclo	7
mulato	7
alvo	5
preto	5
roxo	5
cabo verde	4
escuro	4
	86

Of the fifteen most salient terms, these eleven terms, and three modifications of them, account for fourteen. The remaining term is *araçuabo*, which has two modified forms, *saruabo* and the idiosyncratic *asaruabo*. These eleven terms and their modified forms account for eighty-six of the 116 terms, or seventy-four percent of the corpus. The rest of the total list consists of nineteen terms which have no modified forms, and the following four terms which have one modified form each: *criolo*, *indio*, *louro*, *vermelhaça*. The full list of all 116 terms therefore can be boiled down to thirty-five modifiable terms of which sixteen have a salience of 1/60.

Let me state right now that I believe that skin color and hair form are the two basic components which order this domain. It is precisely at this point in any componential analysis that the game may be won or lost. This is what Wallace and Atkins, following Goodenough, call step three (1960); it is where Lounsbury (1968:130) begins his "inspection" of the corpus and its denotata; it is where Burling (1964) tells us that any number of possible analyses may begin. The identification of the initial components is where the decision between elegance, economy, and prediction on the one hand, or psychological validity on the other, must be made. Having stated my bias, I will now offer evidence to support my hypothesis.

There are reasons beyond the evidence I will offer, however, which led me to select skin color and hair form as the basic discriminants. First, from my reading before going to Brazil, I was certain that these two variables were involved in the meaning of the terms. Second, Harris' picture set contained these two variables, and his selection of the features tested in the set of drawings was based upon his knowledge of Brazilian culture. Third, as a result of the participant observer process, and of many interviews with informants in which I asked exactly which features are most important, I came to feel subjectively that hair form and skin color were the most basic elements of meaning. I think it is worth noting that some knowledge of the culture is always involved in choosing the initial components in any ethnoscientific analysis (cf. Faris 1968). Something more than a mere "inspection" of the corpus inescapably enters the selection process.

A thoroughly uncharitable critic could say that all I have done is show that hair form and skin color are more important components of meaning than lip and nose form (the only variables included in the picture set). I am not entitled to say anything about other parameters, such as hair color and eye color which the questionnaire data show to be important for some, not all, informants in discriminating certain terms from others. Additional features, say facial width or ear size, may be as important, or even more important, components than the two I am suggesting.

I have tried to give some of the justification for choosing skin color and hair form as hypothetically significant prior to designing the test instruments. However, the range of variables and their ranked importance are only to be discovered through the formation of hypotheses and the subsequent interaction of observer's test and informant's response. In designing the questionnaire I discovered that hair color was another variable. In administering the questionnaire, I learned that eye color was still another variable, about which I was not able to ask systemically. Further research based upon hypotheses concerning more than four variables is obviously appropriate. My data represent no more than an increment to a series of studies which has yet to be completed.

I have tried to make explicit the reasons why I chose skin color and hair form as the basic components. Now I will present the evidence which I believe confirms this hypothesis. In doing so I do not wish to deny the measure of ambiguity within the data. I fully accept Harris' characterization of the use of racial vocabulary in Brazil (Harris 1970). Going in the other direction, however, I can also find something informative to say about cognitive structure and psychological validity (both in a modal sense), about how the system is learned and about individual verbal behavioral differences. I believe that Harris' and my own findings are fully complementary.

If skin color and hair form are the two most important components, then high percentages of informants should show their awareness of

Table 1. Appearance of *branco* and *alvo* as responses to the male drawing test

Skin	Hair Form			Skin	Hair Form		
	Straight	Wavy	Kinky		Straight	Wavy	Kinky
Light	153	135	26	Light	37	34	9
Medium	44	51	15	Medium	11	16	3
Dark	0	0	0	Dark	0	0	0
	branco (N=424)				*alvo* (N=110)		

these variables. A good indication of this is the salience in the responses to the male drawing test of terms denoting the logical types in a two variable system: (1) light skin, straight hair; (2) dark skin, kinky hair; (3) light skin, kinky hair; (4) dark skin, straight hair. Four pairs of terms, I contend, fit these logical types: (1) *branco, alvo*; (2) *araçuabo; preto, negro*; (3) *sarará, araçuabo*; (4) *cabo verde, caboclo*.

The second set of data, the forty questionnaires, provide information about the abstract racial types in terms of the five traits about which I asked each informant. I offer a summary of the results of this questionnaire as evidence for the pairings, and for their use as indicators of the four logical types.

(1) *branco-alvo*. Of the forty informants, thirty-eight told me *branco* has white skin. All of them said *branco* has straight hair. The responses for hair color were more ambiguous: about half said *branco* has black hair, and half said blond hair. In describing *alvo*, thirty-eight of the forty merely said *alvo* is the same as *branco*. Only one man identified himself as *alvo*. He had yellowish skin and wavy hair. When he said he was *alvo*, the other people standing around us began laughing and told him, and me, that he was not *alvo*. I conclude that *branco* and *alvo* are synonyms. I can think of no situational or sociological factor which would account for using one term instead of another.

The appearance of *branco* and of *alvo* as responses to the male drawing test is shown in Table 1. The responses to the thirty-six cards were divided on the basis of two variables, three values each. Each of the nine boxes accounts for the responses for four pictures. Each box contains a total of 240 responses altogether (4×6=240). The total responses for all

Table 2. Appearances of *preto* and *negro* as responses to the male drawing test

Skin	Hair Form			Skin	Hair Form		
	Straight	Wavy	Kinky		Straight	Wavy	Kinky
Light	0	0	1	Light	0	0	3
Medium	2	0	3	Medium	0	0	2
Dark	20	35	98	Dark	2	7	50
	preto (N=159)				*negro* (N=64)		

nine boxes is 2160 (9×240=2160). Of the 2160 responses, 424 were the term *branco*, and 110 were the term *alvo*.

(2) *preto-negro.* All forty informants agreed that *preto* has black skin, black hair and thick nose and lips. Of the forty, thirty-six said *preto* has kinky hair, and the other four said he may have either kinky or straight hair. All forty said that *negro* means the same thing as *preto*. It is evident, however, that usage varies. *Preto* is preferred, a more polite form. *Negro* is used more often when referring to a disliked person and may mutate to *nega* a stronger form not used in polite conversation. (*Nego*, however, is used affectionately with children.) Five informants identified themselves to me as *preto*, and only one as *negro*. I conclude that the abstract meaning of the two terms is close, but that situational and sociological variables probably account for differences in verbal behavior. (The appearance of *preto* and *negro* as responses to the male drawing test is shown in Table 2.)

(3) *sarará-araçuabo.* Many informants immediately said "white with bad hair" (*branco do cabelo ruim*) when I came to the term *sarará*. I recorded these responses before asking about the remaining traits. For the forty informants altogether thirty-eight said *sarará* has kinky hair. For skin color, twenty-two of forty said white, and eight others used terms indicating light skin coloring. Of the remaining ten, six said red skin color, two *moreno* and two *moreno escuro*. For hair color, thirty-two said red, six yellow, and two red or black. Answers for lips and nose were about half thin and half thick. Of the forty, fourteen told me that *araçuabo* was the same as *sarará*. Four others did not know the term. Of the twenty-two who provided descriptions of the traits, seventeen said

Table 3. Appearance of *sarará* and *araçuabo* as responses to the male drawing test

Skin	Hair Form			Skin	Hair Form		
	Straight	Wavy	Kinky		Straight	Wavy	Kinky
Light	2	5	141	Light	0	3	22
Medium	2	3	113	Medium	0	0	18
Dark	0	2	7	Dark	0	0	1
	sarará (N=275)				*araçuabo* (N=44)		

araçuabo has kinky hair. The responses for hair color, skin color, nose and lip form paralleled the *sarará* responses. Some people clearly do distinguish *sarará* and *araçuabo*. Six informants told me *araçuabo* means red skin and red hair. The one man who identified himself as *araçuabo* conformed to this description. But such discrimination must be classed as subcultural. For most of my informants the terms *sarará* and *araçuabo* share the components of light skin and kinky hair. Disagreement arises in the other traits. But it is with the first two traits that I am concerned. (The appearance of *sarará* and *araçuabo* as responses to the male drawing test is shown in Table 3.)

(4) *cabo verde-caboclo*. I am arguing that *cabo verde* is the logical obverse of *sarará*. Many informants volunteered the description "black with good hair" (*preto do cabelo bom*) as soon as I mentioned *cabo verde*. Only one informant did not know the term. For skin color, thirty-two of thirty-nine informants gave answers indicating dark coloring, and the rest gave either *moreno*, or darker terms. Of the thirty-nine, thirty-eight said *cabo verde* has straight, black hair. The results for nose and lip form were about half thin and half thick. Thirteen informants told me *caboclo* is the same as *cabo verde*. One said it means *preto*, and three did not know the term. Of the twenty-three who offered descriptions, all said *caboclo* has black hair. For hair form, fifteen of twenty-three responded straight, five kinky, and three either straight or kinky. For skin color, fifteen of twenty-three gave dark terms, and the others varied, although most were between medium and dark. The twenty-three informants responded three to one that *caboclo* has thick lips and nose.

The correspondence between *cabo verde* and *caboclo* is the weakest for

Table 4. Appearance of *cabo verde* and *caboclo* as responses to the male drawing test

Skin	Hair Form			Skin	Hair Form		
	Straight	Wavy	Kinky		Straight	Wavy	Kinky
Light	1	1	0	Light	4	3	0
Medium	20	10	0	Medium	15	12	3
Dark	96	40	2	Dark	35	20	2
	cabo verde (N=170)				*caboclo* (N=96)		

any of the four paired terms, although strong when compared to correspondences between other terms. Consideration of the two features at
issue, however, reveals that about three quarters of the informants agree
that *caboclo*, like *cabo verde*, has dark skin and straight hair. (The appearances of *cabo verde* and *caboclo* as responses to the male drawing test
are shown in Table 4.)

These eight terms had the highest levels of agreement among informants for the features about which I inquired. For the remaining terms
of high salience, the agreement was considerably less than for *caboclo*, as
in the cases of *moreno* and *mulato*. Responses for other terms seem to
indicate that there is agreement, but that it is subcultural; a small number of people make the same discrimination of a term from one of the
more salient terms, *moreno claro* from *moreno*, or *roxo* from *preto*, for
example.

If we consider the salience for the paired terms, that is sum the informants who use either one, the other, or both terms in each pair, in the
male drawing test, the results are this:

Term Pair	Salience (n=60)
branco-alvo	57
preto-negro	56
sarará-araçuabo	51
cabo verde-caboclo	51

In terms of competence, not salience, at least three quarters of the
forty informants on the questionnaire were able to describe consistently
each of these eight terms. Agreement was higher for these terms than for

Table 5. Male drawing test according to three values for hair form and
skin color

Skin	Hair Form		
	Straight	Wavy	Kinky
Light	(1) *branco-alvo* 190 79.8% *moreno* 10 *cabo verde-caboclo* 5 *sarará-araçuabo* 2 *preto-negro* 0	(2) *branco-alvo* 169 70.4% *moreno* 10 *sarará-araçuabo* 8 *cabo verde-caboclo* 4 *preto-negro* 0	(3) *sarará-araçuabo* 163 67.9% *branco-alvo* 35 14.6 *moreno* 8 *preto-negro* 3 *cabo verde-caboclo* 0
Medium	(4) *moreno* 74 30.8% *branco-alvo* 55 22.9 *cabo verde-caboclo* 35 14.6 *moreno claro* 28 11.7 *sarará-araçuabo* 2 *preto-negro* 2	(5) *moreno* 79 32.7% *branco-alvo* 67 27.9 *cabo verde-caboclo* 22 *sarará-araçuabo* 3 *preto-negro* 0	(6) *sarará-araçuabo* 131 54.6% *moreno* 35 14.6 *branco-alvo* 18 *preto-negro* 5 *cabo verde-caboclo* 3
Dark	(7) *cabo verde-caboclo* 128 53.3% *moreno* 46 19.2 *preto-negro* 22 *sarará-araçuabo* 0 *branco-alvo* 0	(8) *cabo verde-caboclo* 65 27.1% *moreno* 54 22.5 *preto-negro* 42 17.5 *sarará-araçuabo* 2 *branco-alvo* 0	(9) *preto-negro* 148 61.7% *moreno* 23 *sarará-araçuabo* 8 *cabo verde-caboclo* 4 *branco-alvo* 0

any others. And disagreement, as I have shown, was in hair color and nose and lip form, not in skin color and hair form.

What the salience figures show, I believe, is that when asked about racial categories, Sitio informants will offer most readily those terms which are most important to them in breaking up the domain of facial appearances. These most salient terms contrast according to skin color and hair form. The higher salience of *branco-alvo* and *preto-negro* would indicate that discriminations based upon color are even more basic than those based upon hair form. I will even go so far as to argue that children learn first to differentiate racial types by color, and then by hair form. I will offer evidence to support this assertion.

Returning to the other terms, *moreno* has a salience of fifty-four, comparable with the four term pairs; these pairs and *moreno* are the core of the system. The next most salient term is *mulato* at twenty-two of sixty. If we expand our two-variable logical domain to conform more with reality, it is obvious that intermediate hair forms and skin colors exist. Such intermediate types expand the domain to dimensions covered in the male drawing test. Table 5 shows the results of this test according to three values for the two variables of hair form and skin color. Terms appearing for at least fifty percent of the responses in a cell are underlined. With the exception of *moreno claro* in cell 4, no term other than the four pairs and *moreno* occurred for more than ten percent of the responses in any cell. The total responses in each cell are 240.

Table 6. Cognitive map of informants

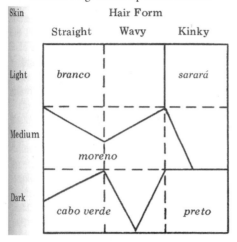

Table 6 shows, in schematic form, what I believe to be the basic cognitive map shared by at least five-sixths of the informants.

The Meaning of Moreno

At this point, I will present the data which pertain to *moreno* from the drawing test and from the questionnaire. I think this will show that on the two-variable, three-value grid, *moreno* does fill the central area where the occurrence of the four term pairs is most limited.

Thirty-nine of forty informants provided descriptions of *moreno*. (One said *moreno* is the same as *claro*.) Of the thirty-nine, some twenty-eight gave words for skin color which indicate medium shades. (Twenty *moreno*, three *côr de canela*, two *media*, one *meio claro*, one *claro* and one *mais preto do mulato*; in this last case, the informant regarded *mulato* as very light, almost the same as *branco*.) Nine other informants gave terms indicating dark coloring. (Six *escuro*, one *escurinho*, one *roxo*, and one *côr de chocolate*; *preto* and *negro* were not given at all for skin color.) Of the remaining informants, one indicated a medium to dark range, and the other gave the enigmatic response "*escuro claro.*"

For hair color, almost all said dark. Twenty-one of thirty-nine informants gave straight for hair form, and ten said kinky. Seven said *moreno* may have either straight or kinky hair. (One said *media* for hair form.) Opinion as to nose and lip form was evenly divided between thick and thin.

Table 7. Appearance of *moreno* in male drawing test

Skin	Hair Form			Skin	Hair Form		
	Straight	Wavy	Kinky		Straight	Wavy	Kinky
Light	10	10	8	Light	17	24	8
Medium	74	79	35	Medium	110	104	40
Dark	46	54	23	Dark	61	76	26
	moreno (N=339)				all *moreno* terms (N=466)		

In terms of the two variables, the pattern of responses that emerges for *moreno* is about three-quarters medium skin, one-quarter dark skin; and two-thirds straight hair, one-third kinky hair. If the four term pairs do tend to occur in the corners of the schematic grid, and *moreno* tends to fill up the central area, then the responses for pictures indicating the central portion of the grid should have the highest proportions of *moreno* responses. And, as corollaries, the association of kinky hair with *moreno* should be greater with medium coloring than with dark, and the association of dark skin should be greater with straight hair than with kinky.

The appearance of *moreno* alone, and of all *moreno*-derived terms as responses to the male drawing test tends to confirm this proposition and the two corollaries (Table 7).

The association with *moreno* and light skin is very slight. The occurrence is greatest with medium skin coloring and straight or wavy hair. *Moreno* occurs less often with dark skin, but here the association is stronger with wavy, or straight hair, than with kinky. Finally, a lesser but significant association with medium skin color and kinky hair appears. This pattern is reflected in Table 6.

Although *moreno* appears in each of the nine cells, and was given at least once for every one of the thirty-six pictures, the appearance in the two cells where *branco* is strongest, and the cells in which *sarará* and *preto* appear most often, is weak compared to the remaining cells. *Moreno* occurs more often in the fourth logical pole, the *cabo verde* area, than in the other three. I think the relatively greater ambiguity in this portion of the domain is attributable to the comparatively small number of individuals possessing the combination dark skin and straight hair. Many more individuals are encountered in Sitio who approach the ideal conceptions of *sarará*, *branco* and *preto*, than who could be called *cabo verde*.

An examination of the pictures most often called *moreno* offers another line of evidence. Seven drawings had from seventeen to twenty-eight (of sixty) *moreno* responses. Of these seven, six have medium coloring and one dark; all had either good or wavy hair. The next five pictures, with thirteen *moreno* responses each, were either of medium or dark skin coloring, and good or wavy hair, with one exception. This drawing had kinky hair, but medium coloring. (This last type is often called *moreno* in Sitio, less often *sarará*. Of the twenty-two informants who identified themselves as *moreno*, at least three fit this description.) Some 83.9% of the *moreno* responses fit the pattern I have described for *moreno*.

A final bit of data suggests that although *moreno* could be used for any set of facial features, it is not felt to be appropriate for dark skin and kinky hair. The most African of my informants identified himself to me as *moreno*. We were alone at the time. I asked other informants what they would call this man. They all replied *"preto."* This man's brother, who had thinner lips and nose than his sibling, identified himself as *preto*. Other people agreed; one told me he was *"bem pretinho*, but a good man."

IV

I administered the set of thirty-six male drawings to 121 children, sixty-three girls and fifty-eight boys, between the ages of five and nineteen. Most of the tests of children under fourteen were conducted in four schools in Sitio. I was able to sit in a room separate from the main classroom, and to give the test to each child individually. The tests for most of the fifteen-to-nineteen-year-olds were collected in the same manner as the adult sample; I gave the tests to as many individuals as I could find.

I have divided the results into four age cohorts: under ten, ten to twelve, thirteen to fifteen and sixteen to nineteen. Only seven of the children tested were either below seven or above eighteen in age (one boy six, three girls five, one boy nineteen, two girls nineteen). Ten of the oldest children formed part of the adult sample of sixty. None of them is married.

In order to consider this data as indicative of how the racial vocabulary is learned, I must first demonstrate that it is learned cumulatively while growing up (and not, for example, learned in a lump at puberty). I

Age Cohort	Male Averages	Female Averages
under 10	3.1 (n=19)	3.1 (n=20)
10–12	3.8 (n=21)	4.3 (n=17)
13–15	5.1 (n=10)	5.3 (n=13)
16–19	7.0 (n= 8)	6.1 (n=13)
adult	8.4 (n=29)	9.0 (n=31)

believe that the average number of terms used by the age cohorts for the male drawing test shows that this vocabulary is in fact learned over time.

I have summarized the children's responses by cohort under four headings:

1. What portion of each cohort makes a distinction between black and white, or dark and light skin color? I use the presence of *preto* and *negro* as indicators that dark skin is discriminated, and *branco* and *alvo* for light skin. (*Alvo* is not used in the under-ten cohort.)
2. How many terms beyond the black/white dichotomy are used?
3. What portion of each cohort makes distinctions on the basis of hair form? On the basis of the results from the adult samples, I use the presence of *sarará*, *cabo verde* and *caboclo* as indicators that hair form discriminations are being made independently of skin color distinction.
4. What terms are used beyond the indicators, and what is their salience?

Under 10 (n=39)

1. Almost all (36) made the black/white distinction. Two others used terms indicating a dark/light discrimination. One used only *moreno*.
2. One-third (12) used only two terms. One-third (13) used only three terms, four of them using *moreno* as the third term. One-third (13) used at least four terms.
3. Less than a third (11) made the hair form discrimination. *Sarará* was used by ten children, and *cabo verde* by two. *Caboclo* did not appear at all.
4. Eight terms were used beyond the indicators. In order of salience they were:

amarelo	6/39
escuro	5
claro	4
vermelho	4
côr de cinza	2
louro	1

mulato	1
verde	1

10–12 (n=38)

1. Almost all (34) made the black/white distinction. The other four used *roxo* or *escuro*, with *branco*, to make a dark/light discrimination.
2. Only three children used no more than two terms. Less than a third (11) used only three terms, nine of them using *moreno* as the third term. Two-thirds (25) used at least four terms.
3. Less than a third (11) made the hair form discrimination. *Sarará* was used by seven children, *caboclo* by four and *cabo verde* by three.
4. Eight terms were used beyond the indicators:

escuro	10/38
claro	7
mulato	5
roxo	5
louro	3
amarelo	1
escurinho	1
vermelhaça	1

13–15 (n=23)

1. All made the black/white distinction.
2. Almost all (22) used at least four terms. All of these used *moreno*.
3. About three-quarters (17) made the hair form discrimination. Fourteen children used *sarará*, five *cabo verde* and three *caboclo*.
4. Fifteen terms were used beyond the indicators:

mulato	5/23
escuro	3
louro	3
claro	2
amarelo	1
escurinho	1
moreno claro	1
moreno escuro	1
nega	1
pretão	1
roxo	1

roxo claro	I
ruivo	I
sarará miolo	I
saruabo	I

16–19 (n=21)

1. All made the black/white distinction.
2. Almost all (20) used at least five terms. All of these used *moreno*. The only children to use more than eight terms were a boy of sixteen (nine terms) and a boy of eighteen (fifteen terms).
3. Two-thirds (14) made the hair form discrimination (seven of eight boys and seven of thirteen girls). *Sarará* was used by all fourteen, *cabo verde* by nine, and *caboclo* by one.
4. Seventeen terms were used beyond the indicators:

escuro	8/21
roxo	8
claro	5
moreno claro	4
mulato	4
escurinho	3
moreno escuro	3
saruabo	2
amarelo	I
araçuabo	I
côr de cinza	I
escuro alvo	I
escuro claro	I
louro	I
mameluco	I
roxinho	I
sarará miolo	I

Several conclusions about how racial vocabulary is learned can be drawn from this data:

1. I believe the data support my hypothesis that a black/white discrimination is learned first. All but one of the under-10 children made at least a light/dark dichotomy of the domain of racial types in their responses to the set of

drawings. The results indicate that at least by seven years of age almost all children distinguish dark people from light people.

2. *Moreno* becomes a more important term in ordering the domain as children grow up. Only a little more than a third of the under-ten cohort used *moreno* at all. Two-thirds of the ten- to twelve-year-olds used *moreno*. Only two of the forty-four children of thirteen years and older did not use *moreno*.

3. Discrimination by hair form seems to be learned later by most children than the color trichotomy. In the under-ten and the ten to twelve cohorts, less than a third distinguish by hair form. Most of the adolescents (thirteen- to fifteen-year-olds) indicate that hair form distinctions are meaningful to them. The sixteen- to nineteen-year-old boys are in line with the trend, but the drop in the sixteen- to nineteen-year-old girls' recognition of hair form is anomalous.[6]

4. The response of the under-ten cohort indicates that during this age period about two-thirds use three terms to break up the racial domain, but only one-third can proceed beyond this. After ten, however, nearly all make at least a trichotomy, and two-thirds use four or more terms. By thirteen almost all are using at least four terms. At sixteen almost all children can use at least five terms.

5. The lists of terms used beyond the indicators show that an increasingly larger corpus of terms is used as children grow up. Several aspects of the lists of terms by cohort are of interest.

   (a) Terms denoting colors are used by the younger children, but less often by the older ones. The salience of *verde, vermelho, vermelhaça, amarelo,* and *côr de cinza* decreases, or disappears in the above-ten cohorts. All of these color terms have very low salience in the adult sample. It would seem young children use the words for color in the wider environmental context to indicate skin coloring, but discontinue this usage as the adult racial vocabulary is learned.

   (b) The words *escuro* (dark) and *claro* (light), which also have a range of meaning in the wider environmental context, are used by children of all ages with a salience about the same or greater than in the adult sample. The salience of *escurinho* increases with age.

   (c) The terms *louro, mulato,* and *roxo* appear to be learned by some children in the ten- to twelve-year-old age range, and continue to be used by some, but not to the extent that the indicator terms are used.

   (d) With the thirteen- to fifteen-year-old cohort a great expansion in the number of terms encountered occurs, but these terms tend to be used by very few individuals. *Nega, pretão, roxo claro* and *ruivo* were used once in the thirteen to fifteen group. *Escuro alvo, escuro claro, mameluco,* and *roxinho* appeared once in the sixteen to nineteen cohort. *Moreno claro, moreno escuro, sarará miolo,* and *saruabo (araçuabo)* appeared first in the thirteen to fifteen cohort, and continued to be used, even more frequently, in the sixteen to nineteen group. These four terms, unlike the other eight just mentioned, have significant salience in the adult sample. These twelve terms show the subcultural and idiosyncratic usage of the adults becoming established among the teenagers.

Although the ability to discriminate in terms of color (*branco-moreno-preto*) is almost universal by age thirteen, some people for certain reasons (lack of interest, lack of intelligence?) never proceed beyond such a comprehension. For example, one informant, a forty-eight-year-old man, gave only these three terms as responses to the male picture set. Another man of about twenty-five used only these three terms before he became too bored to finish the test. I asked him about other terms and he seemed genuinely not to know what I was talking about.

Most people, however, as the drawing test and the questionnaire indicate, do make discriminations on the basis of hair form as well as color. As far as generalizing about shared competence, that is as far as I am prepared to go. Some informants make many more distinctions: *sarará* from *sarará miolo* from *araçuabo,* for example; some have very clear ideas about the meaning of *mulato, roxo, escuro,* or *amarelo;* some make consistent discriminations by modifying *moreno* with *escuro, claro* and other terms. Such subcultural or individual differences do not correlate with sex, age, or social strata, but factors such as family traditions, experience in other communities and acquaintance with others who do make more discriminations may all be relevant.

V

I am reluctant to claim that my analysis extends beyond my sample or, at most, beyond Sitio. Studies within the state of Bahia report terms which I did not find at all (Kottak 1963; Hutchinson 1957), even though I asked deliberately several informants if they knew them. The term *mulato,* which has both low salience and low level of agreement in Sitio, is no doubt of high salience in other parts of Brazil as Harris' data (1970) and a few tests I conducted with the picture set in Salvador and Rio de Janeiro suggest. I should add that several informants in Sitio mentioned in conversations a term which is used for *preto* in Vila do Conde, the nearest community, but which, they said, "we do not use in Sitio."

There are good historical reasons why a dark/light dichotomy should be of primary significance within the Brazilian racial vocabulary. Certainly no one in Sitio has forgotten that the masters were white and the slaves were black. Although I would not even intimate that learning recapitulates history, further ethnohistorical study of the origin and historical development of racial categorizations in Brazil (cf. Harris 1964b) would be interesting in light of the data on how terms are learned in the contemporary situation. Faris (1968), in a very different context, has also suggested that diachronic studies, both of history and learning processes, can only illuminate synchronic emic analysis.

Judging from my acquaintance with ethnoscience, it appears that racial vocabulary in Sitio is a considerably less ordered semantic domain than Subanun disease terms, Hanunoo color categories or most kinship terminologies. It would seem especially valuable to conduct more studies of such relatively unordered domains in order to test fully the limits of componential analysis.

In the absence of a number of quantitative studies, however, such designations as "relatively ordered" or "unordered" are no more than *ad hoc*. Even where minimal quantitative data exist, it appears that such relatively "ordered" domains as American kinship have penumbras of ambiguity and disagreement (Schneider and Homans 1955; Wallace and Atkins 1960; Romney and D'Andrade 1964b; Goodenough 1965; Schneider 1965; Harris 1968:586–588).

Beyond developing rigorous quantitative procedures, it would seem the next step for the New Ethnography is to formulate a series of hypotheses about cultural systems as wholes rather than to hope that series of distinct studies of, say, kin terms, plant names, and color categories will somehow add up to a full ethnography. If anthropologists attempted to formulate logically all the expected semantic domains, and to make hypotheses about distribution and learning, a series of studies could be conducted leading to higher level generalizations about the cognitive organization of the culture and its relation to the environment. I am not arguing for what Mills called Grand Theory. What we need is to un-Abstract our Empiricism and use it to ground and test our Grand Theories. The faults of the New Ethnography lie not in what it is, but in what it is not.

It is currently fashionable to define culture as a "design for living,"

and to leave the study of living itself to sociologists, out-of-bounds ethologists or maverick anthropologists. But even those who accept this
division of labor, or labour, will have to face such questions as: What is
the psychological reality of the analysis? Are there subcultural variants
or alternatives? How many people in the population share the cultural
elements? How does the extent of sharing vary from trait to trait and
from person to person? How and when is the cultural pattern learned?[7]
The very fact that Frake admits that the Subanun may disagree, even if
rarely, means that quantitative procedures are employable and, I would
add, desirable.[8]

Appendix

	Primitive Term	Hair Form	Claro-Escuro	Dim-Aug	Other
23	moreno 54	de cabelo bom 4 de cabelo liso 1 de cabelo escubido 1 de cabelo cachiado 1 de cabelo ruim 1 cabelo sarará 1	claro 21 escuro 13 bem claro 1 bem escuro 1 escurinho 1	*moreninho 3 de cabelo bom 1 escuro 1 cabelo bom 1	alvo 1 cabo verde 1 sarará 1 roxo 1 côr de canela 2 laranjado 1 bronzeado 1
12	branco 52	cabelo bom 1 de cabelo bom 1 de cabelo liso 1 de cabelo ruim 3		*brancozinho 1	legitimo 2 não legitimo 1 limpo 1 louro 1 sarará 1 *pouca brancada 1
7	sarará 46			*sararazinho 1 *sararazão 1	miolo 6 legitimo 1 preto 1 *sararazado 2
7	caboclo 32	cabelo de flecha 1	claro 1	*caboclinho 1	cabo verde 1 araçuabo 1 *caboclado 1
7	mulato 22		claro 4 escuro 1	*mulatinho 1	bem limpo 1 gazo 1 preto 1
7	negro 22	de cabelo bom 1		*negrinho	legitimo 1 *nega 2 da africa 1 da costa 1
5	preto 41	de cabelo bom 1		*pretinho 1 *pretão 1	moreno 1

	Primitive Term	Hair Form	Claro-Escuro	Dim-Aug	Other
5	*alvo* 21	cabelo ruim 1 de cabelo ruim 1		*alvinho 1	bem alvo 2
5	*roxo* 11	de cabelo bom 1	claro 1	*roxinho 3 de cabelo bom 1	
4	*cabo verde* 37		claro 1 escuro 1		legitimo 1
4	*escuro* 14		claro 1	*escurinho 8	alvo 1
3	*araçuabo* 12 (*saruabo*)				*asaruabo 1
2	*louro* 6			*lourinho 1	
2	*criolo* 3			*criolinho afri- cano 1	
2	*indio* 2		mais escuro 1		
2	*vermelhaça* 1				vermelho 1
1	*claro* 7				
1	*amarelo* 3				
1	*mestiço* 3				
1	*côr de cafe com leite* 1				
1	*côr de canela* 1				
1	*côr de cinza* 1				
1	*côr de fomiga* 1				
1	*africano* 1				
1	*chinês* 1				
1	*francêsa* 1				
1	*português* 1				
1	*alemã* 1				
1	*amisturado* 1				
1	*misturo* 1				
1	*gazo* 1				
1	*mameluco* 1				
1	*marrom* 1				
1	*pardo* 1				
1	*ruivo* 1				

The entire corpus is listed. The number preceding each primitive term indicates the sum of the term and its modified forms. The number following each term is its salience, or how many of the sixty informants used it in the male drawing test. The modified terms are listed under four headings: hair form designations, *claro* and *escuro*, diminutives and augmentatives and other modifications. Only the additional element is listed, unless the term is transformed. In those cases, the transformed form is listed and is indicated by an asterisk. Modifications of transformed forms are indented.

Notes

1. For my wife, despite Hymes' hypothesis, advertising, not periodicity of publication, is the element of meaning which distinguishes magazine from book.

2. Perhaps as a result of the nonstatistical work to date, within the New Ethnography the precise boundaries of the "society" or "culture" under consideration have been at best vaguely delimited. As all anthropological fieldwork involves sampling from the behavior stream in one way or another, the relation of sample to universe is critical. Were an operational definition of society and culture (Harris 1964a:182–183) applied in conjunction with quantitative procedures, such indeterminacy would disappear.

3. My preference for a statistical grounding of "social facts" as against intuitive impressions is based upon fieldwork experience as well as my theoretical orientation. The term *vermelhaça* seemed to be very important and consistently defined in the first few conversations I had with my immediate neighbors in Sitio. However, not a single adult used the term in the picture set test, and only two children used it. In the questionnaire results, ambiguity reigned. Those who provided descriptions varied considerably, and a third of the informants did not know the term at all. To complete my point, two said it meant German, and one said it meant gringo. Had I relied upon nonstatistical impressions of what seemed to be the "common knowledge" meaning of the term, I would have been wrong.

4. The research in Brazil was supported by the Columbia-Cornell-Harvard-Illinois Summer Field Studies Program and supervised by Marvin Harris of Columbia University. Fieldwork was conducted in Portuguese, with the help of Ney Dos Santos of Sitio.

5. In terms of this last context, on the basis of her fieldwork in Chile where a similar but less complex system obtains, Sister Jennifer Oberg has pointed out to me that identifying one actor as, say, *moreno*, may indicate merely that he is more *"moreno"* in appearance than others.

6. Anna Lou de Havenon and Judith Shapiro have suggested that the lower proportion of sixteen- to nineteen-year-old girls who make hair form distinctions may be connected to the fact that girls of this age almost all straighten their hair. The small sample size may also be responsible for this odd figure.

7. Cf. the questions Wallace raises about Schneider's generalizations concerning the American kinship system (1969:105–106).

8. The influence of Marvin Harris' teaching and writing is obvious to readers of this paper. The advice of Allen Johnson was indispensable as well. I would also like to thank Georges Condominas and the members of his spring 1969 seminar in fieldwork techniques, and the members of Dr. Johnson's spring 1969 seminar in quantitative methods for hearing portions of this paper and for offering me their ideas. I am grateful to Roy D'Andrade, David Epstein, Daniel Gross, and Joseph Schaeffer for their encouragement and suggestions.

References Cited

Berreman, Gerald D.
1966 Anemic and Emetic Analyses in Social Anthropology. American Anthropologist 68:346–354.

Burling, Robbins
1964 Cognition and Componential Analysis: Gods' Truth or Hocus-Pocus? American Anthropologist 66:20–28.

Colby, Benjamin N.
1966 Ethnographic Semantics: A Preliminary Survey. Current Anthropology 7:3–32.

Conklin, Harold C.
1962 *Comments on* The Ethnographic Study of Cognitive Systems. *In* Anthropology and Human Behavior. W. C. Sturtevant and T. Gladwin, eds. Washington: The Anthropological Society of Washington.

Faris, James C.
1968 Validation in Ethnographical Description: The Lexicon of "Occasions in Cat Harbour." Man 3:112–124.

Frake, Charles O.
1961 The Diagnosis of Disease among the Subanun of Mindanao. American Anthropologist 63:113–132.
1962 The Ethnographic Study of Cognitive Systems. *In* Anthropology and Human Behavior. W. C. Sturtevant and T. Gladwin, eds. Washington: The Anthropological Society of Washington.

1964 Notes on Queries in Ethnography. American Anthropologist 66(3) pt. 2:132–145.

Goodenough, Ward H.
1956 Componential Analysis and the Study of Meaning. Language 32:195–216.
1965 Yankee Kinship Terminology: A Problem in Componential Analysis. American Anthropologist 67(5) pt. 2:259–287.

Hammel, E. A.
1964 Further Comments on Componential Analysis. American Anthropologist 66:1167–1171.

Hammel, E. A., ed.
1965 Formal Semantic Analysis. American Anthropologist 67(5) pt. 2.

Harris, Marvin
1964a The Nature of Cultural Things. New York: Random House.
1964b Patterns of Race in the Americas. New York: Walker.
1968 The Rise of Anthropological Theory. New York: Crowell.
1970 Referential Ambiguity in the Calculus of Brazilian Racial Identity. Southwestern Journal of Anthropology 26:1–14.

Hutchinson, Harry W.
1957 Village and Plantation Life in Northeastern Brazil. Seattle: University of Washington Press.

Hymes, Dell H.
  1964a   Discussion of Burling's Paper. American Anthropologist 66:116–119.
  1964b   A Perspective for Linguistic Anthropology. *In* Horizons of Anthropology. S. Tax, ed. Chicago: Aldine.
  1965   On Hammel on Componential Analysis. American Anthropologist 67:1283.
Kottak, Conrad
  1963   Race Relations in Arembepe. Columbia-Cornell-Harvard-Illinois. Summer Field Studies Program. mimeo.
Lounsbury, Floyd G.
  1956   A Semantic Analysis of the Pawnee Kinship Usage. Language 32:158–194.
  1968   The Structural Analysis of Kinship Semantics. *In* Kinship and Social Organization. P. Bohannan and J. Middleton, eds. Garden City: Natural History Press.
Romney, A. Kimball, and Roy D'Andrade
  1964a   Transcultural Studies in Cognition. American Anthropologist 66(3) pt. 2.
  1964b   Cognitive Aspects of English Kin Terms. American Anthropologist 66(3) pt. 2:146–170.
  1964c   Introduction. Transcultural Studies in Cognition. American Anthropologist 66(3) pt. 2.

Schneider, David M.
  1965   American Kin Terms and Terms for Kinsmen: A Critique of Goodenough's Componential Analysis of Yankee Kinship Terminology. American Anthropologist 67(5) pt. 2:288–308.
Schneider, David M., and George C. Homans
  1955   Kinship Terminology and the American Kinship System. American Anthropologist 57:1194–1208.
Sturtevant, William C.
  1964   Studies in Ethnoscience. American Anthropologist 66(3) pt. 2:99–131.
Wallace, Anthony F. C., and John Atkins
  1960   The Meaning of Kinship Terms. American Anthropologist 62:58–80.
Wallace, Anthony F. C.
  1961   Culture and Personality. New York: Random House.
  1962   Culture and Cognition. Science 135:351–357.
  1965   The Problem of the Psychological Validity of Componential Analyses. American Anthropologist 67(5) pt. 2:229–248.
  1969   *Review of* American Kinship: A Cultural Account, by David M. Schneider. American Anthropologist 71:100–106.

The Potlatch:

A Structural Analysis

Abraham Rosman

Paula G. Rubel

VOL. 74, 1972, 658–671

The Potlatch, as a phenomenon, has gripped the imagination of ethnographer and layman alike.[1] Its elaborate ceremonialism and the large-scale distributions of goods which accompanied it created a scene of high drama. Several crucial features of the potlatch have seemed to observers to involve elements of irrationality which defied explanation. These features included the accumulation of large amounts of property which were subsequently given away reducing the potlatch donor to penury, the shaming of rivals, and the keen competition between rivals which at times even involved the destruction of property.

Several different kinds of explanations have been offered by anthropologists for the potlatch as an institution. The psychological explanation offered by Benedict constitutes one of the earliest. Selecting specific sections out of context from the material on the Kwakiutl collected by Boas, she sought to demonstrate that the Indians in their behavior and value system presented a certain configuration which she likened to megalomania. She placed great emphasis upon the boasting and shaming which took place at potlatches, and attempted to build a picture characterizing the total society as one dominated by a striving for power. Reexamination of the data serves to place this behavior in its proper context and to make explicit the inadequacies of Benedict's psychological approach.

The approach utilized by Herskovits is related to the psychological type of explanation of the potlatch. He sees potlatching as falling into the category of behavior which Veblen characterized as conspicuous consumption and display. Though purporting to be an economic type of explanation, Herskovits' conception requires the assumption of certain underlying universal psychological motivations. Benedict, also, drew the parallel between potlatching and conspicuous display.

A more recent type of approach to the potlatch is that which utilizes an ecological framework. The emphasis here is upon the potlatch as a redistributive system which serves to maintain a relatively uniform level of resource use in the face of uneven distribution of resources. Beginning with a documentation of the unequal nature of the occurrence of resources in time and space they proceed to an explanation of the potlatch as an institution which functions in order to overcome this inequality of resources (Vayda 1961; Suttles 1960; Piddocke 1965).

Barnett (1938) provides a series of generalizations about the potlatch as it occurs throughout the Northwest Coast. He shows the crucial importance that rank plays in the societies in this area and advances the important notion that witnessing at a potlatch is an essential service, providing as it does the means by which rank is validated, and that this service is compensated for by the distribution of goods. However, even here, despite the sociological approach utilized by Barnett, the important variations in the potlatch in the various Northwest Coast societies are not considered nor explained.

The foregoing explanations of the potlatch, in our view, constitute only partial explanations. In these explanations, the potlatch is related to only a particular range of variables. A number of compelling questions remain unasked and unanswered. For example, when do potlatches occur; that is, what are the occasions which demand that a potlatch take place? Who are the guests at a potlatch, and what are their relationships to the hosts? Further, to whom do you redistribute your accumulated resources at a potlatch? Who are your rivals — the ones whom you are intent upon shaming at a potlatch — and whom do you call upon to perform the important service of witnessing at your potlatch?

These are the central questions which have guided our approach and enabled us to relate the potlatch to a different range of variables. We have sought to explain the potlatch in terms of its relationship to social structure.

The central characteristic of the potlatch, for us, is that it represents the most formal and most elaborate of exchange processes in the societies in which it is found. Like all types of exchanges, it defines relationships both within and between groups. Exchanges define the boundaries of groups while at the same time they serve to create and sustain alliances. As in alliances, the exchanges may set groups off as rivals to one another as well as create bonds between groups. The rivalry of the potlatch must be set against this theoretical background. As one examines the links which become manifest through the process of exchange, what one is uncovering are the lines of the social structure. The exchanges can also be seen as reinforcing the relationships which comprise the social structure. As social structures vary in significant ways so do the exchange processes associated with them. Since the societies within the Northwest Coast area exhibit great variations in their social structures, we would expect, therefore, to find variations in the structure of their potlatches. This paper will demonstrate not only the variations in the social structure of societies in this area but the way in which the nature of the potlatch in these societies relates to these variations in the social structure.

Beyond these variations in social structure and in the potlatch which occur in Northwest Coast societies, there are a number of constant features which are invariably present. In all societies where potlatching occurs, rank is intrinsically important, and presence of rank is a constant. However, the way in which rank is manifested varies. For example, in one society marriages may involve individuals different in rank, and this has certain structural implications; in another society rank differences do not enter into selection of a spouse. Similarly, succession to rank position may be fixed; or it may be flexible and open to competition, and this in turn has implications for the structure. In each case, the nature of the potlatch varies accordingly. We have constructed a model of the potlatch-type society which encompasses both the constants and the variables (see Rosman and Rubel 1971).

Our procedure begins with a consideration of the social structural implications of rules. Following Lévi-Strauss, most analysts have constructed models of social structures solely on the basis of marriage rules (Lévi-Strauss 1969). In the course of this paper, we will first construct a model on the basis of a marriage rule, and subsequently we will also construct another model on the basis of a rule of succession.

Where a preferential marriage rule does exist, it can be taken as an ideal statement about the relationships between groups as based upon the exchange of women, and used to build a model of the social structure. Where no specific marriage rule exists, marriage choices are made on the basis of a number of factors. This kind of marriage pattern is referred to by Lévi-Strauss as a complex structure in which personal evaluations of options determine marriage choices. Several of the societies with ambilateral descent on the Northwest Coast have no marriage rule, and instead show a pattern which could be characterized as a marriage strategy and are consequently complex rather than elementary structures. In this situation, we have built our model on the basis of a rule other than the marriage rule — the rule of succession. This model is the same kind of analytical model as those models built upon the basis of rules of marriage, and, as we hope to demonstrate, as useful in comparative analysis. Just as a marriage rule has certain structural implications for the building of analytical models, so too does a rule of succession. As will be shown by our analysis, a rule of succession has direct implications for residence patterns and the nature of descent.

Although we construct our model on the basis of rules, we are equally concerned with actual behavior which we deem to be the verification of our model. We are concerned with the pattern of actual marriages and related kinship behavior, which we use to support our model since it involves the nature of relationships between groups. Chiefs act as the representatives of groups; therefore, the marriages of chiefs are of great significance in expressing relationships between groups. Thus the frequency of marriages conforming to the ideal may be small; yet, if they are the marriages of chiefs, they are sufficient to sustain the system. With this in mind, the examination of the actual marriages of chiefs is a means of verifying the hypothesized social structure.[2] There are other types of data — such as the actual transmission of names, the actual structure of households, and the kinship terminology — which also constitute a means of the verification of the structure. The strongest support, however, comes from the realm of exchange behavior — namely, the potlatch. Potlatches are behavioral events; they occurred at particular points in time and involved real individuals who distributed real currency or blankets on these occasions. The actual behavior of individuals serves as a confirmation and verification of the model of the social structure. These models are analytical constructs whose usefulness is to be evaluated solely in terms of their explanatory power, since they show the interrelationship of behavior in various disparate realms.

In what follows, we will contrast two societies, the Tlingit and the Kwakiutl, on the Northwest Coast. We will show the way in which their social structures differ and the way in which these differences relate to differences in the potlatch. In this paper, we concentrate on the variables in our model of potlatch-type societies and the ways in which they interrelate in two differing potlatch-type societies. Elsewhere, we have demonstrated an identity of structure in the relationships between variables and constants for other potlatch-type societies, the Haida and the Trobrianders (Rubel and Rosman 1970), and the Kwakiutl, Nootka and Maori (Rubel and Rosman 1971).

The Tlingit are matrilineal in descent and avunculocal in residence. The marriage pattern shows a preference for father's sister's daughter marriage. De Laguna notes, "we find that the ideal form of marriage is that which links a man with the sib and lineage of his father. . . . Such a marriage with a woman of his father's line, preferably with the father's sister or her daughter (both are called 'aunt'), is described as a 'royal marriage' . . . (1952:6). On this point, Durlach further notes "the proper marriage for a man was his father's sister: he might, of course, marry her daughter if no members of the older generation were available . . ." (1928:65). In Tlingit kinship terminology, the same term, *at*, is used for both father's sister and her daughter and by extension for the women of father's lineage. As de Laguna has noted, the marriage preference is also extended in this way. A different kinship term, *kalk*, is used for mother's brother's daughter. This kind of marriage pattern, given matrilineal descent, generates Figure 1. Inspection of the diagram reveals a number of general structural features. Each lineage is linked to two others in marriage. A man's father's, wife's, and children's lineage is the same lineage. In every household, there is a core of matrilineally related adult males and adult females from two other lineages. In every matrilineage, the males are divided into two categories in terms of the lineages of their fathers.

These features, as enumerated above, derive from an inspection of the structure. Several types of direct evidence from the ethnographies support these points. Analysis of actual marriages in a nine generation genealogy collected by Durlach supports the preference for marriage with someone in the category of father's sister's daughter (Durlach 1928). The genealogy contains two actual father's sister's daughter marriages, and one with father's sister, but no marriages to mother's brother's daughter. The analysis of the marriages in this genealogy indicates that the lineage of the ego in the genealogy is linked in marriage to two other lineages. Out of twenty-nine possible lineages into which ego's lineage can marry, the genealogy overwhelmingly documents marriages into only two other lineages. This is in conformity with the model which shows each lineage linked to two others in marriage.

The same genealogy indicates the manner in which names, which are lineage possessions and important indicators of rank, are inherited. Out

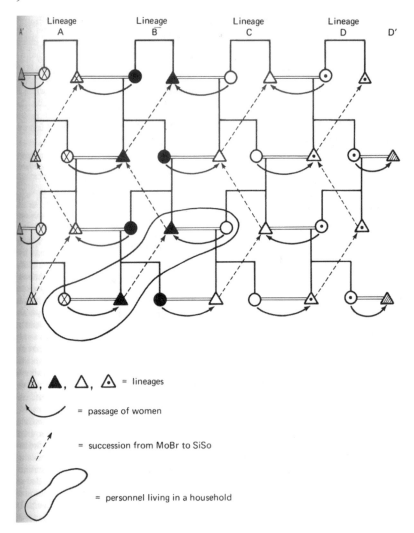

△, ▲, △, △ = lineages

⌣ = passage of women

⟋⟋ = succession from MoBr to SiSo

⬭ = personnel living in a household

Fig. 1. The structure generated by FaSiDa marriage

of eighteen cases of name transmission, two-thirds skip one or three generations. This substantiates the equation of alternate generations which is a characteristic of the structure generated by father's sister's daughter marriage. Five out of nine male names are inherited from mother's mother's brother who is also ideally father's father (see Fig. 1).

The identification of wife's lineage and father's lineage is also implied by the structure. In the Durlach genealogy, in thirteen out of twenty cases where both wife's and father's lineage affiliation was known, wife and father came from the same lineage.

In accordance with the overall structure, within each house there is a clear separation of the members of the same lineage into two groups on the basis of the lineages of their fathers. This is a function of the fact that each lineage is linked to two others in marriage. Durlach (1928:55) comments:

> There seems to have been a certain antagonism between the members of a maternal family, depending on the clan affiliations of the fathers. Thus, in the Finn House we find that one side of the house is occupied by Ganaxtedi sons, i.e., sons of Ganaxtedi fathers, the other side by Luknaxadi sons and that the greatest rivalry existed between the two groups.

Durlach provides us with two Tlingit terms — *akekdax*, one side; *henax*, other party — which refer "to both sides of the house, the two branches of a maternal family" (*Ibid.*:55). This is couched in a somewhat different framework by de Laguna (1952:10) who, instead of emphasizing the rivalry between groups within the maternal family on the basis of clan affiliation of father, notes the positive bonds of sentiment uniting children whose fathers are of the same sib:

> The father-child tie is one which is stressed on all possible occasions. Children of the men of a sib, for example Kagwantan children, are supposed to form a particularly close and happy group, like "brothers." To address or to refer to a group as "Kagwantan children" brings pleased smiles to their faces.

It should also be noted that a moiety division is present among the Tlingit. However, it is clear from the substantive ethnographic data above, that a three-sided structure is the significant ordering structure for the Tlingit. Four parts, at least, are necessary in order for such a system to actually operate. Thus, the moieties are structurally relevant and should be seen as a way of accommodating the three-sided marriage structure with the four parts which are required for it to function. However, the significance of the moieties has been overestimated by previous observers, particularly in their analysis of the potlatch.

Rank among the Tlingit is flexible and operates in the following manner. Internal ranking is flexible; this is exemplified in the flexibility of succession to positions of rank after the death of the previous holder. De Laguna states that the potlatch is the "arena where potential heirs compete for coveted honors and where the victor triumphs over his rival" (1952:6). We shall further develop this point in our discussion of the potlatch. Ranking of groups is not present (see Swanton 1908:408, 414, 427). This lack of external ranking is consistent with the structure generated by the preference for father's sister's daughter marriage. The alternating movement of women is not in accord with the presence of consistent rank differences between the lineage of wife giver and the lineage of wife taker (Homans and Schneider 1956:14).

In our theoretical framework, the potlatch constitutes one of the most important sources of verification for our model. Among the Tlingit, there is only one main type of potlatch — the potlatch held in conjunction with funerary rites. No potlatch sequence can occur without a death, except for two minor types of potlatches involving shaming and loss of dignity. The death of every important male is followed by a potlatch. In addition to its mortuary aspects, the potlatch involves the building or rebuilding of a house to be occupied by the successor to the position, the accession to formal status by children of the deceased's group who receive new names, the formal display of crests and dances which are owned by the deceased's group, and secret society performances.

At a Tlingit potlatch, hosts are of one moiety, and guests are of another. Guests are always separated into two groups which correspond to the two lineages within which the host lineage intermarries. Swanton provides a description of an actual potlatch held at the turn of the century. This account describes a potlatch which took place after the completion of the house of the successor. The stated reason for its occurrence was the secondary reburial of the bones of the previous chief and the erection of a totem pole as a memorial to him. The host lineage was seated in the back of the house and the guests were divided into two distinct groups and ranged along the two sides of the house, separated from one another. Competition and rivalry as well as non-competitive types of behavior are evident at the potlatch. The competition is in the form of eating, dancing, and singing contests between the two groups of guests. There is no competition between either of the guest groups and the host group, and, in fact, members of the host lineage try to keep disputes from getting out of hand. It should be remembered that the competition just described is competition between people of the same moiety. If lineage B (see Fig. 1) makes the potlatch, the competition would be between members of lineage A and lineage C who are both in the same moiety. These two lineages are linked through marriages to lineage B, the host lineage. One represents the lineage of the wife of the donor of the potlatch, and one represents the lineage of the wife of the deceased chief, the predecessor of the donor. The wife of the donor and her lineage are mentioned as present throughout Swanton's account. Swanton also states in a different source describing the speeches at Tlingit potlatches that "the first side to dance is that to which the widower, or widow of the deceased belongs" (Swanton 1909:375), thus also indicating that the lineage of the wife of the deceased is present.

At an earlier point in the potlatch proceedings, to assuage the sorrow of the host group, the two guest groups dance in peace, stating "I am holding your daughter's hand." Swanton explains this statement in a footnote, saying, "the daughter of one Wolf man (moiety) being the wife of another and vice versa" (Swanton 1908:440, footnote b). Referring once again to Figure 1, if lineages A and C who are the guests are members of the Wolf moiety, then they do indeed marry each other's daughters. A term of reference exists to express the relationship between these two groups, members of the same moiety bound to one another by links to a third group. This term, *(ax)Daketqi*, reported by Durlach, is one whose meaning is not clear to her. She cites the text reference and indicates that it is used by "the chief of the Kasqaguedi, a Raven clan, . . . in addressing the opposite Ravens. Just what is meant by this is not clear. Perhaps it means the other Raven clans present" (Durlach 1928:54). Our analysis makes the meaning of this term clear and indicates why such a term is useful in the context in which it occurs.

The only competition evidenced in the Tlingit potlatch is between the two groups who exchange women with the host lineage. The host at a Tlingit potlatch distributes property, $11,000 in this case, but does not directly compete with his guests. The competition at a potlatch recapitulates the competition and rivalry between men whose fathers come from two different groups within a household as noted by Durlach and mentioned above.

The potlatch constitutes a further verification of the structural model built on the basis of a father's sister's daughter marriage rule. The guests at a Tlingit potlatch are the affines of the host group. We have noted above that succession to rank position is flexible and subject to competition. No fixed rule of succession, such as a rule of primogeniture, is present. The validation of any claim to succession is necessary, and it occurs at the public ritual of the potlatch. At that time, the successor to the position of leadership validates his accession to the name associated with that position by a goods distribution. The competition occurs when competing claimants for position vie to accumulate goods in order to carry out the potlatch and succeed to the position, so that, as de Laguna has noted, the potlatch becomes the arena for competition to succession. The guests who come perform the service of witnessing the validation of the claim to title by the new chief. These guests build the house for the new chief and erect a totem pole in honor of the old chief as well as perform the service of witnessing. In exchange, property is distributed to them. The rank system is flexible in that it involves competition over succession and thus the funeral is the occasion for a potlatch. Potlatches occur on occasions which involve flexibility in the structure.

Spouse selection among the Tlingit is not flexible but follows a rule. Given a preference for father's sister's daughter marriage, neither individual rank nor ranking of groups enters into consideration in marriage arrangements. These two factors would then preclude marriage as an occasion for potlatch, and, in fact, the Tlingit do not have marriage potlatches.

The evidence from the Tlingit potlatch constitutes a verification of the structure deriving from the rule of preferred marriage with father's sister's daughter. We have demonstrated that both data concerning the potlatch, as well as other kinds of ethnographic material, provide evidence that verifies the existence of the structure. The gifts distributed at a potlatch serve to link the host group with the two groups to which it is also linked in marriage. However, in the course of one generation the host group will be giving a woman to one of those guest groups and taking a woman from the other. Thus, a lineage will be linked by goods exchange to each of its two partners in every generation though they give and receive women in alternate generations. Viewed over time, a sequence of marriages, deaths, and potlatches succeed one another, and each of these occasions represents another way of reaffirming the structure. Our analysis clearly demonstrates the viability of father's sister's daughter marriage and its capacity to encompass an overall structure. The overall sequence of exchanges of all types points to the fact that there is no necessary relationship between father's sister's daughter marriage and short cycles of exchange, whether conceived of as short in time or in ability to integrate many groups (see Needham 1958; Lévi-Strauss 1969).

The Kwakiutl are another example of a potlatching society. The pattern of their potlatching contrasts sharply with that of the Tlingit. There are many more occasions at which potlatches take place. Shaming of rivals is more pronounced. As we would expect on the basis of our theoretical framework, their social structure is also quite different. The Kwakiutl have ambilateral descent. Although descent groups exist, there is no unilineal rule of affiliation and individuals may have multiple memberships in such groups. However, residential factors usually result in a single primary affiliation. There is no stated rule concerning the selection of spouses. Furthermore, marriages may be contracted with very close relatives including half brother to half sister, and marriage with younger brother's daughter. Although descent groups exist, there is no rule of exogamy; thus, no fixed rules relating to either descent or choice of spouse are present.

One area in which a fixed rule exists is that relating to succession to chiefly office. The Kwakiutl have a rule of primogeniture in which the oldest child, regardless of sex, succeeds to office. This is unlike the usual usage of the term "primogeniture," which refers to succession of the eldest male.

It is this Kwakiutl rule of succession which we shall use to build our analytical model. There are many passages in the corpus of material about the Kwakiutl collected by Boas which can be cited to support the presence of this rule. In the words of George Hunt, Boas' principal Kwakiutl informant: "This office of giving away property never goes to a younger brother; it is only the eldest child that takes the office of giving away property to all the different tribes. Even if a girl is the eldest one of the children of the one whose office is to give away property, she takes it although she is a woman" (Boas 1925:91). Further, in Boas' summary statement on Kwakiutl social organization, he states, "The fundamental principle seems to be that primogeniture, regardless of sex, entitles the first born child to the highest rank held by one of its parents" (Boas 1940:360; see also Boas 1921:924, 1087, 1107; 1966:52). What are the logical implications of the presence of this kind of rule and the absence of a marriage rule, and how does it enable us to build a model? In the following paragraphs we shall indicate what these implications are and at the same time support their presence among the Kwakiutl with ethnographic data.

The office of giving away property referred to above is the office of chief, which is synonymous with highest rank within the group, since the chief in giving away property acts as a representative of the entire group. The office is embodied in a name as well as in a "seat." There are names which carry lesser rank and are associated with lesser "seats." In fact, for every descent group or *numaym* there exists a complete series of ranked names and associated seats. One of the implications of the rule of primogeniture is that birth order is the basis for the bestowal of named ranked positions by the previous generation. There is a complete internal ranking system and every person within a *numaym* occupies a "seat" of different rank.

A further implication is that marriage is always between individuals of different rank whether it is between individuals of the same *numaym* or different *numayms*. In the absence of a fixed rule of marriage specifying a particular category of individuals from which a spouse must be chosen, and given the possibility of choice within or outside of one's *numaym* or tribe, marriage becomes a strategy whose purpose is to maximize the rank possibilities for one's children. Father or mother may be of higher rank. Boas so indicates: "Rank is, on the whole, determined by the order of birth and the noblest line is the line of the first born. The lowest in rank is that of the youngest born. Hence, when the father and mother are of equally high rank, the first born child may be assigned to one *numaym*, the following to another *numaym*" (1940:360). Thus, the implications of the rule of primogeniture are followed out to their logical conclusions. The first born child gets the highest ranked position held by either parent, the next child the next highest position, and so on, birth order reflecting rank order. It should also be kept in mind that individuals may be recipients of ranked positions or seats in more than one *numaym*.

The particular marriage stratagem followed depends upon a number of factors. These include number of sons and daughters born in a family, whether the first born is a son or daughter, and the rank of each parent. There are several options possible. A father may select a mate for his child from within his own *numaym* or tribe or from another tribe. He may seek for his child a spouse whose rank is higher or lower than that child's. There is recognition of these different possibilities. As Hunt points out, "For there are four ways of wooing, going downward, different from the 'obtaining of a slave,' and 'taking hold of a foot,' and 'the exchange marriage.' All of these are different from what we are now finishing, that we call the 'great bringing out the crest in marriage'" (Boas 1925:281). In a footnote, Boas indicates that the phrases are terms for different forms of marriage. In terms of the operation of this system, which is obviously a complex marriage structure from our description, the following example will give some idea of how it operates. If one is a high-ranking chief with a daughter and no sons, it is likely that one would marry that daughter to a lower-ranking husband from outside the group and that the newly married couple would live uxorilocally with the *numaym* of the girl and her father. The chief would thereby retain control over the future offspring of the marriage, thereby providing himself with an heir. There is no fixed rule concerning residence, although Boas notes it is predominantly virilocal.

Although wives may live virilocally, they are not incorporated into the *numayms* of their husbands. As we shall see below in our discussion of the potlatch, there is a marriage purchase by the husband's *numaym* and repurchase by the wife's *numaym* after children are born. At this point, she may leave to return to her natal group.

As should be obvious by this time a pattern of ambilateral descent is a structural implication of the type of rule of primogeniture present among the Kwakiutl and their strategy of marriage. Birth order determines rank and may also determine *numaym* affiliation. The eldest born child, be it a girl or boy, takes the rank and *numaym* affiliation of the highest-ranking parent, be it father or mother. The next born child receives the next highest rank position held by either parent; this may affiliate this second born child with a different *numaym* from the first born child. Thus, another logical implication of this rule is that siblings may be assigned to different *numayms*, as was noted by Boas in the quotation above.

Both men and women form the links in the line of descent of any particular *numaym*. Ordinarily, primogeniture, given unilineal descent, should minimize rivalry between brothers, since succession is fixed and individuals are socialized to accept the position relegated to them by their birth order. However, given primogeniture and a system of ambilateral descent, rivalry between brothers may find full institutional expression since brothers may be chiefs of different *numayms* in opposition to one another.

The characteristics which we have described above constitute features derived from the fixed rule of succession by primogeniture and the corresponding absence of a rule of marriage preference. The internal structure of groups, as derived from the rule, consists of lines of succession to ranked positions. The succession is dependent upon birth order. There is no competition or flexibility in the succession to political office. On the other hand, group affiliation is flexible, membership and residence involve options, and, given the range of marriage choice, affiliation of children is also flexible.

Up to this point we have derived the features of our model solely from the rule of primogeniture. The external relationships of groups operates independently of the rule of primogeniture. Relationship between *numayms* is not phrased in kin terms. There is no conceptualization of a segmentary lineage system. The same is also true of relations between the groups at the next highest level — the tribe. A number of *numayms* compose a tribe and are ranked with respect to one another within the tribe. Tribes are also ranked with respect to one another. The relative rank of *numayms* and tribes is made manifest by the distribution at a potlatch, and changes in this rank system will be reflected in the potlatch. Boas presents data on traditional rivalries between tribes. Boas studied the Kwagul tribes who had moved to live at Fort Rupert after its establishment as a trading post. The Kwagul tribe was very large and was divided into four subtribes which were ranked and were equivalent in size to non-Kwagul tribes. The Kwagul subtribes in order of rank were Gwetela, Qomoyaye, Walas Kwagul, and Qomkutes. The traditional paired rivals presented by Boas were between these Kwagul subtribes and a neighboring cluster of non-Kwagul tribes: the Mamaleleqala, Qweqsotenox, Nimkish, and Lawitses. We have noted the absence of a marriage rule among the Kwakiutl. An analysis of data on Kwagul marriages contracted with other Kwakiutl tribes indicates that for eighty-three such marriages involving fourteen different tribes, sixty percent are with Mamaleleqala, Nimkish, and Lawitses, their traditional rivals (Rosman and Rubel 1971).

We have derived a number of features of Kwakiutl social organization from the rule of primogeniture. The presence of ambilateral descent among the Kwakiutl does not imply that groups which may exchange goods as well as women do not exist among the Kwakiutl. On the contrary, stable *numayms* with rights of ownership of a wide range of properties, including seats and rank positions, are the operative groupings in Kwakiutl society. They interact and compete with one another. Individuals, however, may shift their residence and thereby shift their group affiliation. They do so in terms of their evaluation of the possibilities of maximizing rank and property for themselves, and because, by virtue of the system, people hold options for multiple memberships though they can reside and participate only in one group at a time. The rule which we have stressed involves succession and access to rights and property which are controlled by the *numaym*. Although the right of inheritance is fixed, individuals can inherit through several lines, and therefore the affiliation of individuals to groups is not fixed. The latter is an area of flexibility and competition in the sense that marriage strategy determines future claims over children and in turn the latter's inheritance possibility.

The potlatch constitutes one of the most important sources of verification for our model of Kwakiutl social structure. The Kwakiutl potlatches differ from the Tlingit in frequency of occurrence, occasions upon which potlatches are held, personae participating, and patterns of interaction. This is to be expected since Kwakiutl social structure is so different from that of the Tlingit. We shall use the life history and potlatching career of Lasotiwalis as presented in text material collected by George Hunt (Boas 1925:112–357). Fourteen potlatches are described in the course of this material, beginning with the potlatch made on the occasion of the birth of Lasotiwalis by his father and ending with the potlatch which commemorates the building of a house for Lasotiwalis. Potlatches occur with frequency during the childhood and adolescence of a boy destined to be chief. Each potlatch marks the assumption of a new and more important name and each includes an increasingly larger and more inclusive company of guests who receive larger and larger gifts. A father serves as host during the potlatches given when his son is a child or adolescent. At some point, however, the son begins to be the distributor of gifts in his own right and still later takes charge of the activities involved in the accumulation of the goods for the potlatch. The greatest and most impressive potlatch occurs when the young man takes over the chiefly name of the person whom he succeeds. At this point, the former chief gives up his chiefly name, seat, and position, and retires to a lowly place in the hierarchy. Names are associated with groups as specific properties of those groups. Each time an individual gets a new name at a potlatch he is either more firmly placed within a particular group by the receipt of a more important name, or, if the name comes from another group to which he is related by kinship, that represents a claim on him as well as on his membership in that other group. Thus, the flexibility associated with potlatching in this case relates to group membership. Claims over children are in turn the function of the marriages that produce them. The relative rank of mother and father determines the particular allocation of names, positions, and *numaym* membership to their children.

Marriage involves a lengthy series of exchanges beginning with the purchase of the bride at which time the groom and his family convey a certain amount of goods to the bride's family to "move her." The repurchase of the bride by her family may take place any time after the purchase. It is larger in size than the purchase. In the career of Lasotiwalis, the repurchase of his wife takes place immediately. The sequence of purchase-repurchase may take place up to four times at which point the high rank of the wife is established. Each purchase and repurchase is associated with a potlatch. In the course of a lifetime of a chief, both his mother's and his wife's purchases and repurchases are tied to potlatches. In the potlatching career of Chief Lasotiwalis, after the several potlatches associated with the acquisition of new names during adolescence, he is initiated into the winter ceremonial at a potlatch made by his father with goods from the repurchase of his mother. The same sequence occurs at a second repurchase of his mother when Lasotiwalis takes the highest chiefly name. The central event on this occasion is the breaking of a copper which has come to Lasotiwalis' father as part of the second repurchase of Lasotiwalis' mother. Succeeding potlatches are tied to Lasotiwalis' own marriage and his wife's purchase and repurchase. In his final potlatch, a new house is built for Lasotiwalis; the goods distributed on that occasion come from the second repurchase of his wife. Thus it is clear that marriage is a potlatch among the Kwakiutl.

We have seen that succession to chiefly office takes place during the lifetime of the holder, not at his death. A child is raised successively to higher and higher office and, on achievement of the highest name, becomes the chief while the previous holder retires. When that previous holder dies, his funeral is not the occasion for a potlatch. The mechanism for assuring succession eliminates the possibility of competition between rival claimants for the position of chief. Therefore, the death and funeral of the previous chief does not serve as the focal point for the ritual celebration of succession to office.

The presence of affines as structurally defined opposites, as, for example, among the matrilineal Tlingit, cannot be so derived for the ambilateral Kwakiutl. However, there are pairings of tribes who are rivals and opposites to one another. This opposition finds its primary expression in potlatching activity between groups bound in marriage. Indeed, as we have shown above, the potlatch itself involves, as an integral part of its composition, many aspects of the marriage rites.

The potlatch structure involves affines as opposites and rivals even if the affines are two brothers. Rivalry and challenge loom large in the Kwakiutl potlatch. The symbolism in the potlatch is replete with phrases concerning the challenge to rivals. Our interpretation is that this rivalry is, in effect, rivalry between affines. In numerous speeches, chiefs present pieces of broken coppers to their traditional rivals. It is clear that to be so honored makes the recipient as well as the giver great in renown. A great chief needs great rivals, since their fortunes and rank are bound together in one overall system. Interpretations of the potlatch which see rivalry as aimed at the shaming and ultimately total destruction of one's rival totally misinterpret the overall reciprocal nature of Kwakiutl potlatching.

The competition between groups in the potlatch involves the external ranking of *numayms* and tribes. Continued unreciprocated potlatches on the part of one group enhance their status to the point that their rank relationship with respect to other groups may be shifted. This is made manifest when *numayms* or tribes are seated as guests at a potlatch given by still another group. The order of receipt of gifts by guests is a direct statement of the rank order of the groups to which the guests belong. The shifts in rank of tribes and *numayms* become factors in the selection of mates in marriage and in the selection of group affiliation for children.

Our analysis of the various aspects of the Kwakiutl potlatch shows the direct relationship of the potlatch to Kwakiutl social structure, including those aspects derived from the rule of primogeniture and ambilateral descent. The frequency of potlatching among the Kwakiutl relates to the flexibility in group affiliation among the Kwakiutl. The bestowal of names during the potlatch represents a statement by the group of claims of membership upon an individual. The frequency of potlatching also relates to the increasing elevation in rank of an individual as he matures until he reaches the pinnacle, early in manhood, and succeeds to chiefly office. Among the Kwakiutl, one potlatches to one's affines. Given the absence of a marriage rule which would determine who those affines will be, marriage becomes a game of strategy involving the enhancement of rank. Chiefs of groups therefore potlatch to whomever the affines, as determined by marriage strategy, happen to be. One common form of strategy, involving the most important chiefs, creates marriage alliances between chiefs of certain tribes who are traditional rivals. These competing tribes represent stable groups, despite the possibility of shifting membership. The largest potlatches, the intertribal potlatches, play out the traditional rivalries between these great chiefs.

Conclusion

A comparison of the potlatches of the Tlingit and the Kwakiutl reveals that there are major differences in the occasions for potlatches, the frequency with which they occur, the guests who are invited, and the nature of the exchanges which take place at the potlatch. The following conclusions can be drawn from our analysis. Potlatches occur on occasions which we define as critical junctures which mark the rearrangement of the social structure, when, in the absence of fixed rules relating to structural changes, the outcome of such changes is dependent upon the manipulations of individual actors. Critical junctures always involve the matter of rank and maneuvering with regard to rank. At such points, the potlatch serves as a ritual involving host and guests where the latter serve as witnesses to the statement of the new arrangement of personnel in the structure; their acceptance of gifts from the host validates this new arrangement. Where competition for positions of rank is present and there is an absence of a rule of succession, the transferral of position is a critical juncture. The confirmation of the successful claimant occurs at the funeral of his predecessor, and this critical juncture is the occasion for a potlatch. In similar fashion, when marriage is a matter of strategy and not subject to rules determining choice of spouse, then marriages, particularly those of chiefs, are critical junctures, since they determine for those chiefs who their affines will be. We find therefore that potlatches occur at marriages where this is the case. In the absence of a fixed rule of descent which affiliates each infant at birth, group affiliation is flexible and brings about critical junctures involving affiliation. These junctures are marked by potlatches which publicly acknowledge the claims of a group over an individual for his membership. Potlatches occur at critical junctures and are in effect *rites de passage* for the society.

We have compared two different kinds of structures, the Tlingit and the Kwakiutl. Tlingit and Kwakiutl social structures exhibit significant differences in the points at which flexibility occurs. In the first, there is a rule of marriage — one marries one's father's sister's daughter — but no rule of succession. In the second society, the Kwakiutl, there is a fixed rule of succession but no rule governing the choice of spouse or group affiliation. In the first case, the Tlingit, potlatches concern succession and occur at funerals, but not at any other time. In the second case, the Kwakiutl, potlatches occur which involve the incorporation of individuals into groups, and also at marriages, while funerals are not the occasion for potlatches.

In both of the societies which we have analyzed, potlatching, rank, and flexibility in rank are present and represent constants; however, the critical junctures, points at which flexibility in the rank system occurs, vary. The variations in the occasions for potlatching are directly related to the variations in the occurrence of critical junctures. Critical junctures occur when rules are absent; thus, the two are in complementary distribution. Potlatching to one's affines is a constant, but who those affines are — the guests at one's potlatch — is a variable. The Tlingit and Kwakiutl each represent a particular permutation of the variables, and of the constants, which together comprise our model of potlatch-type society.

Notes

1. This paper is part of a larger research project which has been supported by grants from the Social Science Research Council and the National Science Foundation (Grant Number GS-2567). We would like to thank Bernard Barber, Robert F. Murphy, and Jonathan Friedman for their comments.

2. For a different view of the problem of chiefly marriages and how they are to be evaluated, see Leach (1958:138), Needham (1962:120–121), and Fox (1967:206).

References Cited

Barnett, H.
  1938   The Nature of the Potlatch. American Anthropologist 40: 344–358.

Benedict, Ruth
  1959   Patterns of Culture. New York: Houghton Mifflin. (First published in 1934.)

Boas, Franz
  1921   Ethnology of the Kwakiutl (based on data collected by George Hunt), 35th Annual Report of the Bureau of American Ethnology, Parts 1 and 2, Washington.
  1925   Contributions to the Ethnology of the Kwakiutl. Columbia University Contributions to Anthropology, Vol. III.
  1940   Race, Language and Culture. New York: Macmillan.
  1966   Kwakiutl Ethnology. Helen Codere, Ed. Chicago: University of Chicago Press.

De Laguna, Frederica
  1952   Some Dynamic Forces in Tlingit Society. Southwestern Journal of Anthropology 8:1–12.

Durlach, Theresa M.
  1928   The Relationship Systems of the Tlingit, Haida and Tsimshian. Memoirs of American Ethnological Society, Vol. XI.

Fox, Robin
  1967 Kinship and Marriage. Baltimore: Penguin Books.
Herskovits, Melville
  1952 Economic Anthropology. New York: Alfred A. Knopf.
Homans, George C., and David M. Schneider
  1955 Marriage, Authority, and Final Causes. Glencoe, Ill.: Free Press.
Leach, Edmund
  1958 Concerning Trobriand Clans and the Kinship Category Tabu. *In* The Developmental Cycle in Domestic Groups. Jack Goody, Ed. Cambridge: Cambridge University Press.
Lévi-Strauss, Claude
  1969 The Elementary Structures of Kinship. Revised edition. London: Eyre and Spotteswoode.
Needham, Rodney
  1958 The Formal Analysis of Prescriptive Patrilateral Cross-Cousin Marriage. Southwestern Journal of Anthropology 14:199–219.
  1962 Structure and Sentiment. Chicago: University of Chicago Press.
Piddocke, Stuart
  1965 The Potlatch System of the Southern Kwakiutl: A New Perspective. Journal of Southwestern Anthropology 21:248–264.
Rosman, Abraham, and Paula Rubel
  1971 Feasting with Mine Enemy: Rank and Exchange among Northwest Coast Societies. New York: Columbia University Press.
Rubel, Paula, and Abraham Rosman
  1970 Potlatch and Sagali: The Structure of Exchange in Haida and Trobriand Societies. Transactions of the New York Academy of Sciences, Ser. II, Vol. 32, No. 6 (June, 1970).
  1971 Potlatch and Hakari: an Analysis of Maori Society in Terms of the Potlatch Model. Man 6:660–673.
Suttles, Wayne
  1960 Affinal Ties, Subsistence, and Prestige among the Coast Salish. American Anthropologist 62:296–305.
Swanton, John R.
  1908 Social Condition, Beliefs and Linguistic Relationship of the Tlingit. 26th Annual Report, Bureau of American Ethnology 1904–05.
  1909 Tlingit Myths and Texts. Smithsonian Institution, Bureau of American Ethnology. Bulletin 39. Washington.
Vayda, Andrew P.
  1961 A Re-examination of Northwest Coast Economic Systems. Transactions of the New York Academy of Sciences, Ser. II, Vol. 23, No. 7 (May, 1961).

Prejudice and Its Intellectual Effect in American Anthropology: An Ethnographic Report

Francis L. K. Hsu

VOL. 75, 1973, 1–19

We usually think of prejudice in terms of employment and educational opportunities, and whether a member of some minority racial or religious group can live where he chooses and where he can afford.[1] Or we think of it in terms of equal or unequal treatment before the courts and by the police, and whether the banks grant mortgages and other loans, or foundations make their awards without reference to skin color or national origin.

Under the compulsion of race riots, student unrest, and legal intervention, our businesses and unions are beginning to make some serious moves toward hiring and admitting some minority members as equals. School and residential integration is an ongoing process, however slow. Some universities are actively seeking Black and other minority employees, students, and faculty members, and, after being threatened with the loss of government contracts and other forms of research money, even executive officers.

Beyond Employment

This paper is not aimed at the usual expressions of prejudice and the relatively obvious means for their remedy. Instead I propose to describe some more subtle and not often recognized forms of prejudice and their more obscure effect on the intellectual development of our profession. In this task I shall confine myself to my own experiences and observations as an American of Chinese ancestry, to American anthropology as a field of scholarly endeavor, and primarily to the theory-making behavior of White American anthropologists as members of a profession. I am not, however, writing this paper to prove the existence of prejudice in our midst. Instead, I hope this paper will serve as a stimulus to American anthropologists of other ethnic origins who will be able to compare and contrast my experiences and observations with theirs, some of which are bound to be different from mine. However, whether they agree or disagree with me, we will have begun a process of professional self-examination long overdue.[2]

The central problem is: after a minority person has been admitted to the profession and has attained the exalted position of a faculty appointment, what are his chances of making his intellectual contribution accepted and recognized? In other words, what are his opportunities of helping to shape the intellectual direction of his chosen profession?

In dealing with this problem, I define myself as an ethnographer from China who has for twenty-six years been a participant observer. Anthropologists have for years resorted to the well-known field technique of being accepted by natives as a cousin, as a member of the tribe, as a brother in some secret order, and so forth. They also have made claims to varying degrees of fluency in the language of the native group under study. From this point of view my credentials are not inconsiderable. I am a member of two honored societies among my natives: the American Association of University Professors and the American Anthropological Association. I have for long been on the faculty of a well-known native institution of higher learning. My native colleagues accepted me so well that I was made chairman of our department and held that position for thirteen years. One of my daughters is married to a native, and both of my children are still being educated in native universities. Our whole family commands the native language well in writing and in speech. We have other advantages as fieldworkers, but it will be unnecessary to enumerate them.

Therefore, although I did not come to America as an ethnographer and did not do fieldwork in the usual sense of the term, I do not believe I can be faulted for that. The scope and intensity of my knowledge of my adopted society and culture through reading, observations, and live experiences are, probably at the risk of seeming to be immodest, greater than can be gained through a few years' usual fieldwork. My associations and contacts are wide, with academic groups because of my profession, with other groups as lecturer, consultant, father of school-age children, neighbor, citizen; and with individuals in diverse walks of life as friends and acquaintances.

Several qualifications must be made at the outset. First, the intention of my remarks is not that of negative criticism, and I hope that what follows will bear this out. By necessity I must be specific and some of the details may be uncomfortable to some of my fellow anthropologists. But I believe the time has come for plain speaking, and it is through the latter — not mutual admiration — that we can hope to improve the intellectual climate and products of our discipline. There will be readers who insist that my motive for writing this piece is pique. I have a couple of observations on this. Prejudice is very unpleasant to those at the receiving end. But the extent to which it continues to hurt depends upon how far one's performance has overridden the impediment. This response is unlikely, however, to be convincing to those preoccupied with hidden motives. I can only refer them to one of my recent publications on Psychosocial Homeostasis (Hsu 1971:23–44), and say that I think they are missing the point. They remind me of a parishioner who reacted to his church minister's recent decision to protest the Vietnam War by fasting, that the minister was "obsessed with a death wish" (reported in *Chicago Sun Times*, March 27, 1972). Such a response undoubtedly enabled its originator simultaneously to dismiss the social significance of the minister's action and to feel comfortable about the Vietnam War.

Second, I realize, of course, that there is diversity among White American anthropologists, and that I am not, therefore, speaking of every or any one of them.[3] Instead, my aim is to reveal something of the intellectual *conscience collectif* of White American anthropologists today in the Durkheimian sense. We may, for example, speak of the behavior of our fellow anthropologists as reflected in our official journal, *American Anthropologist*, without reference to individual editors who are changed every few years. The case is not unlike that of the link between Americans and the Vietnam War. Certainly there are many White American critics against the war from the very beginning. Later it has been the object of a flood of White American protests. But the United States of America as a whole made the Vietnam involvement happen and continue.

Third, if some readers find in the content of what follows confirmation of racism in America, they should realize that my purpose is not to expose racism as such. Racism cannot be eradicated and racist attitudes may even be hardened by exposés, although some exposés are necessary to define the problem. Some readers may also point to the fact that I have achieved a degree of "success in the American anthropological fraternity [which] is itself a strong refutation of the thesis of prejudice."[4]

I shall reply to this view by a simple question: are the success stories which grace the pages of *Ebony* magazine all the time and those of *Reader's Digest* occasionally "a strong refutation" of the reality of prejudice against Blacks in American business and industry?

Finally I am not unmindful that prejudice is a complex phenomenon, of which racism is only one variety. Ethnocentrism, the firm belief that one's own culture is all superior, and parochialism, the inability or refusal to see beyond one's own immediate surroundings or concerns, may feed and in turn be reinforced by racism. A man's views and behavior may be influenced by one or another or all of them. We are concerned here with a body of facts which in my view are expressions of or rooted in prejudice, however the term is defined.

In the following pages I shall address myself to three questions: (1) What and how far non-White intellectual contributions have been given a chance? (2) How do my own personal experiences illuminate the picture? (3) What are the intellectual implications to American anthropology, if any, of the answers to questions 1 and 2?

The Treatment of Non-White Intellectual Contributions

To begin with, most or all American anthropologists know something about Peking Man. But how many have heard or seen in print the name of Dr. Pei Wen-chung in the discovery and researches connected with this prehistoric find? Instead, the names they are familiar with here include Davidson Black, Franz Weidenreich, and even Von Konigswald.

For my own curiosity, I examined carefully the scholars cited or referred to in these three works: *Anthropology Today*, prepared under the chairmanship of Kroeber (1953); *Structural Anthropology*, by Lévi-Strauss (1963); and *The Rise of Anthropological Theory*, by Marvin Harris (1968). The first book was planned as an "international symposium" but its seven planners as suggested by its president A. L. Kroeber, were all White Americans.[5] Of the fifty-two invited contributors, thirty-eight were White anthropologists from the United States, eleven White anthropologists from Europe, and two Latin Americans. The one contributor from Indonesia turned out to be a Dutchman (Kroeber 1953:941–947).[6] Lévi-Strauss, author of the second title, is of course a Frenchman. But he has been accorded a leading position by American anthropologists as a whole. This fact is undeniable, not the least by his receipt of the special Wenner-Gren Medal. Both *Anthropology Today* and *Structural Anthropology* have exerted considerable influence in American anthropology. I chose Harris' book because it claims to be a "major new work" which "traces the development of anthropological thought from its beginnings to the present."

The results of my examination are interesting. Only eight references to works by non-Whites are found in the 940-page *Anthropology Today* (Busia, Chiang, Fei and Chang, Yang, and four by Hsu), and only one reference to a work of a non-White in the 398-page *Structural Anthropology* (Ling). Harris can boast of the largest bibliography for a single book. *The Rise of Anthropological Theory* contains a total of some 1,000 items, but only four of them are by non-Whites (Skinner, Imanishi, Li, and Hsu.)[7]

When we examine the nature of the few works by non-Whites which have been noted in the three books, the results are even more interesting. The works referred to are primarily ethnographies by natives of their own cultures. Only one of them enters into any of the central theoretical arguments of one of the three books in question.

In *Anthropology Today* (Kroeber 1953:469), Busia's book *Position of the Chief in the Modern Political System of the Ashanti* (1951) is mentioned as an example of an independent restudy of the Ashanti. The book by Chiang Mon-lin, *Tides from the West* (1947), does not have much to do with the paper that refers to it (Kroeber 1953:668–681). The books *Earthbound China* (Fei and Chang 1945), *A Chinese Village: Taitou, Shantung Province* (Yang 1945), and *Under the Ancestors' Shadow* (Hsu 1948), all studies by natives of their own culture, are merely noted as types of emphasis in fieldwork. Hsu's joint article with Theodora Abel, "Some Aspects of Personality of Chinese as Revealed by the Rorschach Test" (1949) appears twice, once in a footnote (Kroeber 1953:661) and a second time cited as one set of data obtained through a particular projective test. The only exception is Hsu's book *Religion, Science and Human Crises* (1952), which scores a theoretical point in Caudill's chapter on "Applied Anthropology in Medicine" (Kroeber 1953:774–775).

In the other two books, non-White scholars fare even worse. Lévi-Strauss has one footnote (1963:268) in which he refers to an article by Ling Shun-sheng on "Human Figures with Protruding Tongue" (1956). It has nothing to do with any of Lévi-Strauss' theoretical arguments. Of the four works by non-Whites referred to by Harris, that of Elliot Skinner contributes a one-paragraph quotation, while Li An-che is noted for his old and brief criticisms of Ruth Benedict's characterization of Zuni psychological orientation (1937) which for some reason most White anthropologists find convenient to use as ammunition against Benedict. Imanishi's contribution is entitled *Social Behavior in Japanese Monkeys* (1963). The reference to Hsu is by title only (Hsu 1961a:400–456).

In the three books examined, a variety of subjects are discussed or summarized, including magic, religion, linguistics, folklore, culture and personality, and national character. No contributions by non-White anthropologists figure in any of them.

My inevitable conclusion is that, as far as our sample data are concerned, works by non-Whites are either totally ignored or used very marginally.

My Own Experiences

How reliable are these results as indicators of the entire body of American anthropological literature? Could it not be that the three works I examined were accidents which simply did not *happen* to use more non-White contributions?[8]

My answer is that, as far as my own personal experiences are concerned, they are not at all out of character with the true situation.

For example, two of my most important books, *Americans and Chinese: Two Ways of Life* (1953) and *Clan, Caste and Club* (1963) were not even reviewed in the *American Anthropologist*. This, in spite of the fact that the 1953 title was accorded extended reviews in over seventy newspapers, magazines, and journals, including *The New York Times, Saturday Review of Literature, The American Sociological Review*, and even the *Catholic Journal of Sociology*.

On the other hand, *Under the Ancestors' Shadow* (Hsu 1948), *Religion, Science, and Human Crises* (Hsu 1952), *Aspects of Culture and Personality* (Hsu 1954), and *Psychological Anthropology: Approaches to Culture and Personality* (Hsu 1961b) were reviewed in the *American Anthropologist*. The first two of these four deal with my native China; my role in the last two books is that of editor and contributor.

This omission of my two most important books from the review pages of the *American Anthropologist* is, too, no accident.

There are quite a few other pieces which happen to fit the puzzle. For example, in addition to the fact that two of my best books were ignored in the *American Anthropologist*, an event which occurred over ten years before took on additional significance for me. If the reader will look at the back numbers of *American Anthropologist*, he will find one issue devoted to the subject, "The U.S.A. as Anthropologists See It," edited by

Special Editor Margaret Lantis (1955). I was included in the preliminary planning session two years before its appearance during one of our annual conventions. But even though my *Americans and Chinese* had already appeared, my contribution was not invited. The final product featured articles by Conrad Arensberg, Evon Z. Vogt, Alan P. Merriam, David Schneider, George Homans, Walter Goldschmidt, Ethel Albert, Melford Spiro, Cora DuBois, and Leonard Mason. These are distinguished scholars each in his or her own right, but most of them were not noted for their work on the United States. Furthermore, while some of them referred to the observations of David Riesman and Geoffrey Gorer on America, not one of them referred to *Americans and Chinese* even on subject matters over which my views and evidences are diametrically contrary to those given or used.[9]

These pieces of the puzzle in turn articulate well with what Kroeber wrote in 1948:

> Quite likely our civilization has its share of counterparts, which we cannot segregate off from the more practical remainder of the business of living because we are engulfed in this civilization of ours as we are in the air we breathe. *Some centuries may be needed* before the full recognition of our own non-rational couvades and totems and taboos becomes possible [Kroeber 1948:307; italics mine].

The obvious answer to Kroeber's problem is that if the Western anthropologists are too "engulfed" in their own particular civilization to achieve relatively objective views of them, we should train and encourage more non-Western anthropologists to scrutinize the "non-rational couvades and totems and taboos" in the Western way of life rather than waiting for "some centuries" to come. Otherwise we shall never be able to arrive at a time when Western anthropologists will see their own ways objectively, because there will never be a time when Westerners will not be engulfed in their own civilization.

Kroeber was not speaking rationally here. In view of his exalted position in American anthropology, I think it is not fantastic to regard his words as symptomatic of a widespread irrational reluctance on the part of White anthropologists to subject their own ways of life to the same kind of scrutiny by non-Whites they have exercised on non-White ways as a matter of course.

The facts I have presented so far would seem to warrant the following general conclusions:

(1) White anthropologists do not consider their non-White colleagues as intellectual equals.

(2) Since theoreticians enjoy higher professional esteem than mere fact gatherers, they can tolerate non-Whites in the role of the latter far more than that of the former.

(3) Even in the role of fact gatherers, White anthropologists would like non-Whites to confine themselves to their own native non-White cultures, and not to poke into the White preserves where the White anthropologists were born, live, work, and raise their children.

(4) White anthropologists find it most intolerable to accept theories about their White American culture by non-White anthropologists, especially if the theories contradict the ones White anthropologists have already head dear.

Intellectual Consequences of Prejudice

We now come to the most important question. All right, I can imagine some of my White colleagues saying, you have dug up some convincing evidence that we Whites have not bothered with what you non-Whites have had to offer intellectually to our profession, but have we not done very well so far? Have we not gathered a great amount of data and built up an impressive body of theories about this and other societies? Let's face it and, mind you, I am not at all personally prejudiced, but we have gone our own way simply because you non-Whites have little or nothing of scientific significance to offer.

In my opinion, the facts will prove such a view wrong. I think the psychocultural bondage under which White American anthropologists have been operating has seriously constrained their theory-making capabilities. This is evident in many areas, only a few of which can be considered here. The reader will note that in the following analysis I have dealt primarily with areas where my own position differs from those of others. I do so because (1) the issues involved are important; (2) my familiarity with the facts and arguments is considerable; and (3) it is in keeping with my hope stated at the outset, that this paper will stimulate colleagues of other ethnic origins to compare and contrast their experiences and observations with mine.

Witchcraft Studies

In witchcraft studies, theorists today have hardly advanced from the traditional notions that witchcraft and witch-hunting have something to do with law and order, that witchcraft can have serious effects among people who believe it, that the whole phenomenon may serve as an outlet for psychological tensions or as a means of "objectivizing subjective states, of formulating inexpressible feelings, and of integrating inarticulate experiences into a system" (Lévi-Strauss 1963:171–173).

Deeply immersed in their own Western cultural background, our White anthropologists have totally failed to note a most basic contrast between witch-hunting in Europe and America and its counterpart elsewhere. Witch-hunting in the West had generally one outcome: the extermination of the convicted. In Western societies there was no way for witches convicted by whatever means to redeem themselves, or to compensate their victims for their alleged wrongdoing. Their victims also could not resort to counter-witchcraft, for in that case the victims themselves would be subject to persecution as witches.

By contrast, witch-hunting in all non-Western societies is always a relativistic matter. The lives of convicted witches can be spared if the guilty ones or their kinsmen make compensation to the victims, or if the witches make public confession of guilt and a promise to reform. Counter-witchcraft, which consists of the same activities as those allegedly resorted to by witches, is common. It is also not uncommon for honored chiefs to possess counter-witchcraft. (For a fuller treatment of these differences see Hsu 1960:35–38.)

I submit that herein lies a key to the differences between Western societies and those of all of the rest of the world. In the former, compromise has little or no persistence. This is why the Inquisition only appeared in the West.[10] This tendency toward extremes is also why an American would be designated a Negro even if only ¹⁄₆₄th of his ancestry was Negro. But this is also why the so-called Witches' Sabbath, real or fancied, has had such a flourishing existence in Europe but has never been reported elsewhere in the world. Movements of extreme reaction only come about in societies presided over by absolutist repression.

Not realizing this difference between absolutist versus relativist views of things, Raymond Firth, a White British anthropologist whose name is a household word in American anthropology, gave the following account of Christianity in Tikopia in his restudy of that island after some thirty years. He found that although most Tikopians had become Christian by the time of his second visit, they did not allow the new faith to stand in the way of a good traditional marriage. That is, Christians and non-Christians still intermarried with ease. At this point Firth stumbled badly; he went on to conclude:

It might seem that the influence of Christianity would have appeared particularly in marriage preferences. Since in *other* societies it is common in Christian circles for objection to be made to the marriage of Christian with pagan, one might have *expected* this in Tikopia. . . . Here again, Christianity in Tikopia is not *yet* strong enough — or deep enough — to overcome the exercise of personal choice in spouses . . . [Firth 1959:204–205; italics mine].

What Firth has failed to see is that it is indeed common for *Western* Christians to object to intermarriage between Christians and non-Christians but not as a rule for *Asian* and most other Christians to act that way.

Some readers may disagree with my interpretation of Firth's remarks. They may opine, as one anonymous (to me) referee of this paper for the *Anthropologist* did, that Firth was actually "pleased to discover that this prejudiced aspect of Christianity had not suffused Tikopian culture." I would have accepted gladly this view had Firth said so (he did not) or given some evidence for it himself elsewhere (there is no such evidence). The truth is, religious beliefs have rarely divided most of the non-Western world as they have divided Western peoples, not in mate selection only. Hence Westerners have always taken human conflict due to differences in religious beliefs to be part of the order of nature, oblivious to the fact that religious strife is cultural, not pan-human (see Hsu 1970:224–276).

Firth's prediction about Christianity in Tikopia is not unlike Malthus' famous but discredited prediction of population and food. There were unavoidable reasons why a nineteenth century Malthus was so myopic, but there is no excuse for a twentieth century Firth to repeat the same performance. White American anthropologists are in the same intellectual boat as Firth, for, except for my own single paper challenging Firth's conclusion (Hsu 1967:1–19), I have seen no serious note taken of this issue in our American anthropological literature, not even in acculturation studies.

Caste Studies

Another area in which White American anthropology has yet to break out of its psychocultural bondage concerns caste. This is one area in which non-White anthropologists have done some serious intellectual exchange with their non-White counterparts. But the pattern of cooperation conforms well to one of my rules spelled out before: Japanese anthropologists will tell us about their native Japanese *Eta* and Indian anthropologists will write about their native arrangements in *varna* and *jati*, but White American anthropologists will work out theories of caste as a universal phenomenon. An excellent example is *Japan's Invisible Race: Caste in Culture and Personality* (DeVos and Wagatsuma 1966).

The superiority of this volume over many other studies of caste is that its contributions, including those of the two editors, have gone beyond the myopic but still ongoing type of work, in which counting the number of castes in an Indian village, ascertaining the caste hierarchy in that village, and giving an exact bill of the relative statuses of different oc-cupations, caste symbols, and pollution rules, including who will accept food or water from whom, etc., form the major task. This book attempts to relate the phenomenon of caste to some general factors which govern the behavior of the individual on the one hand and the society at large on the other. But its failure is considerable, and its failure comes from the fact that although the vision of the authors is less constricted than that of many others, it is still not wide enough. They would have fared better intellectually had they examined some results of a larger radius — for example, comparative studies of India, China, and the United States. A comprehensive understanding of caste phenomena requires that we not only study it *per se* but also its wider context, not only in societies where it exists, but also where, in comparable situations, it fails to develop.[11]

I can deal here only with one of the issues raised by one of the authors of this book, namely that of Gerald D. Berreman, on whether caste is also an Indian dilemma in the same sense that Gunnar Myrdal spoke of the Negro-White caste situation as an American dilemma (Berreman 1966:297–298). Myrdal, as most of us know, concluded that the inequal-ity suffered by American Negroes is an American dilemma because it is inconsistent with the egalitarian nature of the American culture. Oliver Cox, writing after Myrdal, said that that dilemma is nonexistent in India. "The difference between the racial attitudes of whites and the caste attitude so far as the social ideals of each system are concerned, is that whites *wrongfully* take the position of excluding groups from participat-ing freely in the common culture, while castes *rightfully* exclude out-siders from participating in their *dharma* [moral duty]" (Cox 1945:367).

Berreman disagrees with both views. He argues along two lines. On the one hand, he thinks there is no American dilemma because "discrim-ination against the Negro is not in violation of southern ideal norms." Berreman quotes Spiro in his support (1951:34). On the other hand,

Berreman insists, "If there is an American dilemma, as Myrdal has described it, there is also an Indian dilemma . . . since India's constitution, like America's, espouses principles of equality and among India's intellectual and political elite there is widespread advocacy of and even conformity to these principles — more widespread one might note, than in the elite of the Southern United States today" (Berreman 1966:297). The net result of Berreman's position is that there is no difference between the caste situation in India and the Black-White inequality in the United States.

I think both arguments are wide of the mark. It is perfectly true, as Spiro (1951:34) noted, that "discrimination against the Negro is not in violation of ideal norms" in the Southern United States. But the Southern United States is not the whole of United States society and is not the maker and prime mover of American national policy today. The overall ideal of the United States society is egalitarian, and the developments (legal, educational, economic, and social) in our society within the last twenty years have moved inexorably toward more and more reduction of the customary *de jure* and *de facto* inequality. Both of these are in sharp contrast to what goes on in the South African Union today.

On the other hand, while it is also true that India's modern constitution is egalitarian in principle and that India's elite support that constitution, the entire weight of the Hindu sacred literature is in support of the Hindu caste system. The latter is in sharp contrast to that in the United States. Furthermore, the ideal and reality of life in local communities all over India are in support of the Hindu caste system. This statement holds true whether we look at Sirkanda, according to Berreman's own ethnographic report (Berreman 1960:125) or elsewhere. And, finally, even the Hindu elite who support the egalitarian principles of the Indian constitution tend to adhere to the caste customs where they pertain to personal matters such as dining and marriage.

The difference between the Indian caste situation and the United States Black-White situation is not a matter of degree, as Berreman would have us believe. The American constitution and the principles of equality and freedom embodied in the American legal framework arose from within the Western and American societies, and were not imported from outside. The Civil War was made in America, not inspired by some colonial masters. [Of course, those who championed the cause of racial equality were opposed by others deeply committed to its opposite. This is in the nature of the United States–type of society, in which extreme fissionary and polarizing tendencies are one of its main characteristics, as I explained in *Clan, Caste, and Club* (Hsu 1963:192–231).] The egalitarian principle among free men, not the hierarchical principle of the caste system, is the basis of the American kinship usages, employer-employee relations, and American interpersonal relationships in general.

This is not the case in India. The modern egalitarian Indian constitution is not rooted in India's past but represents a major form of Western intrusion. It has yet to find its psychosocial foundation in India. It is still incommensurate with India's kinship system and interpersonal relationships in general. There simply is no Indian dilemma comparable to its American counterpart.

Had Berreman understood something of China's transformation under Western impact during the last hundred years, he might have seen much more of a parallel between India and China and much less *of anything* in common between India and the United States.

China did not have any caste system, but the weight of her long tradition was heavy upon her shoulders when the West knocked down her doors in the middle of the nineteenth century. The series of new constitutions promulgated in 1913, 1917, and 1936 had no grassroots in Chinese society and culture. Certainly there were houses of parliament in Western style. There were many returned students and others with modern Chinese education who not only supported the new constitutions but also attacked ancestor rites, worship of all traditional gods, the big family ideal, filial piety, and Confucianism. Some members of this elite are even well known in the United States, such as Liang Chi-chao and Hu Shih. But democracy of the Western European and American type in the end has not prevailed in China. Had a caste system been part of China's traditional society, the egalitarian Chinese constitutions also would not have led to any Chinese dilemma comparable to that which Myrdal described for the United States of America.

The Obsession with Economic Determinism

The major weakness in American anthropology is found in its general theories on the determinants of human social and cultural behavior. This major weakness is in my view directly attributable to the failure of White American anthropologists to consider views other than those to which their cultural conditioning has led them.

A principal conclusion of my book *Americans and Chinese: Purpose and Fulfillment in Great Civilizations* (1970; first published in 1953 with the subtitle "Two Ways of Life") is that the traditional Chinese type of society in which the individual is imbedded in the elementary kinship and locality ties tends to predispose its members to weak involvement with things, while the American type of society — whether old or new — in which the individual has no comparable human moorings, tends to compel its members to seek strong defense behind material successes. (Readers should not mistake this contrast for the usual spiritual-materialist dichotomy, for it is also part of my thesis that the Chinese were never seriously involved with their gods, while the Americans, even today, in spite of their materialism, still place high valuation on religious affiliation and services, as witness, for example, the continuing furor about abortion and the most recent controversy over prayer in the schools.)

Thus the American solution to all problems seems to be more money to build better and taller physical external safeguards; law and order? more police and detection devices; strangulating congestion in the legal process? more courts and more prisons; riots and violence? more low-income housing and more employment; danger of Communism and other revolutionary movements? enlargement of the Vietnam conflict by invasion of Cambodia and bigger and better bomb tests; and so on.

I find much evidence which supports this same hypothesis in the theory-making ways of American anthropologists. Having been reared in an individual-centered culture in which men do not form lasting and close ties with each other, American anthropologists seem to avoid delving deeply into the question of how human beings relate to each other. Instead, they resort to what I describe as theoretical escapism. They have not improved on Durkheim's distinction between mechanical and organic solidarity. They repeat Linton's concepts, status and role. They excel in componential analysis of kinship terms. But they leave the entire area of affect — how human beings feel about each other — untouched, except to resort to a Freudian idiom or two now and then.

One of the more recent forms of theoretical escapism is economic determinism of one kind or another. We have, therefore, theories of human behavior variously entitled the "Culture of Poverty" (Lewis); the "Peasant Society" (Foster); "Ecology" (Sahlins, Helm, Conklin, Leeds, and others); "Food Surplus" (Steward); the "Hydraulic Society" (Wittfogel, used by many anthropologists). A brief check of *Current Anthropology* from 1965 to 1971 shows that, out of a total of fifty-one major articles, at least seventeen bear on the influence of technology or ecology or poverty. Lewis' "Culture of Poverty" received the most attention, being the object of no fewer than four major articles and two full-scale "CA Treatment" book reviews.

Just how good are some of these economic deterministic theories? In this article I can only briefly examine two pieces of work. One is by Julian Steward and Louis C. Faron (1959); the other is by Jack M. Potter (1968).

Under the subtitle "Surplus Production and Social Types" Steward and Faron begin by saying:

> While sociocultural types are not determined entirely by the amount or kind of food production, there is an important relationship between the two.
>
> The Araucanians of central Chile also lacked specialists, although they were seemingly capable of potential surplus food production. It would seem therefore that while some societies lacked the minimum productivity necessary to develop an internally specialized society, it does not necessarily follow that the possibility of surplus production will lead to full-time specialists [1959:60].

So far Steward and Faron have not said anything substantial. Then, under the subtitle "Environment and Production in Relation to Types of Chiefdoms," after showing indifferent evidence in support of a link between the two, they observe:

> it seems certain that two factors stimulated cultural development beyond the seeming environmental limitations imposed by the swamps in the unhealthy lowlands and the prevalent rain forests on the mountains. First, Central America had been an avenue of cultural exchange between North and South America for several thousand years. . . . Second, coastal resources supplemented farming among some groups such as the Cuna of Panama [1959:179–180].

However, Steward and Faron find the latter two factors inadequate to account for their facts either, for they maintain: "Some Central American Indians, however, never developed chiefdoms" (1959:180). Again Steward and Faron have not said anything substantial, for the different parts of what they have said cancel each other out. But, they are not giving up the economic factor. Explaining why the Araucanians, though favorably situated according to their food surplus thesis, have never developed the state and chiefdom, Steward and Faron continue:

The actual conversion of "adequate" food production and leisure time into production of surplus foods that supported classes of specialists who were relieved of food production was brought about principally by diffused patterns of warfare and religion. . . . The Araucanians never received the military and religious patterns that led to state formation among the chiefdoms. . . . The chiefdoms resulted from the combination of potential surplus production with factors that amalgamated individual villages into larger units requiring social, military, and political controls of much wider and greater power than anything known among the Araucanians or the tropical-forest villages [1959:185–186].

After such an exhibition of the uselessness of the notion of food surplus or even population density as satisfactory explanations for social development, Steward and Faron grandly conclude:

The chiefdoms and states, like the other cultural types in South America, represented special ways in which people were organized to achieve cultural objectives in particular environments. . . . And yet *the general character of these objectives was ultimately determined by the nature* of food production [1959:199; italics mine].

Jack Potter's views arising out of his study of a village in the New Territory of Hongkong are illuminating of the intellectual effect of White American anthropological prejudice in a different way. H. T. Fei and a number of other Chinese social scientists, together with the British historian, R. H. Tawney, have documented in a variety of ways the deleterious economic effects of foreign domination through the Treaty Ports on China. Potter, partly using his data from a Chinese village in the British Crown Colony of Hongkong, now says that this just is not so. Instead, he maintains, the foreign domination and the Treaty Ports benefited the Chinese peasants and their domestic industries by stimulating their prosperity and growth. In searching for support, Potter makes brief excursions into a number of previous articles and books on agrarian China, and he protects himself by the following sentence:

Furthermore, in discussing the effects of treaty port industry and commerce on the Chinese rural economy, I am talking only about the period from roughly 1900 to the late 1930's, a limited time perspective, and am not making judgments as to the ultimate and long-range effects of the treaty powers on the rural Chinese economy or on Chinese society as a whole [1968:181].

Now, if I were cynical, I would have observed that Potter's position reminds me of a piece I once read in the "Guest Privilege" column of *Life* Magazine entitled something like "Business Needs the Mafia." That writer showed how the Mafia was beneficial to a number of individual business establishments. I cannot but point out that had Potter confined his researches to the Chinese *compradores* who performed such lucrative and efficient services as middlemen between foreign merchants and Chinese farm producers for the period he is talking about, he would have been able to point to even more startling benefits for the Chinese.

If Potter were an economist pure and simple whose concern is with week-to-week variations, or an archaeologist whose attention is often unavoidably confined to the economic factor because of the limits of the data with which he has to deal, I would understand. But is Potter justified in being so near-sighted as to ignore "the ultimate and long-range effects of the treaty powers on the rural Chinese economy or on Chinese society as a whole"? Surely Potter must know that, besides suffering from foreign military presence, political domination, legal privileges, and tariff shackles, China had an adverse trade balance during the very period in question many many times worse than what we are experiencing in the United States today. The sad thing was that China could not then even do anything to remedy the situation, such as the sudden imposition of a ten percent surcharge on all imports, for the Chinese customs service was, too, in the hands of the treaty powers and the rates of levy were determined by the Unequal Treaties.

Had Potter not been so anxious to show the economic benefits for the Chinese, and had he put himself in the place of the Chinese, he might have seen the starker side of the reality described by Marshall D. Sahlins, who says about the Plains Indians and the horse:

> The florescence of Plains culture was a fugitive episode, lasting altogether less than 300 years; and these decisive opening and closing events, as well as the trade that subsidized tribal history in all the time between, were "benefits" of European civilization [1968:41].

There is here room for quite a few Potters to show how the White men showered economic benefits on the Indians. They could also follow Potter's example by burying their self-protection clause in some insignificant place in their texts. Their very limited results could then be used by those so disposed under some such general headline as

"Unequal Treaties Beneficial to Indians, New Discovery by California Anthropologist!"[12]

The Myth of the Changing American Character
In the 1955 all-White symposium on "The U.S.A. as Anthropologists See It" mentioned previously, Conrad Arensberg dealt with the changing patterns of American communities from New England to the South and to the Midwest. Following Lewis Mumford (1937) he saw this change as the result of "the great transformations of the industrial revolution" (Arensberg 1955:1156). Arensberg noted the development of "a new urban life" where, agreeing with David Riesman (1950), "the life of the 'peer groups' of the 'lonely crowd'" prevails. And Arensberg concludes:

> This mosaic of discontinuities of age, class, and ethnicity which is the new metropolitan community is a very different one indeed from the visibly hierarchic and mobile community that preceded it . . . the new cultural form, with its new social and economic traits and problems, is here before us, in the most violent emergence, and the new age has already found its new unit of transmission and organization [Arensberg 1955:1159–1160].

The individual-centered man, having no permanent human moorings, rationalizes his condition of life by placing high premium on the idea of change. In turn, his preoccupation with things to compensate for his deficiency in permanent human relations tends to make him believe that economic factors are the very source of all change. This was why the simple-minded Turner thesis was an instant success among American historians (see, e.g., Taylor 1949; Smith 1950; Billington 1966). This is also why Mumford's and Riesman's observations have become so influential in American sociology.

I submit that the high value Americans accord to the idea of change is not the same as change itself, but that the escalation of material achievements may in fact be merely symptomatic of the real lack of and refusal to change in the American character. The scientific significance of these observations is unlikely to be appreciated by White American anthropologists unless they consciously break out of the bondage of the intellectual vicious circle.

Elsewhere I have shown how David Riesman errs in concluding that the American national character has changed from what he terms "inner-direction" to "other-direction." Instead, I see "other-direction," of which conformity is its outstanding characteristic, as the result of American intensification of "inner-direction," of which individualism is its primary institutional mover. For there are basic differences between conformity in situation-centered societies such as traditional China (where conformity was generally considered good), and in individual-centered societies such as the United States (where conformity is a mere means for peer acceptance, but where it is at the same time resented and protested against) (Hsu 1953:111–118).

We cannot blame American sociologists, prevented as they are by their general unfamiliarity with non-American ways to develop a wider intellectual vision, for mistaking economic and other material changes for real changes (or causes for the changes) in the American character. But is there a good excuse for anthropologists, who are cross-cultural by intention, to commit the same error? Is there a good excuse for them, too, to mistake economic and other material changes for real changes (or causes for the changes) in the American character?

Any casual observer of today's United States of America cannot fail to see our *external* differences (material, institutional, and cultural) from Europe and from our own earlier conditions of existence. The communications networks are faster and more extensive, the buildings are taller and replete with more modern equipment, the suburbia, the vast business empires, the proliferation of colleges and universities, the huge bureaucracy, the new weapons, the welfare system, the increasing casualness of human contacts, the sex explosion in literature, movies, and elsewhere, coeducational dormitories on campuses, to name but a few. But has the American national character changed from its antecedental European and early American counterparts? Has America really created something new for Western man, new in spirit, new in objectives, and new in the way that man treats the world around him and goes about solving his problems?

I submit that America has not — not in the essentials anyway. What America has done is to escalate those values, attitudes, and aspirations held dear by Western man from the beginning of Western history, thereby magnifying their strengths and their weaknesses, their rewards and their punishments. The scenery is new, but the players and what they pursue and how they act are the same as before.

Take the case of the Trojan War, made famous by Homer's *Iliad* and substantiated by the archaeological work of Schliemann and others. *The Iliad, The Odyssey, Agamemnon* — especially the first two — are among the most widely read treasures of Western literature. They are required reading in high schools and colleges. Their popularity is attested to by the fact that they are annotated and interpreted and published in numerous editions. What do they tell their readers?

To secure the return of his seduced sister-in-law, Agamemnon amassed a formidable fleet of some 1200 ships by twisting the arms of many less powerful princes into becoming his allies, sacrificed his first born daughter to get a suitable wind, sailed to far away Asia Minor and besieged the city of Troy for ten years until the stubborn enemy was vanquished and the city laid waste. However, not only were the conquerors beset by quarrels among themselves during the war and on their return journey, but those who made their way home were met by treachery even greater than the initial abduction of Helen, and hostility on the part of those they had left at home years before. Shortly afterwards, the returning heroes and their people were driven out of their homeland by northern invaders such as the Thessalians and the Dorians.

Is there not a parallel between the contents of these Greek tragedies, the Medieval Crusades, and the twentieth century American intervention in Vietnam?

In each case, the leading campaigners were obsessed with one idea and one objective. In each case, tremendous amounts of armed might were mobilized to achieve an objective, the significance of which was either questionable or far outweighed by the expenditure of life and resources. In each case, willing or unwilling allies were pressed into service. In each case, victory on the battlefield did not lead to peace and happiness at home.

Furthermore, the manner in which these Greek tragedies have been approached by our scholars and teachers of English is interesting. They do not as a rule discuss the social and political implications of the Trojan War. Instead they speak of *The Iliad* as the tragedy of Achilleus, dwelling on the sufferings of the Greek forces in his absence, "the story of a great man who through a fault in an otherwise noble character (and even the fault is noble) brings disaster upon himself, since the death of Patroklos is the work of free choice on the part of Achilleus," the vengeance taken by Achilleus on Hektor, and the resolution of Achilleus' anger in a grudging forgiveness by the return of the body of Hektor to the Trojans.

Illicit love, romantic or other intrigues, personal mistakes, personal suffering, personal invincibility, personal triumph, and personal freedom — and more along the same lines — these rather than the individual's role in society have been the mainstay of European and American drama and fiction ever since: Captain Ahab of *Moby Dick* fame, Jesse James of the "westerns," the Old Man in *The Old Man and the Sea,* Lee Harvey Oswald,[13] the assassin of President Kennedy, these are but a few of the many popular American heroes. And more heroes in the same mold are being made before our very eyes. For example, the man who recently (November, 1971) hijacked a Northwest Airlines airplane and parachuted from it with $200,000 ransom money has already been described as a "system-beater" hero in the public media. The "D. B. Cooper, Where Are You?" T-shirt is a rage among many young men in the Pacific Northwest. (D. B. Cooper is the name the hijacker himself gave to the airline.) For that is the American anti-establishmentarian way. What Americans glorify are the courage, determination, and skill exemplified by the individualistic hero's acts, whatever their consequences to the society or societies.

The *structure* of the American society is indeed different from its ancestral European and early American varieties, but its *content* — the pattern of how its people feel about and act toward themselves and each other as well as the rest of the world — is not.[14] Instead, this content has merely been escalated or intensified. The essence of that process of escalation and intensification is the American's search for new places to live, new means of amusement, new communications media, new ways of romance and self-gratification; in short, new worlds. But the newness of the one is the very essence of the oldness of the other.

New Discovery: Neo-Instinctivism
Perhaps as a reaction to the obsession with economic determinism but continuing to avoid focusing on man's relationship with other men, some individual-centered White American anthropologists have recently seemed to gravitate toward what, for want of a better term, I call Neo-Instinctivism. That is, we behave the way we do because of our biological endowment. Hence we have *The Human Animal* (La Barre 1954), *Men in Groups* (Tiger 1969, reviewed by Count 1970), *The Imperial Animal* (Tiger and Fox 1971),[15] *The Hunting Peoples* (Coon 1971), and, of course, *The Naked Ape* (Morris 1967, reviewed by Tuttle 1968).

I shall deal only with one of them, namely, *Men in Groups.* Tiger's thesis begins with the assumption that male bonding is universal from prehistoric hordes to complex modern communities. This male bonding, which is a "spinal cord" of the human community, is probably biologically based. It is still evident among primates. It provides a "definite genetic advantage" (*Ibid.*:99) in hunting. Since the "hunting phase" occupied about 99% of human history, and since the evolution of the "hunting hominid was well under way fourteen million years ago, the selective pressure on human populations existing during (that phase was) of particular and crucial importance in determining the human genotype" (*Ibid.*:98).

Up to this point, Tiger's arguments seem reasonable. What becomes untenable is that he proceeds from here to show that this "biologically" programmed male bonding is the basis of behavior patterns of today's man in politics, in play and work, in religion, in age-grading, and in voluntary associations many of which involve bloody initiations, aggression, and war.

To "prove" his thesis, Tiger's data concern Western man ninety-nine percent of the time. The few non-Western facts he uses are incidental or contradictory. For instance, Tiger points to Madame Sun Yat-sen as an example of a female who could only acquire high office "by being politically active relatives of senior politicians who die" (1969:73). But he does not mention the high positions of Madame Binh at the Paris Vietnam Peace talks, Madame Chiang in Taiwan, and Madame Mao in mainland China whose husbands are alive and in power. Furthermore, these Oriental women did not even gain power by any of the "constitutional and other legal restraints" which according to Tiger might "permit successful dominant females an effective role" (1969:75).

A more basic flaw is Tiger's use of William Golding's *Lord of the Flies* as very important evidence of male bonding and aggression. A less ethnocentric anthropologist might at least have inquired as to whether comparable novels could be found in China, Japan, or India. The author would have received a negative answer, not even in India, and certainly not in Japan or China.

It is not possible here to detail the many differences between Western novels and Asian novels and what they signify. I have treated them elsewhere (Hsu 1970:24–41). The total absence of *Lord of the Flies* type of literature in Asia is basic and critical, and must be faced by Tiger if he is to make his point. As it is, Tiger takes English public school culture and its ethics of violent mastery, hierarchy, and concern about a monotheistic God, to be universal human nature.

This procedure of taking an example of the Western behavior pattern to be the universal human pattern is followed by all the others in the instinctivistic vein. They see violence and aggression as inevitable. They echo the psychologist B. F. Skinner (1971) that all mankind is headed toward self-destruction. Somehow the real cultural differences in which the anthropologists have been claiming to be specialists for so long have been lost. When the chips are down, Western anthropologists are too "engulfed" in their own civilizations "as the air" they "breathe," so that they mistake, after all, their own cultural ways for the ways of the rest of mankind.

With the bombs getting bigger and better every advancing day, mankind is indeed in danger of total destruction, but it is not world self-destruction. Instead, it is a case of self-destruction by Western men who promise to take the rest of mankind with them. From that point of view, these and other instinctivistic, biologically deterministic books, to the extent that they succeed in cautioning individualistic and individual-centered Westerners against further escalation of the forces for self-destruction, will have performed a useful service. But as anthropological theories of human social and cultural behavior, they can only lead to regression, not progression.

For over 300 years, Whites, first European and then American, have been trying to save the rest of the world by asking us to believe in the Virgin Birth and the Resurrection of Jesus. Now some of them are asking us to believe that we are nothing but sub-human apes in human clothing.

Human beings are not born of virgins and they cannot return from the dead; but neither are they sub-human apes. The lack of human trust, the proliferation of aggression and violence in some societies that some anthropologists have mistaken for sub-human behavior are also cultural, but they are manifestations of one variety of culture, and certainly are not universal. For example, there are many societies where it is still safe to walk its streets after dark, where employees are still devoted to their employers, and where friendship among men is still lasting because they are unafraid of being sentimental toward each other.

Human beings everywhere associate primarily with other human beings: they rub shoulders with each other, confide in each other, and compete against each other. We are produced by human beings and mentally shaped by human beings. The major key (though never the only key) as to why we behave like human beings as well as to why we behave like Americans or Japanese is to be found in our relationships with our fellow human beings, not in our instincts or our relationships with animals or things.

Concluding Remarks

The primary purpose of this article is not to attack prejudice or to outline ways and means for its elimination in American anthropology. Instead, it aims at demonstrating the reality of prejudice (racist, ethnocentric, and parochial) and how its mental bondage has in some areas warped the intellectual direction and arrested the intellectual progress of our profession.

To the reader who is still troubled by the fact that I have separated racism from ethnocentrism and parochialism, I can now explain the problem by something familiar. For example, American Blacks were "invisible" until recently to the world of the White American. That phenomenon was not exclusive to the United States. Tom Mboya, the assassinated leader of Kenya, was once a clerk in a telegraph office. An English woman came in when Mboya was alone to receive customers and she called out straight over Mboya's head, "Is there anyone in the office?" What I have dealt with here is not the gross kind of physical "invisibility" White America has for long imposed on the non-Whites, especially Blacks, but the subtler forms of "invisibility," of non-White intellectual presence. From that point of view, ethnocentrism and parochialism merge with racism.

Also, I do not mean White America alone has a monopoly on prejudice, although I claim it possesses some peculiar characteristics (see Hsu 1972:241–266), or that White Americans offer nothing but prejudice. The intellectual and material advantages that the United States society can provide individuals with talent, drive and imagination are great. That is why so many came to her shores, including myself.

However, unless we begin to consider ways and means of breaking out of this mental bondage, all talk of integration, of our progression, or of "cultural transmission . . . across societal lines" (Mead 1966:68) is spurious, and truly universally applicable theories of man can hardly emerge.

Notes

1. Principally based on a paper presented at the 70th Annual Convention of the American Anthropological Association in New York City, 1971. I am indebted to my colleague, Johannes Fabian, and to the anonymous referees consulted by the Editor of the *American Anthropologist*, for constructive criticisms which materially improved this paper.

2. I know of two Black anthropologists who raised questions along similar lines before me. See Delmos Jones (1970) and William S. Willis, Jr. (1970). The Committee on Minorities and Anthropology of our Association, under the chairmanship of Tom Weaver, is now in the process of analyzing the returns to a questionnaire from some seventy American anthropologists of minority origins on many issues, including ones raised in this paper.

3. Many American anthropologists are Jewish in origin. Considering the very great importance Jewish/non-Jewish differences signify in American society, I cannot be sure that such differences have no bearing on the subject of this paper.

4. This is a direct quotation from one of the anonymous referees of this paper consulted by the Editor.

5. The planning group consisted of Wendell C. Bennett, Harry Hoijer, Clyde Kluckhohn, Ralph Linton, David G. Mandelbaum, William Duncan Strong, and S. L. Washburn. Linton was subsequently confined to bed and did not attend the organizing meetings (Kroeber 1953:v–vi).

6. There were some glaring omissions of White anthropologists too. M. J. Herskovits was conspicuous by his absence.

7. Harris' book, which pretentiously claims to be *summa anthropologiae*, suffers also from the omission of significant works by many White Europeans. The following names are a partial list of his omissions: Karl Mannheim, Jacobson, F. Barth, Max Muller, W. Koppers, W. Wundt, Hocart, and, most incredibly, Max Weber. Of the few non-Whites referred to only two are members of the American anthropological fraternity.

8. I am aware of the fact that one man's experiences in a profession are insufficient for generalizing about that profession as a whole. However one man's experiences over twenty-six years in the profession become quantitatively more valid than those over much shorter periods of time. I am offering my personal experiences not alone but in conjunction with other evidences. Readers who do not care for the experiences of one individual or who see only ego tripping in such an account are advised to skip the next few pages, go on directly to the following section and consider the merits and demerits of my arguments on intellectual grounds.

9. See section of this article entitled "Myth of the Changing American Character" for a major disagreement between Riesman's and my positions on American character.

10. Except for Goa in India under the Portuguese.

11. For example, why did *Eta* develop and persist in Japan but not in China when both societies traditionally had slavery? This question is dealt with in Chapter 12 of my book, *Iemoto: The Heart of Japan* (Hsu n.d.).

12. One anonymous referee of the paper advised me to "show more clearly how these theories (economic determinism and others which follow) by white anthropologists function to buttress racism in white societies and in white rule."

Throughout human history those in control of power never relinquish it willingly. It is therefore perfectly conceivable that some forms of theoretical escapism are not unconnected with some hidden wish to reinforce that control or at least to maintain the status quo. Such a desire may have underlined the view that Chinese scholars could not be "objective" about China, a view used as we saw before, to justify their exclusion from any important role in established departments with Chinese concentration. But I am unwilling to speculate on unconscious motives. Besides, I think most of my White fellow anthropologists regard themselves as liberals *vis-à-vis* minorities. Some of them are, for example, actively trying to protect the American Indians.

13. For a report of how well Lee Harvey Oswald's mother and widow have done by selling stories and mementoes, see Anonymous 1967.

14. For the distinction between structure and content see Hsu 1959.

15. Tiger and Fox try to disclaim biological determinism, but that, in my view, is pure window dressing.

References Cited

Abel, Theodora M., and Francis L. K. Hsu
1949. Some Aspects of Personality of Chinese as Revealed by the Rorschach Test. Rorschach Research Exchange and Journal of Projective Techniques 13(3): 286–301.

Anonymous
1967 The Assassination: Scene of the Crime. Newsweek, December 4:31–32.

Arensberg, Conrad M.
1955 American Communities. American Anthropologist 57: 1143–1162.

Berreman, Gerald D.
1960 Caste in India and the United States. American Journal of Sociology 66(2):120–127.
1966 Structure and Function of Caste System. *In* Japan's Invisible Race: Caste in Culture and Personality. George DeVos and Hiroshi Wagatsuma, Eds. Berkeley: University of California Press. pp. 277–307.

Billington, Ray Allen
1966 America's Frontier Heritage. New York: Holt, Rinehart & Winston.

Busia, K. A.
1951 Position of the Chief in the Modern Political System of the Ashanti. London and New York: Oxford University Press for the International African Institute.

Caudill, William
1953 Applied Anthropology in Medicine. *In* Anthropology Today. Alfred L. Kroeber, Ed. Chicago: University of Chicago Press, pp. 771–806.

Chiang, Mon-lin
  1947 Tides from the West. New Haven: Yale University Press.
Conklin, Harold C.
  1961 The Study of Shifting Cultivation. Current Anthropology 2(1):27–61.
Coon, Carleton
  1971 The Hunting Peoples. Boston: Little, Brown and Co.
Count, Earl W.
  1970 Review of Men in Groups, by Lionel Tiger. American Anthropologist 72:869–872.
Cox, Oliver
  1945 Race and Caste: A Distinction. American Journal of Sociology 50:360–368.
DeVos, George, and Hiroshi Wagatsuma
  1966 Japan's Invisible Race: Caste in Culture and Personality. Berkeley: University of California Press.
Fei, H. T., and C. I. Chang
  1945 Earthbound China. Chicago: University of Chicago Press.
Firth, Raymond
  1959 Social Change in Tikopia. London: George Allen and Unwin.
Foster, George
  1965 Peasant Society and the Image of the Limited Good. American Anthropologist 67:293–315.
Harris, Marvin
  1968 The Rise of Anthropological Theory. New York: Thomas Y. Crowell.

Helm, June
  1962 The Ecological Approach in Anthropology. American Journal of Sociology 67:630–639.
Hsu, Francis L. K.
  1948 Under the Ancestor's Shadow. New York: Columbia University Press. (Revised 1967 and 1971).
  1952 Religion, Science and Human Crises. London: Routledge & Kegan Paul.
  1953 American and Chinese: Two Ways of Life. New York: Schuman.
  1954 Aspects of Culture and Personality. New York: Abelard-Schuman.
  1959 Structure, Function, Content, and Process. American Anthropologist 61:790–805.
  1960 A Neglected Aspect of Witchcraft Studies. Journal of American Folklore 73(287):35–38.
  1961a Kinship and Ways of Life. In Psychological Anthropology: Approaches to Culture and Personality. Francis L. K. Hsu, Ed. Homewood, Illinois: Dorsey Press. pp. 400–456.
  1961b Psychological Anthropology: Approaches to Culture and Personality. Homewood, Illinois: Dorsey Press.
  1963 Clan, Caste, and Club. New York: Van Nostrand-Reinhold.
  1967 Christianity and the Anthropologist. International Journal of Comparative Sociology 8(1):1–19.

1970 Americans and Chinese: Purpose and Fulfillment in Great Civilizations. Revised edition. New York: Doubleday and the Natural History Press.

1971 Psychosocial Homeostasis (PSH) and *Jen:* Concepts for Advancing Psychological Anthropology. American Anthropologist 73:23–44.

1972 Psychological Anthropology. 2nd Edition. Cambridge: Schenkman.

n.d. Iemoto: The Heart of Japan. Cambridge: Schenkman. (In press.)

Imanishi, K.

1963 Social Behavior in Japanese Monkeys. *In* Primate Social Behavior. C. H. Southwick, Ed. Princeton: D. Van Nostrand. pp. 68–82.

Jones, Delmos

1970 Towards a Native Anthropology. Human Organization 29: 251–259.

Kroeber, Alfred L., Ed.

1948 Anthropology. Revised Edition. New York: Harcourt.

1953 Anthropology Today. Chicago: University of Chicago Press.

LaBarre, Weston

1954 The Human Animal. Chicago: University of Chicago Press.

Lantis, Margaret, Ed.

1955 The U.S.A. as Anthropologists See It. American Anthropologist 57(6, pt. 1).

Leeds, Anthony, and Andrew P. Vayda, Eds.

1965 Man, Culture and Animals. Washington, D.C.: American Association for the Advancement of Science.

Lévi-Strauss, Claude

1963 Structural Anthropology. New York: Basic Books.

Lewis, Oscar

1966 The Culture of Poverty. Scientific American 215:19–25.

Li, An-che

1937 Zuni: Some Observations and Queries. American Anthropologist 39:62–77.

Ling Shun Sheng

1956 Human Figures with Protruding Tongue Found in the Taitung Prefecture, Formosa, and Their Affinities Found in Other Pacific Areas. Nankang, Taipei: Bulletin of the Institute of Ethnology, Academia Sinica, No. 2.

Mead, Margaret

1966 *Author's precis for* Continuities in Cultural Evolution, by M. Mead. Current Anthropology 7(1):67–68.

Morris, Desmond

1967 The Naked Ape. New York: McGraw Hill.

Mumford, Lewis

1937 The Culture of Cities. New York: Harcourt and Brace.

Nash, Manning

1966 Primitive and Peasant Economic Systems. San Francisco: Chandler.

Potter, Jack M.
   1968   Capitalism and the Chinese Peasant. Berkeley and Los Angeles: University of California Press.

Riesman, David
   1950   The Lonely Crowd. New Haven: Yale University Press.

Sahlins, Marshall D.
   1968   Tribesmen.   Englewood Cliffs: Prentice-Hall.

Skinner, B. F.
   1971   Beyond Freedom and Dignity. New York: Alfred A. Knopf.

Skinner, Elliot
   1964   The Mossi of the Upper Volta. Stanford: Stanford University Press.

Smith, Henry Nash
   1950   Virgin Land. Cambridge: Harvard University Press.

Spiro, Melford E.
   1951   Culture and Personality: The Natural History of a False Dichotomy. Psychiatry 14(34): 19–46.

Steward, Julian, and L. Faron
   1959   Native Peoples of South America. New York: McGraw-Hill.

Taylor, George Rogers, Ed.
   1949   The Turner Thesis. Boston: D.C. Heath.

Tiger, Lionel
   1969   Men in Groups. New York: Random House.

Tiger, Lionel, and Robin Fox
   1971   The Imperial Animal. New York: Holt, Rinehart & Winston.

Turner, Frederick J.
   1920   The Significance of the Frontier in American History. In The Frontier in American History. New York: Henry Holt. pp. 1–39.

Tuttle, Russell H.
   1968   Review of The Naked Ape, by Desmond Morris. American Anthropologist 70:1239–1240.

Willis, William S., Jr.
   1970   Anthropology and Negroes on the Southern Colonial Frontier. In The Black Experience in America: Selected Essays. J. D. Curtis and L. L. Gould, Eds. Austin: University of Texas Press. pp. 33–50.

Wittfogel, Karl A.
   1957   Oriental Despotism: A Comparative Study of Total Power. New Haven: Yale University Press.

Yang, Martin C.
   1945   A Chinese Village. New York: Columbia University Press.

On Key Symbols

Sherry B. Ortner

VOL. 75, 1973, 1338–1346

It is by no means a novel idea that each culture has certain key elements which, in an ill-defined way, are crucial to its distinctive organization.[1] Since the publication of Benedict's *Patterns of Culture* in 1934, the notion of such key elements has persisted in American anthropology under a variety of rubrics: "themes" (e.g., Opler 1945; Cohen 1948), "focal values" (Albert 1956), "dominant values" (DuBois 1955), "integrative concepts" (DuBois 1936), "dominant orientations" (F. Kluckhohn 1950), and so forth. We can also find this idea sneaking namelessly into British social anthropological writing; the best example of this is Lienhardt's (1961) discussion of cattle in Dinka culture (and I say culture rather than society advisedly). Even Evans-Pritchard has said,

> as every experienced field-worker knows, the most difficult task in social anthropological field work is to determine the meanings of a few key words, upon an understanding of which the success of the whole investigation depends [1962:80].

Recently, as the focus in the study of meaning systems has shifted to the symbolic units which formulate meaning, the interest in these key elements of cultures has become specified as the interest in key symbols. Schneider (1968) calls them "core symbols" in his study of American kinship; Turner (1967) calls them "dominant symbols" in his study of Ndembu ritual; I called them "key symbols" in my study of Sherpa social relations (Ortner 1970).

The primary question of course is what do we mean by "key"? But I will postpone considering this problem until I have discussed the various usages of the notion of key symbols in the literature of symbolic analysis.

Two methodological approaches to establishing certain symbols as "core" or "key" to a cultural system have been employed. The first approach, less commonly used, involves analyzing the system (or domains thereof) for its underlying elements — cognitive distinctions, value orientations, etc. — then looking about in the culture for some figure or image which seems to formulate, in relatively pure form, the underlying orientations exposed in the analysis. The best example of this approach in the current literature is David Schneider's (1968) analysis of American kinship; Schneider first analyzes the kinship system for its basic components — nature and law — and then decides that conjugal sexual intercourse is the form which, given its meaning in the culture, expresses this opposition most succinctly and meaningfully. Schneider expresses his debt to Ruth Benedict, and this debt turns out to be quite specific, since the other major work which embodies this method is Benedict's *The Chrysanthemum and the Sword* (1967). The sword and the chrysanthemum were chosen by Benedict from the repertoire of Japanese symbols as most succinctly, or perhaps most poetically, representing the tension in the Japanese value system which she postulated. She did not arrive at this tension through an analysis of the meanings of chrysanthemums and swords in the culture; she first established the tension in Japanese culture through analysis of various symbolic systems, then chose these two items from the repertoire of Japanese symbols to sum up the opposition.

In the second, more commonly employed approach, the investigator observes something which seems to be an object of cultural interest, and analyzes it for its meanings. The observation that some symbol is a focus of cultural interest need not be very mysterious or intuitive. I offer here five reasonably reliable indicators of cultural interest, and there are probably more. Most key symbols, I venture to suggest, will be signaled by more than one of these indicators:

(1) The natives tell us that X is culturally important.
(2) The natives seem positively or negatively aroused about X, rather than indifferent.
(3) X comes up in many different contexts. These contexts may be behavioral or systemic: X comes up in many different kinds of action situation or conversation, or X comes up in many different symbolic domains (myth, ritual, art, formal rhetoric, etc.).
(4) There is greater cultural elaboration surrounding X, e.g., elaboration of

vocabulary, or elaboration of details of X's nature, compared with similar phenomena in the culture.

(5) There are greater cultural restrictions surrounding X, either in sheer number of rules, or severity of sanctions regarding its misuse.

As I said, there may be more indicators even than these of the key status of a symbol in a culture, but any of these should be enough to point even the most insensitive fieldworker in the right direction. I should also add that I am not assuming that there is only one key symbol to every culture; cultures are of course a product of the interplay of many basic orientations, some quite conflicting. But all of them will be expressed somewhere in the public system, because the public symbol system is ultimately the only source from which the natives themselves discover, rediscover, and transform their own culture, generation after generation.

It remains for us now to sort out the bewildering array of phenomena to which various investigators have been led to assign implicitly or explicitly the status of key cultural symbol. Anything by definition can be a symbol, i.e., a vehicle for cultural meaning, and it seems from a survey of the literature that almost anything can be key. Omitting the symbols established by the first approach cited above, which have a different epistemological status, we can cite from the anthropological literature such things as cattle among the Dinka and Nuer, the Naven ritual of the Iatmul, the Australian churinga, the slametan of the Javanese, the potlatch of the northwest coast, the forked stick of Ndembu rituals, and from my own research, the wheel-image in Tibet and food among the Sherpas. We could also add such intuitive examples as the cross of Christianity, the American flag, the motorcycle for the Hell's Angels, "work" in the Protestant ethic, and so on.

The list is a jumble — things and abstractions, nouns and verbs, single items and whole events. I should like to propose a way of subdividing and ordering the set, in terms of the ways in which the symbols operate in relation to cultural thought and action.

The first major breakdown among the various types of symbols is along a continuum whose two ends I call "summarizing" *vs.* "elaborating." I stress that it is a continuum, but I work with the ideal types at the two ends.

Summarizing symbols, first, are those symbols which are seen as summing up, expressing, representing for the participants in an emotionally powerful and relatively undifferentiated way, what the system means to them. This category is essentially the category of sacred symbols in the broadest sense, and includes all those items which are objects of reverence and/or catalysts of emotion — the flag, the cross, the churinga, the forked stick, the motorcycle, etc. The American flag, for example, for certain Americans, stands for something called "the American way," a conglomerate of ideas and feelings including (theoretically) democracy, free enterprise, hard work, competition, progress, national superiority, freedom, etc. And it stands for them all at once. It does not encourage reflection on the logical relations among these ideas, nor on the logical consequences of them as they are played out in social actuality, over time and history. On the contrary, the flag encourages a sort of all-or-nothing allegiance to the whole package, best summed up on a billboard I saw recently: "Our flag, love it or leave." And this is the point about summarizing symbols in general — they operate to compound and synthesize a complex system of ideas, to "summarize" them under a unitary form which, in an old-fashioned way, "stands for" the system as a whole.

Elaborating symbols, on the other hand, work in the opposite direction, providing vehicles for sorting out complex and undifferentiated feelings and ideas, making them comprehensible to oneself, communicable to others, and translatable into orderly action. Elaborating symbols are accorded central status in the culture on the basis of their capacity to order experience; they are essentially analytic. Rarely are these symbols sacred in the conventional sense of being objects of respect or foci of emotion; their key status is indicated primarily by their recurrence in cultural behavior or cultural symbolic systems.

Symbols can be seen as having elaborating power in two modes. They may have primarily conceptual elaborating power, that is, they are valued as a source of categories for conceptualizing the order of the world. Or they may have primarily action elaborating power; that is, they are valued as implying mechanisms for successful social action. These two modes reflect what I see as the two basic and of course interrelated functions of culture in general: to provide for its members "orientations," i.e., cognitive and affective categories; and "strategies," i.e., programs for orderly social action in relation to culturally defined goals.

Symbols with great conceptual elaborating power are what Stephen Pepper (1942) has called "root metaphors," and indeed in this realm the basic mechanism is the metaphor. It is felt in the culture that many aspects of experience can be likened to, and illuminated by the comparison with, the symbol itself. In Pepper's terms, the symbol provides a set of categories for conceptualizing other aspects of experience, or, if this point is stated too uni-directionally for some tastes, we may say that the root metaphor formulates the unity of cultural orientation underlying many aspects of experience, by virtue of the fact that those many aspects of experience can be likened to it.

One of the best examples of a cultural root metaphor in the anthropological literature is found in Godfrey Lienhardt's discussion of the role of cattle in Dinka thought. Cows provide for the Dinka an almost endless set of categories for conceptualizing and responding to the subtleties of experience. For example:

> The Dinkas' very perception of colour, light, and shade in the world around them is . . . inextricably connected with their recognition of colour-configurations in their cattle. If their cattle-colour vocabulary were taken away, they would have scarcely any way of describing visual experience in terms of colour, light and darkness [1961:13].

More important for Lienhardt's thesis is the Dinka conceptualization of the structure of their own society on analogy with the physical structure of the bull. " 'The people are put together, as a bull is put together,' said a Dinka chief on one occasion" (*Ibid.*:23), and indeed the formally prescribed division of the meat of a sacrificed bull is a most graphic representation of the statuses, functions, and interrelationships of the major social categories of Dinka society, as the Dinka themselves represent the situation.

In fact, as Mary Douglas points out, the living organism in one form or another functions as a root metaphor in many cultures, as a source of categories for conceptualizing social phenomena (1966). In mechanized society, on the other hand, one root metaphor for the social process is the machine, and in recent times the computer represents a crucial modification upon this root metaphor. But the social is not the only aspect of experience which root metaphor–type symbols are used to illuminate; for example, much of greater Indo-Tibetan cosmology — the forms and processes of life, space, and time — is developed on analogy with the quite simple image of the wheel (Ortner 1966).

A root metaphor, then, is one type of key symbol in the elaborating mode, i.e., a symbol which operates to sort out experience, to place it in cultural categories, and to help us think about how it all hangs together. They are symbols which are "good to think," not exactly in the Lévi-

Straussian sense, but in that one can conceptualize the interrelationships among phenomena by analogy to the interrelations among the parts of the root metaphor.[2]

The other major type of elaborating symbol is valued primarily because it implies clear-cut modes of action appropriate to correct and successful living in the culture. Every culture, of course, embodies some vision of success, or the good life, but the cultural variation occurs in how success is defined, and, given that, what are considered the best ways of achieving it. "Key scenarios," as I call the type of key symbol in this category, are culturally valued in that they formulate the culture's basic means-ends relationships in actable forms.

An example of a key scenario from American culture would be the Horatio Alger myth. The scenario runs: poor boy of low status, but with total faith in the American system, works very hard and ultimately becomes rich and powerful. The myth formulates both the American conception of success — wealth and power — and suggests that there is a simple (but not easy) way of achieving them — singleminded hard work. This scenario may be contrasted with ones from other cultures which present other actions as the most effective means of achieving wealth and power, or which formulate wealth and power as appropriate goals only for certain segments of the society, or, of course, those which do not define cultural success in terms of wealth and power at all. In any case, the point is that every culture has a number of such key scenarios which both formulate appropriate goals and suggest effective action for achieving them; which formulate, in other words, key cultural strategies.

This category of key symbols may also include rituals; Singer seems to be making the point of rituals as scenarios when he writes of "cultural performances" (1958), in which both valued end states and effective means for achieving them are dramatized for all to see. Thus this category would include naven, the slametan, the potlatch, and others. The category could also include individual elements of rituals — objects, roles, action sequences — insofar as they refer to or epitomize the ritual as a whole, which is why one can have actions, objects, and whole events in the same category.

Further, scenarios as key symbols may include not only formal, usually named events, but also all those cultural sequences of action which we can observe enacted and reenacted according to unarticulated formulae in the normal course of daily life. An example of such a scenario from Sherpa culture would be the hospitality scenario, in which any individual in the role of host feeds a guest and thereby renders him voluntarily cooperative vis-à-vis oneself. The scenario formulates both the ideally valued (though infrequently attained) mode of social relations in the culture — voluntary cooperation — and, given certain cultural assumptions about the effects of food on people, the most effective way of establishing those kinds of relations. Once again then, the scenario is culturally valued — indicated in this case by the fact that it is played and replayed in the most diverse sorts of social contexts — because it suggests a clear-cut strategy for arriving at culturally defined success.

I have been discussing the category of key symbols which I called "elaborating" symbols, symbols valued for their contribution to the sorting out of experience. This class includes both root metaphors which provide categories for the ordering of conceptual experience, and key scenarios which provide strategies for organizing action experience. While for purposes of this discussion I have been led by the data to separate thought from action, I must hasten to put the pieces back together again. For my view is that ultimately both kinds of symbols have both types of referents. Root metaphors, by establishing a certain view of the world, implicitly suggest certain valid and effective ways of acting upon it; key scenarios, by prescribing certain culturally effective courses of action, embody and rest upon certain assumptions about the nature of reality. Even summarizing symbols, while primarily functioning to compound rather than sort out experience, are seen as both formulating basic orientations and implying, though much less systematically than scenarios, certain modes of action.

One question which might be raised at this point is how we are to understand the logical relationships among the types of key symbols I have distinguished. As the scheme stands now, it has the following unbalanced structure:

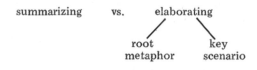

I would argue that this asymmetry follows from the content of the types: the meaning-content of summarizing or sacred symbols is by definition clustered, condensed, relatively undifferentiated, "thick," while the meaning-content of elaborating symbols is by definition relatively clear, orderly, differentiated, articulate. Thus it is possible to make distinctions among the different ordering functions of elaborating symbols, while the denseness of meaning of summarizing symbols renders them relatively resistant to subdivision and ordering by types. Nonetheless, in the interest of systematic analysis, we may raise the question of whether such subdivisions are possible, and in particular whether the thought/action distinction which subdivides elaborating symbols (into root metaphors and key scenarios) also crosscuts and subdivides summarizing symbols.

The important mode of operation of summarizing symbols, it will be recalled, is its focusing power, its drawing-together, intensifying, catalyzing impact upon the respondent. Thus we must ask whether some summarizing symbols primarily operate to catalyze thought or in any case internal states of the actor, while others primarily operate to catalyze overt action on the part of the actor. Now it does seem possible, for example, to see the cross or some other religious symbol as primarily focusing and intensifying inner attitude, with no particular implied public action, while the flag or some other political symbol is primarily geared to focusing and catalyzing overt action in the public world. Yet, intuitively at least, this distinction seems relatively weak and unconvincing compared to the easily formulated and grasped distinction between the two types of elaborating symbols: static formal images serving metaphor functions for thought (root metaphors), and dramatic, phased action sequences serving scenario functions for action (key scenarios). Of course, as I said, root metaphors may imply particular modes of, or at least a restricted set of possible modes of, action; and key scenarios presuppose certain orderly assumptions of thought. But the distinction — the former geared primarily to thought, the latter to action — remains sharp.

Summarizing symbols, on the other hand, speak primarily to attitudes, to a crystallization of commitment. And, in the mode of commitment, the thought/action distinction is not particularly relevant. There may certainly be consequences for thought and action as a result of a crystallized commitment, but commitment itself is neither thought nor action. The point perhaps illuminates the generally sacred status of summarizing symbols, for they are speaking to a more diffuse mode of orientation in the actor, a broader context of attitude within which particular modes of thinking and acting are formulated.[3]

This is not to say that nothing analytic may be said about summarizing symbols beyond the fact that they catalyze feeling; there are a number of possible ways of subdividing the catalog of sacred symbols in the world, some no doubt more useful or illuminated than others. My point is merely that the particular factor which subdivides elaborating symbols — the thought/action distinction — does not serve very powerfully to subdivide the category of summarizing symbols, since the summarizing symbol is speaking to a different level of response, the level of attitude and commitment.

We are now in a position to return to the question of "key" or central status. Why are we justified in calling a particular symbol "key"? The indicators provided earlier for at least provisionally regarding certain symbols as key to a particular culture were all based on the assumption that keyness has public (though not necessarily conscious) manifestation in the culture itself, available to the observer in the field, or at least available when one reflects upon one's observations. But the fact of public cultural concern or focus of interest is not *why* a symbol is key; it is only a *signal* that the symbol is playing some key role in relation to other elements of the cultural system of thought. The issue of keyness, in short, has to do with the internal organization of the system of cultural meaning, as that system functions for actors leading their lives in the culture.

Broadly speaking, the two types of key symbols distinguished above, defined in terms of how they act upon or are manipulated by cultural actors, also indicate the two broad modes of "keyness" from a systemic point of view, defined in terms of the role such symbols are playing in the system; that is, a given summarizing symbol is "key" to the system insofar as the meanings which it formulates are logically or affectively prior to other meanings of the system. By "logically or affectively prior" I mean simply that many other cultural ideas and attitudes presuppose, and make sense only in the context of, those meanings formulated by the symbol. The key role of an elaborating symbol, by contrast, derives not so much from the status of its particular substantive meanings, but from its formal or organizational role in relation to the system; that is, we say such a symbol is "key" to the system insofar as it extensively and systematically formulates relationships — parallels, isomorphisms, complementarities, and so forth — between a wide range of diverse cultural elements.

This contrast between the two modes of "keyness" may be summed up in various ways, all of which oversimplify to some extent, but which nonetheless give perspective on the point. (1) "Content versus form": The keyness of a summarizing symbol derives from its particular substantive meanings (content) and their logical priority in relation to other meanings of the system. The keyness of an elaborating symbol derives from its formal properties, and their culturally postulated power to formulate widely applicable modes of organizing cultural phenomena. (2) "Quality versus quantity": The keyness of a summarizing symbol derives from the relative fundamentality (or ultimacy) of the meanings which it formulates, relative to other meanings of the system. The keyness of an elaborating symbol derives from the broadness of its scope, the extent to which it systematically draws relationships between a wide range of diverse cultural elements. (3) "Vertical versus lateral": The keyness of a summarizing symbol derives from its ability to relate lover-order meanings to higher-order assumptions, or to "ground" more surface-level meanings to their deeper bases. (The issue here is degree of generality of meaning. Whether more general meanings are termed "higher" or "deeper," "ultimate" or "fundamental," by a particular cultural analyst seems a matter of personal preference.) The keyness of an elaborating symbol by contrast derives from its ability to interconnect disparate elements at essentiality the same level, by virtue of its ability to manifest (or bring into relief) their formal similarities.

All of these terminological contrasts — form/content, quantity/quality, lateral/vertical — are really perspectives upon the same basic contrast, for which we have no more general term; that is, when we say a summarizing symbol is "key" to the system, we mean that its substantive meanings have certain kinds of priority relative to other meanings of the system. When we say an elaborating symbol is key to the system, we refer to the power of its formal or organizational role in relation to the system.

But at this point we must stop short of reifying the distinctions, for, in practice, the contrast between the two broad types of key symbols and the two modes of "keyness" may break down. It seems empirically to be the case that an elaborating symbol which is accorded wide-ranging applicability in the culture — played in many contexts, or applied to many different sorts of forms — is generally not only formally apt but also substantively referential to high-level values, ideas, cognitive assertions, and so forth. Indeed, insofar as such high-level formulations are made, a key elaborating symbol of a culture may move into the sacred mode and operate in much the same way as does a summarizing symbol. And, on the other hand, some summarizing symbols may play important ordering functions, as when they relate the respondent not merely to a cluster of high-level assumptions and values, but to a particular scenario which may be replayed in ongoing life. (One may think, for example, of the Christian cross evoking, among other things, not only a general sense of God's purpose and support, but also the particular scenario of Christ's martyrdom.)

Thus we are brought to an important point, namely, that we are distinguishing not only types of symbols, but types of symbolic functions. These functions may be performed by any given symbol — at different times, or in different contexts, or even simultaneously by different "levels" of its meaning. While there are many examples of summarizing and elaborating symbols in their relatively pure forms, the kinds of functions or operations these symbols perform may also be seen as aspects of any given symbols.

To summarize the original scheme briefly, key symbols may be discovered by virtue of a number of reliable indicators which point to cultural focus of interest. They are of two broad types — summarizing and elaborating. Summarizing symbols are primarily objects of attention and cultural respect; they synthesize or "collapse" complex experience, and relate the respondent to the grounds of the system as a whole. They include most importantly sacred symbols in the traditional sense. Elaborating symbols, on the other hand, are symbols valued for their contribution to the ordering or "sorting out" of experience. Within this are symbols valued primarily for the ordering of conceptual experience, i.e., for providing cultural "orientations," and those valued primarily for the ordering of action, i.e., for providing cultural "strategies." The former include what Pepper calls "root metaphors," the latter include key scenarios, or elements of scenarios which are crucial to the means-end relationship postulated in the complete scenario.[4]

This scheme also suggests, at least by the choices of terms, the modes of symbolic analysis relevant to the different types of key symbols. The first type (summarizing symbols) suggests a range of questions pertaining to the cultural conversion of complex ideas into various kinds of relatively undifferentiated commitment — patriotism, for example, or faith. The second type (root metaphors) suggests questions applicable to the analysis of metaphor in the broadest sense — questions of how thought proceeds and organizes itself through analogies, models, images, and so forth. And the third type (key scenarios) suggests drama-tistic modes of analysis, in which one raises questions concerning the restructuring of attitudes and relationships as a result of enacting par-ticular culturally provided sequences of stylized actions.

This article has been frankly programmatic; I am in the process of implementing some of its ideas in a monograph on Sherpa social and religious relations. Here I have simply been concerned to show that, although a method of cultural analysis via key symbols has been for the most part unarticulated, there is at least incipiently method in such analysis. It is worth our while to try to systematize this method, for it may be our most powerful entree to the distinctiveness and variability of human cultures.

Notes

1. This is a revised version of a paper presented at the symposium "Method in Symbolic Analysis," 70th Annual Meeting of the American Anthropological Association, New York, November, 1971.

2. While I am not using the phrase "good to think" precisely in the way in which Lévi-Strauss uses it, there is obviously some parallel between my discussion of root metaphors and Lévi-Strauss' discussion of "the science of the concrete" (1966).

3. Cf. Geertz's discussion of "moods and motivations" in his "Religion as a Cultural System" (1966), which is dealing with similar issues.

4. There are a number of schemes in the literature of semiotics to which this scheme may be compared, although none are isomorphic with it. Probably the closest is the tripartite scheme derived from philosophical psychology, which divides the symbolic functions into the affective, the cognitive, and the conative (cf. Miller 1964).

References Cited

Albert, Ethel
  1956 The Classification of Values: A Method and Illustration. American Anthropologist 58: 221–248.
Benedict, Ruth
  1934 Patterns of Culture. Boston: Houghton-Mifflin.
  1967 The Chrysanthemum and the Sword. Cleveland and New York: World.
Cohen, A. K.
  1948 On the Place of "Themes" and Kindred Concepts in Social Theory. American Anthropologist 50:436–443.

Douglas, Mary
  1966 Purity and Danger. New York: Praeger.
DuBois, Cora
  1936 The Wealth Concept as an Integrative Factor in Tolowa-Tututni Culture. *In* Essays in Anthropology Presented to A. L. Kroeber. Robert Lowie, Ed. Berkeley: University of California Press.
  1955 The Dominant Value Profile of American Culture. American Anthropologist 57:1232–1239.
Evans-Pritchard, E. E.
  1962 Social Anthropology and Other Essays. New York: Free Press.
Geertz, Clifford
  1966 Religion as a Cultural System. *In* Anthropological Approaches to the Study of Religion. Michael Banton, Ed. ASA Monographs 3. London: Tavistock.
Kluckhohn, Florence
  1950 Dominant and Substitute Profiles of Cultural Orientation. Social Forces 28:376–393.
Lévi-Strauss, Claude
  1966 The Savage Mind. Chicago: University of Chicago Press.
Lienhardt, Godfrey
  1961 Divinity and Experience. Oxford: Clarendon Press.

Miller, George A.
  1964 Language and Psychology. *In* New Directions in the Study of Language. Eric H. Lenneberg, Ed. Cambridge, Mass.: MIT Press.
Opler, Morris E.
  1945 Themes as Dynamic Forces in Culture. American Journal of Sociology 51:198–206.
Ortner, Sherry B. (Sherry O. Paul)
  1966 Tibetan Circles. M.A. thesis, University of Chicago.
  1970 Food for Thought: A Key Symbol in Sherpa Culture. Ph.D. thesis, University of Chicago.
Pepper, Stephen
  1942 World Hypotheses. Berkeley and Los Angeles: University of California Press.
Schneider, David M.
  1968 American Kinship. Englewood Cliffs, N.J.: Prentice-Hall.
Singer, Milton
  1958 The Great Tradition in a Metropolitan Center: Madras. *In* Traditional India: Structure and Change. Milton Singer, Ed. Philadelphia: American Folklore Society.
Turner, Victor
  1967 The Forest of Symbols. Ithaca: Cornell University Press.

Sheep in Navajo Culture and Social Organization

Gary Witherspoon

VOL. 75, 1973, 1441–1447

Past accounts of Navajo social organization have made little or no reference to the role of the sheep herd in social organization.[1] Navajos have been described as a pastoral people but no one has described in detail how their pastoral activities and economy relate to social organization. Downs (1964) has provided an account of animal husbandry among the Navajo but he made only minor references to the part animal husbandry plays in social organization. In their most recent work on the Navajo Mountain community, Shepardson and Hammond noted that "the whole value system is integrated about the sheep herds" (1970:242). Building on this observation, this article will attempt to show how not only the value system but also how the ethical and social system are integrated in the operation of the sheep herd.

Concepts of and Attitudes toward the Sheep Herd

When Werner and Begishe asked their informants what a Navajo should think about most, their reply was nearly always "the sheep" (1968:105). Reichard also notes the extent to which sheep occupy the thoughts of Navajos:

> The Navajo, particularly the women, are "sheep-minded." From the first white crack of dawn to the time when the curtain of darkness descends they must consider the sheep. Yes, and even beyond [1936:6].

The beyond to which she made reference is the night time when one must be careful that the sheep do not get out of the corral and wander away or get harmed by coyotes. In addition, the lambing season requires a night vigil when one must make sure the newly born lambs get to suckle properly and do not freeze.

If there is one word which could best characterize this tremendous emphasis upon and concern for the sheep herd, it would be security. The sheep herd provides the Navajo with his best insurance against starvation and poverty. Sheep provide the Navajo with meat for food, wool for clothing, bedding and weaving, and sinew for bows. In the autobiography of the Son of Old Man Hat, the son is instructed by his father to always keep the care of the sheep uppermost in his mind, noting that

> The herd is money. It gives you clothing and different kinds of food. You know that you have some good clothing; the sheep gave you that. And you've just eaten different kinds of food; the sheep gave that food to you. Everything comes from sheep [Dyk 1938:103].

Elsewhere (Witherspoon 1970:55–65) I have noted that the central symbol of Navajo social organization is motherhood, and that the meaning of this symbol is found in the reproduction and sustenance of life. It is not surprising, therefore, that the Navajo find a conceptual relationship between sheep and motherhood, which is articulated beautifully by Werner and Begishe's informant:

(129) dibé wolgheíi nimá át'é
       Those called sheep are your mother.
(130) dibé iiná nilínii át'é
       Sheep are life [1968:96].

Not only does the sheep herd provide the Navajo with an actual sense of security in terms of food and other items of subsistence, but it also provides the Navajo with a psychological sense of security. An incident in the youth of the Son of Old Man Hat illustrates this:

> About this time I began to herd around the hogan in the morning and evening when the sheep came home. But I was so small. I went out with the sheep like a dog. I just walked along with them and stayed right in the middle of the herd. I was afraid to go around them, but while I was in the middle of the sheep I wasn't afraid of anything [Dyk 1938:8].

In commenting on this passage in the foreword of the book, Sapir asks if security has ever been more accurately defined.

Many Navajos also consider the sheep to have some instinctual sense of danger, which can be communicated to the herder if he is sensitive to it. On one occasion the Son of Old Man Hat was warned by the sheep of impending danger. In relating the story, he noted that "the sheep know everything about what's going to happen to them and to us" (Dyk 1938:262).

By providing the Navajo with both a material and psychological sense of security, the sheep herd contributes significantly to a Navajo's physical and mental health, something of great interest and concern to the Navajo. An informant of Shepardson and Hammond stated that "although I am a very old woman, I am still able to get around. I live by livestock. By working with the sheep, cattle, and horses, I stay in a good frame of mind and I think it gives me good health." Another informant said, "I have had a full life because I have sheep" (personal communication).

It is not surprising from the above that the Navajos feel a moral responsibility to give the herd proper care. Anyone who fails to care for their herd properly will not be respected by the community, and will often be singled out for sharp criticism. On occasion, I have observed community meetings in which certain individuals were considered to be unworthy for various positions of leadership and responsibility because it was claimed they had not properly cared for their herds. Shepardson and Hammond report that one man complained to the Navajo tribal court that "his daughter was guilty of illicit cohabitation with a Paiute, that she was drinking excessively and neglecting her children and her sheep" (1970:78). In speaking to his children, another informant said, "I won't be with you too much longer because of my age. I ask you to take good care of the sheep." The implication of this is, as it is sometimes articulated by Navajos: If we take care of the sheep, the sheep will take care of us.

Navajos also have great affection for their sheep. When Navajos are away from home for extended periods of time they often comment in letters about how much they miss the sheep and ask about how the sheep are doing. When they return home, one of the first things they want to do is to herd the sheep:

On several occasions I was asked to drive a Navajo living at a distance from the family home where the sheep were kept and in most instances the reason they gave for wanting to take the trip was to "see the sheep." "I haven't seen the sheep for a long time" was considered sufficient explanation for wanting to visit one's homestead. On one occasion, having taken a woman and her husband to visit her sister, we found that the sheep were still grazing. After waiting for perhaps an hour, we were forced to leave, because of a sudden snow storm, before the herd was brought in. The woman's complaint, "I sure wanted to see them sheep" [Downs 1964:91].

Downs also states that the word "love" is frequently used by informants to describe their feelings toward their sheep.

In summary it can be said that the sheep herd occupies an important place in Navajo thought, that it provides the Navajo with both a material and a psychological sense of security, which contribute to one's mental and physical health, and that the Navajo has a significant affective investment in and responsibility to the sheep herd. The sheep herd is also an important aspect of a Navajo's social identity, and plays an important role in the formation and organization of social groups. To see how this is true, I will now turn to the role of the sheep herd in social life and organization.

The Sheep Herd and Social Organization

The residence group[2] has now come to be recognized as the unit of fundamental importance in Navajo social organization. It is basically an extended family group organized around a matrifocal head (Witherspoon 1970). Its major asset is land which is used primarily for grazing, and its major enterprise is the sheep herd. Members of a distinct residence group put their sheep in a common herd and share in the tasks of caring for the herd; so at the residence group level, social groups correspond to the groupings of sheep into herds. Often when the distance between homes does not clearly indicate which households form distinct residence groups, the matter can be clarified by ascertaining who puts their sheep in which herd.

The sheep herd is an important symbol of social integration within the residence group. The sheep herd is a cooperative enterprise of the individual owners. Nearly everyone in the unit has some sheep, and therefore has an interest in the welfare of the herd. Children are given lambs to begin building their flocks as soon as they are able to share in the tasks of caring for the sheep, and this is usually around five years of age. It is in the sheep herd, more than anywhere else, that the divergent interests of the individual members of the unit are converged into this very meaningful and cooperative endeavor.

The identity, welfare, and status of the residence group is closely linked to the size and well-being of the sheep herd. Community members judge the character and qualities of those within the residence group on the basis of the size and appearance of their sheep herd. No one will be respected in the community or elected to positions of leadership if his family's herd gives the appearance of improper care and attention.

An individual's identity and social position is also closely linked to his sheep. Most often the person who wields the most power and influence within a residence group is the person who has the most sheep in the herd. My data at Rough Rock indicated that the status of people within the residence group and the number of sheep they had in the herd corresponded quite closely, though there was plenty of evidence to indicate that this is changing rapidly and that it was probably more true in the past, especially before stock reduction, than it is now.

Sheep are also an important aspect of the way in which an in-marrying affine is integrated into the residence group of his spouse. The in-marrying affine may bring none or only a few of his sheep to his wife's home at the beginning of their marriage, leaving the majority of his sheep in the herd of his natal group. Later, as children come and his marriage becomes more stable, he will bring more or most of his herd to his wife's home. Sometimes it might not be until after ten or twenty years of marriage that a man will finally have placed all his sheep in his wife's herd (Shepardson and Hammond 1966:90). Having fully tied his identity and loyalty to his new residence group, the in-marrying affine is likely to begin to have more influence over the affairs of the group and may soon become its leader. From this it may be concluded that a person's status within and loyalty to a particular social group or groups largely correspond to the location and position of his sheep in a particular herd or herds.

Because of the close link between a person's sheep and his social identity and status, stock reduction caused a social upheaval of unbelievable proportions. This is profoundly and powerfully indicated by the speech of Tall John when he confronted stock reduction officials:

> Young men who were little more than children during stock reduction can repeat word for word the speeches made by Tall John when he confronted the government agents sent to implement the reduction program. These speeches threatened violent resistance; 'If you take my sheep you kill me. So kill me now. Let's fight right here and decide this thing' [Downs 1944:20].

Sheep are also a means of incorporating children into the life and communal economy of the residence group. As noted above children are given lambs as the nucleus of a future herd. This is an earned right because it comes when they get old enough to share in the tasks of caring for the herd (Shepardson and Hammond 1966:90). Thus children have a direct interest in the welfare of the herd, just like their parents. It is in this corporate enterprise or institution that the child learns the meaning, necessity, and nature of group or communal life. He is initiated into this group at a young age, and it is this experience, more than any other, that forms his social personality.

Although income from the sheep herd amounts to only about a fourth of the current income of Navajos in the Rough Rock area, it remains a basic aspect of the economy of the community. Some residence groups do not have any cattle, wage workers, agricultural fields, welfare assistance, medicine men, or seasonal workers, but they all have a sheep herd. And social life remains organized primarily around the sheep herd. Shepardson and Hammond also found this to be true at Navajo Mountain (1970:112), as did Downs at Pinon and Black Mesa:

> Although in a classic economic sense, livestock is not a dominant factor, it is in fact the directing principle of the lives of almost all the people who live in Black Mesa. Their activities are molded to suit the needs of the herds and their personalities shaped to the life of herdsmen [1964:18].

Broader Implications of the Sheep Herd Enterprise

The operation of the sheep herd enterprise is based on a unique combination of individualism and communalism. Up to this point the emphasis has been on the communal nature of the residence group, so let us now turn our attention to how individualism manifests itself in Navajo social organization and then proceed to a discussion of how communalism and individualism converge in the sheep herd enterprise.

According to Navajo cultural concepts, each being in the world has the right to live, to eat, and to act for itself. These rights to life and freedom extend to plants and animals, as well as to human beings. Only real and immediate human need justifies the killing of an animal or the cutting down of a tree. On such occasions a prayer should be said to the plant or animal explaining one's need and asking for the pardon and indulgence of the soul of the animal or plant.

Reichard observed this respectful attitude toward the life and souls of plants:

> The Navajo have a sentimental attitude toward plants, which they treat with incredible respect. . . . To pick them without taking them into ritual, to let them wither as cut flowers is quite out of order, even dangerous, there being no aesthetic compensation for the fear such sacrilege may engender [1950:22, 144].

With regard to Navajo attitudes toward the unnecessary taking of animal life, Downs notes the following:

> Many observers of the Navajo have commented that in large part their resentment of the stock reduction program was due to the government's allowing thousands of sheep to die in holding pens or en route to the railroads. Such behavior, perfectly understandable in white economic terms, was viewed as utter barbarism by the Navajo and is still spoken of in Pinon [1964:93].

Navajos believe that each person has the right to speak for himself and to act as he pleases. This attitude is manifested in both dyadic and intra-group relations. The mutual rights and duties of kinsmen normally discussed under the concept of jural relations are best described as mutual expectations, rather than obligations. This distinction is a matter of emphasis and degree, but is very real and worth noting. Desirable actions on the part of others are hoped for and even expected, but they are not required or demanded. Coercion is always deplored.

In intra-group relations no individual, regardless of position or status, has the right to impose his will or decision on the group. Likewise, the group does not have the right to impose its will on the individual. Unanimity is the only basis of collective action. Although a system of majority rule has been imposed on the Navajos for half a century, the extent to which the principle of unanimity continues to pervade almost all social and political deliberations is amazing.

Downs described this Navajo attitude as a belief in the "inviolability of the individual." He further discusses some of the social implications of this belief:

> Despite close and absolutely essential familial ties, Navajo remain highly individualistic people. Their primary social premise might be said to be that

no person has the right to speak for or direct the actions of another . . .
[Downs 1964:69].

In searching for a key to the Navajo social system, Shepardson and
Hammond came upon the phrase "it's up to him." They note that "just
as this is a Navajo informant's regular response to questions about
expected behavior, so it is his view of society's patterned relations"
(1970:241). There are, however, patterned expectations in social relations but these expectations are balanced by an emphasis upon individualism and pragmatism.

In the sheep herd operation individualism is manifested in several
ways. First, the sheep are individually owned and one's involvement in
the communal herding is voluntary. He may separate his sheep from the
others at any time, either for the purpose of selling them or for placing
them in a separate or different herd. Second, he is not required to help
with the care of the herd, although he is expected to do so whenever
possible.

Communalism operates not only in the placing of individually owned
sheep into a common herd but also in the sharing of the products of the
herd. Food from the herd is shared among everyone in the residence
group. Usually an informal rotation is followed in the periodic butchering of sheep. The permission of individual owners is not necessary to
butcher their sheep if the meat is to be shared within the residence
group. Wool from the herd is not sacked and sold individually. It is sold
together and the proceeds are used by the head of the group to buy food
and other things for the entire group. The head of the group may also
buy individual things for people in the group but there is no clear attempt to distribute the proceeds either equally or proportionate to the
size of each individual's number of sheep in the herd.

The sheep herd enterprise also provides an interesting convergence
of the ethical concepts of egoism and altruism. John Ladd, a philosopher,
made a study of the Navajo moral code. He provides an insightful discussion of egoism and altruism in Navajo morality (1957:303–304):

> One of the most interesting aspects of the reconstructed Navajo code of
> morality is the light it throws on the relations between egoism and altruism.
> Western moralists have generally assumed that egoism and altruism are in-
> compatible; and therefore, that one of them must be rejected. . . .
> According to the Navajo ethical system which I have outlined, it is impossible

to be a good egoist without at the same time being a good altruist. Although all the moral prescriptions listed here are ultimately based upon egoistic premises, in content they are altruistic. . . .

The basic factual belief which unites egoistic premises with altruistic conclusions is that the welfare of each individual is dependent upon that of every other in the group. What is good for the individual is good for everyone else, and what is good for everybody is good for the individual.

The particular social group in which the concepts of egoism and individualism converge with the concepts of altruism and communalism is the residence group. This convergence occurs most forcefully and profoundly in the operation of the sheep herd. The welfare of one's own sheep is intrinsically related to the welfare of the entire herd. In providing good care for his own sheep, the individual is providing good care for everybody else's sheep and vice versa. The inviolability and inviability of the individual and his sheep are both asserted and demonstrated through putting one's own sheep in the common herd, and the common herd beautifully symbolizes both the individualism and the communalism of the residence group.

The sheep herd provides the major insurance of the group against hunger and starvation. Because food is shared among all members of the group, the increase or decrease of an individual's sheep increases or decreases the food supply for everyone. Thus doing good for oneself is inseparably related to doing good for others. Ladd found this thinking to be basic in Navajo economic theory:

> The Navajo 'economic theory' assumes that there is a potential abundance of goods, and that through cooperation the amount of goods will be increased for everyone; in other words, they would deny the basic assumption upon which much of our own economic theory depends, namely, the scarcity of goods. . . .
>
> No man is thought to be in competition with his fellow. Rather, it is assumed that a neighbor's success will contribute to one's own welfare [Ladd 1957:224, 253].

By putting his sheep in the common herd, the interests of the individual become voluntarily attached to the interests of others in the group. By maintaining individual ownership while at the same time making the sheep herd a communal enterprise, Navajos are able to successfully merge the concepts of individualism and egoism with those of communalism and altruism.

From this discussion of the sheep herd in Navajo culture and social organization, it should be clear why Shepardson and Hammond came to the conclusion that "not only the traditional social interaction patterns, rules of residence, types of groups, forms of marriage and preferred roles, but the whole value system is integrated about the sheep herds" (1970:242).

Notes

1. I wish to express my appreciation to Fred Eggan and David Schneider for their comments, assistance, and encouragement in the development of this paper.

2. In previous works I have used the term "subsistence residential unit" to refer to what others are now calling the residence group. To avoid confusion and for the sake of economy of words I have decided to abandon my term and use the term which most Navajo specialists seem to have adopted.

References Cited

Downs, James F.
  1964 Animal Husbandry in Navaho Society and Culture. Berkeley and Los Angeles: University of California Press.
Dyk, Walter
  1938 Son of Old Man Hat. New York: Harcourt, Brace.
Ladd, John
  1957 The Structure of a Moral Code. Cambridge: Harvard University Press.
Reichard, Gladys
  1936 Navaho Shepherd and Weaver. New York: J. J. Augustin.
  1950 Navaho Religion: A Study of Symbolism. New York: Bollingen Foundation.
Shepardson, Mary, and Blodwen Hammond
  1966 Navaho Inheritance Patterns: Random or Regular. Ethnology 5:87–96.
  1970 The Navajo Mountain Community. Berkeley and Los Angeles: University of California Press.
Werner, Oswald, and Kenneth Begishe
  1968 Styles of Learning: The Evidence from the Navajo. Unpublished working paper.
Witherspoon, Gary
  1970 A New look at Navajo Social Organization. American Anthropologist 72:55–65.

Verbal Art as Performance

Richard Bauman

VOL. 77, 1975, 290–311

We will be concerned in this paper to develop a conception of verbal art as performance, based upon an understanding of performance as a mode of speaking.[1] In constructing this framework for a performance-centered approach to verbal art, we have started from the position of the folklorist, but have drawn concepts and ideas from a wide range of disciplines, chiefly anthropology, linguistics, and literary criticism. Each of these disciplines has its own distinctive perspective on verbal art, and a long tradition of independent scholarship in its study. From at least the time of Herder, however, there has been an integrative tradition as well in the study of verbal art, manifested in the work of such figures as Edward Sapir, Roman Jakobson, and Dell Hymes, scholars who have operated at an intellectual level beyond the boundaries which separate academic disciplines, sharing an interest in the esthetic dimension of social and cultural life in human communities as manifested through the use of language. The present paper is offered in the spirit of that integrative tradition.

In a recent collection of conceptual and theoretical essays in folklore, assembled to indicate a range of new perspectives in the field, it was emphasized in the Introduction that the contributors shared a common concern with performance as an organizing principle (Bauman 1972a). The term performance was employed there, as it was by several of the contributors to the collection, because it conveyed a dual sense of artistic *action* — the doing of folklore — and artistic *event* — the performance situation, involving performer, art form, audience, and setting — both of which are central to the developing performance approach to folklore. This usage accorded well with the conventional meaning of the term "performance," and served to point up the fundamental reorientation from folklore as materials to folklore as communication which characterized the thinking of the contributors. Conventional meanings can carry scholarship just so far, however, before the lack of conceptual rigor begins to constrain analytical insight rather than advancing it. In view of the centrality of performance to the orientation of increasing numbers of folklorists and anthropologists interested in verbal art,[2] the time seems opportune for efforts aimed at expanding the conceptual content of folkloric performance as a communicative phenomenon, beyond the general usage that has carried us up to this point. That is the purpose of this essay.

One orientational and terminological point before proceeding: consistent with the chiefly sociolinguistic and anthropological roots of the performance approach, the terms "verbal art" and "oral literature" provide a better frame of reference, at least as a point of departure for the ideas to be advanced here, than the more diffuse and problematic term "folklore." "Spoken art" might be even better, insofar as this paper is concerned solely with a way of speaking and its attendant phenomena, but the term has never achieved currency in any of the disciplines where it might have served a useful purpose — folklore, anthropology, or linguistics.[3] Many things have been studied under the name of folklore, but verbal art has always been at or near the center of the larger domain, and has constituted the chief common ground between anthropological folklorists and those of other persuasions. Accordingly, the shift from the "folklore" of the preceding paragraph to the "verbal art" of those to follow is neither unprecedented nor arbitrary, but will serve, hopefully, to make somewhat clearer the universe of discourse within which the ideas which follow have been formulated.

Let us make explicit as well that a great deal more is intended here than a convenient relabeling of what is already known. The conception of performance to be developed in these pages is not simply an alternative perspective on the familiar genres of oral literature long studied by folklorists and anthropologists. It is that, but it is more than that as well. Performance, as we conceive of it and as our examples have been selected to illustrate, is a unifying thread tying together the marked, segregated esthetic genres and other spheres of verbal behavior into a general unified conception of verbal art as a way of speaking. Verbal art may comprehend both myth narration and the speech expected of certain members of society whenever they open their mouths, and it is performance that brings them together in culture-specific and variable ways, ways that are to be discovered ethnographically within each culture and community.

The Nature of Performance

Modern theories of the nature of verbal art, whether in anthropology, linguistics, or literature, tend overwhelmingly to be constructed in terms of special usages or patterning of formal features within texts. General formulations identify a primary "focus on the message for its own sake" (Jakobson 1960:356; Stankiewicz 1960:14–15) or a "concern with the form of expression, over and above the needs of communication" (Bascom 1955:247) as the essence of verbal art. Others are more specific about the nature or consequences of such a focus or concern, suggesting, for example, that the touchstone of verbal art lies in a maximized "use of the devices of the language in such a way that this use itself attracts attention and is perceived as uncommon" (Havránek 1964:10). Among certain linguists, the idea has some currency that verbal art "in some way deviates from norms which we, as members of society, have learnt to expect in the medium used" (Leech 1969:56; cf. Stankiewicz 1960:12; Durbin 1971), while others of their colleagues make a point of the "multiplicity of *additional formal laws* restricting the poet's free choice of expressions" (Fónagy 1965:72; italics in original).

Whatever their differences, of focus or emphasis, all of these approaches make for a conception of verbal art that is text-centered. For all, the artful, esthetic quality of an utterance resides in the way in which language is used in the construction of the textual item. To be sure, it may considered necessary, at least implicitly, to assess the text against the background of general linguistic norms, but it is the text itself that remains the unit of analysis and point of departure for proponents of these approaches. This in turn places severe constraints on the development of a meaningful framework for the understanding of verbal art as performance, as a species of situated human communication, a way of speaking.

It is, of course, possible to move from artistic texts, identified in formal or other terms, to performance, by simply looking at how such texts are rendered, in action terms. But this is to proceed backwards, by approaching phenomena whose primary social reality lies in their nature as oral communication in terms of the abstracted textual products of the communicative process. As we shall see, oral literary texts, though they may fulfill the formal measures of verbal art, be accurately recorded, and bear strong associations with performance in their conventional contexts, may nevertheless not be the products of performance, but of rendition in another communicative mode. How many of the texts in our collections represent recordings of informants' abstracts, resumés, or reports of performances and performance forms rather than true performances (cf. Tedlock 1972)? By identifying the nature of performance and distinguishing it from other ways of speaking, we will have, among other things, a measure of the authenticity of collected oral literary texts.

A performance-centered conception of verbal art calls for an approach through performance itself. In such an approach, the formal manipulation of linguistic features is secondary to the nature of performance, per se, conceived of and defined as a mode of communication.

There is a very old conception of verbal art as communication which goes back at least to Plato's insistence that literature is lies. The notion, also manifest in Sir Philip Sidney's oft-quoted dictum, "the poet nothing affirmeth" (Ohmann 1971:5) holds that whatever the propositional content of an item of verbal art, its meaning is somehow cancelled out or rendered inoperative by the nature of the utterance as verbal art. A more recent expression of this conception is to be found in the writings of the British Ordinary Language philosopher, J. L. Austin. Austin maintains, "of any and every utterance," that it will be "*in a peculiar way* hollow or void if said by an actor on the stage . . . or spoken in soliloquy." He continues, "language in such circumstances is in special ways — intelligibly — used not seriously, but in ways *parasitic* upon its normal use — ways which fall under the doctrine of *etiolations* of language" (Austin 1962:21–22; italics in original).[4]

Leaving aside the unfortunate suggestion that the uses Austin mentions exert a weakening influence on language, a product of his particular bias, we may abstract from the cited passage the suggestion that performance represents a transformation of the basic referential ("serious," "normal" in Austin's terms) uses of language. In other words, in artistic performance of this kind, there is something going on in the communicative interchange which says to the auditor, "interpret what I say in some special sense; do not take it to mean what the words alone, taken literally, would convey." This may lead to the further suggestion that performance sets up, or represents, an interpretative frame within which the messages being communicated are to be understood, and that this frame contrasts with at least one other frame, the literal.

In employing the term "frame" here, I am drawing not upon Austin, but on the powerful insights of Gregory Bateson, and the more recent and equally provocative work of Erving Goffman (1974). Bateson first developed systematically on the notion of frame as a defined interpretive context providing guidelines for discriminating between orders of message (1972[1956]:222), in his seminal article, "A Theory of Play and Fantasy" (1972[1955]:177–193). We shall return to aspects of this theory, and of Goffman's, in more detail below.[5]

Although the notion of performance as a frame was introduced above, in connection with Austin's thinking, as contrasting with literal communication, it should be made clear from the beginning that many other such frames besides these two may be identified. For example:

—*insinuation*, in which the words spoken are to be interpreted as having a covert and indirect relation to the meaning of the utterance (cf. Austin 1962:121);

—*joking*, in which the words spoken are to be interpreted as not seriously meaning what they might otherwise mean (cf. Austin 1962:121);

—*imitation*, in which the manner of speaking is to be interpreted as being modeled after that of another person or persona;

—*translation*, in which the words spoken are to be interpreted as the equivalent of words originally spoken in another language or code;

—*quotation*, in which the words spoken are to be interpreted as the words of someone other than the speaker (cf. Weinreich 1966:162).

This is a partial and unelaborated list, which does not even adequately sample, much less exhaust, the range of possible interpretive frames within which communication may be couched. It should be noted, moreover, that frames listed may be used in combination, as well as singly. It should also be stressed that although theorists like Austin suggest that the literal frame somehow has priority over all the others — is more "normal" — this is not necessary to the theory, and in fact biases it in unproductive ways (Fish 1973). The notorious difficulty of defining literalness aside, there is growing evidence that literal utterances are no more frequent or "normal" in situated human communication than any of the other frames, and indeed that in spoken communication no such thing as naked literalness may actually exist (Burns 1972; Goffman 1974). For our purposes, all that is necessary is the recognition of performance as a distinctive frame, available as a communicative resource along with the others to speakers in particular communities.[6]

The first major task, then, is to suggest what kind of interpretive frame performance establishes or represents. How is communication that constitutes performance to be interpreted? The following represents a very preliminary attempt to specify the interpretive guidelines set up by the performance frame.

Fundamentally, performance as a mode of spoken verbal communication consists in the assumption of responsibility to an audience for a display of communicative competence. This competence rests on the knowledge and ability to speak in socially appropriate ways. Performance involves on the part of the performer an assumption of accountability to an audience for the way in which communication is carried out, above and beyond its referential content. From the point of view of the audience, the act of expression on the part of the performer is thus marked as subject to evaluation for the way it is done, for the relative skill and effectiveness of the performer's display of competence.[7] Additionally, it is marked as available for the enhancement of experience, through the present enjoyment of the intrinsic qualities of the act of expression itself. Performance thus calls forth special attention to and heightened awareness of the act of expression, and gives license to the audience to regard the act of expression and the performer with special intensity.[8]

Thus conceived, performance is a mode of language use, a way of speaking. The implication of such a concept for a theory of verbal art is this: it is no longer necessary to begin with artful texts, identified on independent formal grounds and then reinjected into situations of use, in order to conceptualize verbal art in communicative terms. Rather, in terms of the approach being developed here, performance becomes *constitutive* of the domain of verbal art as spoken communication.

Some examples may be useful at this point, to demonstrate in empirical terms the application of the notion of performance we have proposed. In several of her writings on the people of the plateau area of the Malagasy Republic (Keenan 1973, 1974), Elinor Keenan delineates the two major ways of speaking identified by this group. The first, called in native terminology *resaka*, may be loosely defined as informal conversation, described by native elders as "everyday talk," or "simple talk." The other way of speaking, *kabary*, is the one of principal interest to us here. *Kabary* is glossed by Keenan as "ceremonial speech, what we might call oratory." The following are excerpts from Keenan's description:

> *Kabary* as a focal point of tradition and as a focal point of artistic expression is ... regarded with great interest. It is not uncommon to see groups of elders

evaluating the skills and approaches of speechmakers following a *kabary* performance. A speechmaker who pleases his audience is rewarded with praise such as: 'He is a very sharp speechmaker.' 'He is prepared.' 'He is a true speechmaker, a child of his father.' His words are said to be 'well-arranged' and 'balanced.' His performance is described as 'satisfying.' . . . Evaluations are based on both skill in handling winding speech and on one's ability to follow certain rules governing the sequence and content of particular oratory [1973:226–227].

And further, "*kabary* performances . . . are platforms for exhibiting knowledge of traditional oratory" (1973:229). Wedding *kabary*, in particular, "is the most developed art form in the culture and a source of great delight and interest to all participants" (1973:242).

It is clear from this description that *kabary* represents for the plateau Malagasy a domain of performance. To engage in *kabary* is to assume responsibility to one's audience for a display of competence in the traditional *kabary* forms, to render one's speech subject to evaluation for the quality of one's speaking. One is judged as a speechmaker, for the way one's words are arranged. *Kabary* performances are keenly attended to and actively evaluated, with good performances indeed serving as a source of enjoyment and satisfaction to the auditors, for the way they are done. The ethnography of verbal art among the plateau Malagasy thus becomes centrally the ethnography of *kabary*.

Among the Ilongot of the Philippines, by contrast with the above, there are three major speech styles, described by Michelle Rosaldo: the stylistically unmarked "straight speech" (*qube:nata qupu*), invocatory speech (*nawnaw*), and a third style, *qambaqan*, described as "crooked" or witty talk (Rosaldo 1973). It is not wholly clear from Rosaldo's account whether *nawnaw* involves preference, but *qambaqan* very clearly does. *Qambaqan* is "artful, witty, charming," "a language of display, performance, pose" (Rosaldo 1973:197–198). What is especially noteworthy about speaking among the Ilongot, within our present context, is that the telling of tales, always included in *a priori* text-centered definitions of verbal art, is classified as a kind of "straight speech." That is, storytelling for the Ilongot is not a form of performance, thus in culture-specific communicative terms, not a form of verbal art. The domain of speaking among the Ilongot is to this extent, among many others, organized differently from that of the many cultures in which storytelling does involve performance.

Japanese professional storytellers, for example, as described by Hrd-ličková, are certainly performers in our sense of the term. For their audiences, "it is not seldom more important *how* a story is told than *what* the story relates. . . . Storytellers regard the mastery of [storytelling] elements as a necessary preliminary stage prior to any successful practicing of their art in public, since the audience not only expects of them an established manner of interpretation, but also rates them according to the degree of artistry the artists command" (Hrdličková 1969:193; italics in original). That is, storytelling involves a display of competence in the manner of telling the story, which is subject to evaluation for the way it is done. The audience derives enjoyment from the performance in proportion to the skill of the narrator (1969:193).

The point to be emphasized here is that just as speaking itself as a cultural system (or as part of cultural systems defined in other terms) will vary from speech community to speech community, so too will the nature and extent of the realm of performance and verbal art (Bauman 1972b). One of the principal questions one must ask in the ethnography of performance is what range of speech activity is regarded as susceptible to performance and what range is conventionally performed, that is, conventionally expected by members of the community to be rendered in a performance mode.[9] For the St. Vincentians, for example, performance may be invoked across a very wide spectrum of speech activity, from oratory, to storytelling, to gossip — even to speaking with a speech impediment — while the seventeenth century Quakers, because of basic attitudes toward speaking in general, restricted performance to an extremely narrow range of activity (Abrahams 1970; Abrahams and Bauman 1971; Bauman 1974, 1975). In performance terms, it is not possible to assert *a priori* that verbal art consists of "folktales, myths, legends, proverbs, riddles, and other 'literary forms' " defined solely in formal terms (Bascom 1955:245). We will return to the culture-specific nature of verbal art as performance below.

The Keying of Performance

Before embarking upon a discussion of the further implications of the notion of performance put forward above, there is one major element integral to the conception of performance as a frame which must be delineated, i.e., the way in which framing is accomplished, or, to use Goffman's term for the process by which frames are invoked and shifted, how performance is *keyed* (Goffman 1974). Here again, we may draw on Bateson's powerful insight, that it is characteristic of communicative interaction that it include a range of explicit or implicit messages which carry instructions on how to interpret the other message(s) being communicated. This communication about communication Bateson termed metacommunication (Ruesch and Bateson 1968:209). In Bateson's terms, "a frame is metacommunicative. Any message which either explicitly or implicitly defines a frame, *ipso facto* gives the receiver instructions or aids in his attempt to understand the messages included within the frame" (Bateson 1972[1955]:188). All framing, then, including performance, is accomplished through the employment of culturally conventionalized metacommunication. In empirical terms, this means that each speech community will make use of a structured set of distinctive communicative means from among its resources in culturally conventionalized and culture-specific ways to key the performance frame, such that all communication that takes place within that frame is to be understood as performance within that community.

An etic list of communicative means that have been widely documented in various cultures as serving to key performance is not difficult to compile. Such a list would include at least the following:

(1) special codes, e.g., archaic or esoteric language, reserved for and diagnostic of performance (e.g., Toelken 1969; Sherzer 1974);

(2) special formulae that signal performance, such as conventional openings and closings, or explicit statements announcing or asserting performance (e.g., Crowley 1966; Reaver 1972; Uspensky 1972:19; Babcock-Abrahams 1974);

(3) figurative language, such as metaphor, metonymy, etc. (e.g., Keenan 1973, 1974; Fox 1974; Rosaldo 1973; Sherzer 1974);

(4) formal stylistic devices, such as rhyme, vowel harmony, other forms of parallelism (Jakobson 1966, 1968; Stankiewicz 1960:15; Austerlitz 1960; Gossen 1972, 1974; Fox 1974; Sherzer and Sherzer 1972);

(5) special prosodic patterns of tempo, stress, pitch (e.g., Lord 1960; Tedlock 1972);

(6) special paralinguistic patterns of voice quality and vocalization (e.g., Tedlock 1972; McDowell 1974);

(7) appeal to tradition (e.g., Innes 1874:145);

(8) disclaimer of performance (e.g., Darnell 1974; Keenan 1974).

The formal and conventional nature of the devices listed above bears an important relation to the very nature of performance itself. Burke has alerted us to the power of formal patterns to elicit the participation of an audience through the arousal of "an attitude of collaborative expectancy. . . . Once you grasp the trend of the form, it invites participation." This "yielding to the formal development, surrendering to its symmetry as such" (Burke 1969[1950]:58) fixes the attention of the audience more strongly on the performer, binds the audience to the performer in a relationship of dependence that keeps them caught up in his display. A not insignificant part of the capacity of performance to transform social structure, to be discussed at the end of this paper, resides in the power that the performer derives from the control over his audience afforded him by the formal appeal of his performance.

A list of the kind given above, however, is ultimately of only limited utility, for the essential task in the ethnography of performance is to determine the culture-specific constellations of communicative means that serve to key performance in particular communities. Features such as those listed above may figure in a variety of ways in the speech economy of a community. Rhyme, for example, may be used to key performance, or it may simply be a formal feature of the language, as when it figures in certain forms of reduplication, or it may appear in speech play (which may or may not involve performance). It may even be inadvertent. Interestingly, when this happens in English, there is a traditional formula which may be invoked to disclaim performance retroactively: "I'm a poet and I don't know it; my feet show it, they're longfellows." This is an indication that rhyme often does in fact key performance in English.

The basic point here is that one must determine empirically what are the specific conventionalized means that key performance in a particular community, and that these will vary from one community to another (though one may discover areal and typological patterns, and universal tendencies may exit). Let us consider some examples.

The telling of traditional folktales, or "old stories," in the Bahamas, as described by Daniel J. Crowley, characteristically involves performance. Narrators assume responsibility for the way they render their stories, and their performances are attended to for the enjoyment to be derived from the telling, and evaluated as displays of competence (for evidence of this see Crowley 1966:37, 137–139). Old story performances are keyed by a complex system of communicative means.

One of the most distinctive of these is the word "Bunday," which serves as a "trademark" for old stories, "since its mere mention is the

VERBAL ART AS PERFORMANCE 175

sign for an old story to begin. . . . To the Bahamians, 'Bunday ain't nothing, it just mean is old story.' " Crowley identifies five conventional functions served by "Bunday" as a marker of old story performance: (1) as a means of announcing one's intention to tell a story and testing the audience's willingness to hear it; (2) as a means of recapturing audience attention (the better the storyteller, the less often he must have recourse to this device, but all storytellers must use it occasionally); (3) for emphasis and punctuation; (4) as a filler to cover pauses and other gaps in the narration; (5) as a signal that the story is ended.

In addition to "Bunday," storytelling performance is further signaled by opening and closing formulae. Some of these, such as "Once upon a time, a very good time, monkey chew tobacco, and he spit white lime," are stylistically developed in their own right, while others, like "Once upon a time," are more simple. Closing formulae are more individualized, with the closing "Bunday" coming before, between, or after the formula. To take one characteristic example, which brings the narrative back to the occasion of its telling: "I was passing by, and I say 'Mister Jack, how come you so smart?' And he make at me, and I run, causing me to come here tonight to tell you this wonderful story" (Crowley 1966: 35–36).

The keying devices for old story performance further include special words and phrases (e.g., "one more day than all . . ." to begin a new motif), special pronunciations, elaborate onomatopoeia, and a range of metanarrational devices, such as the following of an impossible statement by "If I was going to tell you a story," and then another even more impossible statement (Crowley 1966:26–27). Finally, old story performance is keyed by distinctive paralinguistic and prosodic shifts for the purpose of characterization (e.g., Crowley 1966:67). In sum, this one segment of the Bahamian performance domain is keyed by a complex system of mutually reinforcing means, serving together to signal that an old story is being performed.

As we have noted, the foregoing inventory of keys to old story performance pertains to but a single genre. A full and ideal ethnography of performance would encompass the entire domain, viewing speaking and performance as a cultural system and indicating how the whole range of performance is keyed. Gary Gossen's elegant analyses of Chamula genres of verbal behavior come closest to any work in the literature known to the author to achieving such a description (Gossen 1972, 1974). Within the overall domain of "people's speech" (sk'op kirsano),

Chamula identify three macro-categories of speech: "ordinary speech" (*lo?il k'op*), "speech for people whose hearts are heated" (*k'op sventa sk'isnah yo?nton yu?un li kirsanoe*), and "pure speech" (*puru k'op*). Ordinary speech is conceived of by the people as unmarked, not special in any way. It is not associated with performance. Speech for people whose hearts are heated and pure speech, on the other hand, are strongly relevant to our discussion.

As an overall category, what distinguishes speech for people whose hearts are heated from ordinary speech is that it is stylistically marked by a degree of verbatim repetition of words, phrases and metaphors, and in certain sub-categories, or genres, by parallelism in syntax and metaphorical couplets. Pure speech is distinguished in turn from speech for people whose hearts are heated by its relative fixity of form and the greater density of parallelism, either through proliferation of syntactically parallel lines or the "stacking" of metaphorical couplets.

From Gossen's description, it is evident that repetition and parallelism constitute keys to performance for the Chamula. Both speech for people whose hearts are heated and pure speech involve the display of competence, contribute to the enhancement of experience, and are subject to evaluation for the way they are done. There is a crucial point to be made here, however. Speech for people whose hearts are heated is idiosyncratic, unfixed, and markedly less saturated with those features that signal performance. The user of speech for people whose hearts are heated is less fully accountable for a display of competence, his expression is less intensely regarded by the audience, his performance has less to contribute to the enhancement of the audience's experience than the one who uses the forms of pure speech. The performance frame may thus be seen to operate with variable intensity in Chamula speaking.

It is worth underscoring this last point. Art is commonly conceived as an all-or-nothing phenomenon — something either is or is not art — but conceived as performance, in terms of an interpretive frame, verbal art may be culturally defined as varying in intensity as well as range. We are not speaking here of the relative quality of a performance — good performance versus bad performance — but the degree of intensity with which the performance frame operates in a particular range of culturally defined ways of speaking. When we move beyond the first level discrimination of culturally-defined ways of speaking that do not conventionally involve performance (e.g., Chamula ordinary speech, Malagasy *resaka*) versus ways of speaking that do characteristically involve performance (e.g., Chamula speech for people whose hearts are heated and pure speech, Malagasy *kabary*), we need to attend to the relative saturation of the performance frame attendant upon the more specific categories of ways of speaking within the community.

The variable range of performance in Chamula is confirmed by the metalanguage employed by the Chamula in their evaluation of performance. Because of the importance of the evaluative dimension of performance as communication, such metalanguages and the esthetic standards they express constitute an essential consideration in the ethnography of performance; the range of application of such esthetic systems may be the best indicator of the extent of the performance domain within a community (Dundes 1966; Babcock-Abrahams 1974). Increased fixity of form, repetition, and parallelism, which serve as measures of increasing intensity of performance, also signal for the Chamula increasing "heat." Heat is a basic metaphor for the Chamula, symbolizing the orderly, the good, and the beautiful, by derivation from the power of the sun deity. The transition from ordinary speech to speech for people whose hearts are heated to pure speech thus involves a progressive increase in heat and therefore of esthetic and ethical value in speaking.[10]

The Patterning of Performance

Our discussion of Chamula performance has centered upon the way in which performance is keyed, the communicative means that signal that a particular act of expression is being performed. We may advance our considerations still further by recognizing that it is only as these means are embodied in particular genres that they figure in the performance system of the Chamula themselves. That is, the Chamula organize the domain of speaking in terms of genres, i.e., conventionalized message forms, formal structures that incorporate the features that key performance. The association of performance with particular genres is a significant aspect of the patterning of performance within communities. This association is more problematic than text-centered, etic approaches to verbal art would indicate (Ben-Amos 1969).

In the ethnography of performance as a cultural system, the investigator's attention will frequently be attracted first by those genres that are conventionally performed. These are the genres, like the Chamula genres of pure speech or Bahamian old stories, for which there is little or no expectation on the part of members of the community that they will be rendered in any other way. He should be attentive as well, however, for those genres for which the expectation or probability of performance is lower, for which performance is felt to be more optional, but which occasion no surprise if they are performed. A familiar example from contemporary American society might be the personal narrative, which is frequently rendered in a simply repertorial mode, but which may well be highlighted as performance. There will, of course, in any society, be a range of verbal genres that are not rendered as performances. These will be viewed as not involving the kind of competence that is susceptible to display, not lending themselves for the enhancement of experience. Not to be forgotten are those genres that are considered by members of the community to be performance forms, but that are nevertheless not performed, as when there is no one left who is competent to perform them, or conditions for appropriate performance no longer exist. A related phenomenon is what Hymes calls performance in a perfunctory key (personal communication), in which the responsibility for a display of communicative competence is undertaken out of a sense of cultural duty, traditional obligation, but offering, because of changed circumstances, relatively little pleasure or enhancement of experience. One thinks, for example, of some masses in Latin. Such performances may, however, be a means of preserving performance forms for later reinvigoration and restoration to the level of full performance.

It should be noted, with reference to the native organization of the domain of speaking and cultural expectations for performance, that the members of a community may conceptualize speech activity in terms of acts rather than genres. The St. Vincentians are a case in point (Abrahams and Bauman 1971). Speech acts and genres are, of course, analytically distinct, the former having to do with speech behavior, the latter with the verbal products of that behavior. For an oral culture, however, the distinction between the act of speaking and the form of the utterance tends characteristically not to be significant, if it is recognized at all. Thus a particular performance system may well be organized by members of the community in terms of speech acts that conventionally involve performance, others that may or may not, and still others for which performance is not a relevant consideration.

We view the act of performance as situated behavior, situated within and rendered meaningful with reference to relevant contexts. Such contexts may be identified at a variety of levels — in terms of settings, for example, the culturally-defined places where performance occurs. Institutions too — religion, education, politics — may be viewed from the perspective of the way in which they do or do not represent contexts for performance within communities. Most important as an organizing principle in the ethnography of performance is the event, or scene, within which performance occurs (see, e.g., Kirshenblatt-Gimblett 1974).

There are, first of all, events for which performance is required, for which it is a criterial attribute, such that performance is a necessary component for a particular event to count as a valid instance of the class. These will be what Singer calls "cultural performances" (Singer 1972: 71). They may be organized and conducted primarily for entertainment, such as Bahamian old story sessions or Vincentian tea meetings, or they may have some other stated primary purpose, like Malagasy bride-price meetings, but performance will be as integral a component for the latter as for the former.

As with genres and acts, there are other events for which performance is an optional feature, not necessary or invariably expected, but not unexpected or surprising, as when someone tells jokes at a party. Again, there will be a further range of events in which performance is extraneous, not a relevant variable insofar as people categorize and participate in the events of their culture.

The structure of performance events is a product of the interplay of many factors, including setting, act sequence, and ground rules of performance. These last will consist of the set of cultural themes and social-interactional organizing principles that govern the conduct of performance (Bauman and Sherzer 1974, Sect. III). As a kind of speaking, performance will be subject to a range of community ground rules that regulate speaking in general, but there will also be a set of ground rules specific to performance itself. Basic, too, to the structure of performance events are the participants, performer(s), and audience. Performance roles constitute a major dimension of the patterning of performance within communities.

As with events, certain roles will incorporate performance as a definitive attribute. Performance is necessary to establish oneself in the role, such that one cannot be considered an incumbent of the role without being a performer of verbal art, like the *sgealaí*, the traditional Irish storyteller (Delargy 1945). Other roles may be more loosely associated with performance, such that members of the community have a certain expectation of performance from a person in a particular role, but it is neither required of everyone in the role, nor surprising when it does not occur. Salesmen may serve as an example here, in that there is a loose expectation in contemporary American culture that salesmen are often good performers of jokes, but no one requires or expects this skill on the part of all salesmen. And, as above, other roles will have nothing to do with performance, either as definitive criterion or optional attribute.

Eligibility for and recruitment to performance roles vary cross-culturally in interesting ways. One dimension along which this variation occurs has to do with conceptions of the nature of the competence required of a performer and the way such competence is acquired. Does it, for example, require special aptitude, talent, or training? Among the Limba, storytelling is a form of performance, but it is not considered to require the special talent called for in drumming and dancing. Anyone is a potential storyteller, and it calls for no special training to become one (Finnegan 1967:69–70). By contrast, the Japanese storytellers who perform *rakugo* or *kodan* must undergo a long and arduous period of training and apprenticeship before they are considered ready to practice their art (Hrdličková 1969).

Also to be taken into account in the analysis of performance roles is the relationship, both social and behavioral, between such roles and other roles played by the same individual. We have in mind here the way and extent to which the role of performer and the behavior associated with it may dominate or be subordinate to the other roles he may play. To illustrate one extreme possibility, we may cite Keil's assertion that in Afro-American society the role of bluesman assimilates or overshadows all other roles an adult male may normally be expected to fulfill (Keil 1966:143, 153–155). Sammy Davis, Jr., tellingly reveals the encompassing power of his role as entertainer in his statement that, "as soon as I go out the front door of my house in the morning, I'm on, Daddy, I'm on" (quoted in Messinger et al. 1962:98–99).

The foregoing list of patterning factors for performance has been presented schematically, for analytical and presentational convenience, but it should not be taken as a mere checklist. It should be self-evident that performance genres, acts, events, and roles cannot occur in isolation, but are mutually interactive and interdependent. Any of the above factors may be used as a point of departure or point of entry into the description and analysis of the performance system of a community, but the ultimate ethnographic statement one makes about performance as part of social life must incorporate them all in some degree. It will be useful to consider one extended example here, drawn from Joel Sherzer's description of three major ceremonial traditions of the San Blas Cuna, to give some indication how the organizing features of a performance system fit together in empirical terms (Sherzer 1974).

Abstracting from Sherzer's rich description of the three traditions, we may note that each is associated with a type of event, within which specific functionaries perform particular genres in a characteristic performance mode. Thus, in the type of congress known as *omekan pela* (the women and everybody), the chiefs (*sakla*) chant (*namakke*) long chants called *pap ikar*. The chants, in turn, are interpreted to the assembled participants in the congress house by special spokesmen (*arkar*), whose speaking (*sunmakke*) also involves performance, though different from that of the chiefs. In curing rituals, a special *ikar*-knower (*ikar wisit*) speaks (*sunmakke*) the particular curing chant (each a type of *ikar*) for which he is a specialist and which is called for by the ailment from which the patient is suffering. In the third type of event, the girls' puberty ceremony, the specialist (*kantule*) in girls' puberty chants (*kantur ikar*) shouts (*kormakke*) the chants for the participants. The three performance traditions may be summarized in tabular form thus:

Event	Act	Role	Genre
congress (*omekan pela*)	chant (*namakke*)	chief (*sakla*)	chief's chant (*pap ikar*)
	speak (*sunmakke*)	spokesman (*arkar*)	interpretation
curing ritual	speak (*sunmakke*)	special *ikar*-knower (*ikar wisit*)	medicine chant (*kapur ikar, kurkin ikar*, etc.)
girls' puberty ceremony	shout (*kormakke*)	specialist in girls' puberty chant (*kantule*)	girls' puberty chant (*kantur ikar*)

For each ceremony or ritual to count as a valid instance of its class, the appropriate form must be rendered in the appropriate way by the appropriate functionary. That *namakke*, the *sunmakke* of the *arkar*'s interpretation and the *sunmakke* of the medicine chants, and *kormakke* all represent ways of performing for the Cuna is clear from Sherzer's description. All four roles, *sakla, arkar, ikar wisit*, and *kantule*, are defined in essential part in terms of competence in these specific ways of performing their respective genres. There is thus, in these ceremonial traditions, a close and integral relationship between performance and specific events, acts, roles, and genres, and the configuration created by the interrelationships among these factors must be close to the center of an ethnography of performance among the Cuna.

Constellations such as Sherzer describes, involving events, acts, genres, and roles in highly structured and predictable combinations, constitute the nucleus of an ethnography of performance among the Cuna, and are aptly made the focus of Sherzer's paper. However, it is crucial to establish that not all performance related to the system Sherzer describes is captured within the framework of conventional interrelationships outlined above. We have noted, for example, that the performance of curing *ikar* by the *ikar-wisit* has its conventional locus in the curing ritual; such performance is obligatory for the *ikar wisit* to fulfill the demands of his role and for the curing ritual to be conducted at all. Against this background, then, it is noteworthy that the *ikar-wisit* may also be asked to perform his *ikar* during a chicha festival associated with the girls' puberty rites, purely for entertainment. That is, the performance that has its primary place in a particular context, in which it is obligatory, may be an optional feature of another kind of event, extended to the latter because of the esthetic enjoyment to be derived from it. The association between performer and genre is maintained, but the context, and of course the function, are different.

Though optional, the performance of curing *ikar* at puberty rite festivities is no less institutionalized than the obligatory performance of these chants in curing rituals. There is no surprise or novelty in the performance of curing *ikar* at the chicha festivals. Beyond the institutionalized system, however, lies one of the most important outlets for creative vitality within the performance domain. Consider the following circumstance, involving a group of small girls whom Sherzer was using as linguistic informants. On one occasion, knowing that he was interested in the performance forms of the community, the little girls launched spontaneously into a rendition of an *arkar*'s performance as they were being recorded (Sherzer, personal communication). The remarkableness of this is apparent when one considers that the role of *arkar* is restricted to adult men, and performances of the kind the girls imitated belonged, in conventional terms, to the congress and the congress house. Though the little girls' rendition was framed as imitation, a reframing of the *arkar*'s performance, it constituted performance in its own right as well, in which the girls assumed responsibility to an audience for a display of competence.

Consider one further observation made by Sherzer in his study of the Cuna. The congresses (*omekan pela*) discussed above, in which the chiefs chant their *pap ikar* and the *arkars* interpret them to the audience, are held in the congress house during the evening. During the daytime, however, when congresses are not in session, individuals who find themselves in the congress house may occasionally sit in a chief's hammock and launch into an attempt at a chief's chant, just for the fun of it (Sherzer, personal communication). Here we have what is a conventional performance doubly reframed as imitation and more importantly as play, in which there is no assumption of responsibility for a display of communicative competence, nor any assumption of responsibility for or susceptibility to evaluation for the way in which the act of expression is done.

What are the implications of these two circumstances? The little girls' performance of an *arkar*'s interpretation represents a striking instance of the use of an element from the conventional, structured performance system of the community in a novel, creative, and unexpected way to fashion a new kind of performance. The playful imitation of the chief's chant involves the reframing of what is conventionally a performance genre into another mode of communication — in this case the performance genre is not performed but is rendered in another frame.[11] In both cases, the participants are using the structured, conventional performance system itself as a resource for creative manipulation, as a base on which a range of communicative transformations can be wrought (cf. Sacks 1974). The structured system stands available to them as a set of conventional expectations and associations, but these expectations and associations are further manipulated in innovative ways, by fashioning novel performances outside the conventional system, or working various transformational adaptations which turn performance into something else. This is a very poorly documented aspect of performance systems, but one richly deserving of study, as a key to the creative vitality and flexibility of performance in a community.

The Emergent Quality of Performance

By stressing the creative aspect of optative performance, and the normative, structured aspect of conventional performance, we do not mean to imply that the latter is fixed and frozen while creativity is confined to the former. Rather, the argument developed up to this point to highlight creativity in the use of the performance frame itself as a resource for communication provides the entree for the final theme to be developed in this paper, the emergent quality of all performance.[12] The concept of emergence is necessary to the study of performance as a means toward comprehending the uniqueness of particular performances within the context of performance as a generalized cultural system in a community (cf. Georges 1969:319). The ethnographic construction of the structured, conventionalized performance system standardizes and homogenizes description, but all performances are not the same, and one wants to be able to appreciate the individuality of each, as well as the community-wide patterning of the overall domain.

The emergent quality of performance resides in the interplay between communicative resources, individual competence, and the goals of the participants, within the context of particular situations. We consider as resources all those aspects of the communication system available to the members of a community for the conduct of performance. Relevant here are the keys to performance, genres, acts, events, and ground rules for the conduct of performance that make up the structured system of conventionalized performance for the community. The goals of the participants include those that are intrinsic to performance — the display of competence, the focusing of attention on oneself as performer, the enhancement of experience — as well as the other desired ends toward which performance is brought to bear; these latter will be highly culture- and situation-specific. Relative competence, finally, has to do with relative degrees of proficiency in the conduct of performance.

One of the first works to conceptualize oral literature in terms of emergent structures was Albert Lord's influential book, *The Singer of Tales* (1960), a study of Serbo-Croatian oral epic poetry for the light it sheds on the classic Homeric epic. Consider the following passage:

> Whether the performance takes place at home, in the coffee house, in the courtyard, or in the halls of a noble, the essential element of the occasion of singing that influences the form of the poetry is the variability and instability of the audience.
>
> The instability of the audience requires a marked degree of concentration on the part of the singer in order that he may sing at all; it also tests to the utmost his dramatic ability and his narrative skill in keeping the audience as attentive as possible. But it is the length of a song which is most affected by the audience's restlessness. The singer begins to tell his tale. If he is fortunate, he may find it possible to sing until he is tired without interruption from the

audience. After a rest he will continue, if his audience still wishes. This may last until he finishes the song, and if his listeners are propitious and his mood heightened by their interest, he may lengthen his tale, savoring each descriptive passage. It is more likely that, instead of having this ideal occasion the singer will realize shortly after beginning that his audience is not receptive, and hence he will shorten his song so that it may be finished within the limit of time for which he feels the audience may be counted on. Or, if he misjudges, he may simply never finish the song. Leaving out of consideration for the moment the question of the talent of the singer, one can say that the length of the song depends upon the audience [Lord 1960:16–17].

The characteristic context for the performance of the oral epics that Lord describes is one in which the singer competes for the attention of his audience with other factors that may engage them, and in which the time available for performance is of variable duration. The epic form is remarkably well-suited to the singer's combined need for fluency and flexibility. The songs are made up of ten-syllable, end-stopped lines with a medial caesura after the fourth syllable. In attaining competence, the singer must master a personal stock of line and half-line formulas for expressing character, action, and place, develop the capacity to generate formulaic expressions on the model of his fixed formulas, and learn to string together his lines in the development of the narrative themes out of which his epic songs are built. The ready-madeness of the formulas makes possible the fluency required under performance conditions, while the flexibility of the form allows the singer to adapt his performance to the situation and the audience, making it longer and more elaborate, or shorter and less adorned, as audience response, his own mood, and time constraints may dictate. And of course, the poetic skill of the singer is a factor in how strongly he can attract and hold the attention of the audience, how sensitively he can adapt to their mood, and how elaborate he can make his song if conditions allow. Lord recorded sung versions of the same narratives from the same singer and from different singers that varied in length by as much as several thousand lines.

Ultimately, one of Lord's chief contributions is to demonstrate the unique and emergent quality of the oral text, composed in performance. His analysis of the dynamics of the tradition sets forth what amounts to a generative model of epic performance. Although it has been argued that perhaps all verbal art is generated anew in the act of performance (Maranda 1972), there is also ample evidence to show that rote memorization and insistence on word-for-word fidelity to a fixed text do play a part in the performance system of certain communities (see, e.g., Friedman 1961). The point is that completely novel and completely fixed texts represent the poles of an ideal continuum, and that between the poles lies the range of emergent text structures to be found in empirical performance. The study of the factors contributing to the emergent quality of the oral literary text promises to bring about a major reconceptualization of the nature of the text, freeing it from the apparent fixity it assumes when abstracted from performance and placed on the written page, and placing it within an analytical context which focuses on the very source of the empirical relationship between art and society (cf. Georges 1969:324).

Other aspects of emergent structure are highlighted in Elinor Keenan's ethnography of the Malagasy marriage *kabary*,[13] an artful oratorical negotiation surrounding a marriage request (Keenan 1973). The *kabary* is conducted by two speechmakers, one representing the boy's family and one the girl's. The boy's speaker initiates each step of the *kabary*, which is then evaluated by the speaker for the girl. The latter may indicate that he agrees with and approves of that step, urging his opposite number on to the next, or he may state that the other's words are not according to tradition, that he has made an error in the *kabary*. The boy's speaker must then be able to justify what he has said, to show that no error has been made, or, if he admits error, he must correct it by repeating the step the right way and paying a small fine to the girl's family.

Keenan discovered, however, that there is no one unified concept of what constitutes a correct *kabary* shared by all members of the community. Rather, there are regional, familial, generational, individual, and other differences of conception and style. This being so, how is it decided what constitutes an error? There is, first of all, a preliminary meeting between the families, often with their respective speechmakers present, to establish the ground rules for the *kabary*. These are never fully conclusive, however, and it is a prominent feature of the *kabary* that arguments concerning the ground rules occur throughout the event, with appeals to the preliminary negotiations becoming simply one set of the range of possible appeals to establish authoritative performance.

Much of the impetus toward argument derives from conflicting pressures on the boy's speechmaker, who is obliged to admit to a certain range of errors, out of courtesy to the girl's family, but who is at the same time actuated by the motives of good performance, i.e., to establish his virtuosity as a performer. The girl's speechmaker, desirous of representing the family to best advantage, is likewise concerned to display his own skill as speechmaker.

The arguments, as noted, concern the ground rules for the *kabary* with each party insisting on the obligatoriness of particular rules and features by appeal to various standards, drawn from pre-*kabary* negotiation, generational, regional, and other stylistic differences. Of particular interest is the fact that the strength of the participants' insistence on the rightness of their own way, their structural rigidity, is a function of the mood of the encounter, increasing as the tension mounts, decreasing as a settlement is approached. Ultimately, however, the practical goal of establishing an alliance between the two families involved takes precedence over all the speechmakers' insistence upon the conventions of *kabary* performance and their desire to display their performance skills; if the *kabary* threatens the making of the alliance, many are willing to reject the rules entirely to accomplish the larger goal.

The most striking feature of the marriage request *kabary* as described by Keenan is the emergent structure of the performance event itself. The ground rules for performance, as negotiated and asserted by the participants, shift and fluctuate in terms of what they bring to the event and the way it proceeds once under way. This is an extreme case, in which the competitive dimension and conflicting pressures make for an especially variable and shifting event structure, but here again the question is one of degree rather than kind, for all but the most ideally stereotyped of performance events will have discernibly variable features of act sequence and/or ground rules for performance. The emergent structure of performance events is of special interest under conditions of change, as participants adapt established patterns of performance to new circumstances (Darnell 1974).

In addition to text and event structure, we may uncover a third kind of structure emergent in performance, namely, social structure. To be sure, the emergent quality of social structure is not specific to situations involving performance. Indeed, there is an important line of inquiry in contemporary sociology which concerns itself with the creation of social structures in the course of and through all social interaction.

The principle addressed here is related to Raymond Firth's articulation, some years ago, of the distinction between social structure and social organization, in which the former is an abstract conception of ideal patterns of group relations, of conventional expectations and arrangements, and the latter has to do with "the systematic ordering of social relations by acts of choice and decision" in concrete activity. In Firth's terms, social organization is the domain of "variation from what has happened in apparently similar circumstances in the past. . . . Structural forms set a precedent and provide a limitation to the range of alternatives possible . . . but it is the possibility of alternatives that makes for variability. A person chooses, consciously or unconsciously, which course he will follow" (Firth 1961:40).

What is missing from Firth's formulation is the centrality of situated social interaction as the context in which social organization, as an emergent, takes form. The current focus on the emergence of social structures in social interaction is principally the contribution of ethnomethodology, the work of Garfinkel, Cicourel, Sacks, and others. For these sociologists, "the field of sociological analysis is anywhere the sociologist can obtain access and can examine the way the 'social structure' is a meaningful ongoing accomplishment of members" (Phillipson 1972:162). To these scholars too is owed, in large part, the recognition that language is a basic means through which social realities are intersubjectively constituted and communicated (Phillipson 1972:140). From this perspective, insofar as performance is conceived of as communicative interaction, one would expect aspects of the social structure of the interaction to be emergent from the interaction itself, as in any other such situation. Rosaldo's explication of the strategic role-taking and role-making she observed in the course of a meeting to settle a dispute over brideprice among the Ilongot illuminates quite clearly the emergent aspect of social structure in that event (Rosaldo 1973). The conventions of such meetings and the oratorical performances of the interactants endow the interaction with a special degree of formalization and intensity, but the fact that artistic verbal performance is involved is not functionally related to the negotiation of social structure on the level Rosaldo is concerned with. Rather she focuses on such matters as the rhetorical strategies and consequences of taking the role of father in a particular event, thus placing your interlocutor in the role of son, with its attendant obligations.

There is, however, a distinctive potential in performance which has implications for the creation of social structure in performance. It is part of the essence of performance that it offers to the participants a special enhancement of experience, bringing with it a heightened intensity of communicative interaction which binds the audience to the performer in a way that is specific to performance as a mode of communication. Through his performance, the performer elicits the participative attention and energy of his audience, and to the extent that they value his performance, they will allow themselves to be caught up in it. When this happens, the performer gains a measure of prestige and control over the audience—prestige because of the demonstrated competence he had displayed, control because the determination of the flow of the interaction is in his hands. When the performer gains control in this way, the potential for transformation of the social structure may become available to him as well (Burke 1969[1950]:58–59). The process is manifest in the following passage from Dick Gregory's autobiography:

> I got picked on a lot around the neighborhood . . . I guess that's when I first began to learn about humor, the power of a joke . . .
>
> At first . . . I'd just get mad and run home and cry when the kids started. And then, I don't know just when, I started to figure it out. They were going to laugh anyway, but if I made the jokes they'd laugh *with* me instead of *at* me. I'd get the kids off my back, on my side. So I'd come off that porch talking about myself. . . .
>
> Before they could get going, I'd knock it out first, fast, knock out those jokes so they wouldn't have time to set and climb all over me. . . . And they started to come over and listen to me, they'd see me coming and crowd around me on the corner. . . .
>
> Everything began to change then. . . . The kids began to expect to hear funny things from me, and after a while I could say anything I wanted. I got a reputation as a funny man. And then I started to turn the jokes on them [Gregory 1964:54–55; italics in original].

Through performance, Gregory is able to take control of the situation, creating a social structure with himself at the center. At first he gains control by the artful use of the deprecatory humor that the other boys had formerly directed at him. The joking is still at his own expense, but he has transformed the situation, through performance, into one in which he gains admiration for his performance skills. Then, building on the control he gains through performance, he is able, by strategic use of his performance skills, to transform the situation still further, turning the humor aggressively against those who had earlier victimized him. In a very real sense, Gregory emerges from the performance encounters in a different social position *vis-à-vis* the other boys from the one he occupied before he began to perform, and the change is a consequence of his performance in those encounters.

The consideration of the power inherent in performance to transform social structures opens the way to a range of additional considerations concerning the role of the performer in society. Perhaps there is a key here to the persistently documented tendency for performers to be both admired and feared — admired for their artistic skill and power and for the enhancement of experience they provide, feared because of the potential they represent for subverting and transforming the status quo. Here too may lie a reason for the equally persistent association between performers and marginality or deviance, for in the special emergent quality of performance the capacity for change may be highlighted and made manifest to the community (see, e.g., Abrahams and Bauman 1971, n.d.; Azadovskii 1926:23–25; Glassie 1971:42–52; Szwed 1971:157–165). If change is conceived of in opposition to the conventionality of the community at large, then it is only appropriate that the agents of that change be placed away from the center of that conventionality, on the margins of society.

Conclusion

The discipline of folklore (and to an extent, anthropology as well), has tended throughout its history to define itself in terms of a principal focus on the traditional remnants of earlier periods, still to be found in those sectors of society that have been outdistanced by the dominant culture. To this extent, folklore has been largely the study of what Raymond Williams has recently termed "residual culture," those "experiences, meanings and values which cannot be verified or cannot be expressed in terms of the dominant culture, [but] are nevertheless lived and practised on the basis of the residue — cultural as well as social — of some previous social formation" (Williams 1973:10–11). If the subject matter of the discipline is restricted to the residue of a specific cultural or historical period, then folklore anticipates its own demise, for when the traditions are fully gone, the discipline loses its *raison d'être* (cf. Hymes 1962:678; Ben-Amos 1972:14). This need not be the case, however, for as Williams defines the concept, cultural elements may become part of residual culture as part of a continual social process, and parts of residual culture may be incorporated into the dominant culture in a complementary process. At best, though, folklore as the discipline of residual culture looks backward to the past for its frame of reference, disqualifying itself from the study of the creations of contemporary culture until they too may become residual.

Contrasted with residual culture in Williams' provocative formulation is "emergent culture," in which "new meanings and values, new practices, new significances and experiences are continually being created" (Williams 1973:11). This is a further extension of the concept of emergence, as employed in the preceding pages of this article, but interestingly compatible with it, for the emergent quality of experience is a vital factor in the generation of emergent culture. Emergent culture, though a basic element in human social life, has always lain outside the charter of folklore, perhaps in part for lack of a unified point of departure or frame of reference able to comprehend residual forms and items, contemporary practice, and emergent structures. Performance, we would offer, constitutes just such a point of departure, the nexus of tradition, practice, and emergence in verbal art. Performance may thus be the cornerstone of a new folkloristics, liberated from its backward-facing perspective, and able to comprehend much more of the totality of human experience.

Notes

1. In the development of the ideas presented in this essay I have profited greatly from discussions with many colleagues and students over the past several years, among whom Barbara Babcock-Abrahams, Dan Ben-Amos, Marcia Herndon, Barbara Kirshenblatt-Gimblett, John McDowell, Norma McLeod, Américo Paredes, Dina Sherzer, and Beverly Stoeltje deserve special mention and thanks. My greatest debt, however, is to the three individuals who have stimulated and influenced my thinking most profoundly: Dell Hymes, for imparting to me the ethnographic perspective on verbal art and for his ideas on the nature of performance; Roger D. Abrahams, for focusing my attention on performance as an organizing principle for the study of folklore; and Joel Sherzer for sharing in the intellectual process all along the way.

2. Particularly important for folklorists is the seminal essay by Jansen (1957), and Lomax (1968), and Abrahams (1968, 1972). Two collections which reflect the performance orientation are Paredes and Bauman (1972) and Ben-Amos and Goldstein (1975). Bauman and Sherzer (1974) reflects a wider performance orientation, of which performance in verbal art is one aspect. Singer (1958a, 1958b, 1972) represents the perspective of an anthropologist on "cultural performances." Colby and Peacock (1973) contains a section on Performance Analysis which, however, ignores the work of folklorists in this field, an omission which is

perhaps to be expected in an article on narrative which announces its deliberate neglect of folklore journals.

3. The term "spoken art" was suggested by Thomas Sebeok in discussion of Bascom's ideas on verbal art (Bascom 1955:246, n.9; see also Dorson 1972:9).

4. Richard Ohmann, in two recent articles, employs the same passage from Austin as a point of departure for the formulation of a theory of literature based on Austin's theory of speech acts (Ohmann 1971, 1972). Ohmann's argument is interesting in places, but its productiveness is severely limited by his failure — like Austin's — to recognize that the notion of strictly referential, "literal" meaning has little, if any, relevance to the use of spoken language in social life. For a strong critique of the concept of "ordinary language," and the impoverishing effect it has on definitions of literature, see Fish (1973).

5. The notion of frame, though not necessarily the term, is used in a similar manner by other writers (see, e.g., Huizinga 1955; Milner 1955:86; Smith 1968; Uspensky 1972; Fish 1973:52–53).

6. Concerning the ecological model of communication underlying this formulation, are Sherzer and Bauman (1972) and Bauman and Sherzer (1974).

7. Note that it is *susceptibility* to evaluation that is indicated here; in this formulation the status of an utterance as performance is independent of *how* it is evaluated, whether it is judged good or bad, beautiful or ugly, etc. A bad performance is nonetheless a performance. On this point, see Hymes (1973:189–190).

8. I have been influenced in this formulation by Hymes (1974, 1975), d'Azevedo (1958:706), Mukařovský (1964:19, 1970:21), and Goffman (1974). A similar conception of performance is developed in an unfinished paper by my former colleague Joseph Doherty (Doherty n.d.), whose recent tragic and untimely death occurred before he was able to complete his work, and prevented me from benefiting from discussions we planned but never had. Elli Köngäs Maranda seems to be operating in terms of a conception of verbal art which is similar in certain central respects to the one developed here (Maranda 1974:6). Compare also Fish's conception of literature (Fish 1973).

A special word should be said of the use of "competence" and "performance" in the above formulation. Use of these terms, especially in such close juxtaposition, demands at least some acknowledgement of Noam Chomsky's contribution of both to the technical vocabulary of linguistics (Chomsky 1965:3–4). It should be apparent, however, that both terms are employed in a very different way in the present work — competence in the sense advanced by Hymes (1971), and performance as formulated at the beginning of this paper.

9. The aspect of conventionality will be discussed below.

10. Ethics and esthetics are not always as coterminous as Gossen suggests, in summing up his analysis of the Chamula. In St. Vincent, for example, the domain "talking nonsense" is negatively valued in terms of ethics, but encompasses a range of speech activities with a strong performance element about them that is

highly valued and much enjoyed in esthetic terms (Abrahams and Bauman 1971). Real, as against ideal, moral systems often accommodate more disreputability than anthropologists give them credit for, and the association between performance and disreputability has often been remarked (see Abrahams and Bauman n.d.). Another case that underscores the complexity of the relationship between ethics and esthetics is that of the seventeenth century Quakers, for whom fundamental moral principles against putting oneself forward, speaking things that were in a strict sense "not the truth," and gratifying the earthly man, severely limited the potential and actual domain of artistic verbal performance, leaving but a few very special kinds of outlets for performance at all (Bauman 1970, 1974, 1975). The whole matter of the relationship between ethics and esthetics is one that badly needs investigation from an anthropological point of view.

11. Hymes (1975) applies the term "metaphrasis" to this phenomenon.

12. The concept of emergence is developed in McHugh (1968). The emergent quality of performance is emphasized in Hymes (1975).

13. *Kabary* designates both a way of speaking and the forms in which it is manifested.

References Cited

Abrahams, Roger D.

1968 Introductory Remarks to a Rhetorical Theory of Folklore. Journal of American Folklore 81: 143–148.

1970 A Performance-Centered Approach to Gossip. Man 5:290–301.

1972 Folklore and Literature as Performance. Journal of the Folklore Institute 8:75–94.

Abrahams, Roger D., and Richard Bauman

1971 Sense and Nonsense in St. Vincent. American Anthropologist 73:762–772.

n.d. Ranges of Festival Behavior. *In* The Reversible World: Essays on Symbolic Inversion. Barbara Babcock-Abrahams, Ed.

Austerlitz, Robert

1960 Parallelismus. *In* Poetics, Poetyka, ποετΝΚΑ. The Hague: Mouton.

Austin, J. L.

1962 How To Do Things With Words. New York: Oxford University Press.

Azadovskii, Mark

1926 Eine Sibirische Märchenerzählerin. Helsinki: Folklore Fellows Communication No. 68. English translation by James R. Dow. Austin, TX: Center for Intercultural Studies in Folklore and Oral History (in press).

Babcock-Abrahams, Barbara

1974 The Story in the Story: *Metanarration* in Folk Narrative. Paper delivered at the VI Folk

Narrative Congress, Helsinki, June 17.

Bascom, William
1955 Verbal Art. Journal of American Folklore 68:245–252.

Bateson, Gregory
1972 Steps to an Ecology of Mind. New York: Ballantine.

Bauman, Richard
1970 Aspects of Seventeenth Century Quaker Rhetoric. Quarterly Journal of Speech 56:67–74.
1972a Introduction. In Toward New Perspectives in Folklore. Américo Paredes and Richard Bauman, Eds. Austin: University of Texas Press.
1972b The La Have Island General Store: Sociability and Verbal Art in a Nova Scotia Community. Journal of American Folklore 85: 330–343.
1974 Speaking in the Light: the Role of the Quaker Minister. In Explorations in the Ethnography of Speaking. Richard Bauman and Joel Sherzer, Eds. New York: Cambridge University Press.
1975 Quaker Folk Linguistics and Folklore. In Folklore: Communication and Performance. Dan Ben-Amos and Kenneth Goldstein, Eds. The Hague: Mouton.

Bauman, Richard, and Joel Sherzer (Eds.)
1974 Explorations in the Ethnography of Speaking. New York: Cambridge University Press.

Ben-Amos, Dan
1969 Analytical Categories and Ethnic Genres. Genre 2:275–301.
1972 Toward a Definition of Folklore in Context. In Toward New Perspectives in Folklore. Américo Paredes and Richard Bauman, Eds. Austin: University of Texas Press.

Ben-Amos, Dan and Kenneth Goldstein (Eds.)
1975 Folklore: Communication and Performance. The Hague: Mouton.

Burke, Kenneth
1969 A Rhetoric of Motives. Berkeley & Los Angeles: University of California Press.

Burns, Elizabeth
1972 Theatricality. New York: Harper.

Chomsky, Noam
1965 Aspects of the Theory of Syntax. Cambridge, MA: MIT Press.

Colby, Benjamin, and James Peacock
1973 Narrative. In Handbook of Social and Cultural Anthropology. John J. Honigmann, Ed. Chicago: Rand McNally.

Crowley, Daniel J.
1966 I Could Talk Old Story Good. Berkeley & Los Angeles: University of California Press.

Darnell, Regna
1974 Correlates of Cree Narrative Performance. In Explorations in the Ethnography of Speaking.

Richard Bauman and Joel Sherzer, Eds. New York: Cambridge University Press.

d'Azevedo, Warren
1958 A Structural Approach to Esthetics: Toward a Definition of Art in Anthropology. American Anthropologist 60:702–714.

Delargy, James H.
1945 The Gaelic Story-Teller. London: Proceedings of the British Academy 31:177–221.

Doherty, Joseph
n.d. Towards a Poetics of Performance. Manuscript.

Dorson, Richard M.
1972 African Folklore. New York: Doubleday Anchor.

Dundes, Alan
1966 Metafolklore and Oral Literary Criticism. The Monist 50:505–516.

Durbin, Mridula
1971 Transformational Models Applied to Musical Analysis: Theoretical Possibilities. Ethnomusicology 15:353–362.

Finnegan, Ruth
1967 Limba Stories and Storytelling. Oxford: Oxford University Press.

Firth, Raymond
1961 Elements of Social Organization. Third edition. Boston: Beacon Press (paperback 1963).

Fish, Stanley E.
1973 How Ordinary Is Ordinary Language? New Literary History 5:40–54.

Fónagy, Ivan
1965 Form and Function of Poetic Language. Diogenes 51:72–110.

Fox, James
1974 Our Ancestors Spoke in Pairs. In Explorations in the Ethnography of Speaking. Richard Bauman and Joel Sherzer, Eds. New York: Cambridge University Press.

Friedman, Albert
1961 The Formulaic Improvisation Theory of Ballad Tradition — A Counterstatement. Journal of American Folklore 74:113–115.

Georges, Robert
1969 Toward an Understanding of Storytelling Events. Journal of American Folklore 82:313–328.

Glassie, Henry
1971 Take that Night Train to Selma: an Excursion to the Outskirts of Scholarship. In Folksongs and Their Makers, by Henry Glassie, Edward D. Ives, and John F. Szwed. Bowling Green, OH: Bowling Green Popular Press.

Goffman, Erving
1974 Frame Analysis. New York: Harper Colophon.

Gossen, Gary
1972 Chamula Genres of Verbal Behavior. In Toward New Perspectives in Folklore. Américo Paredes and Richard Bauman, Eds. Austin: University of Texas Press.

1974   To Speak with a Heated Heart: Chamula Canons of Style and Good Performance. *In* Explorations in the Ethnography of Speaking. Richard Bauman and Joel Sherzer, Eds. New York: Cambridge University Press.

Gregory, Dick
1964   Nigger: An Autobiography. New York: Dutton.

Havránek, Bohuslav
1964   The Functional Differentiation of the Standard Language. *In* A Prague School Reader on Esthetics, Literary Structure, and Style. Paul L. Garvin, Ed. Washington, DC: Georgetown University.

Hrdličková, V.
1969   Japanese Professional Storytellers. Genre 2:179–210.

Huizinga, Johan
1955   Homo Ludens. Boston: Beacon.

Hymes, Dell
1962   *Review of* Indian Tales of North America, by T. P. Coffin. American Anthropologist 64: 676–679.
1971   Competence and Performance in Linguistic Theory. *In* Language Acquisition: Models and Methods. Renira Huxley and Elisabeth Ingram, Eds. London and New York: Academic Press.
1973   An Ethnographic Perspective. New Literary History 5: 187–201.
1974   Ways of Speaking. *In* Explo-

rations in the Ethnography of Speaking. Richard Bauman and Joel Sherzer, Eds. New York: Cambridge University Press.
1975   Breakthrough into Performance. *In* Folklore: Communication and Performance. Dan Ben-Amos and Kenneth Goldstein, Eds. The Hague: Mouton.

Innes, Gordon
1974   Sunjata: Three Mandinka Versions. London: School of Oriental and African Studies, University of London.

Jakobson, Roman
1960   Linguistics and Poetics. *In* Style in Language. Thomas A. Sebeok, Ed. Cambridge, MA: MIT Press.
1966   Grammatical Parallelism and Its Russian Facet. Language 42:399–429.
1968   Poetry of Grammar and Grammar of Poetry. Lingua 21: 597–609.

Jansen, William Hugh
1957   Classifying Performance in the Study of Verbal Folklore. *In* Studies in Folklore. W. Edson Richmond, Ed. Bloomington, Indiana: Indiana University Press.

Keenan, Elinor
1973   A Sliding Sense of Obligatoriness: The Poly-Structure of Malagasy Oratory. Language in Society 2:225–243.
1974   Norm Makers, Norm Breakers: Uses of Speech by Men and Women in a Malagasy Commu-

nity. *In* Explorations in the Ethnography of Speaking. Richard Bauman and Joel Sherzer, Eds. New York: Cambridge University Press.

Keil, Charles
1966 Urban Blues. Chicago: University of Chicago Press.

Kirshenblatt-Gimblett, Barbara
1974 The Concept and Varieties of Narrative Performance in East European Jewish Culture. *In* Explorations in the Ethnography of Speaking. Richard Bauman and Joel Sherzer, Eds. New York: Cambridge University Press.

Leech, Geoffrey
1969 A Linguistic Guide to English Poetry. London: Longmans.

Lomax, Alan
1968 Folksong Style and Culture. Washington, DC: American Association for the Advancement of Science.

Lord, Albert B.
1960 The Singer of Tales. Cambridge, MA: Harvard University Press.

Maranda, Elli Köngäs
1972 Theory and Practice of Riddle Analysis. *In* Toward New Perspectives in Folklore. Américo Paredes and Richard Bauman, Eds. Austin: University of Texas Press.
1974 Individual and Tradition. Paper delivered at the VI Folk Narrative Congress, Helsinki, June 20.

McDowell, John
1974 Some Aspects of Verbal Art in Bolivian Quechua. Folklore Annual of the University Folklore Association (University of Texas, Austin), No. 6.

McHugh, Peter
1968 Defining the Situation. Indianapolis, IN: Bobbs-Merrill.

Messinger, Sheldon L.
1962 Life as Theater: Some Notes on the Dramaturgic Approach to Social Reality. Sociometry 25:98–110.

Milner, Marion
1955 Role of Illusion in Symbol Formation. *In* New Directions in Psychoanalysis. Melanie Klein, Ed. New York: Basic Books.

Mukařovský, Jan
1964 Standard Language and Poetic Language. *In* A Prague School Reader on Esthetics, Literary Structure and Style. Paul L. Garvin, Ed. Washington, DC: Georgetown University.
1970 Aesthetic Function, Norm and Value as Social Facts. Ann Arbor: Department of Slavic Languages and Literature, University of Michigan.

Ohmann, Richard
1971 Speech Acts and the Definition of Literature. Philosophy and Rhetoric 4:1–19.
1972 Speech, Literature, and the Space Between. New Literary History 4:47–63.

Paredes, Américo, and Richard Bauman (Eds.)

1972   Toward New Perspectives in Folklore. Austin: University of Texas Press.

Phillipson, Michael

1972   Phenomenological Philosophy and Sociology. *In* New Directions in Sociological Theory, by Paul Filmer, Michael Phillipson, David Silverman, and David Walsh. Cambridge, MA: MIT Press.

Reaver, J. Russell

1972   From Reality to Fantasy: Opening-Closing Formulas in the Structures of American Tall Tales. Southern Folklore Quarterly 36:369–382.

Rosaldo, Michelle Z.

1973   I Have Nothing to Hide: the Language of Ilongot Oratory. Language in Society 2:193–223.

Ruesch, Jurgen, and Gregory Bateson

1968   Communication. New York: Norton.

Sacks, Harvey

1974   An Analysis of the Course of a Joke's Telling in Conversation. *In* Explorations in the Ethnography of Speaking. Richard Bauman and Joel Sherzer, Eds. New York: Cambridge University Press.

Sherzer, Dina, and Joel Sherzer

1972   Literature in San Blas: Discovering the Cuna *Ikala*. Semiotica 6:182–199.

Sherzer, Joel

1974   *Namakke, Sunmakke, Kormakke:* Three Types of Cuna Speech Events. *In* Explorations in the Ethnography of Speaking. Richard Bauman and Joel Sherzer, Eds. New York: Cambridge University Press.

Sherzer, Joel, and Richard Bauman

1972   Areal Studies and Culture History: Language as a Key to the Historical Study of Culture Contact. Southwestern Journal of Anthropology 28:131–152.

Singer, Milton

1958a   From the Guest Editor. Journal of American Folklore 71: 191–204.

1958b   The Great Tradition in a Metropolitan Center: Madras. Journal of American Folklore 71: 347–388.

1972   When a Great Tradition Modernizes. New York: Praeger.

Smith, Barbara H.

1968   Poetic Closure. Chicago: University of Chicago.

Stankiewicz, Edward

1960   Poetic Language and Non-Poetic Language in their Interrelation. *In* Poetics, Poetyka, ποετΝΚΑ. The Hague: Mouton.

Szwed, John F.

1971   Paul E. Hall: a Newfoundland Song-Maker and Community of Song. *In* Folksongs and Their Makers, by Henry Glassie, Edward D. Ives, and John F. Szwed. Bowling Green, OH:

Bowling Green University Popular Press.

Tedlock, Dennis

1972   On the Translation of Style in Oral Narrative. *In* Toward New Perspectives in Folklore. Américo Paredes and Richard Bauman, Eds. Austin: University of Texas Press.

Toelken, J. Barre

1969   The 'Pretty Language' of Yellowman: Genre, Mode, and Texture in Navaho Coyote Narratives. Genre 2:211–235.

Uspensky, B. A.

1972   Structural Isomorphism of Verbal and Visual Art. Poetics 5:5–39.

Weinreich, Uriel

1966   On the Semantic Structure of a Language. *In* Universals of Language. Joseph Greenberg, Ed. Cambridge, MA: MIT Press.

Williams, Raymond

1973   Base and Superstructure in Marxist Cultural Theory. New Left Review 82:3–16.

World Picture, Anthropological Frame

Robert McC. Adams

VOL. 79, 1977, 265–279

Annual meetings ostensibly exist to improve and widen communication within a discipline. No one will question that to some extent they succeed in this purpose. But it is also true, as Devons and Gluckman have matter-of-factly put it, that "reality is complex, and the first task of any scientist is to delimit specific problems within a restricted field of data" (1964:158). Multiple simultaneous program listings therefore confront us with a classic example of conflicting norms. Good intentions to maintain a balance of depth with breadth notwithstanding, it is the densest, narrowest, and most age-stratified networks that seem to dominate our choices in listening to papers and allocating time in the corridors. The reality is that within anthropology, as in the social sciences generally, massive tendencies toward intellectual fragmentation meet little resistance. Subverting their purpose, annual meetings are in some respects tending to become boundary-maintaining mechanisms.

The same is even more true with regard to the essentially artificial lines dividing the social science disciplines from one another. At least at their conceptual margins, the fields continually intergrade with one another. The subtle process of distinguishing centrality from marginality, necessary as it may be in some respects, also reinforces the existing barriers and thus impedes or distorts the study of what is in fact a seamless web of potential research problems. This is the substance of Donald Campbell's criticism of the ethnocentrism of all scientific disciplines, to which he has opposed the ideal image of continuously overlapping microfields as an alternative (Campbell 1969).

To be sure, that criticism applies to all branches of scholarship.

Hence anthropology comes within the shelter of the general rebuttal, that clusters of specialties around even quite artificial cores provide the only practical means yet devised for the collective judgment of academic quality. But it is also worth noting that the lines are more rigidly drawn in the social sciences than elsewhere. Interdisciplinary projects, to us, usually imply no more than the collaboration of specialists in several social science disciplines. Natural scientists seldom apply the same word unless the activities so described span at least the physical and life sciences and often parts of the social sciences and engineering as well (Adams 1977). Similarly, individual specialties are being merged into more broadly integrative departments of biology in a number of institutions, a trend for which there is as yet no social science counterpart.

Proliferating specialization, then, is an increasingly dominant characteristic of our field. In part, the process is surely defensible — or at any rate unavoidable. There is also a more questionable part of it, however, that appears to stem not from the requirements of more complex data or methodologies but from a variety of institutional and societal pressures. Such pressures have their greatest, most disquieting effect on individuals during the vulnerable, early stages of their professional careers. Hence, it is worthwhile to counteract them when we can by taking a perspective that overrides most of the boundaries we have drawn around ourselves. Quite possibly nothing could succeed for long in retarding their growth, and there is certainly little to be gained by merely replacing them with others. But one can constructively use occasions like this to reiterate that communications barriers are largely of our own making, and that there is a basis for real and continuing intercourse beyond them and in spite of them.

There is a connective tissue of differently expressed, but essentially similar, ideas that increasingly characterize not only anthropology but also other social science realms and even the society at large. This breadth of application calls into question the stress we continue to give to older identifying symbols like cultural holism or participant observation. They may be irreplaceable as features of a distinctive anthropological approach, but for the same reason they impede our recognition of the needs and possibilities of wider discourse. More recent orientations that lack this particularism are as yet less commonly acknowledged and formally codified. However, they have already emerged as the decisive guides to research on a number of seemingly disparate problems. Both their wide occurrence and our subdisciplinary fragmentation make it implausible to trace these parallelisms to a common source within anthropology, and their origin must be sought instead in the larger context of contemporary human experience.

As an illustration, let us consider first a phenomenon that most of us apprehend daily — American cities. The "classic" model of the American metropolis that governed both research and planning a generation or two ago was a nucleated, organic one in which radiating transit lines assured the dominance of the central business district over both inner city and suburbs. Immigration from the hinterlands was more or less assumed to be a continuing infusion, an "externality" in economic terms. The primary focus of concern was the processes of neighborhood growth and decay that took place in concentric zones, upon the arrival of successive waves of workers for the industrial plants that energized the system (Park, Burgess, and McKenzie 1925).

It will come as no surprise to anyone that this model has been largely swept away by the subsequent flow of events. Terms like megalopolis, reflecting the fusion of adjoining metropolitan regions, convey the important implication of a progressively expanding scale of lifeways and patterns of interaction that are essentially urban. Urban immigration as a dominant demographic process has ended, on the other hand, and the problem now is not only one of suburban exodus but of the stagnation and incipient decline of entire metropolitan areas in some parts of the country. This is coupled with the unprecedented phenomenon of innercity abandonment. Lateral, shopping center–focused, automobile-dependent movements are completely in the ascendancy, with the increasing preponderance of nationally distributed, home-centered entertainment systems serving further to reduce the centralizing impulses of cultural institutions in individual cities. Major regional shifts are also taking place, impelled by a wide assortment of forces that include differential housing and labor costs, highway construction programs, federally insured mortgages, widespread industrial relocation toward the south and west, and the corresponding attrition in job opportunities, growth of welfare-dependent ghettos, and decay of the urban ambience and municipal services in the older centers (Berry and Dahmann 1977). A very recent overview of these processes ends on an almost unrelievedly gloomy note:

Government jurisdictions may well have to accept as a fact of life the permanence of decay, concentrate on those things it can realistically deal with, and
avoid . . . thinking about recapturing past glories [Sternlieb and Hughes
1976:23].

Faced with this altered reality, students of American cities have correspondingly altered their research orientations. In place of preponder-
antly "natural" processes of growth and decay engendered by market
forces, they must deal with increasingly extensive processes of deliberate
intervention that are largely engineered at the federal level. Cities are
primarily seen today within national networks of ecological and institutional arrangements. These more extensive networks made obsolescent
the older, place-oriented formulations, under which each city more or
less autonomously exemplified parallel evolutionary processes. As a metaphor, we may think of cities as having altogether lost those qualities as
independent *organisms* that were highlighted at an earlier time, and become instead largely dependent *organs* within an embracing national
economy and polity (Handlin 1963:2).

This recitation of trends may seem to concentrate on generalized,
impersonal forces that are largely beyond the reach not only of our own
potentials of participation as citizens, but of anthropological methods
of study. But of course we cannot avoid encountering the changed character of the urban setting as it continually impinges both directly and
indirectly on our own plans and activities. Many aspects of change reach
to the interpersonal level and affect the texture of urban life itself.
Urban heterogeneity, for example, at one time referred primarily to a
mosaic of neighborhoods differentiated with respect to fairly stable, ascribed characteristics — ethnic stock, language, educational and religious
background. Almost everywhere today those neighborhoods have been
severely eroded, with heterogeneity taking new, more volatile forms that
have moved outward to embrace suburbs as well as city. Life style differences with a larger element of personal choice have come to the forefront,
linked to occupational differences, income, age, and family type (Abu-
Lughod 1968). Heterogeneity remains at least as characteristic of urban
populations as it ever was, in other words, but is channeled through less
durable, differently constituted subgroups. And the population identified
as urban, in this as in other respects, no longer is drawn to cities proper
but dominates the national landscape.

Few would argue that these specific features of U.S. urban evolution — or devolution — are already or will necessarily become a part of worldwide urbanization patterns. In most less developed countries today there is instead a strikingly contrastive trend toward hyperurbanization, in which immigrants and resources are drawn to a single primate city and the rural exodus is continuing or even accelerating. To some extent, this different direction of change may be an historic outgrowth of international relations of dominance and dependency. Many commentators on Latin America, for example, have come to regard underdevelopment itself as "not a stage preliminary to capitalism but a consequence and particular form of it — namely, dependent capitalism — which conditions the whole form and logic of a nation's internal development" (Morse 1971:50). But the new, spatially extended nature of urban processes and the alteration in forms of heterogeneity are surely characteristics common to most of the world. Also common is the discovery that cities are not bounded, internally autonomous units but complex, shifting groupings of subsystems. "Rural" and "urban" have almost everywhere come to be recognized as closely interrelated rather than polarized abstractions. The key forces and features of world urbanization, then, are also not confined within urban boundaries or even metropolitan regions. Instead they involve wide-ranging flows of people, information, cultural symbols, capital, innovations, and decision-making authority, within and beyond the entire nations — at any stage of development — that increasingly have come to constitute "urban fields" (Friedmann and Miller 1965).

For present purposes there should be no need further to document these themes of systemic change. While more detailed data would surely disclose considerable variation from country to country and region to region, the general trends are clear. Cities have been the focal points of advanced societies for millenniums — seats of government and of learning, crossroads and markets, repositories of tradition, clusterings of institutions that both sustain and challenge the exercise of centralized authority, dense, unambiguously defined settlements of human beings. Now the scale of what is urban has exploded past all urban boundaries, while the internal articulation of municipal institutions and neighborhoods slips into powerless disarray and even physical decay. There is considerable truth, if also some hyperbole, in Martindale's conclusion that "the age of the city seems to be at an end" (1958:62).

As individuals whose daily lives are caught up in this process, we cannot escape its influence also upon our scholarly work. Herein lies an important if rarely acknowledged root of the cumulatively profound shift that has taken place in anthropology over the past generation or so — away from the study of closed social systems in bounded, isolable communities and toward open, interacting networks of functionally specialized relationships. This is not to deny that the changed orientation of our field also has a number of other roots. Often cited among them are the wartime impetus given to studies of culture and national character "at a distance," increasing sensitivities about a preoccupation with "primitives" that have accompanied the rise of new nations, and the growing recognition by anthropologists that in any case there is no pristine condition of static, isolated traditionalism which might serve as a baseline for the measurement of subsequent changes among the societies we study. However, these and similar explanations for the shift rest to some extent on the common premise that anthropology is itself a closed system, an organized, bounded community. Were this so, it might be adequate to regard our changing theoretical orientations as having been generated by some internal dialectic, or by our having adapted as an autonomous, cohesive body to an altered pattern of constraints, opportunities, and empirical findings. But that premise, as I have already suggested, is increasingly undermined as our intellectual fragmentation continues and as even the older, more "natural" forms of community wither.

There are diverse applications of the concern for open, extended patterns of interaction, but it is the common, underlying shift in approach that is most relevant for this discussion. Perhaps a little tendentiously, Edmund Leach charts the "classical manner" in ethnography which in some respects may be considered the original point of departure for the shift:

> It is assumed that within a somewhat arbitrary geographical area a social system exists; the population involved in this social system is of one culture; the social system is uniform. Hence the anthropologist can choose for himself a locality 'of any convenient size' and examine in detail what goes on in this locality; from this examination he will hope to reach conclusions about the principles of organisation operating in this particular locality. He then generalises from these conclusions and writes a book about the organisation of the society considered as a whole [1965:60].

It was Leach's highly influential observation, of course, that only invalid conclusions would come from the application of such an approach to the Burmese hill region with which he was dealing.

Similar views have come to play an important part in the concerns of a new generation of critical or revisionist anthropologists. In a recent critique of the research priorities that long dominated the African scene, for example, Stephen Feuchtwang calls attention to the tendency to study primitive isolates rather than the larger social systems of which they are also parts. The prevailing absence of study of large-scale, multicomponent systems cannot be satisfactorily explained, he maintains, on the grounds that the latter would not have been amenable to techniques of observation identified with anthropology. He rightly goes on to wonder,

> Why should the particular method of study, so-called participant observation, have been so stressed and celebrated, and the empiricist ideal — inducing social structure only from what was known through the senses of the observer — have been given such currency? Perhaps the method and its stress are concomitants of the study of societies as isolates, not a cause [1975:78].

A slight but significant modification of Leach's perspective was suggested by Robert Redfield in the late fifties, in connection with the first substantial entry of anthropologists into civilizational studies. It was the case prior to that entry, he observed, that,

> The "primitive isolate" was in fact, and was in any event conceived, as a system, a relatively stable arrangement of parts wholly understandable within itself, without seriously disturbing reference to ought outside of it [1962:380].

It was not the convenient but arbitrary bounding of the unit of study that was characteristic, he implied, but the concern for discovering a parsimonious group of organizing principles, a self-enclosed system. This is nothing other than the core of a structural frame of reference, one in which, as again "classically" defined, "a social system can be apprehended as a unity made up of parts and processes that are linked to one another by a limited number of principles of wide validity in homogeneous and relatively stable societies" (Fortes 1953:39). Redfield went on to note with approval some early efforts to transcend this viewpoint. The unit of observation in most of them continued to be the small, face-to-face community, but, in what was then a still incomplete transition from the older approach, they were seen "with extensions" into larger social and cultural entities.

Fredrik Barth's emphasis on the persistence of ethnic boundaries can be regarded as an additional step in the same direction. Boundaries, to Barth, are ongoing relational processes that shape and survive both intergroup conflict and intragroup flux, rather than a self-evident corollary of a group's existence. This considerably softens Redfield's implicit separation between a community and its external relations, in which the latter could be described merely as "extensions" or appendages (Barth 1969:10). What ultimately emerges as a result of the gradual but cumulatively substantial shift in approach is a position persuasively put forward by Sidney Mintz:

> it needs to be stressed that an adequate conceptualization of this kind is not concerned simply with "fitting" or "linking" the community as such to wider systems; to a very substantial degree, it is the nature of that integration which actually *helps to define the community itself*. The view of communities as firmly bounded and isolated groupings, gradually losing their separateness and intactness to outside pressures, while conveying a generally accepted understanding of how change occurs, is not quite adequate, then, in dealing with the reality of larger sociocultural wholes. Surely one reason for the popularity of anthropological marketing studies in recent years has been the growing recognition that the analytical "reality" of communities is no greater than the analytical "reality" of marketing systems; when employed as heuristic devices, these abstractions may even serve in part to define each other [1976:xii–xiii].

Associated with the growing stress on interactional phenomena that transcend local groups has been the introduction of investigative approaches like network analysis. Particularly in urban communities, discriminations of network density at least partly supplant earlier, almost automatic acceptance of urban communities as the unit of study (Barnes 1969:62). In addition, the concept of networks has been employed in the sense of persisting lines of interconnection between spatially detached centers of human activity. The pattern or organization of such lines then forms a basis for the analysis of a hierarchically complex as well as spatially extended form of social system (Redfield 1962:384). It must be borne in mind, however, that considerable differences in outlook may lie hidden behind apparent similarities in network terminology and geometry.

One use of the term is associated with locating an individual within the numerous, different networks of which he or she is a member. At least the purer, more pristine forms of structuralism failed to reckon with the absence of any uniformly prevailing order of precedence among the disparate networks in which an individual participated. Instead anthropologists tended to take a high level of consistency for granted, extracting norms from a compressed and largely unreported mass of divergent individual behavior and informants' statements. Van Velsen's situational analysis has responded to this by directing attention to the choices that continually face individuals in selecting among at least partially conflicting norms (1967:132). Barth carries this stress on personal choice among alternatives further still:

> What we see as a social form is, concretely, a pattern of distribution of behavior by different persons and on different occasions. I would argue that it is not useful to assume that this empirical pattern is a sought-for condition, which all members of the community equally value and willfully maintain. Rather, it must be regarded as an epiphenomenon of a great variety of processes in combination... [1967:662].

The community, the initially most important focus of anthropological study, on this reading has become an ongoing series of disparate, individually selected options that on the whole tend to be both rational and economically motivated. Others, notably Frederick Bailey, have remained more skeptical about the dominance and rationality of an individual's cost-benefit calculus and chosen to concentrate instead on "the acceptable justifications for making choices" (1973:326).

These alternative approaches clearly share a common feature. The stable, integral, self-enclosed character of a system of social relations is no longer assumed. Instead attention is directed toward the at least partly disarticulating effects of change upon primary groups and intergroup relations, change induced by widening patterns of interactions over which a local community's control diminishes and uncertainty mounts. That common if implicit assessment of where the highest priorities of study lie is surely responsive to our declining sense of community as we participate in an exploding urban order. On the other hand, studies taking this form have tended to deal almost exclusively with relatively modest, short-term, purposive innovations, within a social context of prevailing continuity and compromise. Moreover, as Talal Asad has observed, there are strong "Hobbesian" overtones to a dominant concern for processes of individual choice or decision making; a way must be found instead to maintain the distinction "between immediate choice and collective life-chances, between class interest and individual motive" (1972:92). Anthropologists like myself with an historical or evolutionary orientation accordingly are likely to find approaches centering on individual choice unrewarding as a source of insight into long-term, worldwide developmental trends. That is particularly the case, of course, insofar as we operate within the usual limitations of documentary or archaeological sources rather than being able to question and interact with our informants.

A second use of networks relates clusters of spatially segregated or dispersed statuses and activities according to explicit, analytical concepts, seeking to elicit generic features of the social organization of a complex society. To do so requires that attention be focused primarily on the regional lattice of interconnections between communities, rather than assuming that community studies in themselves can somehow represent the larger systems. New methods then are also required: to obtain rapport, to assure adequate sampling, and to isolate key variables for investigation (Olsen 1976:54). This more schematic, generalizing approach presupposes some guiding theoretical orientation, according to which order can be perceived in a reduced range of recorded fact. Hence it provides a better basis for a comparatively based science concerned with principles of lawful progression or evolution, whose general applicability overrides differences in detail that naturally will accompany every occurrence.

The leading early advocate of efforts to relate spatially dispersed centers to the concentration of power in complex social hierarchies was Julian Steward, particularly if one considers research he stimulated not only in ethnology and social anthropology, but in ethnohistory and archaeology as well. His was a pioneering recognition that higher level systems of integration modified the characteristics of their components through the forms of functional dependence that they imposed (Steward 1950), and he led also in seeking ways to apprehend these higher systems through the complementary efforts of teams of fieldworkers.

To some extent, however, it still seems to be the case a generation after Steward's initial essay that its potential remains unrealized in terms of persuasively detailed case material. The study of more embracing systems has proved to be an uncongenial one for most anthropologists. An ambitious formulation of them by Aguirre Beltrán, for example, provides convincing detail on the operation of what he calls the "dominical" mechanisms involved in the subordination of peripheral communities to the more technologically and economically developed centers.

But he is able to draw upon only a comparatively thin body of empirical data even from a well-studied country like Mexico to show how the regional dimensions of social structure were organized and maintained in those centers (Aguirre 1967). Perhaps, as Wolf has implied, the problem is that higher levels of integration cannot be understood without reference to the quite asymmetrical, which is to say often downright unpleasant, relationships of political and economic power on which they ultimately depend (1956:1066). Confronting the exercise of power dangerously undermines the search for homogeneous principles and unifying norms. Apparently that objective retains its emotional attractions for many of us in spite of its increasing artificiality.

Briefly to recapitulate before proceeding further, we tend to give insufficient attention as a discipline to the consequences of the obvious and profound changes in our cognitive, perceptual, and behavioral worlds. The directional trends are rapid and coherent enough to reinforce an unfolding sense of discovery of a "reality" in the worlds of our fieldwork that is radically transposed from that with which anthropology was traditionally associated. It has been convenient to identify the shift here by alluding to the fate of cities, partly because their changing state is generally familiar and can be easily summarized with censuses and other highly aggregated data, and partly because the fate of cities encapsulates so many of the symbolic dimensions of change.

This is not meant to imply that the cognitive maps of an earlier generation of urbanites and urbanologists, or of our own generation for that matter, are entirely faithful in their reflection of the encompassing reality of their time and do not contain a large ideological dimension. In the case of the former, recent quantitative work on American cities in fact strongly suggests that many of the contemporary trends I have adumbrated here already had their remote beginnings much earlier than the autonomous, isolated, centripetal models of the original urban ecologists (e.g., Pred 1975; Jackson 1975). Still less is it implied that changes in settlement form, function, and internal structure necessarily constitute the main, causal axis of sociocultural change more generally. What has happened to cities, however, is so general and decisive that it must influence our choice of causal models to assume or investigate. And it surely provides at least an external framework within which other, equally pervasive and influential, changes are underway in the prevailing character of the interpersonal relationships we perceive and study as well as enter into.

Communities remain, but their place in and power over our lives diminishes. Locational stability declines radically. Boundaries that had seemed stable and unambiguous govern declining numbers of relationships, and expand or contract under the impact of forces external to any recognizable community. Multitiered networks proliferate, with localities losing much of their relevance for the information we need and the interests with which we associate. Those networks vastly extend not only their geographic range but their claims upon our individual time and loyalties. New cellular structures appear, but largely on a time-bound or voluntaristic basis exemplified by the increasing segregation of age-sets and the brittleness of families.

It remains problematical, of course, how far the corresponding trend of thought among many anthropologists, away from an emphasis on unifying norms and toward a preoccupation with contingent choice under divergent patterns of constraint, is an outgrowth of these shifts. Few would argue for complete dependence of disciplined thought on the aggregate of our personal life experiences. But with societal and disciplinary trends so closely convergent, it seems at least equally difficult to argue that the former has not interacted with and powerfully stimulated the latter.

Suggestions of a changing disciplinary orientation have been necessarily impressionistic and perhaps overgeneralized. A brief further illustration, drawn from recent trends in Middle Eastern anthropology, may make them more tangible. The traditional, essentially static picture, prevailing almost without challenge until the last two decades or so, was one of nomads, agricultural villagers, and townsmen as distinct social orders that could best be understood in self-perpetuating autonomy (e.g., Coon 1958). Later fieldwork has dissolved all of these entities as meaningful, self-enclosed units of analysis — or rather, has recast them into larger, interacting systems. Geertz, in fact, has forthrightly suggested that we "discard the community study genre, for both town and villager, in favor of a regional focus that can include both rural and urban systems in a common framework, a larger system" (1972:464). What is involved is not simply a separation of conditions found to be associated with modernization from those that were traditional. Instead there is a growing recognition that interaction may have increased in scale and rapidity but has always been there, that there never was a timeless "traditional" baseline.

A preponderant part of recent and current fieldwork falls into place within this perspective. It is fundamental, of course, to the undertakings of Geertz and a number of his collaborators in Morocco. It is a principal finding of much recent work on nomadism, which both stresses the symbiotic interchange characteristic of peasant-nomad relations and sees the prevailing balance in those relations as heavily influenced by the changing powers and strategies of the central government (e.g., Bates 1971; Marx 1973; Irons 1974). It partly underlies Emrys Peters' elegant analyses of complementary opposition in segmentary lineage systems. He contrasts the contingent loyalties and behavior of his informants with the fixed ideology of lineage theory, showing the former to be part of a wider strategy of alliances that crosses deep, universally acknowledged structural divisions and even extends beyond its home terrain of the steppe into the oases (Peters 1967). The same perspective is clearly central to later work on Lebanese villages, in which local patterns of political rivalry, stratification, and economic specialization are shaped and intensely influenced by ties with urban religious elites, entrepreneurs, officials, and relatives who have emigrated (Peters 1972; Nader 1965). It is found to govern the course of political polarization and the rise of nationalism even in remote, rigidly stratified, seemingly isolated Yemeni towns (Bujra 1971). Any listing of individual works is to some extent a subjective selection, of course, but the shift in orientation among Middle Eastern anthropologists seems altogether too pervasive for anyone to deny.

Our awareness of the interconnectedness of phenomena across broad spatial domains has its corollary in the extension of time dimensions. "A web of group relationships implies a historical dimension," as Wolf puts it. "Group relationships involve conflict and accommodation, integration and disintegration, processes which take place over time" (1956:1066). Similarly, the flat time perspective of a community study developed from a single season's fieldwork ceases to be appropriate when emphasis shifts away from statements of unifying structural principles and toward the eliciting of diverse patterns of choice and action that are responsive to wider contingencies. An important thrust in contemporary economic anthropology, for example, traces the differential perception of, as well as response to, uncertainties, risks, and opportunities in agriculture. In general, these can only be understood through analysis of a community's changing, as well as differentially felt, experience in interaction with its wider natural and social setting over a period of years (e.g., Cancian 1972; Ortiz 1973; Collier 1975). Equally important, the time-frame of groups now increasingly thrown into interaction with one another across traditional boundaries is anything but uniform. A notable evocation of modern Mexico by Octavio Paz conveys this theme in arresting metaphors:

> a variety of epochs live side by side in the same area or a very few miles apart, ignoring or devouring one another. "Catholics of Peter the Hermit and Jacobins of the Third Era," with their different heroes, customs, calendars and moral principles, live under the same sky [1961:11–12].

The trend toward embracing larger and longer fields of interaction in anthropology has a cognate in historical studies that is perhaps most closely identified with the work of Fernand Braudel and his followers. His major work on the Mediterranean, appearing already a generation ago, is the archetype of studies that accept no arbitrary limits but instead identify processes of varying scale and duration. Ultimately the frame of his analysis moves outward through concentric rings to embrace most of the known world of the 16th century, while also distinguishing the rapid fluctuations of individual influences and transitory events from slower underlying rhythms of change and continuity. But what emerges from the Braudel School more generally is a sense of the complementarity of these different levels of analysis. Those that are more inclusive in space and time focus principally on slow tendencies of cultural transmission and accumulation — histories of mining, of agricultural crops and technology, of trade, of sea routes. Others, more localized and volatile, he tends to distrust as mere "surface disturbances, crests of foam that the tides of history carry on their strong backs" (Braudel 1972:I, 21).

This analytical device of distinguishable levels of historical process is in some respects a troubling one for anthropologists. Even worldwide movements and glacial continuities may not represent the implacable movement of forces "underlying" the irregular surface of events but only the generalizations we impose on a stream of historical reality that is sustained by aggregations of small upheavals and unstable relationships. Is the persistence for centuries of initiating "poles of development" in Europe and North America really comprehensible, for example, without reference to the briefer, cyclical alternations of expansion and contraction that were imposed on peasantries in the southern hemisphere, and the corresponding rural dependency on "circulating" elites in urban-based patronage systems (Wolf 1955:464–465)?

Smaller scale, cyclical phenomena also play a part in traditional

China, where Skinner feels that major modifications are needed in Wolf's Latin American peasantry typology. On the one hand, empire-wide fluctuations in dynastic power may be an essentially "external" source of alternating stability and deterioration in local environments, leading not to a stable dichotomy of "open" and "closed" communities, but to widespread oscillation between these conditions. Conversely, the cycles of dynastic growth and decay may be at least partly a consequence of local trends that interact cumulatively to produce alternating integration and compartmentalization of the provincial landscape (Skinner 1971:280–281).

Doubts like these hint at what may be a distinctive anthropological avoidance of Braudel's separation of the phenomenological world into discrete strata, and our predilection instead for pursuing broad historical processes into the immediate range of an identifiable group's experience. Yet in the explicit relativity of his temporal and spatial frames of reference, we can hardly fail to find in Braudel a kindred spirit.

Thus far I have been concerned primarily with the central domain of anthropology, social and cultural anthropology. If nuances have occasionally been misunderstood or misplaced, that is probably because I view the center from one of its more remote and professionally under-populated peripheries. Mention of the work of historians, however, brings me to studies of temporal change in which I can begin to stake a more plausible claim to authority.

It is curious and somewhat disquieting that anthropologists who are also archaeologists and culture historians have for the most part re-garded the main body of professional historians as practitioners of a quite different and in some respects alien enterprise. Yet anthropology itself, as it turns to grapple with widespread, historically developing webs of interrelationship that require command of temporal sequences, can provide no fully acceptable substitute. On the one hand, the time perspective of ethnography is characteristically shallow. To be sure, it is tending less and less to be confined to the observations of a single field season and the unaided memories of informants. But the familiar hori-zon still is generally limited to brief spans of years, and the outer limits of unremembered, unrecorded darkness rarely extend more than a few generations into the past. The wing of archaeology that is concentrated in anthropology, on the other hand, contains only a handful of specialists who concentrate on historically documented peoples and places. And the remainder, while it often deals with long spans of change and continuity, can handle most of them only with the depressing lack of precision associated with a radiocarbon chronology.

Constrained to place their data in a framework of indefinitely defined chronological intervals that always must give or take at least a century, prehistorians purporting to deal with "process" suffer from severe limitations. Hence the frequently heard equation of anthropological archaeology with science, as opposed to history, is one of the more misdirected of anthropology's boundary-maintaining mechanisms. In effect, it rationalizes a prevailing failure to take account of historical research on sequences of change, in which the variable of time is much more adequately controlled. The archaeological tendency is to fall back instead on the assumption that (relatively) well-understood beginning and ending points can be connected by smoothed curves of unidirectional development. This provides at best an artificially narrow and determinate view of evolutionary process as well as historical causality. It is subject to distortion, in particular, through its neglect of rapid shifts, discordant norms and motivational elements, and its corresponding overemphasis on functionally interactive trends and irreversible, adaptive outcomes.

Setting aside at least for the moment the barriers we have ourselves erected, the trend in social anthropology toward a conscious widening of the field of study is at least as characteristic of the archaeologically oriented components of our field. Manipulation and control of the spatial and temporal framework is, after all, fundamental to the most elementary progress in reconstructing the past from its archaeological vestiges. But modes of thought have shifted more than may be apparent from the slow replacement of terminology. Behind the older delimitation of culture areas, horizons, cultures, co-traditions, and even civilizations lay ideal-typical constructs in which traits and norms clustered uniquely and cumulatively. With survey methodologies and sampling as perhaps the most important key, the door has since been opened into a realm in which both change and continuity require explanations that deal with different scales of group interaction. Kent Flannery's recent and provocative book *The Early Mesoamerican Village* (1976) explicitly reflects the new orientation in its organization of a rich and rapidly developing field of research, for it moves successively from analysis at the household level to household clusters, to communities, to catchment areas, to regions, and finally to interregional networks. At each step his and his colleagues' concern is for tracing variation over time within and between progressively larger, more complex social and spatial units. By providing a means for identifying functionally separable subsystems, this highlights divergences in the paths of development that were followed in different settings. Avoiding reification, the nested, progressively larger units of analysis are all treated, not as firmly bounded self-defined entities, but as operationally convenient abstractions.

Yet if this mode of thought now seems inherently natural to many, its elaboration is nonetheless relatively recent. Only within the last decade or so, for example, have archaeologists begun to study widely diffused styles, not as spreading influences that mysteriously appear in many autonomous cultural units, but rather as expressions of reciprocity and symbolic linkage that are limited to specific groups in local and regional social hierarchies (Flannery 1968; Struever and Houart 1972). Little more than a decade ago I still found it reasonable to compare the aggregate development of a number of continuously interacting Mesopotamian urban societies with an interrupted succession of individually dominant Mexican polities whose wider interactional context was largely lacking (Adams 1966). That seemed to advance our evolutionary understanding with the data then readily accessible. In retrospect, however, it has emerged with increasing clarity that those are different orders of reality, the juxtaposition of which may misdirect the search for genuinely comparative features. Fortunately, correctives have not been long in coming, made possible both by perhaps the most intensive program of regional archaeological reconnaissance yet undertaken anywhere and by ongoing reappraisals of the archival and codice sources for particular towns (Wolf 1976; Bray 1972).

This example suggests that archaeology and ethnology have converged in giving greater emphasis to interactional phenomena from quite different, in some respects opposite, points of departure. Ethnology might be said to have begun with holistic reconstruction of the lifeways of primitive isolates, later adding time-ordered dimensions of change and a concern for progressively widened settings within which local groups took on new meanings. Archaeology's initial concern was with monumental centers that promised the most striking discoveries, and that were also more or less automatically regarded as dominating the processes of innovation and ensuing change. Small, dependent settlements and "peripheral" regions — both defined largely with reference to monumentality or the lack of it — only began to receive adequate attention by archaeologists concerned with more complex societies as processual orientations and survey methodologies were introduced. That these latter developments were largely incremental and unplanned is suggested by the fact that changed funding patterns and growing difficulties of access to some areas also played a part.

But in the sequel, paralleling the case of ethnologically recognized communities and culture areas, the unambiguously bounded, self-evident character of archaeological sites and so-called "nuclear" civilizations has come into question. Shifting, far-flung patterns of resource procurement, symbolic exchange, and buffering against political setback or subsistence failure have provoked active discussion if as yet little consensus. The common characteristic of these new patterns is that systemic interaction is central to their very definition. Thus they intersect only accidentally with formerly recognized domains of similarity tied to zones of irrigation, isopleths of population density, generalized cultural co-traditions, or even the cognitive "frontiers" recorded by sedentary urban elites who were largely ignorant of them (e.g., Tosi 1973–1974; Adams 1975; Lamberg-Karlovsky 1975).

It may appear that no equivalent stress on interactional phenomena is attainable as one moves further back into the domain of the prehistorian. No one would question the interpretive advantages conferred by the richness and complexity of the remains that early civilizations have left us, above all by way of written sources and representational art. But while there are obvious differences in the kind and amount of available data, there is something approaching continuity in sense of problem. The dominant ecological approach in prehistory is characterized, in fact, by a concern not merely for human responses to immediate environmental stimuli but for second- and third-order interactions with component subsystems of the social as well as natural environment.

Concepts like niche width and complexity, focusing on the spatial range and variety of resources sought as security against localized variability and unpredictable losses, provide a useful bridge of common contextual concern between prehistoric and ethnographic realms (Hardesty 1975). Equally illustrative of the similarity in trends of thought is a recent paper on Late Pleistocene population fluctuations that stemmed from environmental changes, nonlinear predator-prey relationships, and other sources. Noting that such fluctuations provide for more open systems of migration, exchange, and gene flow, Albert Ammerman (1975) properly questions our predisposition to equate small, primitive hunting and gathering populations with closed, isolated models of stasis or development.

There is no reason to continue a ramble through the forests of recent literature in search of further documentation. Nothing is particularly subtle or obscure about the shift that has occurred. What is remarkable is only its generality, coupled with the apparent absence of a correspondingly general understanding of its impact upon our field. Clearly, a bundle of closely related themes runs through our work, to which we commonly address ourselves only in their particulars — peasant studies, networks, marketing systems, urban-rural relations, situational analysis, regional approaches, levels of integration, cultural brokers, spheres of interaction, ecosystems, and the like. Those particulars are undoubtedly the kinds of limited domains in which we must generally write articles, design good research projects, and advance scholarship. But the responsibility of scholarship, and particularly of anthropological scholarship, is to be an observer as well as a participant. That involves seeking broader perspectives on the work we do, looking for patterns of congruence or the lack of it with related fields, and giving serious, detached attention to the boundaries set by our own conventional research models and their probable consequences. It also involves occasionally taking time to consider the relationship between our premises, models, and research priorities, on the one hand, and the broader context of societal change, debate, and choice, on the other.

The sense of context is critical for us, as Goldschmidt's recent editorial has taken the lead in indicating (1976). Proper concern for it implies that we should identify anthropology's foremost contribution with fitting successively narrower and wider frames, with consciously, continuously shifting the power of the investigator's lens and the field of vision it encompasses. Ours is a share in the science-wide discovery that there are no purely external, passive observers, that we can form no picture which does not include something of ourselves as subjects. But equally important, ours should be a growing awareness that the frame of an *anthropological* picture is neither fixed nor self-evident, but instead constitutes one of the most powerful tools we have with which to analyze the contents of the picture itself.

When we step back to enlarge the field of vision, we do not retreat from phenomena but better perceive their significance. We have tended to define the groups we study largely on the basis of their self-constituted structure, their aspect as independent organisms. Increasingly, however, an approach based on the web of interrelations that individuals as well as groups maintain seems at least equally valid and more consistent with the main course of development of the world we know. The aspect of groups as differentiated organs struggling to maintain themselves in wider, multilevel systems does not present us with merely their external face, but is essential even to an analysis of the core processes that provide for self-identification and continuity. As anthropologists we can only deepen our understanding of our subject matter by stressing a contextual view, by actively seeking the perspectives of the other social sciences and of the society at large.

References Cited

Abu-Lughod, Janet
  1968   The City is Dead — Long Live the City: Some Thoughts on Urbanity. University of California. Center for Planning and Development Research, Monograph 12.

Adams, Robert McC.
  1966   The Evolution of Urban Society: Early Mesopotamia and Prehispanic Mexico. Chicago: Aldine.
  1975   The Mesopotamian Social Landscape: A View from the Frontier. *In* Reconstructing Complex Societies: An Archaeological Colloquium. Charlotte B. Moore, ed. Pp. 1–20. Bulletin of the American Schools of Oriental Research, Supplement 20.
  1977   Social Research and Development. *In* The National Research Council in 1977: Current Issues and Studies (in press).

Aguirre Beltrán, Gonzalo
  1967   Regiones de refugio: el desarrollo de la comunidad y el proceso dominical en mestizo Amé-

rica. Mexico: Instituto Indigenista Interamericano.

Ammerman, Albert J.
  1975   Late Pleistocene Population Dynamics: An Alternative View. Human Ecology 3:219–233.

Asad, Talal
  1972   Market Model, Class Structure and Consent: A Reconsideration of Swat Political Organisation. Man 7:74–94.

Bailey, Frederick G., ed.
  1973   Debate and Compromise: The Politics of Innovation. London: Blackwell.

Barnes, J. A.
  1969   Networks and Political Process. *In* Social Networks in Urban Situations: Analyses of Personal Relationships in Central African Towns. J. C. Mitchell, ed. Pp. 51–76. Manchester: Manchester University Press.

Barth, Fredrik
  1967   On the Study of Social Change. American Anthropologist 69:661–669.
  1969   Introduction. *In* Ethnic

Groups and Boundaries: The Social Organization of Culture Differences. Fredrik Barth, ed. Pp. 9–38. Bergen: Universitets Forlaget.

Bates, Daniel G.
1971 The Role of the State in Peasant-Nomad Mutualism. Anthropological Quarterly 44:109–131.

Berry, Brian J. L., and Donald C. Dahmann
1977 Recent Changes in the Settlement Patterns of the United States. Assembly of Behavioral and Social Sciences, National Research Council (in press).

Braudel, Fernand
1972 The Mediterranean and the Mediterranean World in the Age of Philip II. 2 vols. New York: Harper and Row.

Bray, Warwick
1972 The City State in Central Mexico at the Time of the Spanish Conquest. Journal of Latin American Studies 4:161–185.

Bujra, Abdalla S.
1971 The Politics of Stratification: A Study of Political Change in a South Arabian Town. London: Oxford University Press.

Campbell, Donald T.
1969 Ethnocentrism of Disciplines and the Fish-Scale Model of Omniscience. In Interdisciplinary Relationships in the Social Sciences. Muzafer Sherif and Carolyn W. Sherif, eds. Pp. 328–348. Chicago: Aldine.

Cancian, Frank
1972 Change and Uncertainty in a Peasant Economy: The Maya Corn Farmers of Zinacantan. Stanford: Stanford University Press.

Collier, George A.
1975 Fields of the Tzotzil: The Ecological Bases of Tradition in Highland Chiapas. Austin: University of Texas Press.

Coon, Carleton S.
1958 Caravan: The Story of the Middle East. Second ed. New York: Holt.

Devons, Eli, and Max Gluckman
1964 Conclusion: Models and Consequences of Limiting a Field of Study. In Closed Systems and Open Minds: The Limits of Naivety in Social Anthropology. Eli Devons and Max Gluckman, eds. Pp. 158–261. Chicago: Aldine.

Feuchtwang, Stephen
1975 The Colonial Formation of British Social Anthropology. In Anthropology and the Colonial Encounter. Talal Asad, ed. Pp. 71–100. London: Ithaca.

Flannery, Kent V.
1968 The Olmec and the Valley of Oaxaca: A Model for Interregional Interaction in Formative Times. In Dumbarton Oaks Conference on the Olmec. Elizabeth P. Benson, ed. Pp. 79–110. Washington: Dumbarton Oaks Research Library.

Flannery, Kent V., ed.
  1976 The Early Mesoamerican Village. New York: Academic Press.
Fortes, Meyer
  1953 The Structure of Unilineal Descent Groups. American Anthropologist 55:17–41.
Friedmann, John, and John Miller
  1965 The Urban Field. Journal of the American Institute of Planners 31:312–319.
Geertz, Clifford
  1972 Comments. *In* Rural Politics and Social Change in the Middle East. Richard Antoun and Ilya Harik, eds. Pp. 460–467. Bloomington: Indiana University Press.
Goldschmidt, Walter
  1976 Anthropology as Context. American Anthropologist 78: 519–520.
Handlin, Oscar
  1963 The Modern City as a Field of Historical Study. *In* The Historian and the City. Oscar Handlin and John Burchard, eds. Pp. 1–26. Cambridge: MIT Press.
Hardesty, D. L.
  1975 The Niche Concept: Suggestions for Its Use in Human Ecology. Human Ecology 3:71–85.
Irons, William
  1974 Nomadism as a Political Adaptation: The Case of the Yomut Turkmen. American Ethnologist 1:635–658.

Jackson, Kenneth T.
  1975 Urban Deconcentration in the Nineteenth Century: A Statistical Inquiry. *In* The New Urban History: Quantitative Explorations by American Historians. L. F. Schnore, ed. Pp. 110–142. Princeton: Princeton University Press.
Lamberg-Karlovsky, C. C.
  1975 Third Millennium Modes of Exchange and Modes of Production. *In* Ancient Civilization and Trade. Jeremy A. Sabloff and C. C. Lamberg-Karlovsky, eds. Pp. 369–408. School of American Research. Albuquerque: University of New Mexico Press.
Leach, Edmund R.
  1965 Political Systems of Highland Burma. Boston: Beacon.
Martindale, Don
  1958 Prefatory Remarks: The Theory of the City. *In* The City, by Max Weber. Don Martindale and Gertrud Neuwirth, eds. Pp. 9–62. Glencoe: Free Press.
Marx, Emanuel
  1973 The Ecology and Politics of Nomadic Pastoralists in the Middle East. Paper, IXth International Congress of Anthropological and Ethnological Sciences.
Mintz, Sidney W.
  1976 Foreword. *In* Markets in Oaxaca. Scott Cook and Martin Diskin, eds. Pp. xi–xv. Austin: University of Texas Press.

Morse, Richard M.
1971   Trends and Issues in Latin American Urban Research 1965–1970. Latin American Research Review 6:3–75.

Nader, Laura
1965   Communication between Village and City in the Modern Middle East. Human Organization 24:18–24.

Olsen, Stephen M.
1976   Regional Social Systems: Linking Quantitative Work and Field Work. *In* Regional Analysis. Vol. 2, Social Systems. Carol A. Smith, ed. Pp. 21–61. New York: Academic Press.

Ortiz, Sutti R. de
1973   Uncertainties in Peasant Farming: A Colombian Case. London School of Economics. Monographs on Social Anthropology, Vol. 46.

Park, Robert E., E. W. Burgess, and R. D. McKenzie
1925   The City. Chicago: University of Chicago Press.

Paz, Octavio
1961   The Labyrinth of Solitude: Life and Thought in Mexico. New York: Grove.

Peters, Emrys
1967   Some Structural Aspects of the Feud among the Camel Herding Bedouin of Cyrenaica. Africa 37:261–282.
1972   Shifts in Power in a Lebanese Village. *In* Rural Politics and Social Change in the Middle East. Richard Antoun and Ilya Harik, eds. Pp. 165–197. Bloomington: Indiana University Press.

Pred, Allan R.
1975   Large-City Interdependence and the Pre-Electronic Diffusion of Innovations in the United States. *In* The New Urban History: Quantitative Explorations by American Historians. L. F. Schnore, ed. Pp. 51–74. Princeton: Princeton University Press.

Redfield, Robert
1962   Civilizations as Societal Structures? The Development of Community Studies. *In* Human Nature and the Study of Society. Margaret P. Redfield, ed. Vol. 1. Pp. 375–391. Chicago: University of Chicago Press.

Skinner, G. W.
1971   Chinese Peasants and the Closed Community: An Open and Shut Case. Comparative Studies in Society and History 13:270–281.

Sternlieb, G., and J. W. Hughes
1976   Post-Industrial America: Metropolitan Decline and Inter-Regional Job Shifts. New Brunswick: Rutgers University Press.

Steward, Julian H.
1950   Area Research: Theory and Practice. Social Science Research Council. Bulletin 63.

Struever, Stuart, and Gail L. Houart
1972   An Analysis of the Hopewell Interaction Sphere. *In* Social

Exchange and Interaction. Edwin N. Wilmsen, ed. Pp. 47–79. Museum of Anthropology, University of Michigan. Anthropology Papers, Vol. 46.

Tosi, Maurizio
1973–74 The Northeastern Frontier of the Ancient Near East. Mesopotamia 8–9:21–76.

Velsen, J. van
1967 The Extended-Case Method and Situational Analysis. *In* The Craft of Social Anthropology. A. L. Epstein, ed. Pp. 129–149. London: Tavistock.

Wolf, Eric R.
1955 Types of Latin American Peasantry: A Preliminary Discussion. American Anthropologist 57:452–471.
1956 Aspects of Group Relations in a Complex Society: Mexico. American Anthropologist 58: 1065–1078.

Wolf, Eric R., ed.
1976 The Valley of Mexico: Studies in Pre-Hispanic Ecology and Society. School of American Research. Albuquerque: University of New Mexico Press.

The Anthropologist as Expert Witness

Lawrence Rosen

VOL. 79, 1977, 555–578

Introduction

As scholars and teachers, governmental advisers, and agency bureau-crats, anthropologists play a number of different roles in American so-ciety. Each role entails certain intellectual and moral issues, but there are few roles that confront conscientious anthropologists with more serious scholarly and ethical problems than those posed by their appearance in legal proceedings as expert witnesses. Drawing on specialized knowl-edge and ostensibly attuned to a professional superego that demands an impartial analysis of the data, the expert witness is brought, usually by one of the adversary parties, into a proceeding whose form and goals often appear foreign, if not overtly antithetical, to scholarly capacities and purposes. Although his awareness of the experiences of other expert witnesses — particularly anthropological witnesses — may be limited and his vision of legal proceedings drawn more from popular stereotypes than detailed knowledge, the expert witness will doubtless be aware that American courts have made frequent reference to sociological data and that the expert's testimony may prove significant to the outcome of the case. Regardless of personal affinity to the position argued by the party calling him as a witness, the anthropologist may not understand how expert testimony fits together with judicial reasoning and legal prece-dent, and precisely how the court's investigation of the facts articulates with the form of knowledge he possesses.

The general use of experts in American courts is familiar to almost everyone. We have all seen enough Perry Mason shows to know that the prosecution or defense, or the parties to a civil proceeding, may call expert witnesses to the stand to testify on anything from the findings of a ballistics test or the nature of tire tracks to the medical condition of an accident victim or the blood type of an alleged father. The use of expert psychiatrists in cases involving the insanity defense or competence to stand trial is also widely known. Less familiar are the regulations affecting expert testimony and the historical context of their development.

The use of expert witnesses is nothing new in the Anglo-American system of adjudication. Their role is deeply intertwined with the development of the jury system, and many of the rules governing expert testimony, as well as many of the difficulties posed for it, are associated with the emergence of this distinctive institution of legal fact-finding.

The early English jury was a very different institution than its contemporary successor. In the 12th to 14th centuries, juries consisted of groups of neighbors who were already acquainted with the facts of a case or regarded as easily capable of discovering them. In a sense, jurors in this period were as much witnesses as judges of the facts. In some cases, particularly those involving disputes among tradesmen or other specialists, the jury was drawn from people with expertise in the matter. Occasionally, the court itself summoned an expert to supply information on a given topic. In these instances, the information was probably furnished directly to the court, rather than to the jury, and the judge was apparently left to decide whether and how the jurors should be informed of the testimony (Hand 1901:41–42; Rosenthal 1935:408). It was only in the 16th century, as the jury was transformed from a panel of co-residents or colleagues to a group of uninformed arbiters who, instead of bringing their own knowledge of the facts to bear on a case, waited for evidence to be presented to them in court, that experts were brought in by the contending parties to give testimony.

Special rules have also developed concerning the presentation of expert testimony in court. Whereas ordinary witnesses were increasingly barred from expressing their own opinions on many issues, various jurisdictions created an exception for the expert witness. Although different courts follow significantly different rules, most contemporary American courts permit the judge to exercise substantial discretion in deciding the propriety and qualifications of proffered expert witnesses. None of the uniform rules proposed for the regulation of expert testimony has received widespread acceptance (Travis 1974). However, several jurisdictions, including the federal courts, have encouraged the use of court-appointed experts in addition to those who may be presented by the parties.

Although the general use of expert witnesses is not new and the rules governing their appearance largely ignore special problems attendant on various types of expert testimony, the use of social science by the courts is both more recent and unfamiliar. Sociologists have been called as expert witnesses in cases involving the custody of children of mixed racial parentage (Rose 1956:210), the relationship between race and the application of the death penalty (Wolfgang 1974), and the impact on minorities of segregated schooling (Levin and Hawley 1975). Linguists have testified on the readability of a back-pay agreement in a dispute involving minority employees (United States District Court, Western District of Pennsylvania 1976). Sociologists and social psychologists have applied their studies of social indicators in trademark disputes (Barksdale 1957) and determinations of parental fitness. In addition to actual testimony, courts and attorneys have frequently cited the work of social scientists in their decisions and briefs (Rosen 1972).

Anthropologists, too, have appeared in an astonishingly wide range of cases. As we shall see, they have testified on everything from racial segregation, miscegenation laws, and child custody to the blood types of putative fathers, the nature of religious communities, and the cultural background of criminal defendants. Their predominant role has been in cases involving American Indians. In suits brought before the Indian Claims Commission, they have testified to the nature of aboriginal land titles, the identification of Indian social groupings, and the comprehension by Indians of treaties signed with the federal government. In nonclaims cases, they have testified as to the nature of Indian peyotism, the nature and consequences of acculturation, and the religious significance of Indian ritual artifacts. In all of these different kinds of cases certain general issues present themselves. These issues are shared by many other kinds of expert witnesses, and present questions the individual anthropologist and the profession as a whole cannot and should not avoid.

The first set of problems raised both for the anthropologist and the court concerns the adequacy, context, and form of presentation of anthropological evidence in an adversary proceeding. Does the mere fact that one holds a doctorate in anthropology qualify one as an expert in all aspects of the discipline or one of its subdivisions? In what sense is the anthropologist's testimony adequate to the interpretation of a highly specific issue that often turns on prospective consequences? Is it true for anthropologists — as most psychiatrists and some sociologists argue for their disciplines — that the kinds of questions which they are capable of addressing are not the same as those posed by a legal case, and that their evidence is therefore either inappropriate for or distorted by the context of a courtroom proceeding? What is the expert's relation to the attorney and how have anthropologists viewed the process of cross-examination and the introduction of a contending expert's testimony? In the courtroom setting, as well as in the presentation of depositions and supporting documents, what evidentiary standards do anthropologists appear to set for themselves, and how do the forms of argument used in these situations compare to those employed when writing for a scholarly or popular audience? Indeed, what relationships exist between the "facts" to which anthropologists testify and the theories that inform those facts, and how sensitive are the courts and lawyers to anthropologists' unstated theoretical biases?

A second set of questions revolves around the mutual effect that courts and anthropologists have had on one another. How have anthropologists' own concepts been affected by the experience of such litigation, and how has the experts' testimony shaped judicial thought? Having participated in such proceedings, will the anthropologist be so concerned with the possible legal significance of his work that his future scholarly investigations will be altered in some fashion?

Finally, serious questions are raised about anthropologists' conceptions of their role in such proceedings, and how the courts and the profession may contribute to appropriate reforms in the present system. Are anthropologists really the providers of crucial information from which judgments are actually derived, or are they merely important personages whose presence in court is simply useful for rationalizing judgments that are founded on other, perhaps judicially less palatable, bases? How, if at all, should anthropology as a profession approach the ethical implications of expert testimony? What reforms might appear most useful given the experience of anthropologists and others as participants in the judicial process?

In order to explore these questions within the context of the specific situations in which they arise, a series of cases will be analyzed in which anthropologists have been involved as expert witnesses. In each, the aim is to sharpen understanding of the issues presented and to show that while no incontrovertible answers exist for the questions posed, this fact alone justifies neither the self-serving relativism nor the moral self-righteousness to which both anthropologists and lawyers may fall prey.

Anthropological Testimony and Racial Discrimination

Justice Frankfurter: . . . [W]e are here in a domain which I do not yet regard as
science in the sense of mathematical certainty. This is all opinion evidence.
Mr. Greenberg: That is true, Your Honor.
Justice Frankfurter: I do not mean that I disrespect it. I simply know its
character. It can be a very different thing from, as I say, things that are
weighed and measured and are fungible. We are dealing here with very subtle
things, very subtle testimony [Oral argument in Gebhart v. Belton, in Friedman 1969:172–173].

In the years leading up to the 1954 *Brown v. Board of Education* decision, in which the Supreme Court ruled that segregated education was
inherently unequal, lawyers for the black litigants placed considerable
stress on the writings and testimony of social scientists. As part of
their strategy, lawyers for the National Association for the Advancement
of Colored People (NAACP) sought to use social science testimony to
strengthen their argument that discriminatory classifications are unconstitutional if, among other things, they are lacking in any rational justification (United States Supreme Court 1949:449). The NAACP was well
aware of the implicit psychological and sociological ideas that suffused
the "separate but equal" doctrine announced by the Court's 1896 decision in *Plessy v. Ferguson*. They knew, too, that at least since the introduction of the Brandeis Brief, with its frequent citation of social and
economic indicators, the Court had become familiar with reliance on
sociological data (Rosen 1972). It was not, however, until the desegregation cases that social science testimony took so central a place in constitutional litigation.

Four years before the *Brown* decision, the Supreme Court was called
on to decide whether the education afforded whites at the University of
Texas Law School and that afforded blacks at a separate state institution
could be supported under the separate but equal doctrine. The case,
Sweatt v. Painter, was unusual in that NAACP lawyers called as a witness
one of the leading anthropologists of the day, Robert Redfield. Redfield
was, in many respects, an ideal choice. Trained as a lawyer before coming into anthropology and possessing years of experience in integrated
education as Dean of the Social Sciences at the University of Chicago,
"Redfield proved a brilliant witness whose every word suggested a cool,
considered judgment with great authority behind it" (Kluger 1976:264).

The thrust of Redfield's testimony dealt less with specific anthropological studies of the composition and character of the races than with the
social consequences of segregated education and the possible repercussions of court-ordered integration. His testimony was intended to support the argument that if legislators sought to give a rational, constitutional basis to racial discrimination they would find nothing in the
experience of social science to support their position (cf. Redfield 1963:
165–168).

The following excerpts from Redfield's testimony indicate something
of the force and direction of the anthropologist's direct testimony, as
conducted by the NAACP's Thurgood (now Mr. Justice) Marshall, and the
cross-examination by counsel for the State of Texas, Price Daniel:

> [*On direct examination by Mr. Thurgood Marshall:*]
> Q: Dr. Redfield, are there any recognizable differences as between Negro and
> white students on the question of their intellectual capacity?
>
> Mr. Daniel: Your Honor, we object to that. That would be a conclusion on
> the part of the witness. It covers all negro students and all white students. It
> isn't limited to any particular study or subject or even show what it is based
> on.
> The Court: I suppose his qualifications he has testified to would qualify
> him to draw his conclusions.
> . . . .
>
> A: We got something of a lesson there. We who have been working in the field
> in which we began with a rather general presumption among our common
> educators that inherent differences in intellectual ability of capacity to
> learn existed between negroes and whites, and have slowly, but I think very
> convincingly, been compelled to come to the opposite conclusion, in the
> course of long history, special research in the field.
> . . . .
>
> Q: . . . [W]hat is your opinion as to the effect of segregated education . . . ?
> A: . . . [I]t prevents the student from the full, effective and economical coming
> to understand[ing of] the nature and capacity of the group from which he
> is segregated. . . . It is my view that education goes forward more favorably
> if the community of student, scholar and teacher is fairly representative of
> the whole community. . . . [S]egregation . . . accentuates imagined differ-
> ences between negroes and whites. These false assumptions . . . are given
> an appearance of reality by the formal act of physical separation.

[*Cross-examination by Mr. Price Daniel:*]

Q: Do you think the [segregation] laws should be changed tomorrow?

A: I think that segregation is a matter of legal regulation. Such a law can be changed quickly.

Q: Do you think it has anything to do with the social standing in the community?

A: Segregation itself is a matter of law, and that law can be changed at once . . .

. . . .

Q: . . . [D]o you recognize or agree with the school of thought, that regardless of the ultimate objective concerning segregation, that if it is to be changed in southern communities . . . it must be done over a long period of time . . . ?

A: That contention, I do not think, will be my opinion on the matter scientifically.

Q: Does that represent, scientifically, a school of thought on that, in your science, in the matter?

A: There are some that feel that way.

Q: Yes, sir. You are acquainted with the history of the carpetbagger days in the Civil War?

A: I feel better acquainted with it today, sir, than anybody.

Q: Dr. Redfield, let me get you clearly on that. You are not talking about your own trip down here, are you, to Texas? You say you are acquainted with it today?

A: It just drifted into my mind.

. . . .

Q: Doctor, are you acquainted with the Encyclopedia Britannica, the publication by that name?

A: I have a set. I don't look at it very often.

Q: You are from the University of Chicago?

A: Yes.

Q: Is that publication now published under the auspices of that University?

A: Yes, sir; and it badly needs rewriting.

Q: It is published under the auspices of your University?

A: Yes.

Q: Have you read the article therein on education, and segregation of the races in American Schools?

A: If I have I don't remember it.

Q: You don't remember it. Have you written any articles for the Encyclopedia Britannica?

A: No, we are just beginning a revision of anthropological articles, and it seems there has to be a very drastic change.

. . . .

Q: Could you give us some of the authorities that you think we would be justified in taking as authorities on the subject you have testified to us about? Have you written any books on the subject?

A: Not with respect to the American Negro. I have written on the general subject with respect to other racial groups. Franz Boes [sic], Ruth Benedict, Ashely [sic] Montague, Otto Klineberg. Is that enough?

Q: Give us one more.

A: I will make it a good one. Then, Dr. Leslie White.

Q: Do all of these scientists have the same, share your ideas as to segregation?

A: I don't know.

. . . .

Q: But on your conclusion as to education, you told me there were authorities in the field who disagreed with your conclusion?

A: I think not.

Q: Maybe I am speaking about the gradual change.

A: I don't know who I could cite for that.

Q: That is all.

[United States Supreme Court 1949:192–193, 194–195, 198, 203, 204–205].

Redfield's testimony was an early and important basis for the contention that no rational foundation for segregation could be found in the social science literature.[1] Ultimately, the Supreme Court avoided the implication of Redfield's argument — that separate education is inherently unequal — and simply found that the facilities provided by the segregated law schools of Texas were not, in fact, equivalent (United States Supreme Court 1950). But Redfield's testimony was also read into the record of *Briggs v. Elliott*, a South Carolina case which was joined before the Supreme Court with *Brown* and several other cases, and to which Marshall made frequent reference in his briefs and oral argument. By then, a considerable number of social scientists — most notably the psychologist Kenneth B. Clark — had testified in the various desegregation cases, and a number of scholars, Redfield among them, were signatories to the statement by social scientists that formed an Appendix to Appellant's Briefs (Chein et al. 1955).

When the desegregation cases came before the Supreme Court, the Justices, especially Mr. Justice Frankfurter, pressed counsel on the rele-

vance and implications of the sociological data. Through his questioning, Frankfurter asserted the Court's right to read, as well as hear, what
social scientists have to say (Friedman 1969:63), and responded to counsel's argument that there was no social science support for the segrega-
tionist argument by saying: "But the testimony of a witness is subject to
intrinsic limitations and qualifications and illuminations. The mere fact
that a man is not contradicted does not mean that what he says is so"
(Friedman 1969:172). Expressing the common concern of the Court,
Frankfurter probed for the perceived consequences of an order striking
down the "separate but equal" doctrine, and responded favorably when
the NAACP stuck to its constitutional argument that if the states could
supply no scientific or other basis for their racial classifications blacks
should not have to bear the demonstrated burdens of this discrimination
(Friedman 1969:44–45). The Court also let pass the remarks of John W.
Davis, arguing for the states, that "much of that which is handed around
under the name of social science is an effort on the part of the scientist to
rationalize his own preconceptions. They find usually, in my limited
observation, what they go out to find" (Friedman 1969:59).

When the Court handed down its unanimous decision it adopted the
finding that segregated education does indeed have "a detrimental effect
upon the colored children," that "the policy of separating the races is
usually interpreted as denoting the inferiority of the negro group," and
that "a sense of inferiority affects the motivation of a child to learn"
(United States Supreme Court 1954:494). The Court then formally repudiated the implicit psychology of the "separate but equal" doctrine
and supplied a footnote reference to the writings of Clark, Chein, Myrdal, and other social scientists to support their assertion that the harm of
segregation "is amply supported by modern authority" (United States
Supreme Court 1954:494).

The Court's decision, and particularly its footnote reference to social
science, has sparked great controversy. Some Southern Congressmen
labeled the social scientists as "Commies" and "foreigners" (Garfinkel
1959:37; Rosen 1972:173–175), and Senator Eastland sought to undercut the constitutional basis of the decision by introducing a Senate Resolution that began: "Whereas this decision was based solely and alone on
psychological, sociological and anthropological considerations . . ."
(Greenberg 1956:965). More responsible commentators were also concerned that the Court had indeed relied more on sociology than law in
its decision and that the particular social science findings used were

altogether inadequate (Berger 1957:475; Cahn 1955; Van den Haag 1960). The social scientists defended the relevance and quality of their findings (Clark 1953, 1959–60, 1969), and numerous commentors have attempted to assess the merits of each side's contentions (Garfinkel 1959; Kluger 1976:355–356; Rosen 1972:182–196).

Throughout this controversy, the precise importance of the social science testimony to the Court's decision has remained elusive. Chief Justice Warren said the Court cited the testimony simply to counter the argument in *Plessy* that the harm of discrimination was a figment of the Negro's imagination (Kluger 1976:706). Judge Wisdom has written (1975:142): "The social science evidence was the kind of support a court likes to find in a record to lend factual and scientific aura to a result sustainable by other, purely abstract and sometimes formalistically legal, considerations, but dictated by the moral necessity of changing social attitudes." And one of the NAACP lawyers has asserted that the testimony aided in the general awareness of the adverse effects of segregation, and that if the sociological data were inadequate the defendants had ample opportunity to demonstrate this during cross-examination (Greenberg 1956; see also Clark 1969:xxxvi). Whether, as the NAACP argued, the demonstration of segregation's effects was at "the heart of our case" (Friedman 1969:18) or was simply the only mechanism available for attacking directly the legal issues surrounding racial discrimination, a close reading of the history of the desegregation cases shows that the arguments of Redfield and others not only preempted the pseudo-scientific assertions of the segregationists but supported, and perhaps even compelled, acceptance of the argument that segregation was without constitutional justification.

The desegregation cases are not the only legal actions concerning race in which anthropological evidence has been employed. Physical anthropologists have appeared in cases involving mixed racial marriages (Maslow 1959–60:245), and numerous citations were made to anthropological works in *Loving v. Virginia*, a 1967 case in which the Supreme Court struck down antimiscegenation laws as unconstitutional (Kurland and Casper 1975a:784–785, 874–886, 942–943, 958, 987–991). Recently, an anthropologist testified about racial classifications in the case of an East Indian who claimed to have been dismissed from his job as a result of racial discrimination. In that case the court, obviously confused as to how anthropologists might once have classified some dark-skinned persons as Caucasian but now relied more on blood group data, simply told the jury to ignore the expert testimony and determine the "race" of the plaintiff on the basis of their own perceptions and common sense (Edward Jay, personal communication).

Each of these cases raises serious issues about the adequacy, impact, and appropriate presentation of social science findings. In the desegregation cases, such data and interpretations contributed to a result which is consonant with both the professional and personal positions adopted by virtually every anthropologist. However, agreement on interpretations and the suitability of anthropological knowledge are not invariably so clear. When such knowledge stems mainly from theoretical orientations and is directed toward prospective consequences, the difficulties inherent in expert testimony become more sharply posed.

The Community and the Law

In 1972 the United States Supreme Court, in the case of *Wisconsin v. Yoder*, held that the state had violated the constitutional rights of the defendant Amish parents by requiring them to send their children to school beyond the eighth grade. Arguing that "only those interests of the highest order and those not otherwise served can overbalance legitimate claims to the free exercise of religion" (United States Supreme Court 1972:215), the Court found that the Amish religious faith and their mode of life were so inseparable and interdependent that the social repercussions of compulsory high school attendance would necessarily infringe on the well-being of the community as a religious entity. In reaching its decision, the Court made frequent reference to the testimony given at the trial court level by the anthropologist John A. Hostetler.

Hostetler testified that "as a part of their way of salvation [the Amish] require a church community that is separate from the world" (1970:49). "I think," he said, "that if the Amish youth are required to attend the value system of the high school as we know it today, the church-community cannot last long, it will be destroyed" (1970:51). In response to direct examination, he said that this is because "great psychological harm can be done to the children," and hence the community, as a result of the alienation that can arise from a clash of values (1970:52). In the Amish view, he testified, higher learning is regarded as "wisdom not responsible to the community" (1970:54A). The Amish, he asserted, train their children to be members of a self-sufficient community, and Amishmen never place a burden on American society as a result of delinquency or welfare requirements.

On cross-examination, the state's attorney tried to bring out that the Amish do not object to sending their children to public school through the eighth grade and that Amish children come into contact with outsiders on their occasional trips to town. Hostetler reasserted, in the following testimony, that the prosecutor's approach was not without its own bias:

Q. Are you saying in effect, Professor, that to minority groups, which includes the Amish, that they should govern themselves as far as education; should minority groups, be it Amish or otherwise, would you say be permitted to set up their own rules as to whether they shall or shall not be educated?

A. I think we need to know a great deal more about how to teach the culturally different child, know the poverty children, and I think it is dangerous to put all children through the same type of value orientation.

Q. Isn't that the reason then, Professor, in the institutions of higher learning, high school and up, you will have elective courses so the children won't all have to take the same?

A. The trouble is it is still the same environment, it doesn't matter what courses they take.

Q. The principal purpose to attend school is to get education, is it not, isn't that the primary purpose?

A. Yes, but I think there is a great deal of difference what education means, education for what.

Q. To put it bluntly, education so the child can make his or her place in the world?

A. It depends which world.

Q. This one, the one we live in?

A. I think education — this is one of the myths in American society — all education is good; education must be tied to a culture that emotionally guides the child in the direction he knows he is going to live when he is an adult.

Q. Well in other words, Professor, you are saying that education should be tied in the sense to culture, is that right?

A. Yes. Anthropologists would say there isn't education without culture climate at all.

Q. So if I am in one culture and you another the education we receive should be different?

A. I would say if there is this difference in Amish society we should have a parallel culture in the society to know each other as common Americans but a different heritage [Hostetler 1970:67–68].

Finally, the state raised the issue of the effect of insufficient education on those who later chose to leave the community:

> Q. Is it fair to say, Professor, that an adult who in his childhood might well be an Amish and now decided not to stay with the Amish is at a handicap because he did not receive the education he might have received were he not an Amish?
>
> A. The conclusion is that the skills required to become an adult are such that if one doesn't have an adult high school education, well, normally people are always looking for people to do manual work. I don't believe any segment is deprived by not having education.[2]
>
> Q. Even those who later cease to become members of the Amish faith and find themselves having to compete in the worldly world?
>
> A. No, I don't think they are deprived [Hostetler 1970:69].

In deciding in favor of the Amish the Supreme Court adopted the reasoning, and indeed many of the phrases, contained in Hostetler's testimony. The Court summarized its position in the following terms:

> It cannot be overemphasized that we are not dealing with a way of life and mode of education by a group claiming to have recently discovered some "progressive" or more enlightened process for rearing children for modern life. Aided by a history of three centuries as an identifiable religious sect and a long history as a successful and self-sufficient segment of American society, the Amish in this case have convincingly demonstrated the sincerity of their religious beliefs, the interrelationship of belief with their mode of life, the vital role that belief and daily conduct play in the continued survival of Old Order Amish communities and their religious organization, and the hazards presented by the State's enforcement of a statute generally valid to others. Beyond this, they have carried the even more difficult burden of demonstrating the adequacy of their alternative mode of continuing informal vocational education in terms of precisely those overall interests that the State advances in support of its program of compulsory high school education [United States Supreme Court 1972:235–236].

Only Mr. Justice Douglas dissented from the majority opinion. He pointed out that attrition from Amish communities is often quite high, and he argued that, although the case involved criminal charges against the parents for violation of compulsory school attendance laws, the interests of the children should have been represented in the case. He also objected to granting an exception only to groups whose values had a religious, rather than philosophical, basis (United States Supreme Court 1972:247–249).

Leaving aside the wisdom of the Supreme Court's unprecedented decision to grant the Amish, because of their religious beliefs, an exception from the requirements of a valid criminal statute, the case raises important issues concerning expert anthropological testimony. The Court was correct when it noted that the state had presented no expert to contradict Hostetler's assessment of Amish life. Nor did the state succeed in undermining the expert's contention that religious and social life are inseparable in Amish communities and that an attack on the one was necessarily an attack on the other. And yet, from the testimony alone, it might appear that Hostetler's interpretation of Amish culture rests on an unstated and unexamined theoretical assumption — namely, that Amish society is the sort of homeostatic, functionally integrated, organically constituted entity which can be analyzed in terms of structural-functional theory. Although this theoretical approach does not pervade his scholarly writings on the Amish, does not his statement that "When culturally different children attend a school that teaches an unattainable identity, an identity that would demand the rejection of the values of the home . . . what can be expected but alienation and rebellion?" (Hostetler 1972) ignore the possibilities of growth, development, evolution, or change? Another expert, or another lawyer, might have pointed, as Mr. Justice Douglas did, to Hostetler's own findings concerning drinking patterns and tension among the Amish (Hostetler 1968:281–283; United States Supreme Court 1972:246–247), and might have challenged the view that two years of additional education would have increased the attrition rate referred to only by Mr. Justice Douglas. If the courts are going to balance state and religious community interests, should anthropological witnesses be encouraged, by their profession if not by the law, to become, in effect, experts for the court, presenting a wide range of data and theoretical alternatives, or is cross-examination an adequate safeguard? Indeed, should prospective assessments of the likely impact of a given practice be stated solely in terms of personal opinion or should the expert explain and evaluate alternative interpretations before voicing his own opinion?

A second issue concerns the expert's own affinity to the cause of the side for whom he appears. Hostetler himself was raised as an Amishman and feels very close to the people. At one point in the testimony he even referred to "*our* Amish culture" (1970:71, emphasis added). The attorney for the Amish, on oral argument to the Supreme Court, effectively pointed to Hostetler as an example of someone who was indeed able to make his way in higher education after being raised in an Amish community (Kurland and Casper 1975b:816). This background was not raised at the trial level. John Hostetler is clearly the most conscientious and thorough of scholars, and his deep concern and commitment to the Amish represents the finest in humanistic anthropology. Of what relevance should it be, then, that he was raised an Amishman and what, if any, obligation for disclosure should be imposed as a general rule on all experts?

Finally, a close reading of the Supreme Court opinion clearly demonstrates that the anthropological testimony in this case may well have been indispensable to the Court's assertion that enforcement of the school attendance law would have had an unusually harsh effect on the entire community of Amish people. Moreover, to the extent that Hostetler's enlightened and responsible testimony raises general problems of the structure of expert testimony in American courts it demonstrates that one does not necessarily lose one's scientific distance by becoming a scholar allied with a cause.

The Battle of the Experts

In the desegregation and Amish cases anthropologists appeared on the side of only one of the parties in the case. Quite often anthropologists appear on opposite sides of a case, and one is confronted with what to some is the rather unseemly — and to others the thoroughly delightful — spectacle of two anthropologists, with varying degrees of experience in such proceedings, being delivered up to the tender mercies of the adversary system. In most instances legitimate differences of interpretation exist, and equally competent and honest experts bring their separate perspectives to bear on the legal questions posed. Cases of this type raise major ethical and scholarly issues for the anthropologists involved (Lurie 1956, Manners 1956). I know, because I have been peripherally involved in several such cases concerning American Indians.

During the summer following my second year in law school, while working with an American Indian litigation group, I was asked to prepare the cross-examination of expert anthropologists appearing as witnesses against our clients in several important cases. One of these was the case of *United States v. State of Washington.* The case was one of several suits brought over the past decade involving the fishing rights of Indians along the Northwest Coast. Basically, the State of Washington argued that the Indians are subject to all state conservation laws and fishing regulations when netting salmon off their reservations. The federal government, as trustee of the Indian's rights, argued that the treaty provisions permitting Indians to fish at all their "usual and accustomed" sites exempt the Indians from state control even when the fishing takes place at sites that are no longer part of reservation lands.

One of the arguments put forth in support of the state's case was that the Indians of northwestern Washington have become so acculturated to American life that their tribes have effectively ceased to exist. Since the original treaty rights were granted to the tribes as organized bodies and since the organization of these groups had been fundamentally altered by their contact with whites, the present litigants were not, the state argued, entitled to the rights accorded the pre-existing tribes.

In furtherance of this general line of argument, the state presented the testimony of an expert anthropologist. He noted that by the 1850s, when the treaties in question were signed, the Indians had been so decimated by disease that they could no longer be regarded as solidary units even if some of the groups ever possessed an overall political structure (United States District Court, Western District of Washington 1973:13, 30–31). On the question of Indian acculturation he testified as follows:

Q. What do you mean when you use the term "culture" or "native culture?"

A. Having an historical ethnological orientation, I tend to think in terms of culture rather than in terms of society. I will give a very simple definition of culture: That is totality of learned behavior, the kind of behavior that we learn rather than the behavior that is part of our biological heritage. A "native culture" is the learned behavior of a given group of people, especially that behavior that sets them off from other groups.

Q. Is there a native culture in Western Washington today?

A. At least among groups I have investigated, acculturation has proceeded pretty far. Western Washington Indians wear western clothes, use modern technology, speak English, share in Western religious traditions, are United States citizens, and, generally speaking, look at the world through Western-European eyes. The amount of "Indianness" varies from group to group and certainly between young and old. I wonder how many Western Washington Indians under 21 today really speak native languages [1973:22].

Clearly, this testimony presented substantial difficulties. To argue that the region was characterized by "village autonomy and . . . no tribal

structure" seemed to ignore the whole concept of acephalous organization, the existence of intervillage ties, and the situational nature of group
alliances and leadership in the region (Sahlins 1968:21). I was troubled
by the expert's definition of culture as the "totality of learned behavior,"
and his consequent assertion that the Indians had taken on the culture of
the whites and had come to see the world through their eyes. Wasn't this
behavioristic theory of culture regarded as inadequate by most anthropologists (Singer 1968:540)? Didn't we know that different meanings
might be attributed to similar symbolic forms and that students of the
region had found that "in spite of an almost complete replacement of
material goods and century-long conflict between white and native beliefs and practices, basic features of native social organization remain"
(Suttles 1963:516)? Is it not possible for people to be bicultural, as well as
bilingual, and is "acculturation" capable of scientific measurement?

As I prepared our attorney for his appearance in the case, my sense of
indignation and my resolve in the wisdom of our own arguments grew.
Yet at some point along the way I found myself asking how I, who had no
field experience in the area, could be so sure that our own interpretations
were correct. We had the detailed testimony of a highly qualified expert
appearing for our side, and most of the anthropological arguments in the
case could probably have been rendered secondary to purely legal issues.
I knew that while some of the adverse expert's assertions were subject to
attack, the federal court would not be unmindful of the fact that state
courts in Washington had earlier relied on such testimony when they
referred to Indians as similar to Irish- or Italian-Americans in their
adoption of American culture. In fact, the state supreme court had even
suggested that perhaps the special privileges accorded the Indians were
so excessive as to violate the constitutional prohibition against granting
any citizens titles of nobility! But even in the face of these absurdities,
how could I be so sure that we were right? As I read through the ethnographic literature I could not get a simple yes or no answer as to
whether the groups involved should somehow be characterized as "acculturated." I appreciated that for anthropologists, as for many other
expert witnesses, the categories of law or judicial reasoning were not
always very appropriate to scholarly inquiry. Categories that courts
might regard as conclusory, social scientists might see as shorthand formulations, general glosses, or purposely ambiguous rubrics covering
details that cannot be summed up as categorical responses to certain
kinds of questions. As an anthropologist, I was less certain that I was

right about many of the arguments I was, as a lawyer-to-be, encouraging our counsel to make. I could, of course, rationalize it all by saying that the final determination was for the court and that I was just helping to bring out additional facts, but I found this line of reasoning no more comforting in myself than in the system at large. To say that there are simply different interpretations of social life and history and that I was just engaging in their formulation was equally dissatisfying. This was no mere academic debate but a legal proceeding, and the Indians would have to live with the results for years to come. I was pleased that the court eventually found in favor of the Indians and declared that the anthropological testimony on our side was more credible (United States District Court, Western District of Washington 1974:350). Nevertheless, I began to look at other situations in which anthropological testimony had been used in courts, and wondered what effects such testimony might have not only on the courts but on subsequent scholarly work.

The Reciprocal Effects of Anthropological Testimony

The bulk of anthropological testimony has come in proceedings before the Indian Claims Commission. Established in 1946, the Commission was authorized to hear Indian claims against the government, including those based on treaties or on the harm done by less than "fair and honorable dealings" with the Indians.[3] Under the statute, only a "tribe, band, or identifiable group" was permitted to file suit (Indian Claims Commission 1963). Moreover, in most cases the plaintiffs have been unable to show that a group, as opposed to a collection of individuals, is involved, without demonstrating that the group exclusively occupied a definite territory for a long period of time. From the inception of the Commission, the testimony of anthropologists has been central to these determinations.

In many instances sharply differing interpretations have been given by the experts involved. Julian Steward related one such case:

> An important difference between witnesses concerning the nature of ac-culturation can be illustrated by the Northern Paiute case. Omer C. Stewart, witness for the Plaintiffs, assumed that territorial "bands" and "chiefs" men-tioned by recent informants and by certain early observers were aboriginal features which continued to exist long after White occupation of the area. I, representing the Government, interpreted the same evidence as indicating

that after horses were acquired predatory groups developed and lasted only during a brief phase of acculturation, when the native economy was changed by the presence of livestock and other foods that could be acquired through raiding. These bands had limited cohesion and transient membership, and they operated under "chiefs" whose function was to lead these forays. None of these functions had an aboriginal basis. The Northern Paiute case also illustrated the hopeless inadequacy of using "nation," "tribe," "band" and "chief" to convey any precise meaning [Steward 1955:298].

The legal meaning of such terms as "tribe" and "band" were so peculiar to many anthropologists that, as one writer put it: "When the ethnologist is asked whether a group in question is a fragment of a tribe he is not certain what is intended by these terms" (Lurie 1955:370). Yet the need to formulate more discriminating categories may have helped some scholars to rethink the categories they applied in their studies. Thus, Julian Steward implied that his own distinction between different kinds of bands—patrilineal hunting bands, composite hunting bands, and predatory bands—was further spurred by his involvement in Claims Commission proceedings (Steward 1955:295). Similarly, the question of Indian concepts and practices of property ownership sharpened Steward's conclusion that: "The plain fact is that anthropology has failed to come to grips with this crucially important problem of 'property' in detail and concreteness" (Steward 1955:293–294).

The experience of anthropologists testifying before the Indian Claims Commission marked the real beginning of anthropological expert testimony in this country, and the subsequent impact on the use of such testimony by the courts has been significant. Involvement in Claims Commission proceedings has not only served to educate many anthropologists in the nature of expert testimony but has served to educate courts and lawyers in the use and relevance of anthropological knowledge. Proceedings before the Commission provided support for a great deal of basic research in ethnography and ethnohistory, and provided scholars with "the opportunity and necessity for reappraisal of long-accepted technical and methodological approaches and consequent reaffirmation or abandonment of each of these" (Ray 1955:287). Such proceedings have also placed the anthropologist in a curious role because, as Steward noted: "He himself becomes 'evidence' in that his testimony is based to an incalculable extent upon his theory (explicit or implicit), his experiences among the people, his travels over the territory..." (Steward 1955:300–301). Whatever their impact on developing judicial concepts and doctrine, and whatever the merits of alternative modes of presenting their data to a legal proceeding, it is clear that participation in legal cases has had a reciprocal effect on anthropological thinking. A series of unrelated cases in which anthropologists have sought to apply their concept of culture to various legal cases illustrates this point even more sharply.

The Cultural Argument

Anthropologists are frequently called on to explain to a court of law certain aspects of the culture of those who have sought their help as expert witnesses. The cases, both civil and criminal, present problems of interpreting to the court the language and concepts of the party involved, and the relation between the legal issues posed and the relevance of anthropological findings. Working closely with counsel, anthropologists have also been instrumental in formulating highly creative arguments that may influence the course and result of a case.

Consider, for example, the case of *United States v. Diaz*. The defendant was charged with removing an Apache ceremonial mask from its resting place in a cave on the Indian reservation, in violation of a federal criminal statute forbidding interference with any "object of antiquity" situated on government-controlled lands. Since the mask was only a few years old, the defendant argued that it was not protected by the statute. The government, however, brought to the stand an anthropologist, Keith Basso, who testified that the mask was simply the most recent material vehicle for the perpetuation of a traditional ceremony, and that the "object of antiquity" to be preserved was the ancient ritual of which the mask was an indispensable part. The trial court accepted the argument and decided in favor of the Indians. However, the appellate court reversed this decision, stating that if a recently made artifact could qualify as an "object of antiquity," a person would be unable to know in advance which of his actions might subject him to a criminal penalty. Accordingly, the court held, the statute itself was unconstitutionally vague (United States Court of Appeals, Ninth Circuit 1974).

Similar cultural arguments have been made by several anthropologists involved in litigation surrounding the use of peyote by American Indians. Anthropologists not only appeared in court to explain the relation between peyote and the beliefs of the members of the Native American Church; they also made their views known to legislators working on the problem (La Barre et al. 1951). In time, the courts found that Indian peyotism is immune from governmental interference (United States Court of Appeals, Tenth Circuit 1959; California Supreme Court 1964), and special statutes were passed to protect these religious practices. Anthropological data have played a similar role in cases involving snake-handling cults (Tennessee Supreme Court 1975).

A more difficult issue is raised by attempts to argue that the social and cultural backgrounds of defendants are relevant considerations in a criminal proceeding. Some American courts have recognized that cultural factors may affect the ability of a person to form the intent necessary for criminal culpability or to control and direct his actions in an acceptable fashion (United States Court of Appeals, District of Columbia Circuit 1967:453). Various arguments have been put forth for a social defense similar to the insanity defense. As one commentor has put it:

> [T]he person whose criminal behavior is primarily engendered by poverty or persecution may be motivated by forces which are just as powerful and unrelenting as those which motivate the emotionally disturbed offender [Halleck 1967:211].

Several scholars have argued for the introduction to the law of a concept of "social incapacitation" based on social background (Shuman 1973:853–855; Walker 1969:288–290); others recommend that if extraneous social conditions — ghetto upbringing, a history of discrimination, etc. — are the proximate cause of a defendant's violent acts the jury should be instructed that it could find the defendant guilty of a less serious offense than that charged (Rafalko 1967:96–97). Data on social background are often considered by courts in determining an appropriate sentence (Connecticut Superior Court 1964:38).

Whatever the merits of these approaches, the proffered testimony of anthropologists on the social background of criminal defendants has largely been denied by the courts. For example, in *People v. Poddar*, the court refused to allow an anthropologist to testify on the direct consequences of the cultural background of an ex-untouchable from India charged with the murder of a Berkeley co-ed who had rejected him. The court said that the anthropologist could testify on the cross-cultural aspects of the case but that the testimony could not be directed toward the issue of diminished capacity since only a psychiatrist would be competent on that point (California Court of Appeal, First District, Division Four 1972:88). A similar case arose in *Chase v. United States*, in which a group of antiwar protestors who destroyed draft files argued that, insofar as they could not conform their actions to accepted standards and could not distinguish right from wrong in the same way as others in American society, they should be able to avail themselves of a defense of "cultural insanity." The court refused to allow an anthropologist to testify about the cultural relativity of insanity. In the court's words: "Defendants' proffered definition of insanity, whatever its anthropological or sociological validity, is not determinative of the issue of criminal responsibility" (United States Court of Appeals, Seventh Circuit 1972:149). In some situations and other countries, however, anthropological data have had significant impact on the outcome of murder trials involving "arctic hysteria," witchcraft murders, and the defense of provocation (Goldstein et al. 1974:985–998; Milner 1966).

The range of cases in which anthropologists have testified, or been prepared to testify, is practically as broad as the discipline itself. They have involved the impact of public works projects on ethnic communities (Aswad 1974), the social repercussions of severe facial injuries (Macgregor 1973), and the effect of decisions made by the Department of Defense on the people of Enewetak Atoll (Kiste 1976). Anthropologists are also becoming involved in environmental disputes, especially in the formulation of environmental impact statements under a law which instructs federal agencies to "utilize a systematic, interdisciplinary approach which will insure the integrated use of the natural and social sciences and the environmental design arts in planning and in decision-making which may have an impact on man's environment" (National Environmental Policy Act 1970, Section 4332 (A); Catalano et al. 1975). In all of these cases, as well as those reviewed earlier, common problems of relevancy, form, and ethical implications arise. Let us, then, return to the questions raised at the outset of this discussion and review them in the light of some of the cases mentioned.

Analyzing and Reforming Expert Testimony

Like many other kinds of expert witnesses, social scientists who have appeared in legal proceedings have been deeply troubled by the ethical implications of their work and alienated by some aspects of American trial procedure and tactics (Rose 1956; Wolfgang 1974). Many judges, lawyers, and legal scholars have also been critical of existing relations between expert testimony and the adversary system, and numerous suggestions have been made to reform the rules of evidence and procedure.

Different jurisdictions have the power to establish different rules, and attempts to adopt uniform rules of expert testimony have not succeeded (Travis 1974). Hence, it may be useful for the professions themselves to consider what standards of conduct they would regard as appropriate to expert testimony and to formulate approaches that judges, in their wide discretion on this matter, could adopt in their courtrooms. In time, these standards might also influence the development of formal legislation. The following discussion analyzes several aspects of the process of expert testimony as it applies to anthropologists and suggests certain reforms that could be made in the present system.

Adversary and Court-Appointed Experts

Perhaps the most troubling aspect of American legal procedures encountered by expert witnesses centers around the nature and rationale of the adversary system. Law, it has been said, is not history: one cannot hope to recapitulate on trial the precise occurrences on which a legal case is based. Therefore, the argument continues, one must rely on the parties who have a vested interest in the outcome to present a neutral court with evidence they consider necessary to their case, while the law must determine whether the relevant proofs offered achieve an appropriate level of persuasion. But as Judge Frankel has remarked, "we know that many of the rules and devices of adversary litigation as we conduct it are not geared for, but are often aptly suited to defeat, the development of the truth" (1975:1036). Despite their recognition of legitimate differences of interpretation, scholars appearing as expert witnesses often feel that courts should place less emphasis on trial gamesmanship and more on a sincere search for truth — even that truth which is not fully understood or unchanging.

A frequent suggestion made in this regard is that the law should rely mainly on court-appointed experts rather than experts presented by contending parties. This, it is argued, would have the advantage of decreasing the expert's tendency to be an advocate for one side and would increase the scientific stature of the expert's testimony. For some years, several New York courts have effectively utilized neutral medical experts chosen by local professional societies, and similar processes have been used in various European systems (Travis 1974; Anonymous 1961). Section 706 of the new Federal Rules of Evidence also permits court appointment of experts, a power courts have possessed though rarely exercised for many years (Sink 1956). Critics of the exclusive use of court-appointed experts point out that such a procedure would not lessen bias since the expert would represent only his own point of view or that of a single school of thought, and would be cloaked with a false air of neutrality (Diamond and Louisell 1965; Levy 1961). Similar failings have been noted by others studying the use of appointed experts in France, Germany, and Italy (Ploscowe 1935; Schroeder 1961).

Whether court-appointed experts would, as one lawyer contends (Griffin 1961), be less prone to mislead than adversary experts and whether they seldom represent schools of thought that are widely divergent are doubtful propositions in light of some of the cases reviewed. However, as will be discussed below, appropriate standards of professional conduct might alleviate these problems. For the moment, the question is not whether court-appointed experts should ever be used but under what circumstances and in what ways they might best be presented.

Many commentors have long been struck with the irony that, as Samuel Butler put it, "the public do not know enough to be experts, yet know enough to decide between them." Confronted with this seeming anomaly, Judge Learned Hand, at the turn of the century, said that what juries need is "a deliverance to them by some assisting judicial body of those general truths, applicable to the issue, which they may treat as final and decisive" (1901:55). Recalling early English practice, Hand suggested the use of a board of experts whose findings would be presented as evidence to a jury that could ignore it only at the risk of having the court dismiss their verdict as unsupported by the evidence (Hand 1901:56–57). Hand's proposal, which is of doubtful constitutional merit, never received support, but less categorical suggestions warrant closer attention. Court-appointed masters have long been used in complex commercial litigation. Where the evidence to be presented appears complicated, technical, or inadequate, the court may appoint a master to help with its finding of the facts. The use of masters has basically been limited to nonjury trials, but their use could be extended to any case involving social data. In such instances, they would primarily serve to simplify and hasten the trial by narrowing the issues involved, educating the court on extrinsic social facts, and investigating and reporting on matters to be considered on trial (Beuscher 1941; Anonymous 1948; Silberman 1975a, 1975b). This information could be used at the discretion of the courts, in addition to that supplied by adversary witnesses. Counsel on both sides would retain the right to cross-examine the court-appointed experts.[4]

Whenever one of the parties to a case indicates that social science data constitute an essential element of the evidence to be presented, and particularly when only one side intends to bring an expert anthropologist to the stand, the court should seriously consider the appointment of its own expert or master. It has been argued that the Federal Rules of Civil Procedure wisely leave disclosure of the expert's official status to the judge's discretion and refrain from requiring disclosure of his fee (Travis 1974:520). However, it might be more advisable for the court to indicate to the jury that the witness has been chosen, rather like a consulting physician, to give a second opinion on the issues, and that his status and payment in no way imply that he is more believable than experts presented by the adversary parties. Like all witnesses, the expert would be subject to full cross-examination by both sides after the presentation of his findings.

A final issue concerns the choice of court-appointed experts. The use of a standing panel of experts holds the risk of encouraging the development of an exclusive guild resistant to new approaches. This is particularly true if it is left to a professional association to choose the roster of experts (Wigmore 1914; Travis 1974). It would perhaps be wiser to encourage professional associations to prepare lists of all those persons — whether or not they belong to the association — who voluntarily ask to have their names placed on the roster of available expert witnesses. It would then remain the court's task to choose its own expert. The lists would aid courts and lawyers, who often do not know how to seek such expertise, in much the same way that lists of doctors and lawyers are made available to the residents of a community. No association should seek to certify or otherwise restrict access to the lists. They could, however, apprise those listed of the recommended standards of professional conduct adopted by their colleagues. These standards might include a recommendation that whenever an anthropologist consents to work on a case he or she should have an agreement with the attorneys that the court and opposing counsel will be apprised of the existence of such lists in the event that either chooses to seek additional expert witnesses.[5]

Pretrial Procedures

Once experts have been chosen, by the contending parties and/or the court, there are several pretrial procedures that could increase the quality and efficiency of the legal process. For example, it has been suggested that some form of pretrial conference be held in which all of the experts, representatives of the parties, and perhaps the presiding judge would be involved (Lurie 1955:360; Manners 1956; Ordover 1974b; Travis 1974; Wigmore 1974). The purpose would be to narrow factual issues, to allow the experts to confront one another directly and discuss the nature of their findings and opinions, and to permit the experts themselves to consider whether they wish to prepare a joint report to be filed with the court. Provided that counsel have agreed to such a conference, they should be barred from preventing the preparation of a joint statement of expert findings for presentation at the trial. The advantage to the lawyers of such a conference is that they would be able to prepare more fully for their respective cross-examinations. Moreover, counsel could be required to raise at that time all objections to the proferred testimony. These objections could be ruled on by the court prior to trial. This would not only speed the trial but lessen the interruptions and grandstanding by lawyers when the case comes to trial.

At the very least, there should be full discovery of all expert testimony well in advance of trial (cf. Friedenthal 1962). Following the lead of several jurisdictions, written reports, and even written depositions of pretrial direct testimony similar to that which will be repeated in court, should be made available to both sides and the court. Anthropologists should be encouraged by the recommended standards of professional conduct to insist that these reports or testimony include statements of experience, methods, data limitations, and theoretical foundations. A bibliography of works relied on should also be attached. Like the pretrial conference, this would afford anthropologists the opportunity to tell their full story, to consider each other's assertions, and to provide lawyers and judges with a better understanding of the nature of anthropological knowledge.

The Presentation of Expert Testimony

Usually, the testimony of an expert witness is conducted orally in open court, first through the direct examination of the attorney who has called the witness and then through the cross-examination of opposing counsel.[6] The judge may choose to ask questions of the witness but usually keeps them to a minimum. One of the problems with a question and answer format is that it may interfere with the expert's full explication of his findings and opinions, and may stifle the need to explain why qualified and limited assertions appropriate to much social scientific knowledge are nonetheless informative and important. It has been wisely suggested that experts be permitted to present their testimony in narrative form or to read from the stand all or part of the testimony entered in the record (Diamond and Louisell 1965:1345–1346; Ordover 1974a, 1974b; Wigmore 1914). If court procedures do not explicitly provide for such narrative testimony, the expert should, during preparation with counsel, require that ample opportunity be given on direct testimony to provide a full explanation of assertions before being turned over for cross-examination.

Moreover, the expert must utilize the opportunity to phrase testimony in terms that are no more definite than the data permit. As Marvin Wolfgang has said:

> Conditional clauses should be employed despite the fact that they are more vulnerable to cross-examination. Such words and phrases as "may," "probable," "other things being equal," "holding constant certain variables," and "associated" rather than "cause" are important verbal accouterments of the probabilistic language of science, and should not be neglected when presenting evidence in court [1974:245].

There should also be an understanding with counsel that witnesses will be able to explain in their own terms the research methods, forms of reasoning, data limitations, and contrary viewpoints surrounding their testimony.[7] As we have seen in several of the cases reviewed, neither opposing counsel nor the court can be relied on to be aware of these factors or to explore them adequately.

Finally, it is a common complaint of expert witnesses that they are asked questions that tend to distort or misconstrue the thrust of their testimony (Wolf 1976:112–113; Wolfgang 1974). Before leaving the stand, the court should ask the witness whether the points of his testimony have been adequately conveyed and whether he would like to make any final comments. This would afford the expert witness an opportunity to summarize his testimony without interfering with the right of counsel to present alternative conceptions of the testimony in their closing remarks. Wherever practicable, it might also be advantageous for the court to request that contending experts be brought to the stand soon after one another so that the judge or jury will have the earlier testimony fresh in mind.

The Role of Professional Associations

Early in this century, Lee M. Friedman, in a discussion of the reform of expert testimony, wrote: "The remedy is not in the enactment of any new statute. No act of the legislature will make witnesses learned or honest. The reform must come from the professions themselves . . ." (1910:252). Kenneth B. Clark, whose testimony played an important role in the desegregation cases, has also called for the establishment by professional societies of safeguards against the abuse of their position by social science expert witnesses (1953:9–10). And Judge Frankel has suggested that the ethical standards governing lawyers should not only command loyalty to and zeal for the client, but a positive obligation to aid in the search for truth (1975:1057–1059). Each of these assertions poses difficulties, while highlighting the roles that professional associations can take in restructuring expert testimony.

It is, I believe, valuable for anthropological associations to formulate standards that will help to guide those serving as expert witnesses. These standards should be posed as recommendations rather than as requirements, and should carry no sanctions of any sort. Some ethical issues confronting expert witnesses are already covered by existing ethical standards. Thus, the question of what should be done if one's pre-testimony research runs counter to the interests of those who have commissioned it is partially dealt with by the free publication standard of the American Anthropological Association's code of ethics.[8] More specific standards of good practice have been noted above. The point to be stressed here is simply this: As recommended and nonsanctioned standards develop, and as anthropologists begin to share with one another their experiences in courtroom situations, it is possible to have a substantial influence on changing legal procedures and on the ways in which social science will be used in legal proceedings. Without exaggerating their own importance to the final decisions, anthropologists, using their professional associations, can formulate guidelines that will aid their own constituents as well as the members of the legal profession.

Conclusion

The frequency with which anthropologists appear as expert witnesses is likely to increase in the coming years. Although the Indian Claims Commission will conclude its work in the foreseeable future, anthropologists will doubtless become more involved in environmental, familial, and race-related cases. All of the subfields of anthropology have been represented in such proceedings, but the lack of communication within and beyond anthropology has inhibited the recognition of common problems and the development of potential reforms. Whether anthropological testimony is central to a legal decision or serves to point out the inadequacy of causal assumptions underlying public policies, anthropology can both serve and benefit from appropriate involvement in the legal process.

Obviously, more is involved in such proceedings than the simple presentation of objective data. Difficult factual and ethical issues are also posed, and anthropologists who appear as expert witnesses may find in the courtroom, as they may earlier have found in the field, that their knowledge and commitments cannot be taken for granted. Carl Sandburg once remarked that "an expert is just a damned fool a long ways from home." Perhaps anthropologists in the courtroom can avoid this characterization by understanding the roles that their colleagues have played in similar proceedings and thinking carefully in advance about the nature and form of their contribution to the decision of legal cases.

Notes

Acknowledgments. This paper has profited greatly from the comments and experiences related to me by David Aberle, James A. Boon, Tamie Bryant, Paul Edson, John A. Hostetler, Robert C. Kiste, Elizabeth Loftus, Nancy O. Lurie, Frances C. Macgregor, and A. Kenneth Pye. Support for part of the research came from the Duke University Research Council. The opinions and interpretations expressed in this paper are the sole responsibility of the author, and do not necessarily represent those of the individuals, academic institutions, or legal aid groups with whom the author has been associated.

1. Redfield's actions off the witness stand also demonstrated his opposition to segregation in Texas. "The courtroom was integrated at the beginning," recalls Charles Thompson, who followed Redfield to the witness stand, "but then it began to get more crowded and the whites coming in later on couldn't find room. A big white policeman — this fellow must have been seven feet tall — came in and saw the whites standing against the wall and then started telling our people, 'Come on now, you know better than that.' It was a state court, remember, and so he began to segregate the audience to make room for the whites. But Dr. Redfield and the dean of Penn law school, they wouldn't move when the fellow told them to. They said they wanted to stay right where they were — with us" (Kluger 1976:266).

2. The intended reference in this last statement is to *high school* education. Personal communication from John Hostetler.

3. In fact, the Commission has tended to act more as a court than as a body which, because of its special status, could develop new principles that would be adopted by the appellate courts. Thus, anthropologists have not had an oppor-

tunity to help develop meaningful concepts of "fair and honorable dealings" with the Indians, although their testimony under other provisions of the Act has been more elaborate (See Lurie 1957.)

4. Another suggestion is that a public agency be created that would act as a depository for social and technological data. "Its mission would be to receive and catalogue social impact studies that qualify for judicial attention. The criteria for determining whether a study qualifies for approval would not be agreement or disagreement with its content or recommendations but only a finding that its design and methods fall within the range of accepted standards of scientific inquiry. These standards would be akin to 'standard accounting principles' in financial practice" (Rosenberg 1976:590; see also Anonymous 1948). The authors do not indicate how and by whom accepted standards of inquiry are to be applied in as interpretive a field as social science research.

5. Another issue concerning the impartiality of adversary witnesses is raised by the use of experts' contingent fees. Until recently, bar association rules have generally not permitted lawyers to pay fees to experts contingent on the outcome of the case. However, a federal court in New York has recently invalidated a bar association disciplinary rule to this effect. Such a rule, said the court, means that less affluent or indigent litigants do not have an opportunity equal to that of wealthier litigants to have a full hearing of their case. One cannot automatically assume, the court continued, that experts will bias their testimony because they have been hired on a contingent fee basis; a blanket rule barring such fees is too irrational to withstand constitutional inspection (United States District Court, Eastern District of New York 1976). In the light of this ruling, expert witnesses may want to draw more fully on some of the recommended standards described in this paper when entering into an agreement with the client and his attorney. [This decision was reversed by the appellate court, United States Court of Appeals, 2d Circuit, *Person v. Association of the Bar of the City of New York* (Federal Reporter, 2d Series 554:534–539, 1977). The decision, however, may be appealed to the U.S. Supreme Court. *Ed.*]

6. Expert witnesses have frequently cited, as one of the more annoying and demeaning aspects of their appearance in court, the challenge to their professional credentials by the cross-examining attorney. Cases could, however, be cited in which an ethnomusicologist testified in a child custody case, or a social scientist with a degree in "World Cultures" testified on the archaeological record of a California Indian tribe. Where a challenge to credentials is aimed at putting the witness in a defensive position or leading the witness to make more categorical assertions than might otherwise be made, it is incumbent on the court and the lawyers to gauge their response accordingly. It is, however, the primary responsibility of anthropologists to determine, when first approached, whether their knowledge is truly appropriate to the issue, and to refuse to participate whenever they feel that their studies and experience are not specifically applicable to the

case. Beyond this, anthropologists must recognize that litigants have every right to question the basis of experts' assertions.

7. On the expert's relation to the attorney, and general suggestions to lawyers and experts on the conduct of expert testimony, see Louisell (1955) and Rose (1956).

8. "An anthropologist should undertake no secret research or any research whose results cannot be freely derived and publicly reported" (American Anthropological Association 1973, Section 3[a]). On the problem of reporting contrary findings, see Wolfgang (1974:243). A federal court has recently held that in certain circumstances the research findings of a scholar who is not a party to the case are entitled to confidential status, and a court may not require the scholar to testify or produce documents concerning his research interviews (United States District Court, Northern District of California 1976; Anonymous 1976; Nejelski 1976).

References Cited

American Anthropological Association
1973 Professional Ethics: Statements and Procedures of the American Anthropological Association. Washington: American Anthropological Association.

Anonymous
1948 Social and Economic Facts—Appraisal of Suggested Techniques for Presenting Them to the Courts. Harvard Law Review 61:692–702.
1961 The Present Status of the Impartial Medical Expert in Civil Litigation. Temple Law Quarterly 34:476–486.
1976 U.S. Court Shields Data of Scholar. New York Times, p. 20, col. 8, 8 June.

Aswad, Barbara C.
1974 The Southeast Dearborn Arab Community Struggles for Survival against Urban "Renewal." In Arabic Speaking Communities in American Cities. Barbara C. Aswad, ed. Pp. 53–83. New York: Center for Migration Studies of New York.

Barksdale, Hiram C.
1957 The Use of Survey Research Findings as Legal Evidence. Pleasantville, New York: Printers' Ink Books.

Berger, Morroe
1957 Desegregation, Law and Social Science. Commentary 23: 471–477.

Beuscher, J. H.
1941 The Use of Experts by the Courts. Harvard Law Review 54:1105–1127.

Cahn, Edmond
1955 Jurisprudence. New York University Law Review 30:150–169.

California Court of Appeal, First District, Division Four

1972 People v. Poddar. California Reporter 103:84–93.

California Supreme Court

1964 People v. Woody. Pacific Reporter 394:813–822.

Catalano, Ralph, Steven J. Simmons, and Daniel Stokols

1975 Adding Social Science Knowledge to Environmental Decision Making. Natural Resources Lawyer 8:41–59.

Chein, Isador, et al.

1955 Appendix to Appellants' Briefs: Statements by Social Scientists. Social Problems 2:227–235.

Clark, Kenneth B.

1953 The Social Scientist as an Expert Witness in Civil Rights Litigation. Social Problems 1:5–10.

1959–60 The Desegregation Cases: Criticism of the Social Scientist's Role. Villanova Law Review 5:224–240.

1969 The Social Scientists, the Brown Decision, and Contemporary Confusion. In Argument: The Oral Argument before the Supreme Court in Brown v. Board of Education of Topeka, 1952–1955. Leon Friedman, ed. Pp. xxxi–l. New York: Chelsea House.

Connecticut Superior Court

1964 State v. Rodriguez. Atlantic Reporter 204:37–38.

Diamond, Bernard L., and David W. Louisell

1965 The Psychiatrist as an Expert Witness: Some Ruminations and Speculations. Michigan Law Review 63:1335–1354.

Federal Rules of Civil Procedure

1972 In United States Code Annotated, Title 28, Rule 26(b)(4). St. Paul: West.

Federal Rules of Evidence

1975 In United States Code Annotated, Title 28, St. Paul: West.

Frankel, Marvin E.

1975 The Search for Truth — An Umpireal View. University of Pennsylvania Law Review 123:1031–1059.

Friedenthal, Jack H.

1962 Discovery and Use of an Adverse Party's Expert Information. Stanford Law Review 14:455–488.

Friedman, Lee M.

1910 Expert Testimony, Its Abuses and Reformation. Yale Law Journal 19:247–257.

Friedman, Leon, ed.

1969 Argument: The Oral Argument before the Supreme Court in Brown v. Board of Education of Topeka, 1952–1955. New York: Chelsea House.

Garfinkel, Herbert

1959 Social Science Evidence and the School Segregation Cases. Journal of Politics 21:37–59.

Goldstein, Joseph, Alan M. Dershowitz, and Richard D. Schwartz
  1974 Criminal Law: Theory and Practice. New York: Free Press.
Greenberg, Jack
  1956 Social Scientists Take the Stand. Michigan Law Review 54:953–970.
Griffin, F. Hastings, Jr.
  1961 Impartial Medical Testimony: A Trial Lawyer in Favor. Temple Law Quarterly 34:402–415.
Halleck, Seymour L.
  1967 Psychiatry and the Dilemmas of Crime. New York: Harper and Row.
Hand, Learned
  1901 Historical and Practical Considerations Regarding Expert Testimony. Harvard Law Review 15:40–58.
Hostetler, John A.
  1968 Amish Society. Baltimore: Johns Hopkins Press.
  1970 Transcript of Testimony in Wisconsin v. Yoder. Wisconsin Circuit Court, Green County, Wisconsin. Mimeograph.
  1972 Dr. John A. Hostetler. Temple University News Release.
Indian Claims Commission
  1963 In United States Code Annotated, Title 25, Section 70. St. Paul: West.
Kiste, Robert C.
  1976 The People of Enewetak Atoll versus The U.S. Department of Defense. In Ethics and Anthropology: Dilemmas in Fieldwork. Michael A. Rynkiewich and James P. Spradley, eds. Pp. 61–80. New York: Wiley.
Kluger, Richard
  1976 Simple Justice: The History of Brown v. Board of Education and Black America's Struggle for Equality. New York: Knopf.
Kurland, Philip B., and Gerhard Casper, eds.
  1975a Landmark Briefs and Arguments of the Supreme Court of the United States: Constitutional Law. Vol. 64. Pp. 687–1007. Arlington, Virginia: University Publications of America.
  1975b Landmark Briefs and Arguments of the Supreme Court of the United States: Constitutional Law. Vol. 71. Pp. 803–826. Arlington, Virginia: University Publications of America.
La Barre, Weston, et al.
  1951 Statement on Peyote. Science 114:582–583.
Levin, Betsy, and Willis D. Hawley, eds.
  1975 The Courts, Social Science, and School Desegregation. Law and Contemporary Problems 39:1–432.
Levy, Elwood S.
  1961 Impartial Expert Testimony—Revisited. Temple Law Quarterly 34:416–451.
Louisell, David W.
  1955 The Psychologist in Today's Legal World. Minnesota Law Review 39:235–272.

Lurie, Nancy Oestreich
  1955 Problems, Opportunities, and Recommendations. Ethnohistory 2:357–375.
  1956 A Reply to: "The Land Claims Cases: Anthropologists in Conflict." Ethnohistory 3:72–81.
  1957 The Indian Claims Commission Act. The Annals of the American Academy of Political and Social Science 311:56–70.

Macgregor, Frances Cooke
  1973 Traumatic Facial Injuries and the Law: Some Social, Psychological, and Economic Ramifications. Trial Lawyers Quarterly 9:50–53.

Manners, Robert A.
  1956 The Land Claims Cases: Anthropologists in Conflict. Ethnohistory 3:72–81.

Maslow, Will
  1959–60 How Social Scientists Can Shape Legal Processes. Villanova Law Review 5:241–246.

Milner, Alan
  1966 M'Naghten and the Witch Doctor: Psychiatry and Crime in Africa. University of Pennsylvania Law Review 114:1134–1169.

National Environmental Policy Act
  1970 In United States Code Annotated, Title 42, Sections 4331–4335. St. Paul: West.

Nejelski, Paul, ed.
  1976 Social Research in Conflict with Law and Ethics. Cambridge, Massachusetts: Ballinger.

Ordover, Abraham P.
  1974a Use of Written Direct Testimony in Jury Trials: A Proposal. Hofstra Law Review 2:67–95.
  1974b Expert Testimony: A Proposed Code for New York. New York Law Forum 19:809–831.

Ploscowe, Morris
  1935 The Expert Witness in Criminal Cases in France, Germany, and Italy. Law and Contemporary Problems 2:504–509.

Rafalko, Walter A.
  1967 Sociological Evidence as a Criminal Defense. Criminal Law Quarterly 10:77–98.

Ray, Verne F.
  1955 Anthropology and Indian Claims Litigation: Introduction. Ethnohistory 2:287–291.

Redfield, Robert
  1963 The Social Uses of Social Science: The Papers of Robert Redfield, Vol. 2. Margaret Park Redfield, ed. Pp. 163–168. Chicago: University of Chicago Press.

Rose, Arnold M.
  1956 The Social Scientist as an Expert Witness. Minnesota Law Review 40:205–218.

Rosen, Paul L.
  1972 The Supreme Court and Social Science. Urbana: University of Illinois Press.

Rosenberg, Maurice
  1976 Anything Legislatures Can Do, Courts Can Do Better? American Bar Association Journal 62:587–590.

Rosenthal, Lloyd L.
  1935   The Development of the Use of Expert Testimony. Law and Contemporary Problems 2:403–418.
Sahlins, Marshall D.
  1968   Tribesmen. Englewood Cliffs: Prentice-Hall.
Schroeder, Horst
  1961   Problems Faced by the Impartial Expert Witness in Court: The Continental View. Temple Law Quarterly 34:378–385.
Shuman, S. I.
  1973   The Placebo Cure for Criminality. Wayne Law Review 19:847–872.
Silberman, Linda J.
  1975a   Masters and Magistrates. Part 1: The English Model. New York University Law Review 50:1070–1118.
  1975b   Masters and Magistrates. Part 2: The American Analogue. New York University Law Review 50:1297–1392.
Singer, Milton
  1968   The Concept of Culture. International Encyclopedia of the Social Sciences. Vol. 3, pp. 527–543. New York: Macmillan.
Sink, John M.
  1956   The Unused Power of a Federal Judge to Call His Own Expert Witness. Southern California Law Review 29:195–214.

Steward, Julian H.
  1955   Theory and Application in Social Science. Ethnohistory 2:292–302.
Suttles, Wayne
  1963   The Persistence of Intervillage Ties among the Coast Salish. Ethnology 2:512–525.
Tennessee Supreme Court
  1975   State ex rel. Swann v. Pack. South Western Reporter 527:99–114.
Travis, William J.
  1974   Impartial Testimony under the Federal Rules of Evidence: A French Perspective. International Lawyer 8:492–522.
United States Court of Appeals, District of Columbia Circuit
  1967   Washington v. United States. Federal Reporter, Second Series 390:444–462.
United States Court of Appeals, Ninth Circuit
  1974   United States v. Diaz. Federal Reporter, Second Series 499:113–115.
United States Court of Appeals, Seventh Circuit
  1972   Chase v. United States. Federal Reporter, Second Series 468:141–149.
United States Court of Appeals, Tenth Circuit
  1959   Native American Church v. Navajo Tribal Council. Federal Reporter, Second Series 272:131–135.

United States District Court, Eastern District of New York

  1976 Person v. Association of the Bar of the City of New York. Federal Supplement 414:139–144.

United States District Court, Northern District of California

  1976 Richards of Rockford, Inc. v. Pacific Gas and Electric Co. Federal Rules Decisions 71:388–391.

United States District Court, Western District of Pennsylvania

  1976 Rodgers v. United States Steel Corp. Federal Rules Decisions 70:639–648.

United States District Court, Western District of Washington

  1973 United States v. State of Washington, Transcript of Testimony. Mimeographed.

  1974 United States v. State of Washington. Federal Supplement 384:312–423.

United States Supreme Court

  1949 Briefs and Records, Sweatt v. Painter. Pp. 189–208. Washington, D.C.: United States Supreme Court.

  1950 Sweatt v. Painter. United States Reports 339:629–636.

  1954 Brown v. Board of Education. United States Reports 347:483–496.

1972 Wisconsin v. Yoder. United States Reports 405:205–249.

Van den Haag, Ernest

  1959–60 Social Science Testimony in Desegregation Cases—A Reply to Professor Kenneth Clark. Villanova Law Review 6:69–79.

Walker, Owen S.

  1969 Why Should Irresponsible Offenders be Excused? Journal of Philosophy 66:279–290.

Wigmore, John Henry

  1914 The Bill to Regulate Expert Testimony. Illinois Law Review 9:353–356.

Wisdom, John Minor

  1975 Random Remarks on the Role of Social Sciences in the Judicial Decision-Making Process in School Desegregation Cases. Law and Contemporary Problems 39:135–149.

Wolf, Eleanor P.

  1976 Social Science and the Courts: The Detroit Schools Case. The Public Interest 42:102–120.

Wolfgang, Marvin E.

  1974 The Social Scientist in Court. Journal of Criminal Law and Criminology 65:239–247.

Whatever Happened to the Id?

Melford E. Spiro

VOL. 81, 1979, 5–13

I had intended, when asked to prepare a paper on anthropology and psychoanalysis for this symposium, to write on the problem of hermeneutics, which I see as the important meeting ground for anthropological and psychoanalytic theorizing. Despite my intention, I have instead addressed an old war-horse, the relationship between nature and culture. I have chosen this subject because, in reviewing the literature on structural and symbolic anthropology in preparation for the hermeneutic paper, I came increasingly to realize that the received opinion in many quarters of cultural anthropology holds that the body, or its drives, or the affects and motives to which they give rise — but most especially those related to sex and aggression — are seldom the concern of cultural symbol systems. If the latter appear to be concerned with sex or aggression, it is the job of the anthropologist to uncover the reality behind the appearance. Although examples are abundant, I can here mention only a few.

I would instance, for example, Leach's contention (Leach 1967) that the denial of physiological paternity in Australia and parts of Melanesia, or the denial of a human genitor to Jesus in parts of Christendom, are statements not about biological sex but about rules of descent. Again, I would instance the contention of Mary Douglas that the (widely held) belief that males are endangered by the vagina and vaginal fluids is not a belief about the "actual relation of the sexes" but is, rather, a symbol of the hierarchical structure of the social system (Douglas 1966:4), or that rituals concerning excreta, breast milk, saliva, and other bodily emissions are concerned not with the body but with the "powers and dangers credited to the social structure," for which the body is a symbol (1966:

115); or that rituals of genital bleeding, such as subincision rites, are concerned not with sex, or blood, or the penis but with society; "What is being carved in human flesh [the penis] is an image of society," and when they are performed by tribes with moieties these genital mutilations "are concerned to create a symbol of the symmetry of the two halves of society" (1966:116).

Now, what is even more remarkable than the Leach-Douglas theory itself is that it is widely accepted as received anthropological wisdom. It is all the more remarkable because this counterintuitive theory is presented by its proponents as a self-evident truth requiring no support other than that of assertion. Consider the following examples, taken at random from Douglas. Item: the notion that beliefs concerning sexual pollution may actually be concerned with sexual pollution is simply "implausible" (1966:3). Item: "we cannot possibly" take rituals concerning excreta, milk, and the like to be in fact concerned with these bodily fluids and emissions (1966:115). Item: "I insist" that the seeming "obsession" of the Yurok with notions of pollution must be related to the "fluid formlessness" of their social structure (1966:127). That is all. No argument or evidence is offered in support of those contentions.

It used to be that one had to be a Freudian to believe that *non*sexual themes in ritual and myth might possibly be viewed as disguised expressions of sexual concerns. It now appears that only a Freudian might believe that *un*disguised sexual themes might be expressions of sexual concerns. And not only sexual. For the wide influence of Lévi-Strauss' theory of myth also suggests that only a Freudian might believe that explicitly aggressive themes in myth are really concerned with aggression. Indeed, it was my recent reading of that marvelous book *The Raw and the Cooked* that finally stimulated me to change the topic of this paper from hermeneutics to the cultural relevance of sex and aggression. Since, however, I have dealt elsewhere (Spiro 1968a, b) with the Leach-Douglas denial of sex as a relevant variable in belief systems, I shall concentrate here on Lévi-Strauss' denial of aggression in myth.

Although most readers will doubtless recall the Bororo myth (Lévi-Strauss 1969:35–37) that constitutes the key text for *The Raw and the Cooked*, I shall briefly summarize it. One day, when the women went into the forest to gather palms, a certain youth secretly followed his mother and raped her. Discerning what had happened, and "anxious to avenge himself," the youth's father sent his son on a series of dangerous undertakings intended to cause his death, but the son repeatedly eluded the traps (with the assistance of helpful animals). Finally, the father acted more directly. After ordering his son to climb to the top of a cliff to capture some birds, he overturned the pole by which the son had ascended, abandoning him to death. After many tribulations, the son managed, however, to return to the village. One day, when his father was hunting, the son, "full of thoughts of revenge," saw his opportunity. Donning some false antlers and transforming himself into a deer, he "rushed at this father with such ferocity that he impaled him on the horns." He then galloped to a lake inhabited by carnivorous fish, and dropped his father into the lake, where he was devoured by the fish. Returning to the village, the son then "took his revenge" on his father's wives, including his mother. (We are not told what form the "revenge" took, and we can only guess that it was either rape or murder.)

According to Lévi-Strauss, that myth, the central text of the book, is an etiological myth that explains the origin of cooked food. Conceding that "to all intents and purposes" that theme appears to be absent from the myth, Lévi-Strauss contends (1969:64) that it is nevertheless "concealed" in it, and in a remarkable *tour de force*, combining staggering erudition with astonishing brilliance, he attempts in the remaining 300 pages of his book to demonstrate the truth of this startling interpretation. Briefly, since an older version of this myth ends with the son's declaring that he will take revenge on the entire clan of his father by sending cold, wind, and rain, this indicates, so Lévi-Strauss claims, that on its surface the myth deals with the origin of storms and rain.[1] On the premise, then, that water is (on a number of dimensions) the inversion of fire, he then proceeds to show, by means of a succession of complex and ingenious structural analyses of a corpus of South American myths, that this Bororo myth can be interpreted as a transformation by inversion of a set of Ge myths that explicitly explain the origin of cooking fire.

Now, even granting the validity of that transformational hypothesis,[2] I would nevertheless have thought that violent Oedipal conflict was the central theme of a myth that begins with a son's raping his mother, continues with the father's numerous attempts to kill the son, proceeds to the son's brutally killing his father, and ends with his killing or raping (depending on correct interpretation of the ambiguous term "revenge") his mother and stepmothers. That its central theme is taken instead to be the origin either of cooking fire or of rain — even granting that an etiological theme is one of its elements — is surely a remarkable reversal of figure and ground.[3] At least it seems to be remarkable until one comes to realize that the code constructed[4] by Lévi-Strauss for the translation of these myths precludes the possibility that violence of any kind might be taken as a mythic concern; instead, the code converts all acts of violence into metaphors for nonviolent social structural relationships.

Take, for example, the son's rape of his mother. In the first step in code switching, that episode is classified by Lévi-Strauss as "incest," i.e., its sexual dimension remains but its violence dimension disappears. In the second step the sexual dimension also disappears, for "incest" becomes a metaphor — *voila!* — for the boy's dependent attachment to his mother. Thus, since the palms collected by the women in the myth are of the type used for penis sheaths, that signifies that the son had reached the age of initiation, when boys are expected to transfer from their mother's hut to the men's house. In such a sociocultural context, the mother-son "incest" (the code word for the boy's rape of his mother) signifies the son's objection to the "loosening of the maternal bonds" and his "return to the mother's bosom at a time when other sons are about to be weaned for good" (1969:56).

As if to emphasize that this translation is not a structuralist spoof, Lévi-Strauss clinches his argument with the following *pièce de résistance.* Since the adult hero of a cognate myth, the putative homologue of the boy in the present myth, is nicknamed "Secluded," and since, by structuralist assumptions, the boy can be assumed to have had the same nickname, and since a secluded boy in the sociocultural context alluded to above is one who "refuses to be separated from female society," it follows that the son is "the sort of boy who, as we say, 'clings to his mother's apron strings'" (1969:57).

And what about the behavior of the boy's parents? By a similar technique of code switching, the violent acts in which the mother and father are respectively involved with their son signify the polar differences in their "attitudes" toward him. Thus, having classified the son's rape of his mother as incest, the mother's "incestuous" relationship with the son is taken to be indexical of her "close" attitude to the son, while the father's "murderous" relationship is indexical of his "remote" attitude to him (1969:138–139).

Thus it is that, by the alchemy of code switching, aggression is simply abolished as a mythic category: the son's sexual assault on his mother is transmuted into his dependency upon her, while the mother's victimization by the son's assault as well as the father's assaults upon the son are transmuted into positions on a scale of psychological distance from the son.

Lest I be misunderstood, I hasten to emphasize that I am not unmindful of the fact that Lévi-Strauss is not so much interested in the content of myths, per se, as in their logical structure — "the system of interrelationships to which we reduce them" (1969:12) — and that, since that aim is achieved by the structural comparisons of a large corpus of myths, it must be pursued by means of a code whose concepts are sufficiently abstract to subsume the concrete concepts of the codes employed by the myths themselves. Since, however, his code consists not of the formal and content-free symbols of mathematics and symbolic logic, but of concepts only slightly more abstract than those of the myths he analyzes, the fact that Lévi-Strauss chooses concepts that systematically eliminate every theme of violence from these myths indicates that this consequence is principled rather than fortuitous. An excellent case in point is the conversion of rape ("incest") and murder in the Bororo myth into the attitudes "close" and "remote."

The attitudes "close" and "remote" are attributed to the parents in the Bororo myth in order to show that "family attitudes" is one variable in a set of variables by which this myth can be inferred to be the inversion (and hence the transform) of the Ge myth. In the latter myth, a young boy who is left by his brother-in-law to die in the wilderness is rescued by a jaguar, who then brings him to his own home (thereby becoming his "adopted father"). The jaguar's wife (therefore, the boy's "adopted mother") dislikes the boy and tries to kill him, but, encouraged by the jaguar, the boy kills her instead. As Lévi-Strauss sees it, the parental attitudes exhibited in the Bororo myth are an inversion of those exhibited in the Ge myth: in the former the mother is "close" and the father "remote," whereas in the latter the father is "close" and the mother "remote." The dimension close/remote is a perfectly good dimension for describing attitudes, but there are at least three reasons for rejecting the assumption that this is the dimension along which the opposite-sex parents in these myths sustain the logical relation of binary opposition within each myth and that of identity across the myths.

(a) That the attitudes of the (adopted) Ge parents toward their son exhibit a relation of binary opposition is self-evident: the father saves the boy's life, while the mother attempts to kill him. Nevertheless, even on the dubious assumption that "close" is an appropriate term to character-

ize the attitude expressed in a father's rescue of a son's life, to characterize as "remote" the attitude expressed in a mother's attempt to kill her
son is surely to distort the meaning of the text beyond recognition.
These designations not only distort the meaning of the text but are not
necessary in order to show the binary opposition in the parents' attitudes. Thus, for example, the dimension life-giving/life-destroying (or
some such terms) is not only faithful to the text but denotes much more
effectively the relation of opposition that characterizes the attitudes of
the Ge father and mother to their son.

(b) The dimension close/remote is even less applicable to the Bororo
parents than to the Ge parents. If "remote," which converts lethal intentions into indifference, is an inappropriate designation for the murderous father, "close" is entirely misplaced when applied to the mother.
For, whether we remain faithful to the text (and describe the mother as
the victim of her son's rapacious assault) or distort the text (and describe
her as the object of the son's "incest"), how can the attitude "close" or
any other attitude be applied either to an *involuntary victim* (rape) or a
passive object (incest)? If, nevertheless, the close/remote dimension is still
held to be applicable to the mother, I would have thought that "remote"
would be the more appropriate term because, presumably, one is raped
only after resisting (= "remote") seduction. But if the mother is "remote," the Bororo parents cannot be contrasted along the close/remote
dimension unless we are prepared to designate the father as "close."
Rejecting such sophistry, a relation of binary opposition can be validly
attributed to the Bororo parents only by comparing them (as I suggested
in the case of the Ge parents) along some dimension that is faithful to the
violent themes of the myth itself. That can be done in one of two ways.
Restricting the comparison to the episodes described in the myth, we
can draw a contrast between the mother, as the *victim* of violent (sexual)
assaults *by* her son, and the father, as the *agent* of violent assaults *on* his
son. Or, going beyond the episodes described in the myth, we can contrast the parents along the same dimension employed in characterizing
the Ge parents: the mother (having borne the son) is life-giving and the
father (being murderous) is life-destroying. From a structuralist point of
view, and consistent with Lévi-Strauss' aim of showing that the Bororo
myth is a transform of the Ge, that has the additional advantage of
demonstrating that the attitudes of the parents in the Bororo myth are
an inversion of those exhibited by the parents in the Ge myth.

(c) Contrary to Lévi-Strauss, a comparative analysis of the two myths does not permit the conclusion that the Bororo mother and Ge father sustain the logical relation of identity on the close/remote dimension. For, even granting the dubious classification of incestuous rape as "incest," by what logical criterion is the attitude "close" attributed both to a *passive object* of incest (the Bororo mother) and an *active agent* of nurturance (the Ge father)? If, moreover, the classification of incestuous rape as "incest" is invalid (as I deem it to be), the attribution of an identity relation to the Bororo mother and Ge father would seem to be fallacious. How can the same attitude ("close") be attributed to two parents of which one is the victim of a son's rapacious assault and the other a protector of the son against assault? On either account, when they are compared with respect to the close/remote dimension, it must be concluded that, rather than sustaining a relation of identity, the relation of the Bororo mother and Ge father is one of binary opposition. If they are to be attributed instead with a relation of identity — and if, therefore, the parents of the Bororo myth are to be seen as an inversion of those in the Ge myth — that can only be accomplished by concepts that are faithful to the violent themes found in these myths. Thus, for example, use of the dimension violent/nonviolent (restricting the comparisons to the episodes described in the myths themselves) or the dimension life-giving/life-destroying (going beyond the episodes described in the myths) makes it apparent that the opposite-sex parents sustain a relation of binary opposition within the myths and one of identity across the myths; hence, the relation of the parents in the Bororo myth is an inversion of that of the parents of the Ge myth.

By this time the reader may be wondering why I stated at the outset that I had changed my topic from hermeneutics to the relationship between nature and culture when, thus far, this paper has been devoted entirely to the interpretation of cultural symbol systems. The paradox is more apparent than real, however. It should be evident by now that the two codes examined (one that systematically and totally denies that sex and aggression in ritual and myth really signify sex and aggression and one that allows that they may indeed signify sex and aggression) may seem to differ in hermeneutic assumptions about the role of metaphor in cultural symbol systems, but actually differ in psychological assumptions about the importance of sex and aggression in human nature following the transition to culture.

What might be the assumptions of a code that interprets the Bororo myth (which on its surface explains why it is that a boy became a vicious parricide) to be an origin myth, whether of cooking or of rain, a code by which a boy's rape of his mother signifies his dependent attachment to her, the mother's being the victim of his rape signifies her close attitude to him, and the father's attempts to murder his son signify his (the father's) remote attitude to him? Such a code, I would suggest, can be based only on an assumption that, in a state of culture, aggressive motives of this type are either transcended or markedly muted so that they cannot possibly be the real concern of myths.[5] Hence it is that, if aggression seems to be the dominant theme of the Bororo myth, its aggressive episodes must be interpreted to mean something other than (if not the very opposite of) what they seem to mean.

In making this suggestion, I am aware, of course, that Lévi-Strauss contends (1969:12) that his interpretations of myths refer to their "unconscious formulations." That contention, however, does not affect the validity of my suggestion, because, for Lévi-Strauss, the "unconscious" meaning of a myth or a mythic episode is not its trivial meaning, but its most fundamental meaning. Hence, when he interprets a myth of Oedipal violence as (unconsciously) signifying the origin of cooking fire, he is not making the trivial claim that the latter element is also to be found in the myth; rather, he is making the important claim that this myth, which *seems* to be about violence, is *really* about something else. Consider, then, that in Lévi-Strauss' code, aggression is systematically and gratuitously precluded as the (unconscious) meaning of any of the violent episodes in these myths. Consider, too, that alternative codes (such as those suggested above), whose (unconscious) interpretations are faithful to the violent content of the myths, achieve the aims of structural analysis without the dubious logic and textual distortions often required by Lévi-Strauss' interpretations. Consider, also, that for Lévi-Strauss, their unconscious meanings are the fundamental meanings of myths. Considering all of this, it seems reasonable to conclude that Lévi-Strauss' elimination of violence as a mythic category, although applying to the unconscious meaning of myths, is based on the assumption that violent motives of the type exhibited in the Bororo and Ge myths cannot be their *real* concern.

That conclusion is supported by his contention (1969:164) — although he attributes the notion to native thought — that cooking marks the transition from nature to culture and that the Bororo myth therefore explains the origin not merely of cooking but also (and by that very same fact) of culture. That is not only, he argues, because of the analogy raw:cooked::nature:culture but also because in the Ge myths both useful and ornamental objects are manufactured from the inedible parts of the cooked plants and animals. That he, therefore, interprets all of the aggressive episodes in the Bororo myth metaphorically suggests that this exegetical maneuver is a solution to a painful dilemma. It is as if he were saying that, if this myth is really concerned with filial rape, parricide, and filicide, the origin of cooking cannot represent the transition to culture, because aggressive motives of this kind, although found perhaps in a state of nature, cannot possibly persist in a state of culture; but, on the other hand, if this myth does not explain the origin of cooking, and if cooking does not represent the transition to culture, the entire argument of the book would collapse. It is this dilemma that is resolved by a code that interprets all aggression in the myth as metaphoric.

It will come as no surprise — turning finally to the psychoanalytic dimension of this paper — that the assumptions of Freud concerning the relationship between aggression and culture are the polar opposite of those of Lévi-Strauss. In Freud's view, aggressive motives are as strong in a state of culture as in a state of nature. Given that assumption, the themes of parricide, filicide, and the like, although *really* signifying parricide and filicide, would not in themselves disqualify the Bororo myth from being interpreted by Freud as a myth of the origin of culture. Nevertheless, even granting that this myth explains the origin of cooking fire, Freud would never agree that it depicts the origin of culture, as can easily be seen from even a cursory glance at Freud's own origin myth. That myth (Freud 1971a), although remarkably similar to the Bororo myth (both are concerned with violent conflict between father and son over the sexual possession of the wife-mother), is its structural inversion. In Freud's myth (which, however, he took to be history), the sons desire the father's wives, and since he will not share them, the sons kill the father in order to take possession of them. Following their parricide, however, the sons experience feelings of remorse that lead them to atone for their deed by renouncing their claims on the women and to institute prohibitions against future parricide, fratricide, and incest.

For Freud, then, it is not the acquisition of cooking fire, nor even the manufacture of useful and ornamental objects attendant upon the cooking of food, that marks the transition from nature to culture, but the institution of norms for the control and regulation of aggression (first, within the sibling-group and subsequently to increasingly larger groups). For Freud, moreover, the transition to culture does not mean the transcendence of nature. Hence, although aggressive behavior, regulated as it is by cultural norms, may be inhibited in a state of culture, aggressive motives are not extinguished. Indeed, it is precisely because these motives (including parricide and filicide) persist in and are even exacerbated by culture (Freud 1971b) that the existence of norms for their regulation is a necessary condition for the existence of culture. Necessary, although not sufficient. For, as Freud views it, it is the internalization of these norms (as a result of the infant's prolonged attachment to nurturant parenting figures) that produces the moral anxiety and guilt that, by inhibiting expression of aggressive motives, preclude the return to a state of nature.[6]

We can now see why Freud would never characterize the Bororo myth as marking the transition from nature to culture — not because the son desired his mother, or the father wished to kill his son, or the son wished to kill his father, nor even because they acted upon their wishes, but because they experienced neither moral anxiety about their desires nor guilt about their deeds.[7] Since absence of anxiety and guilt implies an absence of cultural norms prohibiting aggressive behavior, in Freud's view this myth could not possibly represent a transition from nature to culture, even if it were granted that it represents the origin of cooking.

For Freud this myth would, however, represent something else. Holding that the transition to culture, although marking the control of aggressive behavior, does not mark the disappearance of aggressive affects and motives, Freud assumed that aggression is a matter of important concern to social actors in a state of culture. And since, so he further assumed, their important concerns are inevitably represented in their fantasies — the privately constituted fantasy of dreams and the culturally constituted fantasy of myth and religion — it follows that the manifestly aggressive themes in the Bororo myth, like the manifestly sexual themes in the rituals and beliefs analyzed by Leach and Douglas, are just that: aggressive and sexual themes. In short, for Freud, the myths, rituals, and beliefs discussed in this paper are concerned with those very sexual and aggressive wishes and fears that these anthropologists and their many followers, denying that they are of concern to cultural symbol systems, interpret out of existence. It is rather startling that this simpleminded view (which, of course, is hardly original with Freud or restricted to Freudians) must be reiterated to an anthropological audience in 1977.

Notes

Acknowledgments. This paper was prepared for, and a shorter version was read at, the 1977 annual meetings of the American Anthropological Association, as a part of a symposium entitled "Psychological Anthropology: a Perennial Frontier?" organized by Professor Theodore Schwartz. The preparation of this paper was assisted by a grant from the National Institute of Mental Health.

1. In fact, the text itself does not support that contention. When the son, following abandonment by his father, returns to the village, he reveals his identity to his grandmother (who had consistently befriended him against his father), and on that night there occurred a "violent wind, accompanied by a thunder storm which put out all the fires in the village except the grandmother's" (Lévi-Strauss 1969:36). Now, if wind and thunderstorm already occur in the *middle* of the myth (and their occurrence is not attributed to the boy's creation), it is difficult to understand how the older version, which *ends* with the boy taking his revenge by sending cold and rain, can be interpreted as their origin. This would seem to signify, rather, that the boy had the power to control the rains, not that this was their origin. Implicitly aware of this criticism, Lévi-Strauss defends his interpretation by noting (1969:137) that (in their commentary) the collectors of the myth state that the natives themselves claim that the rain that falls in the middle of the myth was the origin of rain. This hardly proves, however, that the origin of rain is the central concern of this myth.

Indeed, to the extent that the text itself has any etiological reference, it has to do with the origin of a certain type of aquatic plant. Thus, after the boy's father was devoured by the carnivorous fish, "All that remained," the text continues, "were the bare bones which lay on the bottom of the lake, and the lungs which floated on the surface in the form of aquatic plants, whose leaves, it is said, resemble lungs" (1969:37).

2. If, as I suggest in the note above, the Bororo myth is not concerned with the origin of rain, the transformational hypothesis is invalid, since it rests on a set of putative structural relationships that obtain between fire and water (rain). Lévi-Strauss, perhaps anticipating this problem, contends (1969:137) that, even without the transformational argument, the Bororo myth in itself can be seen as dealing with the origin of fire. Since the storm extinguished all the fires in the village except that of the boy's grandmother, the boy "becomes the master of fire, and all the inhabitants of the village must apply to him to obtain firebrands with which to kindle the lost fire. In this sense the Bororo myth also relates to the origin of fire, but by a process of omission." That interpretation seems to be adventitious, however, because, even assuming that the boy was living with his grandmother, there is no indication that the villagers applied to him for fire, rather than to his grandmother; indeed, since he was still uninitiated, the former hypothesis would seem unlikely. Nevertheless, fifty pages later, Lévi-Strauss escalates his claim: "The Bororo myth creates water in order to destroy fire

or, more precisely, to allow the hero [the boy] to become the master of fire" (1969:188).

3. It is remarkable for at least three reasons. First, the occurrence of the rain is a minor (two-line) episode in a very long myth concerned primarily with the relationship between the boy and his parents. Second, even if we accept that the natives say that the rain in the myth was the origin of rain, the commentators do not contend that they take the myth to have an etiological aim. Third, even the *pro forma* "And this is the origin of x" (often appended to a myth as a device for attributing didactic inport to an otherwise nondidactive narrative) is not found in this case.

4. I say "constructed" because it is important to emphasize that this code is not discovered by structural analysis of the myths but is an invention of Lévi-Strauss. Although clearly ambivalent about the issue, Lévi-Strauss admits that this may be so. Thus, in addressing the problem, he begins by claiming that his code "has neither been invented nor brought in from without. It is inherent in mythology itself, where we simply discover its presence" (1969:12). (That is reminiscent of Michelangelo's modest claim that, rather than creating a sculpture *ex nihilo*, he merely reveals the sculpture that is inherent in the uncarved marble — which, of course, is true, except that for *n* sculptors there are *n* sculptures inherent in the marble.) In a later passage, however, Lévi-Strauss concedes that that may not be the case: "It is in the last resort immaterial whether in this book the thought processes of the South American Indians take shape through the medium of my thought, or whether mine take place through the medium of theirs" (1969:13).

5. The same assumption underlies Douglas' (though not necessarily Leach's) elimination of sex as a concern of cultural belief systems.

6. That Freud is the (unacknowledged) spiritual descendant of Hobbes, just as Lévi-Strauss is the (acknowledged) spiritual descendant of Rousseau, would seem to be obvious. Freud differs from Hobbes in that the latter believed that the physical authority of the state is necessary to assure compliance with the cultural prohibition on aggression, while Freud believed that the key to the problem is the moral authority of the parents, internalized as the superego and reflected in moral anxiety and guilt.

7. Indeed, rather than experiencing guilt and, thereby, atoning for killing his father by renouncing his claims on his mother and stepmothers, the son continues to take his "revenge" on them.

References Cited

Douglas, Mary
    1966 Purity and Danger. New York: Praeger.

Freud, Sigmund
    1971a Totem and Taboo. *In* The Standard Edition of the Com-

plete Psychological Works of Sigmund Freud, Vol. 13. London: Hogarth Press.

1971b Civilization and Its Discontents. *In* The Standard Edition of the Complete Psychological Works of Sigmund Freud, Vol. 21. London: Hogarth Press.

Leach, Edmund

1967 Virgin Birth. Proceedings of the Royal Anthropological Institute for 1966:39–49.

Lévi-Strauss, Claude

1969 The Raw and the Cooked. New York: Harper and Row.

Spiro, Melford E.

1968a *Review* of Purity and Danger. American Anthropologist 70: 391–393.

1968b Virgin Birth, Parthenogenesis, and Physiological Paternity. Man 3:224–261.

Linguistic Knowledge and Cultural Knowledge:

Some Doubts and Speculations

Roger M. Keesing

VOL. 81, 1979, 14–36

Introduction

Several years ago, I argued that a cognitive anthropology that looked to linguistics for methods and models had been left behind by advances in the formal theory of grammar (1972b). The intervening years have seen both a disintegration of the several post-Chomskyan orthodoxies in grammatical theory and a resurgence of linguistic anthropology. The time has come, I think, to turn the argument around: to suggest that some of the difficulties that beset grammatical theory derive from trying to analyze native speakers' linguistic knowledge as a self-contained system. I will argue that this has obscured the ways in which language rests on and draws on cultural premises about the world in which speech takes place. The cognitive economies that make linguistic communication possible rest on what native speakers know about their world, which they need not then encode directly in utterances. Languages viewed as formal systems, sentences viewed as formal objects, are cut off from these cultural takens-for-granted, which consequently remain hidden and unanalyzed.

I will suggest that attempts by linguists to distinguish native speakers' knowledge of their language from their "knowledge of the world" have too often been based on narrow heuristic strategies rather than principled, cognitively and epistemologically salient distinctions; that they obscure the nature of cultural "knowledge of the world" in treating it as residual and unstructured; and that in so doing they render opaque some of the very linguistic facts that are supposed to be rendered manageable. The illusion that linguistic knowledge can be analyzed as a separate formal system can be sustained most easily if the linguist analyzes a European language: the linguist takes most of the same things for granted as the users of that language, and hence need not render them explicit. And the illusion is most effectively dispelled by examining a language spoken in a very different kind of world.

Using data from the Kwaio of Malaita, Solomon Islands, I will show how a speaker's knowledge of his/her language is contingent on and takes for granted a culturally defined model of the universe. I will show first how, in the realm of lexical semantics, the meanings of lexical items rest on cultural assumptions and symbolic structures in subtle but crucial ways, such that the lexical representations conventional in linguistics became deeply problematic. I will suggest further, using Kwaio examples, that when linguists have explored the "pragmatic" aspects of using and understanding sentences, they have often had too limited a view of how cultural models of the universe in which speech takes place infuse and support language, and too undifferentiated a view of nonlinguistic knowledge. Finally, I will illustrate with Kwaio examples how insufficient appreciation of the range of cultural variation in the uses of speech foils incorporation of the illocutionary force of language into syntactic theory in attempts to extend the philosophical theory of speech acts.

None of the points I will make is radically new and revolutionary. Most of them may seem obvious to anthropologists, working as they do on the "messy" side of the language/culture boundary that linguists avoid as best they can. Linguists, too, may feel that they have taken all this into account.[1] But linguists, I suggest, still have much to learn about cultural analysis, despite the impressive incursions some have made into traditionally anthropological territory; and most anthropologists, despite progress along the border in recent years, are still insufficiently aware of the anthropological implications of contemporary linguistics. The risk of saying the obvious seems well worth taking.

Linguistic Knowledge and Cultural Knowledge: Conceptual Preliminaries

Let me clarify my biases on three conceptual issues, to make clear what I am *not* saying. First, I use the term "culture" in a cognitive sense (Keesing 1974): "a culture" is in this view a system of *knowledge*, a composite of the cognitive systems more or less shared by members of a society. It is not, in this view, a way of life; it is not a system of behavior. Linguistic knowledge is thus *part of*, and on the same epistemological plane as, cultural knowledge (Keesing 1972b, 1974). My questions about the lan-

guage/culture boundary are thus questions about the compartmentalization of one subsystem of knowledge, linguistic knowledge, from other
subsystems.

Second, my references to cultural variations in cosmological premises
do not imply a strong Whorfian argument or any contention that the
thought-worlds of non-Western people are radically diverse. I have in
recent years argued (Keesing 1972b, 1974) that the diversity of thought-
worlds in alien cultures has been greatly exaggerated, and that substantial
universal cognitive structures very probably underlie cultural variations.
I will suggest, however, that these variations may have implications for
linguistics that have not been sufficiently appreciated.

Third, my argument will *not* be the one familiar from the literature of
"ethnoscience" or ethnographic semantics — that the lexically labeled
chunks into which a people segment their physical and social environment reveal the unique structure of their perceptual and conceptual
world. It is probably true that the "things" a language labels are the
things — or some of the things — that its speakers treat as distinct and
culturally salient. But that seems to me to be a trivial and even vacuous
sense in which semantic systems are articulated with other realms of
cultural knowledge.

My view of culture is explicated in some detail in the latter sections of
Keesing (1974). It will be worth recapitulating that position briefly, since
I will build on it in the sections to follow. First, since culture consists of
knowledge (implicit and explicit, unconscious and conscious), its loci are
the minds/brains of individuals (cf. Geertz 1973). At the same time,
cultural knowledge is distributed and transmitted within *communities* and
hence must be learnable and broadly shared, although individuals command variant and partial versions of the community's pool of knowledge.
Cultural knowledge consists of conceptions, implicit and explicit, of
"what is, . . . what can be, . . . how one feels about it, . . . what to do about
it, . . . and how to go about doing it" (Goodenough 1961:522): theories
about the world and the way it is viewed and acted in by members of
one's community.

Cultural knowledge is organized hierarchically, including specific
routines and understandings appropriate to particular contexts and more
general conceptions and assumptions about the social and natural world.
In addition to the intricate hierarchical structuring of cultural knowledge, whose organization has barely been glimpsed, there is strong evidence of a specialization into partly separate subsystems. Our linguistic

faculties seem, on the basis of considerable neurological and cognitive evidence, to constitute one such subsystem. But there is, I believe, considerable crossover between these subsystems. One mode of such crossover is the hierarchical application of more general premises to constrain and render economic the storage, retrieval, and manipulation of specific information in partly specialized subsystems. It is such crossovers in the realm of language that I shall explore.

Linguistic Knowledge and "Knowledge of the World"

One of the major themes in recent linguistics has been a steady expansion in the realm with which linguists are concerned. A recent observation by George Lakoff makes the point well:

> one cannot just set up artificial boundaries and rule out of the study of language such things as human reasoning, context, social interaction, deixis, fuzziness, sarcasm, fragments, variations among speakers, etc. Each time we have set an artificial boundary, we have found some phenomenon that shows that it has to be removed. That is not to say that there are no bounds . . . [to] linguistics, . . . only that . . . the boundaries are disappearing daily (1974a:xi–40).

Although the realm of syntax once seemed relatively self-contained, it has become evident that presuppositions about world-states implied within sentences must be taken into account, along with other considerations that once seemed far from the realm of language. Lexical semantics and particularly sentence semantics have required more and more references to the sociolinguistic contexts of language use.

Lakoff and most of his colleagues, however, hope or assume that information about cultural and sociolinguistic conventions required to interpret grammatical patterns can be incorporated by stretching formal grammatical theory. Thus Lakoff, in discussing rules of "conversational implicature" that would "vary from culture to culture," notes that "there are culture-specific assumptions that have to be characterized in order to understand various aspects of speech acts in a given culture." But, he goes on to observe, "cultural assumptions play the same role in semantic entailment as any other assumptions," so that "we need [not] . . . go beyond the resources of formal semantics to provide an account of speech acts" (Lakoff 1974b:X, 20–21).

In another recent paper (1971), Lakoff argues that the widening of grammatical theory to incorporate, for example, the speaker's assumptions about the mental powers of cats or goldfish does not break down the boundary between a speaker's "knowledge of the language" and his/her "knowledge of the world": it simply widens the boundary of the former. Robin Lakoff, another pioneer in exploring the outermost boundaries of linguistic knowledge, has criticized the view that "pragmatic" phenomena should be excluded from linguistic analysis "since they are not, strictly speaking, grammatical phenomena, but rather reflect all sorts of non-linguistic facts about the speaker, his environment, and the real world." If seemingly synonymous sentences elicit different responses, or are appropriate to different settings, she says, "I must suspect that this is part of my linguistic heritage just as much as it is part of my cultural heritage" (1974:xvi–2).

Where, then, does that leave the boundary between the speaker's "linguistic heritage" and his/her "cultural heritage"? Linguists exploring this frontier have not been very explicit on the point, and that, I will argue, is part of the problem. "Linguistic knowledge" is everything that the linguists find has to be taken into account to interpret sentences; "knowledge of the world" or the "cultural heritage" is that residual wilderness that seems not to have to be taken into account — until some need is perceived to push the frontier back with new linguistic rules. This "wilderness" conception of "knowledge of the world," I will suggest, has led linguists to miss seeing some more pervasive forms of connection between cultural premises and linguistic knowledge.

A glimpse of the assumptions and goals of lexical semantics will underline why linguists (feel they) need to maintain a boundary between a speaker's knowledge of the language and the rest of what he/she knows about the world and will open the way for us to see the problematic of this boundary, from a cultural point of view.

Lexical Representations

In second-generation Chomskyan transformational theory (Chomsky 1965; Katz and Fodor 1963), one of the major components of the linguistic "base" was a *lexicon*. The lexicon consisted of a "list" (hoped ultimately to have some cognitive salience) of the lexical items of the language. For each item, the speaker's knowledge was assumed to include the necessary grammatical marking (to indicate the syntactic slot(s) it could fit into), minimal phonological information (supplemented by subsequent transformational and phonological rules in a derivation), and a *semantic representation*. The semantic representation constituted an analysis, according to semantic features (such as + animate) and other available descriptive devices, of the semantic readings assignable to such a form. (A further set of rules, projection rules, was to provide for the semantic relationships to be interpreted from the deep structures of sentences.) The nature and function of lexical representations has changed considerably in subsequent modifications of this formulation by generative semanticists, Chomskyans, semantic field theorists, ethnographic semanticists, and others. The means have been considerably improved whereby semantic representations can be rendered with maximum formal rigor and economy, where possible in a culture-free and logically coherent metalanguage. The premises that underlie the quest for more effective semantic representations of lexical items, however, remain substantially the same, I think, and can well be made explicit: (1) The speaker's knowledge codified in semantic representations is patently *linguistic* knowledge, not "knowledge of the world." To be sure, the objects, features, percepts, qualities, acts, or events to which semantic analyses refer are situated in the world of experience or imagination: semantic analysis, in this sense, maps linguistic forms onto "the world." Some of the knowledge codified in the lexicon may be pragmatic — Dyirbal "mother-in-law" forms (Dixon 1971) must be marked as such. But these specifications need not differ in their *form* from the marking of semantic and grammatical features. (2) Lexical representations specify the defining or denotative elements of referential meaning, not the connotative shades of meaning that forms may carry or evoke. This further obviates the need to include an amorphous mass of a speaker's "knowledge of the world" in lexical representations. It may be true that the word "marshmallow" conjures up to some English speakers childhood memories of campfires and roasting charred, melting objects on sticks. But such evocations, and whether for particular speakers they happen to be associated with falling in love or a tyrannical Cub Scoutmaster, is irrelevant to the analysis of English. (3) Because linguistic rules specify *outside the lexicon* whatever regularities attach to grammatical classes and phonological realizations, the lexicon constitutes an irreducible residue of idiosyncratic information about particular forms.

It is too simple to see the lexicon as codifying linguistic knowledge in the form of defining features, and shucking off the vague, unsystematically distributed connotations that linguistic forms may evoke.

That leads us, as with the marshmallow example, into the trap of seeing "knowledge of the world" as idiosyncratic, unstructured, and muddled — one of the twin traps into which linguists have too often fallen. The other is the unstated hierarchical structure of cultural assumptions that linguists share about *their* world, assumptions that underlie the semantics (and pragmatics) of English, Russian, German, and most of the other languages on which contemporary linguists have developed their skills.

Lexical Semantics and Symbolic Structures

Now let me turn to Kwaio, a language spoken by about 6,000 people, many of whom still live in the mountainous interior of Malaita Island in the Solomons, with their traditional social structure and ancestral religion still flourishing despite more than a century of European contact.

My first examples deal with the meanings of some common Kwaio surface verbs. Each has a common physical sense and a nonphysical (perhaps metaphoric) sense.[2]

The first few reflect such common — perhaps universal — extensions from the physical-spatial realm to the nonphysical that they are almost fully transparent to English speakers.

	Form	Gloss	Nonphysical Sense
1 (a)	ʔulasi-a	open	open ritually (e.g., by desacralization); open (an event, a procedural sequence, etc.)
(b)	lafu-a	lift, lift up	raise for sacrifice, give up in sacrifice
(c)	faʔabono-a [('cause') ('be shut') — PR OBJ][3]	close	close up, close off ritually; block or shut off (a place, activity)

So far, things seem transparent enough. If we were led to ask questions about such nonphysical usages, they would more probably be questions about their generality, perhaps universality — questions about the human mind, perhaps, but not about Kwaio culture.

If we add to the list we get a bit further into cultural particularities, although, again, the extensions seem transparent enough:

2 (a)	siufi-a	wash	ritually expiate, cleanse symbolic pollution
	(b)	bani-a	wall up (a thatch hut)	close off ritually or magically
	(c)	sifo	descend	become desacralized

And going further from transparent metaphors that one might call "natural," we find:

3 (a)	bibi	press down	magically suppress; magically bury a piglet to acquire power from the spirits
	(b)	fa'ala'u-a	parcel up, wrap	expiate pollution, ritually atone
		[('cause') ('be wrapped') — PR OBJ]	
	(c)	baba	hide, hide from, duck down away from	avoid recognizing relationship to an ancestor
	(d)	ofosi-a	take down, take off	magically cure
	(e)	kwate-a	give	of ancestor, deliver up to malevolent spirits or forces
	(f)	fa'amamu-a	fish by chumming	magically attract wealth
		[('cause') ('attraction by scent') — PR OBJ]	

To go further, there are many terms with nonphysical senses that are opaque to us (although not completely so).

4 (a)	fida	slap, smack	consecrate (pigs) to an ancestor
	(b)	olofi-a	jump on	take possession of a person's mind (of an ancestor)
	(c)	ano-a	bury, cover with soil	hide wild game (magically) from others

Finally, there are many verbs that have no physical meanings (in the senses I have been using) but refer only to events we would class as supernatural or have supernaturally mediated consequences.

5 (a)   dilo-a   cause to be sick,
                            press demands
                            by visiting
                            illness or
                            misfortune (of
                            an ancestor)
  (b)   saka-lia   take possession of
                            (of an ancestor)
  (c)   fa'ageni-a   defile by pollution
           [('cause') ('be female') — PR OBJ]

At this point, let me throw in a few elements of cultural information about the people who speak this language, some of which the reader will have begun to surmise from the glosses in the right-hand column. I will set out briefly some major principles of Kwaio cosmology.

(a) The spirits of ancestors—ancestral members of one's own kin group and more remote and powerful ancestors—control events in the universe that affect human life; they are everywhere, "like the wind," and constantly in direct or indirect communication with the living.

(b) Human life and successful human effort depend on spiritual potency infused by ancestors into objects and events (the Kwaio term is a metathesized form of Oceanic *mana*). Without such ancestrally conferred power, human efforts will fail. Ancestors confer *mana* on their descendants when they are pleased with them—a response induced mainly through proper ritual observances and consecrated offerings (particularly pigs), and proper conduct.

(c) Ancestors (and thus humans) are preoccupied with preservation of proper boundaries between the realms of the sacred, the mundane, and the polluted. The bodies of women are polluted and polluting: menstruation, defecation, urination, and, most of all, childbirth are ritually contaminating and must be kept within proper bounds by scrupulous observation of very detailed taboos. When ancestors are displeased with the living—because of swears, ritual errors, failure to consecrate offerings, or (by far the most common reason) violation of pollution taboos—the ancestors visit sickness, death, or misfortune upon the living. Such breaches of relations between a group and their ancestors (for, by and large, ancestors are only concerned with their own descendants) must be repaired by expiation, usually in the form of sacrificial pigs.

(d) There are no accidents in the Kwaio universe. All events that could concern humans are determined by causal chains: a poisonous snakebite, a tree-felling mishap, etc. These chains are controlled by ancestors — so that a snakebite or fall or wound constitutes evidence of ancestral action whose precise nature and cause must be discovered through divination.

(e) By invoking particular ancestors and following procedural recipes, humans can manipulate these chains of causal connection so as to bring about de-sired results — beneficial results for oneself or one's group, harmful results for one's enemies. What is conventionally called magic — sympathetic and contagious — is an everyday part of human effort to achieve desired ends.

Now let me return to the Kwaio verbs I set out above. The semantic information that a speaker of Kwaio commands presupposes the exis-tence of that kind of universe. If it is possible to construct semantic representations for lexical items in Kwaio, if those representations are going to be manageable in length, and if they are to avoid enormous redundance, it is because such general knowledge of the world is *assumed* in analyzing the semantics of particular forms.

Is such knowledge linguistic? Or is it cultural? One's immediate in-clination is to call it cultural; lexical semantic knowledge concerns the distinctive structures of referential meaning encoded in particular lexical items. Yet that is too simple, I suggest. If cultural knowledge is drawn upon to understand the meanings of particular lexical items, if these conceptions about the cosmos and the forces that guide and govern events motivate linguistic categories and usages, then adequate semantic representations of Kwaio forms may have to be articulated with, predi-cated on, and constructed with reference to such cultural knowledge. Usages such as 2(c) depend on a symbolic association between up and sacredness, and between down and pollution. Must that be explicated as part of the semantic representation? How many times for how many forms? If we include in semantic representations the particularities of particular forms, do we not risk obscuring general patterns of symbolic association? Do we not risk producing a spuriously *ad hoc* list of linguistic idiosyncrasies, where these in fact reflect quite general cultural premises and symbolic systems? Is it possible to assign semantic representations to forms such as 2(a) or 3(b) without reference to culture-specific cos-mological assumptions about pollution and contagion? Can semantic representations deal adequately with 5(c), *faʔagenia,* 'defile,' whose underlying structure is morphologically transparent as 'cause-be female'? To ignore the underlying tree structure expressed in morphology of the surface verb will not suffice; to give a semantic representation such as "cause to be defiled by pollution as the bodies of women are polluted" expressed clumsily what, in the Kwaio world, is a straightforward and simple meaning (something like "female-ize"). And yet, such awkward-nesses will be repeated over and over again in a lexicon if we separate linguistic knowledge from the cultural knowledge presupposed by it. Kwaio understand one another, I presume, by using linguistic signs to evoke a world of meanings they share—meanings that express, pre-suppose, and are motivated by cultural assumptions about ancestors, causality, and pollution.

Let me illustrate two Kwaio terms for magical acts whose meanings, I suggest, can only be intelligible in the kind of universe I have sketched.

6   fa'alaŋaa   dry (v.t.)   perform magic to keep
                                                a fisherman from
        [('cause') ('be dry')—PR OBJ]   catching anything

To understand the semantic association, we need to know that *la ŋa*, 'dry,' has a metaphorical sense 'for nothing, without result.' But that does not eliminate the semantic obscurities. Consider

7 (a)   anoma'ite'enia   perform magic to cause a
                                                person to waste away

Needed here is an excursion into Kwaio verb morphology. Recall

4 (c)   ano-a,   bury   The root of 4(c) and 7(b)
                                                is ground, land.

7 (b)   ano

Affixing the object-pronoun -a we produce 4(c), a transitive verb, 'bury.' However the transitivity can be marked by infixing the transitive suffix -mi-, producing:

7 (c)   anomia   plant (it)

Using another regular morphological device, the transitivity can be heightened (with various semantic shadings) by adding a transitive in-tensifier [(-me'e-), (-te'e-), (-fe'e-), (-ne'e-), (-le'e-)] in addition to the transitive suffix (which in this environment becomes -ni-):

7 (d)   anome'enia   bury (it) (put it be-
                         neath the surface)

But a further morphological device takes the semantic shading so created and renders it intransitive: -me'e- becomes -ma'i, and the transitive
suffix and pronoun object are deleted:

7 (e)   anoma'i   sink beneath the
                      ground

as in   sina ka
          anoma'i   the sun has set

But what, then, of 7(a), anoma'ite'enia? In this case, the detransitivized
form 'sink beneath the ground' has been rendered transitive by the further suffixation of a transitive intensifier plus transitive suffix plus direct
object (-te'enia) producing a form whose literal sense could only be
'cause to sink below the ground,' which can be glossed as 'cause [a
person] to waste away'; i.e., to go down the way the sun sinks below the
horizon. Now, how, I wonder, can the semantics of such a form be
disentangled from the universe of causal connection and its magical
manipulation within which such acts are imaginable?

The same points could be illustrated for nouns and other grammatical
classes in Kwaio: the semantics of lexical items, the contrast sets they
form, the symbolic implications they carry, are infused by cultural assumptions. Thus *kaloŋa* is preeminently the realm of nature. *Kaloŋa* is the
'wild' or natural world; humans own 'land,' but one cannot own *kaloŋa*,
its trees, its wildlife. And pollution is neutralized in *kaloŋa*, in contrast to
clearings or gardens. Thus *kaloŋa* is symbolically loaded, and enters into
semantic contrast with other forms (such as *lalabata*, 'clearing') as a
vehicle for expressing a symbolic opposition of NATURE:CULTURE. This
and many other Kwaio nouns are linked into semantic/symbolic domains whose structure and logic are opaque if we look at their physical or
most literal senses (cf. Fox's analysis, 1975, of parallelism in Rotinese
ritual language). Are these symbolic linkages part of a native actor's
knowledge of the language? Are they to be included in semantic representations? If so, they are likely to emerge as arbitrary particularisms, not
as elements in a symmetrical and elegant mosaic. Kenneth Hale's observations about antonymy in Walbiri illustrate the point:

> Many [semantic] oppositions [used in antonymy] can be fully understood
> only in reference to other aspects of Walbiri culture. The opposition of fire

and water, for example . . . is an important theme in Walbiri ritual and epic. . . . In taboo-laden and culturally loaded areas, equivalences are, from the strictly linguistic point of view, idiosyncratic — e.g., the oppositions semen, coitus/ mulga seed. . . . [But] it is unlikely that the vocabulary which exhibits this seemingly idiosyncratic behaviour is . . . an arbitrary assemblage of lexical items [Hale 1971:482–488].

Walbiri antonymy reveals underlying abstract semantic structures, some unapparent from other evidence, and some reflecting specific symbolic oppositions of Walbiri cosmology rather than obvious semantic associations. Dixon (1975) gives a parallel Australian case in which the logic of Dyirbal noun classes is intelligible only in terms of mythic and symbolic associations. Are such myths and symbolic associations linguistic facts or cultural facts? Can we describe Walbiri or Dyirbal semantics without reference to them?

Cultural "Rules" and Linguistic Analysis

All this remains programmatic and vague if we talk about "cultural premises" and "cosmological assumptions" as if they hovered above linguistic usages and infused them with intelligibility in some magical way. Although cognitive anthropology may have fallen well short of its goals, it has established, I think, that cultural knowledge is coherently structured, and that many of these structures are amenable to formal description. If we are to illuminate Kwaio semantics by cultural analysis, it should ideally be by ethnographically defining a universe within which otherwise opaque linguistic usages are both transparent and natural. Such an ethnographic description must be structured hierarchically; it builds on general assumptions about ancestors, causality, time, *mana*, sacredness, and pollution to which I have alluded, but those assumptions provide only the foundations.

Writing even a sketch of such a partial "grammar" of Kwaio religious principles, cosmological assumptions, ritual, and magic would be an enormous task. Limitations of space preclude even a preliminary sketch version. But a very brief summary of some elements of Kwaio religion as a system of knowledge will enable me to make some more concrete suggestions about what Kwaio speakers know that enables them to command lexical information in an economical way and, correspondingly, how a description of these cultural assumptions might be articulated with semantic analyses.

Some very general cosmological premises are a necessary starting point. Kwaio religion is centrally concerned with what we may call *realms* — that is, with *states* and their concomitant spatial-temporal manifestations. A pervasive first distinction is between a realm we may call PHENOMENAL and one we may call NOUMENAL. The former is the physical, material world, which humans perceive directly; the latter is the parallel plane of invisible spiritual beings and powers. Ancestors are in the NOUMENAL realm, and living humans in the PHENOMENAL. Yet every animate creature has a 'shade' (*nununa*) that is the noumenal counterpart of its 'body' (*to'ofuŋana*): the shadow cast by the body is a kind of phenomenal trace of the noumenal 'shade.' In some states, notably dream, possession, and coma, the 'shade' departs the 'body' and wanders in the noumenal realm, interacting with the 'shades' of the dead.

The NOUMENAL realm is free of many of the constraints of time, space, and physical connection that apply in the PHENOMENAL realm. Thus, the 'shades' of ancestors can see into the future, can be in many places at once, are all-seeing, and can control events through nonphysical interventions.

Another crucial set of realms (in this case, states or qualities that attach to contexts, places, and events) has to do with sacredness and its mirror image. Here we have a tripartite opposition between SACRED (*abu*, the Kwaio reflex of Oceanic *tapu*), POLLUTED (*sua*), and an unmarked middle term, ORDINARY (*mola* = secular). The POLLUTED/ORDINARY/SACRED oppositions characteristically operate in a binary fashion through neutralization of one of the oppositions, so as to form SACRED:PROFANE or POLLUTED:PURE. The "grammar" of sacredness is complex, involving a series of degrees and their spatiotemporal correlates and sociological entailments. Here, a recent summary will have to suffice:

> Sacredness is symbolically associated with an upwards or uphill direction, with shrines and men's houses. Pollution is the mirror-image . . . of sacredness, associated with a downwards or downhill direction, with menstrual huts and the women's latrine and childbirth area. . . . The middle state between the states of sacredness and pollution is *mola*, 'ordinary'. The ancestors . . . are sacred; the living are normally *mola*, except when they have become sacred or are polluted by menstruation or childbirth; death is associated with sacredness, life is normally 'ordinary' . . . [Keesing 1977].

Specification of the states, changes of state, ritual procedures and rules, and their sociological entailments for these and other realms

of Kwaio "religion" is understandably a formidably complex task—
although not, I think, an inconceivable one (perhaps no more impossible
on principle than a linguistic grammar). Kwaio rituals and magical procedures are concerned above all with effecting "grammatical" changes of
state (where the rules were originated by ancestors who also function as
unseen monitors of and participants in their correct enactment). A concomitant concern is with preventing dangerous changes of state (defilement, desecration) and invasion or abandonment of boundaries.

> Kwaio rites use physical acts—descending, opening, closing, sending away—
> as symbols . . . of changes of state. They draw on the fact that a [sacred] state is
> 'closed' and must be progressively 'opened'; that sacredness is 'up' . . . and
> becoming *mola* involves descending to the middle part of the clearing, that
> pollution or evil influences spread and must be 'walled up' or 'shut off', and so
> on. Thus metaphors, and physical symbols, of opening (for example, breaking
> open a coconut), containment, washing to purify, are prominent in Kwaio
> symbolism. . . . Biting into [an areca or] betel nut, and chewing it serves to
> open a channel between the priest and ancestors in prayer, [as] a symbol of . . .
> a channel between the physical, material world and the immaterial world of
> the . . . spirits. . . .
> . . . Planting or burying objects in the ground powerfully expresses continuity
> or stability; other powerful physical [symbols] represent 'sending away' mis-
> fortunes, accusations and illness from the settlement, and 'wrapping' a mantle
> of protection around the group. Another dominant physical [symbol] is the
> irresistible attraction of smell (*mamu*) that draws insects to flowers or fish to
> bait [see 3(f)] [Keesing 1977].

It is in the framework of a grammar of such symbolism that the
nonphysical senses of Kwaio surface verbs such as those examined in the
previous section are natural and transparent in a Kwaio universe. This
dependence of semantic readings on symbolic structures and religious
premises emerges if we look more closely at Kwaio conceptualizations of
mana (what in the Oceanic literature is often described as a kind of
supernatural potentiation akin to electricity). The closest that Kwaio get
to talking about *mana* in even quasi-physical terms is to treat *mana* by
indirection as if it were a kind of mantle with which the ancestors en-
velop the living, their settlements, their gardens, protecting them from
malevolent and dangerous uncontrolled powers of the world of nature.
The ancestors, Kwaio fear, will *kwatega* 'deliver them up' [see 3(e)] to
such lethally malevolent powers if they do not follow pollution rules,

expiate violations, and make adequate propitiatory offerings. For Kwaio, there is no problematic gulf between this usage and *kwatea* 'give it' as an everyday transitive verb. For a linguist who began with the common-sense expectations of Western cultures, this usage would be idiosyncratic, if not completely opaque; its naturalness and transparency derive from nonlinguistic principles. A parallel articulation between semantic readings and the "mantle" conceptualization of *mana* can be illustrated with the quasi-verbal (Keesing 1976:xxix) form

8 (a)   ʾafuia   'around, around the outside of'

In everyday physical senses, this occurs in constructions such as 'pass around the outside of,' or 'stand on each side of me.'

8 (b)   agaʾafuia

is literally 'look around (the outside of),' but

8 (c)   agaʾafuinau

is 'look after me, take responsibility for me.' If the agent of the verb *aga*, 'look,' is an ancestor, the meaning of 8(c) is unambiguous: 'protect me with *mana*' (i.e., maintain my protective mantle). Consider now several usages where the agent is a human actor but where the referent of ʾ*afuia* is the ancestral mantle of protection:

8 (d)   nalu ʾafuia   'sacrifice in expiation on behalf of' (lit., 'wash around the outside of,' but here, 'purify to restore the ancestral mantle around').

  (e)   lii ʾafuia   'consecrate a propitiatory pig to an ancestor to maintain the mantle around.'

  (f)   gama ʾafuia kaloṇa   'ritually eat a sacred taro pudding [the noumenal essence of which goes to the ancestors] to ensure ancestral benefits for the land' [which the ancestors own].

But if the transparency of such forms to Kwaio speakers is at least partly clear once the cultural idiom of *mana* as a protective mantle against malevolent and destructive forces has been explicated, that does not necessarily help the linguist assaying economical semantic representations of Kwaio forms.

A crucial first step is to assume that, in the long run, a "grammar" of a culture and the grammar of a language would be complementary and mutually reinforcing and suppletive — even though neither is yet writ-able. I assume that a single vast system comprises *all* of what any individual knows about his/her world (including knowledge of one or more languages, knowledge about the world, natural and social, and how to act in it, but also knowledge and memories of particular people, places, and life experiences). Cognitive economy and neural specialization entail a partial separation into subsystems. But cognitive economies, as I have argued, also demand that general assumptions about the world not be recoded (metaphorically, we might say "restated") with relation to every segment of knowledge that rests on or is motivated by them. The explorer of some cognitive realm, whether linguist or ethnographer, hopes or assumes that linguistic knowledge or (nonlinguistic) cultural knowledge will turn out to make up (or be describable as) a separate subsystem. But how, then, are we to capture the crossover between subsystems? How are we to draw on or incorporate into linguistic analysis the general cultural assumptions about the world that language describes? Since these assumptions patently *must* be rendered explicit in a description of a culture as a system of knowledge, an ethnography can potentially provide a foundation for linguistic analysis. An ethnographic description of nonlinguistic cultural knowledge inevitably draws heavily on linguistic materials, so that cultural analysis and linguistic analysis become mutually reinforcing. Where the cultural assumptions on which a language builds are alien to the linguist and his/her audience, as with Kwaio, Dyirbal, or Walbiri, at least selective ethnography becomes a prerequisite for grammatical analysis; where they can be taken for granted, it need not be.

But how, then, does a linguistic description incorporate and make reference to a cultural analysis? First, we admit key concepts and categories defined in the cultural grammar as terms and operators in the metalanguage of semantic representation. For Kwaio, *abu, mola, mana,* become terms in the semantic metalanguage, as admissible as the nuclear verbs of Dyirbal (Dixon 1971). Second, we key our semantic analyses to culturally salient distinctions (which may temporarily thwart the quest for universals but in the long run could yield more genuine ones). For Kwaio, we introduce into our semantic metalanguage a notation to indicate whether the agent is human or ancestor. Where [as in 4(b), 5(a), 5(b), 9(a)] the actor is an ancestor, there is an immediate and predictable shift in reference from the PHENOMENAL to the NOUMENAL realm. Given cultural assumptions about the nature and motives of ancestors and the constraints that operate in the NOUMENAL realm, a whole series of Kwaio usages — much longer than I have illustrated — become transparent and in many cases quite predictable. We perhaps need a notation as well to indicate whether alter, or the intended target of the act, is an ancestor — which, similarly, shifts the semantic frame into the logic of the NOUMENAL realm. Through such means, *ʾafuia* could neatly be defined as having a PHENOMENAL SENSE as 'around, around the outside of,' with a NOUMENAL transform as 'surrounding with *mana*.'

Third, we distinguish (for Kwaio) magical vs. nonmagical action. For many Kwaio forms there is only magical sense (which may or not be transparent, at least with regard to the goals of the magical action). More commonly [as with 2(b), 3(a), 3(d), 3(e), 3(f), 4(c) and 6], there is both a nonmagical and magical sense. By marking them as such, and specifying in the cultural grammar the principles and assumptions that guide magical action, we simplify the task of semantic description. Magic entails a human agent following a procedural recipe in the PHENOMENAL realm that leads an ancestor to make a corresponding set of manipulations in the NOUMENAL realm so as to effect desired PHENOMENAL results. By specifying the logic of magical action outside a linguistic grammar but keying semantic descriptions to such an analysis, we begin to systematize the regularities that make many magical senses transparent to Kwaio speakers and begin to reduce a jumbled miscellany of semantic idiosyncracy to roughly the dimensions with which Kwaio speakers, as repositories of esoteric knowledge, must themselves cope. Semantic treatment of the magical senses of Kwaio forms in terms of general cultural principles of magic can illustrate another important point. If a line is to be drawn between what is included in a semantic representation and what is left out, the position of that line will depend in part on cultural principles. To know and perform magic, one must command three components: (1) a physical procedure, using objects or substances; (2) a 'spell,' consisting of naming a sequence of paired objects in a specified order (two coconuts, two cordylines, etc.); and (3) a 'validation,' consisting of the names of a line of ancestors from the one who 'discovered' the magic down to the one who taught it to the person performing it. What is to be included in the semantic representation of a term for a complex of magic such as *faʾalaŋaa?* The procedure? The spell? Only the goal? This, I would argue, is as much a cultural as a linguistic question. It is most appropriate to specify the goals of magical complexes in semantic representations, but not the procedures, spells, or validations, because for Kwaio, the *goal* of a kind of magic is public knowledge, the procedure is known much less widely, and the 'spell' and 'validation' constitute secret knowledge that can be bought and sold. This becomes a principled and general procedure, not an *ad hoc* matter of descriptive convenience.

A further step in the direction of articulating cultural and semantic descriptions can be taken by devising an ethnographic notation for symbolic oppositions and constructions and keying semantic representations to it. That could presumably be done for Walbiri (Hale 1971) or Dyirbal (Dixon 1975); it is certainly possible for Kwaio. Thus, if we code a series of symbolic contrasts (MALE:FEMALE; SACRED:MOLA:POLLUTED; UP:DOWN; RIGHT:LEFT; CULTURE:NATURE; DEATH:LIFE; SUBSTANCE: SPIRIT; NOUMENAL:PHENOMENAL; ANCESTORS:HUMANS; etc.) we can indicate in semantic representations the lexical sets into which forms fit (*kaloŋa* vs. *lalabata*) and the symbolic oppositions (NATURE:CULTURE) for which such pairings are vehicles. Moreover, if we recognize that such symbolic oppositions correspond to realms or states distinguished in Kwaio cosmology, we can introduce into our semantic metalanguage an operator to indicate state-transitions. Thus

9 (a)   fane   'ascend'
                 and
   (b)   sifo   'descend'

can be keyed to the oppositions UP:DOWN, and SACRED:PROFANE/POLLUTED:PURE, and marked to indicate the state-transitions involved (fane = POLLUTED → PURE, sifo = SACRED → PROFANE).

Semantic representations of what otherwise would be an unordered series of lexical items become interlocked, by such means, into culturally meaningful systems of domains or fields. In part, a cultural grammar then becomes a metatheory of semantic fields in a language (see Werner 1970, 1972). Thus, the forms with which

maŋo-na   'breath'

can be paired contrastively, including *beʔu-na* 'corpse,' *nunu-na* 'shade,' *toʔofuŋa-na* 'body,' become crucial vehicles for the expression of Kwaio ideas about orders of existence, the nature of persons, life, death, etc., all of which can at least be tagged in semantic representations with reference to the symbolic designs of Kwaio culture. And for morphological modifications of a single root, we are led to see a logic that might otherwise be hidden. Thus, *toʾofuŋana* is 'body' in the PHENOMENAL realm, in contrast to *nuna-na* 'shade' in the NOUMENAL. It is also 'essence' in contrast to 'appearance,' 'body' as opposed to 'legs' (of, e.g., a carved pig), 'trunk' as opposed to the rest of the human body, and *toʾofuŋaʾa*, an adjective derived by suffixation, is 'real,' designating the unmarked member of a pair (as in *bata toʾofuŋaʾa*, 'real shell valuables,' as opposed to *bata naa faka*, 'cash money,' both of which are *bata* in some contexts). The whole semantic structure ordered by unmarkedness:markedness begins with cultural premises about orders of existence and reality.

By explicitly articulating semantic analysis to ethnography, and hence to pervasive cultural assumptions about the cosmos, causality, time, and being, we begin to capture not only the subtleties of meaning accessible to native speakers but the creative powers of language in metaphor and symbolism as well (Basso 1976). And in doing so, we begin to explore interconnections between cognitive realms that too easily remain hidden if we map a single domain at a time.

Pragmatic Rules and Cultural Knowledge

If linguists analyzing syntactic and semantic patterns have been able to treat pragmatic phenomena as residual and unstructured, sociolinguists have not. In seeking to map the distribution of linguistic variations within communities, the nature and context of speech registers, rules of conversation, and other sociocultural contextualizations of speech, sociolinguistic researchers have been able to find order and structure in phenomena that had long seemed "messy" and peripheral. But in analyzing pragmatic rules, explorers of that frontier will, I believe, increasingly confront the same difficulties I have illustrated for semantics. The conceptual, cognitive, and descriptive problems that will result have not yet been squarely faced. Pragmatic rules are phrased in terms of social groups and categories and cultural standards of formality, distance, etc. But they also assume (and hence need not make explicit) more general assumptions about the social and cultural universe without which they would be meaningless. How, then, to capture these takens-for-granted in our analyses, to render transparent the otherwise opaque?

We must begin by defining the pragmatic realm so that it is not unstructured and residual — whatever has to do with concrete social situations or involves cultural or psychological rather than referential/denotative aspects of meaning.

What is urgent, I believe, is a preservation in the realm of prag-

matics — whatever its bounds — of the epistemological distinction between systems of knowledge and patterns of behavior. To deal with
conversational implicatures or the various aspects of indexicality outlined by Silverstein (such as speech registers and deictic shifters), we
need a theory of *pragmatic knowledge* — not pragmatic behavior (Silverstein 1976). The problem is not so much how Javanese use speech registers in actual situations, what actual Dyirbal say to their mothers-in-law,
or what an English-speaker is thinking when he uses a deictic "this. . . ."
The problem is what Javanese must *know* about linguistic forms, classes
of situations, classes of actors, to move through their ever-changing
world understanding and being understood, and conveying appropriate
or strategic messages about status. If we formulate the question this way,
the interrelationship between denotative, referential meanings, pragmatic knowledge, and other cultural knowledge becomes problematic
but amenable to investigation.

Even if space allowed, I could barely begin to map the pragmatic
knowledge that speakers of Kwaio must command in order to embed
utterances appropriately in social contexts, and to use choices of alternative, referentially equivalent forms to manipulate situations and one another. My point here will be to illustrate: (1) how the relationships between pragmatic "rules of use" and referential-semantic meanings are
not only complex but, as Silverstein (1976) has argued, problematic for
linguistic theory and (2) how the knowledge that enables Kwaio to situate speech events appropriately or successfully in the social world (like
their knowledge of lexical semantics) presupposes, draws on, and is
motivated by hierarchically structured cultural knowledge. Having illustrated this with Kwaio examples, I will suggest, borrowing an example
from Fillmore, that the relationships between cultural premises and
principles and specific pragmatic rules have been obscured or overlooked in linguists' treatment of "pragmatics" and/or "knowledge of the
world" as residual.

I will begin by sketching some of the principles that Kwaio use to
select alternative lexemes that, from the point of view of lexical semantics, have the same referential denotation (in at least some of their
senses). One axis is that of "politeness," especially with reference to
terms related to sex and sexual anatomy. Choice between direct, blunt
forms (as with *la'i* 'fuck,' most of the Kwaio forms happen to be four-
letter words) and many alternative euphemisms (e.g., 'press down on,'
'climb up on,' 'grab around the middle,' 'grab the breasts of,' 'sleep

with,' 'be friends with,' 'ask') depends in part on their varying degrees of polite or ribald connotation. But these choices draw on a highly complex pragmatic grammar that involves: (a) sex and age of speaker and alter; (b) sexual distance of speaker and alter (see Keesing 1965:77–79, 94); (c) presence, and identity, of other hearers; and (d) the situational context, especially whether the conversation is defined as *dooŋa*, 'ribald joking.'[4] Choice of an inappropriate term, especially with reference to alter's (or hearer's) sexuality or sexual anatomy, may be a matter not only of politeness but also of jural entailment: a 'sexual insult,' *kwaisulafiŋaa*, is an offense calling for compensation.

Although such rules of a pragmatic "grammar" are complex, they do not necessarily preclude, or even render unduly complicated, semantic representations of these lexical items (which ideally would mark each lexical item with an index of politeness or bawdiness, geared to the pragmatic rules). Nor do they necessarily refer to more general cultural premises and principles; although their codification requires substantial mapping of Kwaio social structure (Keesing 1965). Most of the burgeoning research in contemporary sociolinguistics deals with social and cultural contextualizations at such levels. But let us look at more problematic aspects of lexical selection.

Some forms must be avoided because they are insults with ritual implications. Thus, *nifo-* 'tooth' (to which pronominal suffixes are directly attached to express grammatically inalienable possession) is used in all forms (*nifogu* 'my tooth,' *nifoga* 'their teeth,' etc.) other than *nifomu* 'your tooth.' The last is grammatically possible but not pragmatically appropriate: *ba'elamu* ('your tooth') is used instead, since 'your tooth' using *nifo-* is, to an adult, a dire insult with supernatural ramifications. Since *ba'ela-* is used correctly *only* to avoid the tabooed form, *ba'elagu* for 'my tooth' is grammatically possible but pragmatically inappropriate. Using *nifomu* is an offense whose nature and dimensions depend on the sex, age, and ritual status of alter and even upon the context (*nifomu* could be used with a young child without consequence). This, again, might seem a simple matter of indicating these pragmatic constraints in the lexicon. But if *nifomu* is used to an adult, and especially a ritually senior man, it is an offense *against his ancestors* as well as against him: it is general principles of Kwaio cosmology and their reflections in the sacredness of parts of one's 'person' that motivate the specific pragmatic rules and their expression in linguistic usages. Contemporary sociolinguistics has dealt less squarely with such manifestations of general cultural principles in pragmatic rules and how they are to be captured in analytical description.

The point can be carried further. A number of euphemisms and circumlocutions are employed to avoid using the name of a decedent (except in special contexts such as genealogical recitation or epic chants). Again, these rules might seem to pose no serious analytical problems until one realizes the premises on which they rest: that the decedents *are parties to the conversation.* Even from a "strictly" linguistic point of view, the complications of these pragmatic conventions are not trivial. A man speaking of events involving his deceased father not only will avoid using his name in most contexts but will use the referential kin term *maʔa ana* 'his father,' rather than *maʔa agu* 'my father.' That can be compared with the "pragmatic metaphors" (Silverstein 1976:31, 38–39) in many languages that express deference to alter by permuting the pronominal system. Defining these rules, and other rules of deference and avoidance in communicating with ancestors or about them (in their "presence"), requires reference to cultural conceptions about ancestors, the NOUMENAL realm, etc., which I sketched in the preceding section; and reference to a cultural mapping of the sociology of the living, of which the sociology of the dead is itself a transform. It is because of what pragmatic rules need not specify (because it is already known) that they can be economically learned and used. To map and formulate these rules, we will have to exploit the same economies.

In Kwaio, words or phrases associated with the names of powerful ancestors (by homonymy or phonological resemblance as well as identity) are tabooed and selectively removed from use or avoided. I have described the linguistic and sociolinguistic aspects of this phenomenon elsewhere (Keesing and Fifi'i 1969). What is most relevant here is that one must have a sociological map of the speech community, almost a Who's Who, articulated with one's lexical knowledge; particular forms are taboo for use with particular people or families. These are often common forms in everyday use within the speech community. Although the seriousness of a violation depends on the predilections of the particular ancestor and the particular descendants involved, it is in general an offense against the ancestor, as party to the conversation in which the form was misused, who (unless satisfied by expiation) will visit punishment (in the form of illness or other misfortune) on the descendants (rather than on the offender). I wonder how the pragmatic rules are to be articulated (if at all) with the semantic representations of the lexical items and phrases to which they are regionally and idiosyncratically applied. I wonder how the pragmatic rules are to be formulated without depicting (as I did in Keesing and Fifi'i 1969) the assumptions about orders of existence, the nature of ancestors, the cultural meanings of names and naming, that motivate and are assumed by them. And in a language pervaded with alternative labels for the same lexical categories, often phonological permutations of the original forms, but often loanwords or lexical innovations, I wonder whether a grammarian would want to consider knowledge of the distribution of taboos within the speech community to be "linguistic knowledge" or "knowledge of the world."

The problem of how pragmatic rules are articulated with referential semantics and with hierarchically structured cultural principles is not unique to Kwaio. Fillmore (1974b) has noted the need to invoke cultural/pragmatic information to show why 'next Friday' is ambiguous (in English) in a way that 'next Monday' is not:

> An account of the ambiguity of one expression and the non-ambiguity of a related expression has required . . . an appeal to knowledge of how the institution of calendar-keeping in our culture works, how the days of the week are organized, when the week cycle begins, and how the choice of a day-of-the-week expression is constrained by the speaker's knowledge of the time of the speech act. I assume that these are pragmatic, and not merely semantic, facts . . . [Fillmore 1974b:v–3].

But what, then, is to define and demarcate the bounds of "pragmatic facts"? Are they simply to include, residually, everything one must know to speak and understand a language that referentially based semantics and syntax cannot incorporate? Does pragmatics deal with all of a speaker's knowledge about the world? Housebuilding techniques? "The institution of calendar keeping"? Religious beliefs? If pragmatics is to incorporate a people's most general cosmological premises, then the most abstract and general forms of cultural knowledge have been misleadingly lumped with principles for using signs in social contexts, obscuring their hierarchical relationships.

I believe that pragmatics is best taken as an analysis of the operating principles for applying general knowledge to particular situations, for communications with signs in social situations and real-world contexts (cf. Silverstein 1976). "Pragmatic knowledge" can in this sense be taken as a shorthand and provisional label for those segments or subsystems of a native actor's cultural knowledge drawn upon in *embedding messages in social contexts*. The interconnectedness of these and other cognitive subsystems remains problematic, although open to investigation.

Just as referential semantics presupposes general systems of knowledge about the world, so too does pragmatics in this narrowed sense — an added reason not simply to label as "pragmatic" everything a speaker knows about the world, in contrast to what he/she knows about the language. To use Fillmore's example, I would want to view "the institution of calendar-keeping," and the more general premises about time that the system codifies, as elements of cultural knowledge that are *assumed* and *drawn upon* in the pragmatic rules for using and talking about times and dates. The point, then, is not to suggest that native actors have separate compartments in their brains/minds, to be labeled "linguistic knowledge," "pragmatic knowledge," and "other cultural knowledge," and that these three respective compartments are the proper disciplinary concern of linguists, sociologists, and anthropologists. That simply puts us back in the present bind of seeing our colleagues' compartments as residual to "ours," and as either mysterious or unstructured. Rather, I am suggesting that referential semantic knowledge is "knowable" by the native speaker precisely because of what does *not* have to be specified because it is assumed. This makes an ethnography of cultural knowledge and a linguistic grammar complementary facets of a single enterprise, even though for some linguistic purposes (and for some languages where the linguist can take a background of cultural knowledge as given) the cultural principles that a language builds on need not be specified. Pragmatic rules, similarly, are knowable and potentially formulable because of what they do not have to specify, but can take as given. To treat the "domain" of pragmatic knowledge as separate and separable disguises precisely the interconnections that need exploration.

Communication in Cultural Perspective

It is possible to view cultures as systems of communicative knowledge, as Silverstein (1976) proposes. Seen in those terms, the exchange of messages within a society is possible not primarily because of the information content of the messages themselves (as referentially based semantics would have it), but because of the knowledge shared by the communicating actors — which does not, for this reason, have to be encoded in message segments, but is presupposed and evoked *by* them, and drawn on to embed them appropriately in social contexts.

Most of this ground is covered, from a rather different direction, by Silverstein's sweeping proposal (1976) that referentially based grammars should be seen as subsystems of wider grammars of communication whose pragmatic functions are primary and demand analysis in their own right. Another example of the articulation between semantico-referential meaning, pragmatic rules, and hierarchically ordered cultural premises, using Kwaio evidence, will suggest how Silverstein's and my mappings fit together. Silverstein, distinguishing semantic/referential and indexical functions of signs in the Peircean sense (Silverstein 1976; Peirce 1932), points out how "shifters" convey both referential and in-dexical meanings. He uses grammatical tense-markers and deictics to illustrate this "duplex" coreference both to a semantically representable referential meaning and the real-world contexts of space and time in which they are uttered. Silverstein suggests that the indexical (situa-tional context-dependent) aspects of meaning have been glossed over by reference-based grammars.

Let me illustrate with a Kwaio example. Kwaio employs deictic point-ers of the "here," "over there" variety. Their meanings can be partly captured in semantic representations, although only with reference to the spatial orientation of the speaker. Thus, *lofo'u* indexically points 'down there'; *lolo'o* indexically points 'up there.' The referential content has to be represented as something like "below the speaker in the direc-tion he/she is indicating." But considering the following:

10 (a)   *falisi lofo'u*   'last year'
    (b)   *falisi lolo'o*   'next year'

Falisi is the term for the annual yam planting and, by extension, the annual cycles marked by those plantings and the units of time so demar-cated. But why 'up there' and 'down there'? From the standpoint of referential semantics, this could be treated as a kind of frozen, idiomatic metaphor in which the indexical deixis is, at most, residual. But, in fact, I would argue that this usage is motivated (as English deictic metaphors of temporality may once have been) by a cultural conception of time: in the Kwaio case, a conception that views the past as having moved forward and downward from the point of reference of the speaker. (For 'next year' Kwaio often use *falisi lolo'o mai*, 'the year coming down from up there'). There is considerable evidence, both linguistic (e.g., the creation of new metaphors; see Basso 1976) and nonlinguistic (e.g., ritual pro-cedure) that this conceptualization is "alive" and productive of new cultural forms; and hence that these usages regarding time are *indexically transparent* as "deictic metaphors" to Kwaio speakers.

The conceptualization of time in Kwaio culture is a permutation of a very widespread (conceivably universal) conception of human life as a line of march. The two critical cycles that probably always serve as paradigms of time are the seasonal cycle (homologous in this respect to the lunar cycle) and the human life cycle and passing of generations. These symbolic conceptions, plus the biologically structured apperception of temporality and experiences of memory, are woven into culturally patterned designs that are much less diverse than they might be. In culture after culture, one's predecessors are viewed as having gone ahead ("before") along a line of march you are following, and one's own life experiences are seen as having been "left behind" ("past" = passed). Kwaio culture permutes this model by conceptualizing the time periods associated with those who have gone before (*taʔa i naʔo* 'people in front') as being in front of and downward from the present. The past in general is *alata i naʔo* 'time in front'; last year can be referred to as *falisi ka liu kau* ('year has passed by away-from-the-speaker'); and, as evidenced by linguistic usages and ritual procedures, it is conceived as having moved downward. If, as I believe, this cultural model of the progression of time is cognitively salient for Kwaio speakers, the indexical transparency of *falisi lofoʔu* is probably as compelling as is our English "up" and "down" for north-south orientation. An ethnography of Kwaio culture that codified this symbolic scheme would not have to treat these deictic metaphors as idiosyncratic idioms. The indexical as well as the referential functions of such usages could be described with reference to their cultural logic, not simply their idiosyncratic particularity.

Silverstein (1976) alludes to the efforts of syntacticians to incorporate into grammatical theory the insights of linguistic philosophers such as Austin and Searle regarding the "work" accomplished by speech acts. He implies that the stretching of transformational syntactic formalisms to accommodate the illocutionary force of "performatives" ("I dub thee Sir Knight") and other speech acts is inadequate, since these phenomena demand an analysis in terms of pragmatics for which syntactic tree-structures are inappropriate. A final set of Kwaio examples will show how an expanded theory of language in culture will require a broadened conception of the pragmatic force of speech acts and the cultural principles that infuse them.

I will take as my texts two Kwaio sentences.

11 (a)   Nau ke feʔesia akwaleʔe umu na adalo agu ma ku
          belia boo ala X.
          'I shit on the ten sacred altar stones of my ancestors
          and steal X's pig.'

  (b)   Wane laʔaua ini ana geni ma ka feea waʔi noʔona.
          'A man steps over [the legs of] his sisters-in-law
          and accepts that marriage payment.'

11(a) illustrates a kind of swear called *taaŋa;* 11(b) illustrates a kind of
ritual injunction called *suluŋa.*[5] There are several other categories of
curses and ritual injunctions generally similar in form and logic.

What is interesting about these and other categories of injunctions
and curses is that they conjoin a clause predicating a drastically forbidden imagined act of defilement, insult, or sexual invasion with a clause
describing a real-world act the speaker wishes to prohibit or to deny
having performed. If the act predicated in the second clause has been, or
is at some future time, actually performed — if proposition B is true —
then the disastrous act predicated in the first clause has, in effect, been
committed by implication: proposition A *becomes* true. More precisely,
the legal entailments and ancestral responses of this imagined world-
state are actualized. In Kwaio terms, the events have occurred in the
NOUMENAL realm, though not the PHENOMENAL. A guilty man who
uttered 11(a) to deny falsely that he had stolen X's pig would by that
speech act have massively defiled the sacredness of his ancestors. (In an
actual swear of denial, he may be forced to curse a whole detailed series
of his most sacred objects and places, contingent on the truth or falsity of
proposition B.) His ancestors will visit death or destruction on him or his
people if he swears falsely, and he cannot purify the curse. Similarly, a
man who accepted the marriage payment after 11(b) had been uttered
would have to pay heavy fines for sexual offenses he "committed" against
his sisters-in-law, actual and classificatory.

  If a person Q said to R

12   Feʔesia feleʔe beʔu i baʔe amu.
     'Shit on the ancestral skulls in your shrine'

there would be no contingency involved. R's ancestral skulls would be as
massively defiled as if a person had actually defecated on them, and R
and his people would be subject to illness or death visited on them by

their outraged ancestors (since another general cultural principle on which these pragmatic rules draw is that ancestors punish their own descendants, not the outsiders who perpetrated the offense). R would have to expiate this offense by sacrificing pigs, perhaps a dozen of them, in purification. R would, of course have a valid jural claim against Q and his kin for compensation: he would in fact demand the needed pigs for purificatory sacrifice. To purify the swear (until the *Pax Britannica* was imposed), Q or one of his close relatives would have been killed as well.

At the very least, to understand such usages we need to know that ancestors are participants (albeit unseen and usually silent ones) in every conversation. This basic sociolinguistic fact may not be part of the "linguistic knowledge" of Kwaio speakers, but the pragmatics of speech can hardly be understood if we lose sight of it; Kwaio pagans cannot afford to. Let us go back to 11(a), the swear denying a pig theft. As a speech act, this assumes a range of facts about the world in which it is uttered: about the logic of causality, about ancestors, about ritual defilement. They are not linguistic presuppositions; but they have pragmatic force. A Kwaio Christian or an ethnographer who uttered 11(a) to deny he had stolen X's pig would do so harmlessly and without the world-establishing force it normally has. It is the same utterance, but he does not live in the kind of world that can be transformed in that manner: he does not have altar stones, he does not have potentially punitive ancestors, or (in the case of a Kwaio Christian) he is assumed to be protected from them by the Christian God (who imposes his own sanctions against theft, etc.). But you are a Kwaio pagan accused of pig theft and utter such a swear of denial. Your interrogators will carefully examine the circumstances to be certain that no loophole has been left. And although they have no legal recourse once such a swear has been made, they may still harbor the suspicion that the denial is false. If the ancestors that convey your powers of pig theft are really strong and supportive, they may intercede with your other ancestors to persuade them to overlook an otherwise devastating curse. To assess the illocutionary force of your curse, your accusers will have to investigate relations in the realm where the consequences of the curse will unfold.

If we reflect on the curious Western ritual of swearing an oath on a Bible in court, these Kwaio curses and injunctions may seem less strange. If you do not assume that "God is listening," taking this oath is no bar to your perjuring yourself. And if we reflect on such residual forms in

English as "I'll be damned" or "I'll be a monkey's uncle," we might suspect that such forms may have once had a pragmatic force in European folk cultures that they now lack.

In Kwaio, speech acts are used to manipulate ancestrally controlled chains of events: to bespell an object, which then acquires magical potency (see Malinowski 1935 and Tambiah 1968) or, as in 11(a) and 11(b), to depict an imagined world-state whose consequences may then be actualized by ancestors. This is a universe where self-claimed monkey's uncles might not actually sprout tails (in deference to George Lakoff, we could call this logical but not fuzzy entailment) but where worlds are created and transformed by words, not merely painted with them.

The force of these Kwaio curses and injunctions, it seems to me, goes well beyond the "work" performed by speech acts imagined by most linguistic philosophers, situated as they are in a world without magic or punitive ancestors. And the chances that yet another stretching of tree-structures and other formal devices of transformational grammar can accommodate such phenomena seem to me remote and perhaps even irrelevant. It is, I believe, a fundamental error about the essential nature of language to imagine that the presuppositional and performative structures entailed *within* sentences can be understood unless one depicts the structures and premises of the culturally defined universe in which they are utterable.

Conclusions

In the Kwaio universe of magic, mana, and pollution, events we would view as "natural," coincidental, or accidental are interpreted as messages from unseen but all-seeing ancestors. Many of the messages Kwaio encode in speech are directed to those unseen actors, seeking to enlist their support, evoke their sympathy, solicit their forgiveness, or draw formulaically on their powers to manipulate events. The messages that the living direct to one another are monitored by those unseen actors and may evoke ancestral responses, punitive or supportive, or actualize imagined world-states through strategic use of language. Ancestors, on their part, may choose to speak *through* the linguistic faculties of the living (in what we would call possession states), so that the speaker of a linguistic message may not be defined as its sender (see Keesing 1978, Chapter 14, for a vivid autobiographical example).

It is scarcely surprising that the meanings of lexical items, the pragmatic conventions of speaking, and the social uses of speech presuppose and are infused by these cultural assumptions about the universe. That does not mean that Kwaio are muddled mystics. It does not mean that the structure of the Kwaio language is radically different from the structures of other languages: it builds on the same universal propositional and logical foundations. What it does mean, I think, is that competence to communicate in the conservative communities of the Kwaio mountains depends on a complex hierarchy of cultural knowledge. What words mean — words for magical acts, ancestrally manipulated events, ritual arrangements, and so on — can be economically learned and organized because of the structures of cultural knowledge that provide the foundations for lexical usage. How to use speech to enlist ancestral support, avoid ancestral wrath, manipulate chains of events, and meet the expectations and demands of human alters can similarly be learned as a code because of the cultural principles that motivate specific "rules." Without those givens, the rules would scarcely be comprehensible, formulable, or learnable.

My critique of the treatment of the language/culture "boundary" in contemporary grammatical theory is thus directed not at the notion that grammatical knowledge is a specialized and partly compartmentalized subsystem but, rather, at the perspective that linguists have taken on this partial separation. I anticipate that, as grammatical theorists increasingly broaden their concern with non-Western languages, they will be forced to face and deal squarely with the gulfs between what the native-speaker takes for granted about the cultural universe within which utterances are uttered, and hence need not incorporate directly into his/her theory of language, and what the linguist can ignore as outside the realm of language. Hence I anticipate that ethnographies of cultural knowledge and linguistic grammars will increasingly emerge as complementary sides of a single enterprise.

Notes

Acknowledgments. Research on Malaita has been supported by the National Science Foundation, the National Institute of Mental Health, the Social Science Research Council, the University of California, and the Australian National University. The initial version of this paper was presented in November 1975, as the final seminar in a series of "Meaning in Anthropology and Linguistics," jointly sponsored by the Department of Linguistics and Department of Prehistory and Anthropology, School of General Studies, Australian National University. That paper, written for an audience of anthropologists and linguists, sought to bridge between and summarize the connections between the preceding papers (cited in the references). For helpful comments and suggestions incorporated into an initial revision, I am indebted to R. Blust, R. M. W. Dixon, K. Hale, J. Haiman, J. B. Haviland, M. Silverstein, and A. Wierzbicka. The anonymous reviewers for this journal and K. Basso and D. Hymes contributed very helpful comments that were drawn on, under difficult circumstances during fieldwork in a remote Solomons community, in a final revision.

1. Professor R. M. W. Dixon's comment in the original seminar — "I agree with everything you said but I don't know why you bothered to say it" — may possibly reflect the reaction of the community of linguists. I suspect, however, that Professor Dixon's own work with Australian Aboriginal languages has forced him, unlike many of his disciplinary colleagues, to take into account the sorts of cultural knowledge with which I am dealing.

2. I go somewhat further in glossing these forms in Keesing (1975); the grammatical patterns I sketch are explicated in greater detail in Keesing (1977).

3. The Kwaio causative construction, which appears again in 6(b) and 7(c), is interesting in terms of the underlying-tree analyses of generative semantics. (For example, 'kill,' which has been so much debated on the linguistic frontier since McCawley's suggestion of an underlying 'cause-be-not-alive,' is rendered in Kwaio with *faʾamaea*, [('cause') ('be dead') — PR OBJ]. The causative prefix (faʾa-), followed by an adjectival root, to which an object pronoun is affixed, creates a surface transitive verb (see Keesing 1975:xix, xxviii; 1977).

4. In 'ribald joking,' normally forbidden sexual references can be made with impunity — up to a certain point. I recently heard a married woman warn a relative who jokingly suggested that she take her pubic apron off that he was going too far: 'in the old days you'd have had to pay compensation for that.' But, although in these joking sessions almost anything goes, a man who finds himself in such a context with a sister-in-law (in a broad classificatory sense) is supposed to withdraw (she is, in Kwaio society, the canonical sexually tabooed affine).

5. The latter invoking the fact that a man has a tabooed relationship with his real and classificatory sisters-in-law that proscribes any sexual elements in their relationship, and the fact that stepping over a woman's legs is symbolic of sexual intercourse with her.

References Cited

Basso, Keith H.

1976 'Wise Words' of the Western Apache: Metaphor and Semantic Theory. *In* Meaning in Anthropology. K. H. Basso and H. A. Selby, eds. Pp. 93–122. Albuquerque, N.M.: School for American Research, University of New Mexico Press.

Chomsky, N.
1965 Aspects of the Theory of Syntax. Cambridge, Mass.: M.I.T. Press.

Dixon, R. M. W.
1971 A Method of Semantic Description. In Semantics: An Interdisciplinary Reader in Philosophy, Linguistics and Psychology. D. Steinberg and L. Jakobovits, eds. Pp. 436–471. London: Cambridge University Press.
1975 Noun Classifiers and Noun Classification. Paper presented at Seminar Series: Meaning in Anthropology and Linguistics, Canberra, Department of Linguistics, Australian National University.

Fillmore, C. J.
1974a Pragmatics and the Description of Discourse. In Berkeley Studies in Syntax and Semantics, Vol. I. C. J. Fillmore et al., eds. Ch. V. Berkeley: Department of Linguistics and Institute of Human Learning, University of California, Berkeley.
1974b The Future of Semantics. In Berkeley Studies in Syntax and Semantics, Vol. I. C. J. Fillmore et al., eds. Ch. IV. Berkeley: Department of Linguistics and Institute of Human Learning, University of California, Berkeley.

Fox, J. J.
1975 The Interpretation of Symbolism. Association of Social Anthropologists of the Commonwealth. Studies 3. Roy Willis, ed. Pp. 99–132. London: Malaby Press.

Geertz, Clifford
1973 Thick Description: Toward an Interpretive Theory of Culture. In The Interpretation of Cultures: Selected Essays. C. Geertz, ed. Pp. 3–30. New York: Basic Books.

Goodenough, W. H.
1961 Comment on Cultural Evolution. Daedalus 90:521–528.

Hale, K.
1971 A Note on a Walbiri Tradition of Antonymy. In Semantics: An Interdisciplinary Reader. D. Steinberg and L. Jakobovits, eds. Pp. 472–482. London: Cambridge University Press.

Katz, J., and J. A. Fodor
1963 The Structure of a Semantic Theory. Language 39:170–210.

Keesing, Roger M.
1965 Kwaio Marriage and Society. Unpublished Ph.D. dissertation, Department of Social Relations, Harvard University.
1972a Simple Models of Complexity: The Lure of Kinship. In Kinship Studies in the Morgan Centennial Year. P. Reining, ed. Pp. 17–31. Washington, D.C.: Anthropological Society of Washington.
1972b Paradigms Lost: The New Anthropology and the New Linguistics. Southwestern Journal of Anthropology 28:299–332.

1974   Theories of Culture. Annual Review of Anthropology, Vol. 3. B. J. Siegel et al., eds. Pp. 73–97. Palo Alto, Calif.: Annual Reviews Press Inc.

1975   Kwaio Dictionary, Pacific Linguistics Series C, No. 35. Canberra, Department of Linguistics, Australian National University.

1976   Cultural Anthropology: A Contemporary Perspective. New York: Holt, Rinehart and Winston.

1977   Kwaio: A Grammatical Sketch. Canberra: Department of Anthropology, Australian National University. (Ms. pending publication)

1978   'Elota's Story: The Life and Times of a Solomon Islands Big Man. St. Lucia, Brisbane: University of Queensland Press; New York: St. Martin's Press.

Keesing, Roger M., and J. Fifi'i

1969   Kwaio Word Tabooing in Its Cultural Context. Journal of the Polynesian Society 78:154–177.

Lakoff, George

1971   Presupposition and Relative Well-Formedness. In Semantics: An Interdisciplinary Reader. D. Steinberg and L. Jakobovits, eds. Pp. 329–344. London: Cambridge University Press.

1974a   Interview with Herman Parret. In Berkeley Studies in Syntax and Semantics, Vol. I. C. J. Fillmore et al., eds. Ch. X. Berkeley: Department of Linguistics.

1974b   Pragmatics in Natural Logic. In Berkeley Studies in Syntax and Semantics, Vol. I. C. J. Fillmore et al., eds. Ch. X. Berkeley: Department of Linguistics.

Lakoff, Robin

1974   What You Can Do With Words: Politeness, Pragmatics and Performatives. In Berkeley Studies in Syntax and Semantics, Vol. I. C. J. Fillmore et al., eds. Ch. XVI. Berkeley: Department of Linguistics and Institute of Human Learning, University of California, Berkeley.

Malinowski, Bronislaw

1935   Coral Gardens and Their Magic: A Study of the Methods of Tilling the Soil, and of Agricultural Rites in the Trobriand Islands. 2 vols. London: George Allen and Unwin.

Morris, Charles William

1949   Signs, Language and Behavior. New York: Prentice-Hall.

Peirce, Charles Sanders

1932   Collected Papers of C. S. Peirce. Vol. 2: Elements of Logic. Charles Hartshorne and Paul Weiss, eds. Cambridge, Mass.: Harvard University Press.

Silverstein, M.

1976   Shifters, Linguistic Categories, and Cultural Description. In Meaning in Anthropology. K. H. Basso and H. A. Selby, eds. Pp. 11–55. Albuquerque: School of American Research, University of New Mexico Press.

Tambiah, S. J.
  1968 The Magical Power of Words. Man 3:175–208.
Wierzbicka, A.
  1972 Semantic Primitives. Frankfurt: Athenaum Verlag.

  1975 Translatability and Semantic Primitives. Paper presented at Seminar Series: Meaning in Anthropology and Linguistics, Canberra, Department of Linguistics, Australian National University.

Tibetan Fraternal Polyandry:

A Test of Sociobiological Theory

Cynthia M. Beall and Melvyn C. Goldstein

VOL. 83, 1981, 5–12

The sociobiological theory of kin selection refines the Darwinian concept of differential individual transmission of genes and adds that the representation of genetic material in the next generation may be either through one's own or one's relatives' reproduction. It hypothesizes that animals maximize their inclusive fitness — their net genetic representation in subsequent generations — and predicts the evolution of altruistic behaviors when such behaviors maximize genetic representation in subsequent generations (Barash 1977).

Sociobiologists' contention that all animal behavior, including that of humans, can be explained by a unified evolutionary biological paradigm has produced lively and often acrimonious debate characterized more by conjecture and plausibility than by empiricism. Most observers now agree that the level of this debate must move from theoretical possibilism to the testing of hypotheses with empirical data. But the testing of sociobiological hypotheses and predictions requires demographic and ecological data and until recently, anthropologists rarely collected such data in a systematic fashion. It is, therefore, not surprising that the debate over human social systems has hardly moved beyond the level of plausible explanations.

The present paper addresses this problem by testing hypotheses derived from kin selection theory in a Tibetan-speaking population practicing fraternal polyandry, the mating system in which two or more brothers jointly share one spouse. At first glance, fraternal polyandry presents a serious challenge to sociobiological theory since it appears to reduce rather than maximize the inclusive fitness of the male practitioners.

Male and female differences in parental investment are fundamental

Table 1. Probability of allele transfer: Probability of passing a given allele from male ego to a given offspring in monogamous and fraternal polyandrous marriages

Marriage form	A Probability of fertilization by ego	B = A × 1/2 Probability of transfer of a given allele by ego	C = 1 − A Probability of fertilization by brothers	D = C × 1/2 × 1/2 Probability of transfer of a given allele by at least one brother	E = B + D Total probability of allele transfer
Monogamy, 1 male	1	.5	—	—	.5
Fraternal polyandry, 2 males	.5	.25	.5	.125	.375
Fraternal polyandry, 3 males	.33	.165	.67	.167	.332
Fraternal polyandry, 4 males	.25	.125	.75	.187	.312
Fraternal polyandry, 5 males	.20	.10	.80	.20	.300

to the evolution of mammalian mating systems (Trivers 1972). Female reproductive strategies generally involve the intensive nurture of a few offspring while the male mating strategy involves maximizing the number of matings. Fraternal polyandry seems an exception since each of the several brothers sexually sharing a single wife substantially lowers his number of matings and his chance to fertilize a female and produce offspring. For example, among Tibetans it is not uncommon for one brother in a polyandrous union of four brothers to split off, marry monogamously, and have the same total number of offspring as his three remaining polyandrous brothers.

Polyandry also reduces the probability of one of ego's alleles appearing in any one of ego's wife's offspring (see Table 1). Assuming full brothers with equal sexual access to the wife and equal fertility, as the number of males in the marriage increases, the probability of ego's being the biological father of his offspring decreases (column B) while the probability of another male (a brother with only a 0.5 probability of possessing ego's allele and a 0.5 probability of passing it on) being the biological father increases (columns C and D). The effect of additional brothers in the marriage is a decrease in the total probability of ego's allele transfer (column E). (If one or more of the brothers is a half brother, then the values in columns D and E are lower.) This strongly suggests that each individual male in a polyandrous union makes considerable sacrifice of his potential to reproduce his alleles in the offspring generation (compared with monogamy). This potential attains a maximum in the case of a monogamously married male and declines regularly as additional males join the union. The decline occurs in the following manner:

$$\text{Total probability of allele transfer} = .25 \left(1 + \frac{1}{n} \right)$$

where n is the number of males in the marriage. The decrement in allele transfer potential is a measure of the "cost" of adding a brother to the marriage indicating again that the selection of the polyandrous alternative seems a case of reproductive restraint of altruism.

Sociobiological theory predicts that altruistic behavior must somehow be rewarding fitness or it would not persist. The existence of fraternal polyandry in Tibetan populations since antiquity thus seems paradoxical. However, a leading sociobiologist (Alexander 1974) has argued that fraternal polyandry is:

> commensurate with predictions from kin selection and parental manipulation . . . [p. 372] [it occurs in societies with] low *and* reliable productivity of farms, with the result that additional labor without additional children . . . has come to be the best route to long-term maximization of reproduction because of the necessity of retaining the minimal acceptable plot of land . . . [p. 317, emphasis in original]. In effect, a parent may dramatically increase the parental care available to its grandchildren by adding parents in the form of nonbreeding offspring. [p. 372]

Other authors use similar arguments to analyze human and avian polyandry (Berte 1977; Jenni 1974; van den Berghe 1979, personal communication). To date, however, attempts to relate sociobiological theory and human fraternal polyandry have not been based on demographic and economic data. This paper tests these and other hypotheses regarding the way fraternal polyandry may enhance inclusive fitness using data from a demographic and ecological study of a polyandrous population undertaken by Goldstein in 1974, 1976, and 1977 in Tsang Village in the Limi Valley of northwest Nepal.

Limi is an indigenous (i.e., not recent refugee) Tibetan culture area of about 518 sq. km. located in the northwest corner of Nepal abutting the Tibetan border. It consists of three villages ranging from 3,688 m. to 3,932 m. in elevation and adjacent pastureland ranging from 3,962 m. to

Table 2. Average number of children ever born, percent of children dying, and mean number of surviving children for females of four marital statuses in Tsang, Limi

Age and marital status	N	Mean number children ever born	Mean percent offspring mortality	Mean number surviving children
20–24				
monogamy	0	—	—	—
polyandry	2	2.0	25	1.5
unmarried	7	0.6	50	0.3
25–29				
monogamy	7	3.3	44	1.9
polyandry	4	3.3	55	1.3
unmarried	4(1)[a]	0.5	50	0.3
30–34				
monogamy	3	4.3	38	2.7
polyandry	2	5.0	40	3.0
unmarried	5(4)	1.2	25	1.0
polygynandry	2	7.0	62	2.5
35–39				
monogamy	3	6.0	41	3.7
polyandry	3	6.0	46	3.3
unmarried	4(1)	0.3	0	0.3
polygynandry	2	6.0	34	4.0
40–44				
monogamy	7	7.0	44	4.1
polyandry	2	7.5	55	3.5
unmarried	2	3.0	20	2.0
45 +				
monogamy	13(12)	7.8	59	4.3
polyandry	4	6.3	69	4.0
unmarried	4(3)	1.8	67	1.0

[a] The bracketed numbers are females with at least one birth. This number is used to calculate mean offspring mortality and survival.

over 5,181 m. in elevation. The population of the area is approximately 800 persons and that of Tsang village is 288.[1]

Theoretically, there are several ways in which fraternal polyandry may enhance the individual and/or inclusive fitness of a male. One hypothesis is that fraternal polyandry enhances fitness because of differential survival of offspring in such unions due to the greater parental investment made possible by multiple brothers supporting a wife and her offspring (see Alexander above).

Table 2 presents the average number of children ever born, percent of children dying, and mean number of surviving children for women of four marital statuses in Tsang. These data describe the entire adult female population of Tsang, not a sample of that population.

The data in Table 2 indicate that monogamously married females do not experience higher levels of offspring mortality than polyandrously mated females. Vital statistics collected by Goldstein between 1973 and 1977 confirm this by indicating no difference in infant mortality between monogamous and polyandrously married females. Mean offspring survival, moreover, is higher for monogamously mated females in all age categories but one (30–34). The greater parental investment of polyandrous males apparently does not pay off in terms of successful child raising.

Applying the potential allele transfer argument developed in Table 1 to the Tsang fertility data, the average number of copies of an allele a male would produce in the offspring generation if he were married polyandrously or monogamously is calculable. Given the fertility of 7.8 and 6.3 for monogamous and polyandrous females over 45 and utilizing the general formula presented in Table 3:

monogamously married: $1 [(7.8) \times (1) (.5) (1)] = 3.9$
polyandrously married: $1 [(6.3) \times (1) (.5) (.46)] + 1.25 [(6.3) \times (.5) (.5) (.46)] = 2.2$

the average number of copies of a gene in the offspring generation is 3.9 for a monogamously married male compared to 2.2 for a polyandrously married male.[2]

Another striking demonstration of the reproductive sacrifice of polyandrously married males is provided by computing the average number of copies of an ego's allele in the offspring generation according to different combinations of marriage types (see Table 3). For example, four brothers could implement seven logically possible combinations of marriage forms, ranging from all four marrying monogamously to all four marrying polyandrously. Using the actual Tsang fertility data and the probability of allele transfer concept (from Table 1), inclusive fitness for a male with three brothers is nearly five times greater if all brothers marry monogamously (9.75) than if they all marry polyandrously (1.97). There is considerable reduction in fitness associated with fraternal polyandry, even if only two brothers opt for polyandry (7.43).

Another possibility, derived from the notion of inclusive fitness, is that polyandrously married brothers recoup the loss of some of their

Table 3. Average number of an ego's hypothetical allele replicated in the total offspring of four brothers according to the marriage form of ego and his three brothers, calculated with respect to the completed fertility of women married monogamously or polyandrously and the probability of allele transfer[a]

A. Ego, 3 brothers each marry monogamously
   $1[(7.8) \times (1) (.5) (1)] + 3[(7.8) \times (.5) (.5) (1)] =$ 9.75

B. Ego, 1 brother each marry monogamously, 2 brothers marry polyandrously
   $1[(7.8) \times (1) (.5) (1)] + 1[(7.8) \times (.5) (.5) (1)] + 2[(6.3) \times (.5) (.5) (.5)] =$ 7.43

C. Ego, 1 brother marry polyandrously, 2 brothers each marry monogamously
   $1[(6.3) \times (1) (.5) (.5)] + 1[(6.3) \times (.5) (.5) (.5)] + 2[(7.8) \times (.5) (.5) (1)] =$ 6.26

D. Ego marries monogamously, 3 brothers marry polyandrously
   $1[(7.8) \times (1) (.5) (1)] + 3[(6.3) \times (.5) (.5) (.33)] =$ 5.46

E. Ego, 2 brothers marry polyandrously, 1 marries monogamously
   $1[(6.3) \times (1) (.5) (.33)] + 2[(6.3) \times (.5) (.5) (.33)] + 1[(7.8) \times (.5) (.5) (1)] =$ 4.02

F. Ego, 1 brother marry polyandrously, 2 brothers marry polyandrously
   $1[(6.3) \times (1) (.5) (.5)] + 1[(6.3) \times (.5) (.5) (.5)] + 2[(6.3) \times (.5) (.5) (.5)] =$ 3.94

G. Ego, 3 brothers marry polyandrously
   $1[(6.3) \times (1) (.5) (.25)] + 3[(6.3) \times (.5) (.5) (.25)] =$ 1.97

---

[a] Calculated according to the general formula:

Completed female fertility (monogamous or polyandrous)	X	Probability of possessing ego's allele	X	Probability of passing on ego's allele	X	Probability of fertilizing wife

reproductive potential through female siblings. Theoretically, the reproductive disadvantage of polyandrously married brothers could be offset if a sufficiently greater proportion of their sisters married and reproduced. The data indicate that this is not the case: about 72 percent of the sisters of both polyandrous and monogamous males marry.

Recent sociobiological theory emphasizes the importance of the environment, including human sociocultural systems, as a selective pressure which must be considered in attempts to explain behavior (Barkow 1978). An understanding of the costs and benefits of alternative strategies lies at the heart of sociobiological research, particularly for humans where sociocultural factors directly affect the opportunity costs of strategic options. This raises the question of why individual brothers initially marry jointly with their brothers and why they remain in these unions. This is not a hypothetical issue, for in Limi and Tibet multiple brothers do not always form polyandrous unions and some polyandrous unions fission when one or more of the siblings split off and establish monogamous nuclear families (Goldstein 1978). However, while monogamy clearly appears the better evolutionary strategy for an individual male to pursue, if brothers face celibacy, not monogamy, when they split off from polyandrous unions (van den Berghe, personal communication), polyandry would enhance rather than reduce fitness.

The Limi data demonstrate that monogamy rather than celibacy is, in fact, the real alternative to fraternal polyandry. There is no female infanticide and no male surplus as has been reported for parts of the Indian Himalayas (Majumdar 1955a, b; Parmar 1975). In fact, there is a large group of unmarried females in Tsang comprising 31 percent of the women over 20 years of age (Goldstein 1976). Rather than a shortage of females (or an excess of males) generating polyandry, fraternal polyandry produces a surplus of unmarried females.

Another concern is whether polyandrously married brothers desirous of fission can economically afford to marry and establish monogamous households. A common explanation of polyandry dating back at least to the Jesuit priest Desideri (DeFillippi 1937) who lived in Lhasa in the early 18th century argues that the "odious" custom of brothers sharing a wife was a necessity in Tibet because of the difficulty of eking out a subsistence existence in the harsh and infertile Tibetan plateau. If fraternal polyandry was (is) in fact a social adaptation to poverty and a last resort to preclude "beggary" as Desideri and others have speculated, it should be more characteristic of the poor in Tibet than of the wealthy. Brothers in wealthier families with abundant resources in land and animals would be able to split from their natal unit, marry monogamously, and set up and sustain neolocal independent households. Thus, one could hypothesize that the higher status/wealthier social strata (including aristocrats and various types of peasant serfs) in Tibet are more likely to opt for monogamy (maximizing individual and inclusive fitness) (Berte 1977; Alexander 1974). In fact, fraternal polyandry in Tsang is more characteristic of the wealthier/high status peasant families where 56 percent opted for polyandry[3] compared with 33 percent of the lower/poorer stratum (when two or more brothers were present in a given generation). Moreover, all brothers who fissioned from their siblings and parents were able to marry, set up independent households and raise families. There are only two unmarried adult males in Tsang; one of these is an old Tibetan refugee celibate monk and the other a middle-aged man who recently split off from his brother.[4]

The political, social, and economic factors underlying the decision to marry polyandrously or monogamously are discussed in Goldstein (1971, 1978) and are only briefly reviewed here. The Tibetans' explanation of fraternal polyandry is highly materialistic. They choose fraternal polyandry to preserve and increase the productive resources (the "estate") of their family corporation across generations. Fraternal polyandry is perceived and consciously selected as a means of concentrating labor and of precluding the division of a family's land and animals among its male coparceners. By virtue of this it is seen as a mechanism for maintaining or improving the wealth, power, and social status of the family. The motivation underlying the selection of fraternal polyandry is economic in nature but is concerned with wealth and social status, not subsistence survival.

Tibetans do not consider fraternal polyandry a highly valued end in and of itself, e.g., something to be encouraged because of a fundamental belief in the value of sibling solidarity. They can articulate quite clearly the negative aspects inherent in it as well as what, for them, are its overriding advantages. Fraternal polyandry, therefore, is not seen to be without problems. Because authority is customarily exercised by the eldest brother, younger male siblings have to subordinate themselves with little hope of changing their status. When these younger brothers are aggressive and individualistic, intersibling tensions and difficulties often occur. Similarly, tension in polyandrous families may derive from the relationship between the wife and her husbands or from the brothers' relationship concerning access to the wife. While the cultural ideal in Tibet calls for equal treatment in terms of affection and sexual access, deviations from this ideal occur and generate intrafamilial tensions, if not outright conflict. Such deviations are particularly common when there is a sizeable difference in age between the partners in the marriage. Thus, while polyandry provides an answer to one type of culturally perceived problem (albeit one which the subjects see as critical), it does generate other types of problems, and the choice facing all younger male siblings is whether to trade personal freedom (monogamy) for real or potential economic security, affluence, and social prestige (fraternal polyandry). Siblings with some reservations about marrying polyandrously must assess their potential for attaining satisfactory income and social status within some reasonable period. While monogamy is clearly an alternative to polyandry, a brother must examine the opportunity cost of fraternal polyandry vis-à-vis fission.

Another dimension to examine is the timing of fission among male siblings. Brothers in Tsang and Tibet do not marry polyandrously with the hope of accumulating sufficient wealth to fission the family later and marry monogamously. Fission normally occurs when younger brothers first reach their early 20s, i.e., the normal marriage age, and fraternal polyandry is clearly not a temporary phase or strategy in a family developmental sequence.

Lastly, the possibility exists that recent environmental changes such as the introduction of modern medicine or new crops have occurred in Limi and made fraternal polyandry appear to decrease fitness whereas under traditional circumstances it actually enhanced reproductive success. However, changes such as these have not occurred. Limi is one of the most inaccessible areas in already remote Nepal. Until 1976, the nearest airstrip (actually a flat pasture area) was a 14-day trek over rugged terrain including two passes over 4,267 m. and one pass over 4,876 m. At the time Goldstein first arrived in Limi (1974), only three Westerners had ever visited the area and since that time only a few have gone for at most several days. No modern medicine is available in Limi and the nearest allopathic physician is a 14-day trek on foot. The Limis, moreover, follow traditional Tibetan cultural patterns in food, dress, language, and social organization. As in traditional Tibet, cultivation of barley and herding of yak and sheep are the economic mainstays. Limi, in fact, was chosen by Goldstein as a research site precisely because it represented one of the last and purest manifestations of traditional Tibetan ecology and society (including contemporary Tibet itself).

In conclusion, this paper presents empirical data testing hypotheses derived from kin selection and parental investment theory for the Tibetan fraternal polyandrous mating system. It presents a number of arguments that could resolve the paradox of polyandrously married individuals reducing their individual fitness by hypothesizing gains they could obtain through inclusive fitness. However, considering the parameters measured, this analysis demonstrates that Tibetan fraternal polyandry does not appear to enhance the fitness of the individuals who practice it and in fact seems to entail substantial reproductive sacrifice. Its perpetuation, therefore, strongly suggests that sociocultural, economic, and political factors can perpetuate mating systems that entail significant reproductive sacrifice, i.e., can perpetuate mating systems that decrease the individual and inclusive fitness of the individuals who practice them.

Notes

Acknowledgments. We thank N. Chagnon, A. Steinberg, P. Tennis, and P. van den Berghe for critical readings of the manuscript, and G. Brittenham for mathematical assistance in deriving the formula on page 310. Research on which this report is based was supported by awards to M. C. Goldstein from the NICHD (Center for Population Research, grant HD 08984-01), the American Council of Learned Societies, the American Institute of Indian Studies, and Case Western Reserve University (Biomedical Fund).

1. For a more detailed description of this group, see Goldstein (1974).

2. Values of the probability of fertilization by ego (.46) and the coefficient of the term expressing the number of alleles ego's brothers may pass (1.25) are weighted averages obtained from Tsang females. Seventy-five percent of the women over 45 in polyandrous marriages have two husbands and 25 percent have three.

3. Two low-hereditary status but exceptionally wealthy families are included in this figure.

4. Note should also be taken that there is no norm of primogeniture in Tibetan society and all males theoretically have equal demand rights to land. Alexander (1974:371) misreads Goldstein (1971) when he cites this article as the source of his polyandry correlate that older brothers have first rights over land and wives.

References Cited

Alexander, Richard D.
   1974   The Evolution of Social Behavior. Annual Review of Ecology and Systematics 5:325–383.
Barash, David P.
   1977   Sociobiology and Behavior. New York: Elsevier.
Barkow, Jerome H.
   1978   Culture and Sociobiology. American Anthropologist 80:5–20.
Berte, Nancy A.
   1977   Polyandry: A Socioeconomic and Evolutionary Mating Strategy. M.A. thesis, Pennsylvania State University, University Park.

DeFillippi, R., ed.
   1937   An Account of Tibet: The Travels of Ippolito Desideri of Pistoia, 1712–1727. London: Routledge and Sons.
Goldstein, Melvyn C.
   1971   Stratification, Polyandry and Family Structure in Tibet. Southwestern Journal of Anthropology 27:64–74.
   1974   Tibetan-Speaking Agropastoralists of Limi: A Cultural Ecological Overview of High Altitude Adaptation in the Northwest Himalaya. Objets et mondes 14:259–286.

1976   Fraternal Polyandry and Fertility in a High Himalaya Valley in Northwest Nepal. Human Ecology 4:223–233.

1978   Pahari and Tibetan Polyandry Revisited. Ethnology 17:325–337.

Jenni, Donald A.

1974   Evolution of Polyandry in Birds. American Zoologist 14:129–144.

Majumdar, E. N.

1955a   Family and Marriage in a Polyandrous Society. The Eastern Anthropologist 8:85–110.

1955b   Demographic Structure in a Polyandrous Society. The Eastern Anthropologist 8:161–172.

Parmar, Y. S.

1975   Polyandry in the Himalayas. Delhi: Vikas.

Trivers, Robert L.

1972   Parental Investment and Sexual Selection. *In* Sexual Selection and the Descent of Man, 1871–1971. B. Campbell, ed. pp. 136–179. Chicago: Aldine.

van den Berghe, Pierre L.

1979   Human Family Systems: An Evolutionary View. New York: Elsevier.

The Golden Marshalltown:

A Parable for the Archeology of the 1980s

Kent V. Flannery

VOL. 84, 1982, 265–278

I am happily too busy *doing* science to have time to worry about philosophizing about it. [Arno Penzias, Nobel Laureate, 1978]

This is a story about archeological goals and rewards, and no one should look for anything too profound in it. It's really just the story of a ride I took on an airplane from San Diego to Detroit. That may not sound very exciting to those of you who fly a lot, but this particular trip was memorable for me. For one thing, it was my first time on a 747. For another, I met someone on that plane who became one of the most unforgettable characters I've ever run across.

The flight was taking me home to Ann Arbor after the Society for American Archaeology meetings in May of 1981. I was leaving San Diego a day early because I had endured all the physical stress I could stand. I didn't particularly feel like watching the movie, so as soon as the plane was airborne and the seat belt sign had been turned off, I went forward to the lounge area of the plane. There were only two people there, both archeologists, and both recognized me from the meetings. So I had no choice but to sit down and have a beer with them.

I want to begin by telling you a little about my two companions, but you have to understand, I'm not going to give their actual names. Besides, their real identities aren't important, because each considers himself the spokesman for a large group of people.

The first guy, I suppose, came out of graduate school in the late 1960s, and he teaches now at a major department in the western United States. He began as a traditional archeologist, interested in Pueblo ruins and Southwestern prehistory, and he went on digs and surveys like the rest of us. Unlike the rest of us, he saw those digs and surveys not as an end in themselves, but as a means to an end, and a means that proved to be too slow. After a few years of dusty holes in hot, dreary valleys he was no closer to the top than when he had started, and in fact, he was show- ing signs of lamentable fallibility. In 50 tries at laying out a 5-ft square, he had never come closer than 4 ft 10 in by 5 ft 3 in, and he'd missed more floors than the elevator in the World Trade Center. And then, just when all seemed darkest, he discovered Philosophy of Science, and was born again.

Suddenly he found the world would beat a path to his door if he criticized everyone else's epistemology. Suddenly he discovered that so long as his research design was superb, he never had to do the research; just publish the design, and it would be held up as a model, a brass ring hanging unattainable beyond the clumsy fingers of those who actually survey and dig. No more dust, no more heat, no more 5-ft squares. He worked in an office now, generating hypotheses and laws and models which an endless stream of graduate students was sent out to test; for he himself no longer did any fieldwork.

And it was just as well, for as one of his former professors had said, "That poor wimp couldn't dig his way out of a kitty litter box."

In all fairness to the Born-Again Philosopher, he was in large measure a product of the 1960s, and there are lots more like him where he came from. And let us not judge him too harshly until we have examined my other companion in the lounge, a young man whose degree came not from 1968, but from 1978. I will refer to him simply as the Child of the Seventies.

Like so many of his academic generation, the Child of the Seventies had but one outstanding characteristic: blind ambition. He had neither the commitment to culture history of my generation nor the devotion to theory of the generation of the 1960s. His goals were simple: to be famous, to be well paid, to be stroked, and to receive immediate grati- fication. How he got there did not matter. Who he stepped on along the way did not matter. Indeed, the data of prehistory did not matter. For him, archeology was only a vehicle — one carefully selected, because he had discovered early that people will put up with almost anything in the guise of archeology.

As a graduate student, the Child of the Seventies had taken a course in introductory archeology from a man I will simply refer to as Professor H. Professor H. worked very hard on the course, synthesizing the literature, adding original ideas and a lot of his own unpublished data. The Child of the Seventies took copious notes. Sometimes he asked questions to draw the instructor out, and sometimes he asked if he could copy Professor H.'s slides. When the professor used handouts, he bound them in his notebook.

At graduation, the Child of the Seventies went off to his first job at Springboard University. The day he arrived, he went directly to Springboard University Press and asked if they would like a textbook on introductory archeology. Of course they did. The Child polished his notes from Professor H.'s course and submitted them as a book. It was published to rave reviews. Today it is the only textbook on the subject that Professor H. really likes, and he requires it in his course. The faculty at Springboard U overwhelmingly voted the Child of the Seventies tenure. Professor H., on the other hand, has been held back because he hasn't published enough. "He's a great teacher," his colleagues say. "If only he could write more. Like that student of his at Springboard U."

To his credit as an anthropologist, the child had merely discerned that our subculture not only tolerates this sort of behavior, it *rewards* people for it. But the story doesn't end there.

The Child of the Seventies had written a six-chapter doctoral dissertation. Now he xeroxed each chapter and provided it with an introduction and conclusion, making it a separate article. Each was submitted to a different journal, and all were published within a year. He then persuaded Springboard University Press to publish a reader composed of his six reprinted works. In that reader, the chapters of his dissertation were at last reunited between hard covers. He added an overview, recounting the ways his perspective had changed as he looked back over the full sweep of his 18 months as a professional archeologist.

His publisher asked him to do another reader. This time, he invited six colleagues to write the various chapters. Some were flattered. Some were desperate. All accepted. He wrote a three-page introduction and put his name on the cover as editor. The book sold. And suddenly, his path to the top was clear: he could turn out a book a year, using the original ideas of others, without ever having an original idea himself. And in the long run, he would be better known and better paid than any of his contributors, even though they worked twice as hard.

I ordered a Michelob, and paid my buck-fifty a can, and sat wondering exactly what I could say to these two guys. It isn't easy when you know that one will criticize any idea you put forth, and the other will incorporate it into his next book. Fortunately I never had to say anything, for it was at exactly that moment that the third, and most important, character of this story entered the lounge.

He stood for a moment with his battered carryon bag in his hand, looking down at the three of us. He was an Old Timer—no question about that—but how old would have been anybody's guess. When you're that tanned and weather-beaten you could be 50, or 60, or even 70, and no one could really tell. His jeans had been through the mud and the barbed-wire fences of countless field seasons, his hat had faded in the prairie sun, and his eyes had the kind of crow's feet known locally as the High Plains squint. I could tell he was an archeologist by his boots, and I could tell he was still a good archeologist by the muscle tone in his legs.

(You see, I have a colleague at Michigan—an ethnologist—who claims that since archeologists have strong backs and weak minds, when an archeologist starts to fade, it's the legs that go first. On the other hand, his wife informs me that when an ethnologist starts to fade, the first thing to go is not his legs.)

The Old Timer settled into the seat next to me, stowed his carryon bag, and turned to introduce himself. I failed to catch his name because the stewardess, somewhat out of breath, caught up with him at that moment and pressed a bourbon and water into his hand. "Thank you, ma'am," he said, sipping it down; and he stared for a moment, and said, "I needed that. And that's the God's truth."

"I know what you mean," I said. "The meetings can do that to you. Six hundred people crammed into the lobby of a hotel. Two hundred are talking down to you as if you're an idiot. Two hundred are sucking up to you as if you're a movie star. Two hundred are telling you lies, and all the while they're looking over your shoulder, hoping they'll meet somebody more important."

"This year it was worse than that, son. Last night my department retired me. Turned me out to pasture."

"I wouldn't have guessed you were retirement age," I lied.

"I'm not. I had two years to go. But they retired me early. Mostly because of an article in the *New York Times Sunday Magazine* by an ethnologist, Eric Wolf. You remember that one?"

"I read it," I said, "but I don't remember him calling for your retirement."

The Old Timer reached into his pocket, past a half-empty pouch of

Bull Durham, and brought out a yellowed clipping from the Sunday
Times of November 30, 1980. I caught a glimpse of Wolf's byline, and
below it, several paragraphs outlined in red ink. "See what he says here,"
said the Old Timer.

> An earlier anthropology had achieved unity under the aegis of the culture
> concept. It was culture, in the view of anthropologists, that distinguished
> humankind from all the rest of the universe, and it was the possession of
> varying cultures that differentiated one society from another. . . . The past
> quarter-century has undermined this intellectual sense of security. The rela-
> tively inchoate concept of "culture" was attacked from several theoretical
> directions. As the social sciences transformed themselves into "behavioral"
> sciences, explanations for behavior were no longer traced to culture; behavior
> was to be understood in terms of psychological encounters, strategies of
> economic choice, strivings for payoffs in games of power. Culture, once ex-
> tended to all acts and ideas employed in social life, was now relegated to the
> margins as "world view" or "values." [Wolf 1980]

"Isn't that something?" said the Old Timer. "The day that came out
my department called me in. The chairman says, 'It has come to our
attention that you still believe in culture as the central paradigm in
archeology.' I told him yes, I supposed I did. Then he says, 'We've talked
about it, and we all think you ought to take early retirement.'"

"But that's terrible. You should have fought it."

"I *did* fight it," he said. "But they got my file together and sent it out
for an outside review. Lord, they sent it to all these distinguished anthropologists. Marvin Harris. Clifford Geertz. And aren't there a couple of
guys at Harvard with hyphenated names?"

"At least a couple," I assured him.

"Well, they sent my file to one of them. And to some Big Honcho
social anthropologist at the University of Chicago. And the letters
started coming back.

"Harris said he was shocked to see that in spite of the fact that I was an
archeologist, I had paid so little attention to the techno-eco-demo-
environmental variables. Geertz said as far as he could tell, all I was doing
was Thick Description. The guy from Harvard said he wasn't sure he
could evaluate me, because he'd never even heard of our department."

"And how about the guy from Chicago?"

"He said that he felt archeology could best be handled by one of the
local trade schools."

There was a moment of silence while we all contemplated the heart-break of an archeologist forced into early retirement by his belief in culture. In the background we could hear our pilot announcing that the Salton Sea was visible off to the right of the aircraft.

"They sure gave me a nice retirement party, though," said the Old Timer. "Rented a whole suite at the hotel. And I want to show you what they gave me as a going-away present."

His hand groped for a moment in the depths of his battle-scarred overnight bag, and suddenly he produced a trowel. A trowel such as no one had ever seen. A trowel that turned to yellow flame in the rays of the setting sun as he held it up to the window of the 747.

"This was my first Marshalltown trowel," he said. "You know what an archeologist's first Marshalltown is like? Like a major leaguer's first Wilson glove. I dug at Pecos with this trowel, under A. V. Kidder. And at Aztec Ruin with Earl Morris. And at Kincaid with Fay-Cooper Cole. And at Lindenmeier with Frank Roberts. Son, this trowel's been at Snaketown, and Angel Mound, and at the Dalles of the Columbia with Luther Cressman.

"And then one night, these guys from my department broke into my office and borrowed it, so to speak. And the next time I saw it, they'd had that sucker plated in 24-karat gold.

"It sure is pretty now. And that's the God's truth."

The trowel passed from hand to hand around our little group before returning to the depths of the Old Timer's bag. And for each of us, I suppose, it made that unimaginably far-off day of retirement just a little bit less remote.

"What do you think you'll do now?" asked the Child of the Seventies, for whom retirement would not come until the year 2018.

"Well," said the Old Timer, "so far the only thing that's opened up for me are some offers to do contract archeology."

The Born-Again Philosopher snickered condescendingly.

"I take it," said the Old Timer, "you have some reservations about contract archeology."

"Oh, it's all right, I suppose," said the Philosopher. "I just don't think it has much of a contribution to make to *my* field."

"And what would that field be?"

"Method and theory."

"No particular region or time period?"

"No. I wouldn't want to be tied down to a specific region. I work on a higher level of abstraction."

"I'll bet you do," said the Old Timer. "Well, son, there are some things about contract archeology I don't like either. Occasional compromises between scientific goals and industrial goals. Too many reports that get mimeographed for the president of some construction company, rather than being published where archeologists can read them. But in all fairness, most of the contract archeologists I know express just as strong an interest in method and theory as you do."

"But they're law *consumers*," said the Philosopher. "I'm committed to being a law *producer*."

The Old Timer took a thoughtful drag on his bourbon. "Son," he said, "I admire a man who dispenses with false modesty. But you've overlooked what I see as one of the strengths of contract archeologists: they still deal directly with what happened in prehistory. If I want to know what happened in Glen Canyon, or when agriculture reached the Missouri Basin, or how long the mammoth hunters lasted in Pennsylvania, often as not I need to talk to a contract archeologist. Because the answers to the cultural-historical questions don't always lie on a 'higher level of abstraction.'"

"No," said the Born-Again Philosopher. "Only the *important* questions lie on that level."

There was an interruption as the stewardess reappeared before us, pushing an aluminum beverage cart. We ordered another round of beer, and she picked up our empty cans, depositing them in a plastic trash bag attached to the cart.

"I'd like to ask a favor," said the Born-Again Philosopher. "Before our 10-minute stopover in Tucson, I'd like to examine the contents of that bag."

"Now I've heard everything," said the stewardess.

"No, it's not a come-on," said the Philosopher. "It's a favor for a friend. I have a colleague, Bill Rathje, who's doing a study of garbage disposal patterns in the city of Tucson [Rathje 1974]. He's got the internal system pretty well mapped out, but he realizes that Tucson is not a closed system: garbage enters and leaves via planes, cars, and backpacks. I promised him if I were ever on a plane landing or taking off from Tucson, I'd sample the refuse on board."

The stewardess struggled to remove all trace of emotion from her face. "Well," she said, "I suppose if you clean up everything when you're done — ."

"I'll be checking the refuse in the tourist-class cabin," said the Philosopher, "while my friend here" (indicating the Child of the Seventies) "will be checking the first-class cabin, and coauthoring the paper with me."

"And what do you call your profession?" she asked.

"Archeology."

"You guys are weird," she called over her shoulder as she and the cart disappeared down the aisle.

The Born-Again Philosopher settled back in his seat with a pleased smile on his face. "Now there's a perfect example of why archeologists should not restrict themselves to the study of ancient objects lying on the surface or underneath the ground. If we're to develop a truly universal set of covering laws, we must be free to derive them from any source we can.

"In my opinion," he said, "the greatest legacy we can leave the next generation is a body of robust archeological theory."

"Well, son, I'll give you my opinion," said the Old Timer. "I don't believe there's any such thing as 'archeological theory.' For me there's only *anthropological* theory. Archeologists have their own methodology, and ethnologists have theirs; but when it comes to theory, we all ought to sound like anthropologists."

"My God, are you out of it!" said the Born-Again Philosopher. "For ten years we've been building up a body of purely archeological laws. I myself have contributed 10 or 20."

"I'd love to hear a few," I said. And I could see I was not the only one: the Child of the Seventies was getting ready to write them down unobtrusively on his cocktail napkin.

"Number One," said the Philosopher: "Prehistoric people did not leave behind in the site examples of everything they made. Number Two: Some of the things they did leave behind disintegrated, and cannot be found by archeologists."

"I don't want to sound unappreciative," I said, "but I believe Schliemann already knew that when he was digging at Troy."

"If he did," said the B.A.P., "he never made it *explicit*. I have made it *explicit*."

"Son," said the Old Timer, "I guess we can all sleep easier tonight because of that."

"I also came up with the following," the Philosopher went on. "Number Three: Objects left on a sloping archeological site wash downhill. Number Four: Lighter objects wash downhill farther than heavy objects."

"Hold it right there, son," said the Old Timer, "because you've just illustrated a point I was hoping to make. So often these things you fellows call archeological laws turn out not to be laws of human behavior, but examples of the physical processes involved in the formation of sites. And son, those are no more than the products of *geological* laws."

The Born-Again Philosopher's face lit up in a triumphant smile. "That objection has been raised many times before," he said, "and it was disposed of definitively by Richard Watson, who is both a geologist and a philosopher. In his 1976 *American Antiquity* article, Watson (1976:65) makes it clear (and here I am paraphrasing) that even when hypotheses are directly dependent on laws of geology, they are specifically archeological *when they pertain to archeological materials.*"

Now it was the Old Timer's turn to smile. "Oh. Well. That's different," he said. "In that case, I guess, archeology just barely missed out on a major law."

"How's that?" asked the Child of the Seventies earnestly, his pencil at the ready.

"Well, following your argument, the Law of Uniform Acceleration could have been an archeological law if only Galileo had dropped a metate and mano from the Leaning Tower of Pisa."

"I don't think you're taking this seriously," the Born-Again Philosopher complained.

"Son," said the Old Timer, "I'm taking it fully as seriously as it deserves to be taken. And as far as I'm concerned, so far the only legitimate archeological law I know of is the Moss-Bennett Bill."

The Born-Again Philosopher drew himself erect. "I think I'd better go back and start my inventory of the tourist-class trash," he said, and he began working his way down the aisle toward the galley.

"You're being awfully hard on him," said the Child of the Seventies. "You have to remember that he's the spokesman for a large number of theoretical archeologists who hope to increase archeology's contribution to science and philosophy."

The Old Timer took a long, slow pull on his bourbon. "Son, do you watch Monday Night Football?" he asked.

"Occasionally," said the Child. "When I'm not correcting page proofs."

"I have a reason for asking," said the Old Timer. "I just want to try out an analogy on you.

"During Monday Night Football there are 22 players on the field, 2 coaches on the sidelines, and 3 people in the broadcast booth. Two of the people in the booth are former players who can no longer play. One of the people in the booth never played a lick in his life. And who do you suppose talks the loudest and is the most critical of the players on the field?"

"The guy who never played a lick," I interrupted. "And the guys with him, the former players, are always saying things like, 'Well, it's easy to criticize from up here, but it's different when you're down on the field.'"

"Well said, son," the Old Timer chuckled. "And I want you to consider the symbolism for a moment. The field is lower than everything else; it's physical, it's sweaty, it's a place where people follow orders. The press box is high, detached, Olympian, cerebral. And it's verbal. Lord, is it verbal.

"Now football is a game of strategy, of game plans (or 'research designs,' if you will), and what are called differing philosophies. In our lifetime we've witnessed great innovations in strategy: the nickel defense, the flex, the shotgun, the wishbone — and the list goes on. How many of them were created in the press box?"

"None," I said. "They were created by coaches."

"By coaches, many of them former players, who are still personally involved in the game, and who diligently study their own mistakes, create new strategies, and return to the field to test them in combat," said the Old Timer.

"I think I see what you're driving at," said the Child of the Seventies, but we knew he was lying.

"There are estimated to be more than 4,000 practicing archeologists in the United States," said the Old Timer. "Most of them are players. Sure, many of us are second- or third-string, but when we're called upon to go in, we do the best we can. And we rely on the advice and strategy of a fair number of archeological 'coaches' — veterans, people we respect because they've paid their dues the same as we have.

"What's happening now is that we're getting a new breed of archeologist. A kind of archeological Howard Cosell. He sits in a booth high above the field, and cites Hempel and Kuhn and Karl Popper. He second-guesses our strategy, and tells us when we don't live up to his expectations. 'Lew Binford,' he says, 'once the fastest mind in the field, but frankly, this season he may have lost a step or two.' Or, 'It's shocking to see a veteran like Struever make a rookie mistake like that.'

"What I worry about, son, is that every year there'll be fewer people down on the field and more up in the booth. There's a great living to be made in the booth, but it's a place that breeds a great deal of arrogance. No one in the booth ever fumbles a punt or, for that matter, misclassifies a potsherd or screws up a profile drawing. They pass judgment on others, but never expose themselves to criticism. The guys in the booth get a lot of exposure, and some even achieve celebrity status. What rarely gets pointed out is that the guys in the booth have had little if any strategic and theoretical impact on the game, because they're too far removed from the field of play.

"But the players know that. Especially the contract archeologists, and those of us who perennially work in the field. Because we have the feeling the guys in the booth look down on us as a bunch of dumb, sweaty jocks. And we're damn sick of it, son, and that's the God's truth."

"But you surely don't deny the importance of theory in archeology," said the Child of the Seventies. "I'm sure you've used what Binford [1977] calls middle-range theory in your own work."

"Of course," said the Old Timer. "I've used it to organize and make sense out of my data. Which is, when you stop to think about it, one of the main purposes for theory. The problem came when the guys in the booth began to think of 'archeological theory' as a subdiscipline in its own right—a higher and more prestigious calling than the pursuit of data on prehistory, which they see as a form of manual labor. As if that weren't bad enough, some of them are now beginning to think of themselves as philosophers of science."

"I find that exciting," said the Child of the Seventies.

"Son," said the Old Timer, "it *would* be exciting, if they were any good at it. Unfortunately, in most cases, it's the only thing they're worse at than field archaeology."

"But some are establishing a dialogue with philosophers," said the Child.

"That's right," said the Old Timer. "Now we're going to have philosophers who don't know anything about archeology, advising archeologists who don't know anything about philosophy."

"They want archeology to make a contribution to philosophy," said the Child.

"I'll tell you what," said the Old Timer. "I'd settle for making a contribution to *archeology*. I guess I'd rather be a second-rate archeologist than a third-rate philosopher."

"But doesn't archeology have more to offer the world than that?"

The Old Timer leaned back in his seat and sipped at his bourbon. "That's a good question," he said. "We hear a lot about archeology's relevance to anthropology in general. To the social sciences. To the world. And of course, we're all waiting for our recently departed friend to come up with his first Great Law. But I'd like to turn the question around and ask, What does the world really want from archeology?

"If I turn on television, or walk through a paperback bookstore, I'll tell you what I see. I see that what the world wants is for archeology to teach it something about humanity's past. The world doesn't want epistemology from us. They want to hear about Olduvai Gorge, and Stonehenge, and Macchu Picchu. People are gradually becoming aware that their first three million years took place before written history, and they look to archeology as the only science — the *only one* — with the power to uncover that past.

"I remember Bill Sanders telling me once that the only legitimate reason to do archeology was to satisfy your intellectual curiosity. And I suspect that if we just try to do a good job at that, the more general contributions will follow naturally. I don't think Isaac Newton or Gregor Mendel ran around saying 'I'm a law producer.' Their laws grew unself-consciously out of their efforts to satisfy their own curiosity.

"Son, if the world wants philosophy, it will surely turn to philosophers, not archeologists, to get it. I'd hate to see us get so confused about what the world wants from archeology that we turn our backs on what we do best. In my opinion, our major responsibility to the rest of the world is to do good, basic archeological research."

"You know," said the Child of the Seventies, "as I listen to you talk, I'm thinking how nice it would be to have you write an overview for the book I'm editing right now. A book on future directions in archeology."

"I'm not sure how excited I am about some of the future directions," said the Old Timer.

"That's why your overview would give us needed balance," said the Child. "Why, you're our link with the past. You've stepped right out of the pages of archeology's rich, much maligned empiricist tradition."

"You overestimate me, son."

"No. You're too modest," said the Child, who was not used to being turned down. "I feel that you may well be the most significant figure of your generation, and I'd consider myself deeply honored to have your overview in my book."

"Horsefeathers," said the Old Timer.

The Child of the Seventies stood up with a gesture of frustration. "I've got to inventory the trash in the first-class cabin, or I won't get to coauthor that article," he said. "But think over what I said. And don't say anything important until I get back."

We watched him disappear through the curtain into the first-class section.

"You must have been inoculated against soft soap," I told the Old Timer.

"Son," he said, "if that young fellow's nose were any browner, we'd need a Munsell Soil Color Chart to classify it."

"If you think he's at all atypical," I suggested, "take a good look around you at the next archeology meeting."

"And you know," said the Old Timer, "we're partly to blame for that. All of us in academic departments.

"We hire a young guy, right out of graduate school, and we give him all our introductory courses to teach. Then we tell him it's publish or perish. His only choices are to write something half-baked, or make an article out of an attack on some already established figure. You take those two kinds of papers out of *American Antiquity*, and you got nothing left but the book reviews.

"What we *ought* to do, if we really want these young people to grow, is give them their first year off, so they can go collect their own data and make their own positive contribution. How can we give them eight courses to teach and then put pressure on them to publish?"

"You're right," I said. "But our two friends here have discovered how to beat the system. One has created a specialty that never requires him to leave his office, and the other has figured out how to get other people to write his books for him. And we reward both of them for it."

"But not without some reservations," said the Old Timer. "You know, archeologists don't really like having a colleague who's so ambitious he'd kick his own grandmother's teeth in to get ahead. Businessmen, or perhaps show-business people, will tolerate it. They'll say, 'He's a real s.o.b., but he gets things done.' But archeologists don't want a colleague who's a real s.o.b. They're funny that way."

The stewardess with the beverage cart paused by our seats for a moment to see if we needed a refill. We did. And I took that opportunity to ask how our friends were coming with their inventory of her garbage.

"The one in the aft cabin seems to have hit a snag," she said thoughtfully. "I think he ran into a couple of airsickness bags."

"Well," said the Old Timer, "nobody said fieldwork was easy."

"What are those guys trying to find out, anyway?" she asked.

"As I understand it," I said, "they're trying to provide us with a better basis for archeological interpretation. Since archeologists study the garbage of ancient peoples, they hope to discover principles of garbage discard that will guide us in our work."

The Old Timer's eyes followed the stewardess as she passed through the curtain into the next cabin.

"Son," he said, "I want to hit you with a hypothetical question. Let's say you're working on a 16th-century Arikara site in South Dakota. There's lots of garbage — bison scapula hoes, Catlinite pipes, Bijou Hills quartzite, cord-marked pottery — you know the kind of stuff. You got to interpret it. You got an 18th-century French account of the Arikara, and you got a report on Tucson's garbage in 1981. Which would you use?"

"I think you already know the answer to that one," I smiled.

"Then why do I have the distinct impression that these two kids would use the report on Tucson's garbage?" he demanded.

"Because *you* still believe in *culture*," I said, "and these kids are only concerned with *behavior.*"

"I guess that's right," he said thoughtfully. "I guess I believe in something called 'Arikara culture,' and I think you ought to know something about it if you work on Arikara sites."

"But suppose, as Eric Wolf suggests in that *Times* article, you're one of those people who no longer looks to culture as an explanation for behavior," I suggested. "Suppose you believe that behavior is explained by universal laws, or psychological encounters, or strategies of economic choice. Then it really doesn't matter whether your interpretive framework comes from tribal ethnohistory or 20th-century industrial America, does it?"

"Nope. And that's sure going to simplify archeology," said the Old Timer. "For one thing, we can forget about having to master the anthropological literature."

He fell silent as the Born-Again Philosopher and the Child of the

Seventies returned to their seats, their notebooks filled with behavioral data and their faces flushed with success.

"Did we miss much?" asked the Child.

"Not much," said the Old Timer. "I was just fixing to ask my friend here where he thinks anthropology will go next, now that it no longer has culture as its central paradigm."

"I'm kind of worried about it," I admitted. "Right now I have the impression that anthropology is sort of drifting, like a rudderless ship. I have the feeling it could fragment into a dozen lesser disciplines, with everybody going his own way. Somehow it's not as exciting as it used to be. Enrollments are down all over the country. The job market sucks. I suspect one reason is that anthropology is so lacking in consensus as to what it has to offer, it just can't sell itself compared to more unified and aggressive fields."

"Doesn't Wolf tell you in his *Times* article what the next central paradigm will be?" asked the Child of the Seventies. He was hoping for a title for his next book.

"No," said the Old Timer. "He mentions other things people have tried, like cultural materialism, cultural ecology, French structuralism, cognitive and symbolic anthropology, and so on. But you know, none of those approaches involves more than a fraction of the people in the field."

"But it's useful to have all those approaches," I suggested.

"That's the God's truth," he agreed. "But what holds us all together? What keeps us all from pursuing those things until each becomes a separate field in its own right? What is it that makes a guy who works on Maori creation myths continue to talk to a guy who works mainly on Paleoindian stone tools?"

"In my department," I said, "they *don't* talk any more."

"Nor in mine," he said. "But they used to. And they *used* to talk because however obscure their specialties, they all believe in that 'integrated whole,' that 'body of shared customs, beliefs, and values' that we called culture."

"That's right," I said. "But now the Paleoindian archeologist would tell you his stone tools were best explained by Optimal Foraging Strategy. And the Maori ethnologist would tell you his creation myths are the expression of a universal logic inside his informants' heads."

"You know," said the Old Timer, "we've got an ethnologist like that on our faculty. He told me once, 'I'm not interested in anything you can feel, smell, taste, weigh, measure, or count. None of that is real. What's real is in my head.' Kept talking and talking about how what was in his head was what was important. For a long time, I couldn't figure it out.

"Then one day he published his ethnography, and I understood why what was in his head was so important. He'd made up all his data."

The Born-Again Philosopher stirred restlessly in his seat. "It's incredible to me," he said, "that you people haven't realized that for more than a decade now the new paradigm has been Logical Positivism. It's hard to see how you can do problem-oriented archeology without it."

Slowly the Old Timer rolled himself a cigarette. The Child of the Seventies sat up momentarily, leaned forward to watch, then slumped back in his seat with disappointment when he realized it was only Bull Durham.

"Have you considered," said the Old Timer deliberately, "the implications of doing problem-oriented archeology without the concept of culture?"

"Now you're putting us on," said the Philosopher.

For just a moment, the Old Timer allowed himself a smile. "Consider this," he said. "An ethnologist can say, 'I'm only interested in myth and symbolism, and I'm not going to collect data on subsistence.' He can go to a village in the Philippines and ignore the terraced hillsides and the rice paddies and the tilapia ponds, and just ask people about their dreams and the spirits of their ancestors. Whatever he does, however selective he is in what he collects, when he leaves the village, it's still there. And next year, if a Hal Conklin or an Aram Yengoyan comes along, those terraces and paddies and fish ponds will still be there to study.

"But suppose an archeologist were to say, 'I'm only interested in Anasazi myth and symbolism, and I'm not going to collect data on subsistence.' Off he goes to a prehistoric cliff dwelling and begins to dig. He goes for the pictographs, and figurines, and ceremonial staffs, and wooden bird effigies. What, then, does he do with all the digging sticks, and tumplines, and deer bones that he finds while he's digging for all the other stuff? Does he ignore them because they don't relate to his 'research problem?' Does he shovel them onto the dump? Or does he pack them up and put them in dead storage, in the hope that he can farm them out to a student some day to ease his conscience? Because, unlike the situation in ethnology, no archeologist will be able to come along later and find that stuff in its original context. It's *gone, son.*"

"It's as if — well, as if your Philippine ethnologist were to interview an informant on religion, and then kill him so no one could ever interview him on agriculture," I ventured.

"Exactly, son," he said. "Archeology is the only branch of anthropology where we kill our informants in the process of studying them."

"Except for a few careless physical anthropologists," I said.

"Well, yes, except for that."

"But hasn't that always been the conflict between 'problem-oriented' archeology and traditional archeology?" asked the Born-Again Philosopher. "Surely you have to have a specific hypothesis to test, and stick pretty much to the data relevant to that hypothesis, rather than trying to record everything."

"And what about other archeologists with other hypotheses?" I asked. "Don't you feel a little uncomfortable destroying data relevant to their problem while you're solving yours?"

"Well, *I* don't, because I really don't do any digging now," said the Philosopher. "I see my role as providing the hypotheses that will direct the research efforts of others. There are lots of archeologists around who can't do anything *but* dig. Let *them* do the digging.

"Look," he said, "I can't say it any better than Schiffer [1978:247] said it in Dick Gould's 1978 volume on ethnoarcheology. To paraphrase him: I feel free to pursue the study of laws wherever it leads. I do *not* feel the need to break the soil periodically in order to reaffirm my status as archeologist."

"Son," said the Old Timer, "I think I just heard 10,000 archeological sites breathe a sigh of relief."

There was a moment of air turbulence, and we all reached for our drinks. The sleek ribbon of the Colorado River shimmered below us, and over the audio system we could hear the captain advise us to keep our seat belts loosely fastened. Hunched in his seat, reflective, perhaps just a little sad, the Old Timer whispered in my ear: "That's what the ethnologists will never understand, son. There's a basic conflict between problem-oriented archeology and archeological ethics. Problem orientation tells you to pick a specific topic to investigate. Archeological ethics tell you you *must* record everything, because no one will ever see it in context again. The problem is that except for certain extraordinary sites, archeological data don't come packaged as 'cognitive' or 'religious' or 'environmental' or 'economic.' They're all together in the ground — integrated in complex ways, perhaps, but integrated. That's why the old concept of culture made sense as a paradigm for archeology. And it still does, son. That's the God's truth."

I wish I could tell you how the rest of the conversation went, but at this point I could no longer keep my eyes open. After all, you wear a guy out at the meetings, and then give him six beers and start talking archeological theory, and that guy's going to fall asleep. So I slept even through those bumpy landings in the desert where the Child of the Seventies and the Born-Again Philosopher retired to their respective universities, and then somewhere between St. Louis and Detroit, I started to dream.

Now, I don't know whether it was because of the beer or the heated discussion we'd had, but my dream was a nightmare. I don't really know what it means, but my friends who work with the Walbiri and the Pitjandjara tell me that Dream Time is when you get your most important messages. So let me talk about it for a minute.

In this dream, I'd been released by the University of Michigan — whether for moral turpitude or believing in culture is really not clear. No job had opened up anywhere, and the only work I could find was with Bill Rathje's Garbage Project in Tucson. And not as a supervisor, just as a debagger. Sorting through the refuse of a thousand nameless homes, Anglo and Chicano, Pima and Papago, hoping against hope for that discarded wallet or diamond ring that could underwrite my retirement program.

And then, one day, I'm standing on the loading dock with my gauze mask on, and my pink rubber gloves, and my white lab coat with "Le Projet du Garbage" embroidered on the pocket, and this *huge* garbage truck pulls up to the dock and unloads a 30-gallon Hefty Bag. The thing is heavy as the dickens, and I wrestle it onto a dolly, and wheel it inside the lab; and we dump it onto the lab table, where the thing splits under its own weight and its contents come out all over the place.

And you know what's in it?

Reprints.

Reprints of *my* articles. Every single reprint I ever mailed out. All of them. And I'm not just talking reprints; I'm talking *autographed* reprints. The kind where I'd written something in the upper right-hand corner like, "Dear Dr. Wiley, I hope you find this of interest."

You know, you can mail 'em out, but you never know whether they *keep* 'em or not.

And I suddenly realize that my whole career — my entire professional output — is in that Hefty Bag. Along with a couple of disposable diapers, and a pair of pantyhose, and a copy of *Penthouse* with the Jerry Falwell interview torn out.

But that's not the worst part.

The worst part is that the form Rathje's people fill out doesn't have a space for "discarded reprints." So my whole career, my entire professional output, simply has to be recorded as "other."

And that's where the nightmare ended, and I woke up on the runway at Detroit. I was grabbing my carryon bag as I bumped into the stewardess on her way down the aisle. "The Old Timer who was sitting next to me," I said. "What stop did he get off at?"

"What Old Timer?" she asked.

"The old guy in the boots and the faded hat with the rattlesnake hatband."

"I didn't see anybody like that," she said. "The only 'old guy' in the lounge was you."

"Have a nice day," I said sweetly. And I caught the limousine to Ann Arbor, and all the way home to my front door I kept wondering whether I had dreamed the whole thing.

Now I'll bet some of you don't think this all really happened. And I was beginning to doubt it myself until I started to unpack my carryon bag, and I was almost blinded by a gleam. A 24-karat gleam.

And there, hastily stuffed into my bag with a note wrapped around the handle, was the golden Marshalltown.

And the note read: "Son, where I'm going, I won't be needing this. I know you and I see eye to eye on a lot of things, so I'm going to ask a favor. I want you to save it for — well, just the right person.

"First off, I don't see any paradigm out there right now that's going to replace culture as a unifying theme in archeology. If some ethnologists want to go their separate way — into sociobiology, or applied semiotics, or social psychology — well, fine, they can call themselves something else, and let *us* be the anthropologists. I sort of felt that the concept of culture was what distinguished us from those other fields and kept us all from drifting apart for good.

"Because of the way our data come packaged in the ground, we pretty much have to deal with all of them to deal with any of them. It's harder for us to abandon the traditional concerns of anthropology, and we can't afford sudden fads, or quixotic changes in what's 'in' this year. We need long-term stability. And because we kill our informants as we question them, we have to question them in ways that are less idiosyncratic and more universally interpretable. And we have to share data in ways they don't.

"Because of that, we have to have a kind of integrity most fields don't need. I need your data, and you need mine, and we have to be able to trust each other on some basic level. There can't be any backstabbing, or working in total isolation, or any of this sitting on a rock in the forest interpreting culture in ways no colleague can duplicate.

"That's why we can't afford too many s.o.b.s. We can't afford guys whose lives are spent sitting in a press box criticizing other people's contributions. Son, all of prehistory is hidden in a vast darkness, and my generation was taught that it was better to light one tiny candle than curse the darkness. Never did I dream we'd have people whose whole career was based on cursing our *candles.*

"In the old days we mainly had one kind of archeologist: a guy who scratched around for a grant, went to the field, surveyed or excavated to the best of his ability, and published the results. Some guys labored patiently, in obscurity, for years. And one day, their colleagues would look up and say, 'You know, old Harry's doing good, solid work. Nothing spectacular, mind you, but you know — I'd trust him to dig on my site.' I believe that's the highest compliment one archeologist can pay another. And that's the God's truth.

"Now that doesn't sound like much, son, but today we got archeologists that can't even do that. What's more, they're too damn ambitious to labor in obscurity. So they've decided to create a whole new set of specialties around the margins of the field. Each defines himself (or herself) as the founder of that specialty, and then sets out to con the rest of us into believing that's where all the action is.

"And because archeologists will believe *anything,* pretty soon you've got a mass migration to the margins of the field. And pretty soon that's where the greatest noise is coming from.

"Now, don't get me wrong. A lot of these kids are shrewd and savvy, and they'll make a contribution one way or another. But that's one out of ten. The other nine are at the margins because things weren't moving fast enough for them in the main stream. You know, some of these kids think archeology is a 100-meter dash, and they're shocked and angry when no one pins a medal on them after the first 100 meters. But I'll tell you a secret: archeology is a marathon, and you don't win marathons with speed. You win them with character.

"Son, after our talk this afternoon, I got to wondering about what archeology needed the most.

"I decided there probably isn't an urgent need for one more young person who makes a living editing other people's original ideas. I decided there probably wasn't an urgent need for one more kid who criticizes everyone else's research design while he or she never goes to the field. And I decided we probably didn't need a lot more of our archeological flat tires recapped as philosophers. There seem to be enough around to handle the available work.

"What I don't see enough of, son, is first-rate archeology.

"Now that's sad, because after all, archeology is fun. Hell, I don't break the soil periodically to 'reaffirm my status.' I do it because archeology is still the most fun you can have with your pants on.

"You know, there are a lot of awards in archeology. The Viking Fund Medal, the Kidder Medal, the Aztec Eagle, the Order of the Quetzal. But those awards are for intellectual contributions. I'd like to establish an award just for commitment to plain, old-fashioned basic research and professional ethics. And that's what this trowel is for.

"So, son, some day when you meet a kid who still believes in culture, and in hard work, and in the history of humanity; a kid who's in the field because he or she loves it, and not because they want to be famous; a kid who'd never fatten up on somebody else's data, or cut down a colleague just to get ahead; a kid who knows the literature, and respects the generations who went before — you give that kid this golden Marshalltown."

And the note ended there, with no signature, no address, and no reply required.

So that, I guess, is what I'm really here for tonight: to announce an award for someone who may not exist. But if any of you out there know of such a kid coming along — a kid who still depends on his own guts and brains instead of everyone else's — a kid who can stand on the shoulders of giants, and not be tempted to relieve himself on their heads — have *I* got an award for *him*.

And that's the God's truth.

References Cited

Binford, Lewis R.

1977 General Introduction. *In* For Theory Building in Archaeology: Essays on Faunal Remains, Aquatic Resources, Spatial Analysis, and Systemic Modeling. Lewis R. Binford, ed. pp. 1–10. New York: Academic Press.

Rathje, William L.

1974 The Garbage Project: A New Way of Looking at the Problems of Archaeology. Archaeology 27:236–241.

Schiffer, Michael B.

1978 Methodological Issues in Ethnoarchaeology. *In* Exploration in Ethnoarchaeology. Richard A. Gould, ed. pp. 229–247. Albuquerque: University of New Mexico Press (for the School of American Research).

Watson, Richard A.

1976 Inference in Archaeology. American Antiquity 41(1):58–66.

Wolf, Eric

1980 They Divide and Subdivide, and Call It Anthropology. The New York Times Sunday Magazine, Nov. 30, 1980.

Types Distinct from Our Own:

Franz Boas on Jewish Identity and Assimilation

Leonard B. Glick

VOL. 84, 1982, 545–565

At the 1908 annual meeting of the American Association for the Advancement of Science, Franz Boas, vice-president of the association and chairman of its section for anthropology, delivered an address entitled "Race Problems in America."[1] A review of his bibliography up to that point indicates heavy emphasis on North American Indian ethnology, with an occasional item on problems of the Black population (Andrews et al. 1943). But at the meeting he chose to speak not primarily about Blacks or American Indians, but rather on the composition of the dominant White American population — "the facts relating to the origins of our nation" (Boas 1909:839) — and the possible impact of southern and eastern European immigration on that population:

> With the economic development of Germany, German immigration has dwindled down; while at the same time Italians, the various Slavic people of Austria, Russia, and the Balkan Peninsula, Hungarians, Roumanians, east European Hebrews, not to mention the numerous other nationalities, have arrived in ever-increasing numbers. There is no doubt that these people of eastern and southern Europe represent a physical type distinct from the physical type of northwestern Europe; and it is clear, even to the most casual observer, that their present social standards differ fundamentally from our own. Since the number of new arrivals may be counted in normal years by hundreds of thousands, the question may well be asked, What will be the result of this influx of types distinct from our own, if it is to continue for a considerable length of time? [ibid.:840]

Boas himself was a German Jewish immigrant who had arrived in the United States in 1884 and had not decided on permanent residence in this country until 1888, when he was already 30 years old. But now at age 50 he considered himself to be an assimilated German-American and, as these remarks suggest, had adopted the perspective of an insider contemplating the potential problems posed by the arrival of outsiders.

This paper is a study, based on published writings, of that perspective — of Boas's sense of personal identity and his views on the nature and desirability of assimilation in American society. Specifically, I shall examine his expressed attitudes toward two linked but conflicting elements in his personal history: his heritage as a German and as a Jew. As I shall try to show, the tension between these two created difficulties, familiar to students of modern Jewish history, which led Boas to adopt attitudes on assimilation that now seem to be paradoxically at odds with fundamental tenets of his professional career. The matter can be summed up by saying that he recognized the right, indeed the duty, of Germans in America to maintain pride in their national origins and cultural heritage, but advocated assimilation to the point of literal disappearance for Jews. Tangentially, it may be noted that in the case of two other ethnic groups with which he has not personally identified — Blacks and American Indians — he seems to have adopted a somewhat intermediate position: he anticipated their ultimate assimilation but recognized and supported their need for a sense of pride in their own heritage.

This entire dimension of Boas's work is marked with the deepest irony, in that his position on these questions was shaped — far more deeply, it would seem, than he recognized — by his own heritage as a German Jew and by formative years which coincided precisely with an eruption of the most explicit and virulent anti-Semitism in Germany prior to Hitler. These matters have been remarked on by other students of Boas's career, most notably Stocking (1968:149–157, 1974, 1979), but I shall maintain that the Jewish element in Boas's personal history and its influence on his intellectual career were greater than anyone has heretofore suggested. For notwithstanding his distinction as a scholar, Boas was in many respects a typical representative of that segment of late 19th-century German Jewry who had in effect abandoned the struggle to integrate Jewish identity with German nationality and had opted for an all-out effort to assimilate themselves out of existence. Some solved the problem — or tried to — by converting to Christianity. For Boas (and others like him) that tactic was clearly out of the question; he turned instead to a personal philosophy compounded of rationalism, cultural relativism, and ethical humanism, and identified himself as an enlightened universalist who had transcended both ethnic provincialism and supernatural religion.

But in much of his writing on ethnic identity and assimilation Boas was not expressing himself in accord with a disinterested rationalism. To the contrary, he was responding, and probably in an only partly conscious manner, to conditions and conflicts that had been integral to his personal experience in Germany during the 1870s and early 1880s. I think it can be argued that he devoted a significant part of his professional career, in a sense the core, to efforts to resolve the very problems that led him to come to America in the first place. That he never wholly resolved these problems is suggested by the inconsistency, and at times one must say incredibility, of some of his statements on assimilation. But that should not be surprising when it is understood that Boas was heir to two generations of Germans and German Jews who had struggled with these questions and reached anything but satisfactory conclusions. In reviewing his particular efforts to confront these matters we shall be focusing on a fragment of a much larger story — but a fragment that had substantial bearing on the history and character of American anthropology.

Kultur and the "Jewish Question" in 19th-century Germany

Jewish identity, as it evolved in Europe through centuries of segregation and oppression, did not rest primarily on theological considerations or questions of religious conviction. First and foremost it meant membership in a well-defined community regulated by ritual laws; more comprehensively it meant identification with a people who were united by a sense of shared history, culture, and destiny (Baron 1952:3–25; Katz 1961:3–34). For the Jews of Germany a turning point came in the early 19th century with their "emancipation" — a term and a process with many dimensions, as it turned out, but essentially signifying the granting of basic civil rights and formal liberation from the more onerous social and occupational restrictions that had been their lot for centuries (Katz 1964; Rürup 1969). Emancipation was bestowed on the Jews of northern Germany (the kingdoms and principalities of the Confederation of the Rhine) and Prussia only as a result of the Napoleonic wars and the French occupation; civil rights were granted grudgingly under orders, and when the opportunity came later they were for the most part dispensed with as despised elements in the legacy of the French Revolution (Sachar 1977:102–103). Everywhere in Germany between 1815 and 1848 there were efforts to roll back the calendar by reinforcing the authority of the traditionally privileged and hedging the influence of the emergent middle class. But restrictions on the Christian middle class were negligible compared to those that were more or less taken for granted with regard to Jews: exclusion from positions of authority in the military and the civil service, strict limits on achievable rank in universities, and so on (Dubnow 1973:36–43). The so-called Revolutions of 1848 were a potential turning point, in that they represented above all the efforts of suppressed sectors of the population (working class and middle class) to reverse these trends. The aims of the revolutionary leadership in Germany, as represented by the men who dominated the Frankfurt Assembly, can be epitomized as establishment of an open constitutional society, liberal in social and political orientation, and favorable to the interests of the emerging bourgeoisie (Hamerow 1958:121–125). Ideals of this sort were obviously compatible with Jewish interests; and even though they were for a time the victims of populist sentiment linking them with privilege and exploitation (Dubnov 1973:255–256), German Jews participated prominently and disproportionately in the revolutionary struggles — so much so that, according to Salo Baron, Jewish emancipation became "intimately identified in the public mind with the revolution" (1949:231). Moreover, in the spirit of the times, they were intent on gaining absolute acceptance as Germans who happened to be Jewish, neither more nor less. Speaking of those who participated in the movement, Sachar says: "The moment Jewish liberals were singled out, even by their friends, as German Jews, or members of the Israelitish 'race,' rather than Germans of the Jewish 'faith' or 'persuasion,' they bristled as if they had been mortally insulted" (1977:109).

The revolutions of 1848 failed, of course, in Prussia as elsewhere, and were followed by more than a decade of reaction. Once again German Jews found themselves struggling for rights which were granted only with such onerous limitations that virtually no German Jew at the time of Boas's birth (1858) could have been described as a completely enfranchised citizen. Only in July 1869 was legislation passed in the North German Confederation abolishing all remaining "limitations of civil and civic rights based on differences of religious creed"; this was incorporated into the constitution of the Second Reich in January 1871 — when for the first time it could have been said that the Jews of Germany had been entirely emancipated (Massing 1949:3–4; Reinharz 1975:5).

The years of Boas's childhood were pivotal in German history. The decade of the 1860s, just prior to the creation of the Second Reich, was a time in which nationalist sentiment reached a high pitch. Nearly every-one, liberal and conservative alike, agreed that the nation's foremost goal must be *Einheit*, unity, even if this meant some surrender of *Freiheit*, freedom. Thus the National Liberal Party, formed in 1867 as the main political organ of moderate middle-class liberals, declared from the start its rejection of traditional liberal values and individual rights when these conflicted with national unification and the immediate interests of the state (Pinson 1966:149, 168; W. E. Mosse 1970:129).

In this atmosphere of nationalism, patriotism, and emerging chauvin-ism, the position of the Jews was ominously uncertain. For nearly a century they had worked at the task of making themselves "presentable": they declared at every opportunity that they recognized no national loyalty other than German; they revised and "reformed" their religious services to eliminate all traces of particularism and messianism, arguing that theirs was a strictly "Mosaic" religion which taught human brother-hood and promoted ethical values over narrowly defined self-interest; they tried (with remarkably little success) to diversify occupationally and to reduce their prominence in commerce — in short, they did everything in their power to convince the German people that, though remaining Jewish, they could assimilate. There is considerable evidence that at no time did they succeed nearly as well as they hoped and perhaps imagined — that even the most assimilated Jews continued to move in social and occupational circles that were disproportionately Jewish. But of all the Jews in Europe surely none tried with more determination to merge with their fellow citizens (Meyer 1967:131–143; Katz 1973:176–215; Sterling 1958).

What stood in their way? The answer in a sentence is that most Germans did not believe that Jews, no matter how long they lived in Germany or how much they asserted their German identity, could ever become genuine Germans. Encounters between the two groups, re-marks Jacob Katz, "continued to be regarded as encounters between members of separate societies that differed in both status and quality" (1973:203). For in line with what was by then a well-established national self-image, most Germans considered themselves to be a unique ethnic group — a *Volk* — with a culture and heritage wholly and exclusively their own.

The term *Volk*, with its dual connotations of genetic identity and shared cultural traditions, is not quite captured by any English transla-tion: "folk" and "people" hardly convey the weight and attraction of the

German. It was introduced into German political philosophy of Herder in his influential *Reflections on the Philosophy of the History of Mankind* (1784–91); there it referred to any culturally distinct nation or people, all of whom, Herder argued, called for recognition and conservation as unique forms of human diversity. But embedded in this positive valuation of individuality was the clear expectation that each people should and must develop along its own particular historical track in order to maintain not only its individuality but its very existence. (It is worth noting, incidentally, that when Herder first used the term, in an early essay on the origins of language, he concluded that the definitive feature of a *Volk* was a common language, and cited the Jews and the Hebrew language as a signal example [Barnard 1965:55–62]).

This perspective on national identity was fundamental to what the German people came to perceive as the shaping principle of their own history. They were a single *Volk*: a racially distinct group, united not only by ties of "blood" but by a shared history reaching back into the prehistoric Teutonic past. And if simple observation contradicted this version of German history—if it was plainly evident, for example, that Bavarians and Prussians did not constitute a single "racial" stock—then it was all the more urgent that everyone believe it.

The place of Jews in this view of things was, to say the least, problematic. Could they be seriously considered part of the German *Volk*, even potentially? Suppose they were to convert and even assimilate to the point of disappearance: would that suffice? During the years prior to about 1875, Germans of a more liberal persuasion were inclined to answer these questions in the affirmative. But even among such people the willingness to accept Jews on terms of absolute equality was contingent on their demonstrating readiness to abandon completely their distinctive social, religious, and cultural characteristics: their attachment to Judaism as the religion of a "chosen people," no matter how that thorny term was to be interpreted and defined; their messianic aspirations for return to a lost homeland; their aversion to intermarriage; their peculiar and immensely disturbing predilection for such occupations as commerce and journalism; and so on. In short, if German Jews could ever become Germans, it would only be when they ceased to be Jews (Cohen 1975:xvi–xxiii; Rürup 1975:18; Pulzer 1980:138–139).

This, it must be emphasized, was the liberal position. Opposed to it, more acceptable to most ordinary Germans, and even more discouraging for Jews who were struggling desperately to achieve simple acceptance as citizens, was a new development in the history of anti-Jewish ideology which is usually characterized as racial or political anti-Semitism (Gurian 1946:227–235; Pulzer 1964). This was not so much a departure from traditional anti-Semitism as an extension of it and a shift in focus, but it represented a new and ominous phase in the life of German Jewry.

The matter was intimately connected to German social and economic history in the 1870s. The first few years after German unification were a time of intensive industrialization, widespread optimism, and financial speculation as Germany set out to realize its massive potential, and the nation progressed more rapidly in industrial development during this period than any in Europe. But the price was high. In 1873 a depression that affected most of Europe struck Germany with particularly disastrous consequences, and there ensued a period of severe economic distress that lasted until 1879 — with expectable consequences for the great mass of Germans constituting the *Mittelstand*, roughly the lower- and middle-income sector of the middle class.

During the latter years of the decade there arose a chorus of protest expressing reactionary sentiments regarding the profound social changes accompanying industrialization, and appealing to workers and the petty bourgeoisie as a dispossessed majority. Along with this went a distinctively chauvinist nationalism, romantic posturing with respect to German culture and identity, and, above all, virulent anti-Jewish declarations by men who were in the forefront of public attention (Massing 1949:5–47; Carsten 1967:22–31, Pulzer 1964:88–102). The core of their ideology was an assumed relationship, permanent and indissoluble, among three fundamental elements of German identity: race, land, and culture. The German landscape was deemed inseparable from the rural folk who farmed it and who were almost literally rooted in it. Indeed such people were the essential Germans, a reminder of what it meant to be genuinely German; they were intrinsic to the land, as much a part of it as any natural feature.[2] The same was true of their culture, which was thought to be part and parcel of their racial and historical identity, inseparable from them as a racially defined community and, of course, wholly inaccessible to any other people. The essential theme here was permanence. The German *Volk* were envisioned as rooted in soil, culture, and tradition, and the connections between racial ancestry, land, and cultural inheritance were perceived not as abstraction or metaphor, but as a literal and absolute bond that could not and must not ever be dissolved (G. L. Mosse 1964:13–28; Tal 1975:54–55).

The German concept of culture calls for particular comment in this connection. In contrast to the English-speaking world, which was tending by this time to merge the terms *culture* and *civilization*, in German the latter word (*Zivilisation*) developed distinctive connotations which established it, somewhat surprisingly, as the precise antithesis of *Kultur*.[3] Whereas *Kultur* evoked images of stability, peasantlike simplicity, and adherence to traditions (real or imagined), *Zivilisation* came to be equated with modernization, cosmopolitanism, and opportunism. It came to signify not the virtues of modern life but its least commendable features: migration of rural people into overcrowded cities; abandonment of traditional values; emergence of a new elite consisting of those who were able to cope with the stresses of urban life and to prosper at the expense of others. And from such a point of departure it was a short step to the ultimate conclusion: civilization was the natural milieu of the one people who were the very antithesis of all that was embodied in the terms *kultur* and *volk*, and indeed the principal threat to their survival. In short, civilization was the Jewish way of life.

The connection between Jews and civilization was taken to be not simply a matter of Jewish penetration into the nation's commercial and industrial life; that was obviously undesirable, but it was only symptomatic of something more profound. The essential problem was that Jews were by nature ethically deficient: their religion, if it could be called that, was nothing more than a fossilized relic of a tribal code of values, in which ethical behavior toward outsiders was neither practiced nor preached, and they had little if any capacity for appreciating cultural morality. Hence their disquieting success in the new realms of industry and commerce which rewarded just such instrumentalism. Hence, too, their absolute disqualification for being accepted into the German nation (G. L. Mosse 1964:126–129, 1970:43–44).

Statements of this sort were appearing as early as 1873, the year in which a journalist named Wilhelm Marr, the man who is generally credited with introducing the term "anti-Semite," published a pamphlet entitled "The Victory of Jewry over Germanism." This appeared in 12 editions over the remainder of the decade, and in 1879 Marr founded an "Anti-Semites' League" with the single declared purpose of "saving our German fatherland from complete Judaization and to make life tolerable there for the descendants of the original inhabitants" (Pulzer 1964:49–51; Massing 1949:6–10).

Much more influential than Marr, however, was a man who identified his principal political constituency as the region of Westphalia in the immediate vicinity of Franz Boas's hometown of Minden. This was Adolf Stoecker, court chaplain to the emperor, a man of considerable political acumen, and the most prominent anti-Jewish agitator of the period (Tal 1975:248–259, Massing 1949:22–31). In 1878 Stoecker organized a Christian Social Workers' Party advocating conservative nationalism along with populist opposition to capitalists who were becoming entrenched as a new elite. At first his message met with only a modest response; but in September 1879 he found his voice with an immensely successful public lecture entitled "What We Demand of Modern Jewry"—a skillfully phrased anti-Jewish diatribe designed to appeal especially to the dispossessed *Mittelstand* (Massing 1949:278–287). The Jews, declared Stoecker, were becoming an increasingly profound threat to Germany, not despite their apparent assimilation but precisely because of it. For in fact they would not and could not become an integral part of the German nation:

> The Jews are and remain a people within a people, a state within a state, a separate tribe within a foreign race. All immigrants are eventually absorbed by the people among whom they live—all save the Jews. They pit their unbroken Semitic character against Teutonic nature, their rigid cult of law or their hatred of Christians against Christianity. We cannot condemn them for this; as long as they are Jews, they are bound to act in this way. But we must, in all candor, state the necessity of protecting ourselves against the dangers of such an intermingling. [ibid.:285–286]

For a problem of such magnitude, he continued, there could be only one solution: "Israel must renounce its ambition to become the master of Germany." The Jews should accept at once the inescapable necessity that their influence in German life be curbed and abridged through strict quotas in every public sector, and through reorganization of the nation's economic structure. "Either we succeed in this," he concluded, "and Germany will rise again, or the cancer from which we suffer will spread further. In that event our whole future is threatened and the German spirit will become Judaized" (ibid.:287).

The impact of this speech on Berlin political life was "extraordinary," says Massing, and for the next five or six years the so-called Berlin movement, led by Stoecker and with anti-Jewish agitation as its definitive characteristic, "kept the capital in a turmoil" (ibid.:30; Boehlich 1965).

In 1881 Stoecker was elected to the Reichstag as representative for Siegen, the constituency immediately adjacent to Minden, and retained this position for many years. He was also by then representative for Minden to the Prussian Diet and is said by one German historian to have been "at that time one of the most popular men in Minden-Ravensberg" (Herzig 1973:125; Pulzer 1964:99). His opponent in the Reichstag election was Rudolf Virchow, the distinguished physical anthropologist and progressive politician with whom Boas soon afterward established close ties. Stoecker distributed an election-eve pamphlet describing Virchow as a defender of Jewish usurers. Moreover, he continued, the Progressives (left liberals) were calling Virchow "the representative of culture," but "I do not want any culture that is not Germanic and Christian" (Massing 1949:41).

That ideas of this sort were not confined to a few isolated crackpots but were in fact finding acceptance among people who stood at the center of German intellectual life is further confirmed by one of the most noteworthy documents of the period, a set of three articles by Heinrich von Treitschke, professor of history at the University of Berlin and one of the most eminent German academics of his time. Published first in the influential periodical *Preussische Jahrbücher* between November 1879 and January 1880, they were immediately reissued as *Ein Wort über unser Judentum*, "A Word About Our Jewry." Author of a multivolume *History of Germany in the Nineteenth Century*, Treitschke was a confirmed nationalist who found Volkish[4] ideology congenial with what he envisioned for Germany, and although his articles included conciliatory gestures, their overall thrust was remarkably hostile and uncompromising. "When the English and French speak with single-minded contempt of German prejudices against Jews," he declared, "we must reply":

> You know nothing about us. You live in fortunate circumstances which render impossible the emergence of such "prejudice." The number of Jews in Western Europe is so inconsequential that they cannot exert noticeable influence on national affairs. But over our eastern frontier there pours in, year after year, from the inexhaustible Polish cradle, a stream of ambitious young pants-peddlers whose children and grandchildren will in time dominate Germany's stock exchanges and newspapers. Immigration is increasing visibly, and the question of how we can blend this alien ethnic type (*Volkstum*) with our own

is becoming ever more serious. [Treitschke 1879, in Boehlich 1965:9–10; my translation]

Native German Jews, he continued, if genuinely possessed of the proper mental set and determination, might assimilate and become genuine Germans:

> What we must insist upon from our Israelitish fellow-citizens is simple: they should become German, should feel plainly and properly German — regardless of their faith and their ancient sacred memories, which are respected by all of us. [ibid.:10]

But there should be no misunderstanding about what was required: complete, unqualified assimilation, not creation of a German-Jewish synthesis that would make a mockery of the entire German cultural tradition. Treitschke was not optimistic:

> Within the most cultivated circles, among men who would reject with abhorrence any thoughts of religious intolerance or national arrogance, one now hears as though from a single voice: The Jews are our misfortune! [ibid.:13]

In the classroom during this same period, his principal biographer reports, Treitschke was even more aggressive: "He indulged uninhibitedly in much crude ridicule of German and East European Jewry" which was regularly rewarded with "frenetic applause" (Dorpalen 1957: 244). The effect of all this on German Jewish university students, not only in Berlin but elsewhere, is difficult to assess at this point. However, there can be no question that, appearing as they did in conjunction with a nationwide eruption of anti-Jewish sentiment, the overall impact of Treitschke's activities on educated sectors of German society was indeed substantial. "After Treitschke," comments Fritz Stern, "there was something virtuous about being anti-Semitic" (1977:572).

On the other side — but speaking for what had by then become a minority — stood the equally distinguished historian Theodore Mommsen, a liberal "in whom the spirit of 1848 lived on" (G. L. Mosse 1964:202). In reply to Treitschke he published "A Further Word About Our Jewry" (*Auch ein Wort über unser Judentum*) arguing that Jews were German citizens and should be accepted as such. Nevertheless, it is interesting to note that in adopting a position that was characteristic of German liberals, Jewish and non-Jewish, Mommsen offered advice to the Jewish community that was virtually indistinguishable from that of Treitschke: Jews, he urged, should do everything possible to hasten their own assimilation, by renouncing whatever was alien about themselves — their *Sonderart*, separate or distinctive manners and style of life (Boehlich 1965:227; Tal 1975:50–54; Liebeschütz 1962).

The public argument — such as it was — resolved, therefore, into disagreement over whether it was a matter of Volkish *Kultur* or "culture" in the sense that would now be called anthropological: could German Jews ever become thoroughly and indisputably German, or was the essence of *Kultur* inaccessible to them? For conservative Germans there could be only one answer: "Jews," remarks George Mosse in his definitive essay on the subject, "could never be men of culture — that was the crux of the matter" (1970:53).

Franz Boas: German-American

But the great majority of German Jews held no such image of themselves. Ever since their "emancipation" from ghetto existence, challenges of this sort had been a fact of life, an inescapable element in their relationship with the non-Jewish world: Do you intend, they had been repeatedly asked, to become wholehearted citizens of this nation; or will you insist on maintaining your claims to peoplehood, your sense of apartness, your longings for a messianic return to an ancient homeland; in short, are you going to be Germans or are you going to persist in being Jews? (Toury 1966:95–96; Pulzer 1980:140). Most Jews felt that this should not even have been a question, and their response, as we have seen, was consistent and determined: they desired nothing but full citizenship in the land of their birth; they aspired to no other nationality or homeland; their Judaism was only a "religious persuasion," a system of ethics and morality based on the teachings of Moses, which had nothing to do with nationality and did not in the least compromise their loyalty as citizens. That many, perhaps most, Germans were not well disposed to these arguments is not surprising in light of what they perceived to be their own needs as a people struggling to achieve national identity. But rejection did not — could not be permitted to — discourage the efforts of German Jews to find acceptance as Jewish Germans. Molded by nearly a century of effort to gain admission into German political and cultural life, deeply influenced by liberal visions of an open society, and desperately anxious to be accepted on terms of absolute equality, they explored every conceivable means of accommodation while struggling against those who would deny them even the right to accommodate. Some simply abandoned the effort and converted, or otherwise buried their Jewish identities as deeply as possible; others formed organizations whose foremost purpose was to argue the case for their right to retain Jewish identity without having to suffer ostracism (Elbogen 1944:190–194; Schorsch 1972:55–59; Rienharz 1975:22–27). It goes without saying that, whatever the particular strategy adopted, these were a troubled people, ambivalent about their own place in the world, able to maintain optimism about the future only by believing in the essential good will of the majority of the German people.

It was in this troubled social environment that Franz Boas grew to young adulthood. Clyde Kluckhohn and Olaf Prufer, writing on his "formative years," have something to say about the intellectual life of the period but make no mention of Volkish ideology. They do note that anti-Semitism was an important problem for Boas: "The letters from Kiel," they remark, "are particularly full of accounts of unpleasant activities among the student body, and of gross personal behavior" (1959:10–11). Commenting on the same period, A. L. Kroeber says that the "non-intellectual aspects" of Boas's university life "may be presumed to have been warm and rich," but he also notes that Boas left with "several deep facial scars from sabre cuts received in duelling." He then refers, somewhat ambiguously, to Boas's self-identification as being of the "Mosaic confession" and to a story about a fight and duel following an anti-Semitic insult (1943:7–8).[5] Stocking states explicitly that the duels were "fought over anti-Semitic remarks" (1979:33).

But whatever one wishes to conclude from these biographical fragments, there can be no question that during the years in which Boas was attending German universities (1877–81) Volkish ideology and anti-Semitism were a pervasive feature of life, something that no Jewish student could ignore. German student associations of the time explicitly excluded Jews from membership, and one, a Union of German Students (*Verein Deutscher Studenten*) openly declared: "Our goal is to fight certain cosmopolitan groups with the national pride of Germany's students" (Dorpalen 1957:246–47; Reinharz 1975:29). By 1883 Jewish university students had begun forming organizations of their own, the principal purpose of which was to develop defensive strategies. As one such group described the situation several years later: "Jewish depravity is put forth with such conviction and zeal, that the young Jew himself begins to doubt the righteousness of his cause and the right of Jewry to exist at all!" (Reinharz 1975:30).

Given these conditions it is not surprising that quite a few German Jews, Franz Boas among them, departed for America. Boas's decision to make this crucial move has received rather little attention from students of his career. The brief and generally superficial biography by Herskovits opens with Boas sailing for the Arctic in 1883, but Herskovits remarks that why he did so "has never been satisfactorily explained" (1953:9). A few pages later Herskovits touches on the decision to settle in the United States: "He found the intellectual atmosphere attractive, and the freedom to choose his own way that was denied him in Germany much to his liking . . . the restrictions of the organization of German intellectual life galled him . . ." (ibid.:12). Stocking's much more penetrating account of the years 1882–84 (1968:133–160) makes it clear that Boas "felt a considerable alienation from the Germany of his own day" (ibid.:150) and was contemplating emigration at least by 1882. It is important to note in this connection that among German Jews Boas was a relative latecomer to America. Most German Jews in the United States at that time were immigrants or descendants of immigrants who had arrived in the mid-19th century, following the collapse of the revolutions of 1848. Boas was a contemporary of immigrants from the initial wave of Russian and Polish Jews who fled to escape oppression that followed the assassination of Czar Alexander II in 1881 (Elbogen 1944:200–231; Glazer 1960:1696–1705). His first 20 years in the United States (1884–1904) corresponded precisely with the period of massive immigration of people from southern and eastern Europe, including millions of Jews — and also, of course, with the intense nativistic reaction that this elicited (Higham 1963:chaps. 3–6).

But it was not only the non-Jewish natives who were hostile. Most German Jews were profoundly ambivalent and at times overtly antagonistic toward the new Jewish immigrants from eastern Europe. In Germany, such people (who, as Treitschke had pointed out, were also appearing on the German scene in uncomfortably large numbers) had been looked on by assimilating Jews as "uncouth, uncultured and offensive" (Cohen 1975:xxiv) — a threat to their own aspirations toward unqualified acceptance as proper Germans. In the United States these attitudes persisted in much the same form, but with the inescapable prospect of long-term coresidence and coidentification as Jews (Rischin 1970:95–97; Sklare 1971:9–13).

The problem of identity for German Jews in the America of Boas's earlier years can be summed up, therefore, as uncertainty and ambivalence in a society in which the balance of influences was steadily changing (Glazer 1960:1709). For example, a study of the history of the German Jewish community of Milwaukee revealed progression from primary identification as German-Americans (encouraged in the earlier years by acceptance from non-Jewish German-Americans) through hesitant and somewhat reluctant recognition of kinship with eastern European Jewish immigrants, to eventual acceptance of identity as American Jews of German Jewish background (Singer 1977). But prior to World War I and even for a time thereafter, self-identification as German-American was relatively easy, even for Jews; one could, after all, be loyal to the Germany that one wanted to remember and dismiss unpleasant matters as transient aberrations or unavoidable lapses.

This was essentially the path that Boas chose. In all the years preceding the emergence of Nazism, he consistently maintained pride in his German-American identity, and indeed, until it became impossible, he was more than ready to defend the homeland, even to the potential detriment of his own career. Thus in 1916 we find him writing a letter to the editor of the *New York Times* protesting American hostility toward Germany, as manifested in what he interpreted as selective application of international law and unwarranted criticism of a nation that should not be expected to follow the same course of political development as that of the United States, desirable though such a course might be; although reluctant to speak out on political matters, he says, he was moved in this case "to express concisely what I, and I believe with me many other German-Americans, feel and think" (Stocking 1974:331). Standing with other German-Americans in defense of the homeland was essential, then, even if this meant defending a political system to which one was opposed in principle.[6]

But if being German posed some obstacles to achieving complete identity as an American, being Jewish might have posed even more. Boas faced the problem with a strategy that was essentially the obverse of his insistence on maintaining his identity as a German-American: he was determined not to be classified as a Jew.

Boas on Jewish Identity in America

It seems probable that Boas never identified himself in his public writings as Jewish, but he had much to say on the subject of his own identity and on the situation of Jews as a social category. Several items in his bibliography are especially instructive, and I want to examine them in some detail. By way of introduction it may be said that, in common with many other Jews, particularly German Jews and others of a strongly assimilationist bent, he did not acknowledge the existence of a specifically Jewish cultural or ethnic identity. That east European Jewish (or "Hebrew") immigrants were a definable population he obviously recognized, but it is important to realize that the definition was exclusively in terms of physical, never cultural, anthropology. To the extent that Jews, in his frame of reference, were possessed of a culture, it was strictly a matter of religious adherence: Jews practiced Judaism, an ancient religion which was essentially incompatible with humanism and individual freedom as he understood those terms.

Looking backward in an essay on his personal "credo," written for *The Nation* in his 80th year, Boas remarked that his early thinking had been conditioned by "a German home in which the ideals of the revolution of 1848 were a living force" (1938a:201). His personal views on religion were shaped, he says, by parents liberated from the burdens of Jewish orthodoxy. The language here, as throughout the essay, it may be noted, explicitly contrasts "freedom" with "tradition"; and the word "shackles," which occurs in this same general connection in his professional writing,[7] appears in this essay first in association with "dogma," then with "tradition":

> My parents had broken through the shackles of dogma. My father had retained an emotional affection for the ceremonial of his parental home without allowing it to influence his intellectual freedom. Thus I was spared the struggle against religious dogma that besets the lives of so many young people.... As I remember it now, my first shock came when one of my student friends, a theologian, declared his belief in the authority of tradition and his conviction that one had not the right to doubt what the past had transmitted to us. The shock that this outright abandonment of freedom of thought gave me is one of the unforgettable moments of my life. [ibid.:201]

The matter continued to concern him for many years thereafter and, in fact, was never to be far from his mind:

The psychological origin of the implicit belief in the authority of tradition, which was so foreign to my mind and which had shocked me at an earlier time, became a problem that engaged my thoughts for many years. In fact, my whole outlook upon social life is determined by the question: how can we recognize the shackles that tradition has laid upon us? For when we recognize them, we are also able to break them. [ibid.:202]

These words may sound strange coming from a man whose professional career centered on rigorous documentation of the cultural traditions of other peoples, including particular attention to their myths and religious beliefs (e.g., 1916, 1930). But as one reads further in the essay it becomes apparent that Boas presents identification of oneself or others with a particular cultural group as a primitive human characteristic, virtually inescapable and therefore provisionally acceptable, perhaps, for such people as the Kwakiutl and the Tsimshian, but deplorable in civilized society—a relic of the past, as it were, to be overcome through education toward progressive panhuman ethical values:

> It is my conviction that the fundamental ethical point of view is that of the ingroup, which must be expanded to include all humanity. . . . The identification of an individual with a class because of his bodily appearance, language, or manners has always seemed to me a survival of barbaric, or rather of primitive, habits of mind. . . . The solidarity of the group is presumably founded on fundamental traits of mankind and will always remain with us. It must be the object of education to make the individual as free as may be of automatic adhesion to the group in which he is born or into which he is brought by social pressure. . . . There is no other way to overcome the herd instinct in man. [ibid.:203]

The arguments of Volkish cultural theorists, by this time (1938) approaching their logical culmination in Germany, come in for brief refutation with the argument for human plasticity and infinite capacity for assimilation, a summation in a few sentences of most of his life's work:

> The belief that a necessary relation exists between the racial position of an individual and his mental attitude has never been proved. . . . On the contrary, we see men of the most diverse descent producing, under proper conditions, similar works of art. We see peoples of diverse descent taking over parts of the folk-poetry, of the literature, of others and making them their own. We see immigrants merging in the people among whom they live. [ibid.]

But despite the insistence on the particular version of human freedom that furnishes the central motif for this essay, Boas ends on a rather surprising and contradictory note of acceptance: we seek to be free, he says, and in a sense we can be; but our personal and social histories ineluctably shape us more than we may realize or desire. As for his own particular traditions, he concludes, "My ideas have developed because I am what I am and have lived where I have lived" (ibid.:204).

His immediate solution to the question of religious identification, to the extent that he accepted this as a question, was to become a member of the Society for Ethical Culture, founded in New York City by Felix Adler, an educator, social activist, and later professor of political and social ethics at Columbia. Adler was the son of the rabbi of the most prestigious Reform congregation in the country, Temple Emanu-El of New York. It was anticipated that he would succeed his father in the same pulpit, but at age 22 he delivered a guest sermon, entitled "The Judaism of the Future," which permanently eliminated that prospect. Judaism, along with all other formal creeds, was on the verge of extinction, he declared, and the only proper course was abandonment of religious particularism in favor of a humanistic faith embracing all humanity: ". . . we discard the narrow spirit of exclusion, and loudly proclaim that Judaism *was not given to the Jews alone, but that its destiny is to embrace in one great moral state the whole family of men* . . ." (Radest 1969:17; emphasis in original). This was, in fact, wholly within the spirit of Reform Judaism, although Adler carried the argument a step further by inviting everyone to join. In his lecture inaugurating the Ethical Culture movement, delivered in 1876, Adler proposed "to entirely exclude prayer and every form of ritual," and declared his primary allegiance to "freedom of thought" as the "sacred right of every individual man" (ibid.:27–28).

The organization prospered and achieved something of a reputation for service in the interests of social reform and humanitarian ideals. The membership was heavily and probably predominantly composed of cultivated German Jews, for whom it gave organizational legitimation to the very same values that Boas summarized as "the ideals of the revolution of 1848," and it is quite apparent why it appealed to him.[8] Although he does not appear to have been deeply engaged with the Society's program, he did travel to London in 1911 to deliver a lecture on "Instability of Human Types" at a Universal Races Congress, sponsored by the Society, which brought together Asians, Africans, and Europeans for what may have been the first such effort to achieve genuine cross-cultural exchange on a formal level (Radest 1969:93–94).

As we have seen, Boas's commitment to assimilation did not mean abandonment of loyalty to one's European homeland and heritage, which in his own case he associated exclusively, of course, with his identity as a German. Jewish identity, however, was clearly another matter: its very existence as an objective reality was questionable, and indeed enlightened individuals were to be expected to want to dissociate themselves from identification as Jews and should be permitted to do so. Quoting again from the "credo" essay:

> Groups as they exist among us are all too often subjective constructions; those assigned to a group often do not feel themselves to be members of it, and the injustice done them is one of the blots on our civilization. Too few among us are willing to forget completely that a particular person is a Negro, or a Jew, or a member of some nationality for which we have no sympathy and to judge him as an individual. [1938a:203]

The association of Jews and Blacks in this passage is characteristic for Boas (see Stocking 1974:314–315; Boas 1945:81), but it can hardly be imagined that he seriously viewed the Black population of America as nothing more than a "subjective construction." It does not seem far-fetched to suggest that the people he had primarily in mind were Jews like himself who were aiming for complete assimilation into the White majority population.

Suggestively similar phrasing appears in a 1931 essay entitled "Race and Progress." Speaking of the individual who is "automatically placed in his class" because of "bodily build," Boas comments:

> The same happens when a group is characterized by dress imposed by circumstances, by choice, or because a dominant group prescribe for them a distinguishing symbol—like the garb of the medieval Jews or the stripes of the convict—so that each individual no matter what his own character may be, is at once assigned to his group and treated accordingly. [1940:15]

He was, of course, well aware that anti-Jewish sentiment was far from uncommon in America; an essay on racial problems originally published in 1925 refers to "the anti-Semitic drift of our times" (1945:21) and it is unlikely that he had only Germany in mind. But he was remarkably resistant to any interpretation other than his own, namely, that this was due to irrational and spurious equation of individuals with categorically disliked groups; or to any proposed resolution other than his own, which came down to absolute assimilation, genetic as well as cultural and social. His most explicit statement on the subject appears, almost as an afterthought, at the end of a 1921 essay on "The Problem of the American Negro," later reprinted as "The Negro in America":

> Thus it would seem that man being what he is, the Negro problem will not disappear in America until the Negro blood has been so much diluted that it will no longer be recognized just as anti-Semitism will not disappear until the last vestige of the Jew as a Jew has disappeared. [ibid.:81; punctuation sic]

When writing specifically about Jews, Boas confined himself almost entirely to physical considerations, pointing out the well-documented fact that by all the accepted criteria of physical anthropology Jews are a very diverse population, and arguing from this that there is "nothing that would indicate the existence of any definite mental characteristics which are the common property of the Jews the world over, or even of a large part of the Jews of any one community" (ibid.:42; originally published 1923). On the subject of the traditional culture of European or other Jews he says nothing. He is prepared to grant that among Jews "there are certain rather small groups" with recognizable "mental characteristics" — "the merchants of Europe and America, the journalists, musicians, etc." But it must be understood, he continues, "that the groups to which these individuals belong represent on the whole a very small, closely inbred portion of the Jewish population of the world" (ibid.:41). "Taken as a whole," he concludes, "the Jews do not show any such traits that cannot be adequately accounted for by the influence of the social environment in which they live" (ibid.:41–42). He does not suggest that being Jewish might in itself operate as a formative element in a social environment.

Among the most revealing illustrations of his almost exclusive concern with physical characteristics are the letters and publications connected with one of his most frequently cited projects, the large-scale and controversial study, funded by the United States Immigration Commission, on the assimilation of immigrant children in New York City (Stocking 1974:203–218; Boas 1911, 1912a, b). Although the Commission had been explicitly charged with collecting and assessing information on social and economic questions (Higham 1963:130, 188–189), Boas framed his proposal from the start in the language of physical anthropology (he was going to study not social behavior but anatomical characteristics) and argued that this was entirely consistent with their mandate. In a letter to one of the Commission members, he remarked that the steadily changing composition of "our immigrant population" was giving rise to an important question: "Instead of the tall blond north-western type of Europe, masses of people belonging to the east, central, and south European types are pouring into our country; and the question has been justly raised, whether this change of physical type will influence the marvelous power of amalgamation that our nation has exhibited for so long a time." His study, he promised, would "settle once and for all the question whether the immigrants from southern Europe and from eastern Europe are and can be assimilated by our people" (Stocking 1974:202, 205).

Although a number of immigrant populations were included in the study as it eventually developed, the focus here, as in several other of his studies, was on the children of east European Jews (who appear under the rubric "Hebrews"). The essential finding in the early phases of the study was that longer residence in America meant more rapid physical and mental development; but the more startling finding was that the head shape of Jewish children ("which race was particularly the subject of our inquiry") was showing "a decided tendency to an increase in length" (ibid.:207).

Supported by several grants from the Commission, the study was eventually extended to a total of about 18,000 persons, including some 5,500 adults; about a third of the total were east European Jews (Tanner 1959:99). In one of his major publications on the results, Boas assessed the significance of his work with a bold and revealingly phrased specula-tion: The fact that head form could change in such a brief time, he declared, was "one of the most suggestive discovered in the investiga-tion, because it shows that not even those characteristics of a race which have proved to be the most permanent in their old home remain the same under the new surroundings; and we are compelled to conclude that when these features of the body change, the whole bodily and men-tal make-up of the immigrants may change" (1912a:5).

That he never advanced beyond physical traits—never took social status and cultural characteristics seriously into account—in his under-standing of the sources of Jewish identity, is indicated also by an un-published study conducted in 1926 and reported in brief by Herskovits. The study, which Herskovits calls "ingenuous," was designed to investi-gate the "quality of 'looking Jewish' " (Herskovits 1960:1505). With the cooperation of people in universities across the country (including Her-skovits at Northwestern) Boas arranged for freshman students, in large classes at the beginning of the academic term, to be engaged in mutual ethnic identification sessions. Each student first provided the following information on a form: place of birth, that of parents and grandparents, language spoken at home, "their 'race' — however they might wish to define this term — and its characteristics as they conceived them." Then each student, identified only by number, stood before the class while they wrote their guesses about "what they thought his origin to be, their degree of certainty in drawing this judgment, and why they classified him as they did" (ibid.:1505–1506). Boas told Herskovits that at one New York college 40% of the Italians were identified as Jews, and vice-versa, and Herskovits recorded several less expectable cross-identifications at Northwestern. But aside from the fact that they did not publish the results, there is nothing in this account to suggest that either man won-dered whether Jewish (or any other) identity was most manifest when a subject stood on mute display before a panel of amateur raciologists.

Finally in this connection may be mentioned an article in one of Boas's favorite periodicals that aroused him to an especially antagonistic response. In 1936, a labor historian named Benjamin Stolberg published an article in *The Nation*, entitled "The Jew and the World," which at-tracted a number of replies from such prominent individuals as The-odore Dreiser, Clifton Fadiman (who found it "brilliant"), and Reinhold Niebuhr (who did not). The article has not worn well; a blend of time-worn "explanations" for anti-Semitism with jauntily optimistic predic-tions for the immediate future, it closes with a swipe at "bourgeois assimilation," which, Stolberg declares, "is not assimilation to social democracy but to bourgeois prejudice. The Jew who becomes assimi-lated to bourgeois society, thereby becomes assimilated to bourgeois anti-Semitism." His solution: "You've guessed it: the answer is Marx-ism!" (Stolberg 1936:769–770).

For Boas this was a red flag in more than one sense, and he responded to what he calls Stolberg's "psychoanalytic verbiage" with the accus-tomed arguments for the right of individuals to stand alone. The blame fell on everyone who would not outgrow ethnocentric traditions.

> We ought to recognize that it is the frequent problem that presents itself whenever a socially segregated or racially recognizable group is considered as a unit in which each individual partakes of all those traits that are more or less

arbitrarily ascribed to it, often merely on the basis of tradition. No matter whether it is a case of Greeks despising barbarians, nobility the common people, Catholics the Protestants, the castes of India one another, whites the Negroes or Japanese, or Gentiles, the Jews; the situation is always the same. [1936:25]

People who want to assimilate, he insists, must be allowed to do so; they must not be forced to remain in a "class":

It becomes particularly acute for the proscribed class when its members come to be conscious of the fact that they are no longer a class but individuals like the rest of the people among whom they live, and when this claim is not recognized but each individual is still looked upon as a member of the despised group. . . . Even our socially privileged classes have not learned the simple fact that they should have learned in school and home, that it is the individual who counts, not the class to which he is assigned. [ibid.]

This use of the term "class" to mean ethnic category was characteristic for Boas, whose sensitivity to ethnic prejudice was paralleled by relative indifference to problems of social class. In a brief discussion of this point Bernhard Stern cites another article, published in a Jewish periodical a year after the reply to Stolberg, in which Boas again expressed the notion that an individual may be arbitrarily and unjustly "assigned to a class with which he himself may have nothing in common" (Boas 1937:232, cited in Stern 1959:238).

The most profound threat to everything that Boas stood for came with the emergence of the Nazis into power, and from evidence that began to appear immediately thereafter that they fully intended to convert the most radical elements of Volkish ideology into public policy. He probably never understood Nazism in adequate historical perspective (Stocking [1979:43] cites a letter of November 1935 in which actions against Jews are described as a threat to "the old cultural values of Germany") but continued to speak and act with his accustomed faith in the power of rationalism to triumph over clannish hatreds and prejudices. His bibliography reflects these developments almost at once: in 1933 he addressed an "open letter" to President von Hindenburg protesting the appointment of Hitler as Chancellor (Herskovits 1953:117), wrote a letter to the editor of the New York *Staats-Zeitung und Herold* commenting on anti-Jewish legislation in Germany, and composed an influential essay, "Aryans and Non-Aryans," which appeared first in a German journal (as *Arier und Nicht Arier*) but was translated into English and Spanish, and widely reprinted over the next year or two in several versions (Andrews et al. 1943:102–103). It is now most readily accessible as a chapter in the collection entitled *Race and Democratic Society*, where it appears as "The 'Aryans'" (Boas 1945:43–53). Herskovits remarks that of all Boas's writings this article "achieved perhaps the widest circulation" (1953:117).

Once again and expectably, the focus is on race, not culture. There is no such thing as a German race, Boas insists; there are only physically diverse populations, with diverse origins and connections. There may be regionally distinctive populations, perhaps, but that is only because of long residence in one environment and tendencies toward local intermarriage; even such populations, however, are by no means fixed or absolutely stable. Jews, too, exhibit a multitude of "local types" impossible of categorical definition, shaped like other people by "the natural and social environment" in which they happen to have been living (ibid.:50). As for the term "Aryan," that is as worthless in this context as the term "Semite": both refer to linguistic groups bearing no consistent relations whatever to racial types. (He seems unaware here of the parallel objections that might have been raised against his own use of "Hebrew.")

The essay closes with a straightforward reiteration of the fundamental principle of his anthropology: race, language, and culture are independent variables, independently determined, and the first of these has no influence whatsoever on "mental characteristics." The final sentence epitomizes Boas's understanding of his own identity, which was not to change in the few years of life then remaining to him: "Just as the Germanized Slavs and French have become German in their culture, as the Frenchified Germans have become French, the Russianized ones Russian; so have the German Jews become Germans" (ibid.:53).

Conclusion

Boas died in 1942, his faith in human malleability and limitless capacity for assimilation apparently undiminished. But looking back over his writing on the subjects of culture, identity and assimilation, one encounters inconsistencies, even outright contradictions, that seem to call for explanation. At times we see Boas the precise ethnographer, patiently recording details of myths and religious beliefs of people in cultural worlds immensely distant from his own. We see him documenting the ineffable uniqueness of other cultures and arguing for the principle, so central to the discipline he established, that every way of life must be not only permitted but encouraged to flourish on its own terms, free of gratuitous interference from outsiders. In line with this, we find him earnestly defending the government, society, and even the military policies of his native land, and insisting that no one has the right to impose externally derived standards on another nation. But at other times we encounter Boas the assimilationist and the exponent of a weighted system of implicit cultural values: a true believer in his adopted nation's amalgamative power who looks forward to the time when everyone — even those most unpromising candidates, Jews and Blacks — will have melted so completely into the American mainstream that ethnic antagonism will disappear for lack of objects. This Boas, well disposed though he is toward people as individuals, has neither interest in nor sympathy for their "traditions," which he seems to dismiss as primitive relics, to be dispensed with as obstacles in the path toward ethical humanism.

The paradox is resolved, however, when one realizes the extent to which Boas maintained bipolar attitudes toward the two fundamental dimensions of his own identity, the German and the Jewish. For when it came to statements reflecting his sense of who he was and where he stood in the ethnic spectrum, Boas seems to have been quite certain of his position and intent on defining it unambiguously: he was a German-American. In this regard, then, his commitment to assimilation did not extend so far as to require that he abandon his own past. But, of course, Boas was also a Jew; and it was from that point of departure — only dimly recognized, it would seem — that he declared his commitment to being identified solely as an autonomous individual, bound by the "shackles" of no tradition, determined not to be classified as a member of any group.

Associated with this disinclination to confront fully the elements of his own identity were Boas's efforts toward defining Jews out of existence through recourse to anatomical studies, epitomized by his research on immigrant children and his conclusions derived from minor changes in head shape. Paradoxically, by concentrating in this manner on physical anthropology, to the virtual exclusion of the historical, economic, and cultural factors that shaped European Jewish identity over nearly two millenia, Boas was employing the very principle to which he was most fundamentally opposed, that "racial" type is the fundamental consideration in national identity, in order to reach conclusions precisely opposite to those of his racist antagonists here and in Germany. Had he carried his analyses one essential step further and given serious consideration to European Jewish history and culture (including its distinguished German variant), he might have reached more penetrating conclusions on assimilation and related questions. But to have done so would have required more candid examination of Jewish identity than he was ever prepared to undertake.

What can one say about the possible impact of German ideas about *Kultur* on Boas's elevation of the concept of culture to a central place in American anthropology? Here I am on less certain ground, but the evidence is so suggestive as to call for some comment. It is evident that Boas's position on the relative importance of race and geography, as compared with history and culture, as molders of human behavior and character, stood in direct antithesis to everything that he and other young German Jewish intellectuals had to contend with in the Germany of the 1870s and 1880s. In particular, his stance on human plasticity and capacity for assimilation represented an absolute reversal of the meaning of *Kultur*. He devoted much of his life to advocacy of the argument that anyone could, as he once expressed it, "partake" of any culture, provided that conditions were favorable in precisely the sense that was not true for the Jews in Germany:

> It cannot be shown by the widest stretch of the imagination that descent makes it impossible to partake of any given type of culture, provided the individual is completely socially one of the people among whom he lives and, what is more important, is considered also by society as one of its members. [1938b:668]

As I have tried to show, however, his writings on the subject of culture and assimilation turn out on critical examination to be not only ambiguous but at times absolutely contradictory; for it could be equally well argued that his ethnographic methods and style — the well-known predilection for publishing long texts, the amassing of "factual" data with a minimum of interpretation, the insistence on trying to see the world "as the natives saw it" (Harris 1968:316) — testify to his irreducible respect for the integrity of each culture. Counterposed against that, however, we find his expectation that Jews, being only "subjective constructions," will disappear into the melting pot; indeed, he seems to say, that is their only sensible option if they are to escape endless antagonism.

Contemplating Boas's career, then, in light of these considerations, the conclusion seems inescapable that the man who led the way to the establishment of cultural anthropology as a discipline could not, or would not, recognize some of the most fundamental determinants of his own perspective on culture, society, and identity—specifically, those elements that were profoundly influenced, if not definitively shaped, by his heritage as a Jew. That this very trait was characteristic of many Jewish immigrants of his generation adds a final note of irony.

Notes

1. Much of this essay can be read as commentary on a recent observation by George W. Stocking, Jr.: "From the perspective of today, one may well question just how far Boas was able to bring the shackles of his own tradition fully to consciousness" (1979:47).

2. One of the most influential proponents of this view of landscape was Freidrich Ratzel, whose related theories on *Anthropo-geographie* were influential in the development of Boas's early approach to environment and culture, but which he eventually rejected (see G. L. Mosse 1964:18; Stocking 1968:145–146).

3. Tylor's *Researches into the Early History of Mankind and the Development of Civilization*, originally published in 1865, illustrates the former point: the term "civilization" appears alone in the opening sentence, which is an earlier version of the well-known definition in *Primitive Culture* ("Culture or Civilization . . ."). But one chapter of the earlier book is entitled "Growth and Decline of Culture," and throughout the book Tylor uses the two terms interchangeably. The subject is treated in depth in Stocking 1968, chapter 4. See also Kroeber and Kluckhohn 1963:81. Their book gives some notion of the complex history of these terms but says very little about the matters under discussion in this paper.

4. I take this term and spelling from G. L. Mosse 1964.

5. The term "Mosaic confession" (or "persuasion") had specific connotations: it meant adherence to the Biblical religion associated with Moses (nominally at least) but rejection of post-Biblical rabbinic Judaism as encoded in the Talmud and later books of commentary. The Talmud, a product of the Diaspora, has been a favorite target of anti-Jewish polemics for some 1,200 years. German Jews anticipated that by identifying their religion as "Mosaic" they might escape at least some of the hostility directed at traditional Judaism. As might be imagined, most Germans failed to grasp the distinction.

6. In 1917 a group calling themselves Society of the Friends of the German Republic invited Boas to become a member. Apparently they intended to make certain that Germany, once defeated, would be reconstituted as a republic. Boas replied that he considered it "impudent and futile for citizens of one State to

arrogate to themselves the right to interfere in any way with the political affairs of another state," and that peace would never be achieved "by the relapse into the Crusading spirit of which you make yourself guilty" (1917).

7. "The data of ethnology prove that not only our knowledge, but also our emotions are the result of the form of our social life and of the history of the people to whom we belong. If we desire to understand the development of human culture we must try to free ourselves of these shackles" (Boas 1940:636). This appears in a revised version of "The Aims of Ethnology," first published in 1889. The original version (in German) has "divest ourselves of these influences" (Stocking 1974:71) where the latter has "free ourselves of these shackles."

8. In an indignant response to a rather heavy-handed monograph by Leslie White (1966), in which it was argued that Boas was the paternalistic founder of a "school" of anthropology dominated by Germans, Jews, and German Jews, Morris Opler advanced the proposition that Boas, being a member in good standing of the Society for Ethical Culture, was not even Jewish — "unless, of course, Dr. White uses the word in other than a religious sense" (1967:741). Opler also interprets White's essay (not without justification) as including "a strong implication that Boas's researches on races and minorities were a self-serving mechanism and little more than a reaction to anti-Semitism" (ibid.:743). They were, of course, much more than that, but White was not as entirely off the track as Opler suggested.

References Cited

Andrews, H. A., et al.
  1943 Bibliography of Franz Boas. In Franz Boas 1858–1942. A. L. Kroeber et al., eds. pp. 67–109. American Anthropological Association Memoir No. 61.

Barnard, F. M.
  1965 Herder's Social and Political Thought. Oxford: Clarendon Press.

Baron, Salo
  1949 The Impact of the Revolution of 1848 on Jewish Emancipation. Jewish Social Studies 11:195–248.
  1952 A Social and Religious History of the Jews. 2nd ed. Vol. 1. New York: Columbia University Press.

Boas, Franz
  1909 Race Problems in America. Science 29:839–849.
  1911 Changes in Bodily Form of Descendants of Immigrants. Senate Document 208, 61st Congress, 2nd Session. Washington: Government Printing Office.
  1912a Changes in Bodily Form of Descendants of Immigrants. New York: Columbia University Press.
  1912b Changes in the Bodily Form of Descendants of Immi-

grants. American Anthropologist 14:530–562.

1916 Tsimshian Mythology. Bureau of American Ethnology, 31st Annual Report, 1909–1910. Washington: Smithsonian Institution.

1917 Each Nation Must Develop as It Deems Best. Letter to Society of the Friends of the German Republic. The American Weekly (Viereck's) 7:171.

1930 Religion of the Kwakiutl. Columbia University Contributions to Anthropology 10. New York: Columbia University Press.

1936 The Individual Counts. Reply to Benjamin Stolberg. The Nation 143:25.

1937 Race and Race Prejudice. Jewish Social Service Quarterly 14:227–232.

1938a An Anthropologist's Credo. The Nation 147:201–204.

1938b Methods of Research. In General Anthropology. F. Boas, ed. pp. 666–686. Boston: D. C. Heath.

1940 Race, Language and Culture. New York: Macmillan.

1945 Race and Democratic Society. New York: J. J. Augustin.

Boehlich, Walter, ed.
1965 Der Berliner Antisemitismusstreit. Frankfurt a/M: Insel.

Carsten, F. L.
1967 The Rise of Fascism. Berkeley and Los Angeles: University of California Press.

Cohen, Gerson D.
1975 German Jewry as Mirror of Modernity. Leo Baeck Institute Year Book 20:ix–xxxi.

Dorpalen, Andreas
1957 Heinrich von Treitschke. New Haven: Yale University Press.

Dubnov, Simon
1973 History of the Jews. Vol. 5: From the Congress of Vienna to the Emergence of Hitler. New York: Thomas Yoseloff.

Elbogen, Ismar
1944 A Century of Jewish Life. Philadelphia: Jewish Publication Society.

Glazer, Nathan
1960 Social Characteristics of American Jews. In The Jews: Their History, Culture, and Religion. 3rd ed. Louis Finkelstein, ed. pp. 1694–1735. Philadelphia: Jewish Publication Society.

Gurian, Waldemar
1946 Antisemitism in Modern Germany. In Essays on Antisemitism. Koppel S. Pinson, ed. pp. 218–265. New York: Conference on Jewish Relations.

Hamerow, Theodore S.
1958 Restoration, Revolution, Reaction: Economics and Politics in Germany, 1815–1871. Princeton, N.J.: Princeton University Press.

Harris, Marvin
1968 The Rise of Anthropological Theory. New York: Thomas Y. Crowell.

Herskovits, Melville J.

1953   Franz Boas: The Science of Man in the Making. New York: Scribner's.

1960   Who Are the Jews? In The Jews: Their History, Culture, and Religion. 3rd ed. L. Finkelstein, ed. pp. 1489–1509. Philadelphia: Jewish Publication Society.

Herzig, Arno

1973   Judentum und Emanzipation in Westfalen. Münster: Aschendorffsche Verlags.

Higham, John

1963   Strangers in the Land: Patterns of American Nativism 1860–1925. 2nd ed. New York: Atheneum.

Katz, Jacob

1961   Tradition and Crisis: Jewish Society at the End of the Middle Ages. New York: Free Press of Glencoe.

1964   The Term "Jewish Emancipation": Its Origin and Historical Impact. In Studies in Nineteenth Century Jewish Intellectual History. Alexander Altmann, ed. pp. 1–25. Cambridge: Harvard University Press.

1973   Out of the Ghetto: The Social Background of Jewish Emancipation, 1770–1870. Cambridge: Harvard University Press.

Kluckhohn, Clyde, and Olaf Prufer

1959   Influences during the Formative Years. In The Anthropology of Franz Boas. W. Goldschmidt, ed. pp. 4–28. American Anthropological Association Memoir No. 89.

Kroeber, A. L.

1943   Franz Boas: The Man. In Franz Boas 1858–1942. A. L. Kroeber et al., eds. pp. 5–26. American Anthropological Association Memoir No. 61.

Kroeber, A. L., and Clyde Kluckhohn

1963   Culture: A Critical Review of Concepts and Definitions. New York: Random House.

Liebeschütz, Hans

1962   Treitschke and Mommsen on Jewry and Judaism. Leo Baeck Institute Year Book 7:153–182.

Massing, Paul

1949   Rehearsal for Destruction: A Study of Political Anti-Semitism in Imperial Germany. New York: Harper.

Meyer, Michael A.

1967   The Origins of the Modern Jew: Jewish Identity and European Culture in Germany, 1749–1824. Detroit: Wayne State University Press.

Mosse, George L.

1964   The Crisis of German Ideology: Intellectual Origins of the Third Reich. New York: Grosset & Dunlap.

1970   Culture, Civilization, and German Anti-Semitism. In Germans and Jews. pp. 34–60. New York: Grosset & Dunlap.

Mosse, Werner E.

1970   The Conflict of Liberalism and Nationalism and Its Effect on

German Jewry. Leo Baeck Institute Year Book 15:125–139.

Opler, Morris E.

1967 Franz Boas: Religion and Theory. American Anthropologist 69:741–745.

Pinson, Koppel

1966 Modern Germany: Its History and Civilization. 2nd ed. New York: Macmillan.

Pulzer, Peter G. J.

1964 The Rise of Political Anti-Semitism in Germany and Austria. New York and London: Wiley.

1980 Why Was There a Jewish Question in Imperial Germany? Leo Baeck Institute Year Book 25:133–146.

Radest, Howard B.

1969 Toward Common Ground: The Story of the Ethical Societies in the United States. New York: Frederick Ungar.

Reinharz, Jehuda

1975 Fatherland or Promised Land: The Dilemma of the German Jew, 1893–1914. Ann Arbor: University of Michigan Press.

Rischin, Moses

1970 The Promised City: New York's Jews, 1870–1914. New York: Harper & Row.

Rürup, Reinhard

1969 Jewish Emancipation and Bourgeois Society. Leo Baeck Institute Year Book 14:67–91.

1975 Emancipation and Crisis— The "Jewish Question" in Ger-

many 1850–1890. Leo Baeck Institute Year Book 20:13–25.

Sachar, Howard M.

1977 The Course of Modern Jewish History. 2nd ed. New York: Delta.

Schorsch, Ismar

1972 Jewish Reactions to German Anti-Semitism, 1870–1914. New York and London: Columbia University Press.

Singer, Catherine

1977 The Sense of Identity and Community of the German Jews in Milwaukee, 1875–1925. Undergraduate senior thesis. Amherst, Mass.: Hampshire College.

Sklare, Marshall

1971 America's Jews. New York: Random House.

Sterling, Eleonore

1958 Jewish Reaction to Jew-Hatred in the First Half of the 19th Century. Leo Baeck Institute Year Book 3:103–121.

Stern, Bernhard J.

1959 Franz Boas as Scientist and Citizen. In Historical Sociology: The Selected Papers of Bernard J. Stern. pp. 208–241. New York: Citadel Press.

Stern, Fritz

1977 Gold and Iron: Bismarck, Bleichröder, and the Building of the German Empire. New York: Knopf.

Stocking, George W., Jr.

1968 Race, Culture, and Evolution: Essays in the History of

Anthropology. New York: Free Press.

1974 The Shaping of American Anthropology 1883–1911: A Franz Boas Reader. New York: Basic Books.

1979 Anthropology as Kulturkampf: Science and Politics in the Career of Franz Boas. *In* The Uses of Anthropology. W. Goldschmidt, ed. pp. 33–50. American Anthropological Association Special Publication No. 11.

Stolberg, Benjamin

1936 The Jew and the World. The Nation 142:766–770.

Tal, Uriel

1975 Christians and Jews in Germany: Religion, Politics, and Ideology in the Second Reich, 1870–1914. Ithaca and London: Cornell University Press.

Tanner, J. M.

1959 Boas' Contributions to Knowledge of Human Growth and Form. *In* The Anthropology of Franz Boas. W. Goldschmidt, ed. pp. 76–111. American Anthropological Association Memoir No. 89.

Toury, Jacob

1966 "The Jewish Question" — A Semantic Approach. Leo Baeck Institute Year Book 11:85–106.

Treitschke, Heinrich von

1879 Unsere Aussichten. Preussische Jahrbücher, November 15. (Reprinted in Boehlich 1965, pp. 7–14.)

White, Leslie

1966 The Social Organization of Ethnological Theory. Rice University Studies 52, No. 4. Houston: William Marsh Rice University.

Other Times, Other Customs:

The Anthropology of History

Marshall Sahlins

VOL. 85, 1983, 517–544

The nature of institutions is nothing but their coming into being (*nascimento*) at certain times and in certain guises. Whenever the time and guise are thus and so, such and not otherwise are the institutions that come into being — Vico, *The New Science.*

Western historians have been arguing for a long time over two polar ideas of right historiography. As opposed to an elite history, narrated with an eye singular to the higher politics, others propose a study whose object would be the life of communities. "For the last fourteen hundred years, only the Gauls, apparently, have been kings, ministers and generals," Voltaire complained, and vowed to write instead a "history of men." The latest "new history" is also of the populist persuasion. Sometimes client of the social sciences, it is concerned with such matters as unconscious structures, collective mentalities, and general economic trends. It tends to be populist in the salience it gives to the practical circumstances of underlying populations. A distinguished historian (Stone 1981:23) invokes Thomas Gray: "Let not . . . grandeur hear with a disdainful smile, / The short and simple annals of the poor." The idea is that history is culturally constructed from the bottom up: as the precipitate, in social institutions and outcomes, of the prevailing inclinations of the people-in-general.[1]

Yet before we congratulate the new history on having finally learned its anthropological (or political) lessons, we should recall that the passage from an elite to a more collective consciousness actually occurred in the history of Western society, as a difference in real-historical practice, and this long before the decline of monarchy in favor of popular democracies and market economies made the mass production of history seem the self-evident truth of our own — should we not say, our bourgeois? — social experience. Jean-Pierre Vernant (1982) brilliantly analyzes the same transformation in the first millenium B.C., in the passage from the sovereignty of Mycenaean god-kings to the humanized institutions of the Greek *polis*. Or is it that we have to do, in society and consciousness both, with a "structure of the long duration": a cyclical alternation between Caesarism and the power of the people, the *gumsa* and *gumlao* of Indo-European history, each social form always pregnant, at least a little bit, with its historic opposite?

Vernant, in fact, begins by comparing Athenian royal traditions with the divine kings of Scythian legend. In repeated quarrels over the succession, the Athenian princes eventually divide between them the functions — priestly, military, and economic — that were characteristically united in Indo-European kingships of the heroic age. So commences the idea of politics as the mutual accommodation of differences, whose more democratic form will be achieved in the *polis*. But in contrast to the Athenian princes, the divinely favored grandson of the Scythian Zeus is alone accorded royal power by his older brothers, as he alone is able to carry off the prototypical golden objects emblematic of the Dumézilian three functions: the libation cup, the war ax, and the plow. Here the sovereign is classically presented "as a person above and beyond the various functional classes that made up society, since he represented them all; and since all equally found in him the virtues by which they defined themselves, he no longer belonged to any one of them" (Vernant 1982:42). At once encompassing and transcending the society, the divine king is able to mediate its relations to the cosmos — which thus also responds, in its own natural order, to his sovereign powers.

In the *polis*, however, an organization constituted by its self-awareness as a human community, the *arche* (sovereign power) "came to be everybody's business" (women and slaves, as usual, excepted). Rotating the authority among the several groups of citizens, thus making domination and submission alternating sides of the same relationships, rendering decisions by public debate among equals in the public square, hence as open convenants openly arrived at, so elevating speech to preeminence over all other instruments of power, speech that was no longer the compelling ritual word pronounced from on high but an argument to be judged as persuasive in the light of wisdom and knowledge verifiable by all as something called truth, the *polis*, by these and many other means, subjected social action to the collective will and made men conscious of their history as human history.

I take up Vernant's thesis as the general point of this lecture: that different cultural orders have their own modes of historical action, consciousness, and determination — their own historical practice. Other times, other customs, and according to the otherness of the customs, the distinctive anthropology that is needed to understand any given human course. For there is no simply "human" course (*devenir*), as Durkheim said, "but each society has its own life, its own course, and similar societies are as comparable in their historicity [or mode of development] as in their structure" (1905–06:140).[2] This mention of structural types is perhaps enough to forestall the idea that I am making merely an idiographic point of historical relativity. Rather I begin with certain reflections on divine kingship, the type of structure from which the *polis* took radical departure, in order to examine the general cultural practice of heroic history.

Heroic History

The idea is from Vico, after Homeric precedents, but as further worked out in the anthropology of archaic kingship by Frazer and Hocart, and tempered in Dumontian concepts of hierarchy.[3] The historical implications follow from the presence of divinity among men, as in the person of the sacred king or the powers of the magical chief. Accordingly, the principle of historical practice becomes synonymous with divine action: the creation of the human and cosmic order by the god.

Of course, I am not suggesting some neolithic form of the great-man theory of history. Nor do I speak of "charisma" — unless it be the "routinized charisma" that structurally amplifies a personal effect by transmission along the lines of established relationships. In a version of the Social Contract that still stands as the philosophic Magna Carta of the General Will, Rousseau argued that "each State can have for enemies only other States, and not men; for between things disparate in nature there can be no real relation." Yet ethnography shows that the Maori chief "lives the life of a whole tribe," that "he gathers the relationship to other tribes in his person" (Johansen 1954:180). His marriages are intertribal alliances; his ceremonial exchanges, trade; injuries to himself are cause for war. Here history is anthropomorphic in principle, which is to say in structure.[4] Granted that history is much more than the doings of great men, is always and everywhere the life of communities, but precisely in these heroic polities the king is the condition of the possibility of community. " 'If I eat,' " says the Kuba man, " 'it is the King; if I sleep, it is the King; if I drink, it is the King' " (Vansina 1964:101).[5] The general life conditions of the people are ordered, as social form and collective destiny, by the particular dispositions of the powers-that-be. Nor is the process a reflexive "ideology" merely, since the general will is not for all that the sovereign interest, except as it is the interest of the sovereign. Hence the pertinent historiography cannot be—as in the good Social Science tradition—a simple quantitative assessment of the people's opinions or circumstances, based on a statistically random sample, as if one were thus taking the pulse of fundamental social *tendencies.* Heroic history proceeds more like Fenimore Cooper Indians—to use Elman Service's characterization: each man, as he walks single-file along the trail, is careful to step in the footprints of the one ahead, so as to leave the impression of One Giant Indian.

So for over a century after their conversion by Methodist missionaries, Fijians could still refer to Christianity as "the religion of Thakombau" (Derrick 1950:115).[6] Thakombau was the ruling chief of the great Mbau confederacy, the dominant power in 19th-century Fiji. On April 30, 1854, he finally declared for Jehovah, after more than 15 years of missionary hectoring. Earlier, in mid-1852, the missionaries had counted only 850 "regular worshippers" in the Mbau area (Methodist Missionary Society: Fiji District, 1952). But directly on Thakombau's conversion, together with certain military successes, "the Holy Ghost was poured out plentifully" in the Mbau dominions, so that by mid-1855 church attendance had increased to 8870 (Williams and Calvert 1859:484). This proves that in the mathematics of Fijian history, $8870 - 850 = 1$. The statistical difference was Thakombau.

On the other hand, the figure of 850 for 1852 by far underestimates the number of Fijians, including Thakombau, who for years had acknowledged the "truth" of the foreigner's god. Even many of the Fijian gods, speaking through priests, had already conceded the supremacy of Jehovah and fled elsewhere, or else indicated they were themselves prepared to become Christians.[7] "Confessing that Christianity was true," Thakombau in 1850 counseled Brother Calvert to have patience, as when he himself turned, "all would follow" (ibid.:445–446). And this proves that the politics of conversion is no simple expression of conviction.

The repeated reference to "truth" in these archives indicates that the widespread disposition to heed Christianity was a matter of Fijian mythopoetics, if not yet of chiefly politics. For the Fijian 'true' (*dina*) is a gloss of *mana*, as Hocart (1914) observed, denoting a power of bringing-into-existence, even as an action that fails for want of *mana* is a 'lie' (*lasu*). So the Fijian chief said to the Methodist missionary, "True — everything is true that comes from the white man's country; muskets & gunpowder are true, & your religion must be true" (Schütz 1977:95, cf. Waterhouse 1866:303). The extraordinary European presence was for Fijians a "to-tal" social fact, "religious" at the same time it was "political" and "economic." More exactly, it could be made intelligible only in the terms of a native theory that stood Marx on his head by its determination "in the final analysis" by the spiritual superstructure. In 1838, the paramount chief of Rewa, soon to be Thakombau's great enemy, but never a professing Christian, admits the missionary's point that "the gods of Fiji are not true: they are like the Tongan gods," he says, of whom it has been shown that "they are not gods; those who trusted them have been destroyed, and those who attended to the religion of the foreigners are prosperous" (Cross: Oct. 22, 1838). If the missionaries labored for years in central Fiji without famous success — save most notably among the sick, who supposed by the same theory that the Wesleyans' god made their medicines work — it was not for lack of credence in popular opinion. Rather, the issue turned on the ruling chiefs, especially of Mbau and Rewa, who had been fighting each other since 1843.

Asked why they did not heed God's word, the people of Viwa Island, subject to Mbau, would tell Brother Cross, " 'I wait for [my chief] Namo-simalua' " (Methodist Missionary Society, District Minutes, 1841). So "the common people wait for their Chiefs," as another missionary complained, "one Chief waits for another [superior chief], one land waits for another land, thus there is in many areas a stalemate" (Jaggar: Oct. 21, 1839). "If Rewa would take the lead," says a third, "we should soon have one hundred thousand *professed* Christians in Fiji" (Williams and Calvert 1859:408). But as one chief thus waited for another, the other was waiting for the right moment. Thakombau was not about to change gods in midwar. And when he finally did change, the same option was precluded for his rival, the Rewa chief: " 'If we all *lotu* [become Christian],' " the latter said, " 'we must give up fighting; as it will not do to pray to the same god, and fight with each other' " (ibid.:356). The conversion came only as a tactic of despair.[8] In the 12th year of war, Mbau was virtually under siege by Rewan forces, even as its European trade was also under embargo by disaffected merchants and its allies were deserting to the enemy by the clan, village, and chiefdom. At this juncture, Thakombau found "the true God" — together with certain windward Christian soldiers, from the Tongan Islands. Aided now by missionary intrigue and the decisive military support of the Christian King of Tonga, Thakombau was able to rout his enemies at the battle of Kamba in 1855. He was indeed saved.

The old religion then gave birth to the new. For as Fijians say, "in olden times, the chief was our god," and Christianity owed something to this ancient conception of divinity. Christianity was destined to become "the religion of Thakombau" because it was won in a battle whose causes were as identified with the chief as the reasons men fought lay in their constituted obligations to serve him, the terms and modes of that service (*nqaravi*) being the same as ritual adoration of the God. Moreover, the same sense of divinity orchestrated the course of battle, with a parallel domino effect on the outcome.

The Fijians fought like Tacitus' Germans: "The chief [*princeps*] fights for victory; the followers [*comites*] for their chief" (*Germ.* XIV).[9] A few weeks before the decisive engagement at Kamba, the paramount chief of Rewa died suddenly of dysentery, without regaining consciousness or passing the charge of war to a successor. Immediately and quasi-totally, the principal Rewan opposition to Mbau disintegrated. The surviving notables sued Thakombau for peace, telling also of their willingness to follow Jehovah. It cannot be that they were merely crypto-rationalists who knew how to find good ideological reasons for extricating themselves from an untenable military situation, since all this happened when they were on the threshold of victory. On the other hand, in the ensuing battle of Kamba, the absence of the main Rewan host proved a serious if not fatal weakness for Thakombau's remaining adversaries. The real correlation of forces and consequent course of events — with effects still visible in the structure of Fijian politics — had turned on the being of the sacred chief, whose sudden removal dissolved the purpose and articulation of his armies.

This really *is* a history of kings and battles, but only because it is a cultural order that, multiplying the action of the king by the system of society, gives him a disproportionate historical effect. Briefly, I recapitulate certain interrelated tendencies of the Fijian case, on the conjecture that they are paradigmatic of a history in the heroic mode. First, the general force of circumstance, such as the European presence, becomes

the specific course of history according to the determinations of the
higher politics. The infrastructure is realized as historical form and
event in the terms of ruling interests, and according to their conjuncture.
Second, this history shows an unusual capacity for sudden change or
rupture: a mutation of the cultural course, developing as the rapid popular generalization of an heroic action. Hence the statistical quantum
leaps. As a corollary, a history of this structural type produces great men,
even geniuses, by transforming the intelligent acts of individuals into
fateful outcomes for the society — consider the brilliant results of Thakombau's conversion. Or more generally, where history thus unfolds as
the social extension of the heroic person, it is likely to present a curious
mixture of tactical geniality and practical irrationality. If Thakombau
consistently exemplifies the first, the collapse of Rewa at the death of its
chief and on the brink of victory makes an example of irrationality that
sorely tries our own native sense of hardheaded surrealism. Still, Chadwick (1926:340–341) found analogous episodes — the capture or death
of the enemy king leading to "destruction of the enemy's organisation"
and "forthwith to the end of hostilities" — a recurrent feature of the
Germanic heroic age, both as poetry and as history. And anthropologists
could come up with many exotic events of the same structural form, if at
the risk of obliterating the distinction between history and ritual.

Consider the incident famous in Zulu annals where the triumphant
army of Shaka's predecessor Dingiswayo suddenly dissolves upon the
abduction and assassination of the latter: a complete reversal of fortune
that elicits from the missionary-ethnographer unflattering comment on
"the innate helplessness of the Bantu people when once deprived of their
leader" (Bryant 1929:166). Indeed, the whole Mtêtwa confederacy fashioned by Dingiswayo broke up at his death, making the opening for
Shaka, leader of the subordinate Zulu "tribe."[10] The rest, as they say, is
history, including the crises of cosmic proportions that attended attempts on Shaka's life, and again at the death of his mother, female
complement of the Ngoni dual sovereignty (see Heusch 1982). The
entire Zulu nation was plunged into paroxysms of internal slaughter,
seeking to forestall, by these massive purges of evil, the conjunction of
Sky and Earth that would naturally follow the fall of the heavenly ruler.[11]

I purposely associate the cosmological catastrophe with the military
debacle on grounds that the two are the same in principle. The disarray
of the victorious army bereft of its leader is an enactment, in the mo-
dality of history, of the same ritual chaos that sets in at the death of the

divine king, well known to ethnography as the return to an original condition of cosmic disorder. In Hawaii, men then wear their loin cloths on their heads, and chiefly women fornicate in public places with commoner men they would otherwise disdain. Giving vent to their grief in various forms of self-mutilation, the people in general so die with their king. The world thus dissolves, until the heir-apparent, who had been kept apart from such pollution, returns to reinstate the tabus and redivide the lands — that is, to recreate the differences that make up the natural and cultural order.[12] Yet we speak of this as "ritual," while holding apart the homologous collapse of armies as "battle," and by such means merely mark our own distinctions between "make-believe" and "reality," while preserving a sense of history as the kingdom of practical reason. Could we remove the praxological scales from our eyes, it would be seen that all these and other events, ranging from the fratricidal strife of the East African interregnum to the seclusion of the king in Polynesian rites of world-renewal, refer to the same system of hierarchy. But I cannot rehearse here the whole text of *The Golden Bough*.

Suffice it to call attention to certain sociological aspects of the kingship as a cosmic principle of order. I mean the various social forms underlying the generalization of heroic action, or the One-Giant-Indian effect. Those I single out — heroic segmentation, hierarchical solidarity, positional succession, division of labor in historic consciousness — are not universal in the heroic societies, but they are probably sufficiently typical.

Old-time students of social structure will appreciate the differences between heroic modes of lineage formation and developmental processes of the classic segmentary lineage system. The segmentary lineage reproduces itself from the bottom upwards: by natural increase among its minimal groups and fission along the collateral lines of a common ancestry. Societies such as Zulu and Hawaiian, however — or the Nguni and Polynesian chiefdoms generally — present also the reverse evolution. The major "lineage"/territorial divisions develop from the top of the system downward, as the extension of domestic fission in the ruling families. Call it "heroic segmentation." Initiated by the centrifugal dispersion of the royal kindred, typically in anticipation of a struggle over succession, the process entails redistribution of the underlying (or defeated) people among members of the ruling aristocracy. The principles of descent are in effect superseded at the higher levels of segmentary order by the privileges of authority. Barnes (1951, 1967) supplies notable examples from the Ngoni: the establishment of "quasi-agnatic" communities around the several royal wives and their respective sons, whose rivalry may issue finally in independent kingdoms. Organized by the relations of power among contemporary princes, rather than by ancestral reference, the main political groups are thus constituted as the social projections of heroic ambitions.[13]

Parenthetically (and speculatively), might not the whole remarkable expansion of Nguni states since the late 18th century, including Zulu, Swazi, and Ndabele, be the historic trace of such heroic processes? The state probably originates as the structural means of some personal project of glory.

We need a notion of "hierarchical solidarity" to go alongside Durkheim's mechanical and organic types. In the heroic societies, the coherence of the members or subgroups is not so much due to their similarity (mechanical solidarity) or their complementarity (organic solidarity) as to their common submission to the ruling power. The corollary of hierarchical solidarity is a devaluation of tribalism as we know it, since the collectivity is defined by its adherence to a given chief or king rather than by distinctive cultural attributes — even as bonds of kinship and relations to ancestral lands are dissolved by such processes as heroic segmentation. Chadwick repeatedly remarks on the absence of "national" sentiment or interest in the European heroic age, by comparison to the prevailing concept of a state apparently "regarded as little more than the property of the individual" (1926:336). And Benveniste observes that, apart from Western Europe, a term for *society* does not appear in the classical vocabulary of Indo-European institutions. Instead, the concept "is expressed in a different fashion. In particular one recognizes it under the name of *realm* [*royaume*]: the limits of society coincide with a certain power, which is the power of the king" (1969 vol. 2:9). In this light, the potential for *déracinement* which we have seen in Africa, and which could be matched for migration and conquest by Germania, Mongolia, or Polynesia, appears as characteristic of the heroic age: the counterpart in historicity of a certain hierarchy.[14]

Beyond personal ambition and glory, the battle royals at the center of these historic maelstroms must also refer to certain structures. I can show this for the fratricidal strife of Fijian chiefly families, and the explication would probably hold for Nguni states, likewise marked by the polygynous alliances of the rulers to ranking women of strategic clans or neighboring states. Such alliances make up the larger set of political relations. But in the event, the sons of a given paramount, as representatives of their respective mothers' peoples, condense in their own persons the entire regional system of political interests. An extensive correlation of social forces is realized in and by the interpersonal relations of royal households, especially the rivalries of paternal half-brothers — and rides on their outcome. Uneasy then lies the head that wears the kingly crown. The structural weight that aristocratic kinship is forced to bear helps explain the Byzantine intrigue, climaxed by cruel scenes of fratricide or parricide, so often told in the annals of heroic history.[15]

And insofar as all the dead generations structurally "weigh like a nightmare on the brain of the living," these struggles may never end. "Yes, 1852," said the Tongan, "that was the year . . . I fought King Ta'ufa'ahau." But, comments the ethnographer, "the actual person who fought King Ta'ufa'ahau was the speaker's great-great-great-grandfather" (Bott 1981:23). We have all heard of the "royal we." Here, as an expression of *positional succession*, is an even more radical "heroic I." Thus a subclan headman of the Luapula Kingdom of Kazembe:

> We came to the country of Mwanshya. . . . I killed a puku [antelope]. . . . We gave some of the meat to Mwanshya. He asked where the salt came from and he was told. So he sent people who killed me. My mother was angry and went to fetch medicine to send thunderbolts. She destroyed Mwanshya's village. . . . Lukoshi then told me to go forward and that he would stay and rule Mwanshya's country. So we came away. . . . Lubunda . . . heard about my strength. He came to see us and married my mother. They went away and I remained. [Cunnison 1959:234, cf. Cunnison 1951, 1957]

All these events, including the narrator's death, transpired before he was born.[16]

By the heroic I — and various complements such as perpetual kinship — the main relationships of society are at once projected historically and embodied currently in the persons of authority. Contemporary ancestors, such heroic figures are structuring simply by being, insofar as the existence of other people is defined by theirs. In European talk this is "power," but "power" then is a positional or systematic value, that may work as well by influence as by coercion. Moreover, the structure as incarnate in such powers-that-be may thereupon prove immune to what other people actually do. At issue is the historical relation between cultural order and empirical practice — which I illustrate again from Fiji.

Dynastic legends tell of the origin of the ruling line from the union of an immigrant prince with a ranking woman of indigenous people.[17] The chiefs henceforth stand as wife-takers and sisters' sons to the people of the land. This helps explain why Fijians say, "The chief is our god." For the paradigmatic privilege of the uterine nephew is to seize the sacrifices made to the god of his mother's people (Hocart 1915, 1936). Consuming the offering—which is to say "tribute" and "trade," in ethnographic pidgin—the chief thus takes the place of the people's god. Now it does not matter, structurally, that certain current marriages between lesser women of chiefly clans and men of the people may run counter to the divine status of the ruling line as wife-takers. Precisely, what ordinary people do is not systematically decisive, in comparison with the higher-order social effects sedimented by aristocratic relationships. And high Fijian chiefs, we have seen, continue to differentially make history by polygynous marriages that amount to systems of intertribal alliance. The structure is not statistical. It is not the expression in institutions of the empirical frequencies of interactions. As the Maori proverb goes, "the great man is not hidden among the many."[18]

Writing of the new history, Barraclough (1978:58) tells us that "all generalizations," including such historical judgments as "significant," are "inherently quantitative"—which presumably also goes for what he just said. For heroic history, then, the effective statistical rule would be something like a Principle of the Significant One: the one who counts. This demonstrates, quantitatively, that "significance" is a qualitative value—in the first place (see Thompson 1977:254–255).

The complement of such heroic statistics is a political division of labor in cultural and historical consciousness. The time of society is calculated in dynastic genealogies, as collective history resides in royal traditions. In the state rituals and political councils of the elite, the cultural schemes are subject to manipulation and comment by specialists, such as priests and genealogists, attached to the ruling interests. Whereas, in the villages, anthropologists encounter a certain indifference to the historic Great Tradition, coupled with an inclination on the people's part to offer improvised pragmatic responses to questions about "custom," in place of the exotic exegeses on the meaning of things their interlocutors had been trained to consider "the culture." The short and simple annals of the poor.

"There are probably no people possessing an equal amount of intelligence," wrote an early White trader among Zulu, "who are less well-acquainted with their history than the Kaffirs" (Fynn in Bird 1888:104).

Judging from Bryant's (1929) success in collecting a detailed Zulu tradition, the assertion must refer to the generality of common folks. Besides, Europeans residing early and late among the equally intelligent Austronesians have run into the same experience, at least in certain quarters. The missionary Hunt said of Fijians that "they know next to nothing of their past. Their origin and history are both a complete mystery to them" (Oct. 28, 1843). Malani of Lakemba (Fiji) was garrulous enough, Hocart found, "but was said to know little because he had been brought up among the common people and not the nobles" (Hocart, n.d.:22). Similarly, a recent notice of Madagascar relates: "History is not evenly distributed because to have it is a sign of politico-religious power and authority" (Feeley-Harnik 1978:402; cf. Fox 1971, on Roti). Examples could be multiplied, but the best would probably remain Cunnison's brilliant analysis of political distinctions in historical consciousness among the Luapula peoples (1951, cf. Cunnison 1957, 1959).

Pocock's well-known article on the anthropology of time-reckoning (1964) makes the differential historical consciousness an aspect of the formal logic of hierarchy. "The larger co-ordination," Pocock writes, or higher level of social system, "subsumes the less." The kingship thus provides a general time indication for the diverse incidents of lineage tradition or personal recollection which, taken by themselves, would be, in a strict sense, socially meaningless and temporally mere duration. Just so, in exemplary expressions of hierarchical encompassment, the old-time Hawaiian figures his own biography in terms of the king's activity: "I was born when Kamehameha conquered O'ahu"; "I was old enough to carry stones when Kamehameha built the fish pond at Kiholo"; and the like.[19] Their own lives are calqued on the king's—

> Upon the king! Let us our lives, our souls,
> Our debts, our careful wives,
> Our children, and our sins, lay on the King!
>
> *Henry V.* IV, i.

At the extreme, the people verge on "historylessness." In Hawaii, the continuous redistribution of lands among the ruling chiefs preempts any local lineage formation, reducing genealogical memories among the common people largely to personal recollections. Having lost control of their own social reproduction, as Bonte puts it for the analogous situation of Tuareg, the people are left without a historical appreciation of the main cultural categories (Bonte and Echard 1976:270ff.). For them, the culture is mostly "lived" — in practice, and as *habitus*. Their lives are run on an unconscious mastery of the system, something like Everyman's control of the grammatical categories, together with the homespun concepts of the good that allow them to improvise daily activities on the level of the pragmatic and matter-of-fact. Such unreflexive mastery of percept and precept is what Bourdieu calls *habitus:* "schemes of thought and expression . . . [that] are the basis for the intentionless invention of regulated improvisation" (1977:79).

The people's code, however, is not altogether so "restricted." True, Hawaiian kings have genealogies going back 963 generations, associated with cosmic myths and royal legends whose telling, especially in political argument, is an express manipulation of the cultural categories. Yet the common people for their part have scores if not hundreds of contemporary kith and kin about whom they endlessly "talk story" — tell the news. Now news is not just anything about anybody; it is likewise a selective determination of what is significant according to canons of cultural value. If "So-and-so, the youngest son of So-and-so, married So-and-so — you know the adopted favorite daughter of the Kealoha folks — and moved inland to take up farming," then a whole series of distinctions and relations between land and sea, agriculture and fishing, junior and senior, birth and adoption — the same sorts of difference that make a difference in royal rite or myth — are being engaged in the recitation of the quotidian and mundane. Besides, the people's gossip often retails enchanted happenings as fabulous as those of myth. It is something of the myth of everyday life.[20] The cultural consciousness objectified in historical forms among the elite appears rather in the practical activities and current annals of the people: a division of cultural labors corresponding to the heroic mode of historical production.

We need not exaggerate the contrast to ourselves, given that the general interest of the bourgeois state is the particular interest of its ruling classes, as Marx taught. But capitalist society does have a distinctive mode of appearance, therefore a definite anthropological consciousness, pervasive also in the theoretical dispositions of the Academy. The native "Boo-jwas" theory is that social outcomes are the cumulative expressions of individual actions, hence behind that of the prevailing state of the people's wants and opinions, as generated especially out of their material sufferings. As if by an Invisible Hand, the society is constructed as the institutional sum of its individual practices. The classical locus of this folklore is, of course, the marketplace, where the relative success of autonomous individual agents, thus the political order of the economy, is measurable by the quantitative shares respectively obtained in the public boodle at the cost of whom it may concern — while at the same time this social process is *experienced* by the participants as the maximization of their personal satisfactions. And since all such satisfactions, from listening to the Chicago Symphony to calling home by a long-distance phone call, require the reduction of diverse social conditions and relations to their lowest common denominator of pecuniary expense to rationally allocate one's finite resources, the impression is given that the whole culture is organized by people's businesslike economizing. This impression is doubled by the democratic political process in which Everyman counts as "one" (vote), so representing the governing powers as "the people's cherce." The prevailing quantitative, populist, and materialist presuppositions of our social science can then be no accident — or there is no anthropology.

On the other hand, the different cultural orders studied by anthropology have their own historicities. Even the kinship orders. Ignoring the passage of time and generation, Crow/Omaha kinship turns contingent events of marriage into perpetual relationships by freezing whole lineages into the familial positions assumed at an initial alliance. Likewise, the elementary marriage systems would reproduce indefinitely the relationships of intermarrying groups; whereas the complex systems, defined negatively by rules against kin marriages, introduce discontinuity in group alliances and their reformulation generation to generation. The Ilongot act on the sense that they invent their own social lives, each generation as it were rediscovering the Philippines (Rosaldo 1980). But do they not thus refer to a system of complex marriage, combined with optative (cognatic) filiation, which besides generates long-term closure of its moments of kindred and residential dispersion? Only that for the Ilongot, as for the Americans, the structure is reproduced as travestied in the aphorisms of the *habitus* — "we follow our hearts" — and through the unreflected mastery of its percepts. The issue is not the absence of structure, but its inscription in *habitus*, as opposed to its objectification as mythopoetics.[21] Here is a main distinction of structures, cross-cutting the others to which I alluded: between those that are practiced primarily through the individual subconscious and those that explicitly organize history as the metaphor of mythical realities. I turn to an extended example of the latter, chosen again for the scandal it makes to a received historiography.

Mytho-Praxis

In his introduction to the *Peloponnesian War,* Thucydides tells of his intention to eliminate all elements of the marvelous from his history since, as he modestly explained: "My work is not a piece of writing designed to meet the taste of an immediate public, but was done to last forever." So begins the Western historiography of the Unvarnished Truth or the triumph of *logos* over *mythos* (see Vernant 1979:196ff.). Curious then that Sir George Grey, in the preface to his *Polynesian Mythology,* tells how he was compelled to gather his great corpus of Maori myth in order to fight a certain Polynesian war. Appointed Governor of New Zealand in the midst of a Maori uprising, Sir George soon discovered that he could not negotiate the critical issues of war and peace with Maori chiefs unless he had a sound knowledge of their poetry and mythology:

> To my surprise ... I found that these chiefs, either in their speeches to me or in their letters, frequently quoted, in explanation of their views and intentions, fragments of ancient poems and proverbs, or made allusions which rested on an ancient system of mythology; and, although it was clear that the most important parts of their communications were embodied in these figurative forms, the interpreters ... could ... rarely (if ever) translate the poems or explain the allusions. ... Clearly, however, I could not, as Governor of the country, permit so close a veil to be drawn between myself and the aged and influential chiefs whom it was my duty to attach to British interests and to the British race. ... Only one thing could under such circumstances be done, and that was to acquaint myself with the ancient language of the country, to collect its traditional poems and legends, to induce their priests to impart to me their mythology, and to study their proverbs. [Grey 1956 (1855): unpaged front matter]

The documented history of the Polynesian wars thus begins where the landmark history of the Peloponnesian wars left off. And if anthropology then inherits a famous collection of myths from the practicalities of battle, it is because the Maori, who think of the future as behind them, find in a marvelous past the measure of the demands that are made to their current existence.

I exemplify by a letter composed in the style of public oratory, in the course of which the author, a chief, sends a threat of war to another chief in the form of a love song (Shortland 1856:189–192). According to the *pakehā* (European) authority to whom the example is due, the threat lies in the refrain, "The hand that was stretched out and returned *tapu* shall become *noa* [i.e., 'free from *tapu*,' 'profane']." The woman in this way tells her previously rejected suitor that if he tries again he will have better success — presumably that what was before untouchable (*tapu*) shall become touchable (*noa*).[22] So the chief is telling his enemy that although last time he came away unscathed, if he dares to return he can expect a warm welcome. Maori will get the allusion since from the beginning of mankind sex has been a battle that women win, turning the death of the man (detumescence) into the life of the people (the child). Maori say, "The genitals of women are killers of men." Behind that too is the myth of the origin of death wherein the trickster Maui, in a vain attempt to win immortality for mankind, is crushed in the vagina of the ancestress-guardian of the underworld (Best 1924 vol. 1:146ff.; 1925: 763–767, 944–948; Goldie 1905; Johansen 1954:228ff.; J. Smith 1974–75).

Clearly, Maori are cunning mythologists who are able to select from the supple body of traditions those most appropriate to the satisfaction of their current interests, as they conceive them. The distinctiveness of their mytho-praxis is not the existence (or the absence) of such interests, but exactly that they are so conceived. The Maori, as Johansen says, "find themselves in history" (1954:163).[23]

Although there are extant examples of such mythic discourse from the very rebellion that brought Sir George (then Captain) Grey to New Zealand, I am rather in the same quandary as he in trying to decode them.[24] Perhaps, then, I may be allowed to make use of a similar speech from John White's (1874) reconstruction of the daily life of the Ngapuhi, the tribe that instigated the uprising in question. The speaker, Rou, a man of some standing in the community, although not the highest, had lost a son in battle and is now protesting the decision of the tribal notables that the enemy victims taken in revenge be buried instead of eaten, because of kinship relations between the warring groups. Rou begins by reciting the legend of the origin of the clan, hence the common descent and character of himself and the elders. This leads into a disquisition on the relation of microcosm and macrocosm: "Man is like this world. . . . He has a voice: the world has its wind. The world has soil: man has a heart," and so forth. Rou acknowledges the chiefs' powers over the cosmos, however, and enunciates the principle of heroic generalization: "Man is like the wind. If the wind blows one way, it all blows that way. If one man praises the chief, all men praise him. . . . As the wind blows in one way, so men blow in the direction you indicate. . . ." But now he sets forth his disagreement, which begins at the origin of the world. He recites the myth of the Children of Rangi (the Heavens)— myth collected by Grey, incidentally, in *Polynesian Mythology*. The story tells of the origin of cannibalism among the divine ancestors, a cannibalism that is also the institution and possibility of human existence. Tū, ancestor and patron of man as warrior, defeats his older brothers, the other sons of Rangi, who are the parents of birds, trees, fish, wild and cultivated foods. To defeat is to render *noa* (without *tapu*) and consumable. Tū is thus able to consume his brothers' offspring, power he passes on to mankind. "If then the gods eat each other," Rou argues, "and they were brothers . . . I ask, why was I not allowed to eat those who killed my child?" Rou goes on to double this mythical argument with another about the divine origin of witchcraft, which explains how evil came into the hearts of men, including his own project of cannibal vengeance. Assuring the chiefs he will not now go against their wishes, he nonetheless concludes by citing two proverbs that signify he will alone and in due time have satisfaction. "You know the proverb that says, 'The anger of relatives is a fire that burns fiercely' [i.e., his own anger at his son's death], and another that says, 'the hand alone can get food to spare for its own body' " (White 1874:185–193).

The Maori past is a vast scheme of life possibilities, ranging from ancient myth to recent memory through a series of epochs parallel in structure and analogous in event, while successively changing in content from the abstract and universal to the concrete and individual, from the divine to the human and on to the ancestral group, from the separation of Heaven and Earth to the delimitation of the clan territories.[25] The kind of transformation between sacred myth and historic legend that Dumézil (1968) finds operating between different branches of the Indo-European stock thus appears within the Maori tradition as a connected succession of stages, with the added consideration that the movement from the cosmic to the "historic" is consummated by the ultimate expression of the same structure as—real life. In the cosmic myths are the generic possibilities. Birth, death, illness, sex, revenge, cannibalism: the elementary experiences are constituted by the deeds of primordial gods/ancestors. But each 'tribe' (*iwi*) also has a humanity specific to itself, arising from the attributes of its particular ancestors and the saga of their migration from Hawaiki, spiritual homeland of the Maori (see the examples in Simmons 1976). The order of social structure is then established by the progression through the New Zealand landscape of tribal and clanic ancestors, leaving their respective traces in the local set of geographic features named from their doings, and in the particular set of persons, both human and "natural," descended from their multiple unions with women of the indigenous 'land people' (*tangata whenua*). In this, social structure is the humanized form of cosmic order. The prototype is the primordial search of the divine ancestor Tāne — Tāne, the Fertilizer — for the *uha*, the female element: search that gave rise, in a series of exotic sexual experiments, to various kinds of birds, trees, insects, waters, and rocks, and eventually to humanity through the mating of the god with a woman fashioned from the *mons veneris* of the Earth Mother (Papa). As Tāne did on an elemental scale, thus did the tribal ancestors in New Zealand. So the main cultural relationships devolve through a series of progressively distinctive and delimited forms, corresponding to the devolution in social sphere or segmentary level, from primordial myths to tribal and clan legends, and from clan legends to family histories, until — as carried forward in the ancestral references of proverbial sayings, proper names or the pronoun "I" — they become the order of present existence. The final form of cosmic myth is current event.

"The life that the ancestors lived forth in history is the same as that active in the living" (Johansen 1954:163). Johansen thus introduces a contrast of the Maori to the Western historical sense analogous to Furet's deft critique of *l'histoire événementielle* as necessarily the client of finalist ideologies, there being no other way of making intelligible events conceived as sudden eruptions of "the unique and the new into the concatenation of time" (1972:54). For Maori, such events are hardly unique or new but are immediately perceived in the received order of structure, as identical with their original. Hence where Western thought struggles to comprehend the history of contingent events that it makes for itself by invoking underlying forces or structures, such as those of production or *mentalité*, the Maori world unfolds as an eternal return, the recurrent manifestation of the same experiences (see Eliade 1954). This collapse of time and happening is mediated for Maori by a third term: *tikanga*, the distinctive action of beings and things that comes of their particular nature. If the present reproduces the past, it is because the denizens of this world are instances of the same kinds of being that came before. This relation of class to individual is the very notion of descent, that is, of the relation of ancestor to descendant, and as is well known the whole universe is for Maori a gigantic kin of common ancestry. Such being the ontological case, we should be wary, as Johansen cautions, of imputing to Maori our own ideas of the individuality of event and experience: "We find it quite obvious that once an event has happened, it never returns; but this is exactly what happens" (1954:161). Hence the very experiences of the past are the way the present is experienced:

> It was *a source of pure, unadulterated joy* for the old time Maori, to be able to say to an enemy, "I ate your father" or "your ancestor," although the occurrence may have occurred ten generations before his time. . . . [Best 1902–03:71; emphasis added]

For Maori, ontogeny "recapitulates" cosmogony. The human sexual act recreates the original union of male Heaven (Rangi) and female Earth (Papa). In particular, the incantations used in conception rites are those that enabled the first parent Tāne to produce human offspring with the Earth-formed woman (Hine-ahu-one) fashioned from Papa. The physiology of birth becomes the saga of creation (see Goldie 1905; Best 1929). The womb is the *pō*. *Pō* in myth is the long night of the world's self-generation, issuing finally in the *ao*, the 'day' or world of humans and gods (*ao marama*). A synonym for the placenta is *whenua*, otherwise 'land' or 'earth,' a reference thus to the primordial mother. The umbilicus attaching this earth to the child, product of the divine male seed, is itself called the *iho*, a term also denoting the heart and strength of a tree (H. W. Williams 1975:75). Here again is Tāne, parent and body of trees, who in myth assumed just this position between the Earth and the sacred Heavens. The "self-extolling," the "degeneration-causing" younger brother of the gods, Tāne stood upon his head, pressed against the Earth Mother and in an act likened to parricide pushed the Sky Father from her embrace. By then propping up the Sky with four poles, Tāne and his divine accomplices — including the warrior Tū, who performed the necessary (human) sacrifice — made it possible for their human progeny to take possession of the Earth (see Grey 1956; Best 1976; J. Smith 1974–75; S. Smith 1913–15; White 1855). Or again, at a later time man 'descends' (*heke*, 'migrates') across the waters from the spiritual homeland of Hawaiki to New Zealand, by means of a canoe fashioned of a tree, another body of Tāne. Creation, migration, and parturition are so many versions of the same story. So the father chants to his newborn son:

It was he [Tāne] who put the poles of heaven above us,
Then you were born to the world of light. [Johansen 1954:161]

We thus return directly to history, in fact to the very uprising that
brought Sir George Grey to New Zealand and (to close the circle) gave
us the canonical texts of this mythology. The whole revolt of 1844–46
was about a certain pole, likewise having to do with possession of the
Earth: the flagstaff flying the British colors above Kororareka in the Bay
of Islands, long the most populous European settlement. I am not speaking figuratively (merely). On four separate occasions between July 1844
and March 1845, the Maori "rebel" Hone Heke and his warriors of the
Ngapuhi tribe cut down that flagpole. And Heke's persistence in down-
ing it was matched only by the British insistence on resurrecting it.
Following the final storming of the pole, British troops, aided by certain
Maori "loyalists," fought three major engagements with Heke and his
allies — in the first two of which the colonials were well and truly beaten.
But throughout, for Heke, the flagstaff itself remained the *putake o te riri*,
the 'root cause of the war,' in the sense also of *the* strategic objective.[26]

"He contends for one object only," reads a contemporary newspaper
account, "the non-erection of the flag-staff" (Carleton 1874 vol. 2: appendix, vi). Nor did Heke condone the interest in plunder that seemed
to motivate certain others. " 'Let us fight,' he told his ally Kawiti, 'with
the flagstaff alone' " (ibid.: xliv). For the fourth assault, of March 11,
1845, Kawiti and his warriors were deployed to make an attack on the
European settlement at Kororareka *as a diversion*, so that Heke could go
up the hill and take the flagpole! Their own mission accomplished, Heke
and his men thereupon sat on the hillside to watch the fracas in the town
below. In May, Heke was discussing with Reverend Burrows the governor's possible terms for peace: " 'One condition,' he said, 'must be that
he [the governor] does not erect another flagstaff' " (Burrows 1886:30).

For their part, the British, if they did not attach exactly the same
finality to the flagstaff, knew how to appreciate its "symbolic" value and
to take the appropriate response — of general panic. Nearly every time
the pole went down, fresh calls for reinforcements were sent to Australia: to show the Maori, as one dispatch urged, that Britons were willing to protect their women from insult and their flag from "dishonour."
But when the Maori insurgents made their attack on Kororareka, the
British, after at first beating them off, precipitously abandoned the town,
to the utter "mystification" of the Maori, who "had never asked for it, or

fought for it," and in their "bewilderment" even hesitated momentarily before they looted it (Carleton 1874 vol. 2:93). About the flagstaff itself, the colonials had always shown a better resolve. The government considered it an imperious necessity to "show the colours" and provided the flag with greater protection upon each occasion of its replacement, the fourth time surrounding the pole with a stockade and blockhouse.

There may have been some working misunderstanding here, since the Maori seem not at all as interested in the flag as they were in the pole. At the third assault, Heke, having toppled the flagstaff, was content to leave the flag itself in the hands of certain Maori "friendlies" who had been set to guarding it. Yet the blockhouse ultimately must have confirmed the rebels' interpretation, for the whole construction now plainly resembled a Maori *tūāhu:* a fenced altar within which were erected one or several poles, such as constituted the sacred precincts of Maori settlements and embodied their ancient claims to tribal lands. Essentially, then, the British would agree with the Maori view. In September 1845 the governor sent a letter to Heke outlining the British terms of peace, which were: first, that the 1840 Treaty of Waitangi yielding "sovereignty" to the Queen be respected; and second, "the British colours to be sacred" (Buick 1926:207). Indeed, in April 1845, when 470 British troops sailed into Kororareka to reestablish "the Queen's sovereignty," their first act upon landing was to hoist the Union Jack on the beach.

Likewise when the ancestors of the Tūhoe and Ngatiawa people landed at the Bay of Plenty, "the first serious task performed by the immigrants was the making and sanctifying of a *tuahu,* or sacred place" (Best 1925:724). Best describes this sacred precinct, also called a *pouahu* or 'post-mound,' as a post or tree set in a low mound. The installation is mimetic of the god Tāne's fructification of the Earth Mother, from which issued mankind, or else of Tāne's primordial separation of Heaven and Earth — Tāne, of course, being a tree. In the ancestral *tūāhu* of the Tūhoe, a physical emblem (*mauri*) was placed, representing the prestige and stability of the tribal group. Descriptions from other areas have an old canoe-end (again Tāne) as the central post of the shrine, and the emblem kept near or in the post was the people's god, likewise housed in its 'canoe' (*waka*) or special container (Skinner 1911:76; Hiroa 1977:480–481). Given this association between the *tūāhu* and the ancestral land claim, one can understand why Hone Heke always said that the British flagstaff meant their possession of the land — else why did they persist in re-erecting it? On the other hand, contemporary chronicles are virtually unanimous in saying that Heke was put up to his attacks by outside agitators, notably the local American consul. Only Reverend Burrows (1886:6) writes that the flag above Kororareka was pointed out to Heke as "a *tohu*," a 'sign' that "their country had gone from them." Otherwise, we are supposed to believe that Heke and other chiefs were being told by certain interested White men that the Maori could put an end to British domination by cutting down the flagpole. One may judge the message as understood by Heke, however, from his own discussion of it:

> I said, "what meaning is there in the flagstaff?" The white people told me, "the *mana* of the Queen is in the flag, there are three tribes [*iwi*] in it." I said, "God made this land for us, and all our children." [Carleton 1874 vol. 2, appendix C:xlvii–xlvii]

The "three tribes" are probably the English, Scots, and Irish.[27] In any event, the Maori had already manifested their own interpretation of similar poles in 1836, when a French man-of-war and two merchant vessels anchored at the Bay of Islands and set up small flags about the harbor for surveying purposes. The local Maori attacked these erections of the "Oui-Ouis" — so the French tribe was known — as they had immediately concluded "that the country was being taken possession of" (Carleton 1874 vol. 2:29).[28]

There are traditional Maori rituals, practiced within or outside the sacred precincts (*tūāhu*), which involve the use of poles set in mounds analogous to the manipulations performed by Heke on the flagstaff set upon the hill. A negative, female pole of death (*toko mate*) called 'Great Mound (or Mons Veneris) of Papa (Earth)' is overthrown, leaving erect a '*Tūāhu* of the Heavens' or male pole of life (*toko ora*), all with appropriate incantations signifying the expulsion of undesirable effects (see Best 1925:1072–1074).[29] But in the myth of Manaia, as rendered in his own *Polynesian Mythology*, Sir George Grey could have found the most exact interpretant of Hone Heke's apparent flagpole fetish. The myth rehearses a common Maori motif of contention over land between successive parties of immigrants from Hawaiki. By a *ruse*, the people of the *second* canoe are able to prove that the local *tūāhu* is theirs, or else that theirs is the older one — "Then they looked at the poles of the *tūāhu*; the poles of the Arawa's *tūāhu* were raw [i.e., still green]; those of the Tainui were cooked by fire in order to speed up their drying" (H. W. Williams 1975:444). In the face of such arguments, the original settlers can do nothing, and are forced to leave their lands, go elsewhere.[30]

The mytho-practical force of the argument is that the sacred precinct, in recreating at the level of community Tāne's original separation
of Heaven and Earth, recreates the act that allowed humans to inherit
the Earth. Such separation of Heaven (Rangi) and Earth (Papa) or darkness (*pō*) and light (*ao*) is, as Johansen says, "the proper substance of
creation, what makes the world fit to live in for a Maori" (1958:85). The
fence or corner uprights of the *tūāhu* are the *toko*, term used in the Tāne
myth to designate the poles propping up the Sky-Father, and meaning as
a verb 'to support,' 'to push to a distance,' and 'to divorce.' *Toko* may be
used for the central pole or posts too; alternately the term is *pou*, which as
a verb denotes 'to fix; to render immovable' (H. W. Williams 1975:297,
434; Tregear 1969:528–529). It follows that the establishment of a *tūāhu*
or *tapu* house of the god amounts to the separation of Heaven and Earth
on the terrestrial plane itself—leaving the better part of that plane free
(*noa*) for human occupation. Hence it is said that "the chief of any family
who discovered and took possession of any unoccupied land"—the
tūāhu, as we have seen, being the sign of such possession—"obtained
what was called the *mana* of the land" (Shortland 1882:89).[31]

In a way, then, Hone Heke's war was already many generations old
before it began. He once tried to explain to the governor that his own
unruliness also was "no new thing" but inherited from his ancestors; a
prominent Maori adversary indeed confirmed that it had been going on
for five generations (Buick 1926:42, 198). The war had immediate precedent, however, in the career of a famous Ngapuhi chief of the previous
generation, Hongi Hika, whose conquests, alliances, and person Hone
Heke sought to assume. Heke's career followed a traditional mode of
usurpation, or at least of upward mobility, by the warrior-chief of demonstrated *mana*, including even Heke's marriage to Hongi Hika's daughter. This respect for precedent extended to Heke's tactical choices of
battle sites, taken in the first instance with a view toward the historic
associations with Hongi. In the event, the tribal alliances and enmities of
the last generation were engaged in the opposition of rebel and pro-
British forces during Heke's uprising, albeit many of these relationships
of the early 19th century were but recent residues of ancient memories
of revenge.[32]

A Ngapuhi chief who fought on the British side has left an enchanted
account of the war, full of the mythopoetic deep structures of Maori
politics, as well as fabulous tales of the battle of the kind Thucydides
taught us to ignore (Anonymous of Ngapuhi, in Maning 1906:220–323;

cf. White 1855:144–146, 175, 176). Such ignorance was indeed one of the problems the British had, according to this account: they were excellent fighters, but they just didn't know a thing about omens. However, one could perhaps take a clue from the received Western historiography and, making a virtue of the limits of time as well as theory, resolve all this mytho-praxis to the basic utilities of the economic conjuncture. The mystical activity must have really been practical—or was it that the practical activity was really mystical?

Between 1840, when the British took over New Zealand, and 1844, the northern part of the country experienced a serious decline in European trade, depriving the Maori of foreign goods to which they had become accustomed. The depression was due in part to *pakehā* depopulation in favor of the new capital at Auckland, in part due to port duties imposed by the new Colonial Government. Still, a simple economic explanation of the 1844 rebellion would be problematic, since many of the Maori loyalists were suffering (if that is the word) as much as Hone Heke's insurgents. The loyalists were led by men of aristocratic lineage opposed in Maori principle to Heke's pretentions, and notably included clans and tribes that had been victims of Heke's predecessor Hongi. But if the structure of the conjuncture cannot be determined directly from material interests, Heke's tilting at the flagstaff does seem logically appropriate to the economic crisis. Or at least, this Maori response to the colonial situation was as mythological as the pragmatics of the European presence were metaphysical. For the Maori, the material crisis was the revelatory sign of something more intangible and enigmatic: of what had happened in 1840 when the chiefs, agreeing to the Treaty of Waitangi, gave up what the British were pleased to call "the sovereignty."[33]

> We all tried to find out the reason why the Governor was so anxious to get us to make these marks. Some of us thought the Governor wanted to bewitch all the chiefs, but our pakeha friends laughed at this, and told us that the people of Europe did not know how to bewitch people. Some told us one thing, some another. . . . We did not know what to think, but were all anxious [the Governor] might come to us soon; for we were afraid that all his blankets, and tobacco, and other things would be gone before he came to our part of the country, and that he would have nothing left to pay us for making our marks on his paper . . . and when when we met the Governor, the speaker of Maori [i.e., the interpreter] told us that if we put our names, or even made any sort of

mark on that paper, the Governor would then protect us, and prevent us from being robbed of our cultivated land, and our timber land, and everything else which belonged to us. . . . The speaker of Maori then went on to tell us certain things, but the meaning of what he said was so closely concealed we never have found it out. One thing we understood well, however, for he told us plainly that if we wrote on the Governor's paper, one of the consequences would be that great numbers of pakeha would come to this country to trade with us, that we should have abundance of valuable goods. . . . We were very glad to hear this. [Anonymous of Ngapuhi, in Maning 1906:223–225]

For sheer mystification, the curious hieroglyphs the Maori chiefs appended to the Treaty of Waitangi could be equaled only by its several provisions. Her Majesty's Government had been moved to intervene by the extensive project of land acquisition announced by the New Zealand Company. Initially, the government meant to forestall the company and protect remaining Maori lands. Hence the treaty was urgently pressed (together with the usual gifts) upon the chiefs as an economic good thing, the assurance of their future prosperity. On the other hand, the combination it offered of yielding the sovereignty to the Queen and keeping the land to themselves would be perfectly unintelligible to Maori: "The speaker of Maori then went on to tell us certain things, but the meaning of what he said was so closely concealed we never have found it out." Just before the Ngapuhi chiefs signed at Waitangi, the Reverend Mr. Colenso respectively intervened to ask the Governor (Hobson) if he thought the Maori understood the terms. " 'I have spoken to some of the chiefs concerning it,' " Colenso said, " 'who had no idea whatever as to the purport of the treaty' " (Buick 1936:155).[34]

The Maori text would be enough to keep its own secrets. In Article One, the "sovereignty" the chiefs agree to surrender is glossed by an adjunctive (or concretive) form of the English loanword for 'govern/ governor,' *kawanatanga*, concept of which the Maori as yet had little or no direct experience. But in Article Two, the Maori are solemnly guaranteed the *rangatiratanga*, the 'chiefship'—or, if you will, the 'sovereignty'—"of their lands, their settlements and all their property" (Buick 1936:360–362).[35] And while the English missionaries, Henry Williams especially, were pleased to think they had on numerous occasions satisfactorily explained the treaty to the Maori, it was precisely the missionaries' deceptions in this regard that Hone Heke brought up when they remonstrated with him about the flagstaff. "Heke did not allow this opportunity to pass without alluding to the Treaty of Waitangi, and of having been deceived by the Archdeacon [Williams] and others in inducing so many chiefs to sign it, when they [Williams et al.] must have known that they (the chiefs) were signing away their lands, etc." (Burrows 1886:9, cf. p. 32). Problem was that the distinction between political supremacy and the occupation of (or "title to") the land was not pertinent to Maori. So long as a chief and his people maintained residence on their ancestral land, and the willingness to defend it, no other chief could rule there. Beyond all Western ideas of property or sovereignty, the land is "the inorganic body of the clan community" (to adopt Marx's phrase). It is the objectified *mana* of the kinship group. Maori and Western concepts on this score are incommensurable. Still, Firth must be right when he says that "the concept of *mana* in connection with land is . . . most nearly akin to the idea of sovereignty" (1959:392; cf. White 1855:190–191). For when Heke determined that the Treaty of Waitangi was proposing some new sacred arrangements of property, he concluded that it must mean for Maori the loss of the *mana* — as occurs in conquest, dispossession, and enslavement. The British were putting up their own *tūāhu*.

In this respect, the economic deprivations that followed upon the treaty were symptomatic merely of a larger issue: the meaning of the British presence; or the fate of the Maori. Maori said that the government claimed to be a parent, but only showed itself to be " 'soldiers, barracks, constables and gaols' " (Sinclair 1972:31). Debate continued among Maori chiefs about what the treaty had signified. Various metaphysical speculations were improvised. The best known, by one Nopera Panakareau, ran to the effect that "the shadow of the land goes to Queen Victoria, but the substance remains to us." That he said in May 1840. Already, by the following January, Nopera had reversed the terms: "The substance of the land goes to the Europeans, the shadow only will be our portion" (cited in Wards 1968: front matter). Whatever the treaty meant, says the Anonymous of Ngapuhi, "this one thing at least was true, we had less tobacco and fewer blankets and other European goods than formerly, and we saw that the first governor had not spoken the truth, for he told us that we should have a great deal more" (Maning 1906:230–231). The whaling and trading ships had nearly stopped coming and the *pakehā* were leaving the northern districts. The government had acted in mysterious and deceptive ways. Or was it not that these adverse effects had made Maori aware that the true issue in the treaty was the *mana*. In this respect, Heke's work on the flagpole was a demystification. It was a reminder that the same had happened before, when the chiefs first came to this New Zealand from Hawaiki, and built their sacred sites (*tūāhu*) on the land, and took control from the original 'people of the land' (*tangata whenna*).

One myth is thus decoded by another (just as Lévi-Strauss says). For the Treaty of the Waitangi was a myth, even in European terms. In one of the most scholarly accounts going of Heke's rebellion — albeit written from a *pakehā* vantage — Wards (1968:171) has to admit that "the Treaty *was* a device to blind and amuse ignorant savages," as contemporary criticism had said. Without undue expense, "quickly and quietly," the Crown had got possession of New Zealand. And if the treaty, in ostensibly providing for the welfare of the Maori, was not an outright deception, since such a purpose could hardly be reconciled with the massive colonization by Her Majesty's White subjects already underway, it was at the least a contradiction, since the government had no means to secure Maori interests and soon abandoned the intention. Moreover, the Colonial Office well knew in advance that the difference between sovereignty and property would not be received by the Maori, as was stated in preliminary drafts of the instructions to Captain Hobson for negotiating the treaty. All these drafts indicate "that it was not believed that the Maoris understood the distinction between sovereignty and property rights" (Wards 1968:28). But no statement to this effect is to be found in the instructions as issued, "clearly because it was not politic to make such a public admission" (ibid.:29). The treaty had been negotiated in bad faith.

Or, in other words, the essential unrealities as well as the impracticalities of the situation had been laid on by the British. Attacking the flagpole, Heke showed he was able to penetrate, become conscious of and objectify the meanings the *pakehā* were prepared to conceal sometimes even from themselves. If the response still seems to us displaced or "symbolic," we should not forget that the decisive issue, as Wards also admits, was equally abstract: Heke "was suffering the inevitable pangs of one who sees, or senses, the eclipse of his own way of life by another" (1968:145).

A Structural, Historical Anthropology
In an oft-cited remark from the preface to *Search for a Method* (1968), Sartre asks, "Do we have today the means to constitute a structural, historical anthropology?" Yes, I have tried to suggest here, *le jour est*

arrivé. Practice clearly has gone beyond the theoretical differences that are supposed to divide anthropology and history. Anthropologists rise from the abstract structure to the explication of the concrete event. Historians devalue the unique event in favor of underlying recurrent structures. And also paradoxically, anthropologists are as often diachronic in outlook as historians nowadays are synchronic. Nor is the issue, or this lecture, merely about the value of collaboration. The problem now is to explode the concept of history by the anthropological experience of culture. The heretofore obscure histories of remote islands deserve a place alongside the self-contemplation of the European past — or the history of "civilizations" — for their own remarkable contributions to an historical understanding. We thus multiply our conceptions of history by the diversity of structures. Suddenly, there are all kinds of new things to consider.

Notes

1. Stone's chapters on historiography (Part I) in *The Past and the Present* (1981) afford an excellent introduction to the "new history." Barraclough (1979) on the same subject also refers to Thomas Gray — a custom of English historians in America? The remarks from Voltaire's *Essai sur les moeurs* are noted by LeGoff (1972) in an essay of his own most pertinent to the present discussion; cf. Braudel (1980), Dumoulin and Moisi (1973), Gilbert and Graubard (1972), Hexter (1972), LeGoff and Nora (1974), Ricoeur (1980).

2. I have translated freely, especially taking liberties with *devenir*, yet I think without altering Durkheim's intent.

3. Besides Frazer (1911–15), Hocart (1927, 1936) and Dumont (1970), the ideas on divine kingship and hierarchy presented here draw especially on recent anthropological studies by Heusch (1962, 1972, 1982), Valeri (1983), Geertz (1980), Tambiah (1976), and Adler (1978, 1982), as well as such earlier classics as Evans-Pritchard (1962 [1948]), Frankfort (1948), Dumézil (1948), Meek (1931), Kuper (1947), Krige and Krige (1943); cf. Sahlins (1981a, b). I make no taxonomic issue of the differences between "divine kings," "sacred kings," "magical kings," and "priest-kings" — or even between "kings" and "chiefs." With regard to the last, I rather agree with Heusch that the state is a creation of the divine king, instead of the other way around, in which case the principal reason for differentiating divine kingship from divine chiefship loses its force. For a discussion of the taxonomic problems surrounding divine kingship, as well as an excellent analysis of Jukun, see Young (1966). No doubt my decision to go with a broad category of heroic polities, without fine regard for the variations, can be

advantageous for present theoretical purposes and over the short run only. I have no illusions about the greater durability or value of the category.

4. Besides, in the Fijian case, quite literally, a chief can be the sister's son to another chiefdom (e.g., *vasu ki Rewa, vasu ki Mbau*, etc.). The personifications of political forces entailed in Fijian *vasu* (uterine nephew) relationships are discussed below.

5. The informant cited, however, is one of the "skeptics" in a fascinating debate among Kuba, reported by Vansina (1964:101–102), concerning the divinity of the king. The skeptics take a functionalist view of the royalty as a necessary condition of order in a society otherwise segmentary, conceding that the king has powerful magic but denying he has divine powers. Apart from such ideological arguments, the Kuba practice a classic set of rituals by which the king, deprived of his natal kinship relations, is placed above as well as outside the clanic order of the society — at once as a force of nature, a representative of the god and an incestuous sorcerer.

6. The usual phrase is *na lotu nei Ratu Cakobau*, in orthodox Fijian spelling. In the present article, I have reverted to an earlier and unorthodox orthography, easier for English speakers to pronounce. When asked once why he did not learn English, Thakombau said it was because he had heard Englishmen speaking Fijian.

7. On the other hand, when certain Mbau gods resisted Christianity even after Thakombau had converted, the chiefs assembled their priests and whipped them (Waterhouse 1866:265–266). The earlier relations of Fijian priests/gods to Jehovah may be followed in the journals of Cross (e.g., Oct. 24, 1840), Hunt (Feb. 18, 1839; May 10, 1839), Calvert (Aug. 15, 1841; Oct. 20, 1841), among others.

8. Thakombau's intelligent resistance to missionary preaching is documented throughout Waterhouse's *The King and People of Fiji* (1866). This includes his indifference to the suggestion of a passing Catholic bishop, who told him that the reason the Methodist missionaries had failed to get access to Mbau was that the Virgin Mary was keeping the place for Catholicism: "Whereupon the king told the bishop to leave him and his city to the care of the Virgin, and to come back again when the Virgin had converted them" (ibid.:196).

Two decades earlier, Protestant missionaries in Hawaii were being subjected to similar experiences as their Fijian colleagues. "'If he [King Liholiho] embraces the new religion,'" Reverend Ellis was told in 1822, "'we shall all follow'" (Ellis 1969:41). One day when the missionary Hiram Bingham went to remonstrate with the royally drunk King, "and told him God was not pleased with such conduct," Liholiho replied, "'I am god myself. What the hell! Get out of my house'" (Hammatt: Jan. 6, 1823). In the ensuing events, which included Liholiho's death, Christianity was taken up as an instrument of rule by the King's foster mother and her brothers, the effective governing group, and as in Fiji it became an overnight sensation (cf. Bingham 1969). Indeed, we seem to be in the presence of a great regularity or law of conversion valid for the Polynesian heroic polities. In New Zealand also there was a quantum statistical leap forward in the conversion process about 1838–39, after a long period of relatively desultory success (notably among Maori slaves). Once again, the lead was taken by the chiefly class (Wright 1959:141ff.).

9. During the Mbau-Rewa war, when an important chief defected to the enemy, as Thokanauto of Rewa, for example, went over to Mbau, a considerable number of clans and villages subordinate to the chief accordingly changed sides. The change was effected without great embarrassment, since, as Reverend Hunt remarks, "whatever party they fought for, they were fighting for their own chief" (Oct. 19, 1845). Derrick likewise paraphrases Tacitus: "As for the common people, their chief's cause was their cause" (1950:73). These defections are a good demonstration of the relation between hierarchical solidarity and "tribal" or "national" consciousness, on which more is said below.

10. The mutations in organization that followed also testify to an heroic historicity, not only by Shaka's capacity to introduce rapid and general change, but in the attention he gave to hierarchical solidarities while reconstituting the conquest state. Repeating the victories of Dingiswago, Shaka was careful not to repeat his predecessor's policies of leaving intact the leadership and organization of the conquered tribes. Liquidating the one with the other, and regrouping the remnants of the enemy armies in the Zulu regimental system, Shaka constructed an order that avoided the faults in Dingiswago's hegemonic ambitions, namely, the confederate system that had divided the interests of the tribes by the existence of their leaders (Bryant 1926; Fynn, in Bird 1888; Isaacs 1970; Krige 1936; Wilson 1969).

11. Firsthand accounts of these incidents are given by Fynn (in Bird 1888:81–84, 91–93) and Isaacs (1970:108ff.). John Kelly has written an excellent M.A. thesis, "Mongol Conquest and Zulu Terror: An Analysis of Cultural Change," with a detailed cultural analysis of the Zulu scheme of heroic dominance (University of Chicago, Department of Anthropology).

12. On the death rites of Hawaiian high chiefs, see Handy and Pukui (1972: 156–157), Kamakau (1961:222), Malo (1951:104–107), Ellis (1969:175ff.), Stewart (1970 [1830]:216). Hawaiian history also shows numerous examples of the collapse (or the incapacity) of a collective response in the absence of the ruling chief. The British naval commander Broughton provides an example from a revolt in 1796, when a rival chief, profiting from the absence of King Kamehameha, easily seized the greater part of Hawai'i Island. Nor could much resistance be expected, according to Broughton, as there was no one to lead it:

He [the rebel, Namakaeha] now possessed four out of [the Island's] six districts, and was approaching near to Karakakooa [Kealakekua], where there was little chance of resistance, as the people were averse to fighting, having no chief in whom they confided to lead them on; indeed the only person of that rank was Mahooa, who had lost his eye-sight. He wished much to go with us to Wohahow [O'ahu] that he might explain what happened To Tamaahmaah [Kamehameha], but the people, having no other chief, would not permit him. [Broughton 1804:69]

13. Gifford's description of heroic segmentation in the Tongan Islands was destined to become a celebrated locus of sociological argument among Polynesianists:

Everything points to the necessity of a line of powerful chiefs as a nucleus about which the lineage groups itself. Without such chiefs it appears to wilt and die and its membership gradually aligns itself with other rising lineages. This process of realignment naturally contravenes the rule of patrilineal descent, which theoretically, and largely in practice, determines lineage membership. [Gifford 1929:30]

The arguments have been laid to rest (or should have been, anyhow) by Elizabeth Bott's (1981) careful description of the Tongan organization, together with excellent examples of the segmentation process in question (pp. 41ff.). One of the lessons of the controversy might be that we should not expect a "lineage consciousness" in the underlying populations of the hierarchical Polynesian societies. Indeed, in Hawaii, where heroic segmentation is taken even further, with the leadership of the districts down to relatively low levels of segmentation redistributed by each ruling chief among his kinsmen at his accession, the local lineage order has been completely eroded. Nor could it be expected that the people would have their own extensive genealogies, hence their own senior lines and collateral relations of solidarity, in opposition to the chiefs constantly being imposed on them. The more subtle ways that Maori "clans" (hapū) are formed by dominant chiefs and as political alliances have been sensitively documented by Schwimmer (1963, 1978).

14. Chadwick writes of "the instability of heroic society":

The military followers of a peace-loving king, unless he was very wealthy and generous, were liable to drift away, while the bulk of the population counted for nothing. In the absence of any truly national organisation or national feeling all depended on the personal qualities of the leaders. Under Theodric the Ostrogoths were the chief power in Europe; but within thirty years of his death they disappear and are not heard of again. Under Dušan the Servians seemed destined to absorb all that was left of the Greek empire; after his death they failed to offer any effective resistance to the Turks. The kingdoms of the Greek Heroic Age seem to have succumbed to much less formidable antagonists. So numerous indeed are cases of this kind that one is perhaps justified in regarding national disaster as the normal ending of such epochs. [Chadwick 1926:461–462]

15. On the royal intrigues of the Fijian states of Mbau and Rewa, see Waterhouse (1866) Derrick (1950), or Wilkes (1845 vol. 3); for Lau, Hocart (1929), Reid (1977). For European analogues, see Chadwick (1926:338ff.).

16. The "heroic I" is found in Maori, Tonga, Fiji, among Yoruba as well as Luapula, and probably numerous other hierarchical orders. This usage is discussed in Sahlins (1981a) as "the kinship I" following Johansen (1954) on Maori. The Maori case is indeed relatively democratic, although the chief is more likely than other people to use the first-person singular in reference to noted ancestors or the clan (*hapū*) as a whole.

17. I have elsewhere (Sahlins 1981a, 1982) analyzed the Fijian polity in greater cultural detail.

18. The long-term constitution of relationships by a "founding marriage," perhaps legendary, is of course characteristic of systems of positional succession. And the differential weight attached to aristocratic marriage generally is a principled reason, valid at least for societies of a certain type, why the distinction between prescriptive and preferential marriage rules need not be received by a structuralist analysis. The rule of generalized exchange, operating sometimes among the highest chiefs, seems as critical in the organization of Tongan society as it is minimal in social practice. In any event, in the Polynesian societies, the ordinary people hardly marry at all, ritually speaking, as opposed to a "living together" (*noho pu*) whose duration and outcome are uncertain until children are born and acknowledged.

19. Excellent examples of this type of autobiographical perception can be found in the testimonies of the Boundary Commission of the Hawaiian Kingdom in the 1860s: Department of Land and Natural Resources, Boundary Commission Books, in the State of Hawaii Archives.

20. The relation between ordinary gossip and, say, royal genealogies is happily illustrated among Luapula peoples by the etymology and fate of the term *ilyashi*, referring to group "affairs" or "traditions." It comes from plateau Bemba where it means mere "gossip," yet latterly has been replaced by the English word *meaning* (Cunnison 1951).

21. The Ilongot historical practice is in so many respects the antithesis of the Maori "mytho-praxis" about to be described that it is necessary to underscore Rosaldo's observation that "even the most brute of brute facts I found to be culturally mediated. . . . Ilongot statements about their past were embodied in cultural forms that highlighted certain facts of life and remained silent about others through their patterned way of selecting, evaluating, and ordering the world they attended to" (1980:17–18). Otherwise the Ilongot ideology might evoke on the ethnographer's part a rabid methodological individualism. Fortunately also, Rosaldo is able to link Ilongot historical consciousness to the system of marriage, a combination of complex and exchange-marriage that uni-

fies each generation while opposing it to adjacent ones, and to show too the cycles of kinship repartition and coalescence (ibid.:199).

22. Or else the meaning is that the male who before preserved his tapu shall next time mix with the woman, and thereby lose it, an interpretation supported by the Maori concept of sexual intercourse as the death of the man (see below).

23. Maoris . . . describe the past as *nga ra o mua,* "the days in front," and the future as *kei muri,* "behind." They move into the future with their eyes on the past. In deciding how to act in the present, they examine the panorama of history spread before their eyes, and select the model that is most appropriate and helpful from the many presented there. This is not living in the past; it is drawing on the past for guidance, bringing the past into the present and the future. [Metge 1976:70]

24. The speeches made by friendly Maori chiefs during a meeting with the government in the course of this war are partly preserved in the correspondence of the then governor, Fitzroy. But the speeches "were so full of allegorical references and responses to ancient Maori customs, that much of them was not understood by the missionaries, who could not render them into English" (Buick 1926:41n.; cf. Carleton 1874 vol. 2:78–79). Just so, Best describes the traditional war councils of chiefs, when "the most stirring and eloquent speeches were made, speeches teeming with strange old saws and aphorisms, with numerous allusions to the famed deeds of ancestors and to the classic myths of the Polynesian race" (1903:46).

25. The ideas on the Maori sense of history presented here were especially stimulated by and are much indebted to Johansen (1954) and an unpublished paper by Gregory Schrempp, "The Pattern of Maori Mythology."

26. The principal sources of the present discussion of Hone Heke's rebellion are: Buick (1926), Burrows (1886), Carleton (1874), Cowan (1922), Sinclair (1972), Wards (1968), W. Williams (1867) and the account given to Maning by an anonymous chief of the Ngapuhi who fought on the British side (Maning 1906:220–323). Unfortunately the books of Rutherford on Heke's war and the Treaty of Waitangi have not been accessible to me at this writing (but see Rutherford 1961:chap. 8).

27. Alternatively, Heke was referring to the British, French, and Americans, all three varieties of *paheka* being pertinent to this period of Maori history; or even to the soldiers, sailors, and settlers, the main divisions of local Europeans during the rebellion, also considered by Maori as distinct ancestral kinds. The Anonymous of Ngapuhi speaks thus of British soldiers and sailors at the first battle with the Maori rebels:

> What a fine-looking people these soldiers are! Fine, tall, handsome people; they all look like chiefs; and their advance is like the advance of a flight of curlew in the air, so orderly and straight. And along with the soldiers came the

sailors; they are of a different family, and not at all related to the soldiers, but they are a brave people, and they came to seek revenge for the relations they had lost in the fight at Kororareka. They had different clothes from the soldiers, and short guns, and long heavy sword[s]; they were a people who talked and laughed more than the soldiers, and they flourished their guns about as they advanced, and ate tobacco. [Maning 1906:248]

28. Conceivably, these poles were taken as tapu signs (*rahui*), which was also a certain Maori opinion of the flagpole at Kororareka, at least while the customs duties were still in effect (before September 1844). Even so, the pole would have essentially the same significance as those of the *tūāhu* and other poles (see below).

29. The existence of a negative (or "dark") pole in the *tūāhu*, by opposition to the positive (or "light") pole, is generally related to the function of preservation by the absorption or neutralization of malevolent effects — thus the female aspect of the negative pole, with analogies to the role of living women in tapu transformations. The chief's hair clippings, for example, might be put in the *tūāhu*, protecting both chief and community against careless exposure of such dangerous substance. Hence the village latrine — notably, the bar on which one squats, separating life (before) and death (behind) — may also be known as a *tūāhu*, being the site of famous rituals.

30. See Shortland 1882:69–70. The twist in Grey's Manaia story is that the original settlers had neglected to construct a *tūāhu*, so that when the newcomers were able to point out the sacred place they had built, Manaia was forced to acknowledge their claims to everything else, including the houses and clearings he and his own people had made (Grey 1956:179–180). Best's Ngati-awa informant provides still another version, perhaps the most pertinent to the present discussion. Pio, who took pride in his descent from the indigenous people of the land (*tangata whenua*), was careful to point out to Best that the *tūāhu* of the immigrants from Hawaiki was really the sacred place (*pouahu*) of the original people, thereby condensing in a phrase the usurpation by aristocratic and violent foreigners (Best 1925:724, 1045).

31. Considering the general and productive value of the Tāne myth, it is not surprising that the ritual erection of poles, in the interest of the preservation of some group or individual, is also found in numerous contexts outside the *tūāhu*. The pole at the right-hand side of the entrance to a Maori fortification might house the *mauri* of the place; called *pou reinga*, it apparently connected the fort with Hawaiki (= Reinga; see Skinner 1911:76; H. W. Williams 1975:297). Tūhoe might set up a pole as the personal *mauri* of a child, analogous to the practice elsewhere of planting the branch used in "baptismal" (*tohi*) rites (Best 1976:365).

32. Hone Heke was certainly a *parvenu* in generational terms, and within the Ngapuhi "tribe" probably also in genealogical terms. It was on such grounds (among others) that Tamati Waka Nene — himself apparently a Ngapuhi chief of the blood (see Wilkes 1845 vol. 2:383–384) — rallied the Maori opposition

against Heke (Burrows 1886:5, 14–15; Davis 1876:80; Shortland 1856:264; Carleton 1874:passim; Rutherford 1961:78). With regard to his famous precursor Hongi Hika, Heke's career is indeed classic, not only in terms of his marriage to Hongi's daughter, but also by the fact that Heke was Hongi's sister's son, or at least a classificatory sister's son, as I judge from Carleton's somewhat unclear remarks (1874 vol. 2:13–14n.). It might be noted that Hongi had sons, who inherited his property, at least two of whom were alive during Heke's rebellion (Carleton 1874 vol. 2:61–62; Davis 1876:56). On the other hand, there is no doubt that Heke assumed Hongi's place or even person, in Maori eyes, hence he also assumed certain of Hongi's enemies: "They came to help Walker [Tamati Waka Nene] in search of revenge against Hongi Ika, for Heke and Hongi are the same" (Anonymous of Ngapuhi, in Maning 1906:241, cf. p. 232). Heke chose to make his first stand against the British where Hongi is supposed to have uttered his dying words, *kia toa! kia toa!*, "Be brave! Be brave!" At this place, Mawhe, Heke built a fort named Te Kahika, "The Ancestor."

The system of alliances and enmities developed during Hongi's time, many of which go back for generations before that, became in turn a *trace structure* (as it might be called) in Heke's revolt (see Smith 1910; Buick 1926:100n.; Wright 1959; Maning 1906). This structure was inherited with all its faults, or geographical divisions cum oppositions within Ngapuhi, since it is clear that the Ngapuhi "tribe" was put together in large measure by Hongi (see Binney 1968:58n.; Carleton 1874 vol. 1:65–68, vol. 2:41–43). Dialectically and selectively, the trace structure was brought to bear in 1844–46 by the conflict between Waka and Heke. Whereas Waka, for his part, and on a traditional Maori model, invoked biographical ties with the *pakehā* ("Europeans") in explanation of his alliance with the Government (Maning 1906; Davis 1876:18–19, 34ff.; White 1887–1890, vol. 5:210–211; Shortland 1856:232–234).

33. The view taken here is close to that of Sinclair, who speaks of the economic depression of 1840–44 as the catalytic, although not decisive, circumstance of the war, by virtue of the revelations it afforded the Maori about the colonial situation (1972:65–66).

34. The hieroglyphic signatures on the treaty are usually said to be attempts of the chiefs to imitate their facial tattoos (for a facsimile of the treaty signatures, see Buick 1936:facing 352). Hone Heke was the first to so sign the Treaty of Waitangi. Whether on the previous day he had also strongly supported the Treaty or vehemently attacked it is a vexed documentary issue (cf. Buick 1936:140n.).

Charles Wilkes, commander of the U.S. Exploring Expedition, was at the Bay of Islands two months after the signing of the Treaty. His remarks on the understanding of it by the Maori chiefs in general and the important Ngapuhi chief Pomare in particular are serving of American interests, no doubt, but the content does not seem any less Maori in character:

So far as the chiefs understand the agreement, they think they have not alienated any of their rights to the soil, but consider it only as a personal grant, not transferable. In the interview I had with Pomare, I was desirous of knowing the impression it had made on him. I found he was not under the impression that he had given up his authority, or any portion of his land permanently; the latter he said he could not do, as it belonged to all his tribe. Whenever this subject was brought up, after answering questions, he invariably spoke of the figure he would make in the scarlet uniform and epaulettes, that Queen Victoria was to send him, and "then what a handsome man he would be!" [Wilkes 1845 vol. 2:376]

35. After these lines had been penned, I was happy to find good anthropological authority for them:

There are two versions of [the treaty], one written by Captain Hobson in English and another, substantially ambiguous one, written by Reverend Henry Williams in Maori. The English version said the Maoris were to cede their 'sovereignty.' The Maori version said they were to cede their 'kawanatanga,' a word coined for the purpose of the treaty and meaningless except in the context of western constitutional law of which the Maori signers were ignorant. The treaty, in English, guaranteed to the Maoris the 'possession' of their land; in Maori this word was rendered as 'rangatiratanga' which may, indeed, mean possession but which may equally well mean 'chief-ship.' A Maori would be hard put, in 1840, to tell the difference between what he gave up (kawanatanga) and retained (rangatiratanga). [Schwimmer 1966:107]

References Cited

Adler, Alfred
1978 Le pouvoir et l'interdit. In Systèmes de signes, 25–40. Paris: Hermann.
1982 The Ritual Doubling of the Person of the King. In Between Belief and Transgression. M. Izard and P. Smith, eds. pp. 180–192. Chicago: University of Chicago Press.

Barnes, J. A.
1951 The Fort Jameson Ngoni. In Seven Tribes of British Central Africa. Elizabeth Colson and Max Gluckman, eds. pp. 194–252. London: Oxford University Press.
1967 Politics in a Changing Society. 2d ed. Manchester: Manchester University Press.

Barraclough, Geoffrey
1979 Main Trends in History. New York: Holmes and Meier.

Benveniste, Émile
1969 Le vocabulaire des institutions Indo-Europeenes. 2 vols. Paris: Les Editions de Minuit.

Best, Elsdon
1902–03   Notes on the Art of War, Parts II, V. Journal of the Polynesian Society 11:47–75; 12:32–50.
1925   Tuhoe: The Children of the Mist. Vol. 1. New Plymouth, New Zealand: Avery.
1929   The Whare Kohanga and Its Lore. Dominion Museum Bulletin, No. 13.
1976 [1924]   Maori Religion and Mythology: Part I. Wellington: A. R. Shearer, Government Printer.

Bingham, Hiram
1969 [1855]   A Residence of Twenty-One Years in the Sandwich Islands. New York: Praeger.

Binney, Judith
1968   The Legacy of Guilt: A Life of Thomas Kendall. Christchurch: Oxford University Press for the University of Auckland Press.

Bird, John
1888   The Annals of Natal, 1495–1845. Vol. 1. Pietermaritzburg: P. Davis and Sons.

Bonte, Pierre, and Nicole Echard
1976   Histoire et histoires: conception du passé chez les Hausa et les Tuareg (République du Niger). Cahiers d'Études Africaines 16:237–296.

Bott, Elizabeth
1981   Power and Rank in the Kingdom of Tonga. Journal of the Polynesian Society 90:7–82.

Bourdieu, Pierre
1977   Outline of a Theory of Practice. Cambridge: Cambridge University Press.

Braudel, Fernand
1980   On History. Chicago: The University of Chicago Press.

Broughton, William Robert
1804   A Voyage of Discovery in the North Pacific Ocean . . . in the Years 1795, 1796, 1797, 1798. London: Cadell and Davies.

Bryant, A. T.
1929   Olden Times in Zululand and Natal. London: Longmans, Green.
1949   The Zulu People. Pietermaritzburg: Shuter and Shooter.

Buick, T. Lindsay
1926   New Zealand's First War, or the Rebellion of Hone Heke. Wellington: Skinner, Government Printer.
1936   The Treaty of Waitangi. 3d ed. New Plymouth, N.Z.: Thomas Avery and Sons.

Burrows, R.
1886   Extracts from a Diary Kept by Rev. R. Burrows During Heke's War in the North in 1845. Auckland: Upton.

Calvert, James
1838–86   Journals of James Calvert, 1838–86. Ms. in Library, School of African and Oriental Studies, University of London.

Carleton, Hugh
1874   The Life of Henry Williams. 2 vols. Auckland: Upton.

Chadwick, H. Munro
1926 The Heroic Age. Cambridge: Cambridge University Press.

Cowan, James
1922 The New Zealand Wars. Vol. 1: 1845–64. Wellington: R. E. Owen, Government Printer.

Cross, William
1837–42 Diary of Rev. William Cross, Dec. 28, 1837–Oct. 1, 1842. *Ms*. Methodist Overseas Mission Papers No. 336, Mitchell Library, Sydney.

Cunnison, Ian
1951 History on the Luapula. Rhodes-Livingstone Paper, No. 21. Manchester: Manchester University Press.
1957 History and Genealogies in a Conquest State. American Anthropologist 59:20–31.
1959 The Luapula Peoples of Northern Rhodesia. Manchester: Manchester University Press.

Davis, C. O.
1876 The Life and Times of Patuone. Auckland: J. H. Field.

Derrick, R. A.
1950 A History of Fiji. 2d ed. Suva: Printing and Stationery Department.

Dumézil, Georges
1948 Mitra-Varuna. Paris: Gallimard.
1968 Mythe et epopée. 3d ed. 3 vols. Paris: Gallimard.

Dumont, Louis
1970 Homo Hierarchicus. Chicago: The University of Chicago Press.

Dumoulin, Jerome, and Dominique Moisi, eds.
1973 The Historian between the Ethnologist and the Futurologist. Paris: Mouton.

Durkheim, Émile
1905–06 Compte-rendu de *Sociologia e Storia*, A. D. Zenopol. L'Année Sociologique 9:140.

Eliade, Mircea
1954 The Myth of the Eternal Return. Bollingen Series XLVI. Princeton: Princeton University Press.

Ellis, William
1969 [1842] Polynesian Researches: Hawaii. New edition. Rutland, Vt.: Tuttle.

Evans-Pritchard, E. E.
1962 The Divine Kingship of the Shilluk of the Nilotic Sudan (The Frazer Lecture, 1948). *In* Essays in Social Anthropology. E. E. Evans-Pritchard, ed. pp. 66–86. London: Faber and Faber.

Feeley-Harnik, Gillian
1978 Divine Kingship and the Meaning of History among the Sakalava of Madagascar. Man, n.s. 13:402–417.

Firth, Raymond
1959 Economics of the New Zealand Maori. Wellington: R. E. Owen, Government Printer.

Fox, James J.
1971 A Rotinese Dynastic Genealogy. *In* The Translation of Cul-

ture. T. Beidelman, ed. London: Tavistock.

Frankfort, Henri
1948 Kingship and the Gods. Chicago: The University of Chicago Press.

Frazer, Sir James G.
1911–15 The Golden Bough. 3d ed. London: Macmillan.

Furet, François
1972 Quantitative History. *In* Historical Studies Today. Felix Gilbert and Stephen R. Graubard, eds. New York: Norton.

Geertz, Clifford
1980 Negara: The Theatre State in Nineteenth-Century Bali. Princeton: Princeton University Press.

Gifford, Edward Winslow
1929 Tongan Society. Bernice P. Bishop: Museum Bulletin, No. 61.

Gilbert, Felix, and Stephen Graubard, eds.
1972 Historical Studies Today. New York: Norton.

Goldie, W. H.
1905 Maori Medical Lore. Transactions of the New Zealand Institute, 1904, 37:1–120.

Grey, Sir George
1956 [1855] Polynesian Mythology. New York: Taplinger.

Hammett, Charles H.
1823–25 Journal of Charles H. Hammett [in the Sandwich Islands, May 6, 1823 to June 9, 1825]. *Ms.* Baker Library, Harvard University.

Handy, E. S. Craighill, and Mary Kawena Pukui
1972 Polynesian Family System in Ka-'u, Hawaii. Rutland, Vt.: Tuttle.

Heusch, Luc de
1962 Le pouvoir et le sacré. Annales du Centre d'Études des Religions, No. 1. Brussels: Institut de Sociologie, Université Libre de Bruxelles.
1972 Le roi ivre ou l'originie de l'État. Paris: Gallimard.
1982 Rois nés d'un coeur de vache. Paris: Gallimard.

Hexter, J. H.
1972 Fernand Braudel and the Monde Braudelien. Journal of Modern History 44:480–541.

Hiroa, Te Rangi (Sir Peter Buck)
1977 [1949] The Coming of the Maori. Wellington: Maori Purposes Fund Board, Whitecoulls.

Hocart, A. M.
1914 Mana. Man 14(46):97–101.
1915 Chieftainship and the Sister's Son in the Pacific. American Anthropologist 17:631–646.
1927 Kingship. London: Oxford University Press.
1929 Lau Islands, Fiji. Bernice P. Bishop Museum Bulletin, No. 62.
1936 [1970] Kings and Councillors. Classics in Anthropology Edition. Rodney Needham, ed. Chicago: University of Chicago Press.
n.d. The Windward Islands of Fiji. Manuscript original of *The*

Lau Islands, Fiji. Turnbull Library, Wellington.

Hunt, Reverend John

n.d. Fiji Journal of John Hunt. Methodist Missionary Society (Box 5, "Biographical"), School of Oriental and African Studies Library, University of London.

Isaacs, Nathaniel

1970 Travel and Adventures in Eastern Africa. Capetown: Struik.

Jaggar, Thomas James

1837–43 Diaries of Thomas James Jaggar, 1837–1843. Microfilm copy of manuscript original in the National Archives of Fiji, Adelaide University Library.

Johansen, J. Prytz

1954 The Maori and His Religion. Copenhagen: Munksgaard.

1958 Studies in Maori Rites and Myths. Historisk-filosofiske Meddelelser 37(4). Copenhagen.

Kamakau, Samuel M.

1961 Ruling Chiefs of Hawaii. Honolulu: Kamehameha Schools.

Krige, Eileen Jensen

1936 The Social System of the Zulus. London: Longmans, Green.

Krige, E. J., and J. O. Krige

1943 The Realm of the Rain-Queen. London: Oxford University Press.

Kuper, Hilda

1947 An African Aristocracy: Rank among the Swazi. London: Oxford University Press.

Le Goff, Jacques

1972 Is Politics Still the Backbone of History? *In* Historical Studies Today. Felix Gilbert and Stephen R. Graubard, eds. pp. 337–355. New York: Norton.

LeGoff, Jacques, and Pierre Nora, eds.

1974 Faire l'histoire. Paris: Gallimard.

Malo, David

1951 Hawaiian Antiquities. Honolulu: Bishop Museum Press.

Maning, F. E.

1906 Old New Zealand. Christchurch: Whitcombe and Tombs.

Meek, C. K.

1931 A Sudanese Kingdom. London: Kegan Paul, Trench & Trubner.

Metge, Joan

1976 The Maoris of New Zealand. Rautahi. 2d ed. London: Routledge and Kegan Paul.

Methodist Missionary Society

1835–52 "Feejee District Minutes and Reports, 1835–1852." *Ms.*, School of Oriental and African Studies Library, University of London.

Pocock, David

1964 The Anthropology of Time-Reckoning. Contributions to Indian Sociology 7:18–29.

Reid, A. C.

1977 The Fruit of the Rewa: Oral Traditions and the Growth of the Pre-Christian Lakeba State. Journal of Pacific History 12:2–24.

Ricoeur, Paul

1980 The   Contributions   of
French Historiography to the
Theory of History. Oxford: Clar-
endon Press.

Rosaldo, Renato

1980 Ilongot   Headhunting,
1883–1974. Stanford: Stanford
University Press.

Rutherford, J.

1961 Sir George Grey. London:
Cassell.

Sahlins, Marshall

1981a The Stranger-King, or Dumézil among the Fijians. Journal
of Pacific History 16:107–132.

1981b Historical Metaphors and
Mythical Realities. Association
for Social Anthropology in Oceania, Special Publications No. 1.

1982 Femmes   crues,   hommes
cuits et autres 'grandes choses'
des iles Fidji. Le Débat 19:121–
144.

Sartre, Jean-Paul

1968 Search for a Method. Hazel
E. Barnes, trans. New York: Vintage Books.

Schütz, Albert J., ed.

1977 The Diaries and Correspondence of David Cargill, 1832–
1843. Canberra: Australian National University Press.

Schwimmer, Eric

1963 Guardian Animals of the
Maori. Journal of the Polynesian
Society 72:397–410.

1966 The World of the Maori.
Wellington: Reed.

1978 Lévi-Strauss and Maori Social Structure. Anthropologica,
N.S., 20:201–222.

Shortland, Edward

1856 Traditions and Superstitions
of the New Zealanders. 2d ed.
London: Longman,   Brown,
Green, Longmans and Roberts.

1882 Maori Religion and Mythology. London: Longmans, Green.

Simmons, David

1976 The Great New Zealand
Myth. Wellington: Reed.

Sinclair, Keith

1972 The Origins of the Maori
Wars. Wellington: New Zealand
University Press.

Skinner, W. H.

1911 The Ancient Fortified Pa.
Journal of the Polynesian Society
20:71–77.

Smith, Jean

1974–75 Tapu Removal in Maori
Religion. Journal of the Polynesian Society (Memoirs Supplement) 83:1–43; 84:44–96.

Smith, S. Percy

1910 Maori Wars of the Nineteenth Century. Christchurch:
Whitcombe and Tombs.

1913–15 Lore of the Ware Wananga. Polynesian Society Memoirs, vols. 3 and 4.

Stewart, C. S.

1970 [1830] Journal of a Residence in the Sandwich Islands
during the Years 1823, 1824,
1825. Honolulu: University of
Hawaii Press.

Stone, Lawrence
    1981 The Past and the Present. Boston: Routledge and Kegan Paul.
Tambiah, S. J.
    1976 World Conqueror and World Renouncer. Cambridge: Cambridge University Press.
Thompson, E. P.
    1977 Folklore, Anthropology and Social History. The Indian Historical Review 3:247–266.
Tregear, Edward
    1969 [1891] The Maori-Polynesian Comparative Dictionary. Oosterhout: Anthropological Publications.
Valeri, Valerio
    1983 Hai Kanaka: The Hawaiian Chief and His Sacrifice. Chicago: The University of Chicago Press. In press.
Vansina, J.
    1964 Le royaume Kuba. Musée Royal de l'Afrique Centrale, Annales, Sciences Humaines, No. 49.
Vernant, Jean-Pierre
    1979 Mythe et société en grèce ancienne. Paris: Maspero.
    1982 The Origins of Greek Thought. Ithaca: Cornell University Press.
Wards, Ian
    1968 The Shadow of the Land. Wellington: A. R. Shearer, Government Printer.

Waterhouse, Joseph
    1866 The King and People of Fiji. London: Wesleyan Conference.
White, John
    1854 Te Rou; or, The Maori at Home. London: Low, Marston, Low, and Searle.
    1855 Maori Customs and Superstitions. In The History and Doings of the Maoris. Thomas Wayth Gudgeon, ed. pp. 95–225. Auckland: Brett.
    1887–90 Ancient History of the Maori. 6 vols. Wellington: Government Printer.
Wilkes, Charles
    1845 Narrative of the United States Exploring Expeditions. Vols. II and III. Philadelphia: Lea and Blanchard.
Williams, Herbert W.
    1975 A Dictionary of the Maori Language. 7th ed. Wellington: A. R. Shearer, Government Printer.
Williams, Thomas, and James Calvert
    1859 Fiji and Fijians. 2 vols. New York: Appleton.
Williams, William
    1867 Christianity among the New Zealanders. London: Seeley, Jackson, and Halliday.
Wilson, Monica
    1969 The Nguni People. In The Oxford History of South Africa. Monica Wilson and Leonard Thompson, eds. Vol. 1. pp. 75–130. Oxford: Clarendon Press.

Wright, Harrison M.

1959 New Zealand, 1769–1840: Early Years of Western Contact. Cambridge: Harvard University Press.

Young, Michael W.

1966 The Divine Kingship of the Jukun: A Re-evaluation of Some Theories. Africa 36:135–152.

Anti Anti-Relativism

Clifford Geertz

VOL. 86, 1984, 263–278

I

A scholar can hardly be better employed than in destroying a fear. The one I want to go after is cultural relativism. Not the thing itself, which I think merely there, like Transylvania, but the dread of it, which I think unfounded. It is unfounded because the moral and intellectual consequences that are commonly supposed to flow from relativism — subjectivism, nihilism, incoherence. Machiavellianism, ethical idiocy, esthetic blindness, and so on — do not in fact do so and the promised rewards of escaping its clutches, mostly having to do with pasteurized knowledge, are illusory.

To be more specific, I want not to defend relativism, which is a drained term anyway, yesterday's battle cry, but to attack anti-relativism, which seems to me broadly on the rise and to represent a streamlined version of an antique mistake. Whatever cultural relativism may be or originally have been (and there is not one of its critics in a hundred who has got that right), it serves these days largely as a specter to scare us away from certain ways of thinking and toward others. And, as the ways of thinking away from which we are being driven seem to me to be more cogent than those toward which we are being propelled, and to lie at the heart of the anthropological heritage, I would like to do something about this. Casting out demons is a praxis we should practice as well as study.

My through-the-looking-glass title is intended to suggest such an effort to counter a view rather than to defend the view it claims to be counter to. The analogy I had in mind in choosing it — a logical one, I trust it will be understood, not in any way a substantive one — is what, at the height of the cold war days (you remember them) was called "anti anti-communism." Those of us who strenuously opposed the obsession, as we saw it, with the Red Menace were thus denominated by those who, as they saw it, regarded the Menace as the primary fact of contemporary political life, with the insinuation — wildly incorrect in the vast majority of cases — that, by the law of the double negative, we had some secret affection for the Soviet Union.

Again, I mean to use this analogy in a formal sense; I don't think relativists are like communists, anti-relativists are like anti-communists, and that anyone (well . . . hardly anyone) is behaving like McCarthy. One could construct a similar parallelism using the abortion controversy. Those of us who are opposed to increased legal restrictions on abortion are not, I take it, pro-abortion, in the sense that we think abortion a wonderful thing and hold that the greater the abortion rate the greater the well-being of society; we are "anti anti-abortionists" for quite other reasons I need not rehearse. In this frame, the double negative simply doesn't work in the usual way; and therein lies its rhetorical attractions. It enables one to reject something without thereby committing oneself to what it rejects. And this is precisely what I want to do with anti-relativism.

So lumbering an approach to the matter, explaining and excusing itself as it goes, is necessary because, as the philosopher-anthropologist John Ladd (1982:161) has remarked, "all the common definitions of . . . relativism are framed by opponents of relativism . . . they are absolutist definitions." (Ladd, whose immediate focus is Edward Westermarck's famous book, is speaking of "ethical relativism" in particular, but the point is general: for "cognitive relativism" think of Israel Scheffler's [1967] attack on Thomas Kuhn, for "aesthetic relativism," Wayne Booth's [1983] on Stanley Fish.) And, as Ladd also says, the result of this is that relativism, or anything that at all looks like relativism under such hostile definitions, is identified with nihilism (Ladd 1982:158). To suggest that "hard rock" foundations for cognitive, esthetic, or moral judgments may not, in fact, be available, or anyway that those one is being offered are dubious, is to find oneself accused of disbelieving in the existence of the physical world, thinking pushpin as good as poetry, regarding Hitler as just a fellow with unstandard tastes, or even, as I myself have recently been — God save the mark — "[having] no politics at all" (Rabinow 1983:70). The notion that someone who does not hold your views holds the reciprocal of them, or simply hasn't got any, has, whatever its comforts for those afraid reality is going to go away unless we believe very hard in it, not conduced to much in the way of clarity in the anti-relativist discussion, but merely to far too many people spending far too much time describing at length what it is they do *not* maintain than seems in any way profitable.

All this is of relevance to anthropology because, of course, it is by way of the idea of relativism, grandly ill-defined, that it has most disturbed the general intellectual peace. From our earliest days, even when theory in anthropology — evolutionary, diffusionist, or *elementargedankenisch* — was anything but relativistic, the message that we have been thought to have for the wider world has been that, as they see things differently and do them otherwise in Alaska or the D'Entrecasteaux, our confidence in our own seeings and doings and our resolve to bring others around to sharing them are rather poorly based. This point, too, is commonly ill-understood. It has not been anthropological theory, such as it is, that has made our field seem to be a massive argument against absolutism in thought, morals, and esthetic judgment; it has been anthropological data: customs, crania, living floors, and lexicons. The notion that it was Boas, Benedict, and Melville Herskovits, with a European assist from Westermarck, who infected our field with the relativist virus, and Kroeber, Kluckhohn, and Redfield, with a similar assist from Lévi-Strauss, who have labored to rid us of it, is but another of the myths that bedevil this whole discussion. After all, Montaigne (1978:202–214) could draw relativistic, or relativistic-looking, conclusions from the fact, as he heard it, that the Caribs didn't wear breeches; he did not have to read *Patterns of Culture*. Even earlier on, Herodotus, contemplating "certain Indians of the race called Callatians," among whom men were said to eat their fathers, came, as one would think he might, to similar views (Herodotus 1859–61).

The relativist bent, or more accurately the relativist bent anthropology so often induces in those who have much traffic with its materials, is thus in some sense implicit in the field as such; in cultural anthropology perhaps particularly, but in much of archeology, anthropological linguistics, and physical anthropology as well. One cannot read too long about Nayar matriliny, Aztec sacrifice, the Hopi verb, or the convolutions of the hominid transition and not begin at least to consider the possibility that, to quote Montaigne again, "each man calls barbarism whatever is not his own practice . . . for we have no other criterion of reason than the example and idea of the opinions and customs of the country we live in" (1978:205, cited in Todorov 1983:113–144).[1] That notion, whatever its problems, and however more delicately expressed, is not likely to go entirely away unless anthropology does.

It is to this fact, progressively discovered to be one as our enterprise has advanced and our findings grown more circumstantial, that both relativists and anti-relativists have, according to their sensibilities, reacted. The realization that news from elsewhere about ghost marriage, ritual destruction of property, initiatory fellatio, royal immolation, and (Dare I say it? Will he strike again?) nonchalant adolescent sex naturally inclines the mind to an "other beasts other mores" view of things has led to arguments, outraged, desperate, and exultant by turns, designed to persuade us either to resist that inclination in the name of reason, or to embrace it on the same grounds. What looks like a debate about the broader implications of anthropological research is really a debate about how to live with them.

Once this fact is grasped, and "relativism" and "anti-relativism" are seen as general responses to the way in which what Kroeber once called the centrifugal impulse of anthropology — distant places, distant times, distant species . . . distant grammars — affects our sense of things, the whole discussion comes rather better into focus. The supposed conflict between Benedict's and Herskovits's call for tolerance and the untolerant passion with which they called for it turns out not to be the simple contradiction so many amateur logicians have held it to be, but the expression of a perception, caused by thinking a lot about Zunis and Dahomeys, that, the world being so full of a number of things, rushing to judgment is more than a mistake, it's a crime. Similarly, Kroeber's and Kluckhohn's pan-cultural verities — Kroeber's were mostly about messy creatural matters like delirium and menstruation, Kluckhohn's about messy social ones like lying and killing within the in-group — turn out not to be just the arbitrary, personal obsessions they so much look like, but the expression of a much vaster concern, caused by thinking a lot about *anthropōs* in general, that if something isn't anchored everywhere nothing can be anchored anywhere. Theory here — if that is what these earnest advices as to how we must look at things if we are to be accounted decent should be called — it is rather more an exchange of warnings than an analytical debate. We are being offered a choice of worries.

What the relativists, so-called, want us to worry about is provincialism — the danger that our perceptions will be dulled, our intellects constricted, and our sympathies narrowed by the overlearned and overvalued acceptances of our own society. What the anti-relativists, self-declared, want us to worry about, and worry about and worry about, as though our very souls depended upon it, is a kind of spiritual entropy, a heat death of the mind, in which everything is as significant, thus as insignificant, as everything else; anything goes, to each his own, you pays your money and you takes your choice, I know what I like, not in the south, *tout comprendre, c'est tout pardonner.*

As I have already suggested, I myself find provincialism altogether the more real concern so far as what actually goes on in the world. (Though even there, the thing can be overdone: "You might as well fall flat on your face," one of Thurber's marvelous "morals" goes, "as lean too far over backward.") The image of vast numbers of anthropology readers running around in so cosmopolitan a frame of mind as to have no view as to what is and isn't true, or good, or beautiful, seems to me largely a fantasy. There may be some genuine nihilists out there, along Rodeo Drive or around Times Square, but I doubt very many have become such as a result of an excessive sensitivity to the claims of other cultures; and at least most of the people I meet, read, and read about, and indeed I myself, are all-too-committed to something or other, usually parochial. " 'Tis the eye of childhood that fears a painted devil": anti-relativism has largely concocted the anxiety it lives from.

II

But surely I exaggerate? Surely anti-relativists, secure in the knowledge that rattling gourds cannot cause thunder and that eating people is wrong, cannot be so excitable? Listen, then, to William Gass (1981:53–54), novelist, philosopher, *précieux*, and pop-eyed observer of anthropologists' ways:

> Anthropologists or not, we all used to call them "natives" — those little, distant, jungle and island people — and we came to recognize the unscientific snobbery in that. Even our more respectable journals could show them naked without offense, because their pendulous or pointed breasts were as inhuman to us as the udder of a cow. Shortly we came to our senses and had them dress. We grew to distrust our own point of view, our local certainties, and embraced relativism, although it is one of the scabbier whores; and we went on to endorse a nice equality among cultures, each of which was carrying out its task of coalescing, conversing, and structuring some society. A large sense of superiority was one of the white man's burdens, and that weight, released, was replaced by an equally heavy sense of guilt.

No more than we might expect a surgeon to say "Dead and good riddance" would an anthropologist exclaim, stepping from the culture just surveyed as one might shed a set of working clothes, "What a lousy way to live!" Because, even if the natives were impoverished, covered with dust and sores; even if they had been trodden on by stronger feet till they were flat as a path; even if they were rapidly dying off; still, the observer could remark how frequently they smiled, or how infrequently their children fought, or how serene they were. We can envy the Zuni their peaceful ways and the Navaho their "happy heart."

It was amazing how mollified we were to find that there was some functional point to food taboos, infibulation, or clitoridectomy; and if we still felt morally squeamish about human sacrifice or headhunting, it is clear we were still squeezed into a narrow modern European point of view, and had no sympathy, and didn't — couldn't — understand. Yet when we encountered certain adolescents among indolent summery seaside tribes who were allowed to screw without taboo, we wondered whether this enabled them to avoid the stresses of our own youth, and we secretly hoped it hadn't.

Some anthropologists have untied the moral point of view, so sacred to Eliot and Arnold and Emerson, from every mooring (science and art also float away on the stream of Becoming), calling any belief in objective knowledge "fundamentalism," as if it were the same as benighted Biblical literalism; and arguing for the total mutability of man and the complete sociology of what under such circumstances could no longer be considered knowledge but only *doxa*, or "opinion."

This overheated vision of "the anthropological point of view," rising out of the mists of caricatured arguments ill-grasped to start with (it is one of Gass's ideas that Mary Douglas is some sort of skeptic, and Benedict's satire, cannier than his, has escaped him altogether), leaves us with a fair lot to answer for. But even from within the profession, the charges, though less originally expressed, as befits a proper science, are hardly less grave. Relativism ("[T]he position that all assessments are assessments relative to some standard or other, and standards derive from cultures"), I. C. Jarvie (1983:45, 46) remarks,

has these objectionable consequences: namely, that by limiting critical assessment of human works it disarms us, dehumanises us, leaves us unable to enter into communicative interaction; that is to say, unable to criticize cross-culturally, cross-sub-culturally; ultimately, relativism leaves no room for criticism at all. . . . [B]ehind relativism nihilism looms.

More in front, scarecrow and leper's bell, it sounds like, than behind: certainly none of us, clothed and in our right minds, will rush to embrace a view that so dehumanizes us as to render us incapable of communicating with anybody. The heights to which this beware of the scabby whore who will cut off your critical powers sort of thing can aspire is indicated, to give one last example, by Paul Johnson's (1983) ferocious new book on the history of the world since 1917, *Modern Times*, which, opening with a chapter called "A Relativistic World" (Hugh Thomas's [1983] review of the book in the *TLS* was more aptly entitled "The inferno of relativism") accounts for the whole modern disaster—Lenin and Hitler, Amin, Bokassa, Sukarno, Mao, Nasser, and Hammarskjöld, Structuralism, the New Deal, the Holocaust, both world wars, 1968, inflation, Shinto militarism, OPEC, and the independence of India—as outcomes of something called "the relativist heresy." "A great trio of German imaginative scholars," Nietzsche, Marx, and (with a powerful assist—our contribution—from Frazer) Freud, destroyed the 19th century morally as Einstein, banishing absolute motion, destroyed it cognitively, and Joyce, banishing absolute narrative, destroyed it esthetically:

> Marx described a world in which the central dynamic was economic interest. To Freud the principal thrust was sexual. . . . Nietzsche, the third of the trio, was also an atheist . . . [and he] saw [the death of God] as . . . an historical event, which would have dramatic consequences. . . . Among the advanced races, the decline and ultimately the collapse of the religious impulse would leave a huge vacuum. The history of modern times is in great part the history of how that vacuum [has] been filled. Nietzsche rightly perceived that the most likely candidate would be what he called "The Will to Power." . . . In place of religious belief, there would be secular ideology. Those who had once filled the ranks of the totalitarian clergy would become totalitarian politicians. . . . The end of the old order, with an unguided world adrift in a relativistic universe, was a summons to such gangster statesmen to emerge. They were not slow to make their appearance. [Johnson 1983:48]

After this there is perhaps nothing much else to say, except perhaps what George Stocking (1982:176) says, summarizing others—"cultural relativism, which had buttressed the attack against racialism, [can] be perceived as a sort of neo-racialism justifying the backward techno-economic status of once colonized peoples." Or what Lionel Tiger (Tiger and Sepher 1975:16) says, summarizing himself: "the feminist argument [for 'the social non-necessity . . . of the laws instituted by patriarchy'] reflects the cultural relativism that has long characterized those social sciences which rejected locating human behavior in biological processes." Mindless tolerance, mindless intolerance; ideological promiscuity, ideological monomania; egalitarian hypocrisy, egalitarian simplisticism — all flow from the same infirmity. Like Welfare, The Media, The Bourgeoisie, or The Ruling Circles, Cultural Relativism causes everything bad.

Anthropologists, plying their trade and in any way reflective about it, could, for all their own sort of provincialism, hardly remain unaffected by the hum of philosophical disquiet rising everywhere around them. (I have not even mentioned the fierce debates brought on by the revival of political and moral theory, the appearance of deconstructionist literary criticism, the spread of nonfoundationalist moods in metaphysics and epistemology, and the rejection of whiggery and method-ism in the history of science.) The fear that our emphasis on difference, diversity, oddity, discontinuity, incommensurability, uniqueness, and so on — what Empson (1955, cited to opposite purposes in Kluckhohn 1962:292–293) called "the gigan-/-tic anthropological circus riotously/[Holding] open all its booths" — might end leaving us with little more to say than that elsewhere things are otherwise and culture is as culture does has grown more and more intense. So intense, in fact, that it has led us off in some all-too-familiar directions in an attempt, ill-conceived, so I think, to still it.

One could ground this last proposition in a fair number of places in contemporary anthropological thought and research — from Harrisonian "Everything That Rises Must Converge" materialism to Popperian "Great Divide" evolutionism. ("We Have Science . . . or Literacy, or Intertheoretic Competition, or the Cartesian Conception of Knowledge . . . but They Have Not.")[2] But I want to concentrate here on two of central importance, or anyway popularity, right now: the attempt to reinstate a context-independent concept of "Human Nature" as a bulwark against relativism, and the attempt to reinstate, similarly, a similar one of that other old friend, "The Human Mind."

Again, it is necessary to be clear so as not to be accused, under the "if you don't believe in my God you must believe in my Devil" assumption I mentioned earlier, of arguing for absurd positions — radical, culture-is-all historicism, or primitive, the-brain-is-a-blackboard empiricism — which no one of any seriousness holds, and quite possibly, a momentary enthusiasm here and there aside, ever has held. The issue is not whether human beings are biological organisms with intrinsic characteristics. Men can't fly and pigeons can't talk. Nor is it whether they show commonalities in mental functioning wherever we find them. Papuans envy, Aborigines dream. The issue is, what are we to make of these undisputed facts as we go about explicating rituals, analyzing ecosystems, interpreting fossil sequences, or comparing languages.

III

These two moves toward restoring culture-free conceptions of what we amount to as basic, sticker-price *homo* and essential, no additives *sapiens* take a number of quite disparate forms, not in much agreement beyond their general tenor, naturalist in the one case, rationalist in the other. On the naturalist side there is, of course, sociobiology and other hyper-adaptationist orientations. But there are also perspectives growing out of psychoanalysis, ecology, neurology, display-and-imprint ethology, some kinds of developmental theory, and some kinds of Marxism. On the rationalist side there is, of course, the new intellectualism one associates with structuralism and other hyper-logicist orientations. But there are also perspectives growing out of generative linguistics, experimental psychology, artificial intelligence research, ploy and counterploy microsociology, some kinds of developmental theory, and some kinds of Marxism. Attempts to banish the specter of relativism whether by sliding down The Great Chain of Being or edging up it — the dog beneath the skin, a mind for all cultures — do not comprise a single enterprise, massive and coordinate, but a loose and immiscible crowd of them, each pressing its own cause and in its own direction. The sin may be one, but the salvations are many.

It is for this reason, too, that an attack, such as mine, upon the efforts to draw context-independent concepts of "Human Nature" or "The Human Mind" from biological, psychological, linguistic, or for that matter cultural (HRAF and all that) inquiries should not be mistaken for an attack upon those inquiries as research programs. Whether or not sociobiology is, as I think, a degenerative research program destined to expire in its own confusions, and neuroscience a progressive one (to use Imre Lakatos's [1976] useful epithets) on the verge of extraordinary achievements, anthropologists will be well-advised to attend to, with various shades of mixed, maybe, maybe not, verdicts for structuralism, generative grammar, ethology, AI, psychoanalysis, ecology, microsociology, Marxism, or developmental psychology in between, is quite beside the point. It is not, or anyway not here, the validity of the sciences, real or would-be, that is at issue. What concerns me, and should concern us all, are the axes that, with an increasing determination bordering on the evangelical, are being busily ground with their assistance.

As a way into all this on the naturalist side we can look for a moment at a general discussion widely accepted — though, as it consists largely of pronouncements, it is difficult to understand why — as a balanced and moderate statement of the position: Mary Midgeley's *Beast and Man, The Roots of Human Nature* (1978). In the Pilgrim's Progress, "once I was blind but now I see" tonalities that have become characteristic of such discourses in recent years, Midgeley writes:

> I first entered this jungle myself some time ago, by slipping out over the wall of the tiny arid garden cultivated at that time under the name of British Moral Philosophy. I did so in an attempt to think about human nature and the problem of evil. The evils in the world, I thought are real. That they are so is neither a fancy imposed on us by our own culture, nor one created by our will and imposed on the world. Such suggestions are bad faith. What we abominate is not optional. Culture certainly varies the details, but then we can criticize our culture. What standard [note the singular] do we use for this? What is the underlying structure of human nature which culture is designed to complete and express? In this tangle of questions I found some clearings being worked by Freudian and Jungian psychologists, on principles that seemed to offer hope but were not quite clear to me. Other areas were being mapped by anthropologists, who seemed to have some interest in my problem, but who were inclined . . . to say that what human beings had in common was not in the end very important: that the key to all the mysteries [lay] in culture. This seemed to me shallow. . . . I [finally] came upon another clearing, this time an expansion of the borders of traditional zoology, made by people [Lorenz, Tinbergen, Eibes-Eibesfeldt, Desmond Morris] studying the natures of other species. They had done much work on the question of what such a *nature* was — recent work in the tradition of Darwin, and indeed of Aristotle, bearing directly on problems in which Aristotle was already interested, but which have become peculiarly pressing today. [1978:xiv–xv; italics in original]

The assumptions with which this declaration of conscience is riddled — that fancies imposed on us by cultural judgments (that the poor are worthless? that Blacks are subhuman? that women are irrational?) are inadequately substantial to ground real evil; that culture is icing, biology, cake; that we have no choice as to what we shall hate (hippies? bosses? eggheads? . . . relativists?); that difference is shallow, likeness, deep; that Lorenz is a straightforward fellow and Freud a mysterious one — may perhaps be left to perish of their own weight. One garden has been but exchanged for another. The jungle remains several walls away.

More important is what sort of garden this "Darwin meets Aristotle" one is. What sort of abominations are going to become unoptional? What sort of facts unnatural?

Well, mutual admiration societies, sadism, ingratitude, monotony, and the shunning of cripples, among other things — at least when they are carried to excess:

> Grasping this point ["that what is *natural* is never just a condition or activity . . . but a certain *level* of that condition or activity proportionate to the rest of one's life"] makes it possible to cure a difficulty about such concepts as *natural* which has made many people think them unusable. Besides their strong sense, which recommends something, they have a weak sense, which does not. In the weak sense, sadism is natural. This just means that it occurs; we should recognize it. . . . But in a strong and perfectly good sense, we may call sadistic behavior *unnatural* — meaning that a policy based on this natural impulse, and extended through somebody's life into organized activity, is, as [Bishop] Butler said, "contrary to the whole constitution of human nature." . . . That consenting adults should bite each other in bed is in all senses natural; that schoolteachers should bully children for their sexual gratification is not. There is something wrong with this activity beyond the actual injury that it inflicts. . . . Examples of this wrong thing — of unnaturalness — can be found which do not involve other people as victims; for instance, extreme narcissism, suicide, obsessiveness, incest, and exclusive mutual admiration societies. "It is an unnatural life" we say, meaning that its center has been misplaced. Further examples, which do involve victimizing others, are redirected aggression, the shunning of cripples, ingratitude, vindictiveness, parricide. All these things are *natural* in that there are well-known impulses toward them which are parts of human nature. . . . But redirected aggression and so on can properly be called *unnatural* when we think of nature in the fuller sense, not just as an assembly of parts, but as an organized whole. They are parts which will ruin the shape of that whole if they are allowed in any sense to take it over. [Midgeley 1978:79–80; italics in original][3]

Aside from the fact that it legitimates one of the more popular sophisms of intellectual debate nowadays, asserting the strong form of an argument and defending the weak one (sadism is natural as long as you don't bite too deep), this little game of concept juggling (natural may be unnatural when we think of nature "in the fuller sense") displays the basic thesis of all such Human Nature arguments: virtue (cognitive, esthetic, and moral alike) is to vice as fitness is to disorder, normality to abnormality, well-being to sickness. The task for man, as for his lungs or his thyroid, is to function properly. Shunning cripples can be dangerous to your health.

Or as Stephen Salkever (1983:210), a political scientist and follower of Midgeley's puts it:

> Perhaps the best developed model or analogue for an adequate functionalist social science is that provided by medicine. For the physician, physical features of an individual organism become intelligible in the light of a basic conception of the problems confronting this self-directed physical system and in the light of a general sense of healthy or well-functioning state of the organism relative to those problems. To understand a patient is to understand him or her as being more or less healthy relative to some stable and objective standard of physical well-being, the kind of standard the Greeks called *aretè*. This word is now ordinarily translated "virtue," but in the political philosophy of Plato and Aristotle it refers simply to the characteristic or definitive excellence of the subject of any functional analysis.

Again, one can look almost anywhere within anthropology these days and find an example of the revival of this "it all comes down to" (genes, species being, cerebral architecture, psycho-sexual constitution . . .) cast of mind. Shake almost any tree and a selfish altruist or a biogenetic structuralist is likely to fall out.

But it is better, I think, or at least less disingenuous, to have for an instance neither a sitting duck nor a self-destructing artifact. And so let me examine, very briefly, the views, most especially the recent views, of one of our most experienced ethnographers and influential theorists, as well as one of our most formidable polemicists: Melford Spiro. Purer cases, less shaded and less circumspect, and thus all the better to appall you with, could be found. But in Spiro we are at least not dealing with some marginal phenomenon — a Morris or an Ardrey — easily dismissed as an enthusiast or a popularizer, but with a major figure at, or very near, the center of the discipline.

Spiro's more important recent forays into "down deep" in the *Homo* anthropology — his rediscovery of the Freudian family romance, first in

his own material on the kibbutz and then in Malinowski's on the Trobri-
ands—are well-known and will be, I daresay, as convincing or unconvincing to their readers as psychoanalytic theory of a rather orthodox
sort is in general. But my concern is, again, less with that than with the
Here Comes Everyman anti-relativism he develops on the basis of it.
And to get a sense for that, a recent article of his (Spiro 1978) summarizing his advance from past confusions to present clarities will serve quite
well. Called "Culture and Human Nature," it catches a mood and a drift
of attitude much more widely spread than its rather beleaguered, no
longer avant-garde theoretical perspective.

Spiro's paper is, as I mentioned, again cast in the "when a child I spake
as a child but now that I am grown I have put away childish things" genre
so prominent in the anti-relativist literature generally. (Indeed, it might
better have been titled, as another southern California–based anthropologist—apparently relativism seems a clear and present danger out
that way—called the record of his deliverance, "Confessions of a Former
Cultural Relativist.")[4]

Spiro begins his apologia with the admission that when he came into
anthropology in the early 1940s he was preadapted by a Marxist background and too many courses in British philosophy to a radically en-
vironmentalist view of man, one that assumed a *tabula rasa* view of mind,
a social determinist view of behavior, and a cultural relativist view of,
well . . . culture, and then traces his field trip history as a didactic parable
for our times, narrative of how he came not just to abandon these ideas
but to replace them by their opposites. In Ifaluk, he discovered that a
people who showed very little social aggression could yet be plagued by
hostile feelings. In Israel, he discovered that children "raised in [the]
totally communal and cooperative system" of the kibbutz and socialized
to be mild, loving and noncompetitive, nevertheless resented attempts
to get them to share goods and when obliged to do so grew resistant and
hostile. And in Burma, he discovered that a belief in the impermanence
of sentient existence, Buddhist nirvana and nonattachment, did not result in a diminished interest in the immediate materialities of daily life.

> In short, [my field studies] convinced me that many motivational dispositions
> are culturally invariant [and] many cognitive orientations [are so] as well.
> These invariant dispositions and orientations stem . . . from pan-human
> biological and cultural constants, and they comprise that universal human

nature which, together with received anthropological opinion, I had formerly rejected as yet another ethnocentric bias. [Spiro 1978:349–350]

Whether or not a portrait of peoples from Micronesia to the Middle East as angry moralizers deviously pursuing hedonic interests will altogether still the suspicion that some ethnocentric bias yet clings to Spiro's view of universal human nature remains to be seen. What doesn't remain to be seen, because he is quite explicit about them, are the kinds of ideas, noxious products of a noxious relativism, such a recourse to medical functionalism is designed to cure us of:

> [The] concept of cultural relativism . . . was enlisted to do battle against racist notions in general, and the notion of primitive mentality, in particular. . . . [But] cultural relativism was also used, at least by some anthropologists, to perpetuate a kind of inverted racism. That is, it was used as a powerful tool of cultural criticism, with the consequent derogation of Western culture and of the mentality which it produced. Espousing the philosophy of primitivism . . . the image of primitive man was used . . . as a vehicle for the pursuit of personal utopian quests, and/or as a fulcrum to express personal discontent with Western man and Western society. The strategies adopted took various forms, of which the following are fairly representative. (1) Attempts to abolish private property, or inequality, or aggression in Western societies have a reasonably realistic chance of success since such states of affairs may be found in many primitive societies. (2) Compared to at least some primitives, Western man is uniquely competitive, warlike, intolerant of deviance, sexist, and so on. (3) Paranoia is not necessarily an illness, because paranoid thinking is institutionalized in certain primitive societies; homosexuality is not deviant because homosexuals are the cultural cynosures of some primitive societies; monogamy is not viable because polygamy is the most frequent form of marriage in primitive societies. [Spiro 1978:336]

Aside from adding a few more items to the list, which promises to be infinite, of unoptional abominations, it is the introduction of the idea of "deviance," conceived as a departure from an inbuilt norm, like an arrhythmic heartbeat, not as a statistical oddity, like fraternal polyandry, that is the really critical move amid all this huffing and puffing about "inverted racism," "utopian quests," and "the philosophy of primitivism." For it is through that idea, The Lawgiver's Friend, that Midgeley's transition between the natural natural (aggression, inequality) and the unnatural natural (paranoia, homosexuality) gets made. Once that camel's nose has been pushed inside, the tent — indeed, the whole riotous circus crying all its booths — is in serious trouble.

Just how much trouble can perhaps be more clearly seen from Robert Edgerton's (1978) companion piece to Spiro's in the same volume, "The Study of Deviance, Marginal Man or Everyman?" After a useful, rather eclectic, review of the study of deviance in anthropology, psychology, and sociology, including again his own quite interesting work with American retardates and African intersexuals, Edgerton too comes, rather suddenly as a matter of fact — a cartoon light bulb going on — to the conclusion that what is needed to make such research genuinely productive is a context-independent conception of human nature — one in which "genetically encoded potentials for behavior that we all share" are seen to "underlie [our universal] propensity for deviance." Man's "instinct" for self-preservation, his flight/fight mechanism, and his intolerance of boredom are instanced; and, in an argument I, in my innocence, had thought gone from anthropology, along with euhemerism and primitive promiscuity, it is suggested that, if all goes well on the science side, we may, in time, be able to judge not just individuals but entire societies as deviant, inadequate, failed, unnatural:

> More important still is our inability to test any proposition about the relative adequacy of a society. Our relativistic tradition in anthropology has been slow to yield to the idea that there could be such a thing as a deviant society, one that is contrary to human nature. . . . Yet the idea of a deviant society is central to the alienation tradition in sociology and other fields and it poses a challenge for anthropological theory. Because we know so little about human nature . . . we cannot say whether, much less how, any society has failed. . . . Nevertheless, a glance at any urban newspaper's stories of rising rates of homicide, suicide, rape and other violent crimes should suffice to suggest that the question is relevant not only for theory, but for questions of survival in the modern world. [Edgerton 1978:470]

With this the circle closes; the door slams. The fear of relativism, raised at every turn like some mesmeric obsession, has led to a position in which cultural diversity, across space and over time, amounts to a series of expressions, some salubrious, some not, of a settled, underlying reality, the essential nature of man, and anthropology amounts to an attempt to see through the haze of those expressions to the substance of that reality. A sweeping, schematic, and content-hungry concept, con-

formable to just about any shape that comes along. Wilsonian, Loren-
zian, Freudian, Marxian, Benthamite, Aristotelian ("one of the central
features of Human Nature," some anonymous genius is supposed to
have remarked, "is a separate judiciary"), becomes the ground upon
which the understanding of human conduct, homicide, suicide, rape . . .
the derogation of Western culture, comes definitively to rest. Some gods
from some machines cost, perhaps, rather more than they come to.

IV

About that other conjuration "The Human Mind," held up as a protective cross against the relativist Dracula, I can be somewhat more suc-
cinct; for the general pattern, if not the substantial detail, is very much
the same. There is the same effort to promote a privileged language of
"real" explanation ("nature's own vocabulary," as Richard Rorty [1983;
cf. Rorty 1979], attacking the notion as scientistic fantasy, has put it); and
the same wild dissensus as to just which language — Shannon's? Saus-
sure's? Piaget's? — that in fact is. There is the same tendency to see
diversity as surface and universality as depth. And there is the same
desire to represent one's interpretations not as constructions brought to
their objects — societies, cultures, languages — in an effort, somehow,
somewhat to comprehend them, but as quiddities of such objects forced
upon our thought.

There are, of course, differences as well. The return of Human Nature as a regulative idea has been mainly stimulated by advances in
genetics and evolutionary theory, that of The Human Mind by ones in
linguistics, computer science, and cognitive psychology. The inclination
of the former is to see moral relativism as the source of all our ills, that of
the latter is to pin the blame on conceptual relativism. And a partiality
for the tropes and images of therapeutic discourse (health and illness,
normal and abnormal, function and disfunction) on the one side is
matched by a penchant for those of epistemological discourse (knowledge and opinion, fact and illusion, truth and falsity) on the other. But
they hardly count, these differences, against the common impulse to
final analysis, we have now arrived at Science, explanation. Wiring your
theories into something called The Structure of Reason is as effective a
way to insulate them from history and culture as building them into
something called The Constitution of Man.

So far as anthropology as such is concerned, however, there is another
difference, more or less growing out of these, which, while also (you

should excuse the expression) more relative than radical, does act to drive the two sorts of discussions in somewhat divergent, even contrary, directions, namely, that where the Human Nature tack leads to bringing back one of our classical conceptions into the center of our attention — "social deviance" — the Human Mind tack leads to bringing back another — "primitive (*sauvage*, primary, preliterate) thought." The antirelativist anxieties that gather in the one discourse around the enigmas of conduct, gather in the other around those of belief.

More exactly, they gather around "irrational" (or "mystical," "prelogical," "affective" or, particularly nowadays, "noncognitive") beliefs. Where it has been such unnerving practices as headhunting, slavery, caste, and footbinding which have sent anthropologists rallying to the grand old banner of Human Nature under the impression that only thus could taking a moral distance from them be justified, it has been such unlikely conceptions as witchcraft substance, animal tutelaries, godkings, and (to foreshadow an example I will be getting to in a moment) a dragon with a golden heart and a horn at the nape of its neck which have sent them rallying to that of the The Human Mind under the impression that only thus could adopting an empirical skepticism with respect to them be defended. It is not so much how the other half behaves that is so disquieting, but — what is really rather worse — how it thinks.

There are, again, a fairly large number of such rationalist or neorationalist perspectives in anthropology of varying degrees of purity, cogency, coherence, and popularity, not wholly consonant one with another. Some invoke formal constancies, usually called cognitive universals; some, developmental constancies, usually called cognitive stages; some, operational constancies, usually called cognitive processes. Some are structuralist, some are Jungian, some are Piagetian, some look to the latest news from MIT, Bell Labs, or Carnegie-Mellon. All are after something steadfast: Reality reached, Reason saved from drowning.

What they share, thus, is not merely an interest in our mental functioning. Like an interest in our biological makeup, that is uncontroversially A Good Thing, both in itself and for the analysis of culture; and if not all the supposed discoveries in what is coming to be called, in an aspiring sort of way, "cognitive science" turn out in the event genuinely to be such, some doubtless will, and will alter significantly not only how we think about how we think but how we think about what we think. What, beyond that, they share, from Lévi-Strauss to Rodney Needham, something of a distance, and what is not so uncontroversially beneficent, is a foundationalist view of Mind. That is, a view which sees it—like "The Means of Production" or "Social Structure" or "Exchange" or "Energy" or "Culture" or "Symbol" in other, bottom-line, the-buck-stops-here approaches to social theory (and of course like "Human Nature")—as the sovereign term of explanation, the light that shines in the relativist darkness.

That it is the fear of relativism, the anti-hero with a thousand faces, that provides a good part of the impetus to neo-rationalism, as it does to neo-naturalism, and serves as its major justification, can be conveniently seen from the excellent new collection of anti-relativist exhortations— plus one unbuttoned relativist piece marvelously designed to drive the others to the required level of outrage—edited by Martin Hollis and Steven Lukes (1982), *Rationality and Relativism*.[5] A product of the so-called "rationality debate" (see Wilson 1970; cf. Hanson 1981) that Evans-Pritchard's chicken stories, among other things, seem to have induced into British social science and a fair part of British philosophy ("Are there absolute truths that can be gradually approached over time through rational processes? Or are all modes and systems of thought equally valid if viewed from within their own internally consistent frames of reference?")[6] the book more or less covers the Reason In Danger! waterfront. "The temptations of relativism are perennial and pervasive," the editors' introduction opens, like some Cromwellian call to the barricades: "[The] primrose path to relativism . . . is paved with plausible contentions" (Hollis and Lukes 1982:1).

The three anthropologists in the collection all respond with enthusiasm to this summons to save us from ourselves. Ernest Gellner (1982) argues that the fact that other people do not believe what we, The Children of Galileo, believe about how reality is put together is no argument against the fact that what we believe is not the correct, "One True Vision." And especially as others, even Himalayans, seem to him to be coming around, he thinks it almost certain that it is. Robin Horton (1982) argues for a "cognitive common core," a culturally universal, only trivially variant, "primary theory" of the world as filled with middle-sized, enduring objects, interrelated in terms of a "push-pull" concept of causality, five spatial dichotomies (left/right, above/below, etc.), a temporal trichotomy (before/at the same time/after) and two categorical distinctions (human/nonhuman, self/other), the existence of which insures that "Relativism is bound to fail whilst Universalism may, some day, succeed" (Horton 1982:260).

But it is Dan Sperber (1982), surer of his rationalist ground (Jerry Fodor's computational view of mental representations) than either of these, and with a One True Vision of his own ("there is no such thing as a non-literal fact"), who develops the most vigorous attack. Relativism, though marvelously mischievous (it makes "ethnography . . . inexplicable, and psychology immensely difficult"), is not even an indefensible position, it really doesn't qualify as a position at all. Its ideas are semi-ideas, its beliefs semi-beliefs, its propositions semi-propositions. Like the gold-hearted dragon with the horn at the base of his neck that one of his elderly Dorze informants innocently, or perhaps not quite so innocently, invited him to track down and kill (wary of nonliteral facts, he declined), such "relativist slogans" as "peoples of different cultures live in different worlds" are not, in fact, factual beliefs. They are half-formed and indeterminate representations, mental stopgaps, that result when, less circumspect than computers, we try to process more information than our inherent conceptual capacities permit. Useful, sometimes, as place holders until we can get our cognitive powers up to speed, occasionally fun to toy with while we are waiting, even once in a while "sources of suggestion in [genuine] creative thinking," they are not, these academic dragons with plastic hearts and no horn at all, matters even their champions take as true, for they do not really understand, nor can they, what they mean. They are hand-wavings — more elaborate or less — of a, in the end, conformist, false-profound, misleading, "hermeneutico-psychedelic," self-serving sort:

> The best evidence against relativism is . . . the very activity of anthropologists, while the best evidence for relativism [is] in the writings of anthropologists. . . . In retracing their steps [in their works], anthropologists transform into unfathomable gaps the shallow and irregular cultural boundaries they had not found so difficult to cross [in the field], thereby protecting their own sense of identity, and providing their philosophical and lay audience with just what they want to hear. [Sperber 1982:180]

In short, whether in the form of hearty common sense (never mind about liver gazing and poison oracles, we have after all got things more or less right), wistful ecumenicalism (despite the variations in more developed explanatory schemes, juju or genetics, at base everyone has more or less the same conception of what the world is like), or aggressive sciencism (there are things which are really ideas, such as "propositional attitudes" and "representational beliefs," and there are things that only look like ideas, such as "there's a dragon down the road" and "peoples of different cultures live in different worlds"), the resurrection of The Human Mind as the still point of the turning world defuses the threat of cultural relativism by disarming the force of cultural diversity. As with "Human Nature," the deconstruction of otherness is the price of truth. Perhaps, but it is not what either the history of anthropology, the materials it has assembled, or the ideals that have animated it would suggest; nor is it only relativists who tell their audiences what they would like to hear. There are some dragons — "tigers in red weather" — that deserve to be looked into.

V

Looking into dragons, not domesticating or abominating them, nor drowning them in vats of theory, is what anthropology has been all about. At least, that is what it has been all about, as I, no nihilist, no subjectivist, and possessed, as you can see, of some strong views as to what is real and what is not, what is commendable and what is not, what is reasonable and what is not, understand it. We have, with no little success, sought to keep the world off balance; pulling out rugs, upsetting tea tables, setting off firecrackers. It has been the office of others to reassure; ours to unsettle. Australopithicenes, Tricksters, Clicks, Megaliths — we hawk the anomalous, peddle the strange. Merchants of astonishment.

We have, no doubt, on occasion moved too far in this direction and transformed idiosyncrasies into puzzles, puzzles into mysteries, and mysteries into humbug. But such an affection for what doesn't fit and won't comport, reality out of place, has connected us to the leading theme of the cultural history of "Modern Times." For that history has indeed consisted of one field of thought after another having to discover how to live on without the certainties that launched it. Brute fact, natural law, necessary truth, transcendent beauty, immanent authority, unique revelation, even the in-here self facing the out-there world have all come under such heavy attack as to seem by now lost simplicities of a less strenuous past. But science, law, philosophy, art, political theory, religion, and the stubborn insistences of common sense have contrived nonetheless to continue. It has not proved necessary to revive the simplicities.

It is, so I think, precisely the determination not to cling to what once worked well enough and got us to where we are and now doesn't quite work well enough and gets us into recurrent stalemates that makes a science move. As long as there was nothing around much faster than a marathon runner, Aristotle's physics worked well enough, Stoic paradoxes notwithstanding. So long as technical instrumentation could get us but a short way down and a certain way out from our sense-delivered world, Newton's mechanics worked well enough, action-at-a-distance perplexities notwithstanding. It was not relativism — Sex, The Dialectic and The Death of God — that did in absolute motion, Euclidean space, and universal causation. It was wayward phenomena, wave packets and orbital leaps, before which they were helpless. Nor was it Relativism — Hermeneutico-Psychedelic Subjectivism — that did in (to the degree they *have* been done in) the Cartesian *cogito*, the Whig view of history, and "the moral point of view so sacred to Eliot and Arnold and Emerson." It was odd actualities — infant betrothals and nonillusionist paintings — that embarrassed their categories.

In this move away from old triumphs become complacencies, one-time breakthroughs transformed to roadblocks, anthropology has played, in our day, a vanguard role. We have been the first to insist on a number of things: that the world does not divide into the pious and the superstitious; that there are sculptures in jungles and paintings in deserts; that political order is possible without centralized power and principled justice without codified rules; that the norms of reason were not fixed in Greece, the evolution of morality not consummated in England. Most important, we were the first to insist that we see the lives of others through lenses of our own grinding and that they look back on ours through ones of their own. That this led some to think the sky was falling, solipsism was upon us, and intellect, judgment, even the sheer possibility of communication had all fled is not surprising. The repositioning of horizons and the decentering of perspectives has had that effect before. The Bellarmines you have always with you; and as someone has remarked of the Polynesians, it takes a certain kind of mind to sail out of the sight of land in an outrigger canoe.

But that is, at least at our best and to the degree that we have been able, what we have been doing. And it would be, I think, a large pity if, now that the distances we have established and the elsewheres we have located are beginning to bite, to change our sense of sense and our perception of perception we should turn back to old songs and older stories in the hope that somehow only the superficial need alter and that we shan't fall off the edge of the world. The objection to anti-relativism is not that it rejects an it's-all-how-you-look-at-it approach to knowledge or a when-in-Rome approach to morality, but that it imagines that they can only be defeated by placing morality beyond culture and knowledge beyond both. This, speaking of things which must needs be so, is no longer possible. If we wanted home truths, we should have stayed at home.

Notes

1. See Todorov 1983:113–144 for general discussion of Montaigne's relativism from a position similar to mine.

2. For materialism, Harris 1968; for "science" and "The Big Ditch," Gellner 1979; for "literacy," Goody 1977; for "inter-theoretic competition," Horton 1982; for "the Cartesian conception of knowledge," Lukes 1982; cf. Williams 1978. For Popper, from whom all these blessings flow, Popper 1963, 1977.

3. The "monotony" example occurs in a footnote ("Monotony is itself an abnormal extreme").

4. Baggish 1983. For another troubled discourse on "the relativism problem" from that part of the world ("I set out what I think a reasonable point of view to fill the partial void left by ethical relativism, which by the 1980s seems more often to be repudiated than upheld" [12]), see Hatch 1983.

5. There are also some more moderate, split-the-difference pieces, by Ian Hacking, Charles Taylor, and Lukes, but only the first of these seems genuinely free of cooked-up alarms.

6. The parenthetical quotations are from the book jacket, which for once reflects the contents.

References Cited

Baggish, H.
  1983 Confessions of a Former Cultural Relativist. In Anthropology 83/84. E. Angeloni, ed. Guilford, Conn.: Dushkin Publishing.
Booth, W.
  1983 A New Strategy for Establishing a Truly Democratic Criticism. Daedalus 112:193–214.
Edgerton, R.
  1978 The Study of Deviance, Marginal Man or Everyman. In The Making of Psychological Anthropology. G. Spindler, ed. pp. 444–471. Berkeley: University of California Press.
Empson, W.
  1955 Collected Poems. New York: Harcourt, Brace and World.
Gass, W.
  1981 Culture, Self, and Style. Syracuse Scholar 2:54–68.
Gellner, E.
  1979 Spectacles and Predicaments. Cambridge, England: Cambridge University Press.

1982 Relativism and Universals. In Rationality and Relativism. M. Hollis and S. Lukes, eds. pp. 181–200. Cambridge, Mass.: MIT Press.

Goody, J.
1977 The Domestication of the Savage Mind. Cambridge, England: Cambridge University Press.

Hanson, F. A.
1981 Anthropologie und die Rationalitätsdebatte. In Der Wissenschaftler und das Irrationale, Vol. 1. H. P. Duerr, ed. Frankfurt am Main: Syndikat.

Harris, M.
1968 The Rise of Anthropological Theory. New York: Crowell.

Hatch, E.
1983 Culture and Morality: The Relativity of Values in Anthropology. New York: Columbia University Press.

Herodotus
1859–61 History of Herodotus, Bk. 3. Chap. 38. New York: Appleton.

Hollis, M., and S. Lukes
1982 Rationality and Relativism. Cambridge, Mass.: MIT Press.

Horton, R.
1982 Tradition and Modernity Revisited. In Rationality and Relativism. M. Hollis and S. Lukes, eds. pp. 201–260. Cambridge, Mass.: MIT Press.

Jarvie, I. C.
1983 Rationalism and Relativism. The British Journal of Sociology 34:44–60.

Johnson, P.
1983 Modern Times, The World from the Twenties to the Eighties. New York: Harper & Row.

Kluckhohn, C.
1962 Education, Values and Anthropological Relativity. In Culture and Behavior. Clyde Kluckhohn, ed. New York: Free Press.

Ladd, J.
1982 The Poverty of Absolutism. In Edward Westermarck: Essays on His Life and Works. Acta Philosophica Fennica (Helsinki) 34:158–180.

Lakatos, I.
1976 The Methodology of Scientific Research. Cambridge, England: Cambridge University Press.

Lukes, S.
1982 Relativism in Its Place. In Rationality and Relativism. M. Hollis and S. Lukes, eds. pp. 261–305. Cambridge, Mass.: MIT Press.

Midgeley, M.
1978 Beast and Man: The Roots of Human Nature. Ithaca, N.Y.: Cornell University Press.

Montaigne
1978 Les Essais de Michel de Montaigne. P. Villey, ed. pp. 202–214. Paris: Universitaires de France.

Popper, K.

1963 Conjectures and Refutations: The Growth of Scientific Knowledge. London: Routledge and Kegan Paul.

1972 Objective Knowledge: An Evolutionary Approach. Oxford: Clarendon Press.

Rabinow, P.

1983 Humanism as Nihilism: The Bracketing of Truth and Seriousness in American Cultural Anthropology. In Social Science as Moral Inquiry. N. Haan, R. M. Bellah, P. Rabinow, and W. M. Sullivan, eds. pp. 52–75. New York: Columbia University Press.

Rorty, R.

1979 Philosophy and the Mirror of Nature. Princeton: Princeton University Press.

1983 Method and Morality. In Social Science as Moral Inquiry. N. Haan, R. M. Bellah, P. Rabinow, and W. M. Sullivan, eds. pp. 155–176. New York: Columbia University Press.

Salkever, S.

1983 Beyond Interpretation: Human Agency and the Slovenly Wilderness. In Social Science as Moral Inquiry. N. Haan, R. M. Bellah, P. Rabinow, and W. M. Sullivan, eds. pp. 195–217. New York: Columbia University Press.

Scheffler, I.

1967 Science and Subjectivity. Indianapolis, Ind.: Bobbs-Merrill.

Sperber, D.

1982 Apparently Irrational Beliefs. In Rationality and Relativism. M. Hollis and S. Lukes, eds. pp. 149–180. Cambridge, Mass.: MIT Press.

Spiro, M.

1978 Culture and Human Nature. In The Making of Psychological Anthropology. G. Spindler, ed. pp. 330–360. Berkeley: University of California Press.

Stocking, G. W., Jr.

1982 Afterword: A View from the Center. Ethnos 47:172–186.

Thomas, H.

1983 The Inferno of Relativism. Times Literary Supplement, July 8, p. 718.

Tiger, L., and J. Sepher

1975 Women in the Kibbutz. New York: Harcourt Brace Jovanovich (Harvest).

Todorov, T.

1983 Montaigne, Essays in Reading. In Yale French Studies, Vol. 64. Gérard Defaux, ed. pp. 113–144. New Haven, Conn.: Yale University Press.

Williams, B.

1978 Descartes: The Project of Pure Enquiry. Harmondsworth, England: Penguin.

Wilson, B.

1970 Rationality. Oxford: Blackwell.

Hominoid Evolution and Hominoid Origins

David Pilbeam

VOL. 88, 1986, 295–312

This lecture is dedicated to the memory of my dearly missed colleague and friend Glynn Isaac.

I shall discuss the broad patterns of hominoid evolution, an exercise made enjoyable by the need to integrate diverse kinds of information, and use that as a vehicle to speculate about hominid origins, an event for which there is no recognized fossil record. Hence an opportunity to exercise some imagination.

When I first became interested in the subject in 1961, the Miocene hominoid fossil record was in something of a mess. Dozens of ape species had been named. Between 1963 and 1965, Elwyn Simons and I reduced this diversity to a much simpler scheme (Simons and Pilbeam 1965). We thought that the middle and late Miocene hominoid *Ramapithecus* was a hominid ancestral to *Australopithecus*, and distinct from the ape *Dryopithecus*. Hominids originated at least 15 M.Y.A. (million years ago). *Ramapithecus* had small canines, and we thought this was functionally associated with tool use and frequent bipedalism (Pilbeam and Simons 1965). The idea for this functional package had of course been around for a long time (Darwin 1871).

Almost all these Miocene hominoids were known essentially just from jaws and teeth; there were few cranial or postcranial parts known. But by 1975 the fossil record was expanding (Pilbeam et al. 1980; Pilbeam 1985). For example, *Ramapithecus* from 8 M.Y. beds in Pakistan and *Australopithecus afarensis* from Ethiopia, about 3 M.Y. old, looked similar, with small canines, large cheek teeth, thick enamel, and robust jaws. This reinforced my view that both were hominids, in contrast to the chimpanzee, for example, which had large canines, small cheek teeth, and thin enamel. I did not consider at the time whether or not the similarities were meaningful, because I had not learned the lessons of one of the most important biological revolutions of the last two decades: phylogenetic systematics or cladism. Cladism is an approach to building evolutionary trees that formally partitions similarity (Wiley 1981). It is worth a brief digression to explain.

Take a character, enamel thickness for example, and divide it into two character states: thick, as in *Ramapithecus* and *Australopithecus*, and thin, as in the chimpanzee. *Ramapithecus* and *Australopithecus* are similar because they share the same character state. We assumed (Pilbeam and Simons 1965) that this was because their immediate common ancestor had thick enamel, while the more distant ancestor of all three had thin enamel, which was retained in the chimpanzee. Thin enamel would be termed "primitive," thick enamel "derived." We had assumed the "polarity" of the character state — that is, the direction of evolution — to go from thin to thick (Figure 1, top).

Similarity can be due to homology — inheritance of a trait in two species like *Ramapithecus* and *Australopithecus* from their ancestor that also had the trait. But it can also be due to parallelism or convergence (homoplasy): two descendants share a trait but their ancestor lacked it. Only homologous similarities are useful in building evolutionary trees. But similarities that are inherited from a more distant ancestor are no good either; it has to be similarity that is relatively derived. So if the actual polarity of enamel evolution was thick to thin (Figure 1, bottom) rather than thin to thick as now seems more likely (Martin 1985), the similarity of *Ramapithecus* and *Australopithecus* relative to the chimpanzee tells us nothing about their relationship. (In fact, *Australopithecus* and the chimpanzee are more closely related than either are to *Ramapithecus*.) Similarity must be relatively derived, or "shared-derived."

Another strong current in evolutionary biology was flowing in the 1950s, the use of genetic comparisons among living species to infer branching patterns and branching times; I am referring particularly to the work of Morris Goodman, Allan Wilson, and Vincent Sarich (see Goodman and Tashian 1975). The patterns, and more significantly, the times inferred from these comparisons differed quite a lot from fossil-based ones.

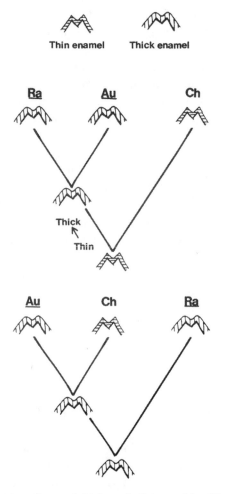

Fig. 1. Distribution of enamel thickness in living and fossil hominoids and alternative evolutionary trees

In particular, hominids clustered with African apes in a monophyletic group, sharing, according to Sarich and Wilson (1967), a recent ancestor. Orangs were a more distantly related outgroup. Sherwood Washburn used these new ideas to propose that the earliest hominids evolved from ancestors that looked like chimps, and that could be characterized as "knuckle-walkers" (Washburn 1968; Tuttle 1967).

So a debate began about the prehominid: when it lived and what it looked like. The debate involved arguments about the reliability of the fossil record, the believability of genetic or molecular patterns, the extent to which "similarity" could be taken at face value. It has been long and often acrimonious.

But what are we after? Whether we focus only on hominid origins or look at broader patterns, the questions are going to be the same: when, where, what, why? When did it happen? Where did it happen? What did the animal in question look like and what can we infer of its biology? And finally, why did change occur? We need, first, an evolutionary framework, and then we need to reconstruct past species as though they were alive today, as though we were watching them from a Time Machine. The great growth in behavioral and anatomical knowledge of living mammals—particularly the living apes, and our deeper understanding of ecological-behavioral principles, now allows us to draw up a kind of checklist of features that adequately describe a species. This reflects the interlocking of ecological, behavioral, and anatomical variables as they are related to the three great problems facing any animal: the pursuit of food, of mates, and of safety.

We know a good deal now about living apes—the gorilla, chimpanzee, and bonobo in Africa, and orangutan and gibbon in Asia. They are quite varied in their behavior, but slowly we begin to understand the patterning of this variation according to socioecological principles (e.g., Wrangham 1982; Hamburg and McCown 1982).

Chimpanzees are forest and woodland apes adapted to an eclectic diet emphasizing ripe fruits. Individual females live generally scattered, and groups of related males monitor the territories of several females. Communities are defended by the males, and males are only 30% bigger than females. Animals are often dispersed, but when together parties generally contain more males than females. Chimpanzees feed mostly in the trees and travel mostly on the ground. Their diverse positional repertoire includes quadrupedal knuckle-walking, but also other important behaviors as well.

Mountain gorillas feed mostly on the ground on a range of herbaceous vegetation that is more or less evenly distributed (as Glynn Isaac often said, they live in a salad bowl!). Social groups consist of a few unrelated females plus infants, focused usually around one much larger male. Intermale competition is fierce, as it is in chimpanzees. Social groups are more compact and stable than in chimpanzees because food distribution is essentially continuous. Bonobos or pygmy chimps are probably on average more arboreal than common chimps (Susman

Table I. Locomotor behavior spectra for various living primates, and inferences for certain fossil hominoids

| | | | Terrestrial | | | Arboreal | | | | Arm-swing | |
	Ter.	Arb.	Bipedal	Quadrup. walk/run	Knuckle-walk	Knuckle-walk	Quadrup. walk/run	Leap/sway	Quadrum. + climb	Brachiate	Bipedal
Colobine	~	100	—	~	—	—	50	40	10	~	~
Baboon	50	50	2	48	—	—	25	20	5	~	~
Gibbon	~	100	—	—	—	—	—	15	20	55	10
Orang	~	100	—	—	—	—	13	15	51	21	~
Bonobo	25	75	3	—	22	1	22	8	22	15	7
Chimp	50	50	2	—	48	3	11	6	15	10	5
Human	100	~	100	~	—	—	—	—	—	—	—
Australopithecus	60	40	55	5	—	—	5	—	15	5	15
"Ancestor"	30	70	10	10	10	1	20	9	20	10	10

— = 0; ~ = approximately 0 but not 0 (<1%).

1984). They feed on both fruits *and* herbaceous vegetation, and because food patch size is often larger than for chimps their social groups are normally larger and more stable. Wrangham has argued plausibly for the evolution of the bonobo pattern from something more chimp-like and more terrestrial (1986). Orangutans are different again: highly arboreal, large, slow, very dimorphic. They are almost asocial in their natural environment, a consequence of being large and living almost exclusively in the trees. These accounts are skeletal, but I hope you can see how understanding the distribution of food begins to explain diverse patterns of social behavior, although it is obviously not the only determinant.

There is one large hominoid we would like to be able to describe in the same way but we cannot. This is the first well-known hominid, *Australopithecus afarensis.* Knowing what it ate and where its food was distributed are essential to understanding its social behavior, but all we have to go on are those ambiguous correlates of behavior, anatomy and paleoecology, and interpretations of both are hotly debated. I shall stick my neck out and go with a picture of *afarensis* as a quite dimorphic species, predominantly vegetarian, mostly but not entirely terrestrial but with a more varied positional repertoire than *Homo.*

Was the protohominid a knuckle-walker? Was it like a chimpanzee? Are those reasonable questions? First, I think it is likely that prehominids (which are the same as prechimpanzees) were uniquely different from all of the above. Second, we must be careful with labels. Let us look at positional profiles (Table 1). Here I have culled and squeezed data to show ground and tree use and positional behavior in various primates, using an approach creatively developed by Rose (1984a). Colobine monkeys and baboons are quadrupedal walkers, runners, leapers almost all the time. "Quadruped" is a good label for them. Humans can do lots of things but we usually do not; mostly we are bipedal. "Biped" is a good label. Gibbons brachiate, but they do other things too, and a good single word label is more difficult to pick. What should we call orangs — other than contortionists? The varied profiles of chimpanzees and bonobos are labeled by single words only at great risk. I have shown chimps as more terrestrial, and I assume that this is not far off the ancestral profile in which their knuckle-walking evolved. Bonobos are in the trees more, where they hardly knuckle-walk at all (Susman 1984). If Wrangham is right and bonobo ancestors were more terrestrial, the knuckle-walking "overprint" is understandable. If this has any substance, it means that we need to know conditions in which features originally evolved, because sometimes conditions might change without the feature changing (see Gould and Vrba 1982).

Early hominids like *A. afarensis* emphasized more the terrestrial portion of the positional repertoire (here I follow Rose 1984a and Susman, Stern, and Jungers 1985). The bipedal portion became more efficient presumably because total anatomical compromises were less restrictive, because of a relative downplaying of arboreal behaviors (Table 1). This is not to say that australopithecines were *Homo*-like — I do not think they were. They probably climbed in trees for food, rest, and protection. But they sought important resources that required efficient ground trekking, and hence the bipedal portion of the repertoire, which had consequences for the total mix. Even if australopithecine bipedalism was more energetically costly than *Homo*-type bipedalism, it was probably still *less* costly than chimp-type knuckle-walking (Rodman and McHenry 1980).

So to ask if the protohominid was a "knuckle-walker" is not phrasing the question correctly. It might have included knuckle-walking in its positional repertoire, and that might be important. But what we need, going back to the Time Machine analogy, is a much fuller picture of feeding behavior, and positional behavior, and social behavior, and we risk losing real complexity when we think with single word labels.

The action over the past two decades has also been exciting in two other areas: "molecular genetics" and paleontology. The initial "molecular" battle was fought over the broad relationships of hominoids. In the late 1950s most primatologists thought that the great apes were a natural group, while hominids diverged much earlier. Morris Goodman used the intensity of immunological responses of serum proteins to look at similarities and differences among living primates (Goodman 1963). He showed that humans and African apes were similar, and differed from orangs and gibbons. These are measures of phenetic or overall similarity; homology and homoplasy, primitive and derived character states are not separated out. Goodman inferred from these patterns of similarity that African apes and hominids were closely related.

This was a surprise. It meant that morphological similarities like those shown by chimp, gorilla, and orang (see Kluge 1983) cannot be shared-derived but must either have evolved in parallel or be homologous but primitive, and further meant that morphologists were not reading morphology well. And that upset morphologists (it still does). One counter to the phenetic patterns was to argue that great apes were indeed monophyletic but that orangs had evolved very rapidly. It is an explanation that is still used (Schwartz 1984), although it has long since been disproved, in an elegant way.

Beginning in the mid-1960s, Vincent Sarich and Allan Wilson (1967) revolutionized "molecular systematics" by developing methods to quantify immunological reaction strengths more easily and to put a number on the differences between a pair of species. They chose to work first with the blood protein albumin, then later with transferrin. Sarich pointed out (1983) that if orangs had indeed evolved more rapidly, this was easily detectable. For example, orangs should be more different from gibbons than humans or African apes were from gibbons. African apes should be more similar to orangs than humans were to orangs. Neither is true. If we look at a matrix (Figure 2) of albumin distances (Cronin 1975) — where smaller numbers mean greater similarity — we see that if we pick an outgroup like the baboon, the distances to each member of the monophyletic group (the hominoids) are roughly equal (data from Cronin 1975). This is the "rate test." It can only be so if the amount of change along independent lineages is about the same, which in turn implies some regular pattern of evolutionary change.

The immunological reaction indirectly measures amino acid differences in the albumins of two species, and the majority of amino acid replacements are approximately selectively neutral. The matrix column values are not exactly equal, as is shown by percentage variation (Figure 2); that is because there is experimental error and some selection-controlled rate variation. But the numbers are reasonably uniform and imply an underlying mechanism that is rather regular. The human-chimpanzee-gorilla triad cannot be resolved because random fluctuations and experimental error obscure the exact pattern. Uniform patterns like these were unfamiliar to morphologists and paleontologists, and were greeted with great skepticism.

Newer ways of comparing proteins and more especially DNA are now producing data patterned even more impressively. Mitochondrial and nuclear DNA of hominids can be both indirectly assayed by restriction enzymes and directly sequenced (see Nei, Stephens, and Saitou 1985). These comparisons show the same general pattern as albumins: humans and African apes are similar, orangs roughly twice as different, and gibbons usually a bit more different than orangs. Single genes often show some rate variation. There is also a problem with resolution of the gorilla-human-chimpanzee triad. One way around that problem is to average together several systems as Sarich and Cronin (1975) did by

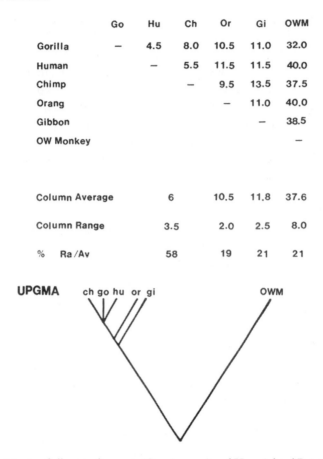

	Go	Hu	Ch	Or	Gi	OWM
Gorilla	—	4.5	8.0	10.5	11.0	32.0
Human		—	5.5	11.5	11.5	40.0
Chimp			—	9.5	13.5	37.5
Orang				—	11.0	40.0
Gibbon					—	38.5
OW Monkey						—
Column Average		6		10.5	11.8	37.6
Column Range		3.5		2.0	2.5	8.0
% Ra /Av		58		19	21	21

Fig. 2. Matrix of albumin distances (Cronin 1975) and Unweighted Pair Group clustering of catarrhines

pooling results from albumin, transferrin, and DNA. In doing this, one expects that evolutionary rate changes in different systems will not co-vary exactly but rather will cancel each other out. The ultimate averaging would come by comparing *all* single copy DNA, both the small fraction expressed as proteins and the more than 90% that is unexpressed. The vast bulk of mutations in both parts will be relatively unaffected by selection. Although each subset of DNA might fluctuate in rate, averaging over all 10^9 plus base pairs should give an average rate for the genomes of related species which is uniform, cancelling out individual

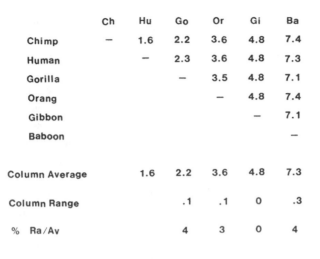

	Ch	Hu	Go	Or	Gi	Ba
Chimp	—	1.6	2.2	3.6	4.8	7.4
Human		—	2.3	3.6	4.8	7.3
Gorilla			—	3.5	4.8	7.1
Orang				—	4.8	7.4
Gibbon					—	7.1
Baboon						—
Column Average		1.6	2.2	3.6	4.8	7.3
Column Range			.1	.1	0	.3
% Ra/Av			4	3	0	4

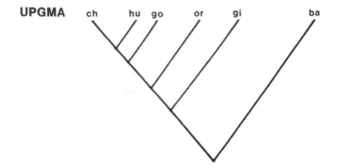

Fig. 3. Matrix of DNA–DNA hybridization distances (Sibley and Ahlquist 1984; Sibley personal communication) and Unweighted Pair Group clustering of catarrhines

fluctuations. This is the "uniform average rate" hypothesis (Sibley and Ahlquist 1984). Its test is the rate test.

DNA annealing or DNA hybridization is an indirect, black box approach to estimating the actual sequence difference between total single copy DNAs of two species (see Benveniste 1985; Sibley and Ahlquist 1984). Several excellent primate data sets now exist, so that we can test the uniform average rate hypothesis using the rate test. Figure 3 shows a matrix of distances—derived from both published and some new unpublished data generously made available by Charles Sibley and Jon Ahlquist. Humans and chimpanzees are most similar. This resolution of the chimpanzee-human-gorilla triad has been hotly debated (see Templeton 1983, 1985; Nei and Tajimo 1985; Ruvolo and Smith 1986), and so has the whole technique (see Farris 1985). But, in my opinion, using the rate test this is an *extremely* regular system in hominoids (note percent variation); humans and chimpanzees are probably closest relatives.

The precise relationship between any of these genetic differences and time is less clear. As Gingerich (1985) has shown, there is no way that relationship can be known except by using geological or paleontological events to estimate splitting times, and results are clearly dependent on the quality of those estimates, few of which are very good. The rate test is not a test of linearity. It is indeed unlikely that any system is linear. But even if they are not linear the local pattern for hominoids over the last 20 million years of evolution is likely to be sufficiently close to linear for us not to have to worry too much. These results have not been accepted without a fight. Many morphologists still react strongly, as though "molecular" systematics puts us all out of a job. Quite the contrary. If we can infer relationships correctly, using whatever methods can be shown as consistent (as DNA hybridization patterns of hominoids are, when judged by the rate test), we have a guide to better interpretation of anatomy.

Given that the branching sequence indeed links hominids and chimpanzees, with gorillas more distant, this may well indicate that protohominids included knuckle-walking in their behavior, but it does not necessarily mean they closely resembled chimpanzees. For example, just from knowledge of living hominoids one would not have predicted *Australopithecus*. This is because not all possible character states are represented in living species, because past species are usually novel combinations of character states, and because we often have only a hazy idea of polarities — what is primitive and what is derived. As an example of difficulties, consider enamel thickness once more. In hominids it is thick, while chimpanzees and gorillas have thin enamel, which was believed to be a derived homology implying a chimpanzee-gorilla link (Figure 4, top). There is histological and fossil evidence that thick enamel is primitive (Martin 1985; Pilbeam 1985), a character state retained in hominids. But if humans and chimpanzees are closest, the thin enamel of chimps and gorillas must be a homoplasy. It looks as though parallelism is widespread among hominoids in many systems.

To reconstruct the protohominid pattern we clearly need both mo-

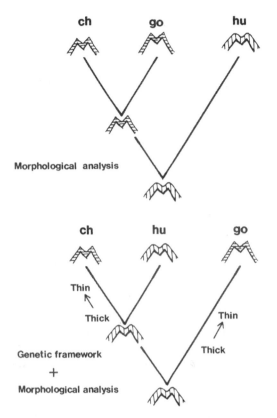

Fig. 4. Alternative evolutionary pathways for enamel thickness

lecular and comparative records, and we need to play those records off against the fossils. So I will turn to them now.

I got involved in Miocene research by chance, but it has been enjoyable. Progress in the last half decade in particular has been phenomenal, but the best-known Miocene hominoids are still barely as well known as the least well known Plio-Pleistocene hominids and, relative to the complexity of the radiations, the Miocene record is an order of magnitude less complete. Much of the new hominoid material is either not properly described or not described at all. The early Miocene record is exclusively African because hominoids did not leave Africa until the middle Miocene (Pilbeam 1985). The middle and late Miocene hominoid records, between roughly 15 and 7 M.Y., are best for Europe and Asia. Few people have seen all or the bulk of the material, and even they do not

agree on everything. And there is an inverse relationship between familiarity and expressed certainty of opinion. . . .

As our knowledge of body parts expands beyond jaws and teeth we are
seeing that Miocene hominoids are indeed heterogeneous: but this time
there is real biological diversity there. I guess that, for any two- or three-
million-year period, ranging over the habitable Old World there would
be over a half dozen large hominoid species, and there would be substantial turnover through time. I would further guess a total of at least 20
different large hominoid species for the Miocene of which we have partial knowledge of less than half. And I think they would all have been
*un*like living apes or *Australopithecus*. Known species present novel configurations of traits and also character states not seen in living apes. The
fossil record until recently consisted mainly of jaws and teeth, which are
not good discriminators in living animals. If you only had jaws and teeth
you would often underestimate true diversity. Also, as with enamel
thickness, we have clearly been led astray over characters, states, and
polarities. So being able to expand the sampling of body parts is bound to
reshape our thinking.

Several facial features show a patterning (Figure 5) that follows the
molecular patterns nicely, for example, the premaxilla and palate (Andrews and Tekkaya 1980; Ward and Pilbeam 1983; Ward and Kimbel
1983). The palate is the bony plate forming the roof of the mouth; the
premaxilla is the lowest portion of the front of the face (it contains the
incisor roots); and the palatine canal runs through the central portion of
the palate, behind the premaxilla, about at the level of the canines. Old
World Monkeys and gibbons have one pattern (A), with a short premaxilla and a large palatine canal. The African apes and *A. afarensis* have
a second pattern (B), with larger premaxilla and smaller canal, which
seems plausibly derived from the first pattern. Humans have a third
pattern (D). We know from the fossil record that this evolved from the
australopithecine configuration (pattern B). The orangutan has another
different derived pattern (C), with canal and contents reduced to a minimum and premaxilla and palate forming an essentially continuous plate.
There is variability in each species, but these patterns are typical and
distinct (Lipson 1985). Polarities can be hypothesized (Figure 6) with
the gibbon primitive (A), the African ape/*Australopithecus* pattern more
derived (B), and the orang pattern more derived still (C). The human
pattern (D) was derived from (B) without any stage resembling

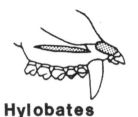

A Hylobates

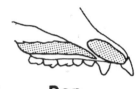

B₂   Pan

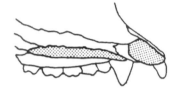

B₁   Gorilla

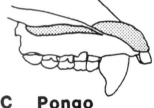

C   Pongo

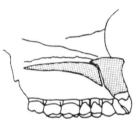

D   Homo

Fig. 5. Premaxillary-palatal morphology in hominoids

(C). Other characters can also be analyzed in similar ways and used to fit fossils onto an evolutionary framework.

Now for a brief and partial review of some of the new fossil information. The best sampled species from the East African Early Miocene, *Proconsul africanus* from Rusinga Island, is approximately 18 M.Y. old, and well known. The skull is now essentially complete (Walker et al. 1983), and restored shows a mixture of primitive and derived features linking it to hominoids rather than to cercopithecoids (Ward and Kim-

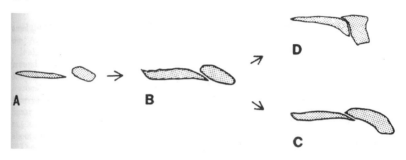

Fig. 6. Hypothetical evolutionary sequence of premaxillary-palatal
morphological patterns

bel 1983; Ward personal communication). The premaxillary region is
primitive, while other cranial features — like sinuses — seem derived.
The 1948 skull is female judging from canine size (Clark and Leakey
1951). Other larger but similar specimens from Rusinga have typically
male large canines (Andrews 1978), and are put in another species, *Proconsul nyanzae*. It has been suggested by Jay Kelley (Kelley and Pilbeam
1986) that *P. nyanzae* and *P. africanus* from Rusinga are males and females
with very size dimorphic cheek teeth — roughly twice as different as
average male and female orangs, the most dimorphic living hominoid.
But Alan Walker's new discoveries at Rusinga suggest to him two species
(personal communication). Postcranially *Proconsul* is an interesting mixture (Walker and Pickford 1983), and was probably a basically arboreal quadruped with a more diverse positional repertoire than any Old
World Monkey. This included perhaps quadrumanous clambering, vertical climbing, arm swinging, and bipedalism, as well as quadrupedal
running and leaping (Rose 1983, 1984a). The lumbar vertebrae are interesting, resembling those of gibbons rather than either Old World
monkeys or large hominoids, and according to Aaron Filler (1981) they
clearly imply non-monkey-like positional behaviors with the body frequently vertical rather than horizontal.

Proconsul-like species postdate (Figure 7) the hominoid-cercopithe-
coid split (Andrews 1985) and the oldest species may be 22 M.Y. old
(Martin 1981; Pickford 1981). But they probably predate the divergence
of large and small hominoids. Evidence for this split comes in particular
from one interesting piece of evidence. This is a lumbar vertebra from
Moroto in Uganda (Walker and Rose 1968; Filler 1981) (Figure 7),
which is associated with a scrappy Early or Middle Miocene fauna (Pick-

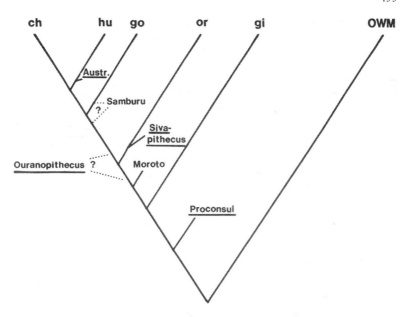

Fig. 7. Evolutionary framework of living catarrhines with certain fossil
hominoids

ford 1981) and is imprecisely and conservatively dated to older than
about 13 M.Y. (Bishop, Miller, and Fitch 1969). It resembles large rather
than small hominoids in the important position of its transverse processes (Filler 1981). African hominoids are poorly known between *Proconsul* at 18 M.Y.A. and *Australopithecus* at 5 M.Y.A., but they seem to be
characterized by extreme tooth size dimorphism, thick tooth enamel,
and facial features that are somewhat derived relative to *Proconsul*. Middle and late Miocene hominoids are better known in Europe and Asia. I
shall discuss only two genera out of several that are now quite well
sampled.

Ouranopithecus from the late Miocene of Greece is known from jaws,
teeth, and a lower face (de Bonis and Melentis 1977, 1978). This shows a
premaxillary pattern (de Bonis and Melentis 1985) similar to chimpanzee or gorilla, which may be primitive for living large hominoids. It
is clearly different from *Sivapithecus*. The cheek teeth are very dimorphic in size. They have thick enamel, and rounded and puffy cusps reminiscent of *Australopithecus* even when unworn (de Bonis et al. 1981).
Ouranopithecus may be part of the large hominoid radiation prior to the

divergence of the orang lineage, or it may be on or close to the clade leading specifically to gorilla, chimp, and hominids (Figure 7). It will be difficult to decide which.

Sivapithecus is the second non-African form. It consists now for me *only* of specimens from Turkey, India, and Pakistan, ranging in age from about 12 to about 7 M.Y.A. (Andrews and Tekkaya 1980; Kelley and Pilbeam 1986). It includes *Ramapithecus* specimens, some of which are females of *Sivapithecus*. I specifically exclude from *Sivapithecus* the *Ouranopithecus* material from Greece; *Rudapithecus* from Hungary (Kretzoi 1975; Kelley and Pilbeam 1986); the so-called *Sivapithecus* and *Ramapithecus* from Lufeng in China (Xu and Lu 1979), which are in my opinion one dimorphic species; *Kenyapithecus* from Kenya (Andrews and Walker 1976; Pickford 1982; Ishida et al. 1984); and the new hominoid from Buluk in Kenya (Leakey and Walker 1985). I do so because *Sivapithecus* in this restricted sense now has well-understood patterns of facial, palatal, dental, and mandibular features (Ward and Pilbeam 1983; Ward and Kimbel 1983; Pilbeam et al. 1980), and these other Miocene hominoids either share only very few or none of them, or also have features — particularly of palate and face — that are definitely different. I should emphasize that we are talking about characters that could not be determined on material until very recently, and in some cases the relevant specimens have yet to be fully or formally described.

In the upper and lower face and palate, *Sivapithecus* and orangutan are very similar (Pilbeam 1982; Andrews and Cronin 1982). I believe these are plausibly viewed as shared-derived homologies, implying a phylogenetic link (Figure 7). The two differ in essentially *all* other known characters. *Sivapithecus* is not an orang, nor is the orang a living fossil. Rather in virtually all features it is highly derived. Nor does the unworn dentition of *Sivapithecus* resemble *Australopithecus*, except in enamel thickness, a character state of questionable phylogenetic value. Dentally, *Sivapithecus* is probably highly size dimorphic (Kelley and Pilbeam 1986). Teeth have thick enamel and are large relative to inferred body size. Yet despite the great contrast in tooth size and enamel thickness relative to chimpanzees, occlusal microwear is essentially identical in the two (Teaford and Walker 1984).

Postcranially *Sivapithecus* is still poorly known, though better represented than other Miocene apes except for *Proconsul*. Michael Rose has thought very creatively about this material (Rose 1983, 1984b; Pilbeam et al. 1980; Raza et al. 1983). Arm and hand bones imply an arboreal hanging, clambering quadruped that was neither orang- nor chimp-like. Lower limbs suggest an arboreal acrobat, but with powerful grasping feet. An active climber, including climbing on vertical supports, is indicated. No single label can adequately describe this repertoire: it would probably have included quadrupedalism, palm and fist walking, quadrumanous scrambling, arm-swinging, bipedalism, leaping and diving. No obvious terrestrial component is present. If orangs are indeed derived from *Sivapithecus*, they have changed substantially.

I will mention just one more Miocene hominoid, a new maxilla from the late Miocene of Samburu Hills of Kenya (Ishida et al. 1984). It is unlike any other hominoid, living or extinct. Its premolars resemble those of gorillas, but its molars differ in having very thick enamel giving a puffy, almost pig-like appearance. If protogorillas indeed had thick enamel then this Samburu Hills fragment could fit in either as an early gorilla, or close to the "African" hominoid ancestor. More material is needed.

If all the ifs are allowed, then we can sketch a hominoid tree (Figure 8) and anchor it around what is in my view the best link: that between *Sivapithecus* and orangs. The oldest *Sivapithecus* is 12 M.Y. old and this could be close to the true splitting time. Our last few seasons' work in Pakistan suggest that *Sivapithecus* is not present in South Asia until then (Barry et al. 1985). Using DNA hybridization patterns and assuming them to be roughly linear over this range of time, we can then predict a chimpanzee-human split at least 5 M.Y.A., gorillas at least 8 M.Y.A., gibbons around 16 M.Y.A., and Old World monkeys about 24 M.Y.A. These are compatible with the fossil evidence.

The basic large hominoid anatomical pattern appears in the middle Miocene 12 to 18 M.Y.A.; and one lineage of that first radiation survives in modified form as the orang. A second radiation begins in the late Miocene 8 to 5 M.Y.A. and produces eventually four lineages, at least one of which, humans, is known to have been considerably modified. Presumably these patterns and changes are mapping environmental change, both abiotic and biotic. The hominoid pattern is similar to those of other herbivore groups, for example, Proboscidea (elephants, etc.). Early Miocene archaic proboscideans are replaced by a more modern radiation at the early to middle Miocene boundary. A portion of this radiation survives, severely edited by late Miocene extinctions, and it also gives rise to a second late Miocene radiation which produces most Pleistocene lineages. We find a similar pattern in bovids. These patterns are monitor-

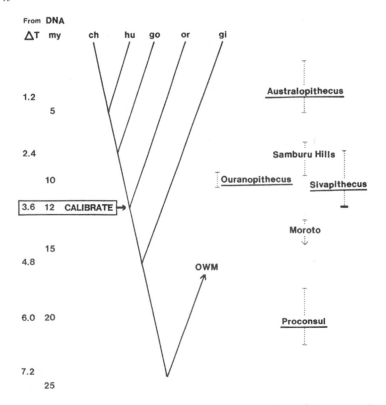

Fig. 8. Evolutionary framework of living catarrhines, and possible stratigraphic ranges of certain fossil hominoids

ing changing climates and habitats, from warmer, less seasonal, more forested to cooler, more seasonal, less forested. The changes happen throughout the last 25 M.Y., but are also pulsed, major shifts occurring 17 to 14 M.Y.A. and 8 to 5 M.Y.A., reflecting changes in continental configurations, mountain systems, oceanic currents, and Antarctic ice (Barry et al. 1985; Vrba et al. 1985).

So let us return again to the ancestor, or rather to that segment of the African hominoid lineage which produced gorillas, hominids, and chimpanzees, and see what molecules, fossils, and the living can tell us. When, where, what, why? When, I have just argued, was 5 to 10 M.Y.A., a time that is still poorly known in Africa, especially West and Central Africa, but that emerges as a critical research focus, one of climatic complexity and correlated changes in habitats and in many mammal groups. Where, seems to have been most likely Africa. But we know that in the late Miocene at least some mammals came into Africa from elsewhere. Remember that *Ouranopithecus* shows a number of similarities to later African hominoids, so perhaps "Africa" should include the southeastern European and western Asian margin as well.

What did this 10 to 5 M.Y. hominoid segment look like? Obviously, like an ape rather than a monkey. Remember that we have no fossil record so we are really "making it up." And remember that even when we do have a fossil record it will probably be at least as ambiguous as *Australopithecus*. But I would guess as follows. It would have had dimorphic canines, thick enameled and very dimorphic cheek teeth. It might have been very size dimorphic like most hominoids except chimpanzees, females weighing around 30 kg, males perhaps twice that. Arms and legs would have been long, chest broad. The lumbar region is a problem: did it have six lumbar vertebrae like early hominids, five like gibbons, or three or four like large apes? Its positional repertoire was mostly arboreal and would have broadly resembled that inferred for *Sivapithecus* (Table 1): in the trees quadrupedalism in palmigrade or fist-walking styles, but perhaps with occasional knuckle-walking, quadrumanous scrambling, vertical climbing, bipedalism, arm-swinging; on the ground did it knuckle-walk or was it bipedal or both?

At least one late Miocene lineage led to the gorilla, became more terrestrial, much larger, and more folivorous. Enamel became thinner, cheek teeth relatively smaller. But feeding in the trees remained important, long hands and grasping feet were retained, knuckle-walking was emphasized. A later hominoid divided into western and eastern parts at least 5 M.Y.A.: western in forests and woodlands, eastern in wooded savannahs and more open habitats. The western segment — protochimps — remained dependent upon arboreal resources, particularly fruits which tended to be scattered and which required an often dispersed and flexible social organization. They also reduced tooth size and enamel thickness. Both terrestrial and arboreal behaviors remained essential: knuckle-walking was emphasized as part of terrestrial movement because long arms and hands and grasping feet were still critical for climbing. Another adaptation, suggested by Peter Rodman (1984), was reduction in male body size because male mobility was at a premium; smaller knuckle-walkers were energetically more efficient than larger ones. If Wrangham (1986) is right, bonobos are descendants of chimpanzees but, because they had no feeding competitors, they were able to broaden their diets, which allowed them to live therefore in larger and less-dispersed groups, with consequent changes in social and sexual behavior. Many of their human-like features would under this scheme be parallelisms but no less interesting for that since parallelisms can give important clues to structure-function relationships.

Early hominids had become committed bipeds, as ground resources became critical. Not much else changed except canines. Male canine height reduced, and in both sexes they became less tusk-like, more incisor-type slicers. Why? Because tools were weapons? But then why the morphological change? I have long thought that this might be a clue to what was being eaten: food that required anterior tooth processing, and a lot of it. I would guess some kind of tougher vegetable food.

So much for when, where, and what. I have made up a protohominid uniquely different from anything we know, and do not forget that I have completely fabricated it. So it would be more than a little crazy to speculate about why the hominids changed. But I shall.

I agree with Mike Rose (1984a) that bipedalism evolved incrementally rather than in one leap. The amount of bipedalism in the repertoire perhaps grew initially as time spent feeding on plant food on the ground did. Food transport may also have been involved, but it is hard to say whether as consequence or cause, and as likely to have been away from as toward conspecifics. By the time bipedalism became a significant portion of the repertoire it would have been "available" for many functions, including transport. Remember (Rodman and McHenry 1980), early hominid bipedalism was probably energetically less costly than ape quadrupedalism (knuckle- or fist-walking) and would convey advantages in several contexts. For example, it would permit more efficient monitoring of non-food sources: one can imagine almost a chimpanzee-like social organization in which bipedalism would allow males to monitor more females, or the same number more widely dispersed, and where bipedalism would not constrain male body size as quadrupedalism evidently does.

This is all good fun, and as we learn more the speculations will become more realistic. As Fleagle et al. (1981) wrote, it is important to speculate about what the hypothetical ancestor might have looked like, even though narrowing the range of options may not mean that we can recognize the ancestor when we find it. We need to know more about the socioecology of apes before they become extinct. And let us get out and find more fossils (especially protogorillas and protochimpanzees). But when we do, do not be surprised if controversy does not go away.

Acknowledgments. I have kept as closely as possible to the text of the lecture in order to save some of its tone and time. Fuller and better documented accounts are referenced or are in preparation. I thank John Barry, Kay Behrensmeyer, Andrew Hill, Steve Ward, Michael Rose, Maryellen Ruvolo, Lawrence Martin, Peter Andrews, Bob Martin, Alan Walker, Richard Leakey, Louis de Bonis, Mahmood Raza, Ibrahim Shah, Eric Delson, Michael Brunet, Larry Flynn, Louis Jacobs, Bernard Wood, Yves Coppens.

References Cited

Andrews, Peter

1978   A Revision of the Miocene Hominoidae of East Africa. Bulletin of the British Museum of Natural History (Geology) 30: 85–224.

1985   Family Group Systematics and Evolution among Catarrhine Primates. *In* Ancestors. Eric Delson, ed. Pp. 14–22. New York: Alan R. Liss.

Andrews, P., and J. E. Cronin

1982   The Relationship of *Sivapithecus* and *Ramapithecus* and the Evolution of the Orangutan. Nature 297:541–546.

Andrews, P., and I. Tekkaya

1980   A Revision of the Turkish Miocene Hominoid *Sivapithecus meteai*. Palaeontology 23:85–95.

Andrews, P., and A. Walker

1976   The Primate and Other Fauna from Fort Ternan, Kenya. *In* Human Origins. G. Ll. Isaac and E. R. McCown, eds. Pp. 279–304. California: Staples.

Barry, John C., Noye M. Johnson, Mahmood S. Raza, and Louis L. Jacobs

1985   Neogene Mammalian Faunal Change in Southern Asia: Correlations with Climatic, Tectonic, and Eustatic Events. Geology 13:637–640.

Benveniste, Raoul

1985   The Contributions of Retroviruses to the Study of Mammalian Evolution. *In* Molecular Evolutionary Genetics. Ross J. MacIntyre, ed. Pp. 359–417. New York: Plenum.

Bishop, W. W., J. A. Miller, and F. J. Fitch

1969   New Potassium-Argon Age Determinations Relevant to the Miocene Fossil Mammal Sequence in East Africa. American Journal of Science 267:669–699.

Clark, W. Le Gros, and L. S. B. Leakey
1951 The Miocene Hominoidea of East Africa. British Museum (Natural History) Fossil Mammals of Africa 1:117.

Cronin, John E.
1975 Molecular Systematics of the Order Primates. Ph.D. dissertation, University of California-Berkeley.

Darwin, Charles
1871 The Descent of Man, and Selection in Relation to Sex. London: John Murray.

de Bonis, L., D. Johanson, J. Melentis, and T. White
1981 Variations Metriques de la deuture chez les Hominoides primitifs: comparaison entre *Australopithecus afarensis* et *Ouranopithecus macedoniensis*. Comptes Rendus des Academies des Sciences, Paris 292:373–376.

de Bonis, L., and J. Melentis
1977 Les primates hominoides du Vallesien de Macedoine (Grece). Etude de la machoire inferieure. Geobios 10:849–885.
1978 Les primates hominoides du Miocene superieur de Macedoine. Annals de Paleontologie (Vertebres) 64:185–202.
1985 Le place du genre *Ouranopithecus* dans l'evolution de hominides. Comptes Rendus des Academies des Sciences, Paris 300:429–432.

Farris, James S.
1985 Distance Data Revisited. Cladistics 6:67–85.

Filler, A. G.
1981 Anatomical Specializations in the Hominoid Lumbar Region. American Journal of Physical Anthropology 54:218.

Fleagle, J., J. Stern, W. Jungers, R. Susman, A. K. Vangor, and J. P. Welks
1981 Climbing: A Biochemical Link with Brachiatian and with Bipedalism. Symposia of the Zoological Society of London 48:359–375.

Gingerich, Phillip D.
1985 Nonlinear Molecular Clocks and Ape-Human Divergence Times. *In* Hominid Evolution: Past, Present, and Future. Phillip V. Tobias, ed. Pp. 411–416. New York: Alan R. Liss.

Goodman, Morris
1963 Serological Analysis of the Systematics of Recent Hominoids. Human Biology 35:377–424.

Goodman, M., and R. E. Tashian, eds.
1975 Molecular Anthropology. New York: Plenum.

Gould, Stephen Jay, and Elisabeth S. Vrba
1982 Exaptation: A Missing Term in the Science of Form. Paleobiology 8:4–15.

Hamburg, David, and Elizabeth McCown
1982 The Great Apes. California: Benjamin Cummings.

Ishida, Hidemi, Martin Pickford, Hideo Nakaya, and Yoshihiko Nakano
1984 Fossil Anthropoids from Nachola and Samburu Hills, Samburu District Northern Kenya. African Study Monographs, #2: Supplementary Issue. Kyoto University.

Kelley, Jay, and David Pilbeam
1986 The Dryopithecines: Taxonomy, Comparative Anatomy, and Phylogeny of Miocene Large Hominoids. (In press).

Kluge, A. G.
1983 Cladistics and the Classification of the Great Apes. *In* New Interpretations of Ape and Human Ancestry. R. L. Ciochon and R. S. Corruccini, eds. Pp. 151–177. New York: Plenum.

Kretzoi, M.
1975 New *Ramapithecus* and *Phiopithecus* from the Lower Pliocene of Rudabanya in North Eastern Hungary. Nature 257: 578–581.

Leakey, R. E. F., and A. Walker
1985 New Higher Primates from the Early Miocene of Buluk, Kenya. Nature 318:173–174.

Lipson, Susan
1985 A Phylogenetic Analysis of the Palatofacial Morphology of *Sivapithecus Indicus*. Ph.D. dissertation, Harvard University.

Martin, L.
1981 New Specimens of *Proconsul* from Koru, Kenya. Journal of Human Evolution 10:139–150.

1985 Significance of Enamel Thickness in Hominoid Evolution. Nature 314:260–263.

Nei, Masatoshi, J. C. Stephens, and N. Saitou
1985 Methods for Computing the Standard Errors of Branching Points in an Evolutionary Tree and Their Application to Molecular Data from Humans and Apes. Molecular Biology and Evolution 2:66–85.

Nei, Masatoshi, and Fumio Tajimo
1985 Evolutionary Change of Restriction Cleavage Sites and Phylogenetic Inference for Man and Apes. Molecular Biology and Evolution 2:189–205.

Pickford, M.
1981 Preliminary Miocene Mammalian Biostratigraphy for Western Kenya. Journal of Human Evolution 10:73–98.

1982 New Higher Primate Fossils from the Middle Miocene Deposits at Majiwa and Kaloma, Western Kenya. American Journal of Physical Anthropology 58: 1–19.

Pilbeam, David
1982 New Hominoid Skull Material from the Miocene of Pakistan. Nature 295:232–234.

1985 Patterns of Hominoid Evolution. *In* Ancestors. Eric Delson, ed. Pp. 51–59. New York: Alan R. Liss.

Pilbeam, D., M. D. Rose, C. Badgley, and B. Lipschutz
1980 Miocene Hominoids from Pakistan. Postilla 181:1–94.

Pilbeam, D., and E. L. Simons
1965 Some Problems of Hominoid Classification. American Scientist 53:237–259.

Raza, S. M., J. C. Barry, D. Pilbeam, M. D. Rose, S. M. I. Shah, and S. Ward
1983 New Hominoid Primates from the Middle Miocene Chinji Formation, Potwar Plateau, Pakistan. Nature 305:52–54.

Rodman, Peter S.
1984 Foraging and Social Systems of Orangutans and Chimpanzees. In Adaptations for Foraging in Nonhuman Primates. Peter S. Rodman and John G. H. Cant, eds. Pp. 134–159. New York: Columbia University Press.

Rodman, Peter S., and Henry W. McHenry
1980 Bioenergetics and the Origin of Hominid Bipedalism. American Journal of Physical Anthropology 52:103–106.

Rose, M. D.
1983 Miocene Hominoid Postcranial Morphology: Monkeylike, Ape-like, Neither, or Both? In New Interpretations of Ape and Human Ancestry. R. L. Ciochon and R. S. Corruccini, eds. Pp. 405–417. New York: Plenum.
1984a Food Acquisition and the Evolution of Positional Behavior: The Case of Bipedalism. In Food Acquisition and Processing in Primates. D. J. Chivers, B. A. Wood, A. Bilsborough, eds. Pp. 509–524. New York: Plenum.
1984b Hominoid Postcranial Specimens from the Middle Miocene Chinji Formation, Pakistan. Journal of Human Evolution 13:503–516.

Ruvolo, Maryellen, and Temple F. Smith
1986 Phylogeny and DNA-DNA Hybridization. Journal of Molecular Evolution. (In press).

Sarich, Vincent M.
1983 Retrospective on Hominoid Macromolecular Systematics. In New Interpretations of Ape and Human Ancestry. R. L. Ciochon and R. S. Corruccini, eds. Pp. 137–150. New York: Plenum.

Sarich, V., and J. Cronin
1975 Molecular Systematics of the Primates. In Molecular Anthropology. M. Goodman and R. E. Tashian, eds. Pp. 141–169. New York: Plenum.

Sarich, V., and A. Wilson
1967 Rates of Albumin Evolution in Primates. Proceedings of the National Academy of Sciences 58:142–148.

Schwartz, J. H.
1984 The Evolutionary Relationships of Man and Orangutans. Nature 308:501–505.

Sibley, C., and J. Ahlquist

1984 The Phylogeny of Hominoid Primates as Indicated by DNA-DNA Hybridization. Journal of Molecular Evolution 20:2–15.

Simons, E. L., and D. R. Pilbeam

1965 Preliminary Revision of the Dryopithecinae. Folia primatologia 3:81–152.

Susman, Randall L., ed.

1984 The Pygmy Chimpanzees. New York: Plenum.

Susman, Randall L., Jack T. Stern, and William L. Jungers

1985 Locomotor Adaptations in the Hadar Hominids. In Ancestors. Eric Delson, ed. Pp. 184–192. New York: Alan R. Liss.

Teaford, M. F., and A. C. Walker

1984 Quantitative Differences in Dental Microwear between Primate Species with Different Diets and a Comment on the Presumed Diet of Sivapithecus. American Journal of Physical Anthropology 64:191–199.

Templeton, Alan R.

1983 Phylogenetic Inference from Restriction Endonuclease Cleavage Site Maps with Particular Reference to the Evolution of Humans and the Apes. Evolution 37:221–224.

1985 The Phylogeny of the Hominoid Primates: A Statistical Analysis of the DNA-DNA Hybridization Data. Molecular Biology and Evolution 2:420–433.

Tuttle, R. H.

1967 Knuckle-Walking and the Evolution of Hominoid Hands. The American Journal of Physical Anthropology 26:171–206.

Vrba, E. S., L. H. Burckle, G. H. Denton, and T. C. Partridge

1985 Palaeoclimate and Evolution I. South African Journal of Science 81:224–275.

Walker, A., D. Falk, R. Smith, and M. Pickford.

1983 The Skull of Proconsul africanus: Reconstruction and Cranial Capacity. Nature 305:525–527.

Walker, A. C., and M. Pickford

1983 New Post-Cranial Fossils of Proconsul africanus and Proconsul nyanzae. In New Interpretations of Ape and Human Ancestry. R. L. Ciochon and R. S. Corruccini, eds. Pp. 325–351. New York: Plenum.

Walker, A., and M. Rose

1968 Fossil Hominoid Vertebra from the Miocene of Uganda. Nature 217:980–981.

Ward, S. C., and W. H. Kimbel

1983 Subnasal Alveolar Morphology and the Systematic Position of Sivapithecus. American Journal of Physical Anthropology 61:157–171.

Ward, S. C., and D. R. Pilbeam

1983 Maxillofacial Morphology of Miocene Hominoids from Africa and Indo-Pakistan. In New Interpretations of Ape and Human Ancestry. R. L. Ciochon and R. S. Corruccini, eds. Pp. 211–238. New York: Plenum.

Washburn, S. L.

1968 The Study of Human Evolution. The Condon Lectures. Eugene: University of Oregon Press.

Wiley, E. O.

1981 Phylogenetics. New York: Wiley.

Wrangham, Richard

1982 Mutualism, Kinship and Social Evolution. *In* Current Problems in Sociobiology. King's College Sociobiology Group, eds. Pp. 269–290. Cambridge: Cambridge University Press.

1986 Ecology and Social Relationships of Two Species of Chimpanzee. *In* Ecological and Social Relationships in Two Species of Chimpanzee. D. I. Rubenstein and R. W. Wrangham, eds. Princeton, NJ: Princeton University Press. (In press.)

Xu, Qinghua, and Qingwu Lu

1979 The Mandibles of *Ramapithecus* and *Sivapithecus* from Lufeng, Yunnan. Vertebrata PalAsiatica 17:1–13.

Culture as Consensus:

A Theory of Culture and Informant Accuracy

A. Kimball Romney, Susan C. Weller, and William H. Batchelder

VOL. 88, 1986, 313–338

The concept of culture has long been the central focus of study in anthropology. Writing in the early 1950s Kroeber (1952:139) observed that "The most significant accomplishment of anthropology in the first half of the twentieth century has been the extension and clarification of the concept of culture." More recently Goodenough (1964:36) has asserted that "the anthropologist's basic task, on which all the rest of his endeavor depends, is to describe specific cultures adequately. . . . Culture, being what people have to learn as distinct from their biological heritage, must consist of the end product of learning: knowledge, in a most general, if relative, sense of the term." In this paper we present a way of describing and measuring the amount and distribution of cultural knowledge among a group of informants in an objective way.

We are reminded of the need for an objective approach to culture and ethnography by the recent controversy generated by the publication of Derek Freeman's book, *Margaret Mead and Samoa* (1983). In the introduction to a special section of the *American Anthropologist*, Ivan Brady (1983:908) commented that "The book has been reviewed all over the world and has raised questions of authenticity and viability in ethnographic research. . . . One broad but undetermined topic of enduring value that emerges from these essays, it seems to me, is the problem of how anthropologists get to know what they know and write in the first place." The model provided in this paper is an attempt to make objective the criteria by which we might measure our confidence in inferring correct answers to cultural questions, i.e., to help answer the epistemological question of "How do we know when we know?"

Despite examples of differing views of ethnographers such as Mead and Freeman in Samoa and Redfield and Lewis in Tepoztlan, Mexico, anthropologists may tend to underestimate the probable effects of the ethnographer in selecting and shaping the data and in forming impressions contained in the final ethnographic report. This points to our need to find more objective ways to investigate culture.

The assumption in fieldwork has been that the investigator is a valid and reliable instrument and that the informant provides valid and reliable information. We suggest that informants' statements should be treated as probabilistic in character. When, for example, an informant states that the name of an object is "X," we should assume that there is some probability (that we can estimate) that the statement is correct. This probability may be close to 1 in the case of a very knowledgeable informant and close to 0 in the case of an uninformed informant. The more informants there are who agree (when questioned independently) on an answer the more likely it is to be the correct cultural response.

Informant interviews are a main source of data for anthropology. Evaluation and analysis of such data, including theory construction and testing, constitute a vital part of the research activity of the profession. Frequent disagreement among informants confronts the investigator with two major problems: first, how can the "cultural knowledge" of different informants be estimated, and, second, how can the "correct" answers to specific questions be inferred and with what degree of confidence? This paper supplies a formal approach that answers these two questions for a variety of cultural information domains that lend themselves to systematic question formats, e.g., true-false, multiple-choice, fill-in-the-blank.

The aspect of culture that our theory attempts to account for is the part that is stored in the minds of its members. Roberts (1964:438–439) has said that "It is possible to regard all culture as information and to view any single culture as an 'information economy' in which information is received or created, stored, retrieved, transmitted, utilized, and even lost. . . . In any culture information is stored in the minds of its members and, to a greater or lesser extent, in artifacts." In a similar vein, D'Andrade has developed the notion of culture as a shared and learned "information pool."

> It is not just physical objects which are products of culture. . . . Behavior environments, consisting of complex messages and signals, rights and duties, and roles and institutions, are a culturally constituted reality which is a prod-

uct of our socially transmitted information pool. . . . In saying that an object —
either a physical object like a desk, or a more abstract object like a talk or a
theorem — is a product of culture, I mean that the cultural pool contains the
information which defines what the object is, tells how to construct the object, and prescribes how the object is to be used. Without culture, we could
not have or use such things. [1981:180]

The size of the cultural information pool virtually dictates that knowledge be distributed and shared. Roberts points out that there is a limit to
what an individual or combination of individuals can learn and that "it is
safe to assert that no tribal culture is sufficiently small in inventory to be
stored in one brain" (1964:439). D'Andrade, in a closely reasoned discussion, places some loose bounds on the possible size of the information
pool that an individual may control. "Upper limits can be obtained by
considering time constraints; e.g., to learn ten million chunks would
require that one learn more than a chunk a minute during every waking
hour from birth to the age of twenty" (1981:180). The large size of the
information pool is also related to the division of labor in society. "One of
the characteristics of human society is that there is a major division of
labor in who knows what" (D'Andrade 1981:180). Clearly we cannot
study all of culture but rather we must have a strategy for sampling
smaller, coherent segments of the total information pool constituting
culture. We also need to make a provision for the possible unequal
distribution of knowledge among "experts" or specialists and nonspecialists in a society.

One segment of culture that provides a reasonable focus derives
from Kroeber's (1948) classic discussion of "systemic culture pattern."
Systemic culture patterns are characterized as coherent subsystems of
knowledge that tend to cohere and persist as a unit limited primarily to
one aspect of culture. A systemic culture pattern has sufficient internal
organization that it may diffuse as a unit. As examples, Kroeber (1948)
discusses plow agriculture and the alphabet. Roberts and his colleagues
have studied such diverse systemic culture patterns as eight-ball pool
(Roberts and Chick 1979), pilot error (Roberts, Golder, and Chick
1980), women's trapshooting (Roberts and Nuttrass 1980), and tennis
(Roberts et al. 1981). They have demonstrated that the relevant behavior
events for each of these domains are coded into what Roberts has called
"high-concordance codes" that cultural participants understand and use
with ease.

Each systemic culture pattern may be thought of as having an associated semantic domain that provides a way of classifying and talking about the elements in the culture pattern. A semantic domain may be defined as an organized set of words (or unitary lexemes), all on the same level of contrast, that jointly refer to a single conceptual sphere, e.g., a systemic culture pattern. The words in a semantic domain derive their meaning, in part, from their position in a mutually interdependent system reflecting the way in which a given language classifies the relevant conceptual sphere. This definition corresponds to Frake's discussion on levels of contrast (1961). Examples of semantic domains include kinship terms, linguistic "tags" for the behavior events in games like tennis (Roberts et al. 1981), manioc names in Aguaruna (Boster 1986), disease terms and characteristics (Weller 1983, 1984a, 1984b), Buang clan membership (Sankoff 1971), and color terminology.

A recent example of ethnographic data that could be analyzed by our theory was collected by Boster (1986) on Aguaruna manioc classification. He asked informants to identify growing manioc plants in a garden. "Data were collected by guiding informants through the gardens, stopping at each plant and asking, *waji mama aita*, 'What kind of manioc is this?' " Boster concluded that the more an informant agreed with others the more knowledge that informant had about manioc. Since he was able to assess differences among informants as to cultural knowledge, he was able to establish that women knew more than men and that women in the same kin and residential groups were more similar to each other in knowledge than nonrelated women.

In a test-retest analysis he found that "within informant agreement is strongly correlated with between informant agreement" (Boster 1986). Since the informants who agree with the group the most on the first test are those who agree most with themselves on the retest, Boster argues that agreement among informants indicates knowledge. The results, he says, "helped confirm the inference of cultural knowledge from consensus." We agree with Boster that knowledge can be inferred from consensus.

The aim of this paper is to derive and test a formal mathematical model for the analysis of informant consensus on questionnaire data that will simultaneously provide the following information: first, an estimate of the cultural competence or knowledge of each informant, and second, an estimate of the correct answer to each question asked of the informants.

The plan for the remainder of the paper is as follows: first, after a brief, informal verbal description of the theory we will present the formal mathematical model for the analysis of true-false, multiple-choice, and fill-in-the-blank profile data. Derivations are kept as simple as possible. Further technical details on the model and related models can be found in Batchelder and Romney (1986). Applications of earlier informal versions of the theory can be found in Romney and Weller (1984), Weller (1984b), and Weller, Romney, and Orr (1986). Second, we apply the model to quasi-experimental data consisting of a general information test where answers are known a priori to illustrate how the model works. We also analyze a small subset of informants and discuss sample size requirements of the model. Third, we apply the model to some field data on disease classification collected in Guatemala. This illustrates the application of the model in a naturally occurring situation where the answers are not known a priori and the results may have important theoretical implications. Finally, we will discuss the implications of the model and relate it to some of the current research concerns in anthropology.

Description and Development of the Formal Model
The central idea in our theory is the use of the pattern of agreement or consensus among informants to make inferences about their differential competence in knowledge of the shared information pool constituting culture. We assume that the correspondence between the answers of any two informants is a function of the extent to which each is correlated with the truth (Nunnally 1978:chap. 6). Suppose, for example, that we had a "perfect set" of interview questions (cultural information test) concerning the game of tennis. Suppose further that we had two sets of informants: tennis players and non–tennis players. We would expect that the tennis players would agree more among themselves as to the answers to questions than would the non–tennis players. Players with complete knowledge about the game would answer questions correctly with identical answers or maximal consensus, while players with little knowledge of the game would not. An insight like this one allowed Boster to identify those informants with the most cultural knowledge in his study of manioc plants.

We are assuming that there exists a "high concordance code" of a socially shared information pool concerning tennis, that informants vary in the extent to which they know this culture, and that each informant answers independently of each other informant. Once we know how "competent" each informant is we can figure out the answers to the questions by weighting each informant's input and aggregating to the most likely answer. That is, we put more weight on the more knowledgeable informants than the less knowledgeable ones. The model we develop is simply an elaboration and formalization of these ideas and their implications.

Although the model and associated data analysis methods are new, we incorporate derivations and concepts from previous well-established theories. The major sources of concepts include the following: the overall structure as well as more general ideas are influenced by signal detection theory (Green and Swets 1966). Approaches used by psychometricians in test construction to study items were adapted to apply to informants rather than items (Lord and Novick 1968; Nunnally 1978). There are structural identities to latent structure analysis (Lazarsfeld and Henry 1968) although again our applications are to informants rather than questions. The relevance of the Condorcet jury trial problem is also important (e.g., Grofman, Feld, and Owen 1983). Techniques common in decision analysis like Bayesian estimation are common in many fields and can be found in any mathematical statistics book (e.g., Hogg and Craig 1978).

At this point we need to introduce some definitions and notation in order to present the formal model. We start with an informant by question Response Profile Data Matrix of the following form:

$$
(1) \qquad \mathbf{X} =
\begin{array}{c}
\text{Informant} \\
 \\
 \\
 \\
 \\

\end{array}
\begin{array}{c}
1 \\ 2 \\ \cdot \\ \cdot \\ i \\ \cdot \\ \cdot \\ N
\end{array}
\overset{\displaystyle \text{Question}}{
\begin{bmatrix}
X_{11} & X_{12} & \cdot & \cdot & X_{1k} & \cdot & \cdot & X_{1M} \\
X_{21} & X_{22} & \cdot & \cdot & X_{2k} & & & X_{2M} \\
\cdot \\
\cdot \\
X_{i1} & X_{i2} & \cdot & \cdot & X_{ik} & \cdot & \cdot & X_{iM} \\
\cdot \\
\cdot \\
X_{N1} & X_{N2} & \cdot & \cdot & X_{Nk} & \cdot & \cdot & X_{NM}
\end{bmatrix}
}
$$

where X_{ik} is the ith informant's response to the kth question. There are N informants and M questions. The model assumes a questionnaire where each question has L possible response alternatives with only one "correct" answer. In a true-false questionnaire $L = 2$ and the response X_{ik} would be "true" or "false" (coded, perhaps, as 1's and 0's, respectively). In a multiple-choice questionnaire, for example, there might be four alternatives so that $L = 4$ and the possible responses X_{ik} might be coded as "A," "B," "C," or "D." A fill-in-the-blank questionnaire can be thought of as a special case of the model with a very large value of L, and X_{ik} would be the actual, possibly edited, written response (possibly blank) of the ith informant to the kth question.

Our notational conventions are:

A. Response Profile Data. $\mathbf{X} = (X_{ik})_{N \times M}$ where X_{ik} is the subject i's response to question k coded as described above.

B. Answer Key. $\mathbf{Z} = (Z_k)_{1 \times M}$ where Z_k is the code for the correct answer to question k (initially unknown to us).

C. Performance Profile Data. $\mathbf{Y} = (Y_{ik})_{N \times M'}$ where

$$Y_{ik} = \begin{cases} 1 \text{ if subject } i \text{ is correct on item } k \\ \\ 0 \text{ if subject } i \text{ is wrong on item } k. \end{cases}$$

D. Response Bias.[1] g_{il} is a bias to respond with an alternative l when informant i does not know answer. The range of g_{il} is between 0 and 1. No bias is $1/L$, e.g., in true-false a bias of $1/2$ means that if the informant does not know the answer to the question that they will choose either alternative with equal probability. In the derivations below we assume no bias.

E. Cultural Competence. D_i is the probability that informant i knows (not guesses) the answer to a question, where $0 \leq D_i \leq 1$, and negative D_i's are not allowed by model. This is a theoretical parameter of the model and cannot be observed directly. We assume each informant has the same D_i for all questions.

Since the notation is crucial to understanding what follows we will review and expand on the above. The response profile data $\mathbf{X}$ is the original raw data from the interviews, and it simply refers to the whole profile data matrix in Eq. 1 consisting of N rows of informants and M columns of questions. The answer key ($\mathbf{Z}$) can be estimated from the model but it is not known a priori, it consists of a single vector or line of data that contains the code for the correct answer. In anthropological work we usually do not know the correct answers a priori and the model provides a method for inferring the answer key from the response profile data. When the response data has been recoded as correct or incorrect based upon an answer key we call it performance profile data denoted by $\mathbf{Y}$. In psychological test theory it is usually assumed that the investigator knows the answers to the questions while in anthropological fieldwork we do not normally know the answers a priori and hence the need for the model.

The assumptions of the formal model may be stated as follows:

Assumption 1. Common Truth. *There is a fixed answer key "applicable" to all informants, that is, each item k has a correct answer,* Z_k, k = 1,2,. . .,M. This simply states the assumption that the informants all come from a common culture, i.e., that whatever the cultural reality is, it is the same for all informants in the sample.

Assumption 2. Local Independence. *The informant-item response random variables satisfy conditional independence, that is,*

$$(2) \quad \Pr[(X_{ik})_{N \times M} \mid (Z_k)_{1 \times M}] = \prod_{i = 1}^{N} \prod_{k = 1}^{M} \Pr(X_{ik} \mid Z_k)$$

for all possible response profiles (X_{ik}) and the correct answer key (Z_k). This assumes that each informant's answers are given independently of each other informant. The correlations among informant's answer patterns are an artifact of the extent to which each is correlated with the "answer key," i.e., **Z**. To the extent that the data fit the model correlations among informants will be high if computed on the response profile data but close to 0 if computed on the performance profile data.

Assumption 3. Homogeneity of Items. *Each informant i has a fixed "cultural competence,"* D_i, *over all questions.* This is a strong assumption that says that questions are all of the same difficulty level. In some situations one might want to make a weaker assumption: namely, that the informants who do better on one subset of the questions will do better on another subset of questions. This generalization might be called the monotonicity assumption and is related to ensuring that the questions are drawn from a coherent domain. Thus, for example, if the tennis experts do better than the nonexperts on one part of the questions concerning tennis, they should to better on another part concerning tennis. The analysis, however, has proven to be very robust in practice under the more restricted homogeneity assumption.

We might note that these assumptions define the ground rules for the operation of our model. They also make it possible to make formal derivations in mathematical terms. It is important to stress that not all response profile data will conform to these assumptions. They require, for example, that all informants are positively correlated with each other (except for sampling variability). In effect this means that our theory assumes that if two people are members of the same culture that they are responding to the questions in terms of a common understanding, i.e., the culture is similar for both informants. By similar we do not mean they will respond identically since there will be misunderstanding of the questions, random guesses, etc. The model measures the shared knowledge of the culture. True negative correlations among informants would mean that they do not have common knowledge in the domain sampled by the questions. Thus when the empirical data show that any of the assumptions are violated then the model does not apply and we infer one of the following: (1) we are not dealing with a culturally defined domain, (2) the informants do not share common knowledge of the cultural domain, or that (3) something else has gone wrong. We will give an example of a violation of the assumptions later.

The formal derivations of the model will be presented in the following steps: first, we derive a method for estimating D_i, the cultural competence, of each informant from the data in the response profile matrix. This estimation is made on the basis of the pattern of shared knowledge (as indexed by proportion of matched responses among all pairs of informants), using the notion that the more consensus the more knowledge. Second, we show how to make inferences as to the correct answers together with statistical confidence levels based on an application of Bayes' Theorem in probability theory (for example, Mosteller, Rourke, and Thomas 1961:146). The model we present is a special case of a more general family of models (Batchelder and Romney 1986) and is referred to there as the High Threshold Model.

Derivations from the Model

We now turn to the task of deriving the cultural competence of the informants from the proportion of matches among them. The parameter D_i is informant i's cultural competence, namely, the probability that informant i "knows" the correct answer to any item ($0 \leq D_i \leq 1$). If the informant does not know the correct answer (with probability $[1 - D_i]$), then they guess the answer with probability $1/L$ of a correct answer, where $(1 - D_i)$ is the probability of not knowing the answer and L is the number of alternative answers to the question. For example, assume an informant's competence is .7 ($D_i = .7$) for a five-item multiple-choice questionnaire. In addition to expecting that the informant will get .7 of the questions correct we would also expect the informant to get some of the .3 ($1 - D_i$) questions correct by guessing. Namely, $1/L$ or $1/5$ of the remaining .3 of the questions or $(1 - D_i)/L$, i.e., $3 \times 1/5 = .06$ would be guessed correctly. We add this to the .7 giving a total expected correct of

.76. More generally the probability of any question k being answered correctly by any informant i is given by

(3) $\quad \mathrm{Pr}(Y_{ik} = 1) = D_i + (1-D_i)/L,$

and the probability of answering incorrectly is given by

$\mathrm{Pr}(Y_{ik} = 0) = (1-D_i)(L-1)/L.$

Note that even if we knew the proportion of questions the informant got "correct" (which we do not usually know) we could not observe the effects of the theoretical parameter D_i directly because the proportion correct includes the proportion the informant got right by guessing. In case the correct answer key is known it is easy to simply count the number of correct responses and divide by M, the number of questions, to obtain the proportion of correct responses T_i for informant i. In order to obtain an estimate of D_i we use the empirically observed T_i in place of $\mathrm{Pr}(Y_{ik} = 1)$ in Eq. 3 and solve for D_i to obtain

(4) $\quad \hat{D}_i = (LT_i - 1)/(L-1),$

where the hat over the D_i is the usual convention to indicate that it is an estimate of the underlying competency D_i. All Eq. 4 does is to adjust the proportion correct for guessing, and this is used routinely in aptitude testing by ETS and other agencies.

The anthropologist, unlike the test-theorist, does not know the correct answers in advance so that we cannot use Eq. 4 to estimate the D_i. Fortunately, and perhaps surprisingly, it is still possible to obtain estimates of the D_i's by examining the proportion of matches among all pairs of informants. The derivation of the procedure follows.

Assume two informants, i and j, whose probabilities for a correct response, from Eq. 3, are:

for informant i,

$\mathrm{Pr}(\text{correct}) = D_i + (1-D_i)/L,$

and for informant j,

$\mathrm{Pr}(\text{correct}) = D_j + (1-D_j)/L.$

Now we want to know the probability of i and j matching responses on any question k in terms of the competence, D_i and D_j, of each. The possible ways of matching are:

1. Both know the answer to the item with probability $D_i D_j$, that is, the probability that i knows the item times the probability that j knows the item.

2. One informant knows the answer to the item and the other guesses the item correctly. This occurs in two ways: i knows the item and j guesses correctly with probability $D_i (1 - D_j)/L$ and j knows the item and i guesses correctly with probability $D_j(1 - D_i)/L$.

3. Neither knows the item but both guess the same response[2] to the item which occurs with probability

$$(1 - D_i)(1 - D_j) \sum_{l=1}^{L} (1/L)^2 = (1 - D_j)(1 - D_j)/L.$$

Let us introduce a random variable for matches,

$$M_{ij,k} = \begin{cases} 1 \text{ if } i \text{ and } j \text{ match on question } k \\ \\ 0 \text{ otherwise.} \end{cases}$$

Then adding all the four possibilities we get

$$\Pr(M_{ij,k} = 1) = \\ D_i D_j + D_i(1 - D_j)/L + D_j(1 - D_i)/L + (1 - D_i)(1 - D_j)/L,$$

which reduces algebraically to

$$(5) \quad \Pr(M_{ij,k} = 1) = D_i D_j + [1 - D_i D_j]/L.$$

Since Eq. 5 does not have the question subscript k on the right-hand side, we can replace $\Pr(M_{ij,k} = 1)$ by the observed proportion of matches, M_{ij}, from the data on all questions and solve for $D_i D_j$ to obtain an estimate of $D_i D_j$ given by

$$(6) \quad \overset{\wedge}{D_i D_j} = (LM_{ij} - 1)/(L - 1).$$

Note that Eq. 6[3] is a close parallel to Eq. 4. Unlike Eq. 4, however, Eq. 6 cannot be used directly to provide separate estimates of D_i and D_j because there are two unknown competencies and only one equation. The key to the method of estimating competencies lies in the fact that the response profile matrix $\mathbf{X}$ provides $N(N-1)/2$ independent equations like Eq. 6, one for each distinct pair of informants. Thus, there are

$N(N-1)/2$ equations in terms of N unknown competencies, so that as long as $N \geq 3$, there are more knowns than unknowns.

In order to write out the entire set of equations for solution, we define

$$(7) \quad M^*_{ij} = (LM_{ij}-1)/(L-1),$$

which is an empirical point estimate of the proportion of matches between informants i and j *corrected for guessing* (on the assumption of no bias).

The set of equations can be written in matrix notation as follows:

$$(8) \quad \begin{pmatrix} D^2_1 & M^*_{12} & \cdots & M^*_{1j} & \cdots & M^*_{1N} \\ M^*_{21} & D^2_2 & \cdots & M^*_{2j} & \cdots & M^*_{2N} \\ \cdot & \cdot & & \cdot & & \cdot \\ M^*_{i1} & M^*_{i2} & \cdots & M^*_{ij} & \cdots & M^*_{iN} \\ \cdot & \cdot & & \cdot & & \cdot \\ \cdot & \cdot & & \cdot & & \cdot \\ M^*_{N1} & M^*_{N2} & \cdots & M^*_{Nj} & \cdots & D^2_N \end{pmatrix} = \begin{pmatrix} D_1 \\ D_2 \\ \cdot \\ D_i \\ \cdot \\ \cdot \\ D_N \end{pmatrix} (D_1, D_2 \ldots, D_j, \ldots, D_N)$$

where, of course, $M^*_{ij} = M^*_{ji}$ for all pairs of informants i and j.

Equation 8 represents an overspecified set of equations and because of sampling variability it is unlikely that they can be solved exactly. However, it is possible to obtain an approximate solution to Eq. 8 and thereby obtain estimates of the individual competencies D_i. The general approach to such problems is to select some criteria of goodness of fit, say least squares, and then to calculate estimates $\hat{D}_i$ that minimize the sum of the squared discrepancies between observed and predicted values of $\hat{M}^*_{ij}$. A least squares fit of the equation above is directly obtainable through the use of a version of factor analysis called the minimum residual method, first described by Comrey (1962). A version that accomplishes the same end is available on SPSS in the PA2 option (Nie et al. 1975:480). In our application we specify just one factor that gives direct estimates of the D_i for each individual. If the assumptions hold there should only be a single factor so that the first latent root should be large with respect to all other latent roots (see Lord and Novick 1968:381–382). We will discuss the criteria for fitting the model later in the paper. In any event, this procedure gives us the estimates of each informant's cultural competence D_i in terms that can be interpreted as the proportion of the questions they actually "know."

We now turn to the problem of how to infer the correct answers to

Table 1. Illustrative data for computing a posteriori probabilities for a single question given two informants with competencies of .8 and .2, respectively

Response pattern	Probability if correct answer		A posteriori probability	
	is true	is false	for true	for false
1 1	.54	.04	.931	.069
1 0	.36	.06	.857	.143
0 1	.06	.36	.143	.857
0 0	.04	.54	.069	.931

the question. We give a formal presentation of a Bayes' Theorem approach to the problem in Appendix A. Now we give an example meant to give an intuitive feel for the approach to be taken.

To illustrate our approach, suppose we have only two informants, 1 and 2, and one true-false question. Suppose we know the competencies to be $D_1 = .8$ and $D_2 = .2$. If we know nothing at all, our a priori probabilities that the question is correctly answered true or false are .5 and .5, respectively. However, when we know the informants' responses, we are in a position to compute a posteriori estimates of the probabilities of the correct answer being true or false. The basic information is given in Table 1. The four logically possible response patterns involving two informants and one question are presented, where 1 codes a "true" response and 0 a "false" response. The probability of each pattern is computed on the assumption the correct answer is "true" and on the assumption the correct answer is "false." For example, assume the correct answer is "true," then the probability of both informants answering true (response pattern [1,1]) is the probability of the first informant being correct times the probability of the second informant being correct. This is computed from the competence using Eq. 3 with $L = 2$. Thus we have $(.8 + [1 - .8]/2) \times (.2 + [1 - .2]/2) = .54$ as shown in Table 1 for a response pattern of $(1,1)$ where the correct answer is "true."

Bayes' Theorem in elementary probability theory provides the machinery for computing the a posteriori probabilities of true and false, respectively, given the a priori probabilities and the "evidence" of the informants' responses. Let X_1 and X_2 be the responses of the two informants, $Pr(T)$ and $Pr(F)$ be the a priori probabilities, and $Pr(T \mid <X_1, X_2>)$, $Pr(F \mid <X_1, X_2>)$ the desired a posteriori probabilities. Then Bayes' Theorem, adapted to our case, requires

(9) $Pr(T \mid <X_1, X_2>) = \dfrac{Pr(<X_1, X_2> \mid T)Pr(T)}{Pr(<X_1, X_2> \mid T)Pr(T) + Pr(<X_1, X_2> \mid F)Pr(F)}$,

where, for example, $\Pr(<X_1, X_2> \mid T)$ is the conditional probability of the evidence if the correct answer is true. Columns 2 and 3 in Table 1 give the conditional probabilities of the evidence given the correct answer is T or F, respectively, and columns 4 and 5 give the a posteriori probabilities from Eq. 9. For example, suppose $X_1 = 1$ and $X_2 = 1$, then

$$ \Pr(T \mid <1, 1>) = \frac{.54 \times 1/2}{.54 \times 1/2 + .04 \times 1/2} = .931 $$

which is the first entry in column 4. The rest of the values in columns 4 and 5 are obtained similarly from Eq. 9 and from the fact that $\Pr(F \mid <X_1, X_2>) = 1 - \Pr(T \mid <X_1, X_2>)$.

In Appendix A, the approach illustrated by this sample example is extended to cover the general case. This requires extension in the following ways: (1) it must handle the case of an arbitrary number of possible answers; (2) it must allow the evidence to come from an arbitrary number of informants; (3) it must handle an arbitrary number of questions; and (4) it must provide a way of using estimated competencies (from solving Eq. 8) in place of true competencies, which are not known. Despite these extensions, the logic behind the Bayes' Theorem applied to the preceding example is the key to the method of inferring correct answers.

Example 1. General Information Test

In this section of the paper we illustrate our procedures with true-false type data from a general information test. We have chosen an illustrative example where we know the answers a priori so that we can compare the results produced by our procedures to known benchmarks. Such a "validation" procedure provides insight into what we could expect in cases where we really do not know the answers ahead of time. In addition we feel that it is important to provide an example with real data so that the reader can better follow the ideas and procedures.

We constructed a 40-item test of general information from questions developed by Nelson and Narens (1980) to study long-term memory phenomena. Their "300 general-information questions were developed from fact books, with the aid of almanacs, atlases, trivia books, friends, and colleagues. All questions pertained to information that was at least 10 years old" (1980:339). We selected 40 of their questions from the median difficulty range and converted them to a true-false format. Roughly half of the correct answers were true and half false (19 true, 21 false). We collected responses to the 40-item questionnaire from 41 randomly selected students in the UCI student union during their leisure time. A copy of the questionnaire appears in Appendix B to facilitate replication.

We do not mean to imply that the General Information Test pertains to a given culture pattern. It probably does not generalize to other areas of culture, and it is meant only as an illustration. In fact we believe that there is great variability in what informants know about various domains of their culture. Informants who may know a great deal about sailing, for example, do not necessarily know much about tennis. We would also expect that there is a greater consensus among informants in some areas than others.

Our main interest in looking at all 41 students is to illustrate how closely our estimates of each student's competence on the test $\hat{D}_p$, computed from the pattern of matches among students by solving Eq. 8, correspond to the estimates of competence computed from the actual proportion of correct answers using Eq. 4. After presenting these results we will provide a detailed numerical example of all our procedures on a small subset of the larger sample.

To obtain estimates of each student's competence on the General Information Test without using our knowledge of the answers, we first construct a 41-by-41-student matrix of the proportion of matches among all pairs of students. This is done by taking each of the $N(N-1)/2$ (820 in our example) pairs of students, and for each pair, counting the number of questions to which the pair had identical responses and divide by the number of questions. We then corrected for guessing by using Eq. 7. The resulting matrix constitutes the system of equations from Eq. 8. We then applied the minimum residual method of factor analysis using the PA2 option in SPSS (Nie et al. 1975:480). This provided us with the estimates of each informant's competence on this set of questions.

These estimates of competence may be interpreted as estimates of the proportion of questions that each student "knew" the answer. Since, in this example, we know the answer key for the questions, we can calculate each student's actual score and correct this score for guessing using Eq. 4. to obtain a traditional estimate of competence. Note that both of these methods only provide us with estimates of competence since guessing and other factors add sampling variability to each student's performance so that their "true" underlying competence is never directly observable. The mean and standard deviation of the estimates based on matches is .54 and .17, respectively, while the corresponding figures estimated from the key are .49 and .19. The correlation coefficient between the two estimates is .93. The two estimates are, for all practical purposes, interchangeable.[4] Thus the estimate obtained without knowledge of the answers is comparable to the estimate based on the knowledge of the answers.

Even though these methods seem robust it is important to note that the original data *must* conform to the assumptions stated earlier or the method may give false or nonsensical answers. The model does not allow for negative true competence, for example. Also, it assumes that the questions are part of a shared belief system, not idiosyncratic preferences, and that the informants are all from a single coherent culture.

How can the researcher know whether the data conform to the assumptions, that the questions are in fact tapping a coherent cultural domain, that the informants are in fact from a single culture, etc.? Fortunately there is a major criterion that normally suffices to ensure that our assumptions are not violated in the structure of the data. The assumptions imply that the matrix of corrected matches in Eq. 8 has a single factor structure. This simply means that a single underlying all-positive factor, in our case competence, accounts for all of the structure in the matrix other than sampling variability. In statistical terms it means that the first factor has all positive values and accounts for several times as much variance as the next factor and that all other factors are relatively small and diminish slowly in size. This is a sufficiently stringent criterion that it normally guarantees that we can assume that the first factor is an estimate of informant competence.

The eigenvalues for each of the first five factors in the General Information Test are 13.95, 2.71, 2.28, 2.06, and 1.96. Note that the first factor, our estimate of competence, is not only all positive but is also over five times as large as the second factor and that the remaining factors are all small and trail off slowly. One can understand why this criterion is crucial if we look at Eq. 8. There we can see only one set of D_i's. If more than one factor were present the system of equations pictured in Eq. 8 would fail to accommodate the surplus data, and to fit the data would require parameters not in the theory. Since the violation of any of the three assumptions affects the factor solution, obtaining an appropriate factor solution is the main requirement in judging the fit of data to the model.

The next task is to infer the correct answers to the General Information Test. To accomplish this we applied the Bayes' Theorem method of estimating the answer key (see Appendix A). This method correctly classified all questions but one as "true" or "false." In fact we found that the a posteriori probabilities were so close to 1 and 0 that they were uninteresting in some sense. This is due in part to the fact that the number of informants is so large. We might note that the one question the method misclassified in the general information test was an item worded as follows: "Burton is the last name of the star of Spartacus." This question is in fact false but the majority of students responded with "true." We can never guard against such errors completely.

Example 2. Subset of General Information Test

We turn now to a detailed numerical example of a small sample of four of the students. In practice anthropologists must often deal with very small samples of informants. We want to illustrate that the method will work with small samples, although there will be a larger error variance than with larger samples. However, based on work reported later (see Table 5), we expect that on high concordance culture patterns samples of six to ten informants will work very well as a base to estimate the answer key. In any event we want to aggregate knowledge across a very small sample of informants to illustrate the possible power of the method.

We picked two high-competence and two low-competence students from the sample of 41 presented above. The response profile data for these four students is given in Table 2.

In order to prepare our system of equations as given in Eq. 8, we go through three simple steps: (1) count the number of matches between each pair of students; (2) divide this count by the number of questions (40) to get proportion of matches; (3) apply Eq. 7 with $L = 2$ to obtain an empirical estimate of the proportion of matches *corrected for guessing*. The results of the three steps are shown in Table 3.

The corrected matches are then analyzed by the minimum residuals method as implemented in SPSS option PA2. The estimates of competence are compared to the solution for all 41 students and to the known answers in Table 4. A comparison of all three columns indicates that the data based on just four informants yielded reasonably accurate competence estimates.

To infer the correct answers, we used the methods presented in Appendix A. In particular, we used Eq. 16 since $L = 2$. Table 5 summarizes the results.

Table 2. Response profile data for four students and 40 questions

```
1 1 1 0 0 1 0 0 0 0 1 1 1 0 0 0 0 1 1 0 0 1 0 1 1 0 1 1 1 1 1 0 1 0 1 1 0 1 0 1
0 1 1 0 0 1 0 0 1 1 1 0 1 1 0 0 1 1 1 0 1 1 1 0 0 1 1 1 1 1 0 0 0 1 0 0 1 0 1
0 1 0 0 0 1 0 0 1 1 1 0 1 1 0 0 1 1 1 0 0 0 1 0 0 1 1 1 1 0 1 0 1 0 1 0 0 1 0 0
0 1 1 1 0 0 0 1 0 0 0 0 0 0 0 0 1 0 1 0 0 0 0 0 0 1 1 1 0 1 1 0 1 1 0 0 1 0 0
```

Table 3. Matches, proportion matches, and corrected matches for four students

	Matches				Proportion				Corrected matches		
...	27	25	22	....	.675	.625	.550	...	.35	.25	.10
27	...	34	21	.675	....	.850	.525	.35	...	.70	.05
25	34	...	23	.625	.850	....	.575	.25	.70	...	.15
22	21	23	...	.550	.525	.575	....	.10	.05	.15	...

Table 4. Three different estimates of competence for the four-student example

Student	Competence from 4	Competence from all 41	Competence from score
2	.36	.33	.35
5	.90	.78	.80
9	.76	.74	.80
29	.12	.18	.25

Table 5 presents the 16 possible response patterns to a given question by the four informants, i.e., the 16 possible patterns of evidence on any questions. The a posteriori probabilities (or confidence levels) for a "true" answer are computed from Eq. 16. The confidence levels for a "false" answer are 1.0 minus the probability of a "true" answer. Since our a priori probabilities are equal for "true" and "false," it is natural to conclude that evidence patterns with values greater than .5 should lead to a reconstructed answer of "true" while patterns with values less than .5 lead to an answer of "false." This is indicated by the break in the table as well as the inference listed in the last column. The number of questions that yielded each response pattern is shown along with the number of questions (3) that were incorrectly classified by the method. It seems remarkable that just four informants, including two rather bad ones, provide enough evidence to correctly classify 37 of the 40 questions.

Note that Table 5 reveals an interesting symmetry, namely, that the values of the a posteriori probability of "true" and "false" are interchanged when the responses of each of the four informants are interchanged (for example, rows 3 and 14). This symmetry is a consequence

Table 5. Bayesian calculations for the 16 logical response patterns for four
informants with D's of .37, .91, .77, and .13, respectively

Response pattern	Likelihood		A posteriori probability of		No.of ques-tions[a]	Inferred answer
	Ratio	Log	True	False		
1 1 1 1	440.362	6.088	.998	.002	8	True
1 1 1 0	264.235	5.577	.996	.004	4	True
0 1 1 1	94.861	4.552	.990	.010	0	True
0 1 1 0	56.920	4.042	.983	.017	6*	True
1 1 0 1	7.731	2.045	.885	.115	1	True
1 1 0 0	4.639	1.534	.823	.177	3**	True
0 1 0 1	1.665	.510	.625	.375	0	True
1 0 1 1	1.001	.001	.5001	.4999	0	True
0 1 0 0	.999	−.001	.4999	.5001	1	False
1 0 1 0	.600	−.510	.375	.625	1	False
0 0 1 1	.216	−1.534	.177	.823	0	False
0 0 1 0	.129	−2.045	.115	.885	0	False
1 0 0 1	.018	−4.042	.017	.983	0	False
1 0 0 0	.011	−4.552	.010	.990	5	False
0 0 0 1	.004	−5.577	.004	.996	5	False
0 0 0 0	.002	−6.088	.002	.998	6	False

[a]No. of questions with this pattern. Each * indicates one error in classification occurred for that pattern.

of the model assumptions of no response bias and the fact that D_i is the probability that informant i knows the correct answer to a question irrespective of whether it is a true or false item. Notice that the first and last three response patterns in the table all give a posteriori probabilities of .99 or better, and 28 questions yielded one of these patterns. The inferred answer to these questions can be accepted with a very high degree of confidence, and in fact, all 28 questions are correctly assigned the correct answer by the method. The three questions misclassified by the method were all assigned lower probability levels. Of the ten questions in which two students answered "true" and two students answered "false," seven were correctly classified by the method and all three misclassified questions came from such a pattern.

Sample Size Requirements

For the General Information example, 41 informants decisively and correctly classified all questions as "true" or "false" (except the Spartacus question discussed earlier). In addition, a selected sample of only four informants correctly classified all but three of the classifiable questions, 28 of which were decisively classified with a confidence level exceeding .99. These extremes ($N = 41$ and $N = 4$) suggest an interesting general question, namely, what is the minimal number of informants needed to describe a cultural domain by our methods? By describe, we mean to be able to confidently infer the answer to most questions.

It is possible to use our model to derive the minimal number of informants, N, needed as a function of a few crucial factors. The factors that determine the number of informants needed are as follows: first, minimum sample size will depend on the cultural competence of the pool of informants used. The higher the average competence of the sample the smaller the sample needed. Second, the investigator must set an appropriate confidence level, that is, the minimal value of an a posteriori probability that will be acceptable to decisively determine the answer to a question. The higher this level is set, the more informants will be needed. Third, the proportion of questions that one wants to decisively and correctly classify, given an average cultural competence and a specified confidence level, affects the number of informants needed. The larger the proportion of questions one wants classified the greater the number of informants needed. Questions not decisively classified will either remain unclassified for the given confidence level or be misclassified. In none of the following calculations do the misclassified items constitute as high as 1%.

Although we do not present the derivations here, we have used the model to derive the minimum number of informants needed to achieve the desired accuracy as a function of these three factors. The derivations assume a true-false ($L = 2$) format and a pool of informants that are homogeneous in competence.[5] The results are presented in Table 6.

Table 6 lists competence levels from .5 to .9 in steps of .1 along the columns. The major row headings list selected confidence levels from .90 through .999. They refer to the lowest acceptable value of the a posteriori probability chosen by the investigator to classify a question as "true" or "false." The minor row heading gives the lowest acceptable proportion of questions that will be decisively classified given various row and column choices. In the body of the table, the integers report the minimal number of informants needed for each of the cells. For example, when average competence is .7, confidence level is .99, and the proportion classified is .95, the minimum number of informants needed is shown to be 9. This means that 9 informants, with mean competence of .7, in response to a true-false questionnaire, have at least a .95 probability of correctly classifying each question with an a posteriori probability or confidence level of at least .99.

Table 6. Minimal number of informants needed to classify a desired proportion of questions with a specified confidence level when average cultural competence is known (confidence levels of .9, .95, .99, and .999 are included)

Proportion of questions	Average level of cultural competence				
	.5	.6	.7	.8	.9
.90 Confidence level					
.80	9	4	4	4	4
.85	11	6	4	4	4
.90	13	6	6	4	4
.95	17	10	6	6	4
.99	25	16	10	8	4
.95 Confidence level					
.80	9	7	4	4	4
.85	11	7	4	4	4
.90	13	9	6	4	4
.95	17	11	6	6	4
.99	29	19	10	8	4
.99 Confidence level					
.80	15	10	5	4	4
.85	15	10	7	5	4
.90	21	12	7	5	4
.95	23	14	9	7	4
.99	*	20	13	8	6
.999 Confidence level					
.80	19	11	7	6	4
.85	21	13	8	6	4
.90	23	13	10	8	5
.95	29	17	10	8	5
.99	*	23	16	12	7

Note: *Well over 30 informants needed.

The most stringent levels in our table are the .999 confidence level and the .99 value of proportion of questions. When these levels are reached, virtually every question is correctly and decisively classified with near-perfect confidence. It is interesting that only 16 informants are needed to achieve this goal if the average competence is .7, and only 12 are needed if it is .8.

What of the questions that are not classified correctly by the method? Our analysis shows that in no case listed in Table 6 is there as much as a 1% chance of misclassification. Thus when the responses of the informants lead to a decisive classification at the selected confidence level, it is essentially always a correct one.

The use of the method with small samples of subjects and items is in rather striking contrast to related psychometric methods. For example, Nunnally (1978:262), among others, recommends sample sizes of 300 to

1,000 and the use of a large number of items with "at least five times as many persons as items." Lord and Novick (1968) present figures based on a sample of 107,234 cases. Lazarsfeld and Henry (1968) use a small number of questions but say we should have samples of subjects of at least 1,000. Are we really justified in using as few as a half-dozen subjects with only a few dozen items? We feel that the answer is yes for the following reasons: (1) we have a very tight theory whose assumptions are very stringent; (2) we are working with very high concordance codes where consensus is high; and (3) we are only trying to find one "correct" answer for a question rather than, say, differentiating questions on a continuous scale of tendency to be "true" or "false."

Example 3. Disease Classification in Guatemala

In a series of recent articles, one of the authors has contributed to the understanding of intracultural variability and the validation of cultural beliefs utilizing data on diseases collected in Guatemala and Mexico (Weller 1983, 1984a, 1984b). In her research she measured "agreement among informants to assess the relative cultural salience of each illness concept. It is assumed that illness concepts with the highest agreement are culturally more salient than those with lower agreement" (1984a:341). In an urban Guatemala setting (population 21,000), she had informants rank order 27 diseases on "degree of contagion" and "those needing the hottest remedy or medicine to those needing the coldest remedy or medicine" (1984a:342). Using a variety of quantitative methods, she demonstrated that informants agreed more among themselves on the concept of contagion than on the concept of whether hot or cold medicines were needed. In a more detailed study using additional data, she added evidence to the lack of informant agreement on the hot-cold concept (1983). Since the results are documented in detail, we feel that the urban Guatemala data represent a good natural situation to analyze with our methods.

To simplify the analysis we used a dichotomous form of the rank order data that was provided by the fact that each informant was asked to divide the diseases into contagious and noncontagious diseases before doing the complete ranking. The same procedure was followed for the hot-cold data. We used this dichotomized data in the following analysis.

We prepared the matrix of adjusted matches for both sets of data as specified in Eq. 8. The minimum residual method of factoring the matrix gave the proportion of variance accounted for in each of the first four

Table 7. Guatemalan disease terms and the number of informants classifying diseases as not contagious and as not cold

Disease	Informants classifying disease as	
	Not-contagious	Not-cold
1. Allergies	20	20
2. Amoebas	8	15
3. Tonsilitis	10	11
4. Appendicitis	23	15
5. Arthritis	24	6
6. Cancer	22	12
7. Colic	24	4
8. Diabetes	24	12
9. Diarrhea	20	10
10. Diphtheria	5	7
11. Kidney pain	24	19
12. Gastritis	24	16
13. Flu	1	1
14. Hepatitis	3	14
15. Intestinal	22	12
16. Malaria	16	5
17. Mumps	1	13
18. Polio	17	11
19. Rheumatism	24	3
20. Rubella	2	13
21. Measles	0	13
22. Tetanus	21	12
23. Typhoid fever	3	10
24. Whooping cough	0	6
25. Tuberculosis	1	6
26. Chicken pox	2	12
27. Smallpox	0	13

factors for contagion as follows: .69, .08, .05, and .03. Since the first factor is all positive and the contagion data is fit with a one-factor solution, it fulfills the assumptions of the model. Thus, we used the Bayes' Theorem method (Appendix A) to classify the diseases as contagious and noncontagious. Results indicated a high level of competence. The average level as estimated by the first principal component was .82 ± .11. Each disease was classified at a very high level of confidence (beyond the .9999 level).

The hot-cold data, on the other hand, produced two factors of about the same size (values for first four are .23, .20, .10, and .10), the first of which had 11 negative values. Thus the data do not satisfy the dominant all positive single factor expected from the model. To check the notion that there might be two separate cultures on hot-cold, we did an analysis of the 12 positive cases. Even this subset of informants did not give a single factor result. The first factor had negative values and the first four

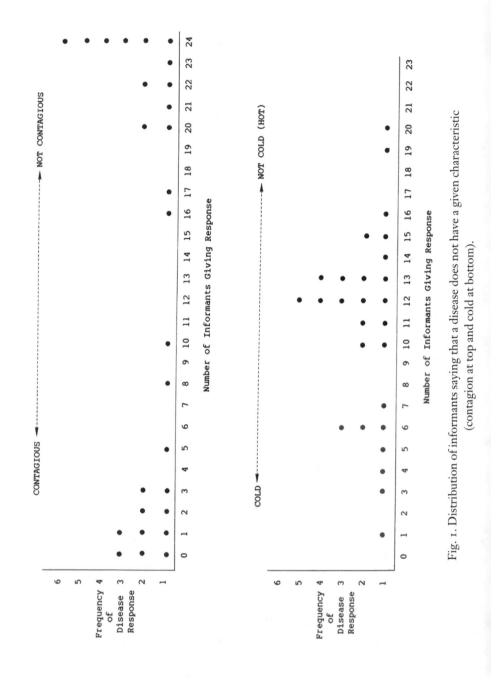

Fig. 1. Distribution of informants saying that a disease does not have a given characteristic (contagion at top and cold at bottom).

factors accounted for the following proportion of variance: .24, .22, .14, and .13. We conclude, therefore, that the informants do not share a coherent set of cultural beliefs concerning what diseases require hot or cold medicines.

One way of getting a graphic idea as to why the method is not appropriate in the case of the hot-cold data is to study the agreement among informants on the raw data. Table 7 lists the 27 diseases studied together with the number of informants classifying each disease as "not contagious" and "not needing cold" medicines. Figure 1 plots the data in Table 7 as frequency distributions. Note that in the case of contagion the data are very bimodal indicating that informants agree on how they classify the disease. All 24 informants agree that six diseases (arthritis, colic, diabetes, kidney pain, gastritis, and rheumatism) were considered noncontagious and three (measles, whooping cough, and smallpox) were contagious.

The hot-cold data are, by contrast, fairly unimodally distributed. None of the diseases is unanimously classified by all informants (there were 23 rather than 24 informants on the hot-cold task). Thus the evidence of consensus analysis reinforces the previous analysis by Weller, and it provides an example of how the violation of the model assumptions by the data is signaled in the analysis.

Summary and Discussion

We have described a model for the analysis of culture knowledge based on the consensus among informants. We illustrated the analysis on data from a general information test on a sample of 41 informants and then focused on a sample of only four informants for a more detailed empirical examination. Finally we reanalyzed some data on the classification of diseases from Guatemala. There remain, however, several important topics that need further clarification and discussion. These topics will be discussed in the following order: (1) The problem of the validity of the method, does it measure what we think it measures? (2) The problem of the reliability of the method, how well do we measure what we measure? (3) How much consensus among informants can be expected and how much is necessary to define culture patterns? (4) How robust is the method and what are some of the dangers and pitfalls? (5) How many informants do we need? (6) Possible directions and prospects for further methodological developments.

1. Validity

The validity of the theory is of prime importance. When we factor the matrix of adjusted matches and obtain estimates of cultural competence represented in the theory by the D_i's (assuming a legitimate single factor solution) do they "really" indicate that informants with high cultural competence "know" more about the domain tested than do less-competent informants? Validity is a complicated concept and difficult to define precisely: however, we take it to mean that our measures relate in known and precise ways to other variables that we accept as measuring substantially the "same" thing as we think we are measuring.

For example, when our competence estimates in the General Information Test correspond closely to the "known" scores on the test we assume that this fact provides evidence for validity. In other words, we found that after going through some rather detailed computations on a matrix of informant-by-informant proportion of matches data, we came out with essentially the same results as simply adjusting the proportion correct. Since we accept at "face value" the idea that competence is related to proportion correct, we then feel that our procedure measures the "same thing." Some might say that our procedure worked in this one case because of chance or because of the special nature of the data which is objective fact (not, for example, a shared cultural belief). Are there other examples that might be interpreted as indicating validity?

In two class examinations of a multiple-choice format,[6] we applied the model in order to test the correspondence between estimates of competence based on "known" answers and those obtained by consensus methods. In the first test, a final in a History of Psychology class with a sample of 60 students, using a five alternative multiple-choice format, the correlation between the two estimates was .978. In the second test, a midterm in a Psychology of Humor class with 35 students, using a four alternative multiple choice format, the correlation between the two estimates was .89. These results fully support the analysis used in the paper, although they are limited to objective test situations in a classroom. Would the results hold up in other areas?

Other research that presents data relevant to the validity of related methods include Romney and Weller's (1984) attempt to predict the accuracy of recall, Boster's (1986) study on consensus and cultural knowledge, and Garro's (1983) finding that older women and curers have more consensus concerning beliefs about diseases than do younger women and noncurers. A final example can be found in Weller, Romney, and Orr

(1986) where individual correspondence to consensual values regarding the appropriateness of discipline techniques was used to predict familial use of corporal punishment.

We feel that the kinds of evidence referred to here demonstrate that the model does have a certain amount of validity in the sense that it does measure what we think it is measuring in those areas so far tested. Of course it remains to conduct more sophisticated tests and to establish how far we can generalize the application of the theory and still obtain valid results.

2. Reliability

The second traditional concern with new methods centers upon the reliability of the results of the analysis. We interpret reliability to be related to the stability and accuracy of the measurement based on criteria such as retesting or internal consistency. In a variety of simulation studies, which we do not have space here to discuss at length, we have some relevant findings that are worth mentioning. We have found that, other things being equal, fill-in-the-blank type questions are more reliable than multiple-choice type, which are in turn more reliable than true-false type. In replicating the General Information Test in a fill-in-the-blank type format, for example, we found that it took about five true-false type questions to produce the same test-retest reliability as one fill-in-the-blank question. Thus the format of questions chosen by Boster to study manioc (1986) was optimal for reliability.

We also found in other contexts that there are two kinds of reliability that need to be distinguished based upon whether one is dealing with *response* profile data or *performance* profile data (see Batchelder and Romney 1986 for formal definitions). In this paper we have dealt solely with *response* profile data, which enables us to measure the reliability of the informants to sort questions into response categories, e.g., "true" or "false." In traditional psychometric work the data are coded "correct" or "incorrect" and so we label it *performance* profile data. Here reliability refers to how well the test items measure differences among the subjects (Nunnally 1978).

In traditional usage, like Cronbach's (1961) alpha, for example, the measure of item reliability would increase as the variability of the subjects increases. For example, it is easier to reliably differentiate between very smart and very dumb people than it is to reliably measure the difference between people almost the same in intelligence. In anthropological fieldwork we frequently deal in high concordance cultural codes so that all of the informants have high cultural competence. The lack of variability makes traditional measures of item reliability based on performance data inapplicable.

A final comment on reliability. There seems to be a limit on the extent to which you can simultaneously have, for a given set of data, both high informant reliability (on the *response* data) and high item reliability (on the *performance* data). The highest possible informant reliability (ability of informant to reliably sort questions) would arise with all informants being totally competent and the same number of questions in each response category. If the informant variability is low, as in this case, then by definition the items cannot reliably distinguish among informants, that is, low item reliability. This phenomenon needs further thought. In particular, anthropologists, unlike psychologists, need not seek high item reliabilities for tests so long as informant reliabilities on response data are high.

3. Consensus

How much consensus does it take to define a culture pattern? In our theory we have built in the assumption that all the informants are reporting on the same culture and that all informants have non-negative competence. One of the problems that we face is how to decide how much consensus is necessary in order for us to infer the existence of a clearly defined culture pattern. In order to get an idea of how much consensus may be expected, we can compare the average correlation among informants in the data sets studied so far. There are $N(N-1)/2$ pairs of informants in any study and by taking the mean of the correlations across all these pairs we can get a good idea of how much consensus exists for that group on that domain. Mean competence could also serve as an indicator. In fact, for a true-false format, it can be shown that the two measures are closely related to each other, the mean informant-by-informant correlation is approximately the square of the mean competence.

In the data reported in this paper the mean of the informant-by-informant correlations was .30 among the 41 informants on the General Information Test, .69 among the 24 informants on the contagion data, and .13 among the 23 informants on the hot-cold data.

The data for the 24 Guatemalan informants on the contagion of diseases clearly stand out. The average informant-by-informant correlation is more than twice as large as any of the other samples. It is the only sample we have that clearly reports on a cultural belief pattern. We feel that Roberts and Chick's (1979) notion of high concordance codes is fully applicable in this situation. In general, we believe that cultural patterns are high consensus codes, and we have shown in Table 7 that a relatively small number of informants is sufficient to correctly classify most questions. Notice that the hot-cold data not only do not satisfy the assumption of a single factor structure but that the informant-by-informant correlations are low.

Even though the General Information Test data do not deal with cultural patterns, they provide crude indicators of what to expect in vaguely coherent domains. The requirement that the first factor is several times as large as the second and all positive will ensure that one is dealing with a single culture. Clearly the lower the level of consensus the more informants one needs to reach the same degree of confidence in the results.

4. Robustness

Just how far can the methods be generalized and how robust can we expect the assumptions to be? One of the important assumptions that we make that is probably frequently violated is that the questions are of equal difficulty. In simulation studies we have found that the method is not very sensitive to even fairly large violations of this assumption. However, there is always a serious danger that a few questions are so different from the others in which they are embedded that the inferences we make about them are wrong. Probably it is unwise to put too much faith in the inferences concerning any particular item since at the moment we do not know how to prove that any particular item belongs in the domain and is of a comparable difficulty level.

In the case of the disease study, for example, we feel very confident that the informants could classify diseases on the basis of contagion. There is a certain parallelism in asking the same question about each disease. In other domains we may not have as good a reason for feeling that the questions all concern the same domain and are of comparable difficulty levels.

The method seems very sensitive, and lacks robustness, with respect to "negative" cultural competence, that is, informants who "know" incorrect answers. This is probably a good feature since it does not make theoretical sense to posit a coherent culture in which, nevertheless, each informant may have an idiosyncratic view. In such a world we could not agree on the meanings of words, symbols, etc. and the cumulation of culture as we know it would not be possible. Other kinds of models need to be constructed to describe such "preference" data.

5. Number of Informants

One of the important findings that needs comment is the ability to estimate the number of informants necessary to classify a given proportion of questions at a specified level of confidence. It should be noted that the numbers given in Table 6 are minimal numbers. Due to the noncontinuous nature of the binomial distribution it is sometimes possible for a larger number of informants to actually classify a smaller proportion of questions at a given level than might be obtained with a smaller number. For this reason it is best not to take Table 6 too literally. The numbers are meant as a rough guide and to illustrate that it is possible to get stable results with fairly small samples.

It may also be noted that Table 7 does not list average competence below $D = .5$. The reason for this is that the model applies to high concordance cultural codes. If the average informant-by-informant correlations fall much below .3 the assumptions of the model probably are not met.

6. Prospects

We have presented the barest outline of a possible theory of cultural consensus. The first and most obvious need is to generalize to a wider variety of question formats. We are currently working to construct models for the analysis of judged similarity data collected using triads, for rank order data (a more difficult problem), judgment of quantitative variables, etc.

We also have more flexible ways of analyzing dichotomous data. Measuring agreement with covariance, for example, completely avoids the problem of response bias as covariance is invariant under different levels of response bias (Batchelder and Romney 1986). Thus in work where one is worried that informants may have differential response biases, one can compare the results from the matching approach (which is sensitive to response bias) to the results from the covariance approach (which is sensitive to proportion "true").

Methods need to be developed that provide better criteria for judging the coherence of the questions to ensure that they apply to a single well-defined cultural domain. Related to this we need to develop measures for the variability in difficulty in the questions and to find if adjustments in the confidence estimates are needed. Further work is also needed on the problem of reliability of both the estimates concerning the informants and the estimates concerning the questions.

Implications

We feel that the consensus model opens up the possibility of measuring the cultural competence of informants in a variety of domains. In addition it allows one to reconstruct the "culturally relevant" answers to the questions posed along with confidence limits on the reconstruction. These abilities of the model have potentially far-reaching implications for the study of anthropology.

Its use enables us to pick out our best (most competent) informants in each area of culture. Clearly no informant masters all the cultural knowledge, so the best set of informants in one area may not be the best set for another area or domain of culture. One of the most important implications is that we can rely on a small number of good informants as shown in Table 6. We do not have to have large samples to objectively ensure that we are confident of the answers. The model is sufficiently well defined and has stringent enough assumptions that we can expect stable results with a half-dozen or so informants in areas of high concordance. This is the first time, to our knowledge, that we can defend at the formal mathematical level the use of such small samples for the aggregation of cultural knowledge.

A closely related implication is that we can objectively distinguish between informants that have specialized knowledge of exotic or specialized cultural domains from those who do not. Garro's (1983) study of curers' versus noncurers' knowledge of disease characteristics in Pichataro, Mexico, is an example. The finding by Boster (1986) that women have more knowledge of manioc names than men is another example. The ability to objectively test the cultural knowledge of different subgroups of informants (without knowing the answers to the questions ourselves) should greatly expand the possibilities of studying intracultural variability.

The model should also contribute to the solution of some questions about what the cultural beliefs actually are in some cases. For example, many writers have assumed that the definition of the hot-cold concepts of medicines and diseases in Latin America are cultural beliefs analogous to severity or contagions (see review in Weller 1983). The model allows an objective comparison between the hot-cold beliefs and other beliefs. Our theory makes it possible to compare the cohesiveness and strength of cultural beliefs from one domain to another.

The theory also facilitates comparisons across cultures. For example, if one believes that the failure of the hot-cold concept to emerge in the Guatemala studies was an accident of the particular cultural group studied, one can replicate the study in any number of societies and make comparisons. One of the valuable features of the theory is that the estimates of the parameters (e.g., cultural competence or D_i's) are always stated in the same metric (proportion of items known) so that one can compare from one culture to the next.

The comparability of results from one study to another raises the possibility that anthropologists could more easily compare results both within and among cultures. A variety of results could be accumulated and greatly facilitate our understanding of the distribution of cultural knowledge both within and among cultures.

Notes

Acknowledgments. The authors would like to thank Tarow Indow who provided the insight in solving Eq. 8 with factor-analytic procedures and to Katie Faust, Kathy Maher, and Ryozo Yoshino who served as research assistants on the project. John Boyd wrote the program to solve Eq. 8. Portions of the work were funded by NSF Grant Number SES-8320173 to Romney and Batchelder.

1. The model becomes more complicated when different informants can have different response biases. Batchelder and Romney (1986) provide methods of handling response bias in case $L = 2$.

2. In this case it is possible for two informants to have matching errors to a question. On the other hand, in the other two cases a match can only occur on a correct response. For a fill-in-the-blank format, it is essential that mutual blanks (no response) not be counted as a match.

3. A practical problem with Eq. 6 is that it can yield a negative value of $\hat{D_i D_j}$. Of course the same problem can occur in Eq. 4, which is the usual formula for correcting for guessing when the answer key is known. The computer solution yielding separate competence estimates described next can tolerate a few negative values of $\hat{D_i D_j}$ and still yield individual non-negative competence estimates.

4. Actually the estimates of competence based on the key average slightly lower than those based on matches. This is probably due in part to a bad question

about the star of Spartacus discussed later. Another factor accounting for the difference in these two estimates is undoubtably sampling variability since the estimates are based on different aspects of the data.

5. It is possible to show that if heterogeneity in competence is allowed, the N will never get higher than provided in Table 7 provided the mean competence in the heterogeneous sample is compared with a homogeneous group of the same competence.

6. The analysis of these two examples was performed by Kathy Maher, a graduate student at UCI, and will be reported in detail in a later manuscript.

Appendix A: Bayes' Theorem Method

Given the response profile data $\mathbf{X}_{N \times M}$ in Eq. 1, we want to reconstruct the correct answers to the M questions with specified confidence levels. We generalize methods based on Bayes' Theorem provided in Batchelder and Romney (1986) and Nitzan and Paroush (1982) for the case of an arbitrary number of possible correct answers, namely, L. The method has several steps as follows: first, we consider a single question and assess our a priori probabilities for each of the L possible correct answers. Second, we assume known competencies of each informant, and given the evidence of the informants' responses, we compute a posteriori probabilities of each of the L possible correct answers using Bayes' Theorem. Third, we replace the informants' competencies in the Bayes' Theorem solution by the estimated competencies from solving Eq. 8. Finally, we note that each question can be classified independently.

First, without knowing the informants' responses to a particular question k, it is reasonable to set our a priori probabilities for each possible response equal, that is, the a priori probability of response l is set to $P_i = 1/L$ for each $l = 1,2,\ldots,L$.

Second, the evidence relevant to our a posteriori classification consists of the kth column of the response profile matrix in Eq. 1 which we denote for convenience by

$$E_k = <X_{ik}> \overset{N}{i = 1}$$

We want to compute a posteriori probabilities denoted by

$$(10) \quad P_l(E_k) = \Pr(Z_k = l \mid <X_{ik}> \overset{N}{i = 1})$$

for each possible $l = 1,2,\ldots,L$. To compute Eq. 10, Bayes' Theorem (see any elementary probability book, e.g., Mosteller, Rourke, and Thomas 1961:146) can be applied. The result is

$$(11) \quad P_l(E_k) = \frac{\Pr(<X_{ik}> \overset{N}{i=1} \mid Z_k = l) \, P_l}{\overset{L}{\underset{z=1}{\Sigma}} \Pr(<X_{ik}> \overset{N}{i=1} \mid Z_k = l) \, P_z}.$$

Since $P_z = 1/L$ for each response z, all that is needed to solve Eq. 11 are the conditional evidence probabilities of the form

$$\Pr(<X_{ik}> \overset{N}{i=1} \mid Z_k = l).$$

To compute these conditional probabilities, first note that the model implies

$$(12) \quad \Pr(X_{ik} = l \mid Z_k = l) = D_i + (1-D_i)/L$$

and

$$\Pr(X_{ik} \ne l \mid Z_k = l) = (1-D_i)(L-1)/L$$

for each response l. Next by the local independence assumption, Eq. 2,

$$(13) \quad \Pr(<X_{ik}> \overset{N}{i=1} \mid Z_k = l) = \overset{N}{\underset{i=1}{\Pi}} \Pr(X_{ik} \mid Z_k = l).$$

To put these facts together we need to introduce the random variables

$$(14) \quad X_{ik,l} = \begin{cases} 1 \text{ if } X_{ik} = l \\ \\ 0 \text{ otherwise.} \end{cases}$$

and also replace the unknown competencies D_i in Eq. 12 by their estimated values $\hat{D}_i$ from solving Eq. 8. The result is

$$(15) \quad \Pr(<X_{ik}> \overset{N}{\underset{i=1}{}} \mid Z_k = l) = \overset{N}{\underset{i=1}{\Pi}} [\hat{D}_i + (1-D_i)/L]^{X_{ik,l}} [(1-\hat{D}_i)(L-1)/L]^{1-X_{ik,l}}$$

$$= \overset{N}{\underset{i=1}{\Pi}} \left[\frac{\hat{D}_i(L-1) + 1}{(L-1)(1-\hat{D}_i)} \right]^{X_{ik,l}} \frac{(1-\hat{D}_i)(L-1)}{L}$$

Note that the quantities $X_{ik,l}$ and $\hat{D}_i$ both can be obtained from the response profile matrix $\mathbf{X}$, namely, Eq. 14 and Eq. 8, respectively. The numerical values of Eq. 15 for each response l can be inserted into Eq. 11 to yield a posteriori probabilities or confidence levels for each possible response l. Finally, we note that from the local independence assumption in Eq. 2, each question k can be decided independently if we are willing to accept the estimated $\hat{D}_i$'s. This step in replacing D_i with $\hat{D}_i$ in the computation is analogous to Lazarsfeld's method of computing recruitment probabilities (see, for example, Lazarsfeld and Henry 1968:69).

In the case of dichotomous response data, it is possible to simplify Eq. 11. If the response data are coded

$$X_{ik} = \begin{cases} 1 \text{ if response of informat } i \text{ to question } k \text{ is "true"} \\ 0 \text{ otherwise,} \end{cases}$$

then by making substitutions in Eq. 15, Eq. 11 becomes

$$(16) \quad P_i(E_k) = \frac{\prod_{i=1}^{N} [(1 + \hat{D}_i)/(1-\hat{D}_i)]^{X_{ik}}(1-\hat{D}_i)}{\prod_{i=1}^{N} [(1 + \hat{D}_i)/(1-\hat{D}_i)]^{X_{ik}}(1-\hat{D}_i) + \prod_{i=1}^{N} [(1-\hat{D}_i)/(1 + \hat{D}_i)]^{X_{ik}}(1 + \hat{D}_i)}$$

$$= 1 / \left[1 + \prod_{i=1}^{N} [(1 + \hat{D}_i)/(1-\hat{D}_i)]^{1-2X_{ik}} \right] ,$$

and, of course, $P_o(E_k) = 1 - P_1(E_k)$ is the a posteriori probability or confidence level for a classification of question k as "false." Naturally we would construct the correct answer for question k as $Z_k = 1$ if and only if $P_1(E_k) > .5$ and this is easily seen to occur in case

$$(17) \quad \prod_{i=1}^{N} [(1 + \hat{D}_i)/(1-\hat{D}_i)]^{1-2X_{ik}} < 1.$$

Taking natural logarithms of both sides of Eq. 17 yields the criterion that $P_1(E_k) > .5$ if and only if

$$(18) \quad \sum_{i=1}^{N} (2X_{ik}-1) \, \ln[(1 + \hat{D}_i)/(1-\hat{D}_i)] > 0.$$

Equation 18 is interesting because it shows that each informant's response coded as $2X_{ik}-1$ can be weighted by $\ln[(1 + \hat{D}_i)/(1-\hat{D}_i)]$ and summed to determine the reconstructed answer key. Further the weighting factor can be interpreted from Eq. 12 as the natural logarithm of the ratio of the probability of a correct response to the probability of a wrong response in case $L = 2$.

Appendix B: General Information Test with Answer Key

1. F   Gyropilot is the name of the navigation instrument used at sea to plot position by the stars.
2. T   Sputnik is the name of the first artificial satellite put in orbit by Russia in 1957.
3. T   Nightingale is the last name of the woman who began the profession of nursing.
4. F   Backgammon is the game in which the standard pieces are of staunton design.
5. F   Brunn is the last name of the man who first studied genetic inheritance in plants.
6. T   Bismarck is the name of Germany's largest battleship that was sunk in World War II.
7. F   Clurmont is the name of the mansion in Virginia that was Thomas Jefferson's home.
8. F   Dodgson is the last name of the author who wrote under the pseudonym of Mark Twain.
9. T   Albany is the capital of New York.
10. T   Shoemaker is the last name of the jockey with the most lifetime winners in horse racing.
11. T   The last name of the man who invented the telegraph is Morse.
12. F   Lock is the last name of the man who wrote the "Star Spangled Banner."
13. T   Frank Lloyd Wright's profession was an architect.
14. T   Hancock is the last name of the first signer of the "Declaration of Independence."
15. F   Burton is the last name of the movie actor who portrayed Spartacus.
16. F   The first country to use gunpowder was Nepal.
17. F   The Italian city that was destroyed when Mount Vesuvius erupted in 79 A.D. was called Herculaneum.
18. T   Nero is the name of the Roman emperor who fiddled while Rome burned.
19. T   The capital of Hungary is Budapest.
20. F   The spleen is the organ that produces insulin.
21. F   Pitchblende is the name of the scientist who discovered radium.
22. T   The Rhine is the river on which Bonn is located.
23. T   Young is the last name of the actor who portrayed the father on the television show "Father Knows Best."
24. F   The unsuccessful auto that was manufactured by the Ford Motor Company from 1957–1959 was the "Model N."
25. F   Sabin is the last name of the doctor who first developed a vaccine for polio.
26. T   Backus is the last name of the man who was the voice of Mr. Magoo.

27. T The mountain range in which Mount Everest is located is the Himalayas.
28. T Burr is the last name of the actor in the role of Perry Mason on television.
29. T The European city in which the Parthenon is located is Athens.
30. F The U.S. Naval Academy is located in the city of Arlington.
31. T The "Nautilus" is the name of the submarine in Jules Verne's "20,000 Leagues Beneath the Sea."
32. F Carrol is the name of the author who wrote "Oliver Twist."
33. F Kane was the last name of the man who was the radio broadcaster for the "War of the Worlds."
34. F Iceland is the largest island excluding Australia.
35. T Chaucer is the last name of the man who wrote "Canterbury Tales."
36. F Ptolemy is the last name of the astronomer who published in 1543 his theory that the earth revolves around the sun.
37. F Buenos Aires is the capital of Brazil.
38. T The collar bone is called the clavicle.
39. F Jefferson is the last name of the man who was president directly after James Madison.
40. F The name of Alexander Graham Bell's assistant was Sanders.

References Cited

Batchelder, W. H., and A. K. Romney
 1986 The Statistical Analysis of a General Condorcet Model for Dichotomous Choice Situations. In Information Pooling and Group Decision Making. B. Grofman and G. Owen, eds. Connecticut: JAI Press. (In press.)
Boster, J. S.
 1986 Requiem for the Omniscient Informant: There's Life in the Old Girl Yet. In Directions in Cognitive Anthropology. J. Dougherty, ed. Urbana: University of Illinois Press. (In press.)
Brady, I.
 1983 Speaking in the Name of the Real: Freeman and Mead on Samoa. American Anthropologist 85(4):908–947.
Comrey, A. L.
 1962 The Minimum Residual Method of Factor Analysis. Psychological Reports 11:15–18.
Cronbach, L. J.
 1961 Coefficient Alpha and the Internal Structure of Tests. Psychometrika 16:297–334.
D'Andrade, R. G.
 1981 The Cultural Part of Cognition. Cognitive Science 5:179–195.
Frake, C. O.
 1961 The Diagnosis of Disease among the Subanun of Mindanao. American Anthropologist 63(1):113–132.

Freeman, D.
 1983 Margaret Mead and Samoa:
   The Making and Unmaking of
   an Anthropological Myth. Cam-
   bridge, MA: Harvard University
   Press.
Garro, L.
 1983 Individual Variation in a
   Mexican Folk Medical Belief Sys-
   tem. A Curer-Lay Comparison.
   Ph.D. dissertation, University of
   California, Irvine.
Goodenough, W. H.
 1964 Cultural Anthropology and
   Linguistics. In Language in Cul-
   ture and Society. D. Hymes, ed.
   New York: Harper & Row.
Green, D. M., and J. A. Swets
 1966 Signal Detection Theory and
   Psychophysics. New York: Wiley.
Grofman, B., S. L. Feld, and G. Owen
 1983 Thirteen Theorems in
   Search of the Truth. Theory and
   Decisions 15:261–278.
Hogg, R. V., and A. T. Craig
 1978 Introduction to Mathemati-
   cal Statistics. New York: Macmillan.
Kroeber, A. L.
 1948 Anthropology. New York:
   Harcourt, Brace.
 1952 A Half-Century of Anthropology. In The Nature of Culture. A. L. Kroeber, ed. Pp. 139–
   143. Chicago: University of Chicago Press.
Lazarsfeld, P. F., and N. W. Henry
 1968 Latent Structure Analysis.
   Boston: Houghton Mifflin.

Lord, F. M., and M. R. Novick
 1968 Statistical Theories of Men-
   tal Test Scores. Reading, MA:
   Addison-Wesley.
Mosteller, F., R. E. K. Rourke, and
   G. B. Thomas, Jr.
 1961 Probability with Statistical
   Applications. Reading, MA:
   Addison-Wesley.
Nelson, T. O., and L. Narens
 1980 Norms of 300 General-
   Information Questions: Accuracy
   of Recall, Latency of Recall, and
   Feeling-of-Knowing Ratings.
   Journal of Verbal Learning and
   Verbal Behavior 19:338–368.
Nie, N. H., C. H. Hull, J. G. Jenkins,
   K. Steinbrenner, and D. H. Brent
 1975 SPSS: Statistical Package for
   the Social Sciences. 2nd edition.
   New York: McGraw-Hill.
Nitzan, S., and J. Paroush
 1982 Optimal Decision Rules in
   Uncertain Dichotomous Choice
   Situations. International Eco-
   nomics Review 23:289–297.
Nunnally, J. C.
 1978 Psychometric Theory. New
   York: McGraw-Hill.
Roberts, J. M.
 1964 The Self-Management of
   Cultures. In Explorations in Cul-
   tural Anthropology. W. H. Good-
   enough, ed. Pp. 433–454. New
   York: McGraw-Hill.
Roberts, J. M., and G. E. Chick
 1979 Butler County Eight Ball: A
   Behavioral Space Analysis. In
   Sports, Games, and Play. J. H.

Goldstein, ed. Pp. 65–99. Hillsdale, NJ: Erlbaum Associates.

Roberts, J. M., G. E. Chick, M. Stephanson, and L. L. Hyde
1981   Inferred Categories for Tennis Play: A Limited Semantic Analysis. *In* Play as Context. A. B. Cheska, ed. Pp. 181–195. West Point, NY: Leisure Press.

Roberts, J. M., T. V. Golder, and G. E. Chick
1980   Judgment, Oversight, and Skill: A Cultural Analysis of P-3 Pilot Error. Human Organization 39(1):5–21.

Roberts, J. M., and S. Nuttrass
1980   Women and Trapshooting. *In* Play and Culture. H. B. Schwartzman, ed. Pp. 262–291. West Point, NY: Leisure Press.

Romney, A. K., and S. C. Weller
1984   Predicting Informant Accuracy from Patterns of Recall Among Individuals. Social Networks 4:59–77.

Sankoff, G.
1971   Quantitative Analysis of Sharing and Variability in a Cognitive Model. Ethnology 10:389–408.

Weller, S. C.
1983   New Data on Intracultural Variability: The Hot-Cold Concept of Medicine and Illness. Human Organization 42(3):249–257.

1984a   Cross-Cultural Concept of Illness: Variation and Validation. American Anthropologist 86(2):341–351.

1984b   Consistency and Consensus among Informants: Disease Concept in a Rural Mexican Town. American Anthropologist 86(4):966–975.

Weller, S. C., A. K. Romney, and D. P. Orr
1986   The Myth of a Sub-Culture of Corporal Punishment. Human Organization. (In press.)

A Discourse-Centered Approach to Language and Culture

Joel Sherzer

VOL. 89, 1987, 295–309

My intention here is to delve into an ancient topic in the history of linguistics and anthropology, the relationship between language and culture. This topic is both so ancient and so basic to these disciplines and yet so thorny that, like other ancient and thorny questions (for example, the origin of language), it is a given of the disciplines, not talked about much in general terms, and even considered by many to be either tabu or else too old-fashioned to speculate about. But, and in some ways like the question of the origin of language, certain developments in anthropology and linguistics make it possible to talk about the relationship of language and culture in new and interesting ways. The development I have particularly in mind is the analysis of discourse that is rooted in social and cultural contexts of language use and considers questions of speech play and verbal art to be central.

Concern with the language-culture relationship finds its best-known modern expression in the writings of Franz Boas, Edward Sapir, and Benjamin Whorf. Boas insisted on the study of language and languages as essential to training and research in anthropology. Part of his reasoning, as expressed in the introduction to the *Handbook of American Indian Languages* (1911), is that language patterns are unconscious and provide access to unconscious cultural patterning otherwise inaccessible to researchers. This position leads rather naturally to what has come to be called the Whorf or the Sapir-Whorf hypothesis, namely that language (that is, grammar) constitutes the means with which individuals think and therefore, especially as stated in its strongest form, language (that is, grammar) conditions or determines cultural thought, perception, and world view.[1]

Since my aim here is to recast the relationship among language, culture, and society, it is necessary to begin with some brief definitions. For the purposes of my argument here and in keeping with conceptions of culture from Sapir to Geertz and Schneider, I view culture as symbolic behavior, patterned organizations of, perceptions of, and beliefs about the world in symbolic terms. According to this definition, the locus of cultural behavior can be a single individual. It is more typically manifested in or shared by groups of individuals. Society is the organization of individuals into groups of various kinds, groups that share rules for the production and interpretation of cultural behavior and typically overlap and intersect in various ways. Language is both cultural and social. It is cultural in that it is one form of symbolic organization of the world. It is social in that it reflects and expresses group memberships and relationships. Language includes grammar, but goes beyond grammar. As a sign system, language has the interesting property of being both unmotivated and arbitrary (purely symbolic in semiotic terms) and motivated (iconic and indexical in semiotic terms).[2] It is unmotivated and arbitrary from the point of view of its properties as a formal, abstract system. It is motivated from the point of view of the meaningfulness and appropriateness that individuals feel about their language as it is used in actual social and cultural contexts. This takes us to discourse.

Like culture, society, and language, different people define discourse in different ways. In my view, discourse is a level or component of language use, related to but distinct from grammar. It can be oral or written and can be approached in textual or sociocultural and social-interactional terms. And it can be brief like a greeting and thus smaller than a single sentence or lengthy like a novel or narration of personal experience and thus larger than a sentence and constructed out of sentences or sentence-like utterances. My definition of discourse is purposely vague. This is because discourse is an elusive area, an imprecise and constantly emerging and emergent interface between language and culture, created by actual instances of language in use and best defined specifically in terms of such instances.

Notice that according to my conception, discourse includes and relates both textual patterning (including such properties as coherence and disjunction) and a situating of language in natural contexts of use. Context is to be understood in two senses here: first the social and cultural backdrop, the ground rules and assumptions of language usage; and second, the immediate, ongoing, and emerging actualities of speech events. Obviously the textuality of a brief greeting is slim, the essence of its structure being the sociocultural and interactional matters lurking behind it. On the other hand the textual structure of a three-hour myth narration will be quite intricate and complicated. Nonetheless it too intimately involves sociocultural and interactional features and these must be attended to analytically.

The Boasian tradition within American anthropology and linguistics did not ignore discourse. Quite the contrary. Boas and Sapir and their students insisted on the collection and publication of texts as part of a three-fold investigation of language, which consisted of grammar-texts-dictionary. But while texts were collected and published, they were not analyzed as discourse per se. They rather served the function of providing both linguistic and ethnological data. Furthermore, this tradition conceives of texts as fixed, inscribed objects and not in terms of text-context, language-in-use relationships.

Taking a discourse-centered approach to the language-culture relationship enables us to reconceptualize the Sapir-Whorf hypothesis. Instead of asking such questions as does grammar reflect culture or is culture determined by grammar, or are there isomorphisms between grammar and culture, we rather start with discourse, which is the nexus, the actual and concrete expression of the language-culture-society relationship. It is discourse which creates, recreates, modifies, and fine tunes both culture and language and their intersection, and it is especially in verbally artistic discourse such as poetry, magic, verbal dueling, and political rhetoric that the potentials and resources provided by grammar, as well as cultural meanings and symbols, are exploited to the fullest and the essence of language-culture relationships becomes salient.

The perspective I argue for here has illustrious predecessors, Sapir and Whorf themselves primary among them. Sapir, in his book *Language*, and elsewhere, views language as a resource for social and expressive usages and notices the poetic potential inherent in grammar. He compares language to a "dynamo capable of generating enough power to run an elevator" but operating "almost exclusively to feed an electric doorbell" (1921:14). Roman Jakobson insists in many places (e.g., 1968) on the intimate association of grammar and poetry. It is in verbally playful and artistic discourse that we find language turned on to its fullest potential and power, possibilities inherent in grammar made salient, potentials actualized. It is where, I believe, we should look for the language-culture-thought intersection. Whorf's concept of "fashions of speaking" goes beyond grammar to include style and some of his examples (e.g., 1956:148–156) include forms of discourse (see Hymes 1961, 1974 for discussions of Whorf). Nonetheless, Whorf, like Sapir and Boas, and in spite of their commitment to the collection and publication of texts, lacks a consistently systematic distinction between language structure and language use.

Dell Hymes's concept of cognitive style moves the Sapir-Whorf hypothesis beyond purely grammatical concerns into the area of verbal style, and his recent work in Native American narrative (1981) focuses on language-culture intersections as manifested in discourse. Paul Friedrich (1979, 1986) reformulates the Sapir-Whorf hypothesis, placing what he calls the "poetic imagination" at its heart. Dennis Tedlock (1983:324) chides anthropologists for dealing with culture as if there were no discourse, as if the natives never speak. The natives Tedlock describes do speak and the narratives they speak are highly poetic.

Erving Goffman (1974) conceives of language, culture, and society as providing resources which take on meaning and structure by means of the communicative frames that activate them. Investigators of such everyday and institutional verbal behavior as face-to-face and telephone conversations, negotiations, interviews, gatekeeping, therapy, and court cases, while not focusing or insisting on verbal art or speech play per se, are very much concerned with the ways in which language-culture-society relationships emerge as pragmatically and strategically salient in discourse (see Erickson 1981; Gumperz 1982; Labov and Fanshel 1977; and Schegloff 1981).

Increasingly, contemporary research in linguistic anthropology takes discourse as its starting point, theoretically and methodologically, for linguistic and cultural analysis. As distinct from viewing texts as metaphors (in the sense of Geertz 1973), an increasing number of researchers, each in quite different ways, analyzes discourse, large and small, written and oral, permanent and fleeting, as not only worthy of investigation in its own right, but as an embodiment of the essence of culture and as constitutive of what the language-culture-society relationship is all about.[3]

My discussion so far has been general. Now to some illustrative examples. My first has to do with the way a grammatical category is used in poetic, magical, and political discourse. Grammatical categories, especially optional grammatical categories, were the focus of much of the discussion in the Sapir-Whorf tradition. Sapir, Whorf, and adherents to the hypothesis associated with them often focused on grammatical categories which are not found in Indo-European languages and are in this sense exotic. These grammatical categories reflect a different way of expressing meaning from "our" ways, and, perhaps, a different unconscious patterning of thought.

It is because grammatical categories are economical and efficient ways of expressing meaning, particularly when compared with the cumbersome translation that rendering in other languages, such as English, requires, that they often have a poetic feel to them and seem to touch at the heart of the genius of a language and especially the language-culture-thought relationship. This is no doubt part of what Sapir meant when he compared Algonquian words to tiny imagist poems. Optional grammatical categories provide speakers with conscious or unconscious decisions, choices, ways of expressing meaning, which, I would say, are actualized in discourse.

This example comes from the language of the Kuna Indians of Panama. It is a grammatical category used to express body position in relation to action. This category, which indicates ongoing action as well as body position, is encoded in a set of four verbal suffixes: *-kwici* (standing, in a vertical position); *-mai* (lying, in a horizontal position); *-sii* (sitting); *-nai* (perched, in a hanging position). Several aspects of this grammatical category are worth noting, as they contribute to or serve as a backdrop to its use in discourse. First, it is an optional category. That is, any verb can be used without necessarily marking it for position. Second, many verbs are associated with one of the set of positionals as the most normal, ordinary, natural, or unmarked usage. Thus:

> *sunmak-kwici* (talking-standing)
> *kam-mai* (sleeping-lying)
> *maskun-sii* (eating-sitting)
> *ua so-nai* (fishing-perched)

Since this category is optional, its use in a particular context is salient, that is noticeable. It becomes all the more salient when it is either used in a marked way (e.g., *kap-sii* "sleeping-sitting," for someone who falls asleep on a bench in the public gathering house) or contrasted with other possibilities in a verbally playful or artistic way, as in the two illustrative cases I will now provide.

The first is a magical chant which is addressed to the spirit of a dangerous snake and is used to raise the actual snake in the air (see

J. Sherzer 1981). The magical power of the chant works in the following way. The spirit, on hearing the chant addressed to it in its special language, immediately does what the narrative of the chant describes and, at the same time, the real, actual snake does so as well. As in all Kuna magical and curing chants, this one is literally teeming with and organized in terms of mosaics of grammatically and semantically parallel lines. Parallel lines are often identical except for a difference in a single word or morpheme. The lines that concern us here occur at the climax of the chant, the moment at which the chanter tells the snake he is raising it in the air. This occurs as follows. The snake is first described as dragging and turning over, in the -*mai* (horizontal) position, that is free on the ground, in two grammatically parallel lines.[4]

> *kali mokimakkemaiye*
> *kali piknimakkekwamaiye*
> The vine (euphemism for snake) is dragging -*mai* (in horizontal position).
> The vine is turning over -*mai* (in horizontal position).

Then there is a magical formula:

> " '*unni na pe onakko*' *anti sokekwiciye*"
> " 'Simply indeed I raise you' I am saying."

during which the snake is raised in the air. Then it is again described as dragging and turning over, but this time in a -*nai* (hanging) position, in two lines which are identical to the two I quoted above except for the change to the suffix -*nai*. They are thus parallel to one another and constitute a couplet parallel to the earlier one.

> *kaliti mokimakkenaiye*
> *kali piknimakkenaikusaye*
> The vine is dragging -*nai* (in hanging position).
> The vine is turning over -*nai* (in hanging position).

The text never explicitly and specifically states its most important meaning, that the specialist has actually succeeded in grabbing and raising the snake. Rather, this is expressed economically and laconically, by means of the simple shift from one verbal suffix of position to another, within a parallel line framework.

There are several points to be made here. First, the *mai/nai* opposition is a basic element in the general poetic structuring of this text. By occurring regularly throughout the text, followed by the suffix -*ye*, the positional suffixes contribute, in conjunction with pauses and musical melody, to the marking of lines within the text, an important aspect of their poetry. These suffixes also enter into and contribute to the parallelistic structure of the text. And the *mai/nai* alteration is, in the terms used by Roman Jakobson, a projection of the paradigmatic axis onto the syntagmatic axis, precisely Jakobson's definition of poetry. Here we have then a good example of what I call the *poeticization of grammar* — the grammatical function of a grammatical element or category is backgrounded, or combined with a poetic one. But in addition, the shift from *-mai* to *-nai*, at the climactic moment of the text, has a very powerful semantic effect crucial to the magic of the chant. When the snake is in the *-mai* position, in the first two lines quoted, it is still on the ground. But when it is in the *-nai* position, in the two later lines, it is "hanging" or "perched" in the air, that is, the chanter has performed the magical action of raising it, precisely through the magic involved in shifting from *-mai* to *-nai*, from horizontal position to hanging position. Through this mini-max solution (Labov 1972:349), this packing of a maximum of meaning into a minimum of form, grammar becomes poetry and poetry becomes magic. Notice that the difficulty, really impossibility, of translating into English these poetic/magical lines which constitute the most heightened moment of the text is an argument for my point that discourse, especially verbally artistic discourse, is the expression of the essence of the relationship, often unconscious, between language and culture.

A completely different usage of the grammatical category of position occurs in the figurative, symbolic language characteristic of Kuna politics, centered in the Kuna gathering house, the meeting place for political leaders together with members of their communities. The particular discourse form I draw on here is the speech performed as an inauguration for a new chief (see Howe 1977 and J. Sherzer 1983:96–97). These speeches are typically bristling with intersecting and overlapping metaphors and other figures — for chiefs and other political leaders — which speakers creatively draw on, manipulate, and create narratives out of. In one speech I have recorded and analyzed, the speaker uses the positional suffixes metonymically, in conjunction with a complex of metaphors, largely drawn from the Kuna plant and animal world, in order to represent Kuna political structure. Chiefs are *-nai* (hanging) because they are perched in their hammocks in the center of the gathering house when they chant myths in public performances, or *-mai* (lying) because they rest or even sleep in these same hammocks while other chiefs are chant-ing or at various times during the day. Chiefs' spokesmen are *-kwici* (standing) because they stand when making speeches in the gathering house or *-sii* (sitting) because they sit on special benches surrounding the chiefs. And ordinary villagers are *-sii* (sitting) because they sit on ordi-nary benches behind both chiefs and spokesmen.

Here the metaphor of chiefs as *-mai* (lying) is combined with the metaphor of chiefs as poles:[5]

walakan mamait, tayleku pel ipya kwinnitik.
The poles who are lying here, it seems all have their eyes alert.

Just as poles rot, chiefs become bad:

immar nunkumai, pe takke tayleku, suar icakkwasaar tayleku nunkumai.
Something is lying rotting, you see it seems, a bad pole it seems is lying rotting.

Here the metaphor of chiefs as *-nai* (perched) is combined with the metaphor of chiefs as animals, again, in this case, in a negative sense, symbolizing chiefs who have turned bad:

usis tulakan taylee simuryapa namaynai pe ittoto pittosursin.
You will hear the *usis* bug people it seems chanting-perched within the knot hole don't you hear.
akkwaser namaynai pe ittotappo.
You will hear the spider chanting-perched there.
iskwir namaynai pe ittotappo takken soke.
You will hear the cockroach chanting-perched there see I say.
tior tayleku tior tatakwat namaynai.
The scorpion it seems Grandfather Scorpion will be chanting-perched.

In this example, the grammatical category of position is poeticized, not by functioning in the creation of line structure and parallelism as in the magical snake-raising chant, but by entering into the figurative com-plex basic to the poetic rhetoric of Kuna political discourse.

Taken together, these two examples demonstrate the ways in which the grammatical category of position is exploited and actualized in the verbally artistic discourse of the Kuna. My point here is not that the Kuna, because of their language, are more aware of position or more capable of perceiving position than are speakers of European languages, as the best-known interpretation of the Sapir-Whorf hypothesis would have it. Heightened awareness, conscious or unconscious, emerges from the multiple inputs provided by language-culture relationships. The grammatical category of position is a resource, a potential, a way of conceiving and perceiving the world which the Kuna language offers and which is made salient by entering into a web and network of associations actualized in discourse, especially verbally artistic discourse. This is Sapir's dynamo. The resulting depth, thickness, and intricacy is what Clifford Geertz finds characteristic of culture.

The Kuna grammatical category of position, especially as manifested in the snake-raising chant, reveals aspects of grammatical and semantic relations and relations between language and culture rarely studied by anthropologists and linguists, precisely because they can only be discovered through attention to actual instances of discourse. Traditional and conventional methods would not reveal the full meaning and potential of this grammatical category. Notice in particular that the shift from *-mai* to *-nai*, from the horizontal to the hanging position, in the crucial, climactic lines of the snake-raising chant, depends on the possibility, in this particular context, of ranking or ordering the suffixes semantically with regard to one another. That is, *-nai* is stronger, more powerful than *-mai* and it is on this fact that both the poetry and the magical power of the text depend. This kind of economical shift to a stronger or more powerful form within a set of grammatical or semantic relations is an instance of a phenomenon widespread in the world, the exploitation of sets of alternatives in discourse. It is often a crucial feature in a set of related forms of dialogic discourse — comebacks, verbal dueling, and bargaining. This takes me to my next extended example.

I draw this example from a short article by K. M. Tiwary dealing with a grammatical process widespread in India and beyond, known as the echo-word construction (Tiwary 1968). The language Tiwary describes is Bhojpuri, spoken in northern India. The echo-word construction is a form of reduplication in which a word is repeated without its initial consonant, sometimes with a vowel change. Thus the word *dudh* (milk) is reduplicated as *dudh-udh*. It is the kinds of meanings this grammatical process takes on and its use in discourse that interests me here. According to Tiwary, the echo-word construction serves as a label for the semantic field in which the base word occurs. Thus *dudh-udh* means "milk and the like" or "dairy products." Notice then that any member of the set of dairy products can be "echoed" to produce a word which can potentially be used as a label for the whole set. For example, *dehi* (curd) or *maTha* (butter-milk). But in actual discourse the selection is by no means neutral, in several ways and for several reasons. First, semantic fields are not absolute givens that are merely reflected in language use. Rather it is language use which creates and develops semantic fields. This is an illustration of what I mean when I say that language does not reflect culture but that language use in discourse creates, recreates, and modifies culture. Meaning, which is at the heart of the symbols-oriented conception of culture I am operating with here is on the one hand a mental construct; but it is a mental construct that is influenced by, as well as it influences, actual language use. Tiwary points out that the echo-word construction can be used as a secret-language of concealment. For example, a child, in the presence of his parents, from whom he wants to conceal the fact that he smokes, can ask someone, for example, a servant, to buy cigarettes for him in the market by overtly asking him to buy *deslai-oslai* (a box of matches and the like). The parents do not know, but the speaker and addressee do, that the semantic field of matches includes in this case cigarettes and that it is really cigarettes that the speaker wants.

Second, the choice of echo-word label for a semantic field is not neutral because the members of the field are often ranked hierarchically in one or another way. Returning to dairy products, the ranking of them depends on social and economic differences between the speaker and the addressee. If the addressee is of the lower income class, it is appropriate to select *maTha-oTha* (buttermilk and the like), since buttermilk is used by those who cannot afford other dairy products. On the other hand, forms such as *dudh-udh* (milk and the like) or *dehi-ohi* (curd and the like) are appropriate for individuals of means, who can afford these items.

It is in bargaining, and the verbal dueling which is at the core of the kind of elaborate bargaining that occurs in India, that we see this grammatical process operating to the fullest. If I am a buyer in a market and want to purchase goods for the lowest possible price, I will call dairy products *maTha-oTha*, thereby indicating that I am the kind of person who uses buttermilk and therefore cannot pay high prices. If on the other hand I am a seller and want to maximize both the politeness I demonstrate to a potential buyer and his or her ability to pay a high price, I will use *dudh-udh* or *dehi-ohi*, thereby showing respect for the buyer as a social person and also expressing my expectations that he or she can pay high prices. Ultimately there is a negotiation of both the linguistic form to be used and the price. With regard to the echo-word construction, Tiwary notes, as I have for the Kuna category of position, that it is impossible to uncover its full meaning without studying naturally occurring discourse in actual social and cultural contexts.

In different parts of Asia such verbal-dueling bargaining occurs in different ways. In Bali, market bargainers use the lexical sets that reflect social caste and social rank, for example, the five or six different ways of expressing the meaning "eat." Sellers will often select forms that are relatively high socially, showing polite respect for potential buyers, but also an expectation of receiving a high price. As in India, buyer and seller verbally duel and negotiate both appropriate linguistic form and price of goods.

In the following example seller (S) and buyer (B) jokingly duel about the price of an item eventually purchased, both of them switching language levels as part of the give and take of language play and barter. Under each word of Balinese I have indicated its level as "a" (relatively high: *alus*) or "b" (relatively low or ordinary: *biasa*).[6] In one utterance, a speaker uses Indonesian, the national language of Indonesia; I have indicated this with "I."

S: *napi   pindang?*
   (a)   (b)
   How about some salted fish?

B: *ji   kuda   niki?*
   (b) (b)   (a)
   What's the price?

S: *niki,   anak   pindang bes   ageng   jié.*
   (a)   (b)   (b)   (b)   (a)   (b)
   This one, is a very big fish.

B: *inggih!*
   (a)
   (Yes)!

S: *kala   nak   ji   tigang   atus, cingakan   dumun,   kéné   nyangluhné,   to   to.*
   (b) (b) (b) (a)   (b)   (a)   (a)   (b)   (b)   (b) (b)
   But the price is 300 [rupiahs], look at this, this is tasty.

B: *tiga   ratus!   bengu   jié   boné   ah.*
   (I)   (I)   (b)   (b)   (b)   (b)
   Three hundred! It smells very rotten.

S: *kanggé?*

   (a)

Do you want it?

B: *tak   éket   nggih?*

   (b)   (b)   (a)

240 ok?

S: *tak telung benang nggih. mamané bé ni angkelé uug basangné, bé grago uluh-uluhe.*

   (b)   (b)   (b)   (a)   (b) (b) (b) (b) (b) (b) (b) (b) (b)

270 ok. The fish got a broken stomach, because it had a small meal.

siki?

   (a)

You want only one?

B: *polih tak   éket?*

   (a)   (b)   (b)

Is 250 enough?

S: *siki siki?*

   (a)   (a)

Just one just one?

B: *kalih-kalih.*

   (a)   (a)

Two-two.

S: *aéng mokoh-mokohné, nasné pempen?*

   (b)   (b)   (b)   (b)

These are big, do you want the head in the bag?

B: *baang apa?*

   (b)   (b)

To give to what?

S: *baang kucit, baang méng.*

   (b)   (b)   (b)   (b)

To give to a pig, to give to a cat.

Notice that after the price has been determined, all the forms used by buyer and seller are relatively low (b).

Tiwary, in his discussion of the Bhojpuri echo-word construction, provides an interpretation that assumes that language is a mirror reflection of culture and society. "This construction reflects certain set expectancies of a society in which the economic distinctions are glaring, quite old, and widely accepted for them to be congealed into linguistic constructions" (1968:36). I do not deny the economic and social distinctions. In both India and Bali they are old and indeed glaringly omnipresent. But I want to offer an alternative interpretation for both the Indian and the Balinese cases, one that sees discourse as the mediation between language and culture. The verbal dueling that is the centerpiece of economic bargaining negotiates status and role as it does price. It functions as if interlocuters either do not know one another's caste and socioeconomic status or else that such status is fluid, to be determined in actual verbal interaction. Both of these propositions are of course false, but nonetheless constitute the assumptions of verbal dueling and bargaining. This informal, colloquial, popular, and fleeting discourse form then is a verbal counterpoint played against the backdrop of the quite real Indian and Balinese social, economic, and verbal worlds, that of sharply defined and expressed caste and status distinctions. Verbal dueling, in its own playful way, also reinforces these distinctions. This is most serious and deep verbal play. In this example, as in the Kuna forms of ritual discourse, we see not an isomorphic matching up of grammar and culture, but rather discourse as a rich, intricate, and dynamic expression of, mediator of, and indeed creator and recreator of the language-culture-society-individual nexus.[7]

One final illustration concerns our own culture and society and the notion of cultural logic, as reflected in narrative. One of Whorf's favorite and best-known examples contrasts Hopi and Indo-European tense-aspect systems. Whorf argued that Hopi grammar is more attentive to verbal aspect than to tense, while Indo-European languages are just the opposite. He suggested that this makes Hopi a more appropriate language, for example, in which to talk about contemporary physics. This was more of a rhetorical stance I feel than an actual belief on Whorf's part, but it makes its point. But again, where is discourse in all of this? Nowhere, or at least surely not prominent in Whorf's discussions.

Whorf's view of Hopi grammar has been challenged recently by Ekkehart Malotki (1983), who provides a massive set of sample sentences in which Hopis talk about tense and time in very concrete terms. But the Whorf-Malotki argument is about grammar, not about the actualization of grammar, in this case, tense and aspect, in discourse. This conflation of grammar and discourse, on the part of both Whorf and Malotki, confuses the issue. If we look, not at grammar, but at discourse, then a deeper correctness of Whorf's insight, namely that it is possible for a language to pay more attention to aspect than to temporality, emerges.

One quite appropriate place to examine tense-aspect systems is in narratives, which are reformulations of previous events. Narratives in English, and indeed in all European languages, whether written or spoken, formal or informal, are essentially a replay of a series of events in temporal sequence. That is, the organizing principle of Western narrative is time (see Genette 1972; Labov and Waletzky 1967; Mitchell 1981; Prince 1973). Notice that I did not say past tense, since the present tense (sometimes called the historical present in such cases) can be used as well to reflect temporal sequences in the past. And in colloquial, spoken narratives, such words and particles as "well," "so," "then," "OK," and "and" are used to move descriptions along in temporal sequence.

Here is a rather typical example of an American English oral narrative, a portion of a hunting-related story told in central Texas about the exploits of a coyote and deer.[8]

> But that little ol', little ol' yearlin', up there, man he threw up that tail 'n' went runnin' off round up through, round the edge of the hill.
> An' uh, when he did, then, the ol' coyote time he creeped on up where the deer was.
> An' he's standin' there, sniffin' the ground, sniffin' the ground. I was watchin' through the binoculars. He's out about a hundred 'n' fifty yards.
> Man all of a sudden, that rascal jus' tore loose a-runnin'. I mean jus' diggin' it like this. He wasn't he didn't start off you know sumthin' that turned round and looked like this 'n' then run. He just took off to runnin'.
> And ah. I was watchin' him run, cause he's runnin' up this sendero.
> About, oh two hundred 'n' fifty yards up there before we got to brush.
> 'N' then what do you think run in run up in them glasses with him while I was watchin' him run goin' this away?
> Whadda you think run in there with 'im?
> That ol' doe.
> That ol' doe run right in there with him an' she could run up close enough to 'im, to where his tail was was between her front legs like this, went running.
> But she had to skip one step to get at 'im with that foot.
> And when she'd skip one step, then he'd gain, he'd gain a step.
> Then she couldn't reach 'im.
> And an' then, then she'd catch up with 'im again, an' when she tried to catch that next step like that, she couldn't git 'im.
> Then ah, she was runnin' 'im like that an' then here them two little ol

yearlin's they come runnin' off out here right on the edge o' the sendero
watchin' mama run the coyote off.

The temporal ordering of events in this narration is identical to their
original, actual ordering, or at least as we as listeners are supposed to
imagine them as having occurred. Given the temporal organization of
most narratives told in European languages, it is not surprising that
narrative theorists, often without knowledge of non-European narrative
traditions, define narrative universally in terms of temporal sequence.
But this is not necessarily so in other languages, cultures, and narrative
traditions. Instead of Hopi, let me return to the Kuna, whose narratives I
am much more familiar with. Kuna grammar offers much more elaboration in aspect than tense. And Kuna narratives, while they do reflect
temporal order, focus much more on aspectual matters, the location,
direction, and ways actions are performed, so much so that Western
readers have difficulty following translations.

Here is a passage that is particularly difficult for English readers, who
tend to find it temporally illogical; but it was not for the Kuna audience
that heard it.[9]

tek ipakwen maskuttasunnoe.

"maskunnar" sokele punorka sokkartasunto sus kepe "muuu   tikkarpa kep
    ainiarsun" soke a.

(visiting chief: *etto so.*)

"ainiarto tiylesat nappa askin ainiarto immar mattutikki ainiar" soke.

(visiting chief: *eee.*)

tey tunkutanisun mu taytisunna i-pi-wa.

(visiting chief: *ipi ainiali?*)

eye.

tey pinna nakkwe ainitani ainitani ainitani tey turpamakkarsunto.

(visiting chief: *ee.*)

tey turpamakkarku e san nakuar takkarku kaa.

(visiting chief: *kaa.*)

mm, "ka" takken soke.

(visiting chief: *ee.*)

tey muu ka, akkwemasunna mukatka kusparsunto kate a. ka ai ok-kin-no-te
    (voice vibrates) *ka kuarku.*

weparte e macikwa purkwisatteka, maskunnalile, sokkartasunto mimmi punorka.

(visiting chief: *ee.*)

"punorye we mu maitse pe anka ka wis ekisna takkenye kapa maskunpiye a."

(visiting chief: *ee.*)

kal ekisnattasunto.

(visiting chief: *ee.*)

tey wepa muka soytapsunnoe "pe ka wis apeye."

(visiting chief: *ee.*)

mu "napir" soke mu kar ka kwannattasunna.

(visiting chief: *ee.*)

ka, kwane tek mu kuti.

tek ipakwenkine, maskunnetkinpali, ekisnatparsunna.

(visiting chief: *ee.*)

wep punoloka soysunna "ka pe kwanna takkenye."

(visiting chief: comment.)

"teki ka kwannapsun" soke.

(visiting chief: *eee muse*, comment.)

teki, muse kwannattasunto, mu ka ipetka kusparsunna.

tek e punoloka na kaa kwannai tule sunmakkarsun nappa yapa.

(visiting chief: *aaa.*)

Well one day always as they were going to eat.

"While they were beginning to eat" it is said the boy always said to his sister
    "near the grandmother's house then there is something growing" he says ah.

(visiting chief: So it is.)

"It was growing on top of the ground something very small was growing" he
    says.

(visiting chief: Yes.)

Well the grandmother saw that it was getting bigger what-was-it?

(visiting chief: what was growing?)

Yes.

Well slowly it rises it keeps growing up keeps growing up keeps growing up
    indeed it produced fruit.

(visiting chief: Yes.)

Well when it produced fruit its flesh got ripe in fact it was pepper.

(visiting chief: Pepper.)

Mm, "pepper," see it is said.

(visiting chief: Yes.)

Well the grandmother is taking care of, a pepper plant and the pepper plant
    belonged to the grandmother ah.

(visiting chief: aah.)

The pepper my friend got-ripe (voice vibrates) that is what happened to the
  pepper.

And as for the boy who had died, while he was beginning to eat, he always
  said to his baby sister.

(visiting chief: Yes.)

"Sister go to that grandmother who is there and ask for some pepper for me
  see I want to eat with pepper ah."

(visiting chief: Yes.)

She would always go to ask her.

(visiting chief: Yes.)

Well she went there and said to the grandmother "I want some of your
  pepper."

(visiting chief: Yes.)

The grandmother says "all right" and the grandmother would always go to
  gather pepper for her.

(visiting chief: Yes.)

pepper, gather well the grandmother was there.

Well one day, while eating again, she went to ask again.

(visiting chief: Yes.)

And she (the grandmother) says to the girl "you go and gather the pepper
  see."

(visiting chief: Comment.)

"Well she went to gather the pepper" it is said.

(Yes to the grandmother's place. Comment.)

Well, she always went to the grandmother's place to gather it, the
  grandmother is the owner of the pepper plant.

Well a person began to speak from inside the ground to the girl who was
  gathering pepper.

(visiting chief: aaah.)

In this passage the narrator constantly jumps back and forth from
place to place, from the home of the brother and the sister to the home of
the grandmother to the grandmother's garden, and in time, from when
the brother was alive to when he had died and was buried under the
pepper plant, always being quite precise about the movement and direction of actions and the ways in which actions are performed. One feature
of this narration that non-Kuna find particularly strange is the fact that
the pepper plant is growing before the boy dies and that the boy is later
found buried under the plant, as if his burial had caused the plant to grow.

There is no doubt that this passage is illogical for a Western European or North American audience or readership. But what we are talking about here is cultural logic, as expressed in discourse. Contemporary, postmodern novelists, in Europe and North and South America, consciously break with Indo-European temporal logic, in order to achieve avant-garde effects, producing texts quite similar in some ways to Kuna narratives (see Dina Sherzer 1986).

Here is a passage from a novel by the most recent nobel prize winning author, Claude Simon (1981:21):[10]

> He is fifty years old. He is general-in-chief of the artillery of the army in Italy. He lives in Milan. He wears a tunic with a collar and breastplate embroidered in gold. He is sixty years old. He oversees the completion of the terrace of his castle. He is shivering, wrapped up in an old military greatcoat. He sees black spots. At night he will be dead. He is thirty years old. He is a captain. He goes to the opera. He wears a three-cornered hat, a blue tunic tight at the waist, and a drawing-room sword.

Notice how difficult it is to follow temporal progression in this text. But as distinct from Simon's text, which is felt to be avant garde by its intended readers, Kuna narratives are not avant garde for the Kuna. Quite the contrary. They are steeped in Kuna tradition and represent a natural and logical intersection between Kuna language and culture. The degree to which the seeming logic of our own narrative structure is also an expression of the intersection of language and culture is best appreciated through comparison with such radically different possibilities as Kuna. And it is important to recognize that this cultural logic is not a result of or an isomorphic reflection of a particular tense-aspect system. Rather, discourse, in this case narrative, draws on tense-aspect, as it draws on other features of the grammar and the lexicon, in the creation of temporal and spatial cultural logical systems.

Both linguists and anthropologists have traditionally treated discourse as an invisible glass through which the researcher perceives the reality of grammar, social relations, ecological practices, and belief systems. But the glass itself, discourse and its structure, the actual medium through which knowledge (linguistic and cultural) is produced, conceived, transmitted, and acquired, by members of societies and by researchers, is given little attention. My stance here is quite different from the traditional one, and reflects a growing interest in discourse in many disciplines. I view language, culture, society, and the individual as all providing resources in a creative process which is actualized in discourse. In my discourse-centered approach, discourse is the broadest and most comprehensive level of linguistic form, content, and use. This is what I mean by saying that discourse and especially the process of discourse structuring is the locus of the language-culture relationship. Furthermore, it is in certain kinds of discourse, in which speech play and verbal art are heightened, as central moments in poetry, magic, politics, religion, respect, insult, and bargaining, that the language-culture-discourse relationship comes into sharpest focus and the organizing role of discourse in this relationship is highlighted.

This is a theoretical position. But it has methodological implications as well, for both anthropologists and linguists. Since discourse is an embodiment, a filter, a creator and recreator, and a transmitter of culture, then in order to study culture we must study the actual forms of discourse produced and performed by societies and individuals, the myths, legends, stories, verbal duels, and conversations that constitute a society's verbal life. But discourse is also an embodiment of language. Grammar provides a set of potentials. Since these potentials are actualized in discourse they can only be studied in discourse.

Notes

Acknowledgments. I am grateful to Greg Urban and Anthony Woodbury for many discussions about the issues raised here. Our joint efforts appear as Sherzer and Urban (1986) and Sherzer and Woodbury (1987). Steven Feld, Dina Sherzer, K. M. Tiwary, Greg Urban, and Anthony Woodbury commented on an earlier version of this paper. I owe a particular debt to Jane Hill for her incisive comments and suggestions on various versions of this paper and especially for provoking me to keep worrying about them.

1. It is important to recognize that Boas, Sapir, and Whorf were clearly each struggling with the question of the relationships between grammar, thought, and culture. Thus seemingly contradictory positions can be found within their own writing on these questions. In particular, the strictly and strongly causal view that language determines thought or culture, often attributed to Whorf, can be found nowhere explicitly in the writings of Boas, Sapir, or Whorf.

2. A point nicely expressed by Emile Benveniste in 1939. See also Friedrich (1979:1–61).

3. Among others, see Ellen Basso 1985; Keith Basso 1979; Bauman 1986; Feld 1982; Gossen 1974; Hanks 1986; Heath 1983; McLendon 1981; Philips

1983; Scollon and Scollon 1979; Tedlock 1985; Urban 1986; and Woodbury 1985.

4. From *The Way of the Snake*, performed by Pranki Pilos of Mulatuppu, San Blas, Panama. For transcription of Kuna discourse, see Sherzer (1983: 41–42).

5. From a speech performed by Muristo Pérez of Mulatuppu, San Blas, Panama.

6. The binary *alus/biasa* distinction is a common way of talking about language levels in Bali. The actual situation is often more complicated and some of the words in the example provided here enter into lexical sets with more than two members (see Kersten 1984; Ward 1973; and Zurbuchen 1981). Notice that the language of the market is not a random mixing of languages and levels, a reflection of speakers' lack of knowledge of their own languages and appropriate language use. Quite the contrary. It is a sophisticated manipulation of the resources provided by the complex Balinese sociolinguistic situation, a manipulation involving economic strategies, politeness, play, and humor.

7. Long and ritualized forms of verbal dueling are extremely common in the world, found among urban Blacks in the United States, Mexican Indians, Mestizo populations in South America, Turkish adolescents, and probably many other places. The basic principle of verbal dueling is for each speaker to provide a comeback which "tops" its predecessor by being maximally semantically more powerful with a minimal economy of formal effort, as defined within an underlying framework of grammatical and semantic relations (see Bricker 1976; Dundes, Leach, and Özkök 1970; Gossen 1976; and Labov 1972). The relationship between verbal dueling and bargaining is an intriguing one, worthy of further exploration.

8. Told by G. H. of Austin, Texas. In this transcription, I use English orthography together with the symbol ', following conventional means of rendering English oral speech in print. In the representation, performance lines begin flush left. They are determined by a long pause coupled with noticeable falling pitch. Within lines, short pauses without noticeable falling pitch are indicated with a comma; short pauses with falling pitch, with a period. A long pause without falling pitch is represented as a long space within a line.

9. From *The Hot Pepper Story*, performed by Mastayans of Mulatuppu, San Blas, Panama. In this transcription and translation, each performance line, determined by pause and intonation patterns, is represented by a line of written text. Pauses within lines are represented by spaces. Stretched out speech is represented by dashes between syllables. The performance is in the form of a dialogue between Mastayans and a visiting chief, whose comments are also represented here (see Sherzer 1987).

10. Translated by Joel Sherzer.

References Cited

Basso, Ellen B.
1985 A Musical View of the Universe: Kalapalo Myth and Ritual Performances. Philadelphia: University of Pennsylvania Press.

Basso, Keith H.
1979 Portraits of "The Whiteman": Linguistic Play and Cultural Symbols among the Western Apache. Cambridge: Cambridge University Press.

Bauman, Richard
1986 Story, Performance, and Event: Contextual Studies in Oral Narrative. Cambridge: Cambridge University Press.

Benveniste, Emile
1966[1939] Nature du Signe Linguistique. In Problèmes de Linguistique Générale. Pp. 49–55. Paris: Editions Gallimard.

Boas, Franz
1911 Introduction. Handbook of American Indian Languages (BAE-B 40, Part 1). Pp. 1–83. Washington, DC: Smithsonian Institution.

Bricker, Victoria Reifler
1976 Some Zinacanteco Joking Strategies. In Speech Play. Barbara Girshenblatt-Gimblett, ed. Pp. 51–62. Philadelphia: University of Pennsylvania Press.

Dundes, Alan, Jerry W. Leach, and Bora Özkök
1970 The Strategy of Turkish Boys' Verbal Dueling Rhymes.

Journal of American Folklore 83:325–349.

Erickson, Frederick
1981 Money Tree, Lasagna Bush, Salt and Pepper: Social Construction of Topical Cohesion in a Conversation among Italian-Americans. In Analyzing Discourse: Text and Talk. Georgetown University Round Table on Languages and Linguistics 1981. Deborah Tannen, ed. Pp. 43–70. Washington, DC: Georgetown University Press.

Feld, Steven
1982 Sound and Sentiment: Birds, Weeping, Poetics, and Song in Kaluli Expression. Philadelphia: University of Pennsylvania Press.

Friedrich, Paul
1979 Language, Context, and the Imagination. Stanford: Stanford University Press.
1986 The Language Parallax: Linguistic Relativism and Poetic Indeterminacy. Austin: University of Texas Press.

Geertz, Clifford
1973 The Interpretation of Cultures. New York: Basic Books.

Genette, Gérard
1972 Figures III. Paris: Editions du Seuil.

Goffman, Erving
1974 Frame Analysis. New York: Harper & Row.

Gossen, Gary H.

1974 Chamulas in the World of the Sun: Time and Space in a Maya Oral Tradition. Cambridge, MA: Harvard University Press.

1976 Verbal Dueling in Chamula. In Speech Play. Barbara Kirshenblatt-Gimblett, ed. Pp. 121–146. Philadelphia: University of Pennsylvania Press.

Gumperz, John J.

1982 Discourse Strategies. Cambridge: Cambridge University Press.

Hanks, William

1986 Authenticity and Ambivalence in the Text: A Colonial Maya Case. American Ethnologist 13:762–775.

Heath, Shirley Brice

1983 Ways with Words: Language, Life, and Work in Communities and Classrooms. Cambridge: Cambridge University Press.

Howe, James

1977 Carrying the Village: Cuna Political Metaphors. In The Social Use of Metaphor. J. David Sapir and J. Christopher Crocker, eds. Pp. 132–163. Philadelphia: University of Pennsylvania Press.

Hymes, Dell

1961 On Typology of Cognitive Styles in Language (with examples from Chinookan). Anthropological Linguistics 3(1):22–54.

1974 Ways of Speaking. In Explorations in the Ethnography of Speaking. Richard Bauman and Joel Sherzer, eds. Pp. 433–451. Cambridge: Cambridge University Press.

1981 "In Vain I Tried to Tell You": Essays in Native American Ethnopoetics. Philadelphia: University of Pennsylvania Press.

Jakobson, Roman

1968 Poetry of Grammar and Grammar of Poetry. Lingua 21: 597–609.

Kersten, J.

1984 Tata Bahasa Bali. Ende: Arnoldus.

Labov, William

1972 Rules for Ritual Insults. In Language in the Inner City: Studies in the Black English Vernacular. Pp. 297–353. Philadelphia: University of Pennsylvania Press.

Labov, William, and David Fanshel

1977 Therapeutic Discourse: Psychotherapy as Conversation. New York: Academic Press.

Labov, William, and Joshua Waletzky

1967 Narrative Analysis: Oral Versions of Personal Experience. In Essays on the Verbal and Visual Arts. Proceedings of 1966 Spring Meeting, American Ethnological Society. June Helm, ed. Pp. 12–44. Seattle: University of Washington Press.

Malotki, Ekkehart

1983 Hopi Time: A Linguistic

Analysis of the Temporal Concepts in the Hopi Language. Berlin: Mouton.

McLendon, Sally

1981 Meaning, Rhetorical Structure, and Discourse Organization in Myth. *In* Analyzing Discourse: Text and Talk. Georgetown University Round Table on Languages and Linguistics 1981. Deborah Tannen, ed. Pp. 284–305. Washington, DC: Georgetown University Press.

Mitchell, W. J. T., ed.

1981 On Narrative. Chicago: University of Chicago Press.

Philips, Susan Urmston

1983 The Invisible Culture: Communication in Classroom and Community on the Warm Springs Indian Reservation. New York: Longmans.

Prince, Gerald

1973 A Grammar of Stories: An Introduction. The Hague: Mouton.

Sapir, Edward

1921 Language. New York: Harcourt, Brace and World.

Schegloff, Emanuel A.

1981 Discourse as an Interactional Achievement: Some Uses of 'Uh Huh' and Other Things that Come between Sentences. *In* Analyzing Discourse: Text and Talk. Georgetown University Round Table on Languages and Linguistics 1981. Deborah Tannen, ed. Pp. 71–93. Washington, DC: Georgetown University

Press.

Scollon, Ronald, and Suzanne B. K. Scollon

1979 Linguistics Convergence: An Ethnography of Speaking at Fort Chipewyan, Alberta. New York: Academic Press.

Sherzer, Dina

1986 Representation in Contemporary French Fiction. Lincoln: University of Nebraska Press.

Sherzer, Joel

1981 The Interplay of Structure and Function in Kuna Narrative, or: How to Grab a Snake in the Darien. *In* Analyzing Discourse: Text and Talk. Georgetown University Round Table on Languages and Linguistics 1981. Deborah Tannen, ed. Pp. 306–322. Washington, DC: Georgetown University Press.

1983 Kuna Ways of Speaking: An Ethnographic Perspective. Austin: University of Texas Press.

1987 Strategies in Text and Context: Kuna Kaa Kwento. *In* Recovering the Word: Essays on Native American Literature. Arnold Krupat and Brian Swann, eds. Berkeley: University of California Press.

Sherzer, Joel, and Greg Urban, eds.

1986 Native South American Discourse. Berlin: Mouton.

Sherzer, Joel, and Anthony Woodbury, eds.

1987 Native American Discourse:

Poetics and Rhetoric. Cambridge: Cambridge University Press.

Simon, Claude
  1981   Les Géorgiques. Paris: Editions de Minuit.

Tedlock, Dennis
  1983   The Spoken Word and the work of Interpretation. Philadelphia: University of Pennsylvania Press.

Tedlock, Dennis, transl.
  1985   Popul Vuh. New York: Simon and Schuster.

Tiwary, K. M.
  1968   The Echo-Word Construction in Bhojpuri. Anthropological Linguistics 10(4):32–38.

Urban, Greg
  1986   Ceremonial Dialogues in South America. American Anthropologist 88:371–386.

Ward, Jack Haven
  1973   Phonology, Morphophonemics and the Dimensions of Variation in Spoken Balinese. Ph.D. dissertation, Cornell University.

Whorf, Benjamin Lee
  1956   Language, Thought, and Reality. Cambridge, MA: M.I.T. Press.
  1985   The Functions of Rhetorical Structure: A Study of Central Alaskan Yupik Eskimo Discourse. Language and Society 14:153–190.

Zurbuchen, Mary
  1981   The Shadow Theater of Bali: Explorations in Language and Text. Ph.D. dissertation, University of Michigan, Ann Arbor.

Knowledge, Power, and the Individual in Subarctic Hunting Societies

Robin Ridington

VOL. 90, 1988, 98–110

Native hunter-gatherers of the North American Subarctic have consistently been described as valuing knowledge, power, and individual autonomy (Black 1977a; McClellan and Denniston 1981; Honigmann 1981; Fiet 1986; Rushforth 1986). Is there something distinctive about the adaptive conditions of subarctic life that brings about an association of knowledge, individualism, and power, or does this patterning suggested by the literature merely reflect a "culture and personality" tradition within North American subarctic scholarship? How do mutual understandings contribute to the communication systems of subarctic people? How can anthropology expand its own language to represent the ideas subarctic hunting and gathering people have about knowledge, power, and individual autonomy?

My reading of the literature on subarctic hunter-gatherers and my own field experience with the Beaver Indians (Dunne-za) lead me to suggest that (1) a complex of knowledge, power, and individualism is a distinctive feature of subarctic adaptation; (2) the social theory of subarctic people themselves has exerted a powerful influence on several generations of anthropologists in formulating their own theories about the individual in society; and (3) an interpretive language (Geertz 1973; Marcus and Fisher 1986; Keesing 1987) is best suited to make sense of the ideas subarctic people have about knowledge and power. I suggest that anthropological theory may, and in some cases should, reflect the thoughtworlds of the people we study as well as those of our own academic traditions (cf. Martin 1987 for a discussion of native thoughtworlds and the writing of history). Conversely, the careless and uncritical application of ideas from academic traditions to the thoughtworlds of subarctic people may produce bizarre and ethnocentric results. For example, such uninformed ethnocentrism dominated much of the debate about the causes of a "windigo psychosis" that was believed to be a culture-bound syndrome peculiar to the Eastern Subarctic (Ridington 1976; Preston 1980). Marano's "Windigo Psychosis: The Anatomy of an Emic-Etic Confusion," carefully documents how social science theory may become ethnocentric when it removes ethnographic information about subarctic people from the context in which it is known, learned, and communicated (Marano 1982).

Traditions of Scholarship in the Subarctic
Despite the relatively small number of ethnographers who worked in the Subarctic until recently (Rogers [1981:22] lists only 58 for the entire Subarctic shield and Mackenzie borderlands area through 1969), many of the first ethnographers made original contributions to anthropological theory in addition to their descriptive ethnographic work. Some of the best-known subarctic scholars wrote about individual knowledge and understanding in relation to culture and the environment. Frank Speck (1935) was one of the earliest of these. His student, A. I. Hallowell (1955), similarly used information about the northern Ojibwa in writing about "the self in its behavioral environment." Later scholarship has continued to describe the individualism of subarctic peoples (Henriksen 1973; Christian and Gardner 1977; Scollon and Scollon 1979; Tanner 1979; Honigmann 1981; Brody 1981; Rushforth 1986; Feit 1986).

Frank Speck
Speck's classic, *Naskapi* (1935), describes a complex native theory of individual thought and action. Speck suggests that, in the anthropology of his day, "thought concerning the effect of environment upon culture-imagination may be scientifically outlawed," but asserts that he will discuss cultural categories and the environment because "in native esteem it calls for consideration" (Speck 1935:242). Speck explains that Naskapi theory is focused on the individual's possession of knowledge about the environment and on his or her personal experience of transformation. He says,

> Existing conditions, the forms and behavior of animals and the geography of the country, are largely the result of *transformation*. Consequently, transformation becomes an abstract principle in the system of thought of the nomads. [Speck 1935:49]

Speck argues that Naskapi hunters experience a powerful transformation in their contact with animals. He refers to the hunt as "a holy occupation" because "the animals pursue an existence corresponding to that of man as regards emotions and purpose in life" (1935:72). Hunter and animal, he says, share an experience of transformation when they come into contact through empowering visions and "hunt dreams."

> The hunting dream is the major object of focus — *kunto' pwa'men*, "he hunt-dreams," (*nto'pwata'm muckw*, "I hunt-dream a bear," *kunto'hun*, "I hunt"). It is part of the process of revelation by which the individual acquires the knowledge of life. It is the main channel through which he keeps in communication with the unseen world. His soul-spirit speaks to him in dreams. [Speck 1935:187]

In Naskapi theory as described by Speck, a person's "active soul," which guides him through life, is called *Mistapeo* ("great man" in Speck's translation). *Mistapeo* reveals itself most directly in dreams. "Every Individual has one," says Speck, "and in consequence has dreams." Because dreams are integral to Naskapi hunting technology, practices such as "fasting, dancing, singing, drumming, rattling, the sweat bath, seclusion, meditation, eating certain foods, as well as drinking animal grease, [and] various kinds of medicine," are used to induce dreaming. "When dreams are obtained," Speck explains, "interpretation is required" (1935:188). This interpretation takes the form of divination. A person's *Mistapeo* directs the interpretive process through *mutone'itcigun*, which Speck translates as "the power of thought." This power allows a person to focus his or her thought on the complex and ongoing pattern of transformations of which each individual's life is a part.

Speck's account of Naskapi divination and hunting strategy examines both its logic and its practice. He consistently presents this and other ethnographic information as part of an organized native system of intelligence that may be apprehended through Naskapi linguistic categories. Speck suggests that Naskapi religion, their "soul philosophy," is integral to their overall adaptive technology. He shows how Naskapi ideas and practices constitute a system of information that guides and empowers the thought, will, and intelligence of individual men and women. According to Speck's presentation of Naskapi theory, human thought and action are part of a more general animating principle of the universe, *tce'mentu*. The spirit of an individual human being, *nic'tu't*, represents the "intellect, comprehension [or] mind" through which he or she may take intelligent action within this animating intelligence of the world at large (Speck 1935:33).

Speck describes Naskapi customs and actions as indications that they experience the world as having an internalized, culturally defined "soul." He says that the Naskapi "perceive the objects of nature . . . as tangible embodiments of volitional beings" (Speck 1935:50). Although later scholars (Preston 1975; Tanner 1979; Armitage 1987) point out alternative interpretations of the Naskapi metaphysical vocabulary, Speck's portrait of Naskapi world view remains an important contribution against which others may be measured. Tanner's *Bringing Home Animals*, for instance, advances Speck's ideas by presenting scapulimancy as part of "a specific ecological and decision-making context" (1979:124) in which the oldest hunters practice divination to "make use of their knowledge of animals and of the environment, a knowledge which is analogous to, and spoken of as, a spiritual power" (Tanner 1979:134–135). Feit (1986:176) similarly describes the world of the James Bay Cree as "analogous to that of some ecological scientists" but based on "a personal metaphor" rather than the organic one of biological science.

Speck's own intellect and comprehension are revealed in the language of his rich ethnography. His work sets out both Naskapi theory and his anthropological understanding of the Naskapi world. He crafts the two into a single statement through the language of his interpretive description. His own theory is implicit in the language through which he represents Naskapi theory. Rather than attempting a theoretical language that would distance the reader from the Naskapi mind and spirit, Speck has adopted one in harmony with Naskapi intellect and comprehension as he understands it.

A. Irving Hallowell

A. I. "Pete" Hallowell is being discovered, or more correctly, rediscovered, as the brilliant thinker he has always been. Brian Morris, in a 1985 article in *Man*, describes him as "a much neglected scholar, whose work has come to be recognized only in recent years" (1985:736). According to Morris, Hallowell is important because he viewed "self and society," as "aspects of a single whole." "Thus," he says, " 'social' existence was [for Hallowell] a necessary condition of the development of the self (or mind) of the individual" (Morris 1985:738). Hallowell's generalizations about "the self in its behavioral environment" grew out of his work on the individual in northern Ojibwa society (Black 1977a, 1977b). His theoretical language seems to have emerged effortlessly from the language of his ethnography.

Hallowell stated explicitly what was understood and implicit in the work of his former teacher. In an essay written for *Culture in History: Essays in Honor of Paul Radin*, he develops the argument that "in the metaphysics of being found among [the Northern Ojibwa], the action of persons provides the major key to their world view" (Hallowell 1960:21). In Ojibwa thought, as described by Hallowell, the concept of a person "is not in fact synonymous with human being but transcends it" (1960:21). Because he viewed the Ojibwa concept of person as more inclusive than that of the culture that produced anthropology, Hallowell warned that "a thoroughgoing 'objective' approach to the study of cultures cannot be achieved solely by projecting upon those cultures categorical abstractions derived from Western thought" (1960:21).

Brown (1986:222) points out that Hallowell described thought categories of the Manitoba Ojibwa as "[leaving] open the possibility of animation in and communication with the totality of the surrounding universe." Ojibwa experience as Hallowell described it, she says, "was individualized, changing, and cumulative" (1986:222). Hallowell's ethnography, Brown says, shows that Ojibwa "concepts of persons and of the world in general" explain why "the private vision or dream was the prime means of access to significant knowledge and power among Northern Algonquians," who treat dream encounters "as seriously as did the Freudian psychologists who 'discovered' the importance and relevance of dreams" (1986:222).

The abstractions that constitute anthropological theory are, according to Hallowell, "a reflection of *our* cultural subjectivity" (Hallowell 1960:21). But the security of anthropological objectivity may be maintained, Hallowell says, by seeking "a higher order of objectivity," which is realized "by adopting a perspective which includes an analysis of the outlook of the people themselves as a complementary procedure" (1960:21). This statement suggests that Hallowell derived his view of culture and personality from the people he studied in the field as well as from the scholars he read during his university education. His focus on self-awareness in the context of a culturally mediated behavioral environment indicates that he found a complementarity between Northern Algonquian phenomenology and that of Western phenomenologists.[1]

Black (1977b:92) cites several pages selected from Hallowell's work that "document his conviction that the ethnographer should strive for an 'inside view' of a people's phenomenal world." She argues that Hallowell appeared "to have solved the phenomenological dilemma in a manner similar to the ethnoscientists" (1977b:93). She says that Hallowell may have been "particularly sensitive to 'cultural factors in the structuraliza- tion of perception'" as a "result partly from his Ojibwa experience" (1977b:99). In effect, Hallowell rationalized and objectified what Speck was doing implicitly through the rich language of his ethnographic de- scription. For both Speck and Hallowell, accurate and objective under- standing of northern hunting peoples requires entering their thought categories, rather than imposing our thought categories upon them to describe their behavior. True objectivity must integrate the perspective of northern hunting people with our own.

Like Speck, Hallowell viewed transformation (which he calls meta- morphosis) as a key to the Northern Algonquian perception of human and nonhuman persons. Transformation helps explain the Ojibwa con- cept of causality which, he says, "directs the reasoning of individuals towards an explanation of events in personalistic terms" (Hallowell 1960:45). Mythic beings are as much causal agents as are the physical instruments of causality. Similarly, "dream visitors" influence the turn of events as much as do the circumstances of waking experience. For the Ojibwa as described by Hallowell, "all the effective agents of events throughout the entire behavioral environment... are selves" (Hallowell 1955:181). The relations a hunter has with his game may thus be seen as interpersonal ones, and therefore subject to the moral obligations that pertain between human persons in Ojibwa society. Success in hunting depends "as much upon a man's satisfactory relations with the superhu- man 'masters' of the different species of game and furbearing animals, as upon his technical skill as a hunter and trapper" (Hallowell 1955:120).

Black (1977b:95) points out that Hallowell's category of "persons... turns out to be what ethnoscientists would term a 'covert category,'" because "the Ojibwa do not recognize this class as such, but the belief system structure is more truly represented by inferring it from his data." Feit (1986:176) cites Hallowell as a reference when he says that knowl- edge is "centrally important in Cree hunting practice" and is "encoded and highlighted by Cree concepts... in what we might call their science of hunting." The Cree concept of power, he says,

> is a coincidence between an internal state of being (thought) and the config-
> uration of the world (event), a congruence which is anticipated by the inner

state and which this anticipation helps to actualize. . . . Power . . . is a relationship in thought and action among many beings, whereby potentiality becomes actuality. . . . We might say that power is truth, rather than that power is control. [Feit 1986:178]

Like Speck, who describes Northern Algonquians as being "ego-istic" but not "egotistic" (1935:245), Hallowell speaks of Ojibwa "ego-involvement" as "the identification of the self with things, individuals, and groups of individuals" (Hallowell 1955:102). Hallowell generalized from his knowledge of Northern Algonquian thought to argue that "the self and its behavioral environment" is a fundamental "feature of human adjustment" (1955:75–110). Although Hallowell grounded his ideas about self-awareness and culture in a phenomenological tradition of Western scholarship, he also credited his Ojibwa friends and informants, particularly Chief William Berens, with teaching him about the phe-nomenology of northern hunting people (Hallowell 1955:120; Black 1977b:91–92). Hallowell's classic 1937 paper, "Temporal Orientation in Western Civilization and in a Preliterate Society," which strikingly par-allels Whorf's "An American Indian Model of the Universe" in its at-tempt to translate native phenomenology (Ridington 1987b), is person-alistic rather than positivistic in its point of reference. Hallowell says:

During the summer of 1932 when I spent most of my time up the Berens River with the Pekangikum Indians, I lost track of the days of the month, since I did not have a calendar with me; the days of the week became mean-ingless . . . the significant fact is that since I remained associated with human beings it was a very simple matter to make their temporal reference points my own. [Hallowell 1955:218–219]

Several later Algonquianists have related their own field experiences to the work of Speck and Hallowell. One of these is Richard Preston, whose monograph, *Cree Narrative: Expressing the Personal Meanings of Events* (1975), is a rich and thoughtful presentation of James Bay Cree ideas about shared meanings expressed in narrative form and ritual prac-tice. Preston, a student of John Honigmann, writes that, like Hallowell, "my point of view and method of approach is not only derived from my intellectual background," particularly Sapir's "insights into the relation-ship of culture and personality," but is equally a reflection of "the ten-dency of Cree individuals to emphasize meaning more than form, to view events personally rather than objectively" (Preston 1975:9). Pres-

ton consciously attempts to understand Cree narratives, "in their meaningful Cree context." This context includes, "conjuring power, autonomy, self-control, hardships and their associated emotional responses,
and the shifting contingencies of the environment" (Preston 1975:13).

Cree Narrative is both more detailed and more reflective than Speck's
Naskapi. It includes extensive and well-contexted narrative texts and a
close description of the shaking tent performance. These serve as vehicles for approaching the Cree meaning of concepts such as *Mistabeo*
(Speck's *Mistapeo*). Preston suggests that *Mistabeo* is best thought of as an
"attending spirit" related allegorically to the spirit of the conjurer, rather
than as a direct manifestation of that person's "active soul" (Preston
1975:92–93). While acknowledging that *Naskapi* is a "pioneering work
of creative ethnology," and that Speck "is on to something of great
importance," Preston feels that Speck's use of a language that contrasts
the Indian "mystical" world with Western "rationality" took him away
from fully entering the world of Northern Algonquian thought and
experience. This limitation, he feels, did not constrain Hallowell, whose
greater understanding is apparent in papers such as his "masterpiece,"
"The Role of Conjuring in Saulteaux Society" (Hallowell 1942; cited in
Preston 1975:162–163).

Preston argues that the key to understanding fundamental Cree practices, such as conjuring, lies in coming to grips with what he calls,
after Sapir, "the psychological reality of the culture pattern" (Preston
1975:164). Because *Mistabeo* is experienced as a psychological reality, it is
literally conjured into consciousness through the media of narrative and
ritual performance. In Preston's view, the psychological reality of Cree
knowledge contributes to its power. Because Cree knowledge is thoroughly contexted in experience, Preston argues that it is most appropriately communicated (following Cree tradition) in the language of
narrative:

> [Cree psychological reality] is not simply an uncritical (prelogical) hodge-
> podge of unconscious patterning, but rather a mixture of partially under-
> stood, partially related events, narratives, beliefs, and suspicions . . . it is not a
> matter for critical analysis and generalization in the fashion of an ethnologist.
> [Preston 1975:168].

As an ethnologist attempting to understand Cree culture from the
inside, Preston concludes that, while *Mistabeo* may appear to the outside
observer as a "mental construct," to the insider it is a "mental percept"

that is experienced directly (Preston 1975:262). Black (1977b) uses strikingly similar language in explaining her own and Hallowell's Ojibwa data. She argues that a key to Ojibwa individualism may be seen in what she calls their "percept ambiguity." The Ojibwa belief system, she says,

> . . . allows the expectation that individuals will 'see' different objects in the same landscape, will 'hear' different sounds; it also allows the expectation that the same entity may appear in different forms from one *time* to another; and it respects the individual's privacy and veracity as to what he has seen or heard and as to which of the entities has appeared to his senses alone and thus in a certain class for him. [Black 1977b:101–102]

Athapaskan Perspectives on Knowledge, Power, and the Individual

Ethnographers have consistently described Athapaskans of the subarctic interior as being individualistic (VanStone 1974; Christian and Gardner 1977; Scollon and Scollon 1979; Brody 1981; Rushforth 1986), but until recently have written little about a rich, culturally based phenomenology (Krech 1980). Honigmann's classic *Culture and Ethos of Kaska Society* (Honigmann 1949), for instance, forcefully presents a portrait of Athapaskan individualism, but contains none of the complex native phenomenology that one finds in the work of Speck and his successors. Honigmann's chapter on Kaska ethos concludes that the Kaska personality is motivated by "egocentricity, utilitarianism, deference, flexibility, dependence, and emotional isolation" (Honigmann 1949:249), but he provides very little information about the cultural context of these psychological characteristics. It is significant, therefore, that even an ethnography that makes little reference to native phenomenology or personality theory describes individual freedom of thought and action as being of paramount adaptive significance.

Honigmann uses the language of an outside observer's "mental constructs," rather than what his student, Preston, calls "mental percepts." It is not surprising that he begins a brief account of Kaska religion with the statement that "religious beliefs are of minor importance in Kaska life" (Honigmann 1949:217). Rushforth (1986:252) suggests that traditional Dene religion is less well known by anthropology than are other aspects of Dene culture, because of "the general difficulty anthropologists have in translating the meaning of religious experience," as well as "the relative lack of formal religious institutions among Dene," and "the deeply personal nature of their religious beliefs, which makes many people

hesitant to discuss them in any detail." From his own experience with the
Bear Lake Dene, Rushforth concludes that "belief in a mythological past
within which the world was formed," and "belief in an inherent power
that pervades the world," explain the knowledge and power required for
both hunting and dreaming. "Through dreams," he says, "individuals
come to 'know a little bit about' things" (Rushforth 1986:253). The
Dunne-za, in my experience, say that a person with power obtained
through dream and vision, "little bit know something."

A recent paper by Jean-Guy Goulet, "Ways of Knowing with the
Mind: An Ethnography of Aboriginal Beliefs," (1987) explores the difference between belief and knowledge in Dene thought. Goulet argues
that the ethnography of Athapaskan religion has been relatively undeveloped because "among Athapaskans a person with religious experience is described not as a believer but as someone who 'knows', " and
because "generally, anthropologists do not share in the kinds of experiences — dreams, visions, power of songs, ceremonies — that are at the
foundation of aboriginal religious experience and knowledge" (Goulet
1987:4). Goulet describes how he developed a deeper level of communication with Dene elders by sharing his own experience of knowing
through dreaming in a discourse conducted in the idiom of Dene linguistic categories. He says,

> As I progressed in the world of the Dene . . . the Elders continued to instruct
> me in increasingly greater depth, through stories, accounts of their own
> experiences, interpretations of objects and songs, and so on. As they did so,
> they would often conclude a session of several hours with the words *wondsdele
> ndedassi edaondihika*, "I tell you a little bit so that you may know." [Goulet
> 1987:25]

The classic literature on northern Athapaskan individualism has been
well summarized by Jane Christian and Peter Gardner (1977). The word
"individualism," they say, "has been used over and over again in the
literature to characterize interpersonal relations in the Subarctic." Beginning with J. Alden Mason's comment in 1913 that among the Great
Slave Lake Dene, "individualism seems to be the keynote to the interpretation of this culture," they cite similar statements about the individualism of interior subarctic Athapaskans from Honigmann, Helm, and
Nelson, indicating an "accord as to the emphasis on individual autonomy in the Subarctic." They use information from their own Slavey
ethnography to ask a key question about "how cognitive sharing is devel-

oped and maintained among such concertedly self-reliant people [who are] quiet, uninterfering, and independent almost to the point of anarchy" (Christian and Gardner 1977:3–5).

Their observations about Slavey individualism are similar to Savishinsky's statement that, among the Hare, "the successful person is . . . a flexible one, an individual who can alter materials and rely on inventive procedures when his situation calls for such adaptations." The Hare, he says, clearly value "the freedom to live as one chooses, to move when and where one pleases, and to schedule, order, and arrange one's life as one wishes." The value they place on freedom "is cognate not only with flexibility, but also with the people's stress upon individualism, antiauthoritarianism, and independence." Savishinsky compares his observations with "the variously individualistic, or 'atomistic' ethos that Honigmann . . . Hallowell . . . Landes . . . and others have found to be characteristic of both Northern Athapaskan and Northern Algonquian groups" (Savishinsky 1974:80–81).

The individualism of Athapaskan people has been particularly striking to ethnographers because it differs so from their own socialization into the authority of an academic tradition. Scollon and Scollon (1979:177–209) focus on this difference when they contrast what they call the Chipewyan "bush consciousness" to the "modern consciousness" of their own academic way of thinking about information. The Scollons comment that "we felt, as others must have felt before us, that we were unable to explain our presence with any conviction except to other Euro-Canadians." They conclude that they, as social scientists, and the Chipewyan, as hunter-gatherers, have profoundly different expectations about the need "to encode knowledge for storage but not for immediate use."

Academic knowledge, they say, following Gumperz (1977), is a "decontextualized [form] of knowledge." In contrast to themselves as academics, they describe the Chipewyan individual as "a fully viable unit of survival." They even go so far as to describe themselves as "a hired sensory apparatus for a knowledge organism" (Scollon and Scollon 1979:185). In contrast to their own academic trust in the written word and the documentary evidence of history, the Chipewyan, they say, regard the written word as hearsay. "Knowledge that has been mediated is regarded with doubt. True knowledge is considered to be that which one derives from experience" (Scollon and Scollon 1979:185). "Far from rejecting order," the Scollons say, bush consciousness "seeks a fully integrated view of world order in which there are no elements felt as foreign. What cannot be assimilated to its worldview is rejected as irrelevant or useless knowledge" (1979:185).

Other scholars (Smith 1973, 1982, 1985; Jarvenpa 1982; Sharp 1986, 1987) have written about cultural categories of Chipewyan phenomenology, in particular the Chipewyan idea of I^nko^nze as an empowering "secret knowledge." Sharp (1986) interprets I^nko^nze as a "subjective paradigm" representing "a pan-Chipewyan system of knowledge." He says that "Relations between men who possess I^nko^nze and the creatures that reveal it to them appear to be controlled by reciprocity" (1986:258). Thus, in native theory, an individual's power is believed to reflect his reciprocity, both with supernatural creatures, and with other humans. "As a plant taken for magical use must have a return given to it in the form of a gift . . . a man with an established reputation for more than the normal amount of I^nko^nze . . . must be paid by those he cures" (Sharp 1986:258). The individualism so evident in observation of how subarctic people behave suggests that similar "mental percepts" operate as unstated assumptions throughout the Subarctic.

Unstated Assumptions and Mutual Understandings in Northern Indian Communication

Jane Christian's chapter, "Some Aspects of Communication in a Northern Dene Community" (Christian and Gardner 1977), is particularly informative in addressing the apparent contradiction between northern Athapaskan individualism and the obvious human need for community and communication. She points out that, among the Slavey, there is an unwritten cultural rule: "don't interfere with someone engaged in a line of thought, a task or other endeavor, but allow him to finish out his intention." The Slavey, she says, will not "stop someone in work or travel without good cause," nor will they "interrupt a speaker or interrupt a deliberate silence" (Christian and Gardner 1977:25). These rules indicate that the Slavey value listening because of a respect for one another's skills and knowledge. Christian concludes with the suggestion that Slavey communication is supported by complex cultural "beliefs, values and attitudes" that are not amenable to quantitative analysis. Although, to an empiricist, these may appear to be a "Pandora's box," she argues that "failing to open this [box] leaves us with a superficial and misleading study" (Christian and Gardner 1977:100–101).

Christian presents the empiricist's dilemma as she sees it, with considerable candor. The dilemma she identifies is inevitable unless attention is paid to the unstated assumptions or "mental percepts" deeply embedded in the culture and experience of subarctic native people.

Subarctic people assume that the events of individual experience are connected to an empowering wealth of cultural tradition. They assume that an individual receives power by acquiring direct knowledge of sentient beings referred to in the mythic language of oral traditions (Ridington 1974; Rushforth 1986). Behind the individualism, flexibility, and autonomy reported for subarctic people lies a complex and well-understood system of interpersonal interdependence. People in subarctic Indian communities share knowledge about these beings as part of communicating what they know about the resource potential of an environment they hold in common. They explore their place in a complex world of other sentient "persons" by following the multiple possibilities of this fundamental "mental percept." They are both autonomous in these negotiations and considered responsible for any consequences that may result. Animals and natural forces know and respond to them and to one another. Because their category of "person" includes sentient animals, animal masters, and forces of nature, northern natives negotiate social relations in the same way that they negotiate relations with animals and natural forces.

The individualism of subarctic people is fundamentally different from that of people in a system of social hierarchy. It is very like the individualism Woodburn describes for what he calls "immediate return" egalitarian societies (Woodburn 1982). In such an egalitarian society the authority of individual judgments requires respect for individual autonomy and nonintervention, while in a system of social hierarchy individualism is viewed as the mechanism by which some people gain the power to intervene in the lives of others. Leaders in the subarctic demonstrate knowledge and the ability to negotiate with human and nonhuman persons, while leaders in hierarchical societies often demonstrate an ability to command and control others. The individualistic form of leadership found among subarctic people is easily misunderstood as a lack of leadership. Leaders communicate by articulating what is commonly known, rather than by giving orders.

Henriksen (1973) gives a particularly good account of reciprocity as a basis for leadership among the Naskapi. The leader, he says, must "be aware of deviating opinions among his followers," and must "voice his own opinion in relation to that of others" (Henriksen 1973:48). "No one," he says, "will either give or take orders from others . . . they are even reluctant to give advice, and when consulted usually answer, '*mokko tchin*'; that is, 'it's up to you' " (Henriksen 1973:44). Autonomy is equally important for both leaders and followers. In order to be well informed, he says, the follower "wants to know all the alternatives." Consequently, "in any Naskapi camp, people are continually 'spying' on each other, trying to find out what everyone is thinking of doing" (Henriksen 1973:48).

My own experience with the Dunne-za illustrates how a leader may instruct without giving orders. After I had spent several years in Dunne-za communities of the Peace River area, their Dreamer, Charlie Yahey, let it be known in one of his talks about Heaven that "the people in heaven" with whom he was in contact knew about me. He said that I could expect to join them there sometime. He said it was good for me to dance during the summer pow-wows. The message he conveyed was complex and "multivocal." It acknowledged that I had spent enough time among the Dunne-za to accumulate a certain amount of shared experience. The story of my life had become one of their stories. The Dreamer's statement articulated our mutual understanding that should I die, my shadow would walk back in the dark of night along the trails I had taken in life. It would not be light enough to rise along *yagatunne*, the "trail to Heaven," until it had passed back through negative events and experiences.

In Dunne-za theory, the presence of a shadow trail near those of the living is considered to be dangerous, especially to the lives of small children, whose own shadows are very light and easily disassociated from their bodies. The ghost's journey backward can only be shortened by dancing with others around a common fire to the "dreamers' songs" (Ridington 1978:24–26). Dancing is a way people demonstrate good will to one another and to the other nonhuman persons of their environment. Charlie Yahey's statement that the people in Heaven knew me thus made sense as part of complex cultural assumptions about the responsibility individuals have in relation to all sentient persons. The statement was his way of explaining to me why I should dance.

It is a common experience of subarctic fieldworkers to "find it virtually impossible to follow a discussion of argument" (Scollon and Scollon 1979:186) because a context of shared experience is missing, or because the culture's mental percepts are not known. But it is possible, also, to follow Hallowell's suggestion that a "higher order of objectivity" may be obtained "by adopting a perspective which includes an analysis of the outlook of the people themselves" (Hallowell 1960:21). Such an order of objectivity requires that the observer understand both the mental percepts of subarctic people, and at least something of the mythic and personal stories within which their subtle and ongoing communication is embedded. He or she must be willing to accept that social life and communication among subarctic hunter-gatherers includes a wider range of "persons" than the language and culture of social science generally admits. The ethnographer must discover concepts within his or her language of description that resonate with those of subarctic people.

Communication based on assumed mutual understandings has been described by sociologist Basil Bernstein (1971:157–158, 200) as a "restricted" as opposed to an "elaborated" code of discourse. Although Bernstein developed his distinction in reference to class differences within a modern urban culture, and there are serious problems with his application of the idea, his terms may be adapted to describe an important quality of communication among northern hunting people. Restricted discourse refers to communication in which the context of communication is taken for granted. Such a social setting provides ample opportunity for references to mutually shared knowledge and experience. When applied to the oral communications of highly individualistic subarctic native communities, Bernstein's "restricted" code might better be called a "reflexive" code, in that discourse depends upon each person placing his or her self within a mutually understood context. Bernstein's distinction would then refer to differences between systems in which the context is assumed, and those in which it must be specified.

Edward Hall has described a similar phenomenon in the distinction he makes between "high and low context messages." According to Hall, "the more information that is shared . . . the higher the context" (1983:56–57). Discourse in small subarctic communities would, in Hall's terms, be highly contexted because of the shared mutual understandings on which it is predicated. Hallowell's "higher order of objectivity" would then be required to develop an interpretive language capable of translating such a highly contexted form of communication.

Ethnographers have described northern hunting people as individualistic because they correctly note that each person is expected to inform and thereby empower his or her self within the mutually understood context of shared knowledge and a shared code of communication.

Their individualism is not, however, at odds with their social context. Indeed, the individualism of Northern Indian people is based upon a fundamental social compact, a trust in the individual's social responsibility and informed intelligence. Northern hunting people trust the individual to be responsible, not only to his or her self, but also to all the other human and trans-human persons of a sentient social environment, in its widest possible context (Hallowell 1960; Scollon and Scollon 1979; Goulet 1987). The intelligence of individual human judgment, and the system of cultural intelligence that informs it, thus define a fundamental resource on which all other adaptations depend.

Northern Hunting Knowledge and Technology
Subarctic hunting people depend fundamentally on knowledge and technique for their successful adaptation to the environment. Although they have been capable of producing elaborate hunting implements such as bows and arrows, traps, and deadfalls (Oswalt 1973:118–119), they also achieve complex interactions with their environment without having recourse to complex material artifacts. Northern hunters have, for instance, traditionally carried out artfully organized communal hunts with a minimum of material possessions. Using artifacts as simple as snares, they have relied on knowledge held in common to work quietly and autonomously toward a common purpose. In some cases "hunt chiefs" (Ridington 1987a) visualize and direct the overall hunt plan through dreaming, but success ultimately depends upon the individual's understanding of human and animal behavior in relation to environmental features. Although the physical *artifacts* required for this form of hunting are minimal, success depends on a complex and sophisticated form of *artifice* and understanding (Ridington 1983). It is easy for an outside observer to interpret information about dreaming and knowledge differently from information about material culture, because of an unexamined assumption that technology *means* material culture. Such an assumption could disguise the full adaptive significance of knowledge for subarctic people and result in what Christian called "a superficial and misleading study" (Christian and Gardner 1977:100–101).

In their *Handbook* article on "Environment and Culture in the Cordillera," McClellan and Denniston describe the technology of Cordilleran Athapaskans as "admirably adapted to mobility" (1981:377). They say that "people carried little with them, since many things could be made rather quickly with materials close at hand." They cite snare and surround hunting to illustrate the mobility, economy, and essentially mental quality of subarctic technology:

> What was absolutely critical was the knowledge of how to use the equipment effectively in varying situations, where best to set the snare or deadfall or to build a caribou surround, where to go on one's snowshoes to locate a moose, how to bait a wolverine deadfall or to disguise the human odor on a beaver net. The successful hunter had to know the landscape, the habits of his prey, and the probable course of the weather. *Equally essential to his mind was the knowledge of how to behave in a personalized universe in which many animal spirits were thought to be more powerful than humans.* [McClellan and Denniston 1981:377; emphasis added]

Northern forest Indians are well aware that their means of production are mental as well as material. Their subsistence technology has emphasized the possession of techniques rather than artifacts. Elsewhere I have suggested that

> In thinking about hunting and gathering people who must move frequently from place to place . . . technology should be seen as a system of knowledge rather than an inventory of objects. . . . The essence of hunting and gathering adaptive strategy is to retain, and to be able to act upon, information about the possible relationships between people and the natural environment. When realized, these life-giving relationships are as much the artifacts of hunting and gathering technology as are the material objects that are instrumental in bringing them about. [Ridington 1982:471]

Conclusions

Knowledge, power, and individual intelligence are keys to understanding the adaptive competence of northern hunting people. The individualism of these people is intelligible only in relation to *their* understanding that an individual's sentient intelligence must make contact with an intelligent organization of the environment at large. Their individualism is sustained by their closely contexted communities, in which a great deal of information about social and natural conditions is held in common. The phenomenology of northern hunting people may be seen as integral to their overall adaptive strategy. Their "religion" may be viewed as social and psychological dimensions of their technology.

Although the traditions of scholarship among Algonquianists and Athapaskanists differ in the attention they pay to native phenomenology and psychology, both indicate that northern native individualism must be understood in relation to empowering cultural theory. A significant number of the anthropologists who studied people of the Subarctic have made contributions to anthropological theory. Many of these contributions seem to have transformed elements of native theory into the language of social science. These contributions correspond to what Hallowell called a "higher order" of objectivity that adopts "a perspective which includes an analysis of the outlook of the people themselves."

Subarctic ethnography is important to anthropological theory as a whole, in that the adaptive conditions experienced by the subarctic native people of North America are in many ways similar to those of northern hunter-gatherers in much earlier times. Fundamental traditions of human thought and practice may have evolved and been sustained in the cultures of northern hunter-gatherers. Their cultures may be understood as systems of information that guide and sustain the intelligence of individual thought and action. The cultural and individual intelligence they have developed are complementary products of a long co-evolutionary process.

Note

1. Lola Romanucci-Ross (1987, personal communication) reports that Hallowell also gave credit to long and intensive conversations about theory with David Bidney as an important source of his thinking about self and environment.

References Cited

Armitage, Peter

1987   Tshekuan issishueu Mitshikapeu?: The Fart Man in Innu Religious Ideology. Paper presented at 1987 CESCE Conference, Quebec City.

Bernstein, Basil

1971   Class, Codes and Control. London: Routledge & Kegan Paul.

Black, Mary

1977a   Ojibwa Power Belief Systems. In The Anthropology of Power. Ray Fogelson and Richard Adams, eds. Pp. 141–152. New York: Academic Press.

1977b   Ojibwa Taxonomy and Percept Ambiguity. Ethos 5(1): 90–118.

Brody, Hugh
  1981 Maps and Dreams. Vancouver: Douglas and McIntyre.
Brown, Jennifer
  1986 Northern Algonquians from Lake Superior and Hudson Bay to Manitoba in the Historic Period. *In* Native Peoples: The Canadian Experience. R. Bruce Morrison and C. Roderick Wilson, eds. Pp. 208–243. Toronto: McClelland and Stewart.
Christian, Jane, and Peter M. Gardner
  1977 The Individual in Northern Dene Thought and Communication: A Study in Sharing and Diversity. National Museum of Man Mercury Series No. 35. Ottawa: National Museums of Canada.
Feit, Harvey
  1986 Hunting and the Quest for Power: The James Bay Cree and Whitemen in the Twentieth Century. *In* Native Peoples: The Canadian Experience. R. Bruce Morrison and C. Roderick Wilson, eds. Pp. 171–207. Toronto: McClelland and Stewart.
Geertz, Clifford
  1973 The Interpretation of Cultures. New York: Basic Books.
Goulet, Jean-Guy
  1987 Ways of Knowing with the Mind: An Ethnography of Aboriginal Beliefs. Paper presented at 1987 CESCE Conference, Quebec City.
Gumperz, John J.
  1977 Lecture to Language Planning Colloquium. Summer Institute of the Linguistic Society of America, University of Hawaii (cited in Scollon and Scollon 1979:185).
Hall, Edward T.
  1983 The Dance of Life: The Other Dimension of Time. Garden City: Anchor/Doubleday.
Hallowell, A. Irving
  1942 The Role of Conjuring in Saulteaux Society. Philadelphia: Publications of the Anthropological Society 2.
  1955 Culture and Experience. Philadelphia: University of Pennsylvania Press.
  1960 Ojibwa Ontology, Behavior, and World View. *In* Culture and History. Stanley Diamond, ed. Pp. 19–52. New York: Columbia University Press.
Helm, June, ed.
  1981 Subarctic. Handbook of North American Indians, Vol. 6. Washington: Smithsonian Institution.
Henriksen, Georg
  1973 Hunters in the Barrens: The Naskapi on the Edge of the White Man's World. Newfoundland Social and Economic Studies No. 12.
Honigmann, John J.
  1949 Culture and Ethos of Kaska Society. Yale University Publications in Anthropology No. 40. New Haven: Yale University Press.

1981 Expressive Aspects of Subarctic Indian Culture. *In* Handbook of North American Indians, Vol. 6. June Helm, ed. Pp. 718–738. Washington: Smithsonian Institution.

Jarvenpa, Robert
1982 Intergroup Behavior and Imagery: The Case of Chipewyan and Cree. Ethnology 21(4):283–299.

Keesing, Roger
1987 Anthropology as Interpretive Quest. Current Anthropology 27(2):161–176.

Krech, Shepard III
1980 Northern Athapaskan Ethnology in the 1970s. Annual Reviews in Anthropology, Vol. 9. Pp. 83–100. Palo Alto: Annual Reviews Inc.

Marano, Lou
1982 Windigo Psychosis: The Anatomy of an Emic-Etic Confusion. Current Anthropology 23(4):385–412.

Marcus, George, and Michael Fisher
1986 Anthropology as Cultural Critique. Chicago: University of Chicago Press.

Martin, Calvin
1987 The American Indian and the Problem of History. New York: Oxford University Press.

McClellan, Catherine, and Glenda Denniston
1981 Environment and Culture in the Cordillera. *In* Handbook of North American Indians, Vol. 6.

June Helm, ed. Pp. 372–386. Washington: Smithsonian Institution.

Morris, Brian
1985 The Rise and Fall of the Human Subject. Man 20(4):722–742.

Oswalt, Wendall
1973 Habitat and Technology: The Evolution of Hunting. New York: Holt, Rinehart and Winston.

Preston, Richard J.
1975 Cree Narrative: Expressing the Personal Meaning of Events. National Museum of Man Mercury Series No. 30. Ottawa: National Museums of Canada.

1980 The Witiko: Algonkian Knowledge and Whiteman Knowledge. *In* Manlike Monsters on Trial. M. Halpin and M. Ames, eds. Pp. 111–131. Vancouver: University of British Columbia Press.

Ridington, Robin
1976 Wechuge and Windigo: A Comparison of Cannibal Belief among Boreal Forest Athapaskans and Algonquians. Anthropologica 18(2):107–129.

1978 Swan People: A Study of the Dunne-za Prophet Dance. Canadian Ethnology Service Mercury Series No. 38. Ottawa: National Museums of Canada.

1979 Sequence and Hierarchy in Cultural Experience: Phases and the Moment of Transformation.

Anthropology and Humanism Quarterly 4(4):2–10.

1982 Technology, World View and Adaptive Strategy in a Northern Hunting Society. Canadian Review of Sociology and Anthropology 19(4):469–481.

1983 From Artifice to Artifact: Stages in the Industrialization of a Northern Native Community. Journal of Canadian Studies 18(3):55–66.

1987a From Hunt Chief to Prophet: Beaver Indians and Christianity. Arctic Anthropology 24(1):8–18.

1987b Models of the Universe: The Poetic Paradigm of Benjamin Lee Whorf. Anthropology and Humanism Quarterly 12(1):16–24.

Rogers, Edward S.

1981 History of Ethnological Research in the Subarctic Shield and Mackenzie Borderlands. In Handbook of North American Indians, Vol. 6. June Helm, ed. Pp. 19–29. Washington: Smithsonian Institution.

Rushforth, Scott

1986 The Bear Lake Indians. In Native Peoples: The Canadian Experience. R. Bruce Morrison and C. Roderick Wilson, eds. Pp. 243–270. Toronto: McClelland and Stewart.

Savishinsky, Joel S.

1974 On the Trail of the Hare. New York: Gordon and Breach.

Scollon, Ronald, and Suzanne B. K. Scollon

1979 Linguistic Convergence: An Ethnography of Speaking at Fort Chipewyan, Alberta. London: Academic Press.

Sharp, Henry S.

1986 Shared Experience and Magical Death: Chipewyan Explanations of a Prophet's Decline. Ethnology 24(4):257–270.

1987 Giant Fish, Giant Otters, and Dinosaurs: "Apparently Irrational Beliefs" in a Chipewyan Community. American Ethnologist 14(2):226–235.

Smith, David

1973 I^{n}ko^{n}ze: Magico-religious Beliefs of Contact-traditional Chipewyan Trading at Fort Resolution, NWT, Canada. National Museum of Man Mercury Series No. 6. Ottawa: National Museums of Canada.

1982 Moose-Deer Island House People: A History of the Native People of Fort Resolution. Ottawa: National Museum of Man Mercury Series Paper No. 6.

1985 Big Stone Foundations: Manifest Meaning in Chipewyan Myths. Journal of American Culture 18:73–77.

Speck, Frank

1935 Naskapi: The Savage Hunters of the Labrador Peninsula. Norman: University of Oklahoma Press.

Tanner, Adrian

1979 Bringing Home Animals: Religious Ideology and Mode of Production of the Mistassini Cree Hunters. Social and Economic Studies No. 23. St. John's: Memorial University Institute of Social and Economic Research.

VanStone, James W.

1974 Athapaskan Adaptations: Hunters and Fishermen of the Subarctic Forests. Arlington Heights: AHM Publishing.

Woodburn, James

1982 Egalitarian Societies. Man 17(3):431–451.

Theories of Social Honor

Elvin Hatch

VOL. 91, 1989, 341–353

The topic of social honor — or prestige, esteem, standing, distinction — is a perennial in the social sciences. Some writers deal systematically with the issue: Max Weber (Gerth and Mills 1958:186–194) and Thorstein Veblen (1953)[1899] are two examples from an earlier age, and Ortner and Whitehead (1981), Schwartz (1981), Turner (1984:124–143), and Frank (1985) represent four fairly recent instances, while a vast number of studies comment on the question indirectly.

Those who have written about status systems tend to assume that the idea of prestige is relatively self-evident, and so they tend to leave it unanalyzed. This in turn leads them to smuggle a number of assumptions into their analyses, including assumptions about what motivates people when they participate in prestige hierarchies and about the way those systems work. The elements that are smuggled into the account are often among the most interesting and important aspects of the study.

This article is an analysis of a variety of approaches to social honor or status systems, and it has two purposes. First, I argue against the common view that status systems can be explained in terms of material inequality, and I do so on the grounds that these approaches operate with a mistaken assumption about the motivation behind prestige systems and therefore about the way they work. Second, I show that a variety of nonmaterialist approaches have been employed in interpreting status systems, and I suggest that the differences among these nonmaterialist approaches reflect different assumptions about the nature of the individual. I also argue that one of these schemes is more tenable than the others.

I begin by discussing the materialist approaches to social honor, which attempt to explain status systems in terms of differences in economic resources and material power within society. I analyze two materialist approaches, starting with the isomorphic.

Materialist Approaches

What distinguishes the isomorphic approach is the postulate that the system of material inequality and the hierarchy of social honor tend to be isomorphic. This scheme rests upon several principles, the first of which is the assumption that wealth and power are cognitively salient: these are matters that people everywhere care about very much, and individuals are oriented by and large toward such material goals as securing and improving their own material well-being. These same individuals also tend to notice those who are wealthier or more powerful than they. Second is the assumption that people confer social honor on a person because of the place that he or she occupies within material systems of wealth and power. Since people find wealth and power desirable, they respect or envy those who have more than they; hence, an individual's position within the economic and political order is the basis for his or her standing within the hierarchy of social honor.

C. Wright Mills's criticism of Thorstein Veblen (Mills 1953:xvi–xvii) illustrates both of these assumptions. Mills takes Veblen to task for merely making fun of the leisure class and for failing to fully comprehend how sinister the matter is. What Veblen missed, according to Mills, is that "prestige buttresses power, turning it into authority, and protecting it from social challenge." Mills's argument rests on the premise that those who enjoy wealth and power also enjoy the respect and adulation of their inferiors, hence the insidiousness of the problem. Not only is society governed by a power elite, but those who are dominated come to admire those who dominate them.

A second illustration of the isomorphic thesis is found in Richard Lee's monograph on the !Kung (1979:242–248). Lee suggests that the !Kung employ a leveling mechanism, called "insulting the meat" (1984:48–50, 151–157), which deters the successful hunter from developing an attitude of arrogance and pridefulness. This is a pattern of rudely criticizing a hunter for failing to bring in more and better game, regardless of how much and excellent the catch might be. Lee's analysis assumes that if a man is successful in the economic sphere of hunting he will almost certainly enjoy the respect of the others, so differences in hunting ability should normally lead to a hierarchy of social honor among the !Kung. But this does not happen because of the leveling mechanism.

The reason the isomorphic thesis has such strong appeal is that it is a Western folk belief with which laypeople and anthropologists alike operate in their everyday lives. If one were to ask the typical American or European why the owners of large corporations have greater prestige than professors, he or she would almost certainly say that it is because the businessman makes more money, and implicitly the person would assume that people find wealth and power so desirable that they look up to those who possess them.

The third defining feature of the isomorphic thesis is that social honor is assigned a relatively unimportant role in society. Systems of social honor are dependent upon systems of wealth and power, and therefore one can usually infer the hierarchy of standing from the system of material inequality. It is true (according to the isomorphic thesis) that a degree of cultural lag may appear, in that people may confer social honor according to elements of a material hierarchy that no longer exists, such as when an aristocratic family continues to be accorded high standing after it has lost its wealth. But such incongruities are eventually overcome, and the current system of material inequality soon prevails.

The isomorphic thesis places little importance on social honor because it assumes that, at bottom, people care more about material wealth and power than they do about social standing, for indeed the one motivation is a by-product of the other. People bestow honor on those above them in the system of material inequality because they find wealth and power so desirable.

A fourth defining feature is epistemological. This is that the essentials of the hierarchy of social honor can be directly perceived by the senses: it is possible directly to observe that some people have more land than others, for example, and that some exercise greater power. A corollary is that there is no significant difference between the perspective of the observer and that of the individual within the system, for both look to the same objective phenomena — wealth and power — in grasping the status hierarchy. In principle, the members of society should see the same hierarchy by viewing it from their perspective as the observer does by using the frame of reference of the social scientist.

The isomorphic thesis faces serious empirical difficulties, for systems of social honor are not always isomorphic with systems of material inequality, and the discrepancies that appear cannot reasonably be explained in terms of cultural lag. Louis Dumont's (1980) analysis of the Indian caste system is illustrative. Another example is again the result of research in India, but whereas Dumont wrote chiefly about the Hindu, this is a case of Muslims living in a suburb of Madras City (Mines 1975). Mattison Mines found that these Muslims differentiate themselves from the more numerous Hindu by means of dress, language, and religious orthodoxy, even though they gain no political or economic advantages in doing so. Their motivation, rather, is a desire for status. Whereas wealth and political power serve as markers of success and standing by the standards of the majority society, they do not do so among the Muslims, for among the latter a man distinguishes himself by adhering to austere standards of orthodoxy. A wealthy Muslim in Madras City may be considered low in status, whereas a poor religious leader will enjoy high status (Mines 1975:413–414). A third case is the Tiwa-speaking Pueblos (Smith 1983), who exhibit little material inequality but significant differences in status. What is more, the hierarchy of standing is based largely on differences in the capacity for "right thinking," or in the qualities of mature wisdom and knowledge. Material inequalities are not the basis for the Tiwa system of social honor, and the latter is governed largely by its own principles.

A second materialist approach to status systems is contained in Maurice Bloch's analysis of the development of the state in central Madagascar (1977a). The hierarchy of material inequality there was characterized by the dominance of a small ruling elite, while the large majority of the population provided labor for the military and agricultural operations and for the construction of dikes. Yet this was not the way the people themselves viewed the system, for they conceived it in terms of a cultural idiom based upon the concept of *hacina*, a mystical power that was possessed to varying degrees by individuals. The relative status of each deme corresponded to the amount of *hacina* its members possessed. Since human fertility and the productivity of the land depended on *hacina*, this supernatural essence was essential to all members of society. *Hacina* was also linked to the political order, for the lives of even the lowliest subjects and the productivity of all the land were dependent on the bestowal of *hacina* by the rulers during the national rituals. In addition, superiors of various kinds (not only the rulers) conferred blessings of fertility and efficacy on those below them, and the latter reciprocated by giving deference and gifts.

The status hierarchy (which was the way the people perceived the hierarchical order) bore a certain relationship to the hierarchy of power (the system of inequality seen from the observer's point of view), in that the deme to which the rulers belonged was near the top of the hierarchy of standing. But the sharp cleavage separating rulers from the ruled was not mirrored in the system of status, for the cultural ideas produced a continuous gradation of rank. What is more, the rulers consisted of but a fraction of their deme, yet all the members of that deme — even those who were among the ruled — enjoyed the same high rank.

According to Bloch, the system of rank in central Madagascar was a mechanism that enabled the superior class to extract a surplus from their inferiors. On one hand it served to hide the reality of exploitation by blurring the line between the rulers and the ruled, and on the other, the supernatural essence made the dominated segment of society dependent on the rulers for the power of fertility they controlled.

Bloch's approach resembles the isomorphic scheme in minimizing the significance and autonomy of the hierarchy of standing, and it does so by building upon the same motivational principle that is fundamental to the isomorphic thesis. This is that people care more about material considerations than social honor. For example, why did the dominated class submit to the power of those who dominated them? In Bloch's analysis, it was largely because the subordinates believed that their material well-being was dependent on the mystical powers of their superiors. The interest in standing as such does not enter into Bloch's account. Indeed, he refers to the system of class domination as "real" and to the hierarchy of honor as a "pseudoreality" (1977a:146). The status system was insubstantial because the people really did not care about social standing as such, or at least not enough that this could be a dynamic element behind the system of rank.

This analysis forces a belief system to carry an enormous theoretical load. Bloch is no relativist in his thinking about reality (cf. Bloch 1977b), and he would have no difficulty applying a general standard of truth to say that the beliefs about *hacina* were mistaken. Yet the people held these beliefs with sufficient conviction that they were willing to submit to the demands of the hierarchy of rank and to endure the alienation of their own labor by working for the state. The beliefs led the people to see the system of rank as serving their material interests when in fact (when viewed from the observer's perspective) it controverted those interests.

The virtual elimination of the interest in standing as such, and of the relative autonomy of hierarchies of status, is as problematic for Bloch's scheme as it is for the isomorphic approach. Status systems cannot reasonably be explained by reference to their obfuscatory role in class domination, and the determination with which the people engage in them cannot be accounted for simply by the fact that the individual adheres to mistaken beliefs about the world.

The Theoretical Divide

Pierre Bourdieu's *Distinction* (1984) is another work that focuses on class domination, but the analysis in this book runs in a radically different direction from Bloch's. What is important about Bourdieu's study in the present context is that it is an example of a nonmaterialist approach to status systems; in particular, it reveals that when systems of inequality are seen from the perspective of social honor they assume a very different character — or operate according to a different logic — from what they do when they are approached from a materialist point of view. Bourdieu's book serves to instantiate the divide between the materialist and nonmaterialist perspectives.

Distinction is an examination of French taste in the 1960s, and an essential element of Bourdieu's analysis is the concept of capital, by which he means resources of different kinds that give some people advantages over others (1984:114). The two types of capital that he emphasizes in the book are economic and cultural. They are linked (1984:53–56) inasmuch as economic capital is a requisite for cultural capital: a person must have certain economic resources in order to have the freedom to cultivate the tastes of the dominant class. Another connection is that both have scarcity value (1984:133). Economic capital is scarce because the demand exceeds the supply, whereas taste (at least highbrow taste) is scarce because it requires cultivation or training that is not easily achieved. It is because of the element of scarcity that both types of capital can serve as distinguishing criteria for ordering people within a hierarchy of standing.

Material considerations enter into Bourdieu's analysis in an important way, and an example is his account of what he calls the taste of luxury that characterizes the dominant class. This taste, or lifestyle, rests upon the fact that the bourgeoisie are farther removed from economic necessity than the dominated classes. Yet the reason the bourgeoisie care so strongly about this feature of bourgeois life is not because it implies greater material benefits for them — greater creature comforts, greater freedom from physical labor, or more agreeable working conditions — but because it distances them from their inferiors. What is important is the symbolic role that these features play in the system of social honor.

It follows that something other than material considerations could be substituted as the principle underlying the distinction between the dominated and the dominant classes. Virtually any principle would do, such as degrees of religious knowledge, so long as it subdivides the society by virtue of its differential distribution among the population. In Bourdieu's analysis, the goal of domination is not to control material resources for purely material ends, but rather to enhance or affirm social standing through the exclusiveness of taste.

Consider his discussion of the chiastic structure of the dominant class (e.g., Bourdieu 1984:114–125, 260–295), which is made up of several fractions, one of which has a large volume of economic capital but a relatively low volume of cultural capital; this fraction is best exemplified by major industrial and commercial employers. Another fraction has a relatively low volume of economic capital, but owes its position to a large volume of cultural capital. This is best exemplified by artists and professors. While artists and professors are members of the dominant class, they are part of the dominated fraction of that class. According to Bourdieu, both of these fractions are engaged in a struggle with the other over the criteria by which to define their standing, and while those who are high in economic capital have been more successful, the implication seems to be that it could have turned out otherwise — the norms and values of the professor and artist could conceivably have prevailed, with all that would mean for the course of modern Western history.

If we push the implications of Bourdieu's analysis to their logical conclusions (which perhaps is farther than he himself would care to take them), we arrive at the position that material considerations enjoy the importance they do in modern France only because those who possess a large volume of this capital have managed to prevail in what Bourdieu calls the classification struggle (Bourdieu 1984:483). Modern industrial society presumably takes the form it does because one definition of significance and distinction has come to prevail over others that in principle are equally possible; presumably the process of industrialization itself was a historical result of the successes of the commercial and industrial sections in past classification struggles. The economic history of Western society is not the result of the unfolding of economic principles per se, but of the struggles among fractions of the dominant class over the criteria to be used for defining social honor.

Bourdieu was not the first to operate with the assumption that the interest in standing or achievement is a central motivation behind systems of inequality. One antecedent was Adam Smith, according to whom "it is not economic motivation that prompts a man to work, but status, respect, esteem, moral mettle, qualities which would allow him to be a man of worth and dignity" (Bell 1981:54, note 2). Another was Thorstein Veblen. But Bourdieu reveals the theoretical implications of this view with particular clarity.

This difference in assumption about motivations — between the materialist and nonmaterialist assumptions — constitutes the single most important divide in the study of status systems. A person becomes committed to a different analysis of social honor (and of systems of inequality in general) depending on the assumption that is used. The materialist assumption leads to the view that prestige systems can be explained in terms of the more basic system of material inequality, whereas the nonmaterialist assumption leads to the view that prestige systems are at least as important as systems of material inequality, and that they are governed by principles of their own.

If one grants the nonmaterialist thesis about the relative autonomy and importance of hierarchies of standing, then another issue comes into view. This is that the interest in social honor that underlies status hierarchies can itself be subdivided into a variety of subforms. There is not one way to conceive this nonmaterialist interest in standing, but several, and the way one conceives it will inform the analysis that is produced.

It must be made clear that I am not calling for a psychological explanation of hierarchies of standing. Motivations alone cannot account for the structures that appear or the strategies in which people engage; these are genuinely emergent systems. In addition, the kind of understanding I suggest is not one that looks for explanations in the scientific sense, for status hierarchies need to be understood interpretively. These are meaningful systems in that they are constituted by cultural ideas, and a central problem for the observer is to interpret the meanings that the agents employ. These are meaningful systems in another sense, in that the agents' actions are purposive, and in order to grasp what the individual is doing interpretive procedures must be used. The motivational assumptions used in apprehending these matters do not enable us to predict the kinds of hierarchies we will find, nor do they enable us to say why these hierarchies take the forms they do. But they do enable us to "see" these hierarchies and to interpret the actions of the participants within them.

One might argue that interpretive procedures are called for in the study of social honor but not for systems of material inequality, because the former is an immaterial system whereas the latter is not. By this view, social honor is immaterial in two ways: the question of who stands higher than whom is a matter of subjective judgment, and status symbols only exist as a matter of cultural definition. By contrast, systems of material inequality are made up of material phenomena that can be directly perceived by the senses, with the result that interpretive procedures are not called for. Yet this line of reasoning is mistaken for two reasons. On one hand, systems of material inequality are rooted in or constituted by cultural ideas in the same way as status systems. Property — land — is illustrative. This has a very material aspect, yet property as such does not exist apart from the cultural conceptions that define it. Among these are conceptions of ownership or entitlement, and the conceptions of person or group that are the property-holding entities. To understand inequalities in property-holding is as much an interpretive exercise as understanding a status hierarchy. On the other hand, the actions of individuals within a system of material inequality — such as the attempts of the members of a class to improve their material conditions, or even such seemingly transparent actions as those of an individual who is busy laying in food for the winter — are purposive. Here again, the process of understanding what these people are up to is an interpretive exercise requiring the use of hermeneutic procedures.

Nonmaterialist Approaches

Probably the most common nonmaterialist approach in the literature on social honor is that of the calculating prestige seeker, which views the human agent as a rational calculator whose goal is to maximize prestige. At least two versions of this notion — the cynical and the benign — can be distinguished.

The benign version is represented by George Homans (1961) and William Goode (1978), and a central feature of their approaches is that the individual acquires esteem by doing something or exhibiting some quality that others approve of, such as conforming to the norms of the group or presenting an outstanding musical performance. Consequently it is to the individual's advantage to express those forms of behavior or to exhibit those qualities, for in doing so he or she acquires the respect and admiration of others.

The element of calculation is more clearly illustrated in Goode's work, since Homans (in conformity with his firm behaviorism) attempts to avoid considerations about the individual's state of mind. Where this process is clearest in Goode's work is in an assumption that he borrows from classical economics, namely, that "Other things being equal, people will seek better terms for their social exchanges, as presumably they do for their economic exchanges" (1978:98–99). For example, a talented violin player will assess the degree of acclaim he or she can hope to achieve as a violinist, measure this prestige against both the risks and costs of entering that profession, and then decide whether or not to do so.

Yet Goode (like Homans) does not develop the image of the self-interested calculator as far as he might. Calculation occurs when the agent chooses among alternative courses of action while trying to maximize prestige, but it is missing from the agent's attitude toward the standards by which prestige is achieved or ascribed. This is particularly manifest in Goode's interpretation of the observing other (the member of society who rewards the prestige seeker with social esteem), who cheerfully confers prestige on the prestige seeker when the latter has earned it according to the rules. To hear an excellent violin performance, or to observe an individual adhering to particularly difficult social norms under trying conditions, stimulates an honest feeling of respect on the part of other members of society.

A more fully developed image of the calculating prestige seeker, the cynical version, is found in the works of a number of other writers, including such British social anthropologists as Malinowski and Leach. For example, the individual in Malinowski's society did not hesitate to manipulate the rules of the game if it was to his or her advantage and if it was possible to get away with it (Malinowski 1934, 1959[1926]; Hatch 1973:290–295).

Leach's *Political Systems of Highland Burma* (1954) presents a systematic analysis of the manipulation of rules for the purpose of maximizing social honor. In the opening pages of the book (1954:10) Leach implies that this is a study of power, but it is more accurately described as an analysis of a prestige system. For example, the *gumsa* chief receives little material advantage from his nominal ownership of the land (Leach 1954: 155–156), and while he can claim tribute from his subjects, what he receives is of very little economic importance. Nor does he enjoy significantly greater decision-making power than a number of other luminaries in his village (1954:183–190). What distinguishes the chief, rather, is his prestige or standing. Similarly, the range of differences in material wealth among the classes in a *gumsa* community is not very significant, although the range of differences in social honor is considerable (1954: 162, 163). The stake in this system is social standing, not material advantage.

In theory, *gumsa* conceptions define a rigidly hierarchical order, but in fact the rules are imprecise, which makes it possible to manipulate them for the purpose of improving one's standing. For example, the rules of succession to chiefship are clear and unambiguous, inasmuch as the youngest son succeeds to office. Yet the chief normally has several wives who were married under different circumstances, and consequently more than one "youngest son" may have a claim to office (1954:166). Change among the Kachin — from *gumsa* principles of organization to *gumlao*, and vice versa — is also a product of interested individuals manipulating the system for advantage. What happens when the *gumlao* revolt takes place, for example, is that certain people see that it is to their advantage to change the rules by which prestige is constituted. When a sufficient number of the chief's supporters conclude that their own interests would be better served by opting for an egalitarian *gumlao* system, the change occurs.

If we push the conception of the rational calculator to its logical conclusion we arrive at the view that the individual has no moral commitment at all to the prevailing system of norms, but adheres to them ultimately because of the personal benefits they offer. This was very nearly Malinowski's view (Hatch 1973:295–297), and Leach seems to come close to it as well when he suggests that the Kachin exchange one form of society (*gumsa* or *gumlao*) for the other when it is to their advantage (1954:197–263).

A second nonmaterialist approach to social honor is the ludic approach, and one of the clearest examples is the work of Johan Huizinga. In *Homo Ludens* (1949), Huizinga argues that the playful spirit is one of the main features of the human character, for human beings everywhere are interested in sport, contests, games, and performances. What is more, this ludic quality has played an important role in history, for it underlies the origin of such institutions as law (which initially was a type of contest [1949:76 ff.]) and warfare (1949:89 ff.). He writes that "pure play is one of the main bases of civilization" (1949:5).

This playful interest, according to Huizinga, also underlies the individual's striving for social honor, and it is not the high regard of others
that people seek when they engage in prestige systems, but the enjoyment of the game. The contrast between Huizinga's position and both
Malinowski's and Leach's is clear. From the latter perspective prestige is
the end that people seek, and prestige symbols (such as political office or
wealth) are tokens of prestige. From the ludic perspective the end that
people seek is the challenge of the contest, and prestige is the token.
Since prestige is a scarce good it may turn any valued activity into a
contest.

An example of Huizinga's interpretation of prestige systems is his
discussion of the potlatch (1949:58–62, 66). The potlatch dominates the
"communal life" of the Kwakiutl, and "everything connected with it
hinges on winning, on being superior, on glory, prestige, and . . . revenge" (1949:59). But prestige is not the goal, for the potlatch is a kind of
game. The players of course are hardly light-hearted about winning: this
is "serious play, fateful and fatal play, bloody play, sacred play," but play
nonetheless (1949:61).

Huizinga's scheme contains a patently objectionable feature, which
is that he sees competition as an inherent characteristic of play: he
implies that the playful impulse necessarily entails the "urge to be first"
(1949:105). Yet it is possible to cite a number of cases that Huizinga
would accept as play that are not necessarily competitive, such as cross-
word puzzles and the games that long-distance drivers make up to amuse
themselves. The activities of the artist fit here as well, to the extent
that he or she attempts to improve upon or elaborate a set of esthetic
principles.

Instead of competition, Huizinga should have placed his emphasis on
another feature that in his view is a central element of play. This is
the element of tension (1949:10–11), which involves the "uncertainty,
chanciness" that is associated with playful activities. In play, the success
of a certain course of action is never assured at the start, but is achieved
only by some element of skill, ability, ingenuity. "The player wants
something to 'go,' to 'come off'; he wants to 'succeed' by his own exer-
tions" (Huizinga 1949:10). Play—as Huizinga himself uses the term—
cannot exist where tension of this kind is absent, but it can exist in
situations without competition. Yet we can see why Huizinga emphasized the element of competition, for the latter increases the chanciness
of any course of action: in a contest with others the player is pitted

against not only the difficulty of the game, but the abilities of the other contestants as well.

A. L. Kroeber's notions about culture and the individual were very close to Huizinga's (Hatch 1973:91–112), and the play impulse in Kroeber's work had as its central feature what Huizinga called the element of tension. To Kroeber, people are drawn toward those areas of life where some course of action requires a measure of skill, or at least luck. For example, the successful businessman or -woman (in Kroeber's thinking) is not simply making a living or striving for prestige; he or she is engaged in a creative enterprise. The person's intellect is stimulated by the sport of success in a competitive and difficult milieu.

The line of thought that Kroeber and Huizinga pursued accounts for both ambitiousness and social hierarchies in human societies. Ambitiousness reflects the urge to participate successfully in an enterprise in which a degree of tension is found, and this creative urge draws people together in collective, creative activities, including competitive ones; hence the participants become ranked within a common hierarchy of achievement. Even if the element of competition is absent hierarchies will still form, because the qualities of the participants' achievements are noticed and evaluated by others.

The two nonmaterialist approaches to status systems that I have described provide radically different interpretations of systems of social honor. First, the very point of the individual's endeavors is different in the two cases. According to the logic of play the object is the experience of tension together with its successful resolution, whereas the logic of prestige takes the achievement of esteem as the goal. Second, the quality of the participants' actions is different in the two cases. On one hand the agent is conceived as creative and playful, and on the other as cynical, manipulative, and self-interested. Third, according to the logic of the calculating prestige seeker, competition is a necessary accompaniment of the achiever's efforts, inasmuch as his or her actions are oriented toward acquiring more prestige than others. But according to the logic of play, achievement need not entail competition, since it is possible to find the challenge of success in a variety of undertakings that do not involve outdoing anyone else. Fourth, the two frameworks evoke different values on the part of the observer. In Western society, at least, a person is not proud to be interested in prestige, but creativity is another matter. For example, one does not present a flattering picture of an American farmer if it is said that the great energy he devotes to increasing his wealth and improving his farm is motivated by the desire for prestige. But to say that farming has tapped the man's creative energies, and that he devotes himself wholeheartedly to it because he finds the work challenging, is to present his efforts in a very positive light.

A third nonmaterialist approach may be called the self-identity theory, and what is essential about it becomes clear when it is contrasted with the image of the calculating prestige seeker. According to the latter, since the individual's underlying motivation is to maximize prestige, his or her attention is focused outward toward other people, or toward their judgments about his or her accomplishments or other qualities. By contrast, the self-identity theory assumes that the agent's focus is primarily inward upon his or her own sense of self-worth. The underlying motivation is to achieve a sense of personal accomplishment or fulfillment, and the individual does so by engaging in activities or exhibiting qualities that are defined by the society as meritorious. Self-identity resides in the recognition that one's actions, indeed one's life, are important as judged by criteria that transcend one's personal self-interest.

Geddes (in Barkow 1975:565; see also Isichei, in Barkow 1975:566) provides the paradigmatic example of the self-identity theory. Geddes reacts against the perspective of the cynical prestige seeker, for in his view a successful undertaking may be fulfilling regardless of what others may think. "Competitive achievement" may seem important from the Euro-American point of view, yet other societies place at least as great an emphasis on the "pleasure of achievement for its own sake, especially important where aesthetic values are involved" (Geddes 1975:565). This motivation is "at least equal with status achievement . . . in the case of Dayak priests" (1975:565). Geddes is suggesting that the Dayak priest carries out his role largely because doing so provides him with the sense that his life is both meaningful and well-spent.

If the individual's actions are oriented toward achieving personal identity, how do we explain hierarchies of standing, which rest on the principle that people look outward in making judgments about others? Even if I am truly unconcerned about how others regard my actions, those others will still evaluate what I do. Even the Dayak priest who devotes himself single-mindedly to religious matters will find that he has a definable position within a local hierarchy of honor, and that his religious devotion plays an important role in people's judgments about where he stands in it. The observing other is ubiquitous, and hierarchies of standing are virtually inevitable. What is more, even though my orientation is inward, toward my own self-identity, the prevailing cultural system defines what is meritorious and therefore what it takes for me to achieve a meaningful life. We are faced with the paradox that I cannot pursue my own self-identity independently of the opinions of others, for the prevailing values provide me with the model for my actions.

The self-identity approach to social honor underlies Bourdieu's *Distinction*. For example, the classification struggle within the dominant class between the fraction with a large volume of cultural capital and the fraction with a large volume of economic capital is not merely a struggle over prestige, but over the definition of the meaningful life. From the perspective of the industrial and commercial employers, the values and lifestyle of artists and professors are spurious and supercilious, whereas their own way of life is right-minded and genuine; the reverse is true from the perspective of the artists and professors. Bourdieu writes (1984:57),

> At stake in every struggle over art there is also the imposition of an art of living, that is, the transmutation of an arbitrary way of living into the legitimate way of life which casts every other way of living into arbitrariness. The artist's life-style is always a challenge thrown at the bourgeois life-style, which it seeks to condemn as unreal and even absurd by a sort of practical demonstration of the emptiness of the values and powers it pursues.

Much later in the book he writes (1984:478),

> In short, what individuals and groups invest in the [social classifications that reflect differences in life-style] . . . is infinitely more than their "interest" in the usual sense of the term; it is their whole social being, everything which defines their own idea of themselves, the primordial, tacit contract whereby they define "us" as opposed to "them," "other people," and which is the basis of the exclusions ("not for the likes of us") and inclusions they perform. . . .

The self-identity approach to social honor also appears in the work of both Max Weber and Thomas Mann. Harvey Goldman (1988) has recently analyzed the concept of personality or personal character that Weber and Mann had in common, and the *concept of "calling"* plays a central role in Goldman's analysis. A "calling" is work that is something more than a purely practical response to material needs. To engage in a calling, rather, is to engage in the service of a higher principle, and therefore it entails discipline and sacrifice, but above all a striving toward achievement. The calling is linked in turn to the individual's sense of self. The calling confers meaning on a person's life by justifying the lines of action in which he or she engages. And it rests on the principle that the individual is interested not simply in the approval of others, but in achieving a sense of self-worth.

The notion of calling was central to Weber's analysis of capitalism, and with capitalism (according to Goldman's analysis of Weber) came a new type of character or person. The older nobility judged itself not in terms of what it did, but in terms of its station in life. The new aristocracy, however — the Calvinist entrepreneurs — had no sense of self-worth apart from their work.

Mann's novels and essays focus on the relationship between the artist and bourgeois society, and they make a point that is very similar to Weber's. The artist in Mann's work is engaged in a selfless devotion to a higher creative goal which provides a sense of identity. Yet the artist's sense of self is fragile, because the artist's life and accomplishments are not truly appreciated by bourgeois society, which values business, politics, professional degrees, and the like. *Tonio Kröger* is illustrative. Tonio feels himself called to the life of the intellect and becomes a writer, which demands complete sacrifice. Yet his calling is also an affliction, because it cuts him off from the ordinary people with whom he identifies — they share neither his insights nor his artistic interests. The ones who appreciate his work are rather those whom he considers crippled and vengeful — the victims of life who are not truly a part of bourgeois society. Tonio has found his calling, but he never fully succeeds in achieving a sense of self-worth because the calling he has chosen does not receive the social validation he needs.

Tonio Kröger illustrates a crucial point that is implicit in Goldman's analysis. The notion of calling is intensely social, in that the individual feels compelled to seek the validation of others for what he or she does. This ratification surely was not all that is needed to make the calling meaningful. For example, Tonio does overcome self-doubt through his art; he is able to experience and feel as normal people cannot. His art provides him with a standard for judging his own self-worth that to a degree is independent of others' opinions. Yet their opinions are not irrelevant, for he remains lonely and alienated from the bourgeois society that simply does not value the artist's work.

In Weber's view the concept of calling is associated with both Calvinism and capitalism and virtually never appears in traditional societies. But it would not be difficult to frame the notion in sufficiently general terms to make it apply to cases as disparate as French taste, Kachin *gumsa* status seeking, and Muslim standards of religious orthodoxy. What is unique to capitalism need not be the element of striving, or a unique attitude toward work, but rather a unique attitude toward the accumulation of wealth as a *kind* of work. In other societies the individual's ambitions may be directed toward such activities as gift-exchange or the expression of religious purity, but the goal would be the same as the Calvinist entrepreneur's, the achievement of a sense of identity.

Conclusion

Earlier I suggested that attempts to explain status systems by reference to patterns of material inequality are inadequate because analyses of that kind do not give sufficient recognition to the force and independence of the interest in social honor. Materialist approaches seriously misconstrue the dynamics of status systems. Granting this, however, we are now faced with another, similar problem, which is to choose among the several nonmaterialist approaches that are in use.

The approach of the calculating prestige seeker has flourished in anthropology since about the 1950s, perhaps in conjunction with the growing cynicism of modern society. As the mood in general turned more cynical, and as political alienation grew, the idea that the members of society are manipulative seekers after their own self-interest, and that they take a calculating attitude toward the cultural and social systems in which they participate, became increasingly appealing. By contrast, the ludic point of view seems untenable in light of the traumatic political and economic events of recent decades. The ludic approach suffers another difficulty of similar order, for it is hard to accept that the creative, playful impulse could be the impetus behind prestige systems that incorporate significant amounts of violence, such as Plains Indian warfare. Can it truly be that such sober and fearful activities are in truth a form of play?

Yet the approach of the calculating prestige seeker also faces difficulties. These are the ones that Durkheim and Talcott Parsons identified in relation to the theories of such individualistic writers as Herbert Spencer (see Hatch 1973:168–169). Put simply, social order is impossible if the individual is governed by unfettered self-interest, for such a system must eventually lead to the Hobbesian war of all against all. The same point can be made in relation to status systems. If we assume the approach of the calculating prestige seeker, then we are led to expect that the higher a person's standing, the greater the stake he or she has in the system. It follows that the relative losers in the struggle — the low-ranking Trobrianders or Kwakiutl — should find it in their interest to subvert or reject the system outright since it offers them virtually no advantages. The point perhaps is arguable, but the ethnographic record does not suggest that this has often occurred. The low-ranking Trobrianders or Kwakiutl may have expressed grievances and frustrations over their social positions, but they seem to have remained committed to the status systems in which they found themselves.

While both the ludic approach and that of the calculating prestige seeker are difficult to defend, the self-identity theory is highly credible and produces a very compelling account of prestige systems. For example, it is not confounded by the problem of why low-ranking people often seem to feel that they have a stake in the hierarchy. What is most important from their perspective is not where they stand vis-à-vis one another. Consequently, the value of the system to them is not contingent on how high a position they have within it. A low-ranking Trobriand man may not enjoy high prestige, but he may experience a strong sense of fulfillment from his activities as a craftsman, fisherman, or gardener, and from his contribution to the matrilineage. A lowly position and a strong sense of duty are neither incompatible nor contradictory.

In addition, while the self-identity approach may not be fully compatible with the cynical image of human action that has come to occupy such a prominent place in the social sciences, unlike the ludic approach it has no difficulty accounting for the dead seriousness that is sometimes expressed in status systems or the violent turn that they sometimes take. For example, Plains Indian warfare — or warfare that is carried out with the goal of advancing Muslim or Christian principles — can be interpreted as attempts to assert one view of the meaningful life over others. What is at stake in these struggles (among other things) is the individual's sense of the value and importance of life itself.

Acknowledgments. An earlier version of this article was presented at the meetings of the American Anthropological Association in Chicago in November 1987, and I am grateful for the comments of those who attended the session. I am also grateful for comments from Richard Feinberg, Mary Helms, Bill Jankowiak, Herbert Lewis, Mattison Mines, M. Estellie Smith, and Jon Turner. I profited as well from comments by the Breakfast Club, particularly from Catherine Albanese, Manthia Diawara, Roger Friedland, Elliot Jurist, A. F. Robertson, Eric White, and Mayfair Yang.

References Cited

Barkow, Jerome H.
   1975   Prestige and Culture: A Bio-
      social Interpretation. Current
      Anthropology 16(4):553–572.
Bell, Daniel
   1981   Models and Reality in Eco-
      nomic Discourse. *In* The Crisis
      in Economic Theory. Daniel
      Bell and Irving Kristol, eds.
      Pp. 46–80. New York: Basic
      Books.
Bloch, Maurice
   1977a   The Disconnection be-
      tween Power and Rank as a Pro-
      cess: An Outline of the Develop-
      ment of Kingdoms in Central
      Madagascar. Archives Euro-
      péenes de Sociologie 18(1):107–
      148.
   1977b   The Past and the Present
      in the Present. Man 12(1):278–
      292.
Bourdieu, Pierre
   1984   Distinction: A Social Cri-
      tique of the Judgment of Taste.
      Richard Nice, transl. Cambridge,
      MA: Harvard University Press.
Dumont, Louis
   1980   Homo Hierarchicus: The
      Caste System and Its Implica-
      tions. Mark Sainsbury, transl.
      Chicago: University of Chicago
      Press.
Frank, Robert H.
   1985   Choosing the Right Pond:
      Human Behavior and the Quest
      for Status. New York: Oxford
      University Press.

Gerth, H. H., and C. Wright Mills
   1958   From Max Weber: Essays
      in Sociology. H. H. Gerth and
      C. Wright Mills, eds. and transls.
      New York: Oxford University
      Press.
Goldman, Harvey
   1988   Max Weber and Thomas
      Mann: Calling and the Shaping of
      the Self. Berkeley: University of
      California Press.
Goode, William J.
   1978   The Celebration of Heroes:
      Prestige as a Social Control Sys-
      tem. Berkeley: University of Cal-
      ifornia Press.
Hatch, Elvin
   1973   Theories of Man and Cul-
      ture. New York: Columbia Uni-
      versity Press.
Homans, George Caspar
   1961   Social Behavior: Its Elemen-
      tary Forms. New York: Harcourt,
      Brace & World.
Huizinga, Johan
   1949   Homo Ludens: A Study of
      the Play-Element in Culture.
      R. F. C. Hull, transl. London:
      Routledge & Kegan Paul.
Leach, Edmund
   1954   Political Systems of High-
      land Burma. Cambridge, MA:
      Harvard University Press.
Lee, Richard
   1979   The !Kung San: Men,
      Women, and Work in a Foraging
      Society. New York: Cambridge
      University Press.

1984 The Dobe !Kung. New York: Holt, Rinehart and Winston.

Malinowski, Bronislaw

1934 Introduction. *In* Law and Order in Polynesia, by H. Ian Hogbin. Pp. xvi–lxxii. New York: Harcourt Brace.

1959[1926] Crime and Custom in Savage Society. Patterson, NJ: Littlefield, Adams & Company.

Mills, C. Wright

1953 Introduction to the Mentor Edition. *In* The Theory of the Leisure Class, by Thorstein Veblen. Pp. vi–xix. New York: Mentor Books.

Mines, Mattison

1975 Islamisation and Muslim Ethnicity in South India. Man 10(3):404–419.

Ortner, Sherry B., and Harriet Whitehead

1981 Introduction: Accounting for Sexual Meanings. *In* Sexual Meanings: The Cultural Construction of Gender and Sexuality. Sherry B. Ortner and Harriet Whitehead, eds. Pp. 1–27.

Cambridge: Cambridge University Press.

Schwartz, Barry

1981 Vertical Classification: A Study in Structuralism and the Sociology of Knowledge. Chicago: University of Chicago Press.

Smith, M. Estellie

1983 Pueblo Councils: An Example of Stratified Egalitarianism. *In* The Development of Political Organization in Native North America (1979 Proceedings of the American Ethnological Society). Elisabeth Tooker, ed. Washington: American Ethnological Society.

Turner, Jonathan H.

1984 Societal Stratification: A Theoretical Analysis. New York: Columbia University Press.

Veblen, Thorstein

1953[1899] The Theory of the Leisure Class. Introduction by C. Wright Mills. New York: Mentor Books.

Kalapalo Biography:

Psychology and Language in a South American Oral History

Ellen B. Basso

VOL. 91, 1989, 551–569

The study of personal narratives is becoming more and more popular, as symbolic-interpretive anthropologists have followed anthropological linguists in changing their analytic focus from structure to discourse, and as those attending to psychological matters recognize the need to understand how ideas of emotion and subjectivity (or the "self") are realized in and through discourse. We hear an insistent call for consideration of the stories people tell about themselves so as to learn about what is significant to them about their experiences of life, and for understanding the rhetorical and poetic strategies they use to speak about those experiences. It would seem that the discourse-focused study of personal narratives challenges anthropologists, as the editors of a recent book on Native American discourse claim, to recast the relations between language, culture, society, and the individual.[1]

Yet, while several writers have already made plain how crucial to an anthropological understanding of local histories are biographical and autobiographical narratives, these are often treated as if they were "microhistories," exemplifying generalized and personally decontextualized trends and processes. Anthropologists seem to continue to search these stories about individual experiences in the past for clues about collective experiences in time, evidence about the origins of particular concepts, or changing notions of role and of moral identity that serve as models for contemporary people to follow.[2] Important as such conclusions have been, they tend to obscure those ideas of *personal* process best realized through narrative. As long as history is treated merely as a context that surrounds the progress of individuals, discourse forms in which there is considerable attention paid to private interests will have a secondary status for understanding historical consciousness, still regarded as primarily a *collective* consciousness. A closer look might help us to recognize in those narratively constituted ideas of emotional events, individual agency, and personal development some important testimony about historical processes themselves.

Ideology and History in the Upper Xingu River Basin

In the Upper Xingu River Basin of central Brazil are nine local communities, speaking (generally, monolingually) at least four mutually unintelligible languages. They share a common technology, a large number of key symbols, an extensive oral tradition, and very similar ritual activities (in some of which several settlements participate jointly). In 1982, each settlement was named and territorially autonomous, specialized with respect to a commodity produced for trade with other groups, and said to be descended (although sometimes vaguely and imprecisely) from common leader-ancestors. Upper Xingu settlements consist of a number of communal family households, each of which is organized around two families related to each other through kinship or marriage or both; there are no descent units or ceremonial moieties such as are found among other central Brazilian peoples. Household and settlement groups depend considerably for their maintenance upon the ties between individuals. All settlements in fact include at least some people who were born elsewhere, and most people participate in multiple and cross-cutting kinship and affinal relationships, both within and outside their communities. Consequently, individuals throughout the region are united by an extensive network of these relationships that includes every Upper Xingu settlement (cf. Basso 1973). Although members of particular settlements sometimes express a sense of their own uniquely pure and rigorous adherence to Upper Xingu values, epitomized by the demeanor of their hereditary leaders, there is also a notion of the moral whole (called *kuge* by the Carib-speaking Kalapalo with whom I lived), made to stand in marked contrast to the geographically marginal and frequently hostile groups (called *angikogo* by the Kalapalo) who seemed — before many were displaced by Brazilian ranchers — to surround the Upper Xingu Basin.

Kalapalo Historical Narratives

When I first visited the Kalapalo in 1966, I was impressed with the strong and repeatedly stated conviction they held about the importance of something they called *ifutisu*. They presented themselves to me as people valuing a "distanced" personal composure involving peaceful and respectful calm in one's relations with others, expressed in generosity and cheerfulness. In certain contexts, *ifutisu* can also mean bashfulness, shame, and the aloof withdrawal of affines from one another. People repeatedly told me that what distinguished them (and others in the Upper Xingu area) from all other native people (especially the club-carrying Ge and the marauding Txicão) was simply that they were not "fierce" (*itsotunda*) but "controlled" (*ifutisunda*). The Kalapalo also distinguished themselves from others by the fact that they refrained from eating game animals. The practice of hunting game must have been discarded fairly recently, though, since quite a few Kalapalo stories contained vivid descriptions of people hunting, butchering, and smoking meat. The Kalapalo took considerable notice of what people ate, since eating only the "right" things was a significant public demonstration of individual responsibility for engendering qualities of restraint (*ifutisu*).

I thought at first these were simply ways the Kalapalo expressed their fear and scorn of people who lived on the margins of the Upper Xingu Basin, particularly at a time when the Brazilian *chefe do posto* administrators showed greater admiration for the rugged character of the more flamboyantly aggressive Ge communities to the north. But I now think that in these practices and attitudes about themselves the Kalapalo are making a contrast with their own past. In stories they tell about how their ancestors lived, they reveal that in certain ways the past is abhorrent to them; just as they have gladly (they say) given up eating most meat, so have they freed themselves from activities of the kind they see continued by their violent neighbors.

Many narratives about the past focus upon individuals who are called ancestors (*ĩfugu*) of living people, or more correctly (since direct family connections are absent) of contemporary communities. These ancestors seem to have lived precariously, frequently being attacked by *angikogo* and in turn leading attacks of their own. In contrast to the large, long-settled communities of today, these ancestors—living in small groups and moving about with some frequency—were suspicious and often hostile toward one another. Many were refugees, fleeing from attacks by other *angikogo*. Some tried to create ties with *angikogo*, but the consequences were often grim. The stories Kalapalo tell about such encounters meticulously describe cannibal feasts and grotesque mutilation of the victims of war.

The narratives thus describe a state of affairs that is substantially different from the present life of Upper Xingu peoples. It is as if a dramatic and drastic ideological shift—at once social and deeply personal in meaning—occurred. From perceiving neighbors as strangers at best but more frequently as dangerous enemies, to whom one could respond only with a corresponding ethic of ferocious aggression, these people come to understand that one participates in a moral sphere of action extending beyond one's own settlement, and that there are others who share a sense of common purpose as manifested by the mutually valued ideal demeanor called *ifutisu*. While people outside this moral sphere of action are called *angikogo*, the possibility of incorporating them into a community of shared interests against outsiders' incursions into the region arises with greater frequency and is often the subject of narrative.[3]

What we learn from stories about the past is that some of the persons most involved in warfare attempted to alter patterns of cannibalistic blood-feuding by expanding the locus of ethical judgment so as to redefine themselves and their enemies as members of a single moral community. These people seem to have become memorable because they were concerned about refashioning critical ideological forms. Although these ways of modeling experience did not achieve fully new and regularized shape until much later (long after these individuals ceased to live), their words registered subtly new understandings of self and of identity and engaged new themes in social life. Such newer ideological forms are developed more fully in stories about the origins of communities, which involve individuals from different places who attempt successfully to marry, trade, and make musical ritual together much like contemporary Upper Xingu people. From the point of view of stories about the past, the end of warfare had less to do with the physical extinction of enemies than with an ideological shifting of the boundaries of the moral community to include people in different communities (even strangers). Relations between individuals belonging to different communities became more personalized in two interrelated senses. First, they were no longer so exclusively constrained by local community identities. Second, individual ties were developed and evaluated in keeping with a set of values about "good" behavior and "correct" action in a great variety of shared experiences (such as ritual, marriage, trade, the diagnosis and treatment of illness), whose meanings also came to be shared. In keeping with this increasing "personalization" and attendant development of a network of relationships, witchcraft accusations, involving complex political relations that cross-cut settlements and always focusing upon individuals, replaced blood feuding between communities. And warriors — men who were earlier trained to protect their fellows against enemies — came to be regarded more and more as "great hunters" until, with the appearance of firearms, male puberty seclusion came to be focused less on skills associated with feuding and with hunting, and more upon agriculture, fishing, and wrestling. With these changes came new variations in the use of words that formerly referred to "enemy," "fierce people," and "warrior."

The Bow Master

At the center of Kalapalo biographies is the remarkable figure of the warrior. The *tafaku oto* or "bow master" was a man who had undergone special training from an early age. If a parent had dreamed about the sparrow hawk it was felt that the next male child would, if properly prepared, become a *takafu oto*. Specialists instructed parents who had dreamed appropriately in the art of creating a morally and physically beautiful person, one whose intelligence was oriented toward war and whose virile presence surpassed that of other men. The novice underwent an arduous and lengthy period of ascetic training that went far beyond the usual activities of puberty seclusion. During his early years, his hands and arms were scraped every few days with a gourd implement set with dogfish teeth, after which chili water was rubbed into the scrapings so as to eventually impart strength and a lethal aim. Later, the boy would be secluded in his father's house, where he would live for many years inside a chamber walled off from the rest of the household space. Here, he was from time to time scraped over his entire body, and made to "cleanse his insides" by drinking and regurgitating gallons of herbal medicines, practices designed to strengthen and purify the body. Other practices were supposed to ensure that his eyes remained focused but aware of subtle peripheral movements, while he remained invisible to enemies.

The future bow master also followed an extremely limited diet in which many things that were normally relished as food were avoided. And like all secluded youths, he was expected to remain strictly celibate, lest all his body work be undone and he exit seclusion a weakling of no consequence. His food was made by a young girl or a woman past menopause, and he was supposed to have no contact (even through speech) with a sexually active woman. When he emerged from seclusion, his personal beauty, deadly aim, powerful strength, and visual acuity were all embraced by the dreaming symbol: the sparrow hawk.

Today, no one is trained to be a bow master. But in a less intense manner, young men and women still undergo the experiences of puberty seclusion. Those who follow such practices correctly under the guidance of their elders are said to be acting responsibly in developing their own bodies by learning to consummate insistent physical demands (for food, sex, sleep, elimination) only within strictly defined limits. Thus, they emerge from seclusion not only physically beautiful but morally beautiful as well, proving themselves capable of controlling potentially destructive feelings that would otherwise jeopardize their families, serving as active icons of the community's own moral worth.

The bow master was held responsible for protecting his community by cultivating fierceness so as to overcome a real, threatening enemy; his aggressive manliness was expected to be directed outwardly, toward *angikogo*. Thus he served as a kind of scout and as a military guard, accompanying his fellows upon request to dangerous places. He also led people to take revenge on enemies after weaker persons had been killed. Not surprisingly, while still a youth he was distinguished by those very enemies as the special target for their attacks. But the ideal image of the beautiful, intensely capable young man, which the Kalapalo ascribed to their techniques of raising boys, resulted in some other inclinations that were perhaps unintended but which were certainly understood and remarked upon. These other qualities of the warrior's character — which fall outside the Kalapalo image of the morally good person developed out of puberty seclusion practices — became the focus of the warrior biographies.

Since the warriors in these stories all share certain characteristics, it is clear that a special kind of "person" is being described, with particular configurations of insight and understanding that emerge from distinctive habits of speech. These are not stereotypes, however. Through representations of their distinctive habits of speech in conversations and declarations, we learn about the unusual decisions and choices made by warriors that made them so interesting to their contemporaries. In their emergent development through narrative, these speech-centered experiences are precisely what make warriors memorable individuals.

A Reader of Signs

The Kalapalo now say that the bow master was very different from his peers by virtue of his special beauty and his enormous size and strength. Even more consistently, and in a way that always lends cohesion to his story, a bow master is distinguished by the fact that he is an interpreter of signs for the others. The bow master's physical condition and his constant activities with signs are closely related, since they arise from the conditions of his training. In the stories, signs not only constitute the messages he receives about his own life, the beginning and end of his existence are marked by them; it was from his parents' dreaming signs that he was selected to become a warrior, and from his own that the way he was to die became known to him. In the story of Tamakafi, it is through the signs of the fallen *atanga* flutes that others learn of his death (only a strong and virile man is supposed to play the *atanga* flutes during public rituals). In "Afuseti" (a story about the abduction of a woman), the warriors are able to trace their sister's abductor by noticing and interpreting a series of signs she has deliberately created in the expectation that they will search for her. These heroes often interpret signs correctly, while their companions misinterpret what they see, or cannot interpret signs at all.

Sign-readership typically has a developmental quality, occurring periodically in stories and contributing in some way to a change of status or to a powerfully intensified or utterly different point of view. It is as if these pragmatic skills were developed in puberty along with the more expected moral and physical qualities. I propose that the elaborate preparation of a warrior from childhood resulted in a "reader of signs," an interpreter and teacher who could readily anticipate the course of his own action, a man who could project forward in his dreaming and in his day-to-day experiences so as to give meaning to his future experience.

Distancing of Relations with Others

The voices of warriors are ironic and embittered, their speech coming in tones of defiant assertion and disgust with the stupidity or incompetence of those around them. Awe and fear and shame respond from all sides: Tamakafi's mother knows that he will die, and suffers from that knowledge; all warriors have older male relatives (fathers or uncles) who really have no regard for them at all, defiantly acting against the good judgment and even strongly worded requests of the bow masters. Friends are lesser men astonished by their power, cowed by the apparent singleminded dedication of the bow master. Tamakafi is remembered as an arrogant and contemptuous person who (even as his friends were dying) sneered at the lack of care they had taken during their own training. And even more fatal was his deeply insulting disdain for the mutilated remains of his former father-in-law, whose sons, themselves bow masters, might have helped him during his battle against fierce people. Following the death of his father, Tapoge never weeps, but brutally takes revenge in a manner reminiscent of executions by collateral relatives of witchcraft victims. This arrogant detachment from social relations is an important element in the bow master character, one that I believe assisted him in killing and in making the kinds of decisions to separate from his own relatives that we see in the stories. This detachment does not mean he is incapable of emotional action: on the contrary, there are numerous references (made by quoting the warrior's speech) to his anger, grief, and guilt at the death of his friends. Also, he is clearly capable of taking responsibility for what happens. The point is that the warrior can simultaneously act as if such emotions were not being enacted: in "Wapage-pundaka" and "Tamakafi" warriors lead their friends to their death, and in the case of Tamakafi, when his jealous uncle insists that they go to cut arrow cane in a dangerous place, the warrior acts against his own dreaming and his mother's urging that he remain at home, in effect committing suicide.

Testimonial: "Let my life be told to succeeding generations . . ."

At moments of the most intensely painful decisions to act, "trembling with grief" (as one storyteller put it), the hero charges his friends to "Let my life be a story to tell," or to "Let us be as we are," and "Let our lives continue in this way." These self-conscious, testimonial expressions appear to be a way of taking responsibility for fatal actions that involve other people. The heroes thus seem to achieve insight into the ambiguities and difficulties of their lives as warriors during these decisive moments. In the story about Tapoge, for example, the young bow master decides to ally himself with a group that is about to attack his father's own people. The testimonial utterance occurs toward the end of the awful slaughter of his father's relatives, when Tapoge spares five of them with the words, "Let them go away to tell the others what happened." In another story, the bow master Tamakafi has a developing sense of being irrevocably drawn along toward a terrible death first anticipated by his dreamings. This is not simply fatalistic, however, but is rather governed by his own periodic, repeatedly stated recognition before others that he has elected to die that way. Each of his statements occurs at a moment of decision when he chooses not to save himself and his companions, and involves a variant of the testimonial, "Let us remain as we are."

When warriors declare their lives should be known to future generations, they are hoping that the full thrust of those decisions to act in certain ways be carried out to the expected, anticipated conclusions, thus leaving behind a reminder and a warning. Since the warriors are telling stories about themselves through the actions they self-consciously perform before others, the stories are somewhat autobiographical.

Performance and Presence

Kalapalo usage suggests the title "bow master" stands as much for action in a "body-technical" mode, a constant active agency, and a kind of acutely alert yet calmly focused, murderous intelligence, as it does for a "status" or a "role." One way of describing this is to say that bow masters perform continuously by being present in many of the senses of that word. Their sheer strength, size, and beauty creates a presence, a feeling in lesser men that they face a model of what (and how) they should have been; bow masters are present in their constant signaling of their presence to others; they are present in their alertness, their palpable activity. But the bow masters are present in other ways as well. They offer themselves to their people as leaders in battle, protectors, advisors, men who avenge the murdered, devoured dead. And they are present in their indictment of the life they must lead: always aware that they might die and be eaten, always on guard, never at peace, never able to fully enjoy the love of women, and forced to constantly persuade people of their sincerity.

Ideological Shifts

More positively, however, it is from this personal situation of detachment and continuous performance that the warriors expanded the locus of ethical judgment beyond their own group. They seem to be pragmatically more flexible in this particular way because of their "sign-readership," because they have learned to pay especially close attention to their own role in giving meaning to external events. This became of utmost importance when the warrior found himself with unusual insights into the character of those events, which others around him did not always find easy to share.

The day-to-day relations between people in the settlement were at least in part defined in terms of the opposition of the community as a whole to outsiders, who were understood to be dangerous, potential (if not actual) murderers. However, the warrior (although trained to be a leader in this aggressive orientation to the outside) came to see the possibility of peaceful contacts — especially marriage, but also ritual and trade — with strangers. He thus stood in contrast to the inflexible attitudes of his relatives, for whom strangers were by definition enemies. In the Wapagepundaka story, there is a clear progression from an initial state of affairs in which the community of shared ethical judgment remains within the local settlement, to one in which Wapagepundaka has successfully expanded his community of personal ethics to include people he had earlier called "strangers." These people initially feared him, thinking he had come to kill them all. Similarly, in "Afuseti" the bow master brothers anticipate they will have to return their sister by force, but ultimately resolve to accept her abductor's payment, leaving Afuseti behind in the stranger's settlement. Stories of more recent encounters with fierce people tell of successful marriages between Kalapalo women and potential enemies (the Dyaquma) who become temporarily integrated (as "brothers" and the sources of riches) into Upper Xingu society.

The Distinctiveness of Evidentials in Warrior Speech

Evidentials appear in the speech of warriors most commonly during moments of heightened tension: in situations of doubt, potential discord, and actual disputes, and especially in situations of dialogue where persuasion and resistance to persuasion take place. They occur on the one hand when a shared meaning is sought, or on the other hand where it is being thwarted: during initial contact between persons hesitant or even overwhelmed by doubt about the propriety of such contact; during moments of poor insight (when someone can't seem to understand what is happening), of negotiation, of resistance to an interpretation, or during outright denial of shared experience. The persistent, repeated, and occasionally flamboyant use of evidentiality in warriors' speech — especially in sequences of dialogue where the testimonial is coupled with irony and sarcasm occurs — makes that speech virtually unique in Kalapalo narratives.

Kalapalo evidentials serve to "contextualize" (Gumperz 1984) relationships, to qualify the psychological mood that emerges from interpersonal contact. Another way to describe this is to say that evidentials help to create an intersubjective experience falling somewhere along an axis between fully shared imaginative intimacy and self-isolating resistance. Evidentials are used when speakers perceive the need to isolate themselves from others, create new boundaries around groups (to which they choose, or do not choose, to belong), or join themselves to people in newly significant ways.

The variety and explicitness of evidentiality coupled with the unresolved or poorly clarified moral identity of participants in Kalapalo warrior narratives may be related to the challenges those men made to an order that no longer worked, a situation of blood feuding in which the categories "we people" and "fierce people" concealed both the real ties between people who fought each other and the murderous tendencies among persons who were the closest of kin. Such an order was apparently in need of replacement through a renewal of the interpretive motive. This need to interpret anew led to recontextualization through shifts in the conventional uses of category labels and through the expanded use of evidentiality, both of which were involved in marking resistance to the old, and an opening up of new ways of understanding. Thus, through his attempts at clarification of his relations with others, the warrior, although trained to kill, actually opened the way to formation of an entirely new society such as we see in the Upper Xingu Basin today.

"Tapoge the Bow Master"

I first heard the story called "Tapoge the Bow Master" from the leader Madyuta, who told it to his wife Ugaki and me on a hot dry afternoon in the Kalapalo settlement of Aifa. Madyuta had recently heard this story from his sister's husband, a Kuikuru man descended from the (Tafununu) Lake Community people mentioned in the narrative. For several years this man had gone during the dry season with his younger relatives to farm beside Tafununu Lake. When he visited the Kalapalo just prior to such a trip, Madyuta's brother-in-law told the story as a gift to his hosts. (He may also have been occupied with the thought of encountering strangers there, since he had once asked me if I had seen any people as I flew over the lake on my way to Brasilia.) About a month later, Madyuta asked me to have him record it. Ugaki's daughter-in-law Kefesugu and two of her adult sons (the leader Muluku and his younger unmarried brother Faidyufi) were also listening to the story.

The setting was typical of Kalapalo occasions for story telling. People were relaxing after a day's work, waiting for Kefesugu's husband to return from a nearby lake. Ugaki and I sat together in the doorway while Madyuta drew up a wooden seat and began his story. While Kefesugu silently attended to the boiling manioc soup during the telling (she was extremely *ifutisunda* with her mother-in-law), the others frequently interrupted. Muluku even tried to take over the story telling. Such interruptions and comments were characteristic of all but the most formal Kalapalo story telling.[4]

The story begins as Madyuta separates the narrative from some preliminary talk about where we are going to put the tape recorder, when he says, "Listen now." He follows with an introductory orientation, letting us listeners know who the main characters are, and their significant characteristics.

> Do listen now.
>> There was a person called Januasi.
>> Tapoge was still a youth.
>>> Still a youth.
> 5   Tapoge.
>> Januasi had already taken a wife from the Lake Community people.
>>> Yes, the Lake Community.
>>> That's all.
>> However, Januasi made his plantation at a place far from there,
> 10   his plantation.
>>>> Yes, his plantation.
>> Where he grew a lot of corn, manioc, and all kinds of plants.
> So, his son was very beautiful.
>> Beautiful.
> 15 "Child of mine," he said to his son.
>> "Child of mine," he said.
>> "Tomorrow we'll go look at our crops, tomorrow."
> "All right," he answered.
>> "If you say so, we'll go."
> 20   "Let's go."
> Prior to their doing that, his brothers-in-law spoke up:
>> "Did we hear correctly you two are going?" they asked.
>> "That just what I said," he answered.

25 "You must not go any longer," they answered. "You must not go any longer. Since you need to guard this son of yours all the time, this son of yours.

Your son."

"You're wrong," he answered.

"You're wrong.

Does anything ever happen to us?

30 In my experience, there's never been any problem, even though we go time after time. Like that."

"You're wrong. Why do you persist in going against our wishes?"

"Now listen to me," he said to his younger brothers.

Tapoge's uncle spoke.

"Listen to me now."

35 "Let's accompany our nephew's father.

Be with our nephew's father."

"Let's go," they answered.

"Let's go."

"We always have to be careful our nephew isn't murdered by fierce people.

40 We have to be careful."

"All right," they answered.

"If you say so, let's go.

If you say so, let's go."

Then when dawn appeared, food for their journey was prepared. When it was ready, they all left.

45 "Let's go," they said.

"Let's go."

"We'll travel by canoe," he said. [*that is, the oldest brother spoke*]

"By canoe.

By canoe," he said.

50 "As for your nephew and I," the father answered, "We'll go in that other direction. That way. By the trail."

"No, it's too far that way. Too far.

It would be better if we all went together in one canoe, all together," they said.

"All together."

"All right," he answered.

55 "All right."

So they went away, shooting many fish as they did so: *tsik, tsik.*

Now their spirits rose,
> they were smiling while they did that.
>> They kept shooting fish.

60   One of them went, *tsik*.
> Another of their party, *tsik*.
>> They were smiling at one another.

"Let's roast the fish right now, come on," their older brother said.
> "Come on, let's roast the fish right now," he said.

65   Tapoge was with them,
> Tapoge.

So they ate, "As soon as you get here you'll eat."
> Their nephew was still with them.

Then as they all ate,

70   "Listen to what I say," he told them, the father spoke.

"Listen to what I say."

"What's that?"

"Since we're getting close, your nephew and I will begin walking.
We're getting close."

"No. We must all go together as I said before, all together.

75   Your son does have to be carefully guarded all the time," he
answered.
> Then that was all.

"Why are you going against our wishes?" he said. "Why? It's best
that we stay together the way we started out. All together.
We have to be careful now that they aren't successful when they try
to murder your son."
> "Very well," he said.

80   Then they all went on.
> That was all.

"We're going now," he said to them. "We're going now."

"Go then," the oldest answered. "Go then.

You must come to us right away if they try to murder your son.

They will want to kill you both.

85   They will kill you both.

We certainly don't want them to do that to you and capture your
son," they told him.

"Nothing of the sort will happen," he answered.
> So he left ahead of the others.

They went upstream in that direction, while he took the route of
the path.
90   Those two walked away along the path. Along the path.
They walked on *tititi*, while the others kept doing as before, *tsik*
they kept shooting at fish.
          They were killing a great many fish,
                his uncles were.
Then they went on as before.
95 As for that relative of theirs, the father was up ahead when they
arrived at the path that led to the place where water was drawn,
          at the path that led to the place where water was drawn.
"Well, it looks as if they were right." Being first, the father ran
quickly ahead until he reached the path ahead of his son *tikii*.
          "Child of mine, I feel someone's here" he said.
          "Child of mine."
100   "It looks as if your uncles have arrived here.
          Your uncles have already arrived here."
"Have they?" he answered. "Have they?"
          "Yes," his father said to him. "Yes, those men up there are your
          uncles.
We shouldn't wait any longer to go see," he said to him.
105 But his son didn't hurry at all.
          He didn't.
          He stayed some distance from his father.
So then they went closer toward the water's edge.
          They could see some other men. "See what's there, my child,
110 I don't understand why you should feel frightened of that.
There's no reason. I assure you, what that is up there is the older
brother's bow, adorned with a piece of the tail of a yellow-headed
cacique bird.
          Adorned with a piece of the tail of a yellow-headed cacique bird.
And that's their younger brother up there, whose bow is adorned
with a piece of toucan's tail,
          the tail of a toucan.
115 That's what your uncles have done up there, with pieces of the red-
rumped cacique's tail."
"You're wrong," Tapoge answered. "You're wrong."
          "You're completely wrong about this. These aren't my uncles,
          not at all.

They're still far away.

They're still far away."

120   "You're wrong. I'm not waiting any longer to go,

I'm not waiting any longer to go."

(E. B.: The father spoke.)

The father spoke.

"I'm not waiting any longer to go."

His father glanced behind him.

125   The path must have been clear and wide.

He was like this he was looking behind him. [*Madyuta shows us how the father walked with his head turned around,that is,* very *carelessly.*]

Finally, as it gradually widened into a place like this, he reached the plaza.

"Now, children, children," he said. "Children," he said.

"Children, there wasn't any reason to take a share of what your nephew shot, was there? Since we've yet to join you," he said.

130   Bok. The others stopped talking.

(E. B.: The fierce people.)

The others stopped talking.

"Those who have come by the path do hungrily approach you, your nephew and I," he said to them.

"Fuuh, hoh, kaw kaw," they shouted out.

Tetulu, so, he ran away.

(E. B.: His son ran away.)

135   his son ran away,

tututu. The father had not taken his bow with him.

His bow.

Tititi tututu, so he was done for.

(E. B.: The father died.)

Tututututututu . . . .

140   When the sun was here, at its height,

"Ha ha ha," now he heard his uncles laughing.

"Here are my dear uncles." *Tuk*, right away he ran back the way he had come.

Tututututu.

As he went on, he saw that they walked with tightly drawn bows.

With their bows kept drawn in his direction,

145   with their arrows aimed at him.

"There's a club carrier, a fierce person."

They looked at him,

and they saw his shell collar. "Oh. That's our nephew," they said.

" 'Let's wait,' weren't we saying that to him?" he asked.

150 " 'Let's wait,' weren't we saying that?"

"Our nephew's right here. Let's go join him," he said.

"Uncle. We aren't well with Father," he said. "Uncle. I'm certain Father is no longer alive."

" 'Let's wait,' we were saying that, weren't we?" he said.

"Let's go." They left the canoe and entered the path.

155 They entered the path.

Ti ti ti ti.

A short distance.

"We should paint ourselves here right now, we'll paint ourselves with charcoal."

That was done. They were with Tapoge. Tapoge.

160 When they were finished, they walked to the path that led to the place where water is drawn.

To the path that led to the bathing place.

"I'll go first from now on," that was Tapoge speaking. "From now on I'll be the first. So I'll be able to see ahead," he said.

"So I'll be able to see ahead."

"Very well," his uncles answered.

165 Then they came on the path, *tiki*. From that spot the fierce people's footprints continued to the house.

Tapoge examined them. "This isn't what I thought. These look like some of my own people," he said to them.

"Our people, not yours."

(E. B.: Who spoke?)

Tapoge spoke.

(E. B.: Tapoge spoke.)

Yes.

170 "These are people just like us.

These are people just like us.

My own people."

(Ugaki: Those were the fierce people, weren't they?)

Indeed they were.

"See for yourselves. Their footprints go over from here up that way. Look at them.

175 These are the stinking people.
From now on you'll call them 'stinking people.'
They are finished," he said to them.
"So they will remain, I say.
Even though they are my own people, I say, let us remain as we
people are. Even though they are my own people.

180 They should be made to chew on wild gourds and nothing more,"
he said. "Wild gourds.
Until their stomachs are filled with wild gourds. They will chew
hard on them. So, that must be our food, our food."
"Let's do it."
That was all.
"But who should be the advance guard?" one of them asked.

185 "It would be best for you to wait here," Tapoge answered.
"Very well."
"It would be best for you to wait here," he said. "Very well."
"It would be best for you to wait here," he said. To the youngest
brother. "It would be best for you to wait here."
To this one, to their fourth brother.

190 The fifth one in their group, the last one, was Tapoge.
Tapoge.
"They won't come with drawn bows.
So don't cry out.
That's a deception.

195 Believe me, that's how we walk," he said.
"Believe me, that's how we walk on our way to murder people.
To another settlement, this way," he said. " 'Hoh hoh hoh,' we call
when we go to drink,
'Hoh hoh hoh.'
When we do that we're moving about with our bows drawn,"
he said to them.

200 "This way," he said to them.
"This way," he said, "This way. This way. This way. This very
way," he said to them. [*As he speaks, Madyuta gestures to suggest a
man quickly and alertly shifting his drawn bow in various directions.*]
"So that way they can frighten you and me. It's a deception.
They move very quickly.
Very quickly."

205   "Very well," one by one they agreed with what he told them. "Very well.

     Very well."
Then they waited, waited, waited for the others to come. When the sun was setting, just as it is now,
   "Kah kah kah koh," the others shouted loudly.

               (Ugaki: The fierce people?)
   They did indeed.

210   Now they were coming to drink.

              (Ugaki: All right, I understand.)
Once again, "Kah kah kah kah koh!"
Once again, four times.
"They're really coming now!" he shouted. "They're really coming now!

     There they are!"

215 *Hum hum*, one of them came out of the water. The first one came out of the water.
He came towards them just as Tapoge said he would, with drawn bow,

   with drawn bow.

              (Ugaki: A bow master?)
   The bow master came.
"Hoh hoh hoh hoh hoh," this was how he was coming. "Hoh hoh hoh," with his bow drawn. [*The utterance is an aggressive signal to enemies that they have been seen; this is the "deception."*]

220   He walked by them one by one.

       (Faidyufi: Others were coming from the watering place?)
                  (Muluku: Yeah.)
Next the one behind him came in their direction,

   the one behind him came in their direction. Each man's bow was tightly drawn. The others stayed where they were for a long time without moving. But they were beginning to feel frightened of the fierce people.
"Hoh."

225   They rose up right up from the water.
Now they were frightened. They kept shooting at them . . . they . . .

             (Ugaki: Watching them.)
[*laughs as Ugaki corrects him*]

kept watching them . . . they kept watching them from their hiding places, for a long time all the men of that group remained motionless with their bows drawn.

That was a deception.

(Muluku: That was a deception, what they did.)

[*Excitedly, Muluku tries to tell the story:*]

Their arrows were aimed at the other men as they walked by.

230   But just after that one of those men who had come up from the water . . . he looked, "Hoh," and one of Tapoge's group jumped with fright.

[*Madyuta regains control of the story:*]

Bok! Someone jumped with fright, and began to shoot wildly, without aiming.

All the time this way.

(Faidyufi: At that same one, the fierce person?)

Yes, the fierce person.

(Muluku: They weren't anything special. He was a bow master.)

"'Let's wait a while longer,' didn't we just say that?"

(E. B.: Tapoge spoke.)

235   Tapoge spoke as the other man ran back.

"'Let's wait a while longer,' didn't we just say that?" he said.

"Why aren't you paying attention to what I say?" he asked.

Tururu, a fierce person, was still up in the plaza.

(E. B.: Still in the plaza.)

(Ugaki: Still there.)

Only one more had yet to pass by them. They still stood like this, with drawn bows, because they were still afraid.

240 But now some fierce people were still going this way, toward the water's edge.

(Muluku: When they reached the others, they tried to shoot them.)

But unfortunately for them, the moment they reached Tapoge and the others, they couldn't shoot them even though they tried.

(Ugaki: How did that happen?)

"Kah kah" *buhruru* some of them scattered to one side. *Tsuhruru* "Kah kah kah."

Shouting, others scattered to the other side. Those by the water's edge *tuk! tuk! tsok! tsok!*

(Faidyufi comments excitedly: Those men really knew how to fight. There were bow

masters among them. Tamakafi was one
they killed. Listen.) [*By this last word, he
signals to Madyuta that it is all right
to resume the story.*]
(E. B.: Yes.)

Mbisuk! Those by the bathing place were all done away with.

(Muluku: [laughing] That's what they intended to happen.)

245   Then on the other side, *tuk.* "Kah kah kah kah kah kah" as they
shot them all.

Tuk tuk tuk.

Their arrows were used up. The bow master's arrows were all gone.

"Every one of our arrows is gone.

We don't have any arrows left at all," they said to him.

"We don't have any arrows left at all."

250   "Every one of our arrows has been used up," they said.

Our arrows are all used up."

"I still have a few," he said. (That's right, I'm mistaken about that.)

"Very well," he answered. "Very well."

"Let me next," he said to them. "Let me next," Tapoge spoke.

255   "Let me next," he said to them.

Then Tapoge took up a heavy branch — a war club — and clubbed
them *tuk tuk tuk tuk tuk tuk.*

He clubbed a good many of them.

There were only five of them left, five.

(E. B.: Five.)

Five.

260   Those on the other side *tuk tuk tuk tuk* were all gone. They were
done away with.

"That's enough," he said to them. "This way, those who are left will
go away to tell about us."

"This way, those who are left will go away to tell about us."

That's all.

Discussion

An approach to the biographical content of this story that uses specification of names, labels, and other categorical differences between identities and relations per se is merely a first and perhaps superficial step
because this content is precisely what is problematic, what is *emerging*

through (rather than being *represented by*) narrative. Like most Kalapalo stories, "Tapoge the Bow Master" consists of extensive conversations and other quotations of speech acts. (Just about half of all the lines — 143 of 263 — are quoted speech.) Since most of the events are of speech-centered and generally dialogical actions that result in distinctively individual versions of reality developed within and through particular social configurations, one needs to become more deeply involved in a search for the individual voices and the cohesion and coherence that is created between them: how descriptions of action are connected to each other to form an intersubjective, emergent narrative process and where and how these voices are repeatedly, yet variously, heard. Thus a discourse-focused approach that investigates temporal organization and developmental processes seems particularly appropriate. Insofar as this approach reveals the special ways that individuals develop within (and thereby change) their social configurations, it is especially suited to searches for implicit forms of historical consciousness in stories.

As he told this story, Madyuta played with symbols of community and personal identity, changing our expectations about the kinds of people he was telling us about. At first, he developed a contrast between the hero's local community and a nearby, hostile group, variously called *angikogo*, "fierce people," *i oto*, "club people," or *tifitsengekiñe*, "the stinking people" (the last, according to Kalapalo, from the palm oil with which they anointed themselves). But later, as we learn that these people were actually known to the hero and were perhaps even his father's relatives, we become unsure of who really are those ferocious, stinking, treacherous, club-carrying cannibals. Are they a separate and distinct enemy community, with a distinctly different way of life? Or are they in fact the hero's own people, whose hurt pride and notions of personal honor we are initially supposed to accept? The answers to these questions are never as clear as we would like, and the fact is that these crucial moral issues are left unresolved.

Developmental Relations

Madyuta's story focuses upon how the warrior attempts to clarify his ambiguous identity. Most of the narrative consists of a meticulous step-by-step portrayal of the events leading to Tapoge's particular manner of assuming the title of "warrior," which occurs in connection with fixing his identity. Tapoge is presented in an ambiguous light because his father is said to have married into a Lake Community group. So part of Tapoge's clarification of identity is a process through which he becomes firmly associated with Lake Community. Also involved is his maturation, by which I mean his manner of enacting the potential achieved through his puberty training. A third element in his clarification of identity involves achievement of an intensive agency that becomes increasingly more powerful throughout the story, until we realize why he is not just any bow master, but a memorable person, someone with a compelling story that must be told to those who are yet to be born.

We first hear of a man named Januasi who has married into Lake Community (a group of people within the moral community of the speaker) but who apparently comes from a group of outsiders, as suggested by the fact that his plantation is located far from his wife's home. Januasi is the father of a "beautiful one" (lines 13–14), that is, a youth recently emerged from puberty seclusion. Januasi's brothers-in-law appear concerned about the fact that he persists in traveling to this distant plantation. Now that their nephew is grown, they are worried that he will be captured and killed by *angikogo*. But Januasi isn't worried and argues with them about the danger. The brothers-in-law then discuss what to do; the oldest proposes that they accompany Januasi, and the others agree. From the start, we hear Januasi's argumentative voice contrasting with his brothers-in-law, which compares unfavorably with the casual ease with which the brothers-in-law validate their oldest brother.

When Januasi's brothers-in-law suggest the group travel by canoe, he wishes to go by way of the trail. But he agrees when they tell him it is too far that way. Later, in lines 70–75, Januasi argues again and more forcibly with his brothers-in-law, even to the extent of anticipating disagreement. Januasi begins by saying, *tsatue ukili,* "Listen to what I say" (line 73), a formulaic utterance that indicates deep sincerity and a commitment to the proposition in the statement that follows. This utterance functions as an appeal to validation by the listeners. Januasi tells the others that he wants to separate from them now, since they are "getting close." The brothers-in-law reply angrily (line 77), and Januasi appears to agree they should stay together. But in lines 82–87, he states for the fourth time his wish to leave the brothers and go his own way, and so (this being the fourth time), the brothers let him go, cautioning him to be careful and hurry back if danger threatens. Januasi, however, is (if anything) even more confident than before, dismissing their concerns with the comment, "Nothing of the sort will happen" (line 87).

When Januasi and Tapoge arrive at the distant settlement, the father is surprised to find that people have arrived ahead of them. He immediately identifies these people as his brothers-in-law, using the counter-expectation evidential *maki* (lines 97, 100). Now, Tapoge speaks for the first time, expressing uncertainty about what his father has just said (using the uncertainty evidential *nika*) (line 102). The father responds with more assurance, even impatiently: "Yes, those men up there are your uncles. We shouldn't wait to go see" (lines 103–104). This tentative disagreement between father and son becomes more fixed when shortly after in lines 109–115, the father insists that what he sees are the decorated bows of his bow master brothers-in-law. Now, in line 116, Tapoge (who is beginning to take shape as a distinct person) directly disputes his father's interpretation of what is going on. By his caution and his responses to his father in lines 105–107 and 116–119, he demonstrates that acute sensory awareness that, among other features of his character, indicate his potential to be a true bow master. His father, on the other hand, continues to resist his son, and stupidly advances forward, not only weaponless, but actually trying to joke about their being late. He walks right into the enemy camp, and is killed.

With a shift in focus marked by Madyuta's reference to the sun being at its height (line 140), attention turns to Tapoge and his relations with his uncles, considerably more developed than his feelings toward his father. Tapoge's subsequent development as a warrior significantly takes place in the presence of the uncles. Tapoge's later actions seem less a consequence of his mourning his father's death than connected to his concern to serve his uncles when they decide to retaliate.

Upon their arrival, the uncles mistake Tapoge for an enemy, but correct themselves when they see that he wears the distinctive shell ornament used by men of their own group. From their point of view, he is different from Januasi, whom they treated more as a stranger come to live among them than one of them. Tapoge is clearly one of them. In lines 158–159, all decide to paint themselves with charcoal, a prelude to battle. The narrator takes care to emphasize that Tapoge, too, painted himself this way, thereby declaring his willingness to kill. In what follows, Tapoge begins to more actively take on this warrior-killer identity, by telling his uncles he will lead the way, "so I'll be able to see ahead." He does this even though they are experienced bow masters. In what follows his warrior agency becomes even more powerful.

But now the horror of his choice begins to become apparent. He identifies the footprints of the enemy as belonging to people of his own (that is, his father's) group; use of the exclusive "we" (*tisuge*) is strikingly apparent in this section, because he is clearly insulting and cursing that same "we." In lines 175–176 he uses the expression "stinking people," thereby labeling his father's killers as enemies by an insulting expression. In line 177, Tapoge first curses the enemy by declaring that they "are finished." In lines 178–179, he curses them even more strongly, saying *latafa itsanini*, "So they will remain." (Here, the third person pronoun is used.) In other words, they will die as they lived (without having a chance to change their ways). And finally, there is the grotesque business about wild gourds, in which the exclusive "we" appears once more. Madyuta suggested that the enemy corpses were to lie unburied with the wild plants twining in and out of their rotted stomach cavities.

As the final episode begins, Tapoge plans the ambush, explaining strategy to his uncles and essentially giving away the martial secrets of the fierce people, "his" people. Here too is that bitter exclusive "we." His description and justification of the entire plan is validated by the others in lines 205–206; again we might think of this relationship of shared interpretation and goals as standing in marked opposition to Januasi and his brothers-in-law, who were never successful at living as a moral community. Next, Tapoge even more assertively takes on his warrior role by criticizing his uncles for their impatience after they fearfully begin shooting at the wrong time. (As the story was about to culminate in the slaughter of the enemy, Muluku and Faidyufi intruded more and more in the telling of the story; their agitation anticipated the final murderous blows of Tapoge himself.) Finally, Tapoge's warrior agency is most fully achieved as he kills the last of the enemy with a war club, arrogantly permitting five men to live so that "those who are left will go away to tell about us" (line 262).

Both the warrior actions of Tapoge and the incompetent behavior of his father Januasi are highly speech-centered. What is special in this regard is that their conversations with one another and with their relatives are replete with various forms of evidentials (such as *maki* and *nika*) and a set of conventional utterances ("Very well," "I see," "I can't agree," "Is that what you say?") that indicate validation or disapproval of propositions. In this story, evidentials are constitutive of independence, individuality, and open conflict (Januasi and his brothers-in-law), but in other cases (involving Tapoge and his uncles) they help to form the most intensive kinds of solidarity of which the Kalapalo are capable. In all cases, claims are being made about shared interpretations of experience.

Moral boundaries and personal allegiances are being drawn through these claims.

A numerical pattern of nine connected events is achieved by the separate contexts in which Tapoge reveals himself through speech in this story. Kalapalo use this number in extended narrative to indicate a process leading to successful accomplishment of a goal. When a "motivated" number of instances is reached (and I have noticed both tellers and listeners counting on their fingers), reinforcement, intensification, and completeness are the results (in the case of things done four, or during a long story eight times) and ultimate success and closure (when things are done five or nine times). That a certain action is *repeated*, or that a person — through activity — is himself part of a pattern, is a significant matter in any Kalapalo psychological description. In Januasi's case, his need to travel alone, and in his own fashion, is only agreed to after his fourth insistent request. As for Tapoge, the ninth activity is a culmination of a process of increasingly intensified warrior action, until he actually has the chance to kill *angikogo*.

Biography and Ideology

By characterizing certain Kalapalo stories as biographical, I am rejecting claims that the "biographical attitude" is absent outside of Western societies, and that biography is not a traditional (or indigenous) Native American literary form.[5] Yet the stories about warriors told by Kalapalo are probably *not* biographical in the ways I think we would most anticipate if we use as models the work of notable Western biographers.

Contrary to the Western idea that biography should be "life-historical," tending toward closure, Kalapalo biographies describe events occurring over very short periods of time: a single lunar period, or (as in the story discussed in this essay) the course of only one horrible day. Although the time depth is very shallow, the details of each story create strikingly personal versions of reality.

Western biographers often configure their subject with regard to implicit programs arising from early childhood experiences. Sometimes these are important in Kalapalo stories, but more generally they represent individual persons "in the here and now" as socially contextualized, action-oriented, and discourse-centered processes, engaged with the practical immediacy of incompatibilities and paradoxes in their understandings of who and what they are. Because these situations of disorientation involve pragmatic difficulties in the practice of warfare, to the extent that warriors become more explicitly concerned with making decisions about their social identity, the foundations underlying roles and relationships within particular communities are made out to be insecure, in danger of collapse when specific ties between individuals fail.

Although ideological ferment is associated most often with modern society, with its rapid changes in traditional structures and challenges to traditional authority,[6] we should expect to find evidence of this "pervasive sense of disorientation"[7] elsewhere. In lowland South America, centuries of brutal invasion and occupation by Europeans has sometimes resulted in new ethnic allegiances and identities, as people from very different kinds of communities, often speaking different kinds of languages, fled from centers of European expansion to form new societies. This must have involved extended and patient efforts during which notions of personal commitment and obligation with respect to membership in a moral community were subjected to particularly intense scrutiny. It was not only Europeans who were present to be resisted and commented upon. Native people also focused attention upon one another as well, and also inwardly, upon their own communities.[8]

Evidence for ideological ferment has been preserved in narratives like "Tapoge the Bow Master," which have much to tell us about what happened to people during such times of disorientation. From the stories, we learn how people tried to reorient themselves, contributing thereby to a very gradual and subtle construction of ideological shifts. The importance of these stories about the past for the Kalapalo rests, however, not in the fact that they represent a new ideology, a set of collectively accepted images that animate social life. Rather, it is precisely in their biographical character, the fact that they describe experiences of individuals taking chances, exploring alternatives to their lives, when conditions forced them into new and untried situations. No longer being able to "go back" to the old ways, often literally forced into an unknown environment by enemies, these men made decisions to act that have reference to their particular abilities to give meaning to the conditions around them, and thus to project forward, clearly imagine, and take responsibility for the course of their futures. For the Kalapalo, close attention to the relevance of local values due to continual confrontation with outsiders seems to motivate the telling of these stories about people who, in the past, tried to reformulate or recontextualize certain basic values central to their particular designated roles as warriors. The actions of warriors thus transcend the time of cannibalism and blood-feuding, of desperate migrations in search of a place to live peacefully. They are relevant to the present because, even now, the Kalapalo find the need to engage one another as individuals, just as they must engage new and unknown peoples — this time non-Indians — in hostile contexts that in some ways are not very different from those of the past.

When we look at the more personal features of historical narratives — their biographical character — we come face to face not with the monological functions of "distortion," "legitimation," "justification," "integration," and "identification" typically associated with ideology (and a narrator's voice), but emotionally charged dialogical processes of challenge, resistance, debate, and the negotiation of meaning, with the struggles that take place as people try to understand and experience anew. In this way, the rhetoric of conflict that is developed within stories about the past becomes merged with the rhetoric of conventional ideology in the practice of contemporary life, so that the usual authoritative resources for telling about "how people were" project a voice struggling for dominance, a voice projecting that "sideward glance" at the voices of others with which Mikhail Bakhtin and his circle were so concerned.

Notes

Acknowledgments. This article was first presented at a session entitled "The Self in Discourse," held during the annual meetings of the American Anthropological Association, Chicago, 1987. I am grateful for the many helpful comments made by the session's discussants (Raymond Fogelson, Emiko Ohnuki-Tierney, and Douglas Price-Williams) and by members of the anthropology departments at the universities of Arizona, Chicago, Pennsylvania, Texas, and Virginia, where later versions were read. My work among the Kalapalo during 1978–80 and 1982 was supported by National Science Foundation, the Wenner-Gren Foundation for Anthropological Research, and the University of Arizona.

1. See Sherzer and Woodbury 1987.

2. Ohnuki-Tierney 1987; Rosaldo 1980; Sahlins 1981, 1985; Taussig 1987.

3. People *do* challenge one another's adherence to this common purpose, and difficult and delicate maneuvers have to be made when relatives in different communities are forced to take sides as conflicts arise.

4. My translation of Madyuta's story is arranged to show the line structure that he created together with his listener-responders (*tiitsofo*), whose most common response is *eh* ("Yes"). (I have omitted "eh" responses in this presentation.) The position of lines is arranged according to Madyuta's voice quality. Lines appearing near the left margin were spoken with relative force, while those

arranged near the right margin were spoken rather softly. A Kalapalo narrative begins a rhetorical segment ("verse") with a relatively loud voice, which during ensuing lines becomes softer and lower-pitched. Subsidiary units within the larger segment usually add more information to the proposition given initially in the segment; these are also spoken rather loudly and with a higher pitch than the opening line of the verse (see Basso 1985, 1987).

5. Brumble 1987; Clifford 1978; Krupat 1987.

6. See discussion in Ricoeur 1986 (especially Part 1) and Thompson 1984.

7. Geertz 1973:223.

8. Numerous discussions of native South American resistance and reorientation to European culture make plain the importance of reformulation of ideas about local power relations (Guss 1986; Hendricks 1988; Hill 1988; Wright and Hill 1987). Hendricks explores most explicitly the relevance of ideology for understanding a particular lowland South American rhetoric.

References Cited

Basso, Ellen B.

1973 The Kalapalo Indians of Central Brazil. New York: Holt, Rinehart and Winston.

1985 A Musical View of the Universe. Philadelphia: University of Pennsylvania Press.

1987 In Favor of Deceit. Tucson: University of Arizona Press.

Brumble, H. David III

1987 Sam Blowsnake's Confession: Crashing Thunder and the History of American Indian Autobiography. In Recovering the Word: Essays on Native American Literature. Brian Swann and Arnold Krupat, eds. Pp. 537–551. Berkeley: University of California Press.

Clifford, James

1978 "Hanging Up Looking Glasses at Odd Corners." In Studies in Biography. Daniel Aaron, ed. Pp. 45–61. Cambridge, MA: Harvard University Press.

Geertz, Clifford

1973 "Ideology as a Cultural System." In The Interpretation of Cultures. Pp. 193–233. New York: Basic Books.

Gumperz, John

1984 Discourse Strategies. Cambridge: Cambridge University Press.

Guss, David

1986 Keeping it Oral: A Yekuana Ethnology. American Ethnologist 13:413–429.

Hendricks, Janet

1988 Power and Knowledge: Discourse and Ideological Transformation among the Shuar. American Ethnologist 15:216–238.

Hill, Jonathan D., ed.
1988 Rethinking History and Myth. Urbana: University of Illinois Press.

Krupat, Arnold
1987 For Those Who Come After: A Study of Native American Autobiography. Berkeley: University of California Press.

Ohnuki-Tierney, Emiko
1987 The Monkey and the Mirror. Princeton, NJ: Princeton University Press.

Ricoeur, Paul
1986 Lectures on Ideology and Utopia. New York: Columbia University Press.

Rosaldo, Renato
1980 Ilongot Headhunting. Stanford: Stanford University Press.

Sahlins, Marshall
1981 Historical Metaphors and Mythical Realities. Ann Arbor: University of Michigan Press.

1985 Islands of History. Chicago: University of Chicago Press.

Sherzer, Joel, and Anthony C. Woodbury, eds.
1987 Native American Discourse: Poetics and Rhetoric. Cambridge Studies in Oral and Literary Culture 13. Cambridge: Cambridge University Press.

Taussig, Michael
1987 Shamanism, Colonialism, and the Wild Man. Chicago: University of Chicago Press.

Thompson, John B.
1984 Studies in the Theory of Ideology. Cambridge: Polity Press.

Wright, Robin M., and Jonathan D. Hill
1987 History, Ritual, and Myth: Nineteenth Century Millenarian Movements in the Northwest Amazon. Ethnohistory 33:31–54.

The Making of the Maori:

Culture Invention and Its Logic

Allan Hanson

VOL. 91, 1989, 890–902

"Traditional culture" is increasingly recognized to be more an invention constructed for contemporary purposes than a stable heritage handed on from the past. Anthropologists often participate in the creative process. Two distinct inventions of New Zealand Maori culture are analyzed, together with the role of anthropologists in each of them. The conclusion expores the logic of culture invention and some of its implications for the practice of anthropology.

Anthropologists and historians have become acutely aware in recent years that "culture" and "tradition" are anything but stable realities handed down intact from generation to generation. Tradition is now understood quite literally to be an invention designed to serve contemporary purposes, "an attempt," as Lindstrom put it (1982:317), "to read the present in terms of the past by writing the past in terms of the present."

Those contemporary purposes vary according to who does the inventing. When people invent their own traditions it is usually to legitimate or sanctify some current reality or aspiration, be it as momentous as the Greek national identity, Quebec nationalism, or the Hawaiian renaissance (Handler 1984; Handler and Linnekin 1984; Herzfeld 1982; Linnekin 1983), or as uncontroversial as the relatively new form of dual social organization that Borofsky (1987) encountered on the Polynesian island of Pukapuka. People also invent cultures and traditions for others, and then treat them as if their inventions were the actual state of affairs. When the inventors are politically dominant, as has been the case between Western nations and their colonies, the invention of tradition for subordinate peoples is part of a cultural imperialism that tends to maintain the asymmetrical relationship of power (Fabian 1983; Ranger 1983; Said 1978).

It is becoming clear that anthropologists too are inventors of culture. The evolutionary ideas of Sir Henry Maine and Lewis Henry Morgan were major sources for the invention of the Fijian system of land tenure (France 1969; Legge 1958). Although it contains misinterpretations, A. B. Deacon's 1934 book, *Malekula: A Vanishing People in the New Hebrides,* has been adopted by the people of the region as the final arbiter of disputes about traditional culture (Larcom 1982:334). The present intellectual climate has even spawned the notion that the quintessential anthropological activities of ethnographic research and writing inevitably produce cultural inventions (Clifford and Marcus 1986; Geertz 1988; Wagner 1981). This raises fundamental questions about the nature of cultural reality and whether the information that anthropologists produce can possibly qualify as knowledge about that reality.

New Zealand Maori culture forms an excellent context in which to frame these issues. The invention of Maori culture has been going on for more than a century, taking at least two distinct forms in that time, and anthropological interpretations and misinterpretations have joined the contributions of other scholars, government officials, and Maoris themselves (including some Maori anthropologists) in the inventive process. The two historical moments described below are the period around the turn of the 20th century—when the primary aim was to assimilate Maoris into White life and culture—and the present day, when Maoris seek to maintain their cultural distinctiveness and to assume a more powerful position in society. Following that discussion we will be ready to consider more thoroughly the theoretical implications of the invention of culture for the enterprise of anthropology.

The Whence of the Maori

Anthropology's contribution in the early decades of this century to the construction of New Zealand Maori culture stems from that great stream of now-discredited anthropological theory: diffusionism and long-distance migrations. This mode of thinking was largely responsible for the birth and nurturance of two major understandings about traditional Maori culture that, in some quarters, still lead a robust existence. One of these is a set of traditions about the settlement of New Zealand that may conveniently be grouped under the rubric of the "Great Fleet."

The other is the idea that pre-European Maori culture featured an eso-teric cult dedicated to a supreme being named Io.

The rudiments of the discovery and settlement theory are these. New Zealand was discovered in A.D. 925 by Kupe, a man from Ra'iatea in the Society Islands. The first settlers, Toi and his grandson Whatonga, ar-rived from Tahiti in about the middle of the 12th century. Finally, a fleet of seven canoes—Tainui, Te Arawa, Mataatua, Kurahaupo, Tokomaru, Aotea, and Takitumu—set out in about 1350 from a homeland named Hawaiki, which was probably Ra'iatea or Tahiti. After a stop in Raro-tonga, the fleet arrived in New Zealand and the migrants dispersed to populate the various parts of the country. Most Maori tribes trace their origin to one or another of the canoes that formed the Great Fleet (Hiroa 1950:5–64; Simmons 1976:3–106; Sorrenson 1979:44–57).

As for the Io cult, it has been claimed that although the Maori pan-theon contained many gods, over them all presided Io: an eternal being, itself uncreated, and the creator of the other gods, the universe, and all things (Smith 1913:110–112). The cult of Io was philosophically sophis-ticated and esoteric, knowledge and worship of the high god being re-stricted to a few ranking chiefs and high priests. "It is quite probable, indeed, that this superior creed may have been too exalted for ordinary minds" (Best 1973:24).

Before examining how anthropology contributed to their develop-ment and promulgation, it is important to know that scholarship in recent decades had thrown both the cult of Io and the Great Fleet story into serious question. The primary source for the Io cult is part 1 of *The Lore of the Whare-wananga*. This is a compendium of religious and mythological lore of the Kahungunu tribe, arranged and translated by S. Percy Smith (1913). After a careful examination of the manuscript material on which the volume is based, David Simmons and Bruce Biggs concluded that chapter 2, which contains the material on the Io cult, is derived from manuscripts whose status as pre-European Maori tradition is questionable (Simmons 1976:382). Te Rangi Hiroa, a half-Maori an-thropologist also known as Peter H. Buck, observed that Io's creative activities—bringing forth light from primordial darkness, dividing the waters, suspending the sky, and forming the earth—had rather too much in common with Genesis for their purely Maori provenance to sound convincing (Hiroa 1950:526–536; see also Johansen 1958:36–61).

As far as the Great Fleet is concerned, in 1840 Horatio Hale, a lin-guist with the United States Exploring Expedition, collected a legend at the Bay of Islands about a fleet of four canoes that were blown off course during a voyage between, he presumed, Samoa and Tonga, and which eventually arrived at New Zealand (Sorrenson 1979:35–36). The army historian A. S. Thomson, writing at mid-century, was also told that migrants to New Zealand set out in a fleet of canoes (Thomson 1859:I:57–68). As with the Io cult, however, Percy Smith was perhaps the key early proponent of migration stories of Kupe, Toi, and the Great Fleet. These are set out particularly in part 2 of *The Lore of the Whare-wananga* (Smith 1915) and *History and Traditions of the Maoris of the West Coast* (Smith 1910).

Simmons and Biggs found the textual material in part 2 of *The Lore* to be a late compilation from a variety of sources (Simmons 1976:386). Simmons conducted an exhaustive study of European writings and Maori traditions from many tribal areas with the aim of ascertaining what Maori traditions actually say about the discovery of and migrations to New Zealand. He concluded that the stories about Kupe, Toi, and Whatonga as summarized above are not authentic Maori tradition (1976:59, 100). In this regard Simmons echoes William Colenso, who, a century before, had written that traditions such as Kupe's discovery of New Zealand and subsequent return to Hawaiki are "mythical rhapsody" that, while entirely believed by some Europeans, were not (at that time) taken as historical fact by the Maoris themselves (Sorrenson 1979:44–45).

While it is undeniable that Maori tribes tell of the arrival of their ancestors in migration canoes, the notion of an organized expedition by a Great Fleet in about 1350 seems to have been constructed by European scholars such as Smith in an effort to amalgamate disparate Maori traditions into a single historical account (Simmons 1976:316). Dating the fleet at 1350 was a particularly blatant work of fiction, since Smith simply took the mean of a large number of tribal genealogies that varied from 14 to 27 generations before 1900. "The date of 1350," Simmons concludes, "has validity only as an exercise in arithmetic" (1976:108; see also Smithyman 1979 for further evaluation of Smith's work).

If the Io cult and the Great Fleet are fabrications about indigenous Maori society, the question arises as to why European scholars so enthusiastically embraced them as fact. The answer pertains to the 19th-century fascination with tracing the various peoples of the world back to a few cradles of civilization. Well before the Great Fleet and Io entered European discourse this penchant of thought produced, as one of the earliest foreign inventions of Maori culture, the idea of the Maoris as

Semites. Samuel Marsden, who in 1819 was the first missionary to visit New Zealand, opined that the Maoris had "sprung from some dispersed Jews." He advanced as evidence for this proposition their "great natural turn for traffic; they will buy and sell anything they have got" (Elder 1932:219).

By the late 19th and early 20th centuries scholars were using the Great Fleet and Io theories to suggest kinship between the Maoris and New Zealand's European settlers. The skin color, physical features, and often amorous hospitality of Polynesians had appealed to Europeans since the days of the 18th-century explorers. Now, diffusionist and migration-minded European scholars in New Zealand were pleased to discover in the Maori race the capacity for sophisticated philosophy, as demonstrated by the Io cult, and a history of heroic discoveries and migrations that included the Great Fleet, Kupe, and, in even more remote epochs, intrepid voyages through Indonesia, India, and beyond. This ennobled Maoris in European eyes to the point where it became possible to entertain the possibility of a link with themselves.

Doubtless that possibility became more palatable to British migrants when, as the 19th century drew to a close, the idea emerged that the Maoris were of Aryan stock. Edward Tregear, a high-level civil servant and amateur ethnologist and linguist who participated in the founding of the Polynesian Society, elaborated this thesis in his 1885 book *The Aryan Maori*. Rejoicing that "Comparative Philology and Comparative Mythology are the two youngest and fairest daughters of Knowledge" (1885:1), Tregear seduced from them a dazzling array of associations between Maori language and lore and that of, among other places, India, ancient Greece, Rome, and Britain. He even demonstrated that although Maori people had long since forgotten the cattle that their ancestors herded in the steppes of Asia and as they migrated through India, the memory remained embalmed in their language. So he found the Sanskrit *gau*, for cow, in several Maori terms containing *kau*. For example, a Maori weapon consisting of "sharp teeth of flint lashed firmly to a piece of wood" was called *mata-kautete* because its shape is reminiscent of a "cow-titty" (1885:30–31). Drunk with power of comparative philology, Tregear uncovered similar memories in the Maori language of pigs, wolves, tigers, bows and arrows, and frogs (1885:30–37).

Such research was beginning to reveal the dim outlines of perhaps the most splendid chapter in human history: the great Aryan migration. Enthused Tregear of the Maori forerunners,

No free-booting Huns or Vandals, mad for plunder and the sack of towns were they but colonists seeking new homes beneath strange stars. We of Europe have set out on the same quest. Encircling Africa, the two vast horns of the Great Migration have touched again; and men whose fathers were brothers on the other side of those gulfs of distance and of time meet each other, when the Aryan of the West greets the Aryan of the Eastern Seas. [1885:105]

Building on Renan's (1889:84) remark that Io is one of the many variants of the name Jehovah, Elsdon Best advanced the same theory (Best 1924:1:90).

The notion of Maoris as Aryans was pertinent to race relations and nation building in fledgling New Zealand. R. Studholme Thompson — who held that the Maoris belonged to the Alpine section of the Caucasian race and came originally from the Atlas mountains of North Africa — explained that his work on Maori origins

"had a large object in view, viz., the demonstration that the highly-civilized Britain and the Maori, just emerging from barbarism, are one in origin; that in fraternising with the Maori the European undergoes no degradation; in intermarrying with the race he does no violence to the claims of consanguinity. It is thought that when this is thoroughly known there will arise a more cordial feeling between the peoples inhabiting the colony, both equally the subjects of one King." [quoted in Sorrenson 1979:29]

"What better myth could there be for a young country struggling for nationhood and for the amalgamation of its races," asks Sorrenson (1979:30), "than this reunification of the Aryans?"

No one talks seriously anymore about ultimate Maori origins as Aryan or Semitic, but the two most prominent features of the tradition — the cult of Io and the discovery and migration stories concerning Kupe, Toi, and the Great Fleet — remain very much alive. Although they are largely of European construction they have been embraced by Maoris as their authentic heritage. Te Rangi Hiroa accepted the traditions concerning Kupe, Toi, and the Great Fleet (1950:4–64); in his mind the last of these was so significant that it "ranks in historical and social importance with the Norman Conquest" (1950:36). Sir Apirana Ngata, longtime Member of Parliament and probably the most influential and respected Maori of the 20th century, promoted the idea of a sextennial celebration in 1950 to commemorate the arrival of the Great

Fleet (and, not coincidentally, to dwarf the mere centennial of the signing of the Treaty of Waitangi, which the New Zealanders of European descent had celebrated in 1940) (Sorrenson 1979:52). From their discourse, it is clear that Maori authors of today such as Maharaia Winiata (1967:25), Douglas Sinclair (1975:118–19), and Ereura Stirling (Stirling and Salmond 1980:83–84) also accept the tradition of the Great Fleet as historical fact.

Io too lives in Maori minds, as is evident from a recent essay on Maori religion and cosmology by Maori Marsden, chaplain in the Royal New Zealand Navy and Te Aupouri tribal member. Relying solely on sources he has encountered in Maori contexts, such as the transmission of tribal lore and orations at Maori gatherings, Marsden depicts Io as an authentically Maori concept of a creator-god who verbally called the universe into being from a primal void and differentiated light from darkness, the earth and waters from the sky (Marsden 1975:210–211).

Maori reasons for affirming Io and the Great Fleet have not, however, been the same as those of Pakeha (Maori for European or White) New Zealanders. If Maoris have always been willing to accept any qualities of racial greatness that Pakeha scholars might attribute to them, it was not so much to believe themselves worthy of assimilation into the White population and culture as it was to bolster a sense of their own ethnic distinctiveness and value. This sense has grown dramatically in strength and stridency of expression in recent years. That development, indeed, lies at the heart of the second chapter in the invention of Maori culture and tradition that we have to consider.

Maoritanga

The movement known as Maoritanga (Maoriness) or Mana Maori (Maori Power) is one of the most important developments in New Zealand society today. As with any large social movement, Maoritanga includes diversity, and not all of the tenets discussed below would be endorsed by all of its supporters. What unites them and, interestingly, what they share with turn-of-the-century scholars such as R. Studholme Thompson, is the goal to secure for Maoris a favorable place in the nation being built in New Zealand. Yet the current and earlier images of that place and of the national culture to emerge, are quite different. The earlier vision was to create one culture, European in form, into which Maoris would be successfully assimilated. To promote this goal it was necessary to identify *similarities* between Maori and European. As we have seen, the invention of Maori culture promulgated by Percy Smith and his contemporaries did just that by using the Io cult as evidence of the Maori capacity for sophisticated thought and the Great Fleet to demonstrate the mettle of Maori ancestors and even to identify them as fellow Aryans.

Maoritanga's vision is different. Its image of the future New Zealand is a bicultural society, in which Maoris are on a par with Pakehas politically and economically and Maori culture is respected as equally valid but distinct from Pakeha culture (see, for example, Sciascia 1984:162). To promote that image, it is necessary to stress the unique contribution that Maori culture has made to national life — different from but no less valuable than the Pakeha contribution. Thus, the Maori tradition that Maoritanga invents is one that *contrasts* with Pakeha culture, and particularly with those elements of Pakeha culture that are least attractive. In New Zealand as in the United States, human relations among Pakehas are often thought to lack passion and spontaneity; the Pakeha approach to things is detached and coldly rational; Pakehas have lost the appreciation for magic and the capacity for wonder or awe inspired by the unknown; Pakeha culture is out of step with nature — it pollutes the environment and lacks a close tie with the land.

Maori culture is represented as the ideal counterbalance to these Pakeha failings. Maoris cherish the dead, speaking to them and weeping freely over open caskets, while Pakehas mute the mourning process and hide the body from sight (Dansey 1975:177). The Maori has a "close, spiritual relationship with the land"; he "loved his land and identified with it perhaps more closely than any other race" (Sinclair 1975: 115). Maori thought appreciates the mystical dimension and transcends reason:

> Abstract rational thought and empirical methods cannot grasp the concrete act of existing which is fragmentary, paradoxical and incomplete. The only way lies through a passionate, inward subjective approach. Only a few foreigners alien to a culture, men like James K. Baxter with the soul of a poet, can enter into the existential dimension of Maori life. This grasp of a culture proceeds not from superficial intellectualism but from an approach best articulated in poetry. Poetic imagery reveals to the Maori a depth of understanding in men which is absent from the empirical approach of the social anthropologist. [Marsden 1975:218–219]

The times have changed a great deal since 1922, when no less respected and proud a Maori than Sir Apirana Ngata could say of a Pakeha scholar, "There is not a member of the Maori race who is fit to wipe the boots of Mr. Elsdon Best in the matter of the knowledge of the lore of the race to which we belong" (quoted in *Journal of the Polynesian Society* 1932:31). Today Maoris are no longer willing to tolerate being told by Pakehas what is good for them, and even how to be Maori (Rangihau 1975). The notion that the rational Pakeha mind is unsuited to grasp Maori life, together with Maoritanga's major objective of drawing power into Maori hands, have encouraged many Maoris to insist that they, not Pakehas, be the proper custodians and managers of knowledge about the Maori heritage.

This sentiment is strong enough that some advocates of Maoritanga have invited Pakeha scholars out of Maori studies. Michael King, a Pakeha who has written extensively on Maori topics, observed that in 1971 Maori radicals insited that Pakecha historians write more about Maori subjects, but by 1983 the demand was that they should not write about them at all (1985:161). King's own 1983 book, *Maori—A Photographic and Social History*, has been negatively received by Maori reviewers, who stated the preference that such topics be addressed by Maori writers (King 1985:163). In the university, a Maori student complained that it is ethically wrong to be taught his own heritage by a Pakeha (Mead 1983:343–344).

Pakehas have not been routed from Maori studies. Indeed, because virtually all scholars who deal in Maori topics actively support the goal of Maoris to secure a better position in society and share the objective of creating a bicultural New Zealand, they have been active participants in the invention of the tradition that Maoritanga presents to the world. Michael King himself, for example, served as editor of the important collection of works by Maori authors that articulated many of the cardinal principles of Maoritanga (King 1975).

A number of writers have fostered the present invention of Maori culture by lending the weight of Pakeha scholarship to the movement. This often takes the form of according special authority to Maoris in matters pertaining to Maori culture. The Pakeha historian Judith Binney acknowledged the premise that Maoris are best equipped to understand and write about Maori topics when, in the preface to her excellent study of the Maori prophet Rua Kenana, she expressed misgivings about her grasp of the material and recorded the hope that one day a Maori scholar would produce a more authoritative account (Binney, Chaplin, and Wallace 1979:11). Anthropologist Anne Salmond has made it one of her professional objectives to promulgate and interpret Maori concepts of knowledge with the aim of incorporating them more fully into a bicultural New Zealand society (Salmond 1982; Stirling and Salmond 1980).

Steps have been taken to avoid offending Maori sensibilities. Preserved and tattooed Maori heads from the early 19th century, only 15 years ago a staple of museum exhibits, are no longer to be found on display in New Zealand institutions. Pakeha scholars have softened critiques of the Io cult and the Great Fleet, primarily, it seems, because many Maoris accept these traditions as authentic. The first edition of anthropologist Joan Metge's *The Maoris of New Zealand*, published in 1967, contains the following passages about Io: "The existence of a supreme god, Io, was allegedly revealed to those who reached the upper grades of the school of learning" (1967:30), and, from the glossary, "Io: Supreme Being whose existence and cult are claimed to have been revealed to initiates of the pre-European 'school of learning'" (1967:223). The corresponding passages in the second edition of the work, published in 1976, are: "The existence of a supreme god, Io-matua-kore, was revealed to those who reached the upper grades of the school of learning" (1976:23), and "Io: Supreme Being whose existence and worship were revealed to initiates of the pre-European 'school of learning'; identified by many Maoris with the Supreme Being of Christianity and used instead of or in alternation with the name Jehovah" (1976:337). A reference to Io as "the Supreme Being of Classic Maori cosmology" also appears on page 55, in a new chapter written for the second edition. Beyond the generally more positive attitude toward the Io cult, an increased concern about highlighting the views of contemporary Maoris is visible in a change of citation in the glossary entry on Io from Hiroa's skeptical account of the cult in *The Coming of the Maori* (1950) to the 1975 essay by Maori Marsden, discussed above, which accepts Io as authentic tradition.

Something similar is happening with the Great Fleet myth. New Zealand archeology has made great strides in recent years, and most discussions of the time and material conditions of early settlement (now established to have occurred by at least the 11th century) rely on archeological evidence. However, in a scholarly presentation of that evidence, Agnes Sullivan carefully states that, while the notion of an organized fleet seems discredited, archeology has produced nothing that disallows the possibility of migrant canoes arriving in New Zealand from East

Polynesia up to about the 14th century. This has the effect of muting any archeological challenge to the magic date of 1350 for the arrival of ancestral canoes although, it will be recalled, Smith's settling upon that date is one of the most contrived components of the Great Fleet story. "In traditional terms," Sullivan concludes, "there appear to be no good grounds at present for suggesting that the central themes of most Hawaiki canoe traditions are to be interpreted other than straightforwardly" (1984:62).

One of the most effective projects to publicize Maoritanga's invention of Maori culture was the exhibition "Te Maori: Maori Art from New Zealand Collections" (see Mead 1984b). Anthropology's role in the project is mainly to be found in the person of Sidney Mead, a Maori anthropologist who was one of the central organizers of the exhibition. "Te Maori" was shown in New York, St. Louis, San Francisco, and Chicago in 1984–86, and subsequently toured New Zealand in a triumphant homecoming. Through a stroke of genius in the presentation of the exhibition, Mead and the other Maoris involved in it managed to clothe the objects with more than simply artistic value. In each city the exhibition opened with a dramatic dawn ceremony in which Maori elders (brought from New Zealand specifically for the purpose) ritually lifted the *tapu* ("taboo") from the objects and entrusted them to the care of the host museum. The ceremony received extensive media coverage in each city, and it conveyed the Maori idea that the objects were infused with a spiritual power that derived from the ancestors and linked them in a mystical union with the Maoris of today. As a result the objects were viewed as more than examples of fine and exotic workmanship, and the notion was inserted into the minds of many Americans who saw or were involved with the exhibition that the Maori people have access to primal sources of power long since lost by more rational cultures (see O'Biso 1987).

The special meanings that became associated with "Te Maori" in the United States also had an impact in New Zealand. Vincent Crapanzano has cogently pointed out (1980:49, 81–87) that it is much easier to believe something about oneself if one succeeds in convincing someone else of it. As the standing of Maori art skyrocketed in international recognition as a result of the exhibition, Maori and Pakeha New Zealanders alike took greater interest and pride in it and became more receptive to the idea of a nonrational, spiritual quality in Maori culture. While the point should not be overemphasized, the exhibition did have some effect in both strengthening Maori identity and increasing Pakeha respect for the Maori people and Maori culture. In this way "Te Maori" advanced the agenda of Maoritanga and the notion of a bicultural New Zealand. Indeed, this was one of the prime purposes and major benefits of the entire project (Mead 1984a:29; 1986:27, 74, 78, 104).

Maoris insisted that art objects produced by their ancestors are tribal treasures (*taonga*), with the result that tribal proprietary rights became an important issue in the mounting of "Te Maori." In the planning stages of the exhibition a distinction was made between the legal ownership of the objects, vested in the museums that hold them, and the cultural ownership, which remained with the tribes. It was decided that no object could leave New Zealand unless the cultural owners agreed. Intense debate raged among elders of the various tribes over this issue, and ultimately the art of the Whanganui region was not included in the exhibition because of tribal disapproval. The concept of cultural ownership of art objects, which had not been enunciated prior to "Te Maori," has enriched the significance of tribal membership for Maori people and represents an important step toward Maoritanga's goal of bringing the Maori heritage under Maori control (Mead 1986:99).

Anthropologists and other scholars throughout New Zealand are also attempting to further the cause of Maoritanga by encouraging the growth of Maori Studies programs in the schools and universities, the involvement of program staff in assisting the Maori people with land claims and other projects, and greater Maori university enrollment. The aim is more ambitious than just increasing knowledge of and respect for Maori culture among Pakehas and making the benefits of Pakeha-style education more available to Maoris. As Anne Salmond articulates it, the imperative is to expand social institutions and modes of thinking in New Zealand to the point where they become truly bicultural, so that Maori concerns and Maori epistemology may be included in the national discourse on an equal footing with Pakeha concerns and epistemology. She has registered satisfaction that signs of this are emerging in the university, in the form of a series of master's theses written in Maori by Maori students about the traditional histories of their own tribes, and often presented from the perspective of Maori epistemology. Her main disappointment is that the response from the Pakeha side has been inadequate, for academic anthropology has offered little relevance to this much-needed injection of Maori ways of thinking and knowing into university-based Maori studies.

It could be that the anthropology we have inherited from Europe and America is simply not used to epistemological experiments of this sort, because it does not confront the experience of bicultural living, day by day, in the university as well as in the field. The questions of who are "we" and who are the "others" is anything but clear-cut when those who sit in lecture theatres and seminars and those who teach in them, those who write books, theses and articles and those who read them are inextricably both Maori and European; and in such a situation anthropology must change or be discarded. [Salmond 1983:323]

Moving still further along the same road, Sidney Mead has suggested that Maori Studies be elevated from its current program or department status in New Zealand universities to the level of a school; indeed, that a whole University of Aotearoa (the name for New Zealand favored by Maoritanga) be founded. The point is quite radical. It apparently aims to transform Maori Studies from a field of inquiry within the Pakeha-defined university to a general and distinctively Maori epistemological perspective from which not only Maori language and culture but also subjects such as anthropology, sociology, history, education, geography, linguistics, art history, and economics would be investigated (Mead 1983:343–346). Such a school would have a *marae* (in Maori villages, the plaza where visitors are received and community matters are discussed) as its central feature, instruction would be in the Maori language, and most of the staff would be Maori. Although Mead does not specify it, he is certainly not oblivious to the prospect that a University of Aotearoa would command more prestige — and much more substantial government funding — than the various *whare wananga* (traditional Maori schools) sponsored by different tribes. Echoing Maoritanga's cardinal demand for more power in Maori hands, Mead contends that the establishment of a Maori university would make it "possible to repossess our heritage, hold on to it, and to exercise a measure of control over it" (1983:346).

The Logic of Cultural Invention

The image of Maori culture that developed around the turn of the 20th century was constructed in the main by scholars who were predisposed to analyze institutions in terms of long-distance migrations, and who cherished the political desire to assimilate Maoris to Pakeha culture. The present image has been invented for the purpose of enhancing the power of Maoris in New Zealand society, and is largely composed of those Maori qualities that can be attractively contrasted with the least desirable aspects of Pakeha culture.

Taken together, these case studies might incline one to the pessimistic view that the reality of traditional culture and history is so irredeemably shrouded behind multiple veils of distortion, some woven from imported fabric and others homespun, that no effort at objectivity could be sufficient to strip them away. But that would miss the distinctive feature of both examples: that the "distortions" have been accepted by Maoris as authentic to their heritage. Io and the Great Fleet have been incorporated into Maori lore and are passed from elders to juniors in storytelling, oratory, and other Maori contexts. Today Maoris, and also those Pakehas who desire to incorporate both sides of bicultural New Zealand into their own experience, make it a conscious point to practice the tenets of Maoritanga. They learn the Maori language and Maori history. They are careful to show respect for elders. They open themselves to the emotional and mystical impact of charisma and the nonrational, and they heighten their appreciation for Maori lore and Maori art. As a result, these and other elements of the current invention of Maori culture become objectively incorporated into that culture by the very fact of people talking about them and practicing them.

Therefore, the fact that culture is an invention, and anthropology one of the inventing agents, should not engender suspicion or despair that anthropological accounts do not qualify as knowledge about cultural reality. Inventions are precisely the stuff that cultural reality is made of; as Linnekin (1983) and Handler (1984) have convincingly demonstrated by means of Hawaiian and Quebecois examples, "there is no essential, bounded tradition . . . the ongoing reconstruction of tradition is a facet of all social life" (Handler and Linnekin 1984:276).

To entertain the notion of a historically fixed tradition is to affirm what Jacques Derrida calls the "metaphysics of presence" (1978:281) or "logocentrism" (1974:12). He argues that since Nietzsche, Freud, and Heidegger, among others, it has been necessary to replace the metaphysics of presence with a more fluid, decentered view.

> Henceforth, it was necessary to begin thinking that there was no center, that the center could not be thought in the form of a present-being, that the center had no natural site, that it was not a fixed locus but a function, a sort of nonlocus in which an infinite number of sign-substitutions came into play.

This was the moment when . . . in the absence of a center or origin, everything became discourse . . . that is to say, a system in which the central
signified, the original or transcendental signified, is never absolutely present. . . . The absence of the transcendental signified extends the domain and
the play of signification infinitely. [Derrida 1978:280]

Applied to our examples, a logocentric view would hold that traditional Maori culture existed in determinate form, say, at the moment of
effective Western contact by Captain Cook in 1769. That cultural essence was then distorted in one way or another by turn-of-the-century
anthropologists as well as by contemporary proponents of Maoritanga —
although all of them claim to be holding fast to it. Derrida would maintain, on the contrary, that Maori culture has always been "a sort of
nonlocus in which an infinite number of sign-substitutions come into
play." From this perspective, discourse about the philosophically sophisticated cult of Io and the arrival in 1350 of a Great Fleet of migrant
canoes represents not really a distortion of traditional Maori culture but
one set of sign-substitutions in the play of signification that is itself the
essence (if we may be allowed to use that word) of Maori culture. Other
sign-substitutions include the warmth, passion, and mysticism stressed
by Maoritanga. Indeed, they also include whatever lore, conventions,
and institutions were in play among Maoris in New Zealand in 1769 on
the eve of Cook's visit, for there is no reason to privilege them with some
sort of fixed (logocentric) authenticity absent from the other inventions
or sign-substitutions that we have considered. Certainly Maoris of the
1760s, no less than contemporary Maori activists, were moved by their
own political agendas to appeal selectively and creatively to the tradition
of their ancestors; and the same can be said for those ancestors, and so on
indefinitely.

It follows from this that the analytic task is not to strip away the
invented portions of culture as inauthentic but to understand the process
by which they acquire authenticity. Social reproduction — the process
whereby people learn, embody, and transmit the conventional behaviors
of their society — is basically a matter of interpersonal communication.
Any conventional act, such as greeting someone on the street, is learned
by observing how other people do it, modeling one's own behavior on
that, and being assured that it is done properly (or alerted that it is not)
by the reactions of other people to the behavior. Moreover, each person
is teacher as well as learner in the process, because his or her behavior

also serves as a model upon which still other people construct their behavior (see Bourdieu 1977; Hanson and Hanson 1981). No one bit of behavior can be said to have ultimate authenticity, to be the absolute and eternal "right way" of which all the others are representations. All of the bits of behavior are models: models of previous bits and models for subsequent ones.

Described like this, the process of ordinary social reproduction is a case of sign-substitution in a play of signification. But, as we have already seen, the invention of culture is also that. This demystifies the process whereby cultural inventions acquire authenticity in the eyes of members of society because the invention of culture is no extraordinary occurrence but an activity of the same sort as the normal, everyday process of social life.

While it is essential to recognize this point, there must nevertheless be something distinctive about culture invention. It is, after all, much too strong a phrase to use for everyday social reproduction. As a first approximation, it might be said that inventions are sign-substitutions that depart some considerable distance from those upon which they are modeled, that are selective, and that systematically manifest the intention to further some political or other agenda. This criterion would authorize us to classify as inventions those sign-substitutions that rework Maori migration canoe legends into a chapter of the great Aryan migration, or that stress Maori respect for the elders and the dead without mentioning that such respect operated within tribes only and was matched by a tendency to revile and cannibalize the elders and dead of other tribes.

Very often, however, the inventive quality of sign-substitutions is recognizable only from outside and when they form clusters. Percy Smith, Edward Tregear, and Elsdon Best worked ingenuously within the tradition of diffusionist anthropology. When compared with the other two, the theories (or sign-substitutions) advanced by any one of them are not radical departures, and certainly they did not consider those theories to be inventions. The same may be said of contemporary advocates of Maoritanga. But when detached observers consider these two movements as wholes, and compare the images of Maori culture they advance and the political agendas they espouse, their status as inventions becomes obvious. Indeed, this highlights one of the main values of the Maori case for the study of culture invention: the fact that there have been two quite distinct inventions of Maori culture makes it much easier to get a clear view of each of them.

We conclude, then, that inventions are common components in the ongoing development of authentic culture, and that producers of inventions are often outsiders (including anthropologists) as well as insiders. This conclusion has a reflexive dimension that pertains to anthropology itself. No less than any other cultural enterprise, anthropology is a discourse consisting of sign-substitutions, of which the present essay is one. To claim otherwise — that anthropology occupies some fixed perspective outside the play of signification of other discourse — would be to sponsor a grotesque mating of logocentrism with professional ethnocentrism.

Granted that this essay is a sign-substitution, but does it qualify as an invention? The comments above distinguishing between the inventive status of individual contributions as opposed to larger aggregates pertain here. Within the rest of the "invention of tradition" literature, which constitutes a kind of paradigm in Kuhn's (1962) sense, this essay is not an invention. But that literature or paradigm, taken as a whole, does make a radical departure from earlier anthropological thinking about tradition, and thus is an invention. Moreover, this anthropological invention belongs to a larger set of inventive sign-substitutions in contemporary Western social thought, represented by thinkers such as Derrida and described by Clifford (1988:9) as "a pervasive condition of off-centeredness in a world of distinct meaning systems, a state of being in culture while looking at culture, a form of personal and collective self-fashioning."

To acknowledge the presence of inventions in anthropology may appear to jeopardize its capacity to locate truth and contribute to knowledge. But that would be to miss the point of the entire argument. It would assume the existence of some other form of discourse that trades in fixed rules and eternal verities — in short, that logocentrism reigns. To the contrary, the thesis of this essay is that invention is an ordinary event in the development of all discourse, which therefore never rests on a permanent foundation.[1] From this point of view truth and knowledge stem — and always have stemmed — from inventions in the decentered play of sign-substitutions.

Notes

Acknowledgments. Thanks are due to Rob Borofsky and Alan Howard for the original impetus to write this essay, to John Massad for insights that contributed to the theoretical sections, and to Louise Hanson for contributions to the whole. Oral versions of this paper were presented at Columbia University and at the

Bob Scholte Memorial Conference on Critical Anthropology, the University of Amsterdam.

1. Obviously this thesis is closely tied to anthropology's long-standing if ambivalent affair with cultural relativism. The issue of relativism is treated more explicitly in another essay which arrives at a similar conclusion by a different path (Hanson 1979).

References Cited

Best, Elsdon
   1924 The Maori. 2 vols. Wellington: Polynesian Society Memoirs, Vol. 5.
   1973 [1922] Some Aspects of Maori Myth and Religion. Wellington: Dominion Museum. Monograph No. 1.

Binney, Judith, Gillian Chaplin, and Craig Wallace
   1979 Mihaia: The Prophet Rua Kenana and His Community at Maungapohatu. Wellington: Oxford University Press.

Borofsky, Robert
   1987 Making History: Pukapukan and Anthropological Constructions of Knowledge. Cambridge: Cambridge University Press.

Bourdieu, Pierre
   1977 Outline of a Theory of Practice. Cambridge: Cambridge University Press.

Clifford, James
   1988 The Predicament of Culture. Cambridge, MA: Harvard University Press.

Clifford, James, and George E. Marcus, eds.
   1986 Writing Culture: The Poetics and Politics of Ethnography. Berkeley: University of California Press.

Crapanzano, Vincent
   1980 Tuhami: Portrait of a Moroccan. Chicago: University of Chicago Press.

Dansey, Harry
   1975 A View of Death. In Te Ao Hurihuri: The World Moves On — Aspects of Maoritanga. Michael King, ed. Pp. 173–189. Wellington: Hicks Smith and Sons.

Deacon, A. B.
   1934 Malekula: A Vanishing People in the New Hebrides. London: George Routledge and Sons.

Derrida, Jacques
   1974 Of Grammatology. Baltimore: Johns Hopkins University Press.
   1978 Writing and Difference. Chicago: University of Chicago Press.

Elder, J. R., ed.
   1932 The Letters and Journals of Samuel Marsden. Wellington: Reed.

Fabian, Johannes
 1983 Time and the Other: How An-
 thropology Makes Its Object.
 New York: Columbia University
 Press.
France, Peter
 1969 The Charter of the Land:
 Custom and Colonization in Fiji.
 Melbourne: Oxford University
 Press.
Geertz, Clifford
 1988 Works and Lives: The Anthropologist as Author. Palo Alto,
 CA: Stanford University Press.
Handler, Richard
 1984 On Sociocultural Disconti-
 nuity: Nationalism and Cultural
 Objectification in Quebec. Current Anthropology 25:55–71.
Handler, Richard, and Jocelyn Lin-
 nekin
 1984 Tradition, Genuine or Spu-
 rious. Journal of American Folk-
 lore 97:273–290.
Hanson, F. Allan
 1979 Does God Have a Body?
 Truth, Reality and Cultural Relativism. Man 14:515–529.
Hanson, F. Allan, and Louise Hanson
 1981 The Cybernetics of Cultural
 Communication. In Semiotic
 Themes. Richard DeGeorge, ed.
 Pp. 251–273. Humanistic Studies, No. 53. Lawrence: University
 of Kansas Publications.
Herzfeld, Michael
 1982 Ours Once More: Folklore,
 Ideology and the Making of

Modern Greece. Austin: University of Texas Press.
Hiroa, Te Rangi (Peter H. Buck)
 1950 The Coming of the Maori.
 2nd edition. Wellington: Whitcombe and Tombs.
Johansen, J. Prytz
 1958 Studies in Maori Rites and
 Myths. Copenhagen: Munksgaard.
Journal of the Polynesian Society
 1932 The Late Elsdon Best. Journal
 of the Polynesian Society 41:1–
 49.
King, Michael
 1975 [ed.] Te Ao Hurihuri: The
 World Moves On—Aspects of
 Maoritanga. Wellington: Hicks
 Smith and Sons.
 1985 Being Pakeha: An Encounter
 with New Zealand and the Maori
 Renaissance. Auckland: Hodder
 and Stoughton.
Kuhn, Thomas
 1962 The Structure of Scientific
 Revolutions. Chicago: University
 of Chicago Press.
Larcom, Joan
 1982. The Invention of Convention. Mankind 13:330–337.
Legge, J. D.
 1958 Britain in Fiji, 1858–1880.
 London: Macmillan.
Lindstrom, Lamont
 1982 Leftamap Kastom: The Political History of Tradition on
 Tanna, Vanuatu. Mankind 13:
 316–329.

Linnekin, Jocelyn S.

1983 Defining Tradition: Variations on the Hawaiian Identity. American Ethnologist 10:241–252.

Marsden, Maori

1975 God, Man and Universe: A Maori View. *In* Te Ao Hurihuri: The World Moves On — Aspects of Maoritanga. Michael King, ed. Pp. 191–219. Wellington: Hicks Smith and Sons.

Mead, Sidney (Hirini) Moko

1983 Te Toi Matauranga Maori mo nga Ra Kei Mua: Maori Studies Tomorrow. Journal of the Polynesian Society 92:333–351.

1984a Nga Timunga me nga Paringa o te Mana Maori: The Ebb and Flow of Mana Maori and the Changing Context of Maori Art. *In* Te Maori: Maori Art from New Zealand Collections. Pp. 20–36. New York: Harry N. Abrams.

1984b [ed.] Te Maori: Art from New Zealand Collections. New York: Harry N. Abrams.

1986 Magnificent Te Maori: Te Maori Whakahirahira. Auckland: Heinemann.

Metge, Joan

1967 The Maoris of New Zealand. London: Routledge and Kegan Paul.

1976 The Maoris of New Zealand, Rautahi. London: Routledge and Kegan Paul.

O'Biso, Carol

1987 First Light. Auckland: Pan Books.

Ranger, Terence

1983 The Invention of Tradition in Central Africa. *In* The Invention of Tradition. Eric Hobsbawm and Terence Ranger, eds. Pp. 211–262. Cambridge: Cambridge University Press.

Rangihau, John

1975 Being Maori. *In* Te Ao Hurihuri: The World Moves On — Aspects of Maoritanga. Michael King, ed. Pp. 221–233. Wellington: Hicks Smith and Sons.

Renan, Ernest

1889 Histoire du peuple d'Israel, Vol. 1. Paris: Calmann Levy.

Said, Edward

1978 Orientalism. New York: Pantheon.

Salmond, Anne

1982 Theoretical Landscapes: On Cross-Cultural Conceptions of Knowledge. *In* Semantic Anthropology. David Parkin, ed. Pp. 65–87. A.S.A. Monograph 22. London: Academic Press.

1983 The Study of Traditional Maori Society: The State of the Art. Journal of the Polynesian Society 92:309–331.

Sciascia, Piri

1984 Ka Pu te Ruha, ka Hao te Rangatahi: As the Old Net Piles up on Shore, the New Net Goes Fishing. *In* Te Maori: Maori Art from New Zealand Collections. Sidney M. Mead, ed. Pp. 156–166. New York: Harry N. Abrams.

Simmons, D. R.
  1976 The Great New Zealand Myth: A Study of the Discovery and Origin Traditions of the Maori. Wellington: Reed.
Sinclair, Douglas
  1975 Land: Maori View and European Response. *In* Te Ao Hurihuri: The World Moves On — Aspects of Maoritanga. Michael King, ed. Pp. 115–139. Wellington: Hicks Smith and Sons.
Smith, S. Percy
  1910 History and Traditions of the Maoris of the West Coast, North Island, New Zealand. New Plymouth, NZ: Polynesian Society Memoirs, Vol. 1.
  1913 The Lore of the Wharewananga, Part 1: Te Kauwaerunga. New Plymouth, NZ: Thomas Avery.
  1915 The Lore of the Wharewananga, Part 2: Te Kauwaeraro. New Plymouth, NZ: Thomas Avery.
Smithyman, Kendrick
  1979 Making History: John White and S. Percy Smith at Work. Journal of the Polynesian Society 88:375–414.

Sorrenson, M. P. K.
  1979 Maori Origins and Migrations: The Genesis of Some Pakeha Myths and Legends. Auckland: Auckland University Press.
Stirling, Eruera, and Anne Salmond
  1980 Eruera: The Teachings of a Maori Elder. Wellington: Oxford University Press.
Sullivan, Agnes
  1984 Nga Paiaka o te Maoritanga: The Roots of Maori Culture. *In* Te Maori: Maori Art from New Zealand Collections. Sidney M. Mead, ed. Pp. 37–62. New York: Harry N. Abrams.
Thomson, Arthur S.
  1859 The Story of New Zealand. 2 vols. London: John Murray.
Tregear, Edward
  1885 The Aryan Maori. Wellington: Government Printer.
Wagner, Roy
  1981 The Invention of Culture. Chicago: University of Chicago Press.
Winiata, Maharaia
  1967 The Changing Role of the Leader in Maori Society: A Study in Social Change and Race Relations. Auckland: Blackwood and Janet Paul.

Facing Power — Old Insights, New Questions

Eric R. Wolf

VOL. 92, 1990, 586–596

In this essay I engage the problem of power and the issues that it poses for anthropology. I argue that we actually know a great deal about power, but have been timid in building upon what we know. This has implications for both theory and method, for assessing the insights of the past and for raising new questions.

The very term makes many of us uncomfortable. It is certainly one of the most loaded and polymorphous words in our repertoire. The Romance, Germanic, and Slavic languages, at least, conflate a multitude of meanings in speaking about *pouvoir* or *potere*, *Macht*, or *mogushchestvo*. Such words allow us to speak about power as if it meant the same thing to all of us. At the same time, we often speak of power as if all phenomena involving it were somehow reducible to a common core, some inner essence. This conjures up monstrous images of power, Hobbes's Leviathan or Bertrand de Jouvenel's Minotaur, but it leads away from specifying different kinds of power implicated in different kinds of relationships.

I argue instead that it is useful to think of four different modes of power. One is power as the attribute of the person, as potency or capability, the basic Nietzschean idea of power (Kaufmann 1968). Speaking of power in this sense draws attention to the endowment of persons in the play of power, but tells us little about the form and direction of that play. The second kind of power can be understood as the ability of an *ego* to impose its will on an *alter*, in social action, in interpersonal relations. This draws attention to the sequences of interactions and transactions among people, but it does not address the nature of the arena in which the interactions go forward. That comes into view more sharply when we focus on power in the third mode, as power that controls the settings in which people may show forth their potentialities and interact with others. I first came across this phrasing of power in anthropology when Richard Adams sought to define power not in interpersonal terms, but as the control that one actor or "operating unit" (his term) exercises over energy flows that constitute part of the environment of another actor (Adams 1966, 1975). This definition calls attention to the instrumentalities of power and is useful for understanding how "operating units" circumscribe the actions of others within determinate settings. I call this third kind of power tactical or organizational power.

But there is still a fourth mode of power, power that not only operates within settings or domains but that also organizes and orchestrates the settings themselves, and that specifies the distribution and direction of energy flows. I think that this is the kind of power that Marx addressed in speaking about the power of capital to harness and allocate labor power, and it forms the background of Michel Foucault's notion of power as the ability "to structure the possible field of action of others" (Foucault 1984:428). Foucault called this "to govern," in the 16th-century sense of governance, an exercise of "action upon action" (1984:427–428). Foucault himself was primarily interested in this as the power to govern consciousness, but I want to use it as power that structures the political economy. I will refer to this kind of power as structural power. This term rephrases the older notion of "the social relations of production," and is intended to emphasize power to deploy and allocate social labor. These governing relations do not come into view when you think of power primarily in interactional terms. Structural power shapes the social field of action so as to render some kinds of behavior possible, while making others less possible or impossible. As old Georg Friedrich Hegel argued, what occurs in reality has first to be possible.

What capitalist relations of production accomplish, for example, is to make possible the accumulation of capital based on the sale of marketable labor power in a large number of settings around the world. As anthropologists we can follow the flows of capital and labor through ups and downs, advances and retreats, and investigate the ways in which social and cultural arrangements in space and time are drawn into and implicated in the workings of this double whammy. This is not a purely economic relation, but a political one as well: it takes clout to set up, clout to maintain, and clout to defend; and wielding that clout becomes a target for competition or alliance building, resistance or accommodation.

This is the dimension that has been stressed variously in studies of imperialism, dependency, or world-systems. Their questions are why and how some sectors, regions, or nations are able to constrain the options of others, and what coalitions and conflicts occur in the course of this interplay. Some have said that these questions have little relevance to anthropology, in that they don't have enough to say about "real people doing real things," as Sherry Ortner put it (Ortner 1984:114); but it seems to me that they do touch on a lot of what goes on in the real world, that constrains, inhibits, or promotes what people do, or cannot do, within the scenarios we study. The notion of structural power is useful precisely because it allows us to delineate how the forces of the world impinge upon the people we study, without falling back into an anthropological nativism that postulates supposedly isolated societies and uncontaminated cultures, either in the present or in the past. There is no gain in a false romanticism that pretends that "real people doing real things" inhabit self-enclosed and self-sufficient universes.

I address here primarily the relation between tactical (or organizational) power and structural power. I do this because I believe that these concepts can help us to explain the world we inhabit. I think that it is the task of anthropology — or at least the task of some anthropologists — to attempt explanation, and not merely description, descriptive integration, or interpretation. Anthropology can be different things to different people (entertainment, exotic *frisson*, a "show-and-tell" of differences), but it should not, I submit, be content with James Boon's "shifting collage of contraries threatening (promising) to become unglued" (Boon 1982:237). Writing culture may require literary skill and genre, but a search for explanation requires more: it cannot do without naming and comparing things, and formulating concepts for naming and comparison. I think we must move beyond Geertz's "experience-near" understandings to analytical concepts that allow us to set what we know about X against what we know about Y, in pursuit of explanation. This means that I subscribe to a basically realist position. I think that the world is real, that these realities affect what humans do and that what humans do affects the world, and that we can come to understand the whys and wherefores of this relationship. We need to be professionally suspicious of our categories and models; we should be aware of their historical and cultural contingencies; we can understand a quest for explanation as approximations to truth rather than the truth itself. But I also believe that the search for explanation in anthropology can be cumulative; that knowledge and insights gained in the past can generate new questions, and that new departures can incorporate the accomplishments of the past.

In anthropology we are continuously slaying paradigms, only to see them return to life, as if discovered for the first time. The old-time evolutionism of Morgan and Engels reappeared in ecological guise in the forties and fifties. The Boasian insistence that we must understand the ways "that people actually think about their own culture and institutions" (Goldman 1975:15) has resurfaced in the anthropology of cognition and symbolism, now often played as a dissonant quartet in the format of deconstructionism. Diffusionism grew exhausted after biting too deeply into the seductive apple of trait-list collecting, but sprang back to life in the studies of acculturation, interaction spheres, and world-systems. Functionalism overreached itself by claiming to depict organic unities, but returned in systems theory as well as in other disguises. Culture-and-personality studies advanced notions of "basic personality structure" and "national character," without paying heed to history, cultural heterogeneity, or the role of hegemony in shaping uniformities; but suspiciously similar characterizations of modern nations and "ethnic groups" continue to appear. The varieties of ecological anthropology and the various Marxisms are being told by both user-friendly and unfriendly folk that what they need is "the concept of culture." We are all familiar, I trust, with Robert Lowie's image of "diffusionism laying the axe to evolutionism." As each successive approach carries the ax to its predecessors, anthropology comes to resemble a project in intellectual deforestation.

I do not think that this is either necessary or desirable. I think that anthropology can be cumulative, that we can use the work of our predecessors to raise new questions.

Three Projects

Some of anthropology's older insights into power can be the basis for new inquiry. I want to briefly review three projects that sought to understand what happens to people in the modern world and in the process raised questions about power, both tactical and structural. These projects yielded substantial bodies of data and theory; they opened up perspectives that reached beyond their scope of inquiry; and all were criticized in their time and subjected to reevaluation thereafter. All three were efforts toward an explanatory anthropology.

The first of these projects is the study of Puerto Rico in 1948–49, directed by Julian Steward; the results are in the collective work, *The People of Puerto Rico* (Steward et al. 1956). The original thrust of the project stemmed from Steward's attack on the assumptions of a unitary national culture and national character which then dominated the field of culture-and-personality. The project aimed instead at exhibiting the heterogeneity of a national society. It was also a rejection of the model in which a single community was made to stand for an entire nation. It depicted Puerto Rico as a structure of varied localities and regions, clamped together by islandwide institutions and the activities of an insular upper class, a system of heterogeneous parts and levels. The project was especially innovative in trying to find out how this complex arrangement developed historically, by tracing out the historical causes and courses of crop production on the island, and then following out the differential implications of that development in four representative communities. It promised to pay attention to the institutions connecting localities, regions, and nation, but actually confined itself to looking at these institutions primarily in terms of their local effects. It did carry out a study of the insular upper class, which was conceived as occupying the apex of linkages to the level of the nation. The project's major shortfall, in terms of its own undertaking, was its failure to take proper account of the rapidly intensifying migration to the nearby U.S. mainland. Too narrow a focus on agricultural ecology prevented it from coming to grips with issues already then becoming manifest on the local level, but prompted and played out upon a much larger stage.

While the Puerto Rico project averted its eyes from the spectacle of migration, another research effort took labor migration to the towns and burgeoning mines of Central Africa as its primary point of reference. This research was carried out under the auspices of the Rhodes-Livingstone Institute, set up in 1937 in what was then Northern Rhodesia and is now Zambia. Its research goal was defined by the first director, Godfrey Wilson, whose own outlook has been characterized as an unconscious effort to combine Marx and Malinowski (Brown 1973: 195). Wilson understood the processes affecting Central Africa as an industrial revolution connected to the workings of the world economy. The massive penetration of the mining industry was seen as causal in generating multiple conflicts on the local and regional scene. Then Max Gluckman, the director from 1942 to 1947, drew up a research plan for the Institute which outlined a number of problem-oriented studies, and enlisted a stellar cast of anthropologists to work on such problems as the intersections of native and colonial governance, the role of witchcraft, the effects of labor migration on domestic economy, and the conflicts generated by the tension-ridden interplay of matrilineal descent and patrilocal residence. Dealing with an area of considerable linguistic and cultural diversity, the researchers were able to compare their findings to identify what was variable and what was common in local responses to general processes. But where the project was at its most innovative was in looking at rural locations, mining centers, and towns not as separate social and cultural entities but as interrelated elements caught up in one social field. It thus moved from Wilson's original concern with detribalization as anomic loss toward a more differentiated scenario of variegated responses to the new behavior settings of village, mine, and urban township. In doing so, it opened perspectives that the Puerto Rico project did not address. Its major failing lay in not taking systematic and critical account of the colonial structure in which these settings were embedded.

The third project I want to mention was directed by Richard Adams between 1963 and 1966, to study the national social structure of Guatemala. It is described in the book *Crucifixion by Power* (Adams 1970). The project took account of the intense growth of agricultural production for the market, and placed what was then known about life in localities within that context. Its specific innovation, however, lies in the fact that it engaged the study of national institutions in ways not broached by the two other projects I have referred to. Adams showed how local, regional, and supranational elites contested each other's power, and how regional elites stabilized their command by forging ties at the level of the nation. At that level, however, their power was subject to competition and interference by groups operating on the transnational and international plane. The study of elites was followed by accounts of the development of various institutions: the military, the renascent Guatemalan Church, the expanding interest organizations of the upper sector, and the legal system and legal profession. Adams then showed how these institutions curtailed agrarian and labor demands in the countryside, and produced individualized patron-client ties between the urban poor and their political sponsors in the capital. What the project did not do was to bring together this rich material into a synthesis that might have provided a theoretical model of the nation for further work.

It seems clear now that the three projects all stood on the threshold of a promising new departure in anthropological inquiry, but failed to cross it. They were adventurous, but not adventurous enough. First, in my view, they anticipated a move toward political economy, while not quite taking that next step. The Puerto Rico project, in its concentration on agriculture, failed to come to grips with the political and economic forces that established that agriculture in the first place, and that were already at work in "Operation Bootstrap" to transform the agricultural island into an industrial service station. We did not understand the ways in which island institutions, supposedly "national" but actually interlocked with mainland economics and politics, were battlegrounds for diverse contending interests. Thus, the project also missed an opportunity to deal with the complex interplay of hegemonic and subaltern cultural stances in the Puerto Rican situation. In fact, no one has done so to date; the task remains for the doing.

The Central Africa project was similarly confined by its own presuppositions. Despite its attention to conflicts and contradictions, it remained a captive of the prevailing functionalism, especially when it interpreted disjunctions as mere phases in the restoration of continuity. There was a tendency to take the colonial system as a given and thus to mute both the historical implications of conquest and the cumulative confrontations between Africans and Europeans. New questions now enable us to address these issues. Colonialism overrode the kin-based and tributary polities it encountered. Their members were turned into peasants in the hinterland and into workers in mine and town; peasantization and proletarianization were concomitant processes, often accompanied by force and violence. New ethnic and class identities replaced older, now decentered ties (Sichone 1989). Yet research has also uncovered a multiplicity of African responses in labor and political organization (Epstein 1958; Ranger 1970), in dance societies (Mitchell 1957; Ranger 1975), in a proliferation of religious movements (Van Binsbergen and Schofeleers 1985; Werbner 1989), in rebellion and resistance (Lan 1985). These studies have reemphasized the role of cultural understandings as integral ingredients of the transformation of labor and power.

Adams's project came very close to a new opening. It embodied an historical perspective, it understood the relations among groups as conflict-ridden processes, and it included the operations of multinational and transnational powers in this dynamic. It did not, however,

move toward a political economic model of the entire ensemble—
perhaps because Adams's own specific interests lay in developing an
evolutionary theory of power. It thus also neglected the complex interplay of cultures in the Guatemalan case. Such a move toward synthesis
still awaits the future.

The significance of these three projects lies not only in their own
accomplishments but in the new questions they lead us to ask. First, they
all call attention to history, but not history as "one damned thing after
another," as Leslie White used to say. "History," says Maurice Godelier,
"does not explain: it has to be explained" (1977:6). What attention to
history allows you to do is to look at processes unfolding, intertwining,
spreading out, and dissipating over time. This means rethinking the
units of our inquiries—households, localities, regions, national entities—seeing them not as fixed entities, but as problematic: shaped, reshaped, and changing over time. Attention to processes unfolding over
time foregrounds organization—the structuring arrangements of social
life—but requires us to see these in process and change. Second, the
three projects point us to processes operating on a macro-scale, as well as
in micro-settings. Puerto Rico was located first in the Hispanic orbit,
then in the orbit of the United States. Central Africa was shaped by
worldwide industrialization, as well as by the policies of colonial governance. Guatemala has been crucified by external connections and internal effects at the same time. The point continues an older anthropology
which spoke first of "culture areas," then of oikumenes, interaction
spheres, interethnic systems, and symbiotic regions, and that can now
entertain "world-systems." Macroscopic history and processes of organization thus become important elements of a new approach. Both involve considerations of power—tactical and structural.

Organization

Organization is key, because it sets up relationships among people
through allocation and control of resources and rewards. It draws on
tactical power to monopolize or share out liens and claims, to channel
action into certain pathways while interdicting the flow of action into
others. Some things become possible and likely; others are rendered
unlikely. At the same time, organization is always at risk. Since power
balances always shift and change, its work is never done; it operates
against entropy (Balandier 1970). Even the most successful organization
never goes unchallenged. The enactment of power always creates fric-

tion — disgruntlement, foot-dragging, escapism, sabotage, protest or outright resistance, a panoply of responses well documented with Malaysian materials by James Scott (1985) in *Weapons of the Weak*.

Granted the importance of the subject, one might ask why anthropology seems to have relinquished the study of organization, so that today you can find the topic more often discussed in the manuals of business management than in our publications. We structure and are structured, we transact, we play out metaphors, but the whole question of organization has fallen into abeyance.

Many of us entered anthropology when there were still required courses in something called "social organization." It dealt with principles of categorization like gender, generation, and rank, and with groupings, such as lineages, clans, age sets, and associations. We can now see in retrospect that this labeling was too static, because organization was then grasped primarily as an outcome, a finished product responding to a cultural script, and not visualized in the active voice, as process, frequently a difficult and conflict-ridden process at that. When the main emphasis was on organizational forms and principles, it was all too easy to understand organization in architectural terms, as providing the building blocks for structure, a reliable edifice of regular and recurrent practices and ideas that rendered social life predictable, and could thus be investigated in the field. There was little concern with tactical power in shaping organizations, maintaining them, destabilizing them, or undoing them.

If an idea is judged by its fruitfulness, then the notion of social structure proved to be a very good idea. It yielded interesting work and productive insights. It is now evident that it also led us to reify organizational results into the building blocks of hypostatized social architectures, for example, in the concept of "the unilineal descent group." That idea was useful in leading us to think synoptically about features of group membership, descent, jural-political solidarity, rights and obligations focused on a common estate, injunctions of "prescriptive altruism," and norms of encompassing morality. Yet it is one thing to use a model to think out the implications of organizational processes, and another to expect unilineal descent groups with all these features to materialize in these terms, as dependably shaped bricks in a social-structural edifice.

How do we get from viewing organization as product or outcome to understanding organization as process? For a start, we could do worse than heed Conrad Arensberg's advice (1972:10–11) to look at "the flow of action," to ask what is going on, why it is going on, who engages in it, with whom, when, and how often. Yet we would now add to this behavior-centered approach a new question: For what and for whom is all this going on, and—indeed—against whom? This question should not be posed merely in interactionist terms. Asking why something is going on and for whom requires a conceptual guess about the forces and effects of the structural power that drives organization and to which organization on all levels must respond. What are the dominant relations through which labor is deployed? What are the organizational implications of kinship alliances, kin coalitions, chiefdoms, or forms of state? Not all organizations or articulations of organization answer to the same functional requisites, or respond to the same underlying dynamic.

Furthermore, it behooves us to think about what is entailed in conceiving organization as a process. This is an underdeveloped area in anthropological thinking. Clearly dyadic contracts, networks of various sizes and shapes, kinship systems, political hierarchies, corporations, and states possess very different organizational potentials. Understanding how all these sets of people and instrumentalities can be aggregated, hooked together, articulated under different kinds of structural power remains a task for the future.

In the pursuit of this task we can build upon the past by using our concepts and models as discovery procedures, not as fixed representations, universally applicable. For example, Michel Verdon developed a strong critique of lineage theory in his book on the Abutia Ewe (Verdon 1983). Yet the critique itself is informed by the questions raised by that theory and by the demands for evidence required for its corroboration. Verdon investigated the characteristics and distribution of domestic units, residential entities, and matrimonial practices, treating these as prerequisites for defining linkages by kinship. He then used the model of lineage theory to pose further queries about the relation of kinship to political synchronization, taking this connection as a problem, rather than an assumption a priori. The model served as a method of inquiry, rather than an archetype.

A similar redefinition of the problem has taken place in the study of chiefdoms, where interest, as Timothy Earle has said, "has shifted from schemes to classify societies as chiefdoms or not, towards consideration of the causes of observed variability" (Earle 1987:279). Social constellations that can be called chiefdoms not only come in many sizes and shapes (Feinman and Neitzel 1984), but they are now understood as "fragile negotiated institutions," both in securing compliance within and in competition with rivals outside. Emphasis in research now falls on the mixes of economic, political, and ideological strategies that chiefdoms employ to these ends, as well as on their variable success in shaping their different historical trajectories (Earle 1989:87). Similarly, where people once simply spoke of "the state," the state is now seen less as a thing than as "a process" (Gailey 1987). A new emphasis on state-making processes takes account both of the "diversity and fluidity of form, function and malfunction" and of "the extent to which all states are internally divided and subject to penetration by conflicting and usually contradictory forces" (Bright and Harding 1984:4).

Signification

Finally, I want to address the issue of power in signification. Anthropology has treated signification mainly in terms of encompassing cultural unities, such as patterns, configurations, ethos, eidos, epistemes, paradigms, cultural structures. These unities, in turn, have been conceptualized primarily as the outcomes of processes of logico-aesthetic integration. Even when the frequently incongruous and disjointed characteristics of culture are admitted, the hope has been — and I quote Geertz — that identifying significant symbols, clusters of such symbols, and clusters of clusters would yield statements of "the underlying regularities of human experience implicit in their formation" (Geertz 1973: 408). The appeal is to the efficacy of symbols, to the workings of logics and aesthetics in the movement toward integration or reintegration, as if these cognitive processes were guided by a *telos* all their own.

I call this approach into question on several grounds. First, I draw on the insight of Anthony Wallace, who in the late 1950s contrasted views of culture that emphasize "the replication of uniformity" with those that acknowledge the problem of "the organization of diversity." He argued that

> all societies are, in a radical sense, plural societies. . . . How do societies ensure that the diverse cognitions of adults and children, males and females, warriors and shamans, slaves and masters articulate to form the equivalence structures that are the substance of social life? [Wallace 1970:110]

This query of Wallace's continues to echo in many quarters: in a feminist anthropology that questions the assumption that men and women share the same cultural understandings; in ethnography from various areas, where "rubbish-men" in Melanesia and "no-account people" on the Northwest Coast do not seem to abide by the norms and ideals of Big Men and chiefs; in studies of hierarchical systems in which different strata and segments exhibit different and contending models of logico-aesthetic integration (India furnishes a telling case). We have been told that such divergences are ultimately kept in check and on track by cultural logic, pure and simple. This seems to me unconvincing. It is indeed the case that our informants in the field invoke metaphoric polarities of purity and pollution, well-being and malevolence, *yin* and *yang*, life and death. Yet these metaphors are intrinsically polysemic, so abundant in possible signifiers that they can embrace any and all situations. To put them to work in particular scenarios requires that their range be constricted and narrowed down to but a small set of referents. What Lévi-Strauss called "the surplus of signifiers" must be subjected to parsimonious selection before the logic of cultural integration can be actualized. This indexing, as some have called it, is no automatic process, but passes through power and through contentions over power, with all sorts of consequences for signification.

Wallace's insights on the organization of diversity also raise questions about how meaning actually works in social life. He pointed out that participants in social action do not need to understand what meanings lie behind the behavior of their partners in interchange. All they have to know is how to respond appropriately to the cues signaled by others. Issues of meaning need not ever rise into consciousness. This is often the concern only of certain specialists, whose specific job or interest it is to explore the plenitude of possible meanings: people such as shamans, *tohunga*, or academics. Yet there are also situations in which the mutual signaling of expectations is deranged, where opposite and contradictory interests come to the fore, or where cultural schemata come under challenge. It then becomes apparent that beyond logic and aesthetics, it is power that guarantees — or fails.

Power is implicated in meaning through its role in upholding one version of significance as true, fruitful, or beautiful, against other possibilities that may threaten truth, fruitfulness, or beauty. All cultures, however conceived, carve out significance and try to stabilize it against possible alternatives. In human affairs, things might be different, and often are. Roy Rappaport, in writing on sanctity and ritual (Rappaport 1979), has emphasized the basic arbitrariness of all cultural orders. He argues that they are anchored in postulates that can neither be verified nor falsified, but that must be treated as unquestionable: to make them unquestionable, they are surrounded with sacredness. I would add that there is always the possibility that they might come unstuck. Hence, symbolic work is never done, achieves no final solution. The cultural assertion that the world is shaped in this way and not in some other has to be repeated and enacted, lest it be questioned and denied. The point is well made by Valerio Valeri in his study of *Kingship and Sacrifice* in Hawaii. Ritual, he says, produces sense

> by creating contrasts in the continuum of experience. This implies suppressing certain elements of experience in order to give relevance to others. Thus the creation of conceptual order is also, constitutively, the suppression of aspects of reality. [Valeri 1985:xi]

The Chinese doctrine of "the rectification of names" also speaks to this point of the suppressed alternatives. Stipulating that the world works in one way and not in another requires categories to order and direct experience. According to this doctrine, if meanings multiplied so as to transcend established boundaries, social consensus would become impossible — people would harm each other "like water and fire." Hence, a wise government would have to restore things to their proper definitions, in clear recognition that the maintenance of categories upholds power, and power maintains the order of the world (see Pocock 1971:42–79).

I have spoken of different modes of structural power, which work through key relations of governance. Each such mode would appear to require characteristic ways of conceptualizing and categorizing people. In social formations that deploy labor through relations glossed as kinship, people are assigned to networks or bodies of kin that are distinguished by criteria of gender, distinct substances or essences of descent, connections with the dead, differential distributions of myths, rituals, and emblems. Tributary formations hierarchize these criteria and set up distinct social strata, each stratum marked by a distinctive inner substance that also defines its positions and privileges in society. Capitalist formations peel the individual out of encompassing ascriptive bodies and install people as separate actors, free to exchange, truck, or barter in the market, as well as in other provinces of life. The three modes of categorizing social actors, moreover, imply quite different relations to "nature" and cosmos. When one mode enters into conflict with another, it also challenges the fundamental categories that empower its dynamics. Power will then be invoked to assault rival categorical claims. Power is thus never external to signification — it inhabits meaning and is its champion in stabilization and defense.

We owe to social anthropology the insight that the arrangements of a society become most visible when they are challenged by crisis. The role of power also becomes most evident in instances where major organizational transformations put signification under challenge. Let me offer some examples. In their study of the Plains Vision Experience, Patricia Albers and Seymour Parker (1971) contrast the individualized visions of the egalitarian foragers of the Plains periphery with the standardized kin-group-controlled visions of the horticultural village dwellers. Still a third kind of vision, oriented toward war and wealth, emerged among the buffalo-hunting nomads who developed in response to the introduction of horse and gun. As horse pastoralism proved increasingly successful, the horticulturalists became riven by conflicts between the personal-private visions of young men involved in buffalo hunting, and the visions controlled by hereditary groups of kin.

The development of the Merina state in Madagascar gives us another example (see, for example, Berg 1986; Bloch 1986). As the state became increasingly powerful and centralized around an intensified agriculture and ever more elaborate social hierarchy, the royal center also emerged as the hub of the ideational system. Local rites of circumcision, water sprinklings, offerings to honor superiors, and rituals ministering to group icons and talismans were increasingly synchronized and fused with rituals of state.

The royal rituals of Hawaii furnish a third case. Their development was linked to major transformations that affected Hawaii after 1400, when agriculture and aquaculture were extended and intensified (see, for example, Early 1978; Kirch 1985; Spriggs 1988). Local communities were reorganized; lineages were deconstructed; commoners lost the right to keep genealogies and to attend temples, and were assigned as quasi-tenants to nonlocal subaltern chiefs. Chiefs and aristocrats were raised up, godlike, into a separate endogamous stratum. Conflicts within the elite brought on endemic warfare and attempts at conquest: both fed the cult of human sacrifice. Innovations in myth and ritual portrayed the eruption of war and violence by the coming of outsiders, "sharks upon the land." Sahlins (1985) has offered the notion of a cultural structure to interpret how Hawaiians understood such changes and re-valued their understandings in the course of change. But reference to a cultural structure alone, or even to a dialectic of a structure of meaning with the world, will not yet explain how given forms of significance relate to transformations of agriculture, settlement, sociopolitical organization, and relations of war and peace. To explain what happened in Hawaii or elsewhere, we must take the further step of understanding the consequences of the exercise of power.

I have put forward the case for an anthropology that is not content merely to translate, interpret, or play with a kaleidoscope of cultural fragments, but that seeks explanations for cultural phenomena. We can build upon past efforts and old insights, but we must also find our way to asking new questions. I understand anthropology as a cumulative undertaking, as well as a collective quest that moves in ever expanding circles, a quest that depends upon the contributions of each of us, and for which we are all responsible.

References Cited

Adams, Richard N.

1966 Power and Power Domains. America Latina 9:3–5, 8–11.

1970 Crucifixion by Power: Essays on Guatemalan Social Structure, 1944–1966. Austin: University of Texas Press.

1975 Energy and Structure: A Theory of Social Power. Austin: University of Texas Press.

Albers, Patricia, and Seymour Parker

1971 The Plains Vision Experience: A Study of Power and Privilege. Southwestern Journal of Anthropology 27:203–233.

Arensberg, Conrad M.

1972 Culture as Behavior: Structure and Emergence. Annual Review of Anthropology 1:1–26. Palo Alto, CA: Annual Reviews.

Balandier, Georges

1970 Political Anthropology. New York: Random House.

Berg, Gerald M.

1986 Royal Authority and the Protector System in Nineteenth-Century Imerina. In Madagascar: Society and History. Conrad P. Kottak et al., eds. Pp. 175–192. Durham, NC: Carolina Academic Press.

Bloch, Maurice

1986 From Blessing to Violence: History and Ideology in the Circumcision Ritual of the Merina of Madagascar. Cambridge: Cambridge University Press.

Boon, James A.

1982 Other Tribes, Other Scribes: Symbolic Anthropology in the

Comparative Study of Cultures, Histories, Religions, and Texts. Cambridge: Cambridge University Press.

Bright, Charles, and Susan Harding, eds.

1984 Statemaking and Social Movements: Essays in History and Theory. Ann Arbor: University of Michigan Press.

Brown, Richard

1973 Anthropology and Colonial Rule: Godfrey Wilson and the Rhodes-Livingstone Institute, Northern Rhodesia. *In* Anthropology and the Colonial Encounter. Talal Asad, ed. Pp. 173–197. London: Ithaca Press.

Earle, Timothy K.

1978 Economic and Social Organization of a Complex Chiefdom: The Halelea District, Kauai, Hawaii. Anthropological Papers, No. 63. Ann Arbor: Museum of Anthropology, University of Michigan.

1987 Chiefdoms in Archaeological and Ethnohistorical Perspective. Annual Review of Anthropology 16:279–308. Palo Alto, CA: Annual Reviews.

1989 The Evolution of Chiefdoms. Current Anthropology 30:84–88.

Epstein, A. L.

1958 Politics in an Urban African Community. Manchester: Manchester University Press.

Feinman, Gary M., and Jill Neitzel

1984 Too Many Types: An Overview of Sedentary Prestate Societies in the Americas. *In* Advances in Archaeological Method and Theory, Vol. 7. Michael B. Schiffer, ed. Pp. 39–102. New York: Academic Press.

Foucault, Michel

1984 The Subject and Power. *In* Art after Modernism: Rethinking Representation. Brian Wallis, ed. Pp. 417–432. Boston/New York: David R. Godine/New Museum of Contemporary Art.

Gailey, Christine Ward

1987 Kinship to Kingship: Gender Hierarchy and State Formation in the Tongan Islands. Austin: University of Texas Press.

Geertz, Clifford

1973 The Interpretation of Cultures. New York: Basic Books.

Godelier, Maurice

1977 Perspectives in Marxist Anthropology. Cambridge Studies in Social Anthropology, No. 18. Cambridge: Cambridge University Press.

Goldman, Irving

1975 The Mouth of Heaven: An Introduction to Kwakiutl Religious Thought. New York: Wiley Interscience.

Kaufmann, Walter

1968 Nietzsche: Philosopher, Psychologist, Antichrist. Princeton, NJ: Princeton University Press.

Kirch, Patrick V.

1985   Feathered Gods and Fishhooks: An Introduction to Hawaiian Archaeology and Prehistory. Honolulu: University of Hawaii Press.

Lan, David

1985   Guns and Rain: Guerillas and Spirit Mediums in Zimbabwe. Berkeley/Los Angeles: University of California Press.

Mitchell, J. Clyde

1957   The Kalela Dance. Aspects of Social Relationships among Urban Africans in Northern Rhodesia. Rhodes-Livingstone Paper No. 27. Manchester: Manchester University Press for Rhodes-Livingstone Institute.

Ortner, Sherry B.

1984   Theory in Anthropology since the Sixties. Comparative Studies in Society and History 26:126–166.

Pocock, John G. A.

1971   Politics, Language and Time: Essays in Political Thought and History. New York: Atheneum.

Ranger, Terence O.

1970   The African Voice in Southern Rhodesia, 1898–1930. London: Heinemann.

1975   Dance and Society in Eastern Africa, 1890–1970: The Beni Ngoma. Berkeley/Los Angeles: University of California Press.

Rappaport, Roy A.

1979   Ecology, Meaning, and Religion. Richmond, CA: North Atlantic Books.

Sahlins, Marshall D.

1985   Islands of History. Chicago, IL: University of Chicago Press.

Scott, James

1985   Weapons of the Weak: Everyday Forms of Peasant Resistance. New Haven, CT: Yale University Press.

Sichone, Owen B.

1989   The Development of an Urban Working-Class Culture on the Rhodesian Copperbelt. In Domination and Resistance. Daniel Miller, Michael Rowlands, and Christopher Tilley, eds. Pp. 290–298. London: Unwin Hyman.

Spriggs, Mathew

1988   The Hawaiian Transformation of Ancestral Polynesian Society: Conceptualizing Chiefly States. In State and Society: The Emergence and Development of Social Hierarchy and Political Centralization. John Gledhill, Barbara Bender, and Mogens Trolle-Larsen, eds. Pp. 57–73. London: Unwin Hyman.

Steward, Julian H., et al.

1956   The People of Puerto Rico. Urbana: University of Illinois Press.

Valeri, Valerio

1985   Kingship and Sacrifice: Ritual and Society in Ancient Hawaii. Chicago, IL: University of Chicago Press.

Van Binsbergen, Wim M. J., and Matthew Schofeleers, eds.

1985 Theoretical Explorations in African Religion. London: Kegan Paul International.

Verdon, Michel

1983 The Abutia Ewe of West Africa: A Chiefdom that Never Was. Studies in the Social Sciences, No. 38. Berlin/New York: Mouton.

Wallace, Anthony F. C.

1970 [1961] Culture and Personality. New York: Random House.

Werbner, Richard P.

1989 Ritual Passage, Sacred Journey: The Form, Process and Organization of Religious Movement. Washington, DC: Smithsonian Institution Press.

Evolution of the Human Capacity for Beliefs

Ward H. Goodenough

VOL. 92, 1990, 597–612

Beliefs are propositions about the relations among things to which those who believe have made some kind of commitment.[1] Commitment may be for pragmatic or emotional reasons. A proposition's credibility may appear obvious from experience, or a proposition may seem to be the most prudent assumption on which to act. In either case, the commitment has a pragmatic basis. Emotional commitment to a proposition occurs when a person wants or feels a need for it to be true because of what its truth implies about things that matter.

Consideration of the evolution of the human capacity for beliefs, therefore, requires that we consider the emergence in hominine phylogeny of the ability to formulate propositions, to evaluate their worth as bases for action, and to make emotional attachments to them.

Propositions

Propositions are statements about relations among things and events, including how people feel. They may be descriptive or they may be expressions of opinion. In any case, they are ultimately rooted in people's experiences of their environment and of the effects of their responses to those experiences.

As here defined, propositions involve language, but experience of environment and neural organization of that experience go back a long way in mammalian phylogeny. If every sensory input were registered as new and phenomenally unlike any previous one, it would be impossible for an organism to develop the associations needed to learn adaptive responses to its environment. An organism's sensory equipment, moreover, is incapable of discriminating among the infinite variety of actual inputs. The senses necessarily serve as a filter. What the inputs are phenomenally for the organism is limited by what the organism is capable of discriminating and by what it has learned to discriminate in the course of experience.

We humans certainly do not learn to make all of the discriminations of which we are capable. When we learn a second language, we discover that there are discriminations we must make that we had not had to make before — discriminations of both sound and meaning. Years ago I was told by a blind student who had lost his sight in World War II how it was that blind persons knew they were coming to a street intersection. He told me that the air pressure on a person's face is different on the side where there are buildings from what it is on the open side where the street lies (actually a difference in sound). On coming to a break in the row of buildings, one can feel the air pressure change. As routes become familiar, a blind person learns when these changes in air pressure indicate intersections as distinct from vacant lots.

It is evident, then, that we ignore some sensory inputs entirely, we lump others together as the same when they are actually different, and we become habituated to making those discriminations we need to make in order to accomplish our purposes in the physical and social arenas in which we live. In this humans are not alone, for we know that many animals can be trained to discriminate cues and perform in ways that differ from what they do in the wild.

So we conclude that the materials from which propositions are made are categorizations of experience, whatever the cognitive processes of categorization may be.[2] The phenomenal world in which we live is necessarily a cognitively structured world; and fundamental to this cognitive structuring is categorization. This is so not only for humans, but for all animals that have to *learn* to respond to things and events in their environment in ways appropriate to survival. Nonhuman primates often behave as if they are seeking conscious goals with "mental maps" of how to reach them (Oates 1986:206); chimpanzees, at least, are capable of planning ahead in relation to fairly immediate goals (Cheney, Seyfarth, and Smuts 1986:1364). The ability to categorize both objects and relationships between objects is necessary to such behavior. This ability, associated with intentionality, appears to be manifested in humans very early in infancy (Bower, Broughton, and Moore 1970; Gelman 1983; also Bower 1974, Fantz 1961). The many parallels in the development of young chimpanzees raised in human homes with that of human infants testify eloquently to their having many similar cognitive abilities (Premack 1976).

Categorization, essential to perceiving things as alike — and essential, therefore, to the development of learned responses — does not ordinarily involve discriminations along only one sensory dimension. Usually, several such discriminations are made simultaneously or nearly so. In language, for example, we respond to words and short phrases as wholes rather than to their constituent categories of sound separately. Similarly, most other things that have stimulus value for us are complex structures of elementary categories. They are, in short, configurations or *gestalts*.[3] Such configurations can in turn be perceived as components of larger structures, as in our perceptions of spatial arrangements. We popularly associate the word "intuition" with the grasping of complex arrangements of arrangements; but we should note that the cognitive processes to which we give this blanket term are involved in perception generally. These processes are as essential to the successful life of monkeys as they are to the life of humans.

The ability to perceive structural arrangements, whole gestalts, as similar is essential to analogy. In making analogies, we equate gestalts on the basis of the similarity of their arrangement alone when we perceive their constituent components as unlike. Many of the propositions humans formulate are based on analogy, especially in the bodies of linked propositions we call belief systems (Jardine and Morgan 1987). In this regard, it is reported that laboratory experiments with chimpanzees indicate that they can be trained to "solve problems of transitivity, use analogical reasoning, and develop deliberate deception of others" (Cheney, Seyfarth, and Smuts 1986:1363). Evidence suggesting the perception of analogous social relationships among monkeys and apes in the wild is provided by the observation that adult females among vervet monkeys tend to respond actively to the screams of their own juvenile offspring, but when another female's offspring screams they tend to look at its mother. Even more suggestive is the observation that when two vervet monkeys fight, a close kin (associate) of one may attack a close kin (associate) of the other.[4]

We must distinguish, however, between the ability to perceive analogous structures in basic social relationships and the ability to analogize more freely. It is noteworthy that the analogical reasoning observed in chimpanzees occurred after they had learned to use a number of fairly arbitrary signs to represent things and to use these signs in communication with human experimenters. Also relevant is the ontogenetic process of becoming able to perceive relationships among others to which a child is not a party as analogous to those in which the child actually participates.[5] Is there a similar ontogeny among monkeys and apes? The evidence just cited about fighting behavior suggests that there may be. How far it is possible to analogize without the use of a system of representational signs remains an open question, but it is clear that the ability to discriminate among gestalts is prerequisite to that process and that some primates, monkeys and apes certainly, are capable of making such discriminations and of classifying and responding to phenomena accordingly. What remains a question has to do with the extent of their ability to perceive structures as analogous when the similarity of constituent elements decreases and the similarity of arrangement is increasingly all that remains as a basis for such perception. There is also the question of the ability of monkeys and apes to perceive analogous structures involving relations among inanimate objects as distinct from analogous relationships among conspecifics or relations of conspecifics to objects. In my own view, such ability is greatly facilitated by the kinds of mental operations that language (or a comparable system of representational signs) makes possible and must remain largely undeveloped without it.

To perceive similarities of arrangement when the component elements are perceived as dissimilar is to make an abstraction. Abstraction makes higher-order categories out of lower-order categories on the basis of some shared characteristics, including shared structural arrangements. I have just indicated that there is some question as to the ability of monkeys and apes, in the absence of language, to make abstractions based on shared structural arrangements alone, the components of the gestalts under comparison being otherwise entirely different. What about abstractions based on other shared characteristics, such as in discriminating between red and blue poker chips in some tasks but discriminating chips, as such, from other things, regardless of color, in other situations? Here one is ignoring the one feature that distinguishes between two otherwise similar gestalts. The result is a higher-order classification that is not based on analogy. The capacity to abstract in this way seems also to be attested in the performance of monkeys in the wild, for they respond to strange monkeys in a way that differs from their response to fellow members of their troop, while at the same time their behavior in relation to monkeys within their troop differs consistently from individual to individual (Cheney, Seyfarth, and Smuts 1986).

In the evolution of the capacity for belief systems, then, we may conclude that a number of the necessary capabilities were already in place before the emergence of the earliest hominids. Some of them, moreover, were already in place further back in mammalian and vertebrate phylogeny.[6]

These capabilities are: (1) categorization of experience; (2) perception and categorization of things in structural arrangements; (3) abstraction of higher-order categories from lower-order ones on the basis of common features, while overlooking a perceived difference; (4) potential for analogizing, largely undeveloped in the absence of language; (5) intuitive grasping or perceiving of relationships that would, if expressed in language, constitute propositions; and (6) the ability to act on these perceptions in the definition and pursuit of goals.

These capabilities have presumably become more highly developed in some animal species than in others; but they seem to have already achieved considerable development among the higher primates prior to the beginning of the hominid line. They are all prerequisite to the emergence of beliefs. What language allows us to objectify as propositions, however, can, in its absence, be no more than subjective or intuitive understandings. An additional prerequisite for the emergence of beliefs, one that is peculiar to humans, is a system of manipulable signs capable of representing categories of thing (including self and other) and categories of feeling, quality, act, and relationship.

Language

The most significant development that set the hominid line on a course different from that of the ancestors of the modern apes seems to have been bipedalism and upright posture. The earliest fossil hominids of the genus *Australopithecus* show this major anatomical change to have occurred before any discernible increase in relative size and complexity of the brain. Upright posture promoted a restructuring of the oral passage that made possible the development of the articulations necessary to produce the number and kinds of distinctive sounds found in human speech (Hill 1972). Later on, with the emergence of *Homo erectus*, roughly 1.6 million years ago, we find a significant increase in the size and complexity of the brain. It is still a matter of disagreement among paleontologists and paleolithic archeologists as to whether language began to emerge with *Homo erectus* or with *Homo sapiens*. Important in this regard is the finding that the structural organization of the vocal tract or upper respiratory region in *Australopithecus*, especially in the position of the larynx, is like that of monkeys and apes, whereas that of *Homo erectus* is intermediate between that of *Australopithecus* and *Homo sapiens* (Laitman 1983).

There are those who argue that even within what is recognized as *Homo sapiens*, language cannot be attributed to the Neanderthal subspecies but only to *Homo sapiens sapiens* (as represented by types like Cro Magnon), whose appearance is associated with the elaboration of stone technology and with cave art and other material evidence of symbolic representation (e.g., Davidson and Noble 1989). The apparent elaboration of tool types in the Mousterian or Middle Paleolithic, associated in Europe with *Homo sapiens neanderthalensis* and previously taken as evidence of language use, has recently been shown to be a result of resharpening, each reduction in size and shape in the process automatically producing the range of what had been presumed to be an intentionally differentiated and specialized tool kit (Dibble 1987, 1988, 1989). While this finding eliminates Mousterian tool differentiation as evidence of the presence of language, it cannot be taken as evidence of its absence.

Those who argue the position that language first appeared with *Homo sapiens sapiens* confuse the first material evidence of a behavioral capability with the earliest emergence of that capability. We take it for granted, for example, that the genetic capacity for composing music of the kind that developed in Europe in the last few hundred years was present in humans long before the realization of that capacity under historical and social circumstances favorable to it. Indeed, there is reason to think that the elaboration of technology reflected in tools and art represents a relatively late application of the possibilities inherent in language to purposes quite different from the social and expressive ones with which language was probably originally associated. The proper inference is that language — in the grammatically developed form we find among all living peoples today — must have been in place by the beginning of the Upper Paleolithic, about thirty thousand years ago, *at the latest*. How much earlier it was in place, and how long it was in process of development and elaboration before that time, remains, on the basis of only the evidence of tool complexity and art, entirely unknown. The fact that it is found in fully developed form among all Amerindians and Australian Aborigines, who were isolated from other humans from the late Pleistocene until fairly recent times, is another fact to be reckoned with, but it does not necessarily take its emergence back before *Homo sapiens sapiens*.[7]

Circumstantial evidence of another kind, however, allows us to push back the time for the presence of language in a developed form to the latter part of the Middle Pleistocene, prior to 125,000 years ago, when archeology indicates that human penetration of temperate and possibly subarctic climatic zones by archaic *Homo sapiens* had occurred. Early hominids, like their nearest primate relatives, were adapted to life in the tropics and subtropics, and through most of their existence were confined to these climatic zones in the Old World. For hominids to survive the winters of the temperate zone, to say nothing of the subarctic zone, required two things. One was an appropriate technology that would provide clothing (however simple in design), shelter, and the making and husbanding of fire for warmth. The other was the ability to plan ahead for changes in seasonal conditions. To begin preparing the skins (or other means) needed to protect the body from the cold only after the cold weather arrives is to act too late. Response must be made not to the weather as it is changing but to what one anticipates the weather to be. This requires planning for the future and a sharing of understandings about and plans for unseen, not-yet-present conditions.

Humans have been using language to accomplish such things from as far back as we have records. To argue that they were managing these preparations for the changing seasons the way squirrels do — presumably because they are genetically programmed for it — flies in the face of everything we understand about biological evolution. Such genetic programming would not have been selected for in the tropical environment in which hominids evolved. Once humans had made a successful adjustment to living in temperate or even colder climatic zones, natural selection would then have begun to operate in favor of such things as body-builds more efficient for heat retention. But the initial human adjustment to living in temperate zones took place in too short a time for natural selection to account for it. We must presume that the means by which humans have adapted socially and technologically to radically changing circumstances in recorded history, which rely heavily on the use of language, are the means that humans have been using for as long as we have evidence of such adaptation. Evidence of successful adaptation to survival in temperate and subarctic zones is, for this reason, presumptive indication of the existence of language with developed syntax as of that time. Moreover, language in such form had already to be in existence to make this adaptation possible. I conclude, therefore, that grammatically elaborated language goes back at least to the time when archaic *Homo sapiens* began to emerge from *Homo erectus.* The evidence from Chou-k'ou-tien in China suggests the possibility of an even earlier date, approximately 460,000 years ago (Chiang 1986:42).[8]

The foregoing is consistent with the view that language did not evolve in connection with toolmaking, contrary to what has long been assumed by many anthropologists, but in social interaction within familial and coresidential groups and the planning and coordination of activities by members of such groups. Simple toolmaking, even to a clearly conceived pattern, can be learned by imitation and, when instruction is necessary, can be taught by example and positive and negative indicators. It does not need syntactically developed language. From this point of view, while language and symbolic behavior played an important role in the adaptive and social behavior of Middle Paleolithic hominids, it did not yet reflect itself in the stone tools they made, which constitute the major part of the archeological record for that period, as observed by Chase and Dibble (1987). Consistent with this view is growing evidence that nonhuman primates, like human infants, are more sensitive and responsive to social than to nonsocial stimuli (Essock-Vitale and Seyfarth 1986:459).

Relevant is the recent report that *Paranthropus robustus,* an early hominid that developed in parallel to the line leading to the genus *Homo,* may have had hands adapted for precision grasping and might therefore have made and used the crude stone tools that were contemporaneous with its remains (Susman 1988). Existing about 1.8 million years ago with a small brain and large jaw and teeth that are not consistent with the presence of language, even in its early stages, *Paranthropus* provides evidence — if this report is verified — that language did not develop in association with making and using simple stone tools. On the contrary, making and using such tools appears to have developed independently, a conclusion that is consistent with the evidence of even more rudimentary tool-making and use by chimpanzees in the wild (Goodall 1986:535–564).

It follows from what I have been arguing that the Middle Paleolithic Neanderthals are better considered to have been language users than not. It has been suggested that they could not have had language because their vocal tracts were so structured that they could not readily make distinctive vowel sounds (Lieberman, Crelin, and Klatt 1972). The argument assumes that vowel distinctions are necessary to spoken language, whereas, in fact, they are not. All that is needed is an undifferentiated continuent between differently articulated consonants, as some modern languages with very few distinctive vowel phonemes attest. Furthermore, many languages, including spoken English, use nasal and liquid consonants like *m*, *n*, *l*, and *r* as continuents, as if they were vowels. There is, in short, no convincing anatomical evidence to support the idea that Neanderthals were incapable of language.

We must note, however, that the shape of the human vocal tract has changed in the course of hominid evolution, including the evolution of *Homo sapiens*. This change has included a considerable reduction in the size of the palate and, perhaps, a change in the articulation of the front teeth (Hockett 1985). We must infer that the range of easily made and even possible speech sounds was not the same 100,000 years ago as it is today. There must have been considerable overlap in the earlier and later ranges, but they were clearly not identical. Such difference, however, is not pertinent to the existence of language, however pertinent it may be to the phonological evolution of languages after language, as such, came into being.

The argument that Neanderthals were probably language users is not controverted by increasing evidence that *Homo sapiens sapiens* emerged in Africa perhaps as early as 90,000 years ago, while still using stone tools of Middle Paleolithic type, and coexisted with Neanderthals for a long time (Stringer and Andrews 1988; Stringer 1988; Valladas et al. 1988). The coexistence of geographical races of the same species must have emerged much earlier following the spread of *Homo erectus* out of Africa. That *Homo sapiens sapiens* subsequently spread into areas formerly occupied by Neanderthals, thanks to new developments in technology, does not imply that the latter were replaced without any input into the later European gene pool any more than the disappearance of Native Americans as a recognizable racial type in most of New England in the past 350 years means that they made no contributions to the gene pool of New England's present population. A number of "White" New England families claim a Native American in their ancestry. Sackett (1988) has pointed out that there is not a sharp break, even in Western Europe, between Middle and Upper Paleolithic archeological remains, but a phasing of one into the other. It may not be a coincidence that the genetic allele for Rh negative blood is statistically most heavily concentrated in the region of

Europe that was occupied for so long in apparent isolation during the last glacial period by the "classic" Neanderthals.

The position taken here is not controverted by widely publicized inferences from recent work relating to mitochondrial DNA (mtDNA), which is transmitted only through women (Cann, Stoneking, and Wilson 1987; Mahler 1973). Mutations accumulate in this DNA faster than in the DNA of a cell nucleus and give rise to different maternal "lineages" based on their shared mutations.[9] Comparison of the mtDNA of a small sample drawn from widely scattered parts of the world has revealed a number of these lineages whose similarities and differences allow them to be ordered in a genealogical tree. The date for the convergence of these lineages in an ancestral population has been roughly estimated at 140,000 to 225,000 years ago, about the time of the emergence of early forms of *Homo sapiens;* and it has been inferred from this that all modern humans derive from a dispersal of *Homo sapiens* out of Africa that in time replaced other hominid forms (Cann, Stoneking, and Wilson 1987; Foley 1987; Stringer and Andrews 1988). This inference is at variance with the paleontological evidence, which supports the view that the several geographical races of *Homo erectus* contributed to the ancestry of *Homo sapiens* (Wolpoff 1988), although it would be erroneous to assume that they all did so equally. In a cogent review, Spuhler (1988) points out that the dating evidence suggests an earlier time of divergence and that the distribution of the oldest branches in the lineage tree is more consistent with the view that the major continental races of *Homo sapiens* had their origin in transitions from *Homo erectus* in at least three different regions than with the view that there was a global replacement of the latter by *Homo sapiens* through a migration from a single region.

From this perspective, the apparent spread of technologically superior modern forms in the late Pleistocene out of Africa into areas inhabited by Neanderthals and other technologically less developed races of *Homo sapiens*, as argued by Stringer and Andrews (1988), can be compared with more recent spreads of technologically or militarily advantaged peoples into areas occupied by less-advantaged peoples in many parts of the world, such as are well attested in recorded history and in the prehistoric record of the past ten thousand years, as well. These spreads did not involve the total replacement of one local gene pool by another. Moreover, in none of them, either historic or prehistoric, have we had reason to assume that the presence or absence of language in a fully developed form was a factor. It need not have been a factor in the spread of people with Upper Paleolithic tool assemblages, either. Indeed, there is increasing archeological evidence of the coexistence and social interaction of Middle and Upper Paleolithic tool users in Europe and elsewhere (Mellars 1989).

The Evolutionary Development of Language and Its Uses
It is highly unlikely that language in its developed form, with grammatical markers and syntactic structure, emerged from nothing in a sudden, great evolutionary leap. Language, moreover, is more than just a communicative system. It has pragmatic, expressive, referential, narrative, task-rehearsing, and reflective uses. As Derek Bickerton (1981:217) has observed, "it must consist of a number of interacting systems." We must posit at least two major stages of development, each based on the crossing of a threshold that led to subsequent elaboration of the possible uses thus opened up, as circumstances and human (as well as primate) propensities for play and exploration stimulated them.

Some things necessary to language were already in place before language emerged at all. Experimental studies reveal that monkeys can discriminate auditorily among the same phonologically different speech sounds that human infants can discriminate among (Kuhl 1978; Stebbins 1970, 1973). We must infer, therefore, that the ability to make the kinds of auditory discriminations involved in human languages is older evolutionarily than the ability to produce them vocally, having arisen in connection with the advantages of being able to respond selectively to a wide range of sounds generally. We must similarly assume that the ability to produce vocal sounds that were distinct intonationally — involving prosodic as distinct from segmentary phonological features — was already in place before the first threshold to spoken language was crossed. Human infants learn to reproduce short intonation sequences characterizing utterances they hear before they can reproduce these utterances phonologically (Crystal 1978). Such abilities were already involved in the kinds of calls and other vocalizations that characterize communication among nonhuman primates. Finally, studies of these primates indicate that vocalizations were already used to some degree in ways that required learning before language emerged. Their use was presumably pragmatic: to communicate and implement intentions in social interaction. Such vocalizations, especially in conjunction with eye movements and gestures, could have referential meaning as well, but were not used for purely referential communication. This inference is consistent with the observed priority of pragmatic over purely referential usage of words in human ontogeny (de Villers and de Villers 1978; Nelson 1978).

The first threshold to human language, then, involved the development of phonologically segmented verbal signs that were used referentially as well as pragmatically to represent objects, persons, acts, and feeling states. I assume that it served mainly to enable speakers to identify things of social importance for one another more precisely and to allow them to make utterances of one or two words of the kind manifested by human children in early stages of language learning. A limited vocabulary of arbitrary signs that can be freely combined in two-word utterances allows for a great deal of communication (Schaerlaekens 1973). It enables individuals to make wants clear to others and to communicate intentions and internal feeling states. Some intentions and feeling states are communicable without such rudimentary language, as is clearly shown in the behavior of chimpanzees.[10] Nevertheless, the possibilities for such communication are expanded considerably by a very limited set of verbal symbols. Wants for things that are not in view and that cannot be pointed to cannot be communicated without such symbols, for example. Two-word utterances do not require grammatical rules other than to make clear, when not contextually evident, what is topic and what is comment, as in the "pre-grammatical rules" discussed by Givón (1989:247–249).

Noteworthy in this regard is the apparent separation of function in different areas of the brain of memory for lexicon (words and their meanings) and memory for how to construct grammatically acceptable sentences (Goodglass and Kaplan 1983). Aphasia affecting the latter leaves a person able to use lexicon but having to do so "telegraphically" in the kind of pre-grammatical, two-word mode just referred to. Aphasia affecting the lexical memory leaves a person able to construct grammatically well-formed sentences but with words largely divorced from their referential meanings. This separation of function is consistent with an evolutionary priority of the kind posited here, the development of lexicon for pragmatic and referential purposes taking place before the emergence of elaborated grammatical organization (Danziger 1988).

What such a level of language development greatly facilitates, especially combined with the use of gestures, is communication of a kind relevant to social interaction within a domestic group, such as a mother and her several not-yet-mature offspring. Given the prolonged dependence of human children on mothers and the bonding with both mother and siblings that results, we can expect that language first emerged within such familial groups.[11] Its advantages must have given such groups a definite survival edge over those that lacked it. Again this inference accords well with what is being learned about the development of language competence in children. Such competence, it is now clear, is developed in familiar social contexts, where situational and behavioral cues are plentiful as aids to learning meaning and syntax (Nelson 1978).

This view sees language as having emerged as a tool, a means to helping accomplish purposes with others in much the same way that gestures do. It accords well with recent work in the ontogeny of language acquisition, which shows that in its early stages children use language primarily instrumentally, as a tool, and only later in purely referential and propositional modes (Moore and Meltzoff 1978). Ontogenetic evidence is relevant not because "ontogeny repeats phylogeny" but because ontogeny gives indication of what kinds of things have to be in place before other things can build developmentally and, by inference, evolutionarily upon them.[12]

Paleoneurological evidence of lateralization of the brain has been used to infer that the development of language at this level, at least, may have occurred with the emergence of an early form of the genus *Homo*.

> By roughly 1.8–2.0 million years ago, there is clear evidence for a *Homo* lineage showing brain endocast patterns suggestive of a more modern and enlarged third inferior frontal convolutional complex, expanded brain size (e.g. 750+ ml), and cerebral asymmetries that are strong and seemingly identical to those known for modern *Homo sapiens* (i.e. left-occipital-right-frontal petalias). In so far as these patterns correlate with right-handedness and a left-right asymmetry of cognitive functioning regarding symbolic language behavior (left) and visual-spatial integration (right), it is possible to speculate that early [*Homo*] cognitive patterns were similar, albeit less advanced. [Holloway 1983:113]

Right and left hemisphere lateralization is found in other primates and even in birds (Kuhl 1978:229–230). This finding suggests that it is associated not so specifically with speech behavior as with performance functions on the one hand (left hemisphere) and monitoring functions on the other (right hemisphere). Performance involves putting acts together sequentially in relation to an intended goal. Speech is just this kind of behavior. Monitoring involves the grasping of situational gestalts and of where the self is in relation to other elements of the situation from moment to moment. Such differentiation of function would seem to have obvious adaptive advantages for arboreal creatures, whether primates or birds.

Of interest are the observations that monkeys in the wild use calls not only expressively but denotatively to indicate the presence of different kinds of things (Seyfarth 1986). Research is now under way to see to what extent specific denotative usages are transmitted by learning (Cheney, personal communication, 1988). If learning is significantly involved, it will mean that the capacity to use vocal calls as arbitrary signs for denotative purposes is already present in rudimentary form in monkeys. The step to achieving the first level of language development may have required only increasing articulatory facility within the vocal tract. I presume that it had occurred by the time *Homo erectus* had emerged. More significant in this regard than evidence of lateralization is the considerable enlargement of the brain in *Homo erectus* to a size intermediate between that of modern humans and that of *Australopithecus*.

It may have taken a long time, once this first threshold had been crossed, for language use to be developed to the extent of its possibilities at this level. Even with two-word utterances, simple propositions can be verbally expressed. "Baby hurt" can be offered as a descriptive statement of fact or, with altered intonation, turned into a question. One can say the words "Baby hurt" at some other time in connection with recall or in anxious or even pleasurable anticipation. But if one wishes to communicate to someone else who was not present that the baby has been hurt, something more is needed. When, where, how, and perhaps by whom become things to be indicated.

Efforts to inform others about events to which they were not a party, I am presuming, were what led to the kind of elaboration that marked the second important threshold in the evolution of language, in which constructions could be made that marked subject and object (or agent and patient, as in ergative languages) and allowed for indications of such things as time, place, reality and unreality, beneficiary, and different kinds of relations among things. To do these things a language must have organizational conventions that use some combination of lexical markers and word order — conventions of the kind that constitute grammar and syntax. The development of these conventions, I am suggesting, occurred in connection with reportorial and narrative uses of language, in which it is necessary to provide contextual information for hearers. (For a similar view see Givón 1979:303–308.)

We cannot rule out pragmatic uses as providing impetus for the beginning of grammatical marking, however, for crosslinguistic studies of language acquisition by small children show that, regardless of grammatical differences in language, children begin to use grammatical markers to indicate the object or patient of an action in connection with verbs meaning such things as 'give,' 'grab,' 'take,' 'hit,' which are said to have apparent salience for small children (Slobin 1985:6). They are indeed prominent in the interactions of small children with mothers and older siblings.

The development of grammar and syntax, whose advent I am assuming coincided roughly with the emergence of *Homo sapiens*, circa 250,000–300,000 years ago, provided the tools with which beliefs could be developed and elaborated into systems of belief. This development and elaboration, I presume, did not take place overnight. It takes time to realize possibilities, but all of the necessary capabilities were now in place. What remained for their realization was for them to be explored and used so that possibilities could be discovered and played with. What remained, in short, was the learning that comes from the cumulative, shared experience that language makes possible. Whatever genetic modifications may have been required for hominids to be able to cross the two thresholds I have postulated, once the capacity for developing grammar and syntax was in place, no further genetic changes were needed.

At the phonological level, as I have indicated, it is probable that languages have undergone some further modification as a result of genetic changes affecting the size and shape of the vocal tract. Aside from this, however, once the second threshold was crossed, the way languages and their uses evolved can be seen as the product of other than genetic change, however much the course of evolution was constrained by such human cognitive abilities and predilections as were already present. If there have been genetic changes affecting human cognitive capacities since the emergence of *Homo sapiens*, they, like those involving the oral cavity, have been diffused through the species generally. Natural selection has worked in these matters in much the same way pan-specifically. Since any human infant from anywhere in the world readily learns whatever language is spoken where he or she happens to be reared, it is clear that differences in existing languages are a result of other than biological differences among human populations. Such must have been the case ever since the threshold to grammatically developed language was effectively crossed.

The use of language reflectively and for task rehearsal purposes must have come in the wake of its syntactic elaboration in relation to reportorial and narrative uses. Recent studies are providing support for the thesis of Vygotsky (1962) that "private" speech, as in reflection and task rehearsal, arises ontogenetically as a development out of "social" speech (Diaz 1986). There is a dramatic rise in the use of audible private speech between the ages of three and five and then a tapering off into whispered and "inner" speech by age seven. The earliest use of private speech is associated with activity and comes after the action with which it is associated. Later, it is used to accompany action, and only later still to precede action, thus gradually developing the task-rehearsing uses by which people plan and guide their activity. It is in this latter context that beliefs are especially significant; and it is in this context, also, I have suggested, that language came to be applied to the elaboration of toolmaking and technology. Private speech is also inextricably involved in the reflective use of language, a use in which speech is now divorced from activity. Reflective use is presumably indispensable to the elaboration of beliefs and belief systems.

The Evolutionary Development of Beliefs

The evidence is increasingly clear that monkeys and apes have understandings about relationships between things and actions and expectations deriving from those understandings. Whether or not we are prepared to call such subjective understandings and expectations beliefs, we must accept that they are the stuff of which beliefs are made. Beliefs, in a more formal sense, come into being when these understandings are mapped into words and expressed as propositions. Thus, what is otherwise subjective is objectified. It can be communicated to others and can be an object of scrutiny and critical examination. With the calculus of language, its implications can be explored.

At what I am supposing to be the earlier stage of language evolution, the capability for such objectification in the form of propositions remained severely limited. Two-word utterances are not readily up to it. They facilitate interaction within the framework of subjective understandings that are shared on the basis of similar or shared experiences; and in the family units within which language presumably first emerged, much experience was shared. With the emergence of grammar and syntax in the later stage of language evolution came also the capability for stating propositions easily and for articulating beliefs. With these developments, moreover, came a number of other capabilities that allowed for propositions about things that were totally outside of experience. Let me review briefly some of these most pertinent capabilities.

Without language, categorizations of experience are entirely subjective. Even with language, many categories, like those of color, for example, remain so. We cannot define "red" to our children except by pointing to something we perceive as red. We define what is "hot" and what is "cold" similarly by having examples demonstrated to us. Categories of this kind are perceptual. We assign new stimuli to one or another category according to which it seems to be most like in overall gestalt, having reference to stereotypes based on past experience, now evoked in memory in acts of recognition. Use of the words that encode perceptual categories serves also as a stimulus to recall and recognition. Thus it greatly facilitates vicarious experience and thereby increases the rehearsals of experience that seem to contribute importantly to the consolidation of long-term memory (Squire 1986:1616). Language not only encodes and objectifies perceptual categories, it opens up the possibility of developing conceptual categories, such as "aunt" and "uncle," "right" and "wrong," as well.

Conceptualization draws heavily on the use of analogy. With the advent of language, the ability to analogize, already present in limited form, was enormously enhanced. Once there are names for things, qualities, relationships, and actions, and once these can be put together in statements that describe arrangements and events in actual experience, it becomes possible to play with these statements by substituting other words of similar grammatical type into the same grammatical slot in a propositional frame. "George is eating carrots" can be played with by substituting the name of any other kind of object for "carrots" in the sentence. The absurd, the statement as fact of what is contrary to experience or what is abhorred, immediately becomes possible. We are all familiar with how children of four and five play with words in just this way. Imagination is thus given enormously increased range. We can imagine "purple cows." Statements such as "George is roaring because George is angry," deriving from experience of human behavior, may well evoke the inference when it thunders that "The sky is roaring because the sky is angry." Such anthropomorphisms follow naturally out of analogy. In science most theory derives from using what we understand about one phenomenon as an analogue for helping us understand another. For example, what we understand about intentionality in humans from the ways they behave leads us to attribute similar kinds of intentionality to animals when they seem to behave in similar ways. Analogy also underlies metaphor; and it plays a major role in logical inference.

Logic begins with the mapping of our experiences of things and relationships into words and with generalizations about relationships that can be rendered into propositions. There was, for example, a great debate among Europeans after the discovery of the New World as to whether its native inhabitants were fully human. The proposition that humans had been endowed with immortal souls by God logically implied that if Native Americans were human, they, too, had immortal souls; and the proposition that it was the duty of the Church to save all human souls through proselytizing implied that the Church had a duty to proselytize Native Americans. Such reasoning is not peculiar to the European cultural tradition. My own experience and that of others who have lived and worked intimately with what used inappropriately to be called "primitive" people, learning to speak their language and to communicate with them in their terms, is that these people draw analogies and make deductive inferences in ways thoroughly familiar to us. For this to become apparent, however, one needs to know the limits of experience within which others are operating and the premises from which they are reasoning. My favorite example illustrating the point comes from a comment before World War I by a Micronesian navigator in defense of his belief that the sun goes around the earth.

> "I am well aware," [he said], "of the foreigner's claim that the earth moves and the sun stands still, as someone once told us; but this we cannot believe, for how else could it happen that in the morning and evening the sun burns less hot than in the day? It must be because the sun has been cooled when it emerges from the water and when toward setting it again approaches the water. And furthermore, how can it be possible that the sun remains still when we are yet able to observe that in the course of the years it changes its position in relation to the stars?" [Girschner 1912:173, my translation]

With the ability to imagine things comes the ability to think about the future, to consider alternative possibilities. The development of expressions or grammatical markers for "what if," "suppose," "maybe," "make believe that," and the like, follows inevitably. We are now fully into the linguistic tools from which human belief systems — and also our scientific theories — have been and continue to be made.

Commitment

Beliefs, we have noted, involve more than simply the statement of propositions. Minimally, belief involves a commitment to accepting a proposition as a basis for decision and action. A decision has to be made as to the proposition's fit with reality, as reality is understood. Beyond this, moreover, a decision has to be made as to whether to take seriously the individual stating the proposition. One might do so if it comes from one person but not if it comes from another. In this regard, it is noteworthy that vervet monkeys will take cover in response to a call indicating the presence of a predator if it comes from an adult, but may have a look first and not take cover if the same call is made by a juvenile that is still learning the system of calls. In short, the monkeys appear to be making credibility judgments (Nishida 1986:473).

Over and above pragmatic commitment is emotional commitment. "True believers" are people who have an emotional commitment to a proposition's absolute "truth." There are many reasons for such emotional commitment; they need not concern us here.[13] The question we must consider is whether or not the capacity for such emotional commitment is peculiarly human or is, like so many other things we have considered, also present in monkeys and apes and presumably, therefore, prehuman in evolutionary time.

Emotional attachments to one's fellows are clearly manifested in the behavior of chimpanzees. Emotional attachments — indeed fixations — to objects by monkeys have been evoked experimentally, as in the well-known experiments with "terry-cloth mothers" (Harlow and Zimmerman 1959; Harlow 1971). Emotional fixations are also found in chimpanzees in the wild, as exemplified by one young male's apparently obsessive attachment to his mother and his pining away and dying shortly after his mother's death (Goodall 1986:66).

Among monkeys and apes there are no propositions to be emotionally attached to. But the capacity for emotional attachment to things within their cognizance similar to that displayed by humans seems clearly to be present. With language, propositions become things within human cognizance and thus objects available for such attachment.

Conclusion

I conclude, then, with the observation that there is increasing evidence that most of the capabilities necessary for human belief systems were already in place in primitive evolution before the emergence of the hominid line.[14] The major new capabilities peculiar to hominids were those that made possible the emergence of language. With the advent of language, new selective pressures may well have been exerted on the other, evolutionarily older capabilities, leading to their enhancement. Such development, along with enhancement of linguistic capability, presumably accompanied further specialization of function in the brain and increase in complexity and number of neural pathways associated with increase in brain size in the genus *Homo* over the past two million years.

What has been involved in the evolution of language and the human capacity for beliefs has, necessarily, been equally involved in the human capacity for culture generally, of which beliefs are an integral part.

Our focus on belief provides evidence for the widely held view that what sets humans apart cognitively from their primate relatives is what is involved in the use of language. An older generation of anthropologists saw tool use as the significant difference. In the view taken here, the use and manufacture of simple tools occurred prior to and independently of the emergence of language. Language began as a kind of tool for implementing intentionality in social interaction. Its expanded use increased the content of memory storage, and its elaboration made possible the formulation in words of propositions. This, in turn, made it possible to plan for contingencies in the future, to imagine things, to develop beliefs and systems of beliefs. An eventual by-product of these developments was the greatly elaborated tool kit and the materially attested symbolic behavior we associate with the Upper Paleolithic era. Thus language, in its grammatically elaborated form, became the prime tool on which most else that we think of as peculiarly human depends.

Notes

Acknowledgments. This article is an expanded version of a paper presented at the annual meeting of the American Association for the Advancement of Science in 1986 in a symposium entitled "Genes and Culture," sponsored by the Institute on Religion in an Age of Science. For helpful discussion of issues and comments on earlier drafts I am indebted to Dorothy Cheney, Eve Danziger, Harold Dibble, Simon Holdaway, Alan Mann, Robert Seyfarth, Michael Speirs, and colleagues in the PARSS Seminar on Human Nature, University of Pennsylvania.

1. For an extensive review of the study of belief systems by anthropologists, both theoretically and methodologically, see Black (1973).

2. See, for example, the important examinations of categories by Lakoff (1987) and Givón (1989).

3. Registering and organizing experience by small children takes place in terms of gestalts (Gelman 1983). Categorization of phenomena by single traits and the organization of phenomena into hierarchies based on such traits come in older children, apparently in conjunction with language use in the process of learning.

4. Cheney, Seyfarth, and Smuts (1986:1364) conclude that if this observation is confirmed, "it would indicate that primates, in the recognition of social alliances, solve problems that are functionally equivalent to laboratory tests of analogical reasoning."

5. See the discussion of "decentration" in human children by Hy Van Luong (1986).

6. A similar conclusion, that many of the cognitive capabilities that characterize humans were already present before the hominid line emerged, is drawn by Hill (1972).

7. For a persuasive argument that Amerindians had entered the New World well before the end of the last glacial period and while still equipped with a Lower Paleolithic stone technology, see Gruhn (1988).

8. Laitman (1983) has indicated that the degree of basicranial flexion permits inference regarding the position of upper respiratory structures as they relate to speech functions. He infers that these structures were similar to those of modern humans in archaic *Homo sapiens* and were well on the way toward the modern condition in *Homo erectus*. Argument that the larynx had not yet descended in adults of *Homo erectus* and Neanderthal types as far as it has in modern humans, and that, therefore, these earlier hominids could not have had speech, fails when we consider that modern children are already speaking when the larynx is still in an intermediate position.

9. If 20% of the women in any generation who reach childbearing age have no daughters who reach childbearing age, then only 11% of the women in a given generation will have descendants who carry their mtDNA ten generations later, and a fraction over 1% of these women will have such descendants twenty generations later. This reduction toward the asymptote, given the mode of inheritance of mtDNA, must exacerbate the effect of genetic drift in small populations. Moreover, it inevitably works in favor of reducing within-population variance in mtDNA over time in the absence of population mixing, while at the same time making for wide within-population variance when there is population mixing. (See Spuhler 1988.)

10. See, for example, the interaction that occurred when a young chimpanzee insisted on being carried by its mother in spite of its mother's efforts to terminate her carrying him, recorded by Goodall (1986:66).

11. Holloway (1983:113) concludes similarly that sexual dimorphism in the structure of the brain, as it evolved in the genus *Homo*, suggests that "natural selection favored an increased degree of cognitive task specialization relative to

both social nurturance and parental investment of relatively immature offspring" in females, while it favored "relatively more skill in visuospatial integrative tasks" for males, and that, in consequence, females retain "a socially-sophisticated edge over males in communicative skills and social structural knowledge."

12. Givón (1979, 1989:261) has proposed that the process of children's acquisition of grammar follows the same developmental paths as the process by which grammar has evolved in human language.

13. For a review of such reasons see Goodenough (1963:157–171). See also Black (1973).

14. Bickerton (1981:221) also has argued that such human mental attributes as consciousness and volition are present in animals as well as humans, and that theory regarding the origin and evolution of language must take account of it.

References Cited

Bickerton, Derek
  1981 Roots of Language. Ann Arbor, MI: Karoma.
Black, Mary
  1973 Belief Systems. In Handbook of Social and Cultural Anthropology. J. J. Honigmann, ed. Pp. 509–577. Chicago, IL: Rand McNally.
Bower, T. R. G.
  1974 Development in Infancy. San Francisco, CA: W. H. Freeman.
Bower, T. R. G., J. M. Broughton, and M. K. Moore
  1970 Demonstration of Intention in the Reaching Behaviour of Neonate Infants. Nature 228: 679–680.
Cann, Rebecca L., Mark Stoneking, and Allan C. Wilson
  1987 Mitochondrial DNA and Human Evolution. Nature 325:31–36.

Chase, Philip G., and Harold L. Dibble
  1987 Middle Paleolithic Symbolism: A Review of Current Evidence and Interpretations. Journal of Anthropological Archaeology 6:263–296.
Cheney, Dorothy, Robert Seyfarth, and Barbara Smuts
  1986 Social Relationships and Social Cognition in Nonhuman Primates. Science 234:1361–1366.
Chiang, Kwang-chih
  1986 The Archaeology of Ancient China. 4th edition. New Haven, CT: Yale University Press.
Crystal, David
  1978 The Analysis of Intonation in Young Children. In Communicative and Cognitive Abilities: Early Behavioral Assessment. F. D. Minifie and L. L. Lloyd, eds. Pp. 257–271. Baltimore, MD: University Park Press.

Danziger, Eve

1988 Language and the Brain: Questions of Interest to Anthropology. (Unpublished manuscript in author's possession.)

Davidson, Iain, and William Noble

1989 The Archaeology of Perception: Traces of Depiction and Language. Current Anthropology 30:125–155.

de Villers, Jill G., and Peter A. de Villers

1978 Semantics and Syntax in the First Two Years: The Output of Form and the Form and Function of Input. In Communicative and Cognitive Abilities: Early Behavioral Assessment. F. D. Minifie and L. L. Lloyd, eds. Pp. 309–348. Baltimore, MD: University Park Press.

Diaz, Rafael M.

1986 The Union of Thought and Language in Children's Private Speech. Quarterly Newsletter of the Laboratory of Human Cognition 8:90–97.

Dibble, Harold L.

1987 The Interpretation of Middle Paleolithic Scraper Morphology. American Antiquity 52:109–117.

1988 Typological Aspects of Reduction and Intensity of Utilization of Lithic Resources in the French Mousterian. In Upper Pleistocene Prehistory of Western Eurasia. Harold L. Dibble and Anta Montet-White, eds. Pp. 181–197. Philadelphia: University Museum, University of Pennsylvania.

1989 The Implications of Stone Tool Types for the Presence of Language during the Middle Pleistocene. In The Human Revolution. Paul Mellars and Chris Stringer, eds. Pp. 415–432. Princeton, NJ: Princeton University Press.

Essock-Vitale, Susan, and Robert M. Seyfarth

1986 Intelligence and Social Cognition. In Primate Societies. Barbara B. Smuts et al., eds. Pp. 452–461. Chicago, IL: University of Chicago Press.

Fantz, Robert L.

1961 The Origin of Form Perception. Scientific American 204(5): 66–72.

Foley, Robert

1987 Hominid Species and Stone-Tool Assemblages: How They Are Related. Antiquity 61:380–392.

Gelman, Rochel

1983 Recent Trends in Cognitive Development. In The G. Stanley Hall Lecture Series, vol. 3. C. J. Schierer and A. M. Rogers, eds. Pp. 145–175. Washington, DC: American Psychological Association.

Girschner, Max

1912 Die Karolineninsel Namoluk und ihre Bewohner. Baessler-Archiv 2:123–215.

Givón, T.

1979 On Understanding Grammar. New York: Academic Press.

1989 Mind, Code, and Context. Hillsdale, NJ: Lawrence Erlbaum Associates.

Goodall, Jane

1986 The Chimpanzees of Gombe. Cambridge, MA: Belknap Press of Harvard University Press.

Goodenough, Ward H.

1963 Cooperation in Change. New York: Russell Sage Foundation.

Goodglass, H., and E. Kaplan

1983 The Assessment of Aphasia and Related Disorders. Philadelphia, PA: Lea and Febiger.

Gruhn, Ruth

1988 Linguistic Evidence in Support of the Coastal Route of Earliest Entry into the New World. Man 23:77–100.

Harlow, H. F.

1971 Learning to Love. New York: Ballantine Books.

Harlow, H. F., and R. R. Zimmerman

1959 Affectional Responses in the Infant Monkey. Science 130:421–432.

Hill, Jane H.

1972 On the Evolutionary Foundation of Language. American Anthropologist 74:308–317.

Hockett, Charles F.

1985 Distinguished Lecture: F.

American Anthropologist 87:263–281.

Holloway, R. L.

1983 Human Paleontological Evidence Relevant to Language Behavior. Human Neurobiology 2:105–114.

Jardine, David W., and Griffith A. V. Morgan

1987 Analogical Thinking in Young Children and the Use of Logico-Mathematical Knowledge as a Paradigm in Jean Piaget's Genetic Epistemology. Quarterly Newsletter of the Laboratory of Comparative Human Cognition 9:95–101.

Kuhl, Patricia

1978 Predispositions for the Perception of Speech-Sound Categories: A Species-Specific Phenomenon? In Communicative and Cognitive Abilities: Early Behavioral Assessment. F. D. Minifie and L. L. Lloyd, eds. Pp. 229–255. Baltimore, MD: University Park Press.

Laitman, Jeffrey T.

1983 The Evolution of the Hominid Upper Respiratory System and Implications for the Origins of Speech. In Glossogenetics: The Origin and Evolution of Language. Eric de Grolier, ed. Models of Scientific Thought, vol. 1. Pp. 63–90. Paris: Harwood Academic.

Lakoff, George

1987 Women, Fire, and Dangerous Things: What Categories Reveal about the Mind. Chicago, IL: University of Chicago Press.

Lieberman, Philip, Edmund S. Crelin, and Dennis H. Klatt

1972 Phonetic Ability and Related Anatomy of the Newborn and Adult Human, Neanderthal Man, and the Chimpanzee. American Anthropologist 74: 287–307.

Luong, Hy Van

1986 Language, Cognition, and Ontogenetic Development: A Reexamination of Piaget's Premises. Ethos 14:7–46.

Mahler, Henry R.

1973 Mitochondria: Molecular Biology, Genetics, and Development. Module in Biology No. 1. Reading, MA: Addison-Wesley.

Mellars, Paul

1989 Major Issues in the Emergence of Modern Humans. Current Anthropology 30:349–385.

Moore, M. Keith, and Andrew M. Meltzoff

1978 Object Permanence, Imitation, and Language Development in Infancy. In Communicative and Cognitive Abilities: Early Behavioral Assessment. F. D. Minifie and L. L. Lloyd, eds. Pp. 151–184. Baltimore, MD: University Park Press.

Nelson, Katherine

1978 Early Speech in Its Communicative Context. In Communicative and Cognitive Abilities: Early Behavioral Assessment. F. D. Minifie and L. L. Lloyd, eds. Pp. 443–473. Baltimore, MD: University Park Press.

Nishida, Toshisada

1986 Local Traditions and Cultural Transmission. In Primate Societies. Barbara B. Smuts et al., eds. Pp. 462–474. Chicago, IL: University of Chicago Press.

Oates, John F.

1986 Food Distribution and Foraging Behavior. In Primate Societies. Barbara B. Smuts et al., eds. Pp. 197–209. Chicago, IL: University of Chicago Press.

Premack, Ann J.

1976 Why Chimps Can Read. New York: Harper and Row.

Sackett, James B.

1988 The Mousterian and Its Aftermath: A View from the Upper Paleolithic. In Upper Pleistocene Prehistory of Western Eurasia. Harold L. Dibble and Anta Montet-White, eds. Pp. 413–426. Philadelphia: University Museum, University of Pennsylvania.

Schaerlaekens, A. M.

1973 The Two-Word Sentence in Child Language Development. The Hague: Mouton.

Seyfarth, Robert M.

1986 Vocal Communication and Its Relation to Language. In Primate Societies. Barbara B. Smuts et al., eds. Pp. 440–451. Chicago, IL: University of Chicago Press.

Slobin, Dan I.

1985 Introduction: Why Study Acquisition Crosslinguistically? *In* The Crosslinguistic Study of Language Acquisition, vol. 1. Pp. 3–24. Hillsdale, NJ: Lawrence Erlbaum.

Spuhler, J. N.

1988 Evolution of Mitochondrial DNA in Monkeys, Apes, and Humans. Yearbook of Physical Anthropology: Yearbook Series Volume 31, pp. 15–48.

Squire, Larry R.

1986 Mechanisms of Memory, Science 232:1612–1619.

Stebbins, W. C.

1970 Studies of Hearing and Hearing Loss in the Monkey. *In* Animal Psychophysics: The Design and Conduct of Sensory Experiments. Pp. 41–66. New York: Plenum Press.

1973 Hearing of Old World Monkeys. American Journal of Physical Anthropology 38:357–364.

Stringer, Chris

1988 The Dates of Eden. Nature 331:565–566.

Stringer, C. B., and P. Andrews

1988 Genetic and Fossil Evidence for the Origin of Modern Humans. Science 239:1263–1268.

Susman, Randall L.

1988 Hand of *Paranthropus robustus* from Member 1, Swartkrans: Fossil Evidence for Tool Behavior. Science 240:781–784.

Valladas, H., J. L. Reyes, J. L. Joron, G. Valladas, O. Bar-Yosef, and B. Vandermeersch

1988 Thermoluminescence Dating of Mousterian "Proto-Cro-Magnon" Remains from Israel and the Origin of Modern Man. Nature 331:614–616.

Vygotsky, L. S.

1962 Thought and Language. Boston: MIT Press.

Wolpoff, Milford H.

1989 Multiregional Evolution: The Fossil Alternative to Eden. *In* The Human Revolution. P. Mellars and C. Stringer, eds. Pp. 62–108. Princeton, NJ: Princeton University Press.

Art, Science, or Politics?

The Crisis in Hunter-Gatherer Studies

Richard B. Lee

VOL. 94, 1992, 31–54

Hunter-gatherer studies have had a rather stormy history. The field has always been marked by controversy, and even the concept of hunter-gatherers itself has waxed and waned in importance. There have been periods in the history of anthropology when the very concept was tabooed, others when it was popular. Within the discipline today, the idea of hunter-gatherer has radically different receptions. Some see it as totally absurd, a derivative of outmoded evolutionary theory, while others see it as an eminently sensible category of humanity with a firm anchor in empirical reality. I noted a strong tendency toward the latter view at the Sixth Conference on Hunter-Gatherers (CHAGS) at Fairbanks, May–June 1990. At least no one advocated canceling the sixth CHAGS for lack of subject matter.

Even if it is agreed that hunters and gatherers exist, almost everything else about them is a matter for contestation. While some fields have crystallized a canon, there is no danger of that in hunter-gatherer studies; the field remains as fractious and controversy-prone as ever. And in recent years a new element has been added to the many voices within the field, a body of opinion that would call into question the entire enterprise and abolish the concept of hunter-gatherers altogether. It would be hard to imagine a more fundamental challenge. Therefore, the purpose of this article is to define the range of anthropological practices that constitute hunter-gatherer studies today and to explore the roots — social, ideological, and epistemological — of the field's crisis in representation.

Some of these difficulties become apparent at the outset when we try to define what we mean by hunter-gatherers.[1] *Economically* we are referring to those people who have historically lived by gathering, hunting, and fishing, with minimal or no agriculture and with no domesticated animals except for the dog. *Politically* gatherer-hunters are usually labeled as "band" or "egalitarian" societies in which social groups are small, mobile, and unstratified, and in which differences of wealth and power are minimally developed.

Obviously there is a degree of fit between "forager" subsistence strategies and "band" social organization, but the fit is far from perfect. Strictly economic definitions of foragers will include a number of peoples with ranking, stratification, and even slavery — the Northwest Coast groups — while the notion of "egalitarian bands" will include a number of small-scale horticultural and pastoral societies — in Amazonia, for example, and some Siberian "small peoples."

Recent attempts to clarify these ambiguities have led to the useful distinction between "generalized" and "complex" hunter-gatherers (Price and Brown 1985; see also Woodburn's immediate/delayed return distinction [1980], and Testart 1988). It is the first category — peoples who hunted and gathered and who were organized into egalitarian bands — that will be the main focus of this discussion, though both simple nonforagers and complex foragers will be referred to from time to time.

The fluctuating fortunes of hunter-gatherer studies are tied as well to ambiguities that lie at the root of the field of anthropology itself; not the least of which revolves around the much debated concept of the primitive. Many would argue along with Stanley Diamond (1974:118) that the "search for the primitive" is the heart of anthropology's unique role in the human sciences. And much of the history of hunter-gatherer studies is linked to our multifaceted understandings of the primitive, either in Diamond's sense, in the quest for origins and fundamentals, or in what Lévi-Strauss terms anthropology's deeper purpose "to bear testimony to future generations of the ingeniousness, diversity, and imagination of our species" (1968:349).

But for other anthropologists the preoccupation with the primitive is an anachronism. For some the primitive is an illusion, an arbitrary construction of the disembodied "other" divorced from history and context (e.g., Clifford 1983; Sperber 1985; Wagner 1981). The result of this ambiguity is that there is a body of opinion in anthropology — not unconnected to views in other disciplines about "the end of history" and particularly among postmodernists — which would find anthropology's preoccupation with the primitive an acute embarrassment; as a consequence, the concept of hunter-gatherers becomes moot (Wilmsen 1989:xi–xviii, 1–6).

A second area of ambiguity is the nature of the anthropological enterprise itself. Anthropology has never declared itself unequivocally on the matter of whether it is a particularizing, historical discipline interested in understanding unit cultures, or whether it is a generalizing, nomothetic science searching for the broadest possible explanatory frameworks. Hunter-gatherer studies broadly defined has vigorous adherents of both these tendencies, going right back to Boas (1935, 1966) and Kroeber (1925) exemplifying the first tendency, and Steward (1936, 1938) and Radcliffe-Brown (1922, 1931) the second.

The history of hunter-gatherer studies, especially since the "Man the Hunter" conference in 1966 (Lee and DeVore 1968), illustrates both anthropology's ambiguities and the problematic role of hunter-gatherer studies within it. Among the persistent issues of the 1970s, 1980s, and 1990s have been debates on the following:

1. Evolutionism. The use and misuse of hunter-gatherer data to understand the fossil record and/or the evolution of human behavior has long been a contentious issue, as has been the concept of evolutionism itself. Hunter-gatherer studies have tended to enjoy respectability among some evolutionists (Isaac 1978; Lancaster 1978; Tanner and Zihlman 1976) and to be viewed with suspicion by others (Wobst 1978; Foley 1988).

2. Optimal Foraging Strategies. Modelers of the behavioral ecology of hunter-gatherers have continued to advocate a nomothetic research strategy and to refine quantitative methodologies at a time when much of the field was moving in the opposite direction. It has been the focus of notable research (Winterhalder and Smith 1981; Hawkes, Hill, and O'Connell 1982; Hill and Hawkes 1983) but also of some pointed critiques (Keene 1983; Martin 1983).

3. Woman the Gatherer. Feminist agendas and priorities have entered hunter-gatherer discourse initially through the ecological issue, raised in "Man the Hunter," of whether women's work in gathering plant foods is not more important to subsistence than men's hunting. This has led to a number of books and articles on gender, women's work, and women's power in foraging society. A significant segment of feminist anthropology has drawn heavily on hunter-gatherer studies (Slocum 1975; Begler 1978; Dahlberg 1981; Hunn 1981; Leacock 1981; Sacks 1979; Tanner and Zihlman 1976).

4. World View and Symbolic Analysis. Studies of the systems of meaning that

give shape and coherence to hunter-gatherer identity and cosmology have
been increasingly in evidence as a countercurrent to and implicit critique of
the predominant ecological orientation of much of hunter-gatherer studies
(Myers 1986b; Ridington 1990; Brody 1981; Endicott 1979).

5. Hunter-Gatherers in Prehistory. Archeologists have always had a strong in-
    terest in hunter-gatherer ethnography and its uses for interpreting the past
    (Binford 1978; Yellen 1977; Keene 1991). Currently, archeological interest
    in foragers exceeds by a wide margin interest by social and cultural anthro-
    pologists. Increasingly, archeologists are working directly with contempo-
    rary gatherer-hunters under the rubric of ethnoarcheology, and the ques-
    tions archeologists ask are often quite different from the problematics
    within which social anthropologists work (Binford 1980; Paynter 1989;
    Yellen 1990; Wiessner 1982).

6. Hunter-Gatherers in History. The links of foraging peoples with the wider
    world, both in the present and in the past, have been a growing focus
    stimulated in part by world-systems analysis and by the publication of
    Wolf's *Europe and the Peoples without History* (1982; see also Schrire 1984;
    Wilmsen 1988, 1989; Headland and Reid 1989). One effect of this move
    toward historicizing has been to call into question the very idea of hunter-
    gatherers, and to argue seriously that they are a noncategory, a construc-
    tion of the observers.

Two Cultures, or Three, or Four?

What analytical frameworks would be most useful and productive in
sorting out the complex currents and countercurrents in the study of
hunting and gathering peoples today? It might be helpful to recall C. P.
Snow's famous essay, "The Two Cultures" (1959), in which he explored
the eternal conflict between two irreconcilable academic subcultures:
the *humanistic* and the *scientific*.[2] In the first, scholarship was devoted to
the study of meanings and interpretations in great works of art and
literature. In the second, scholarship was dedicated to systematic and
rigorous investigation of natural laws and general principles governing
the natural and human world.

Anthropology is an apt example of a discipline that finds itself strad-
dling the boundaries of C. P. Snow's two cultures. Within the discipline
today there is a powerful current moving toward the view of anthropology as essentially a humanistic, even literary discipline, where truth,
apart from the poetic variety, is unattainable. An equally strong current
moves in the opposite direction, embracing the promise and moral au-

thority of science and strengthening its commitment to improved techniques of data collection and measurement, coupled with more (not less) rigorous application of theory. The first sees itself as modeled after literature and literary criticism, the second draws its inspiration from theoretical biology and evolutionary ecology as well as an updated and recharged structural-functionalism.[3]

Within hunter-gatherer studies, the struggles and contradictions between the humanistic and scientific cultures are played out in a number of ways. While the scientists are gathering data for the construction of mathematical models of forager predator-prey behavior, the humanists, working sometimes among the same people, are collecting life histories of elders and recording and interpreting cosmologies and religious beliefs.

But there is a third culture embedded in current anthropological practice. This school sees neither humanistic nor scientific discourses as adequate to account for the past, present, and future of anthropological subjects. Raising issues of context and history, and placing foragers in regional systems, some scholars focus on the overriding issue of the relations of foragers with the world system. I will call this the "culture" of *political economy*.

The first anthropological perspective draws its inspiration from the interpretivist, structuralist, and hermeneutic traditions of Clifford Geertz (1973), Claude Lévi-Strauss (1963), Mary Douglas (1966), Victor Turner (1969), and James Clifford (1988; Clifford and Marcus 1986); the second from the positivist and adaptationist current of Julian Steward (1936, 1938), Lew Binford (1978, 1980), and others (e.g., Harris 1979); and the third from the critical Marxist tradition in which Eric Wolf and Sidney Mintz are situated (Wolf 1982; Mintz 1985; Leacock 1981; see also Roseberry 1989, Patterson and Gailey 1987). Each approach has a distinctive methodological stance and each has made important contributions to hunter-gatherer studies. In fact, however much one may profess allegiance to one or another of the three cultures, in practice elements of all three approaches are frequently employed in contemporary research projects (for a classic example of synthesis, see Sahlins 1968).

My first intention in writing this paper was to give a critical appraisal of research contributions to hunter-gatherer studies from each of the anthropological traditions. But a prior question must be addressed, an issue that poses a challenge to the entire collective enterprise so fundamental that to ignore it would be to fiddle while Rome burns.⁴ Following the lead of Foucault, Derrida, and the French poststructuralists, several anthropologists have declared hunter-gatherers a noncategory, a construction of observers mired in one or another brand of romantic idealism. The claims of this group are so far-reaching and so ill-contained within the paradigm space of the three cultures that they could be said to constitute a fourth culture rendering irrelevant large parts of the other three.

Revisionism, as it has been called, combining *some* elements of political economy with *some* elements of poststructuralism, presents a fundamental challenge to the way that anthropologists have looked at hunter-gatherers for the past 30 years. It posits that foragers are not what they appear to be; and it proposes a drastic rethinking of our subject. Schrire poses the revisionist challenge in these terms:

> There can be no doubt that, one way or another, all [ethnographies of hunter-gatherers] describe societies coping with the impact of incursions by foreign forces into their territories. . . . The big question that arises is, are the common features of hunter-gatherer groups, be they structural elements such as bilateral kinship systems or behavioral ones such as the tendency to share food, a product of interaction with us? Are the features we single out and study held in common, not so much because humanity shared the hunter-gatherer life-style for 99% of its time on earth, but because the hunter-gatherers of today, in searching for the compromises that would allow them to go on doing mainly that, have reached some subliminal consensus in finding similar solutions to similar problems? [1984:18]

And Wilmsen, writing of the Kalahari San, puts it this way:

> the current status of the San-speaking peoples on the rural fringe of African economies can be accounted for only in terms of the social policies and economies of the colonial period and its aftermath. Their appearance as foragers is a function of their relegation to an underclass in the playing out of historical processes that began before the current millennium and culminated in the early decades of this century. *The isolation in which they are said to be found is a creation of our view of them, not of their history as they lived it.* This is as true of their indigenous material systems as it is of their incorporation in wider spheres of political economy of southern Africa. [1989:3, emphasis added]

There are two components to the revisionist critique, and it is essential to recognize the distinction between them. First there is the argument from history (see, e.g., Myers 1988:262–264; Headland and Reid 1989) that accuses past ethnographers of misreading or ignoring history and political economy and hence of treating the society in question as more bounded, more isolated, and more pristine than it really is. Political-economic revisionism argues that foragers have been integrated into larger regional or even international structures of power and exchange for so long that they can reveal nothing about the hunter-gatherer way of life. Evidence of trade and political domination is cited in support of this thesis. Linked to this line of critique is the purported discovery in hunter-gatherers of relations of domination and wealth accumulation previously associated with class societies (Price and Brown 1985; Flanagan 1989; Legros 1985).[5]

These critiques raise important issues, yet in terms of method, the argument remains on familiar terrain: one examines the historical, archeological, or other data and tests the merits of competing hypotheses against these data. Were the hunter-gatherers in question isolated? What does archeology reveal? What is the most parsimonious explanation for the observed facts? This is what Jacqueline Solway and I did in a recent *Current Anthropology* article titled "Foragers, Genuine or Spurious" (1990), meeting the issues raised by revisionists with empirical data that refuted their position.

The poststructuralist criticism, by contrast, takes a much more radically skeptical line. This view, linked to some versions of postmodernism, to deconstruction, and to a variety of other current schools, argues that there is no truth, only regimes of truth and power, and that all anthropology is powerfully shaped by the cultural constructions of the observer. Thus, ethnographic writing (about foragers or anybody else) has more in common with the historical novel and other works of fiction than it has with a scientific treatise. Therefore, the task of ethnography becomes immeasurably more problematic; truth is at best partial, flawed, obscured, and above all *relative*.[6]

This argument has radical implications for methodology. The production of knowledge has left the realm of empirical investigation and analytical methods of the past can no longer be relied upon. One can no longer utilize, for example, the etic/emic distinction because science after all is really only "Western emic" (Marcus and Fischer 1986:180–181). The use of Occam's Razor or the law of parsimony to choose between the merits of two competing explanations is no longer admissible because all are "true" at some level.

What impact does this have on the study of foragers? Political economists and post-structuralists have tended to make the same critique of ethnographic practice, but as we shall see, for rather different reasons. Both argue the extraordinary proposition that the natives are "Us," and both put into question the assumption that hunter-gatherers, whatever they may be, represent the "Other." The political economists argue that the natives are to all intents like Euro-Americans, because relations of domination and/or merchant capital reached the Arctic or the Ituri Forest or Sarawak long before ethnographers did and, therefore, tributary or mercantilist or capitalist relations of production have transformed foragers into people like ourselves, as parts of larger systems with hierarchies, commodities, exploitation, and other inequities and all their accompanying social consequences (Schrire 1984:18). Poststructuralists take the view that because anthropologists (like everyone else) are prisoners of their own ideology, as a consequence they can see in the "other" only a flawed perception of themselves. Thus, in either scenario, the "other" is declared a noncategory.

If the revisionist/poststructuralist position merits serious consideration — and the sheer volume of journal articles on these topics suggests that it does — then a major tenet of anthropology from Boas forward — that anthropology is the study of difference — becomes untenable. Or if "difference" is to be preserved as an anthropological problematic, then anthropology becomes the study of difference mutually constructed by powerful masters and powerless subalterns within a single world system.

In what follows I will explore the roots of the curious proposition that the natives are only different in surface features and that in truth they are "us." I see it as a peculiar expression of the intellectual culture of Late Capitalism. Anthropological revisionism lies at the intersection of two major tenets of contemporary Western thought: Proposition 1 — *Nothing is real*; and Proposition 2 — *The "system" is all-powerful*.

Nothing Is Real

We live in an era in which the line between real and nonreal has become dangerously blurred. What is real has become a scarce commodity and the pursuit of the "real" sometimes becomes a desperate search. Under capitalism, as Marshall Berman (quoting Marx) titles his book, "all that is solid melts into air" (1983). We don't have to search far for evidence of this proposition. The Disney corporation produces and distributes in a single fiscal year, perhaps in a single week, more fantasy material to more people than entire archaic civilizations could produce in a century. States of the Left, Right, and Center and their bureaucracies also produce prodigious volumes of fantasy, and through advertising and other media elites deploy enormous manipulative power (Ewen 1976). A recent ad for cigarettes (typical of the thousands that bombard Euro-Americans daily) has a picture of a carefully posed professional model, turned out as a fashion photographer, pretending to photograph another professional model herself posing, surrounded by other posed models in postures of forced gaiety. The caption: "Real People/Real Taste."

To protect the psyche from this type of assault, consumers and citizens in the West (and East) can be forgiven for erecting a shell of cynicism as a survival strategy under conditions of extreme debasement of the currency of reality. In fact it is hard to imagine keeping your sanity by any other means. This position of cool detachment and ironic distanciation has been considered the hallmark of the "postmodern condition" (Lyotard 1984; Sloterdijk 1987; Jameson 1984).

The world of scholarship has not escaped these massive social and psychological forces. In *The Invention of Tradition* (1983) Hobsbawm and Ranger and others show how allegedly hallowed customs handed down from the past are in fact the product of recent history. In his method of deconstruction, Derrida has argued that history is akin to a literary text and, like all texts, is ultimately unknowable (1976, 1978). It seems a short step to extending a critical and debunking discourse to all anthropological subjects.

But along the way there has been a slippage. The tools of deconstruction, developed to debunk and call into question the high and mighty, are now being applied to the powerless. Where the invention-of-tradition perspective was initially deployed to deconstruct the public rituals of the 19th-century British monarchy or pomp and circumstance in colonial India, it was now being generalized to question the claims to authenticity of small peoples. In his influential work, *The Predicament of Culture*, James Clifford shows how the Mashpee Indians construct their identity *de novo* in order to meet the exigencies of a court case (Clifford 1988). Similar arguments (but with less sympathy for the subalterns) have been made for the Maori by Hanson (1989) and for the ancient Hawaiians by Bergendorff, Hasager, and Henriques (1988; see also the reply by Sahlins 1989).[7]

The situation within anthropology is paralleled by the impact of poststructuralism on the broad front of the social sciences. Foucault's famous dictum (1976a, 1976b) that there is no truth, only regimes of truth and power, was originally intended as a critique of arbitrary power, but by showing the fragility of all truth-claims it has had the effect of undermining the legitimacy as well of oppositional movements for justice against these same powers (Taylor 1984; Habermas 1987).

There is a kernel of truth to the idea that all societies in the world are products of interaction with other societies and world society. Modern ethnography is a product of the Enlightenment and is a form of practice in which members of our academic subculture observe the other; as the late Kathleen Gough reminded us, anthropology is a child of imperialism. And then there are cases like the Philippine Tasaday, where a perfectly reasonable Southeast Asian semi-hunter-gatherer group, of which many examples exist, was seized on by the *National Geographic* and other media and popularized as the "Lost Stone Age" find of the century. Their recent exposure, and the media circus surrounding them, certainly fuels the cynicism that is itself the source of postmodernist sensibilities (Lee 1992; see also Dumont 1988; Berreman 1991; Duhaylungsod and Hyndman 1992).

Nevertheless, to succumb to the enticements of the poststructuralists or revisionists would be a disaster. Where I part company with the poststructuralists is in the view that our knowledge of the other — being filtered through perceptions, language, and culture — is so suspect that subjects can only be provisionally and arbitrarily constructed. It is striking how the largely male, White, and Western poststructuralists are proclaiming the death of the subject, precisely at the moment when alternative voices — women, people of color, Third World and aboriginal peoples — are struggling to constitute themselves as subjects of history, as the makers of their own history (Mascia-Lees, Sharpe, and Cohen 1989; see also Spivak 1988).

I do not believe that anthropologists are nearly so powerless before the awesome task of representing the other's reality, or that the ethnography of the 1960s or 1970s was so flawed that it has to be discarded. Adam Kuper, in a recent critique of postmodernism, points out that the methodologies of the 1960s were not so very different from those of the present,[8] and that their results were subjected to the critical scrutiny of peer review and comparative evidence. Kuper argues, and I would agree, that the view that ethnographic writing is more akin to fiction than it is to science does not accord with the history of the discipline. If the ethnographers of that not-so-distant era had passed their fiction off as science their readership and their peers would not have stood for it (Kuper 1990). (For other critiques of "postmodernism" that attempt to reconstruct the "realist" foundations of social science epistemologies see Mascia-Lees, Sharpe, and Cohen 1989; Roth 1989; Sangren 1988; Gellner 1988; Lovibond 1989; Soper 1991; see also Bhaskar 1979, 1986.)

Strictly speaking, the position taken by poststructuralists is not that *nothing* is real, since all take as given the existence of the power elite, of the state and its bureaucracies, and of the world system and its awesome power and reach. Therefore it would be more accurate to represent Proposition 1 as "Nothing is real . . . except power," which brings us directly to the second of our Propositions.

The "System" Is All-Powerful

The core proposition, "nothing is real," is reinforced by and reacts synergistically with the proposition, "the 'system' is all-powerful." We are living through a time in which history is accelerated; as the modern system continues to grow, things are moving faster and faster. Events and processes that unfolded over centuries are compressed into decades or years, and what transpired on a scale of years now unfolds in the space of months or weeks (Piel 1972:17–48; Harvey 1985:6–35). We need to put the revisionist debate in the context of this recent history.

Not everyone within hunter-gatherer studies has paused to reflect on the titanic forces that are transforming the world before our eyes. The era of Late Capitalism is witnessing the accumulation of capital on an unprecedented scale, the rise of the multinational corporation, and the phenomenal growth of the state as an apparatus for shaping and controlling human behavior (Chomsky 1989; Hardison 1989). In addition, one must try to comprehend the accelerating and expanding networks of information transfer on a world scale. Through television, e-mail, modems, cellular phones, fax, and other technologies it is possible to touch any part of the world in seconds, and through these same media we can dispose of all the world's accumulated knowledge and images with the push of a button — what Frederic Jameson has called "a decentered global network of microcircuits and blinking lights."

It is not surprising that this power of instantaneous communication, combined with the vast output of the culture industries mentioned above, and the centralizing power of the state, leads to fantasies of omniscience and omnipotence for the small minority of the world's population that has access to such tools (Berman 1983). Late Capitalism consumes the past with amazing rapidity, spews it out with such dizzying speed that it has the effect of obliterating the past, including the past of even 20 years ago.[9] All these processes tend to endow the force of capitalism with a mystique of enormous reach and totalizing power.[10]

Externally, the spread of worldwide capitalism, sporadic and localized in the 18th century, a flood in the 19th and early 20th century, has become a veritable avalanche in the last third of the 20th century.[11] As John Bodley, Shelton Davis, and others have pointed out, the world's tribal peoples are sitting directly in the path of the world's largest multinational corporations (Bodley 1982, 1988; Davis 1977; see also Jorgensen 1990). The scale of this penetration has increased in many cases by orders of magnitude in 10 or 20 years. To take an example, when I first arrived in Maun, Botswana, in 1963 there was a single tour operator taking tourists into the Okavango Swamps. Today there are over 80 operators; many of them offer to take clients to the last of the River Bushmen, a man who now gets "discovered" 40 or 50 times a year. The Dobe area in 1963–64 was even more isolated than the Okavango Swamps. In that era it received one motor vehicle visit every four to six weeks, for a total of 9 to 13 vehicles per year. In 1987 I counted a vehicle *every four to six hours* for an annual total of 1,400 to 2,100, a one- to two-hundredfold increase. Tom Headland notes that at the turn of the century there were 500 agriculturalists in the vicinity of his Agta communities in northeastern Luzon. Today there are 30,000 (personal communication, 1990).

The Penan (or Punan) of Sarawak carried on regular long-distance trade with the coastal Dyak for hundreds of years; the impact of this trade on Penan institutions is the subject of another intense revisionist debate (Hoffman 1986; Brosius 1988).[12] But whatever their links to the coast may have been historically, they are nothing compared to the impact of the Japanese multinationals clear-cutting the rain forest at a rate faster than that in the Amazon. The Penan are now fighting for their lives as the multinationals, in conjunction with the state government (many of whose ministers hold logging concessions), clear-cut the Penans' traditional foraging areas, leaving them destitute and forcing them into government resettlement schemes. The Penan have mounted roadblocks to stop the bulldozers, and hundreds of Penan have been arrested, but the logging goes on (Burger 1990:94–95; Colchester 1989; CBC 1990; see also Hong 1987). Similar examples could be drawn from virtually any part of the First, Second, or Third Worlds. This is the context of accelerating and massive change in which the field of hunter-gatherer studies is situated, and this is the source of the crisis of representation that the field is undergoing.

The point I want to emphasize is that fieldworkers who arrive in the 1980s and 1990s and observe these appalling conditions find it unbelievable that 30, 20, or even 10 years earlier, observers could have found societies with band structure, kinship, and subsistence patterns still functioning. Instead of reflecting on the magnitude of the changes in that 10- or 20-year period, these revisionists immediately assume that the earlier studies were wrong and they go on to blithely project the contemporary patterns of destruction or outside domination back into the past.

Universalizing the present is the obverse of the equally flawed history that postulates pristine hunter-gatherers roaming the forest the year before the anthropologist arrives. While the latter view has correctly come in for a wave of criticism, it could be argued that the revisionists' willingness to project the present onto the past indicates an enchantment with the power of Capital that is, at base, no less romantic and uncritical than the much-criticized enchantment with the pristine or primitive order.

Mythologizing Pre-Revisionist Ethnography

It would be foolish to argue that studies of hunters and gatherers prior to, say, 1970 were above reproach and therefore immune to criticism. Just as it would be equally foolish to argue that prior to 1970 all hunter-gatherers lived a pristine existence. Scholars working in that era made mistakes, and that includes myself. My own thinking has undergone continual reassessment, and it might be appropriate at this point to dispel some of the myths that have grown up about exactly what Kalahari ethnographers stand for.

One misconception is that pre-revisionist ethnographers believed the San were pristine hunter-gatherers (Wilmsen 1989:3, 6, 10, 33–43ff.; Wilmsen and Denbow 1990:503–507). But as early as 1965 I pointed out that the great majority of the ethnic San — about 80% — were herders or farmers, or were existing as clients or servants on Black cattle posts and on commercial ranches (Lee 1965:20). Also in the 1960s I wrote in detail about the impact on the Dobe !Kung of European hunters and traders going back to the 1870s (Lee 1965:53–68).

A second myth concerns the notion that despite recognizing changes elsewhere, ethnographers have maintained a vision of the Dobe !Kung as unchanging in the face of overwhelming evidence to the contrary (e.g.,

Wilmsen and Denbow 1990:520; Gordon 1984). At all stages of field-work Kalahari ethnographers have grappled with this issue and have tried to give a scrupulous accounting of the non-!Kung elements present in the Dobe area, including the Herero presence, the Tswana presence, and the "European" presence. Any illusions I might have harbored about !Kung pristine conditions were dispelled by the late 1960s when new information came to light. When it became apparent, for example, that the actual economic circumstances of the !Kung had been misread, I was at pains to correct first impressions (note that even in 1976 the word "pristine" appears in quotation marks):

> As our field work continued, a more realistic picture of the "pristine" nature of the Dobe Area began to emerge. Most of the men of the Dobe area had had some experience at some point in their lives of herding the Bantu cattle, and about 20 percent of the young men were working on the cattle at any one time. Some had even owned goats or cattle in the past. Similarly the !Kung were not total strangers to agriculture. Many had learned the techniques by assisting their Bantu neighbors in planting, and in years of good rainfall some had planted small plots themselves and had harvested crops. [1976:18]

Far from holding a rigid and unchanging view of hunter-gatherers, there is evidence that many (but not all) students of the subject have changed their thinking over the years, and these changes have taken the field away from the position of the 1960s: that studies of contemporary hunter-gatherers are primarily a tool for understanding the evolution of human behavior. Two of these changes in particular are worth noting.

Recognizing that foragers have coexisted with farmers sometimes for centuries, *yet have remained foragers*, has moved a number of scholars toward a much more complex understanding of the historical position of foragers. Some of the same evidence that led revisionists to discard the very concept of hunter-gatherers led the editors and authors of *Politics and History in Band Societies* (Leacock and Lee 1982:1–20) in a different direction. The book was structured around the argument that hunter-gatherers can only be understood by seeing how some of them have been involved with farmers for a long time yet have retained their cultural identity.[13]

Understanding hunter-gatherer ecology, however important, is not enough. One has to look at the internal dynamics and the articulation of this internal system with wider histories. This has led to a second change in the thinking of a number of anthropologists, a shift away from an emphasis on hunting and gathering as modes of subsistence, toward the broader concept of "communal mode of production."

From Subsistence Ecology to Mode of Production

As I have discussed elsewhere (Lee 1981, 1988, 1990), communal relations of production are a widespread and well-documented phenomenon. Yet, despite their ubiquity, the subject has been woefully undertheorized. Communal relations of production are observed among the !Kung as well as among a number of hunter-gatherers in a wide variety of historical settings. They are also found among peoples with mixed economies of foraging and horticulture, such as the Iroquois (Trigger 1987, 1990), the Sharanahua (Siskind 1980), and the Batek (Endicott 1979). They are found even among former foragers in peripheral capitalism, such as aboriginal fringe dwellers in Darwin, Australia (Sansom 1980).[14]

Accepting the *existence* of communal relations of production in diverse settings among foragers and (some) nonforagers, the next question is how this is to be explained. I find it extremely difficult to accept that all these diverse instances are to be seen, as revisionists have argued, strictly as societal impoverishment resulting from exploitation by larger and more powerful societies (Schrire 1984:18; Gordon 1984:220; Wilmsen 1983, 1989).

The explanation lies, rather, in one remarkable organizational principle shared by band societies and peoples like them: the ability to reproduce themselves while limiting the accumulation of wealth and power. Such societies operate within the confines of a metaphorical ceiling and floor: a ceiling above which one may not accumulate wealth and power and a floor below which one may not sink. These limits on both aggrandizement and destitution are maintained by powerful social mechanisms known as leveling devices (Lee 1990:242–245). Such societies therefore have social and political resources of their own and are not just sitting ducks waiting to adopt the first hierarchical model that comes along. Clastres (1989) said it best when he said that for these kinds of societies the main problem was resisting becoming a state; by this he meant resisting not only the imposition of a state from outside but also resisting the pressures building up within, pressures leading toward accumulation and concentration of wealth and power.

Clastres did not imply that the nonstate societies lived in a state of perfect equality, nor would I. Hunter-gatherers may exhibit differences in wealth and power and they are certainly *not* nonviolent.[15] I prefer to follow the argument developed by Harriet Rosenberg in her recent research on !Kung aging and caregiving (1990). Rosenberg uses the term "entitlement" to account for the ways in which !Kung elderly were cared for by relatives and nonrelatives alike, such that no one, not even childless people, would be denied access to support in old age. This was part of a general phenomenon in !Kung society in which everyone claimed and was recognized as being "entitled" to the necessities of life, by right of being a member of the society.

> !Kung elders do not see themselves as burdens. They are not apologetic if they are not able to produce enough to feed themselves. They expect others to care for them when they can no longer do so. Entitlement to care is naturalized within the culture. Elders do not have to negotiate care as if it were a favor; rather it is perceived as a right. [Rosenberg 1990:29]

Will the "Real" San Please Stand Up?

The Kalahari revisionists claim to be restoring the San *to* history, but it is a curious view of history that the only way you can historicize foragers is to make them into pastoralists (or serfs) in the past! This seems to be an instance of life imitating art — of granting all agency to the dominating society whether capitalist or tributary, and making the histories of these diverse societies entirely reactive.[16] Solway and I (1990) have shown that while some San peoples did become peasants and serfs of Black overlords, others did not. The !Kung San of the Dobe area lay outside of the main routes of trade and spheres of tributary power. They defended their lands against incursions from Blacks and Whites, and when they entered into client relations with Black patrons they did so on terms that were more favorable than those prevailing in other parts of the Kalahari. The result is that when systematic ethnographic study began in the 1950s and 1960s, observers found a society with a number of key institutions — language, kinship, ritual practices — intact, while other institutions — land tenure, dispute settlement, political dynamics — were clearly in a state of flux (Marshall 1976; Lee and DeVore 1976; Lee 1979; Shostak 1981; Solway and Lee 1990; Yellen 1977).

Why did these distinctive institutions persist? They should not be seen simply as holdovers or survivals from the past kept in place by the weight of tradition. This trivializes their significance. These institutions are essential elements of cultural survival and they must be reproduced anew in each generation. Their presence is as good an index as any of the cultural viability and vitality of peoples like the !Kung.[17]

What is at issue here is whether foragers broadly represent a diverse but nevertheless identifiable form of human society with characteristic social and economic properties, or whether the foragers' identity dissolves and merges with that of serf, servant, client, slave, or rural proletariat.

What is the !Kung view of their own history? The !Kung see themselves as a people, increasingly circumscribed and threatened, but a people nonetheless with a strong sense of themselves. When told that they were really tributary appendages, long integrated into the economies of their more powerful neighbors, they were surprised and not a little offended.[18]

History and Identity of Hunter-Gatherers: Two Views

This brings us to two views of history and identity. One starts from cultural difference and postulates that there are cultures out there, which exist independent of academic constructions of them; for hunter-gatherers there is a lived reality regardless of whether or not they trade or render tribute to their neighbors. The other view sees historical status as constituted *only* by membership in a regional trading bloc, by subject status in a chiefdom or state, or by the production of a commodity for exchange; in other words, historical visibility can only be achieved through a relationship with *other* systems. The question that arises is whether that part of their history is the only thing or even the main thing that we want to know about hunter-gatherers.

Leacock and I (1982) argued that foraging societies can only be understood as the product of a triple dynamic: first, the internal dynamic of communal foraging relations of production; second, the dynamics of their historical interactions with farmers, herders, and states; and third, the dynamic of articulation and incorporation within the modern world system. The difference between this position and the revisionist one is the latter's privileging the operation of the second and third dynamics at the expense of the first. The revisionist position accords minimal reality to foraging as a distinct mode of life, what Tim Ingold (1990:130) has recently called "a radically alternative mode of relatedness."[19]

These two views of hunter-gatherers inscribe alternate discourses about the current conjuncture. The first says we are living in a time when the world is young, in flux, and still in the process of formation; some of the antecedent societal forms are still there to be observed and experienced. The people we have come to call hunter-gatherers are examples, to varying degrees, of alternative ways of life, examples of difference. The other discourse says no, the world is old, what you are seeing is not difference, it is just another aspect of us, created by the same forces, the same "system" that created us. In my view this second discourse contains a number of unexamined assumptions about the transformative power of commodities, and about the ability of mercantile and tributary systems to project their power and to impose their will on the peoples on their periphery.[20]

How will we ever sort out the conflicting claims of the differing schools of thought in hunter-gatherer studies? Given the enormous load of ideology in hunter-gatherer studies, along with most branches of scholarship, I want to reiterate a plea for the importance of empirical evidence; I am as much opposed to mindless empiricism as anyone, but without empirical evidence debates will disintegrate into ideological name-calling.

What is urgently needed in this era of disillusion is the middle path: a working discipline that sees science, humanism, and critical reflection as three components of a single field; scholars need empiricism tempered by reflexivity and a dialectic between the two. All of this should be framed within a sense of history and political economy, to ensure that a scholar's situated history and the relationship between scholar and subject are not lost. Scholars must interrogate assumptions as the poststructuralists suggest, but after that, I for one would like to get on with it. If sound methods demonstrate that hunter-gatherers are historically serfs or pastoralists or whatever, then so be it. But the current crop of revisionist arguments are dubious, to say the least.[21] The task of situating hunter-gatherers historically has barely begun, and there remains a great deal of scope for archeological, ethnographic, and ethnohistoric investigations to resolve the question of to what degree hunter-gatherers can be said to be culturally autonomous or integrated into larger systems at various points in their histories.[22] I also suggest that these questions will motivate the production of the kinds of knowledge that will be used by future generations, sifted and resifted long after the debates of this decade fade into the past.

To recover a link to the real world, to empirical reality, is precisely what some scholars tried to do in the 1960s with the work diaries, demography, subsistence ecology, and careful ethnography (e.g., Helm 1965; Hiatt 1965; Marshall 1961; Rose 1960). This is a scholarly tradition that many are carrying on today, while constantly improving their methods. But empiricism, however critically informed, is not the whole story. Self-definitions change. In the 1960s, many anthropologists saw themselves as crusading empiricists, replacing speculation with facts, but it is now possible to recognize that, like all scholars in the human sciences, the ethnographers of the 1950s and 1960s were also storytellers, weavers of narratives (after all, the origin of the word "text" is from "textiles"). It was not only a question of *what* they had to say but also *how* they said it. To this extent those who emphasize anthropology's affinities to literature *do* have a point.[23]

As Donna Haraway has noted (1989), one of the master narratives constructed (in part) from hunter-gatherer data has been the story of human nature and life in the "state of nature": who we are as a species, our past, and by implication our future. The post-structuralist project focuses our attention almost exclusively on the "constructedness" of these narratives. But just because they are constructed doesn't mean that they have no claim to empirical validity or that the search for knowledge of the past is an illegitimate enterprise. Ethnographic analogy to the past does involve leaps of extrapolation and therefore must be treated with extreme caution, but the archeological record can and does provide direct knowledge of the distant past.

The problem remains, however, that like ethnography archeological interpretations of the past are no less shaped by the ideological forces of the present. This highlights the critical need for maintaining and enlarging the sphere of knowledge — in both archeology and ethnography — that transcends the ideological battles of each era: the need for a version of anthropology that is both critical and empirical (cf. O'Meara 1989; Carrithers 1990).

Given the difficulties of living up to the demands of doing this kind of work and the many pitfalls, it is surprising how much good work is being done in hunter-gatherer studies. Rejecting the view of foragers as timeless primitives *or* as rural proletarians, there are those who would see hunting and gathering as a way of life that exists in the present yet is different from Western urban modes of life. To varying degrees these students attempt to maintain a sense of balance and proportion between the reality of their scholarly world and the reality of their subjects, and between the methodological demands of the three cultures.[24]

One trend that seems to be present in all three methodological currents is a move by some (but by no means all) away from seeing hunting and gathering peoples as *objects* of anthropological inquiry, to a situation in which they become the *subjects* of their own history and often the directors of their own research. This has paralleled the development of political consciousness among indigenous people. As foragers and former foragers have become more involved in struggles for their rights, hunter-gatherer studies have become much more of a collaborative enterprise: working *with* the people in their struggles to determine their futures.[25]

Perhaps the most significant development of the last decade is indigenous peoples speaking to us in their own voices; for example, the Canadian Innu, Lubicon, Teme-Augama, and others in Richardson (1989). The Gitksan and Wet'suet'en people of British Columbia are good examples of former (and continuing) foragers who have addressed the larger public directly in a variety of voices and settings, including the courts (Sterritt 1989; People of 'Ksan 1980; Gisday Wa and Delgum Uukw 1989). Increasingly, indigenous peoples are making political alliances with environmentalists, feminists, youth groups, and peoples of color.

On this new and expanded political terrain an interesting question concerns how hunters and gatherers themselves regard hunter-gatherer studies. Clearly the cultural renaissance under way in a number of native communities has generated considerable interest in "traditional" ethos and world view, governance, subsistence, arts, crafts, ethnobotany, and healing; for these and other spheres of knowledge, the elders and anthropological texts are the main sources of information.[26]

Conclusion

This article has delineated the crisis of representation in hunter-gatherer studies and has attempted to comprehend the underlying epistemological and ideological roots of the crisis. The field of hunter-gatherer studies has been undergoing a series of transformations and the original raison d'être has required reassessment. Yet, despite the fundamental challenges of the "revisionists," it can be argued that a core of relevance to both scholarly and indigenous peoples' agendas remains in hunter-gatherer studies; that the field is responding to this challenge is indicated by the shift away from simplistic evolutionary arguments toward more nuanced, historically sensitized, and critical understandings. In this respect the altered contours of hunter-gatherer studies represent a successful incursion by humanists and political economists on a terrain that had been largely dominated by natural science–oriented methods and philosophies.

In the preface to *Man the Hunter*, DeVore and I wrote, "We cannot avoid the suspicion that many of [the contributors] were led to live and work among the hunters because of a feeling that the human condition was likely to be more clearly drawn here than among other kinds of societies." (Lee and DeVore 1968:ix). I now believe this is wrong. The human condition is about poverty, injustice, exploitation, war, suffering. To seek the human condition one must go, as Wolf and Hansen (1975) did, to the barrios, shantytowns, and palatial mansions of Rio, Lima, and Mexico City, where massive inequalities of wealth and power have produced fabulous abundance for some and misery for most. When anthropologists look at hunter-gatherers they are seeking something else: a vision of human life and human possibilities without the pomp and glory, but also without the misery and inequity of state and class society.

Almost all of humanity lives today in highly organized bureaucratized societies of enormous scale and systematic inequalities. Hunter-gatherers, in spite of the inducements (or threats?) to become incorporated, choose for whatever reasons to resist and to live lives very different from that of the majority. The pace is slower, technology simpler, numbers smaller, inequality less, and the relationship to land and resources — the sense of place — is on a radically different basis. Following Clastres, I have argued that what sets hunter-gatherers apart is their ability to reproduce themselves *while severely limiting* the accumulation and concentration of wealth and power. This feature they share with a number of simple horticultural and pastoral societies. Since the accumulation of wealth and power (and resistance to it) is the driving force of much of human history, it follows that societies that don't have this dynamic must have a dynamic of a different sort: what Tim Ingold has called a "different kind of sociability" (1990:130–131).

If indigenous peoples want to adopt a Western (or Soviet) way of life, the door is open; in fact, the pressures to conform are immense. The fact that this has not happened, that some foragers still pursue alternative lifeways not in isolation but in full awareness of alternatives, is a persuasive argument against the two propositions that framed the present essay. *There is something out there beyond the reach of the world system (capitalist or otherwise). The "system" is powerful but not omnipotent.* Pockets of resistance persist and show us that even in this hard-bitten postmodern age other ways of being are possible.

Since so many of the world's intractable problems derive from the gigantic maldistribution of wealth and power, it stands to reason that societies that can reproduce themselves without exploitation have a great deal to teach us. As the world's peoples struggle to redefine alternative visions in the aftermath of the Cold War, I am convinced that hunter-gatherer studies, far from being the fantasy projection of uncritical romantics, have a role to play: in the movement for justice for indigenous peoples, and as part of a larger movement to recapture wholeness from an increasingly fragmented and alienating modernity.

Notes

This paper was presented at the Sixth International Conference on Hunting and Gathering Societies (CHAGS), Fairbanks, Alaska, May 27–June 1, 1990, and is published here with permission of the CHAGS organizing committee, chaired by Linda Ellanna. The author would like to thank the following colleagues and friends for useful input in the development of this paper: Michael Asch, Victor Barac, John Barker, Alan Barnard, Liz Cashdan, Julie Cruikshank, Richard Daly, Pat Draper, I. Eibl-Eibesfeldt, Bion Griffin, Matthias Guenther, Henry Harpending, Bob Hitchcock, Tim Ingold, Dick Katz, Tom Patterson, Nick Peterson, Phillip Smith, Harriet Rosenberg, Jackie Solway, Eric Smith, Verna St. Dennis, Polly Wiessner, Eric Wood, and John Yellen. These critics are not responsible, of course, for any errors of facts or interpretation. Versions of this paper have been presented at seminars at the Universities of British Columbia, Victoria, Simon Fraser, and Washington. Critical comments by colleagues and students at these institutions were instrumental in further clarifying the issues presented here.

1. Whether hunter-gatherers are more accurately called gatherer-hunters to acknowledge the predominance of gathered foods over game is an issue I have addressed in detail elsewhere (Lee 1979). The term "foragers" is an economical shorthand that does not prejudge the issue either way (e.g., Lee 1981).

2. Snow's position in turn can be traced back to a 19th-century critical Romanticism, which saw science as providing an ideological basis for the spread and destructive effects of capitalism. (I thank Victor Barac for this observation.)

3. The first draft of this paper had been completed before I became aware of Michael Carrithers's (1990) article, which also develops the figure of the "two cultures" as a means of comprehending contemporary anthropology.

4. While work from this perspective still constitutes only a small fraction of hunter-gatherer research, it would be a serious error to ignore, as many within the field have, its profound implications, not only for researchers but, more important, for the anthropological subjects themselves.

5. For a thoughtful and balanced discussion of this issue see Paynter 1989.

6. For a late conversion to relativism see Leach 1989; on the fallacy of "hyper-relativism" see Trigger 1989.

7. Wilmsen uses the Hobsbawm and Ranger thesis to the same effect in a section of his book entitled "The Invention of 'Bushmen'" (1989:24–26).

8. As a case in point, Wilmsen, after stating that his "book is . . . not an ethnography" and proclaiming the end of "the ethnographic era of anthropology" (1989:xii), goes on to devote several hundred pages to the presentation of "ethnographic" data on the San in the form of ethnohistory, genealogies, demography, economic anthropology, and subsistence ecology.

9. David Lowenthal (1985) has offered a provocative discussion of how both selective cultural amnesia and an obsession with the past characterize contradictory contemporary views of history.

10. The feeling of omniscience and instant global communication was nowhere more clearly expressed than in the television coverage of the first days of the war in the Persian Gulf, where major developments were seen as they occurred during North American prime time.

11. Many of these ideas are drawn from the works of Ernest Mandel (1978), Fred Jameson (1984), and the thought of Marshall MacLuhan.

12. Hoffman has argued, like Wilmsen, that the Penan were locked into the coastal trade centuries ago and had long since become subjects of coastal suzerains. Brosius and others have made the case for a greater degree of Penan autonomy.

13. Of this volume Bender and Morris write: "The publication of *Politics and History in Band Societies* . . . demolish[ed] the notion that contemporary gatherer-hunter societies were in any sense 'pristine'" (1988:6). A similar point is made by John Wright (1989:535) and by Donna Haraway (1989:194–197, 227), who clearly locates Lee as a member of the "revisionists." The revisionists for their part seem to prefer to retain a 1960s image of hunter-gatherer studies as a more convenient straw-person.

14. Some would argue, along with Phillip E. L. Smith, that communal relations and other aspects of foraging lifeways can be discerned in frontier European populations like the transhumant English settlers in Newfoundland from the 18th century on (Smith, personal communication, 1991).

15. For example, the appearance of slavery in complex foraging societies like those of the Northwest Coast (Donald 1983), and of other forms of inequality elsewhere (e.g., Legros 1985; Flanagan 1989), need to be seriously studied. And Clastres's own treatment of several topics — for one, gender — leaves much to be desired.

16. Bender and Morris in their introduction to Volume 1 of *Hunters and Gatherers* (Ingold, Riches, and Woodburn 1988a) perceptively make a similar critique of the revisionist view of history (1988:7–14):

> Above all the message of [*Politics and History in Band Societies*] must be that gatherer-hunters have their own history. An understanding of the processes of encapsulation has to work in tandem with an understanding that gatherer-hunter variability, past or present, has an internal dynamic. Change in gatherer-hunter societies does not wait upon the arrival of land-hungry farmers, nor upon capitalist penetration. [1988:13–14]

17. Having said this, there is still room to accommodate Alan Barnard's (1988) arguments that ethnicity and identity of San peoples are constructed in part from their mutual accommodations and antagonisms with other peoples.

18. Not only is the assertion of their "subjugation" vehemently denied by the !Kung themselves, but their view of the timing of the entrance of non-!Kung into their lands directly contradicts the "revisionist" position. When !Kung elders were asked to identify which of their African neighbors — the Hereros, Tswanas, or Ba Yei — first came into their land, they insisted it was none of them: the Europeans came first, followed by other Africans (Solway and Lee 1990:115). Since the Europeans only arrived in the 1870s, this renders moot the revisionist argument that the !Kung of the Dobe area were subjugated in the 1st millennium A.D. !Kung oral histories of the colonial period are presented in Lee (1991).

19. In fact, Ingold has argued that hunter-gatherer sociality is of such a different order that the term "society" is inappropriate with reference to them and should be reserved for describing post-forager peoples (1990:130–131).

20. In the Kalahari, for example, there are a number of problems in applying 20th-century patterns of power-holding and projecting them back into the past of the Dobe !Kung. For over 90% of the centuries of San/Black interaction, the putative overloads were not capitalists or even mercantilists, but African kin-ordered and tributary formations. In order for the revisionist model to work in this prehistoric context one has to endow 1st- and 2nd-millennium chiefdoms (if that is what they were) with the same predatory impulses and the same ability to exercise power across great distances that the historic Tswana chiefdoms briefly possessed in the 19th century, under the intense pressure of the Boer military threat and the competition of the British traders and imperialists. Despite the claims of the revisionists (e.g., Wilmsen and Denbow 1990:449–503), there is no convincing evidence that any group in what is now northwestern Botswana had that kind of power before the late 19th century, least of all the Tawana chiefdom,

the weakest of the eight major tribes that made up the Tswana nation (Tlou 1985).

21. For a critique of revisionist historiography in the Kalahari see Lee and Guenther (1991).

22. For two excellent examples of how this can be done see Trigger (1990) and Hunn (1990).

23. As I wrote in 1979:

Modern anthropology no longer believes that the scientist of culture is neutral: today's epistemology includes *the observer along with the "natives" in the field of view.* When acknowledged and used creatively the observer's likes and dislikes, his [*sic*] prejudices and enthusiasms, become an instrument of discovery, a part of the learning process itself and not external to it. [Lee 1979:8, emphasis in original]

24. While an inventory of recent work in hunter-gatherer studies is far beyond the scope of this paper, a few examples from two of the "paradigms" are appended to illustrate the abundance of work in the 1980s and 1990s (see also Note 23).

"Scientists": Ingold (1986a, 1986b), Woodburn (1980, 1982, 1988), and Wiessner (1982); Winterhalder (1990), Smith (1988); see also Winterhalder and Smith (1981); Smith and Boyd (1990), Vierich (1982), Cashdan (1987, 1990), Griffin (1989), Kent (1989), and the Harvard Pygmy project (Bailey and Peacock 1988, Bailey et al. 1989).

"Humanists": Brody (1981), Myers (1986b), Ridington (1990), Shostak (1981), Cruikshank (1991), Bird-David (1990). For some interesting recent work on Western perceptions and constructions of hunter-gatherers see Dumont (1988), Sponsel (1992), Armitage and Kennedy (1989); see also Myers (1986a). (For various combinations of all three paradigms see Ingold, Riches, and Woodburn [1988a, 1988b].)

25. This renegotiated ethnographic ethic can be seen clearly in the work of some of the "political economists": Asch (1984), Chance (1990), Daly (1988), Duhaylungsod and Hyndman (1992), Feit (1985, 1991), Hitchcock (1977, 1988), Hitchcock and Brandenburgh (1990), Hunn (1990), Kidd (1990), Peterson (1982, 1985), Peterson and Matsuyama (1991), Sansom (1985), and Tanner (1979). Special mention should be made of the work of Megan Biesele and John Marshall, who have been working with the !Kung San of Namibia through the most dramatic changes in their history (Biesele and Weinberg 1990).

26. On this score I found it instructive that so many members of indigenous Alaskan organizations endorsed the 1990 Fairbanks Conference on Hunting and Gathering Societies, not only contributing papers and workshops but also supporting CHAGS financially. These sponsors included Bering Straits Native Corporation, NANA Regional Corporation Inc., Interior Fish Processors of Alaska, and the Interior Mayors' Association of Alaska.

References Cited

Armitage, Peter, and J. C. Kennedy
1989   Redbaiting and Racism in Labrador and Quebec. Canadian Review of Sociology and Anthropology 18(4):798–817.

Asch, Michael
1984   Home and Native Land: Aboriginal Rights and the Canadian Constitution. Toronto: Methuen.

Bailey, R., and N. Peacock
1988   Efe Pygmies of Northeast Zaire: Subsistence Strategies in the Ituri Forest. In Uncertainty in the Food Supply. G. A. Harrison and A. Boyce, eds. Pp. 88–117. Cambridge: Cambridge University Press.

Bailey, R. C., G. Head, M. Jenike, B. Owen, R. Rechtman, and E. Zechenter
1989   Hunting and Gathering in Tropical Rain Forest: Is It Possible? American Anthropologist 91:59–82.

Barnard, Alan
1988   Cultural Identity, Ethnicity and Marginalization among the Bushmen of Southern Africa. In New Perspectives on the Study of Khoisan. Rainer Vossen, ed. Pp. 9–27. Hamburg: Helmut Buske Verlag.

Begler, E.
1978   Sex, Status, and Authority in Egalitarian Society. American Anthropologist 80:571–588.

Bender, Barbara, and Brian Morris
1988   Preface. In Hunters and Gatherers, Vol. 1: History, Evolution and Social Change. T. Ingold, D. Riches, and J. Woodburn, eds. Pp. 4–14. London: Berg.

Bergendorff, Steen, Ulla Hasager, and Peter Henriques
1988   Mythopraxis and History: On the Interpretation of the Makahiki. Journal of the Polynesian Society 97:391–408.

Berman, Marshall
1983   All that is Solid Melts into Air. New York: Simon and Schuster.

Berreman, Gerald
1991   The Incredible "Tasaday": Deconstructing the Myth of a "Stone-Age" People. Cultural Survival Quarterly 15(1):3–46.

Bhaskar, Roy
1979   The Possibility of Naturalism: A Philosophical Critique of the Human Sciences. Brighton, UK: Harvester Press.
1986   Scientific Realism and Human Emancipation. London: Verso.

Biesele, Megan, and Paul Weinberg
1990   Shaken Roots: The Bushmen of Namibia. Johannesburg: EDA Publications.

Binford, Lewis R.
1978   Nuniamiut Ethnoarchaeology. New York: Academic Press.

1980 Willow Smoke and Dogs' Tails: Hunter-Gatherer Settlement Systems and Archaeological Site Formation. American Antiquity 45:4–20.

Bird-David, Nurit
1990 The Giving Environment: Another Perspective on the Economic System of Gatherer-Hunters. Current Anthropology 31(2):189–196.

Boas, Franz
1935 Kwakiutl Culture as Reflected in Mythology. New York: Memoirs of the American Folklore Society, 28.
1966 Kwakiutl Ethnography. Helen Codere, ed. Chicago: University of Chicago Press.

Bodley, John
1982 Victims of Progress. Menlo Park, CA: Cummings.
1988 Tribal Peoples and Development Issues: A Global Overview. Mountain View, CA: Mayfield.

Brody, Hugh
1981 Maps and Dreams. Harmondsworth: Penguin.

Brosius, Peter
1988 A Separate Reality: Comments on Hoffman's *The Punan: Hunters and Gatherers of Borneo.* Borneo Research Bulletin 20(2): 81–105.

Burger, Julian
1990 The Gaia Atlas of First Peoples: A Future for the Indigenous World. New York: Doubleday.

Carrithers, Michael
1990 Is Anthropology Art or Science? Current Anthropology 31: 263–282.

Cashdan, Elizabeth
1987 Trade and Its Origins on the Botetli River. Journal of Anthropological Research 43:121–138.
1990 [ed.] Risk and Uncertainty in Tribal and Peasant Economies. Boulder, CO: Westview Press.

CBC (Canadian Broadcasting Corporation)
1990 The Fate of the Forest. Toronto: CBC "Ideas" Programme Transcript.

Chance, Norman A.
1990 The Inupiat and Arctic Alaska: An Ethnography of Development. Fort Worth, TX: Holt, Rinehart and Winston.

Chomsky, Noam
1989 Necessary Illusions: Thought Control in Democratic Societies. The Massey Lectures. Montreal: CBC Enterprises.

Clastres, Pierre
1989 Society against the State: Essays in Political Anthropology. New York: Zone Books.

Clifford, James
1983 On Ethnographic Authority. Reflections 1:118–145.
1988 The Predicament of Culture: Twentieth Century Ethnography, Literature, and Art. Cambridge, MA: Harvard University Press.

Clifford, James, and George Marcus, eds.

1986   Writing Culture: The Poetics and Politics of Ethnography. Berkeley: University of California Press.

Colchester, Marcus

1989   Pirates, Squatters and Poachers: The Political Ecology of Dispossession of the Native Peoples of Sarawak. London and Kuala Lumpur: Survival International and INSAM Malaysia.

Cruikshank, Julie

1991   Life Lived Like a Story: Lifestories of Three Yukon Native Elders. Lincoln: University of Nebraska Press.

Dahlberg, Frances, ed.

1981   Woman the Gatherer. New Haven, CT: Yale University Press.

Daly, Richard

1988   Land Ownership among British Columbia First Nations. Paper presented to First Nations Land Ownership Conference, Vancouver, B.C., Justice Institute, Oct. 1988.

Davis, Shelton

1977   Victims of the Miracle: Development and the Indians of Brazil. New York: Cambridge University Press.

Derrida, Jacques

1976   Of Grammatology. Baltimore, MD: Johns Hopkins University Press.

1978   Writing and Difference. Chicago: University of Chicago Press.

Diamond, Stanley

1974   In Search of the Primitive: A Critique of Civilization. New Brunswick, NJ: Transaction Books.

Donald, Leland

1983   Was Nuu-chah-nulth-aht (Nootka) Society Based on Slave Labor? In The Development of Political Organization in Native North America. Elisabeth Tooker, ed. 1979 Proceedings of the American Ethnological Society. Pp. 108–119. Washington, DC: American Ethnological Society.

Douglas, Mary

1966   Purity and Danger. New York: Praeger.

Duhaylungsod, Levita, and David Hyndman

1992   Behind and Beyond the Tasaday: The Untold Struggle over Resources of Indigenous Peoples. In The Tasaday Controversy. Tom Headland, ed. Washington, DC: American Anthropological Association Special Publication. (In press.)

Dumont, Jean-Paul

1988   The Tasaday, Which and Whose? Towards the Political Economy of an Ethnographic Sign. Cultural Anthropology 3: 261–275.

Endicott, Kirk
  1979 Batek Negrito Religion. Cambridge: Cambridge University Press.
Ewen, Stuart
  1976 Captains of Consciousness: Advertising and the Social Roots of Consumer Culture. New York: McGraw-Hill.
Feit, Harvey
  1985 Legitimation and Autonomy in James Bay Cree Responses to Hydro-Electric Development. *In* Indigenous Peoples and the Nation-State. Noel Dyck, ed. Pp. 27–66. St. John's, Newfoundland: Memorial University Press.
  1991 Gifts of the Land: Hunting Territories, Guaranteed Incomes and the Construction of Social Relations in James Bay Cree Society. *In* Cash, Commoditisation and Changing Foragers. N. Peterson and T. Matsuyama, eds. Senri Ethnological Studies No. 30. Pp. 223–268. Osaka: National Museum of Ethnology.
Flanagan, James
  1989 Hierarchy in Simple "Egalitarian" Societies. Annual Review of Anthropology 18:245–266.
Foley, Robert
  1988 Hominids, Humans and Hunter-Gatherers: An Evolutionary Perspective. *In* Hunters and Gatherers, Vol. 1: History, Evolution and Social Change.

T. Ingold, D. Riches, and J. Woodburn, eds. Pp. 207–221. London: Berg.
Foucault, Michel
  1976a Truth and Power. *In* Power/Knowledge. C. Gordon, ed. (*Reprinted in* The Foucault Reader, P. Rabinow, ed., pp. 51–75, Random House, 1984). New York: Pantheon.
  1976b The Archaeology of Knowledge. New York: Harper and Row.
Geertz, Clifford
  1973 The Interpretation of Cultures: Selected Essays. New York: Basic Books.
Gellner, Ernest
  1988 The Stakes in Anthropology. American Scholar 57:17–32.
Gordon, Robert
  1984 The !Kung in the Kalahari Exchange: An Ethnohistorical Perspective. *In* Past and Present in Hunter-Gatherer Studies. Carmel Schrire, ed. Pp. 195–224. Orlando, FL: Academic Press.
Griffin, P. Bion
  1989 Hunting, Farming, and Sedentism in a Rain Forest Foraging Society. *In* Farmers as Hunters: Implications of Sedentism. Susan Kent, ed. Pp. 60–70. Cambridge: Cambridge University Press.
Habermas, Jürgen
  1987 Modernity: An Incomplete Project. *In* Interpretive Social Science: A Second Look. Paul

Rabinow and William M. Sullivan, eds. Pp. 141–156. Berkeley: University of California Press.

Hanson, Allan
1989   The Making of the Maori: Culture Invention and Its Logic. American Anthropologist 91: 890–902.

Haraway, Donna
1989   Primate Visions: Gender, Race and Nature in the World of Modern Science. New York: Routledge, Chapman and Hall.

Hardison, O. B., Jr.
1989   Disappearing through the Skylight: Culture and Technology in the Twentieth Century. Baltimore, MD: Penguin.

Harris, Marvin
1979   Cultural Materialism: The Struggle for a Science of Culture. New York: Vintage.

Harvey, David
1985   Consciousness and the Urban Experience: Studies in the History and Theory of Capitalist Urbanization. Baltimore, MD: Johns Hopkins University Press.

Hawkes, Kirsten, Kim Hill, and James O'Connell
1982   Why Hunters Gather: Optimal Foraging and the Ache of Eastern Paraguay. American Ethnologist 9:379–398.

Headland, Tom, and Lawrence Reid
1989   Hunter-Gatherers and Their Neighbors from Prehistory to the Present. Current Anthropology 30:43–66.

Helm, June
1965   Bilaterality in the Socio-Territorial Organization of the Arctic Drainage Dene. Ethnology 4:361–385.

Hiatt, Les
1965   Kinship and Conflict: A Study of an Aboriginal Community in Northern Arnhem Land. Canberra: Australian National University Press.

Hill, Kim, and Kirsten Hawkes
1983   Neotropical Hunting among the Ache of Eastern Paraguay. In Adaptive Responses of Native Amazonians. R. Hames and W. Vickers, eds. Pp. 139–188. New York: Academic Press.

Hitchcock, Robert
1977   Kalahari Cattle Posts. Gaborone: Government of Botswana.
1988   Monitoring Research and Development in the Remote Areas of Botswana. Gaborone: Government Printer.

Hitchcock, Robert, and Rodney Brandenburgh
1990   Tourism, Conservation and Culture in the Kalahari Desert, Botswana. Cultural Survival Quarterly 14:20–24.

Hobsbawm, Eric, and T. O. Ranger, eds.
1983   The Invention of Tradition. Cambridge: Cambridge University Press.

Hoffman, Carl
1986 The Punan: Hunters and Gatherers of Borneo. Ann Arbor: UMI Research Press.

Hong, Evelyne
1987 Natives of Sarawak: Survival in Borneo's Vanishing Forest. Pulau Pinang, Malaysia: Institut Masyarakat.

Hunn, Eugene
1981 On the Relative Contribution of Men and Women to Subsistence among Hunter-Gatherers of the Columbia Plateau: A Comparison with *Ethnographic Atlas* Summaries. Journal of Ethnobiology 1:124–134.

Hunn, Eugene, with James Selam and family
1990 Nch'i-Wána, "The Big River": Mid-Columbia Indians and Their Land. Seattle: University of Washington Press.

Ingold, Tim
1986a The Appropriation of Nature: Essays on Human Ecology and Social Relations. Manchester: Manchester University Press.
1986b Evolution and Social Life. Cambridge: Cambridge University Press.
1990 *Comment on* "Foragers, Genuine or Spurious: Situating the Kalahari San in History," by J. Solway and R. Lee. Current Anthropology 31:130–131.

Ingold, Tim, David Riches, and James Woodburn, eds.
1988a Hunters and Gatherers, Vol. 1: History, Evolution and Social Change. London: Berg.
1988b Hunters and Gatherers, Vol. 2: Property, Power and Ideology. London: Berg.

Isaac, Glynn
1978 The Food-Sharing Behavior of Protohuman Hominids. Scientific American 238(4):90–108.

Jameson, Frederic
1984 Postmodernism, or the Cultural Logic of Late Capitalism. New Left Review 146:53–92.

Jorgensen, Joseph
1990 Oil-Age Eskimos. Berkeley: University of California Press.

Keene, Art
1983 Biology, Behavior, and Borrowing: A Critical Examination of Optimal Foraging Models in Archaeology. *In* Archaeological Hammers and Theories. A. Keene and J. Moore, eds. New York: Academic Press.
1991 Archeology and the Heritage of Man the Hunter. Reviews in Anthropology 16:133–147.

Kent, Susan, ed.
1989 Farmers as Hunters: Implications of Sedentism. Cambridge: Cambridge University Press.

Kidd, Dorothy
1990 Ikajurti, The Helper: Midwifery in the Arctic (film). Ottawa: Inuit Broadcasting Corpo-

ration, and Pauktuutit, the Inuit Women's Association.

Kroeber, A. L.

1925   Handbook of the Indians of California. Washington, DC: Bureau of American Ethnology Bulletin No. 78.

Kuper, Adam

1990   Ethnographic Practice. Unpublished ms., Department of Human Sciences, Brunel University, Uxbridge, Middlesex, England.

Lancaster, Jane

1978   Carrying and Sharing in Human Evolution. Human Nature 1(2):82–89.

Leach, Edmund

1989   *Review of* Works and Lives, by C. Geertz. American Ethnologist 16:137–141.

Leacock, Eleanor

1981   Myths of Male Dominance. New York: Monthly Review Press.

Leacock, Eleanor, and Richard Lee, eds.

1982   Politics and History in Band Societies. Cambridge: Cambridge University Press.

Lee, Richard

1965   Subsistence Ecology of !Kung Bushmen. Doctoral dissertation in Anthropology, University of California, Berkeley. Ann Arbor: University Microfilms.

1976   Introduction. *In* Kalahari Hunter-Gatherers: Studies of the !Kung San and Their Neighbors.

R. Lee and I. DeVore, eds. Pp. 3–24. Cambridge, MA: Harvard University Press.

1979   The !Kung San: Men, Women and Work in a Foraging Society. New York: Cambridge University Press.

1981   Is There a Foraging Mode of Production? Canadian Journal of Anthropology 2:13–19.

1988   Reflections on Primitive Communism. *In* Hunters and Gatherers, Vol. 1: History, Evolution and Social Change. T. Ingold, D. Riches, and J. Woodburn, eds. Pp. 252–268. London: Berg.

1990   Primitive Communism and the Origins of Social Inequality. *In* The Evolution of Political Systems: Sociopolitics in Small-Scale Sedentary Societies. Steadman Upham, ed. Pp. 225–246. Cambridge: Cambridge University Press.

1991   Solitude or Servitude: !Kung Images of the Colonial Encounter. Paper presented in the symposium, "Narratives of Resistance: History, Ethnography and Power." Meetings of the Canadian Anthropology Society, London, Ontario, May 1991.

1992   Making Sense of the Tasaday. *In* The Tasaday Controversy. Tom Headland, ed. Washington, DC: American Anthropological Association Special Publication. (In press.)

Lee, Richard, and Irven DeVore, eds.
1968 Man the Hunter. Chicago: Aldine.
1976 Kalahari Hunter-Gatherers: Studies of the !Kung San and Their Neighbors. Cambridge, MA: Harvard University Press.

Lee, Richard, and Mathias Guenther
1991 Oxen or Onions: The Search for Trade (and Truth) in the Kalahari. Current Anthropology 32. (In press.)

Legros, Dominique
1985 Wealth, Poverty, and Slavery among 19th Century Tutchone, Athapaskans. Research in Economic Anthropology 7:37–64.

Lévi-Strauss, Claude
1963 Structural Anthropology. New York: Basic Books.
1968 The Concept of Primitiveness. In Man the Hunter. R. Lee and I. DeVore, eds. Pp. 349–352. Chicago: Aldine.

Lovibond, Sabrina
1989 Feminism and Postmodernism. New Left Review 178:5–28.

Lowenthal, David
1985 The Past Is a Foreign Country. Cambridge: Cambridge University Press.

Lyotard, Jean François
1984 The Postmodern Condition: A Report on Knowledge. Minneapolis: University of Minnesota Press.

Mandel, Ernest
1978 Late Capitalism. London: New Left Books.

Marcus, George, and Michael Fischer
1986 Anthropology as Cultural Critique: An Experimental Moment in the Human Sciences. Chicago: University of Chicago Press.

Marshall, Lorna
1961 Talking, Sharing and Giving: Relief of Social Tensions among the !Kung Bushmen. Africa 31:231–249.
1976 The !Kung of Nyae Nyae. Cambridge, MA: Harvard University Press.

Martin, J.
1983 Optimal Foraging Theory: A Review of Some Models and Their Applications. American Anthropologist 85:612–629.

Mascia-Lees, Frances, Patricia Sharpe, and Colleen Ballerino Cohen
1989 The Post-Modernist Turn in Anthropology: Cautions from a Feminist Perspective. Signs 15(1):7–33.

Mintz, Sidney
1985 Sweetness and Power: The Place of Sugar in Modern History. New York: Viking Press.

Myers, Fred
1986a The Politics of Representation: Anthropological Discourse and Australian Aborigines. American Ethnologist 13:430–447.
1986b Pintupi Country, Pintupi Self: Sentiment, Place and Pol-

itics among Western Desert Aborigines. Washington, DC: Smithsonian Institution Press.

1988   Critical Trends in the Study of Hunter-Gatherers. Annual Review of Anthropology 17:261–282.

O'Meara, J. Tim

1989   Anthropology as Empirical Science. American Anthropologist 91:354–369.

Patterson, Tom, and Christine Gailey, eds.

1987   Power Relations and State Formation. Washington, DC: American Anthropological Association.

Paynter, Robert

1989   The Archaeology of Equality and Inequality. Annual Review of Anthropology 18:369–399.

People of 'Ksan

1980   Gathering What the Great Nature Provided: Food Traditions of the Gitksan. Vancouver: Douglas and McIntyre.

Peterson, Nicholas

1982   Aboriginal Land Rights in the Northern Territory of Australia. In Politics and History in Band Societies. E. Leacock and R. Lee, eds. Pp. 441–462. Cambridge: Cambridge University Press.

1985   Capitalism, Culture and Land Rights. Social Analysis 18:85–101.

Peterson, Nicholas, and Toshio Matsuyama, eds.

1991   Cash, Commoditisation and Changing Foragers. Senri Ethnological Studies No. 30. Osaka: National Museum of Ethnology.

Piel, Gerard

1972   The Acceleration of History. New York: Knopf.

Price, T., and J. Brown, eds.

1985   Prehistoric Hunter-Gatherers: The Emergence of Social Complexity. Orlando, FL: Academic Press.

Radcliffe-Brown, A. R.

1922   The Andaman Islanders. Cambridge: Cambridge University Press.

1931   The Social Organization of Australian Tribes. Sydney: Oceania Monographs, 1.

Richardson, Boyce, ed.

1989   Drumbeat: Anger and Renewal in the Indian Country. Toronto: Summerhill Press/Assembly of First Nations.

Ridington, Robin

1990   Little Bit Know Something: Stories in a Language of Anthropology. Vancouver: Douglas and McIntyre.

Rose, Frederick G. G.

1960   Classification of Kin, Age Structure and Marriage amongst the Groote Eylandt Aborigines: A Study in Method and Theory of Australian Kinship. Berlin: Akademie Verlag.

Roseberry, William

1989   Anthropologies and Histories: Essays in Culture, History, and Political Economy. New Brunswick, NJ: Rutgers University Press.

Rosenberg, Harriet G.

1990 Complaint Discourse, Aging, and Caregiving among the !Kung San of Botswana. In The Cultural Context of Aging. Jay Sokolovsky, ed. Pp. 19–41. New York: Bergin and Garvey.

Roth, Paul A.

1989 Ethnography without Tears. Current Anthropology 30:555–569.

Sacks, Karen

1979 Sisters and Wives. Urbana: University of Illinois Press.

Sahlins, Marshall

1968 Notes on the Original Affluent Society. In Man the Hunter. R. Lee and I. DeVore, eds. Pp. 85–89. Chicago: Aldine.

1989 Captain Cook at Hawaii. Journal of the Polynesian Society 98:371–423.

Sangren, Steven

1988 Rhetoric and the Authority of Ethnography: "Postmodernism" and the Social Reproduction of Texts. Current Anthropology 29:405–435.

Sansom, Basil

1980 The Camp at Wallaby Cross: Aboriginal Fringe Dwellers in Darwin. Canberra: Australian Institute of Aboriginal Studies.

1985 Aborigines, Anthropologists and Leviathan. In Indigenous Peoples and the Nation-State.

Noel Dyck, ed. Pp. 67–94. St. John's, Newfoundland: Memorial University Press.

Schrire, Carmel, ed.

1984 Past and Present in Hunter-Gatherer Studies. Orlando, FL: Academic Press.

Shostak, Marjorie

1981 Nisa: The Life and Words of a !Kung Woman. London: Allen Lane.

Siskind, Janet

1980 To Hunt in the Morning. New York: Oxford University Press.

Slocum, Sally

1975 Woman the Gatherer. In Towards an Anthropology of Women. R. Reiter, ed. Pp. 36–50. New York: Monthly Review Press.

Sloterdijk, Peter

1987 Critique of Cynical Reason. Minneapolis: University of Minnesota Press.

Smith, Eric A.

1988 Risk and Uncertainty in the "Original Affluent Society": Evolutionary Ecology of Resource-Sharing and Land Tenure. In Hunters and Gatherers, Vol. 1: History, Evolution and Social Change. T. Ingold, D. Riches, and J. Woodburn, eds. Pp. 222–251. London: Berg.

Smith, Eric A., and Robert Boyd

1990 Risk and Reciprocity: Hunter-Gatherer Socioecology and the Problem of Collective Action. In Risk and Uncertainty in Tribal and Peasant Economies. E. Cashdan, ed. Pp. 167–195. Boulder, CO: Westview Press.

Snow, C. P.
1959   The Two Cultures and the Scientific Revolution. New York: Cambridge University Press.

Solway, Jacqueline, and Richard Lee
1990   Foragers, Genuine or Spurious: Situating the Kalahari San in History. Current Anthropology 31:109–146.

Soper, Kate
1991   Postmodernism, Subjectivity and the Question of Value. New Left Review 186:120–128.

Sperber, Dan
1985   On Anthropological Knowledge. New York: Cambridge University Press.

Spivak, Gayatri C.
1988   Can the Subaltern Speak? In Marxism and the Interpretation of Culture. Cary Nelson and Lawrence Grossberg, eds. Pp. 271–313. Urbana: University of Illinois Press.

Sponsel, Leslie
1992   Our Fascination with the Tasaday: Anthropological Images and the Image of Anthropology. In The Tasaday Controversy. Tom Headland, ed. Washington, DC: American Anthropological Association Special Publication. (In press.)

Sterritt, Neil J.
1989   Gitksan and Wet'suwet'en:

Unflinching Resistance to an Implacable Invader. In Drumbeat: Anger and Renewal in the Indian Country. B. Richardson, ed. Pp. 265–294. Toronto: Summerhill Press/Assembly of First Nations.

Steward, Julian
1936   The Economic and Social Basis of Primitive Bands. In Essays in Anthropology in Honor of A. L. Kroeber. R. H. Lowie, ed. Pp. 331–350. Berkeley: University of California Press.

1938   Basin-Plateau Aboriginal Sociopolitical Groups. Bureau of American Ethnology Bulletin No. 120. Washington, DC: Smithsonian Institution.

Tanner, Adrian
1979   Bringing Home Animals: Religious Ideology and Mode of the Production of the Misstassini Cree Hunters. London: Hurst.

Tanner, Nancy, and Adrienne Zihlman
1976   Women in Evolution 1: Innovation and Selection in Human Origins. Signs 1:585–608.

Taylor, Charles
1984   Foucault on Freedom and Truth. Political Theory 12(2): 152–183.

Testart, Alain
1988   Some Major Problems in the Social Anthropology of Hunter-Gatherers. Current Anthropology 29:1–21.

Tlou, Thomas
1985   A History of Ngamiland

1750 to 1906: The Formation of an African State. Gaborone: Macmillan.

Trigger, Bruce
1987 The Children of Aetaentsic. Revised edition. Montreal: McGill-Queens University Press.
1989 Hyperrelativism, Responsibility and the Social Sciences. Canadian Review of Sociology and Anthropology 26(5):776–797.
1990 Maintaining Economic Equality in Opposition to Complexity: An Iroquoian Case Study. *In* The Evolution of Political Systems: Sociopolitics in Small-Scale Sedentary Societies. Steadman Upham, ed. Pp. 109–146. Cambridge: Cambridge University Press.

Turner, Victor
1969 The Ritual Process. Chicago: Aldine.

Vierich, Helga
1982 Adaptive Flexibility in a Multi-Ethnic Setting. *In* Politics and History in Band Societies. E. Leacock and R. Lee, eds. Pp. 213–222. Cambridge: Cambridge University Press.

Wa, Gisday, and Delgam Uukw
1989 The Spirit in the Land: The Opening Statement of the Gitksan and Wet'suwet'en Hereditary Chiefs in the Supreme Court of British Columbia. Gabriola, BC: Reflections Press.

Wagner, Roy
1981 The Invention of Culture. Chicago: University of Chicago Press.

Wiessner, Polly
1982 Risk, Reciprocity and Social Influences on !Kung San Economics. *In* Politics and History in Band Societies. E. Leacock and R. Lee, eds. Pp. 61–84. Cambridge: Cambridge University Press.

Wilmsen, Edwin
1983 The Ecology of Illusion: Anthropological Foraging in the Kalahari. Reviews in Anthropology 10:9–20.
1988 We Are Here: The Politics of Aboriginal Land Tenure. Berkeley: University of California Press.
1989 Land Filled with Flies: A Political Economy of the Kalahari. Chicago: University of Chicago Press.

Wilmsen, Edwin, and James Denbow
1990 Paradigmatic History of San-Speaking Peoples and Current Attempts at Revision. Current Anthropology 31(5):489–524.

Winterhalder, Bruce
1990 Open Field, Common Pot: Harvest Variability and Risk Avoidance in Agricultural and Foraging Societies. *In* Risk and Uncertainty in Tribal and Peasant Economies. E. Cashdan, ed. Pp. 67–87. Boulder, CO: Westview Press.

Winterhalder, Bruce, and Eric A. Smith, eds.

1981 Hunter-Gatherer Foraging Strategies: Ethnographic and Archeological Analyses. Chicago: University of Chicago Press.

Wobst, Martin

1978 The Archaeo-Ethnology of Hunters and Gatherers, or, The Tyranny of the Ethnographic Record in Archaeology. American Antiquity 43:303–309.

Wolf, Eric R.

1982 Europe and the People without History. Berkeley: University of California Press.

Wolf, Eric, and Edward Hansen

1975 The Human Condition in Latin America. New York: Columbia University Press.

Woodburn, James

1980 Hunters and Gatherers Today and Reconstruction of the Past. In Soviet and Western Anthropology. E. Gellner, ed. London: Duckworth.

1982 Egalitarian Societies. Man (n.s.) 17:431–451.

1988 African Hunter-Gatherer Social Organization: Is It Best Seen as a Product of Encapsulation? In Hunters and Gatherers, Vol. 1: History, Evolution and Social Change. T. Ingold, D. Riches, and J. Woodburn, eds. Pp. 31–64. London: Berg.

Wright, John

1989 Review of Politics and History in Band Societies, edited by E. Leacock and R. Lee. Journal of Southern African Studies 15:535–536.

Yellen, John

1977 Archaeological Approaches to the Present. New York: Academic Press.

1990 The Present and Future of Hunter-Gatherer Studies. In Archaeological Thought in America. C. C. Lamberg-Karlovsky, ed. New York: Cambridge University Press.

Empowering Place:

Multilocality and Multivocality

Margaret C. Rodman

VOL. 94, 1992, 640–656

A critique could be carried out of this devaluation of space that has prevailed for generations. Space was treated as the dead, the fixed, the undialectical, the immobile. Time on the other hand, was richness, fecundity, life, dialectic. If one started to talk in terms of space that meant one was hostile to time. It meant, as the fools say, that one "denied history," that one was a "technocrat." They didn't understand that to trace the forms of implantation, delimitation, and demarcation of objects, the modes of tabulation, the organisation of domains meant the throwing into relief of processes — historical ones, needless to say — of power. [Foucault 1980:70]

Place is a problem in contemporary anthropological theory. The problem of place arises, paradoxically, because the meaning of place too often seems to go without saying. As anthropologists and as ordinary people living in the world, we are as situated in place as we are in time or culture. The people we study in non-Western, less industrialized countries may have even more immediate and full relationships with place insofar as time-space relations are less fragmented and they retain more local control over their physical and social landscapes. Yet anthropologists who take pains to lead students through the minefields of conceptualizing culture often assume that place is unproblematic. It is simply location. It is where people do things. This article takes the kind of hard look at place that others have taken at culture. It suggests how anthropologists can learn from current thinking about place in geography. And it applies anthropological thoughts on voice and place, especially multivocality and multilocality, using examples from Melanesian ethnography and field research in Vanuatu (the ex–New Hebrides).

The article approaches the anthropological problem of place from two vantage points, exploring in the process some of the terrain between them. The first is that of places as anthropological constructions. Places in anthropological writing have been equated with ethnographic locales. As such, they could be taken for granted. They were just space, "the dead, the fixed, the undialectical, the immobile" in Foucault's lament above. They became the settings, albeit often exotic ones, where things happened.[1] Anthropologists have critiqued places as localizing strategies (Fardon 1990) or ideas (Appadurai 1988a; 1988b); for example, India has exemplified the concept of hierarchy. Others have objected to the use of places as metonyms in which one locale stands, inappropriately, for a whole area (Fernandez 1988), as, for example, Andalusia has been made to stand for all of Spain. But insufficient attention has been paid to conceptualizing place in anthropology as something other than a physical setting or a passive target for primordial sentiments of attachment that flow from life's "assumed 'givens'" (Geertz 1973:259).[2]

Places are not inert containers. They are politicized, culturally relative, historically specific, local and multiple constructions. Anthropologists have accepted the polyphony of the voices they hear and represent ethnographically. What Appadurai (1988a:17) has called "the problem of voice ('speaking for' and 'speaking to')" may intersect with "the problem of place ('speaking from' and 'speaking of')," but the former has certainly received more critical attention. One goal of this article is to show that place as an anthropological concept is as complex as voice.

A further problem is that place and voice are not, or not just, academic creations. Places are not defined simply by researchers or by the topics that preoccupy them in particular settings. Places in the world of our research are not totalized, essentialized Western creations.

This leads to the second point of view in the article, namely, that of places as socially constructed. Here the emphasis is on places in the world, on the agency of individuals and of forces beyond individual control. Places have multiple meanings that are constructed spatially. The physical, emotional, and experiential realities places hold for their inhabitants at particular times need to be understood apart from their creation as the locales of ethnography. While anthropologists indeed create places in ethnography, they hold no patent on place-making.

I advocate a different approach to place than the traditional ethnographic focus on setting. I argue for a more critical usage of place than is common in contemporary anthropology and take seriously the attendant dimensions of power. I raise questions (and do not try to answer all of them) about how the anthropological study of place relates to experiences of living in places. In so doing, I explore the idea of multilocality as one way of "constructing regional worlds in experience," to borrow Nancy Munn's (1990) evocative phrase.

Organizationally, the article begins with a selected overview of the study of place in contemporary geography, emphasizing work that seems especially appropriate to anthropology. I go on to evaluate new approaches to place and the related concept of region in anthropology. The next section of the paper pays particular attention to place as lived experience. Using recent studies in Melanesia concerning power and social landscapes (esp. Lindstrom 1990), I point to some ways that the work of Foucault applies to understanding multivocality ethnographically. I suggest how Giddens's (1990) views on space-time distanciation also can be helpful for understanding multivocality and multilocality in non-Western places. Examples from my own fieldwork in Vanuatu illustrate a multivocal, multilocal approach to understanding the social construction of place anthropologically.

Geographers and Place

To some extent, the concept of place and, on a larger scale, that of region have languished even in geography. "Chorology," the study of region and place, was marginalized as a theoretical subject in the 1950s and 1960s as geographers, like anthropologists of the period, sought to make their discipline more scientific. This does not mean that regional studies disappeared. Even within Melanesia their continued contribution remained evident into the 1970s (see, e.g., Brookfield with Hart 1971). But regional studies became a largely descriptive field.

Geographers now are expressing renewed interest in the theoretical concepts of place and region.[3] Entrikin (1989:40) regards this interest as part of attempts to "redirect geographical research toward a concern for the richness of human experience and an understanding of human action. . . . [T]hey are taking seriously the cultural significance of everyday life."

In his recent introduction to systemic regional geography, Dov Nir (1990:59–60) observes that there are two opposing views of "region" in contemporary geography. For some, "region" is just a concept, a mental construct or analytical tool. For others, regions are realities that exist in space. Anthropologists similarly hold these two seemingly opposing views with regard to place, as the two viewpoints from which this article is organized suggest — that is, place as (1) an anthropological construct for "setting" or the localization of concepts and as (2) socially constructed, spatialized experience.[4] Nir (1990:10) proposes that both views can be compatible insofar as regional studies are in fact studies of places, spatial relationships (Claval's [1984] "social space"), and values attached to places and relationships. Others would call this concatenation "lived space."

Berdoulay (1989:130) defines "lived space" (*l'espace vécu*) to include living space (territory, activity areas), social space, and the values attached to both. He notes that current interest in lived space, especially among French writers, grows out of the contribution of Vidal de la Blache's (1917) possibilism to the development of regional studies and analyses of place. One aspect of Vidalian geography focused on the tensions between the influence humans exert on their environments and, reciprocally, the impacts their environments have on them. Berdoulay suggests (1989:126) that "the Vidalian thrust in geography is compatible with the current interest in place. It was very attentive to the environment as experienced by people. The concern for people's plans, worries, initiatives, and efforts gave this geography the highly humanistic overtones which have frequently been noted by non-French commentators" (such as Buttimer [1971], and Ley and Samuels [1978]).

In this sense, places not only feature in inhabitants' (and geographers') narratives, they are narratives in their own right: "a place comes explicitly into being in the discourse of its inhabitants, and particularly in the rhetoric it promotes. Thus the geographer's discourse uses the same ways as the people who define their own place" (Berdoulay 1989:135; see also Tuan 1991). Entrikin (1991:3) suggests that such discourse productively blends distinctions between place as an analytical concept, on the one hand, and as "situatedness" in a real world, on the other: "We understand the specificity of place from a point of view, and for this reason the student of place relies upon forms of analysis that lie between the centered [subjective, experiential] and decentered [objective, transcendent] view; such forms may be described as narrative-like syntheses." Entrikin's book, *The Betweenness of Place*, goes on to advocate a position interstitial to the two viewpoints, one that could suggest a resolution of their apparent contradiction for anthropologists as well:

This divide between the existential and naturalistic conceptions of place appears to be an unbridgeable one, and one that is only made wider in adopting a decentered [objective] view. The closest that we can come to addressing both sides of this divide is from a point in between, a point that leads us into the vast realm of narrative forms. From this position we gain a view from both sides of the divide. We gain a sense both of being "in a place" and "at a location," of being at the center and being at a point in a centerless world. To ignore either aspect of this dualism is to misunderstand the modern experience of place. [1991:134]

One problem here is the tendency to privilege verbal communication. Ironically, while this has been common in anthropology, it has been rare in geography until recently. Lack of attention to speech now troubles geographers interested in narrative. Tuan (1991:684) points to the neglect of speech as a "curious gap in the extensive and growing literature on place." He advocates an expansion of human geography to include speech and writing as integral to both place-making and geographic inquiry. One approach he favors "is cultural — the varying ways by which different societies use speech and/or the written word to realize place" (1991:695).[5] But places come into being through praxis, not just through narratives. One should also be wary of the assumption that the geographers' and the inhabitants' discourses will be consistent and that all inhabitants (and all geographers) will share similar views. The briefest glance at recent anthropological writing on ethnography and on rethinking culture would cast doubt on those assumptions. Entrikin, but not Tuan, seems well aware of recent work in this area.

In a comment reminiscent of the Foucault quote at the beginning of this article, the Marxist urban geographer David Harvey (1989) notes that time-space relations are fundamental to social relations, yet time has tended to receive much more attention than space.[6]

> The priority given to time over space is not in itself misplaced. Indeed, it mirrors the evolution of social practices in important ways. What is missing, however, is an appreciation of the practices that underlie the priority. Only in such a light can we understand those situations in which location, place, and spatiality reassert themselves as seemingly powerful and autonomous forces in human affairs. And such situations are legion. [1989:175]

Harvey quips that "the question of space is too important to be left exclusively to geographers." In the next section, I explore what anthropologists have had to say about the topic recently, beginning with the matter of voice and returning later in the section to the question of time.

New Approaches to Place in Anthropology

Despite considerable reappraisal of "voice" in anthropology, "place" has received surprisingly little attention and virtually no critical reassessment. There is little recognition that place is more than locale, the setting for action, the stage on which things happen. Anthropologists would do well to follow geographers' renewed interest (Agnew and Duncan 1989b:2) in reunifying *location* (i.e., the spatial distribution of socioeconomic activity such as trade networks), *sense of place* (or attachment to place), and *locale* (the setting in which a particular social activity occurs, such as a church) to yield a more rounded understanding of places as culturally and socially constructed in practice.

The idea, well-established in geography, that places produce meaning and that meaning can be grounded in place, has yet to attract much theoretical interest in anthropology. Denise Lawrence and Setha Low's (1990) article in *Annual Reviews in Anthropology* begins to redress this neglect, although their concern is with studies of the built environment rather than place more broadly. They and others involved in the Place and Space group have made important contributions to the anthropological study of place and space. This work deserves more critical theoretical attention.[7]

Place too often is subsumed as part of the problem of voice, so that geography becomes purely metaphorical. For example, Rosaldo speaks of "Miami Vice" TV episodes as places that are the "site of the implosion of the Third World into the First" (1988:85).

Alternatively, places have come to stand for particular problems in anthropology. Thus, for example, Melanesianists as "areal specialists" are likely to study adoption or the invention of tradition. Appadurai (1988a:16) defines this "problem of place" as "the problem of the culturally defined locations to which ethnographies refer." In his view, ethnographic places become metonyms for certain anthropological images and ideas. As an example, he traces the attachment of the idea of hierarchy to India. In urging anthropologists to contest such "topological stereotypes," Appadurai is in effect advocating a regional approach. The ideas that seem to represent the essence of certain places would be recognized, in this approach, as merely momentary localizations or coales-

cences of ideas from all over (Appadurai 1988b:46). Further, he encourages "the production and appreciation of ethnographies that emphasize
the *diversity* of themes that can fruitfully be pursued in *any* place"
(1988b:46, emphasis in original).

The "problem of place," as Appadurai defines it, is well addressed in a
theme issue of *Cultural Anthropology* (1988). My complaint is that the
"problem," as defined, misses one larger point. It is time to recognize
that places, like voices, are local and multiple. For each inhabitant, a
place has a unique reality, one in which meaning is shared with other
people and places. The links in these chains of experienced places are
forged of culture and history.

Recent writing, as evident in the *Cultural Anthropology* theme issue
on place and voice, suffers from a failure to be critical of place as an
anthropological concept. Place is at best seen purely as locale, and the
"problem" is defined as if place were entirely an anthropological creation, a metonymic prison that incarcerates natives, in Appadurai's
terms (1988b:37). In his view, such a prison is produced when certain
images come to stand for particular areas. To be sure, there are dangers
in reifying place (A. Strathern 1990:376). The hegemony of particular research topics, such as exchange, is as evident in Melanesian ethnography as in the Indian example of hierarchy that interests Appadurai. But it would be arrogant and naive to assume that places exist
only as localizations of totalized anthropological voices. Anthropologists need to become more aware of Western bias and not assume that
"place" means those places foreign ethnographers or metropolitan theory define.

Returning control over the meanings of place to the rightful producers requires reconsideration of questions of power and agency that
implicate both anthropology and the people we study. It requires coming to terms with Entrikin's (1991) "betweenness of place" in anthropological contexts, as both subject and object. "What has to be cancelled,"
argues Marilyn Strathern (1988:94), "is the basis of the comparison" so
that we, as Westerners, no longer privilege our own vantage point and
peripheralize all other places. Rather than places becoming exemplars of
our concepts, they should be seen as, to varying degrees, socially constructed products of *others'* interests (material as well as ideational) and
as mnemonics of *others'* experiences. The contests and tensions between
different actors and interests in the construction of space should be

explored. We should consider what Munn (1990) has called "construct-ing regional worlds in experience."

Ironically, Munn's real interest in her stimulating article on regional worlds is in time more than space. She traces the incorporation of an episode from a *kula* transaction into the construction of events else-where in the region some six years later. She wants to understand how people become aware of and use past, distant events as horizons that can inform present action:

> My intent is to stress that for the subject a regional world is not given but lived, as Williams (1977:129) has put it, "in singular and developing forms" and created in the "living." Instead of considering the formation of a regional order through the structure and functioning of given social forms such as types of social organization, exchange or communication (see for example Werbner 1977; Smith 1976), I am concerned with its ongoing formation in certain experiential syntheses that actors create in practices, and the events that transpire in their terms. [Munn 1990:2]

Space is only a frame for the action in Munn's article. But at least it is a frame that is locally made. Place could be taken more seriously by broad-ening her approach. What if we look at places as well as actors and at the ongoing formation of experience that occurs in a particular place or net-work of places? In other words, instead of confining the analysis to the *actor's* view of a wider *social* milieu, as Munn does, let us consider how specific *places* implicate each other in a wider *geographical* milieu as well. Landscapes, too, can be "listening posts" to somewhere else (cf. Munn 1990).

Her "event history" is similar enough to the geographer Berdoulay's idea of the narrativity of place to suggest a synthesis of their approaches. Both are phenomenological, culturally shaped constructions. For Munn, "the relations between events are developed in the practice of everyday life through infusing the experience of a given event with pasts (or possi-ble pasts) and futures" (1990:13). As well, one could argue that regional relations between *lived spaces* are developed through infusing experience in one place with the evocation of other events and other places.

Rabinow's defense of anthropology as nominalism elaborates on the idea of "horizons" in a way that would have been useful to Munn's argu-ment, had she considered it. The task of anthropology, as passed down from Kant to Foucault to Rabinow (1988:356), is to elucidate the language of social relations through which people create the world as they know it:

As these worlds appear only from the horizon of the present, whose frontiers they form, they function as limits to who we are and what we can know, hope, do. These worlds, along with the structures of our reason, constitute the limits of our experience. For that reason, anthropology taken pragmatically occupies that place where humans learn to recognize their own culture as "l'école du monde," . . . in which universality and particularity are joined in a single relationship. [Rabinow 1988:356]

But how do we decenter this approach so that the "school of the world" is not dominated by *our* (Western) schools of thought and *our* worlds? How do we deal with the problem of multivocality and with the differential power relations implicit in such cultural constructions of place? Munn conveys no sense of contested, competing views in the social construction of regional, lived space. How were various actors' interpretations of Gawa events smoothed into the single narrative she presents? Depending on the placement of the observer, the horizons of the regional world could be quite different. Munn does not deal with this phenomenological problem of constructing a shared narrative from individually unique experiences. Nor does she deal with associated doubts that could be raised concerning the future of comparison and generalization.[8]

The "true defining horizon" of our concepts of "otherness" and "difference," in Edward Said's (1989:217) view, is the fact of empire. We can only understand the world from within our culture, he argues, if we understand the imperial contest that shaped and continues to shape it. Thus an anthropology grounded in place would have to be historically as well as geographically constituted. Then, like Berdoulay's grounded narratives and Munn's regional worlds, cultures may

> be represented as zones of control or of abandonment, of recollection and of forgetting, of force or of dependence, of exclusiveness or of sharing, all taking place in the global history that is our element. Exile, immigration, and the crossing of boundaries are experiences that can therefore provide us with new narrative forms or, in John Berger's phrase, with *other* ways of telling. [Said 1989:225]

How do we restore agency to the people we study while remaining keenly aware of their imperial historical (and contemporary) contexts? "Multi-locale ethnography" is George Marcus's term for one way to solve this problem. "The idea is that any cultural identity or activity is constructed by multiple agents in varying contexts, or places, and that ethnography must be strategically conceived to represent this sort of multiplicity and to specify both intended and unintended consequences in the network of complex connections within a system of places" (Marcus 1989:25; see also Marcus and Fischer 1986:94). The goal is to reconceptualize regional ethnography in a way that eliminates distinctions between macro- and microlevels. Marcus wants to preserve the ethnographic concern with place but push it further. He seeks "an ethnography that while it encompasses local conditions, is aimed at representing system or pieces of system" (1989:25). This decentered discourse has ethnographic locale at its heart. It is constrained by the limited notion of place as nothing more than locale. It is also constrained by the notion of system, which needs further definition in his article. Presumably, Marcus does not mean to suggest that such local systems are self-contained or homogenous. But it is not clear how he means to apply the idea of "system" to contemporary cultural analysis.

As for "locale," Giddens (1979:206) has developed the concept to link the individual to what Marcus might call "the system" through human agency, but Marcus does not cite Giddens, so this seems not to be the usage he has in mind. By locale, Giddens means "the physical settings of social activity as situated geographically" (1990:18; see also 1984:ch. 3). The emptying of time integral to modernity, Giddens argues, leads to a concomitant "emptying of space" or separation of space from place. Localized activities dominated the shaping of space into place in what Giddens calls "traditional" or "premodern" societies. But distanciated relations predominate in the world today and provide the basis for new spatial as well as temporal zones and boundaries:

> The advent of modernity increasingly tears space away from place by fostering relations between "absent" others, locationally distant from any given situation of face-to-face interaction. In conditions of modernity, place becomes increasingly *phantasmagoric:* that is to say, locales are thoroughly penetrated by and shaped in terms of social influence quite distant from them. [1990:18–19, emphasis in original]

Like geographers Entrikin and Berdoulay, anthropologists Marcus and Munn, and other scholars (notably Said) discussed so far, Giddens sketches an analytic framework that dissolves macro-micro oppositions. Multilocality, like multivocality, becomes a theme to be explored. For Giddens, place is "phantasmagoric" in that we experience it as a constantly shifting, complex succession of images. The extent to which space-time distanciation prevails varies, ironically, in space and time. In places such as Melanesia today, local identity defined by and expressed through place remains stronger than in much of the West. But place is still fragmented and multilocal in its construction to some degree. This is evident in the commodification of land, its use for cash cropping that relies on foreign markets, the use of such media as radio and newspapers to talk about land and national identity, the construction of an urban identity in terms of a place one no longer lives in, and so on.

The fragmentation of place in Melanesia is not nearly so startling as the postmodern landscapes, epitomized by Los Angeles, that fascinate postmodern geographers. Edward Relph, best known to anthropologists for his *Place and Placelessness* (1976), considers such landscapes in his recent work. Postmodern landscapes confuse and juxtapose times and places. Relph asks (1991:104), "[W]hat happens when the imagineered logic of Disneyworld becomes the logic of the rest of the world?" The resulting landscapes he calls "heterotopias." The term originated with Foucault (1970:xviii), who contrasted the imagined places of utopias, which directly reflect or invert "real" societies, with heterotopias, which are "a kind of effectively enacted utopia in which the real sites, all the other real sites that can be found within the culture, are simultaneously represented, contested, and inverted" (1986:24). Foucault's examples of heterotopias include cemeteries, museums, libraries, brothels, carnivals, and gardens. For Relph, heterotopias are not so orderly:

> Heterotopia is the geography that bears the stamp of our age and our thought — that is to say it is pluralistic, chaotic, designed in detail yet lacking universal foundations of principles, continually changing, linked by centre-less flows of information; it is artificial and marked by deep social inequalities. [Relph 1991:104–105]

Foucault's (1980:24) first principle of "heterotopology" is that "there is probably not a single culture in the world that fails to constitute heterotopias," but by far the greatest impact of this notion has been in geographers' study of Western, urban, postmodern landscapes. As we shall see, anthropologists working in other places could use the concept productively.

Heterotopias are sites. Multilocality is a way of experiencing those and other places. Building on Giddens and Marcus, I see multilocality as having a number of dimensions. First, it assumes a decentered analysis, not in Entrikin's sense of "objective" analysis but in seeking to understand the construction of places from multiple, non-Western as well as Eurocentric viewpoints. Multilocality in this sense means looking at places from the viewpoint of Others, while recognizing that there really are no "others" in a world in which everyone can potentially suffer from one agent's actions (as, for example, in oil spills or nuclear accidents). As Gupta and Ferguson (1992:16) argue, anthropologists should be willing to question "the apparent 'given' of a world in the first place divided into 'ourselves' and 'others.'"

Second, multilocality can refer to comparative or contingent analyses of place. Marcus advocates paying attention to this dimension. Some activities (e.g., markets, social movements) arise from the actions of multiple agents in different places and can only be understood by identifying "both intended and unintended consequences in the network or complex connections within a system of places" (Marcus 1989:25).

Third, multilocality can refer to reflexive relationships with places. An anthropologist, traveler, or anyone whose place has been transformed, for example, by a natural disaster or suburban development — in other words, anyone dislocated from his or her familiar place, or from the possibility of local identity — is keenly aware of contrasts between the known and the unfamiliar. In such situations, people often see a new landscape in terms of familiar ones. This is a multilocal way of sorting out meaning. Alternatively, as Basso (1988) has observed, strange landscapes can baffle and silence observers just as strange languages can.

Finally, a single physical landscape can be multilocal in the sense that it shapes and expresses polysemic meanings of place for different users. This is more accurately a multivocal dimension of place, but multilocality conveys the idea that a single place may be experienced quite differently.

All these dimensions of multilocality are predicated on connections, on the interacting presence of different places and different voices in various geographical, anthropological (cultural), and historical contexts. I agree with Fabian (1990:771) that our goal should be "to transform ethnography into a praxis capable of making the Other present (rather than making representations predicated on the Other's absence)." The way that Fabian proposes to do this is through a concern with performance and the writing of ethnography. But there are other ways. For our purposes, let me sketch the outlines, or "horizons," of a view toward empowering place as a critical concept in anthropology. Application to Melanesia of recent anthropological and geographical theorizing about place illustrates how place reciprocally shapes individuals and society through human agency.

The first step is to recognize that space is socially constructed, and contested, in practice. The sociocultural construction of space has received considerable attention from Marxist urban geographers (e.g., Castells 1977; Gottdiener 1985; Harvey 1973, 1989). For many scholars, urban space has been of primary interest. In North America and Europe, the development of capitalism and the "local state" have been crucial in structuring space (e.g., Logan and Molotch 1987). Confrontation between entrepreneurs concerned with exchange values and residents concerned with use values, such as quality of life, must focus on "the complex articulation between symbolic universes of meaning, capital accumulation and space" and are crucial for the analysis of urban development (Gottdiener 1985:155).

In my research on Toronto housing cooperatives with Matthew Cooper (Cooper and Rodman 1990, 1992; Rodman and Cooper 1989), we have shown that when exchange-value considerations are removed, as in nonprofit housing cooperatives, other social processes involved in the creation and manipulation of the use values of urban space come into sharper focus. By use values I mean such noncommodified dimensions of place as quiet enjoyment or feeling at home. Hypothetically, the same may be true of the social construction of space in Melanesia. There capitalism has less impact and use values remain of central importance to most rural islanders, although exchange-value considerations enter the picture through mining, forestry, tourism, and even cash cropping. Very little research has been conducted on the social construction of space outside of the urban centers of the capitalist world. Studying the social construction of place in Melanesia enriches our understanding of people for whom, individually and collectively, places remain integral to social life.

Empowering Place: Examples from Contemporary Melanesia

Margaret Jolly has addressed this issue ethnographically, pointing to the inseparability of place and people in Vanuatu identity.[9] She and I have each written about the powerful condensation of person and place in the concept of *man ples* (Jolly 1990:17; Rodman 1987:35–36). As she aptly remarks, "such imagery was not only crucial in reclaiming the land as inalienably attached to the people of the place, but proclaiming the people as necessarily in control of the place" (Jolly 1990:17). Giddens

(1990:88) might consider this a form of re-embedding, an attempt to counter the space-time distanciation initiated through the colonial process. In Vanuatu, this was accomplished less by face-to-face contact than by a rhetorical emphasis on the rootedness of people in place, or autochthony.

Jolly notes the primordialism, or evocation of an original state in which people and place were one, that runs through Vanuatu constructions of place. This expression of connectedness between people and places creates what Giddens (1990:102) refers to as an "environment of trust" in kin relations, local communities, cosmology, and tradition, which is place-based. The strong assertion of the inalienability of land in Vanuatu no doubt responds to the extensive alienation of land for plantations in the colonial period, which only ended in 1980. It also harkens back to the insecurity of pre-pacification life (prior to about 1930). Warrior leaders might seize their followers' land, as well as that of their enemies, and hold it for a lifetime or longer. The connection between place and voice was direct. Followers who lacked the power to voice their objections also lacked the power to regain their land.

Jolly contrasts the meaning of place in contemporary Fiji and Vanuatu. Fijian "custom" is less fused with concepts of place — although it is called *vakavanua*, "the way of the land." Jolly argues that the British valued Fijian traditional culture and tried to blend it with colonial administrative practice. In Vanuatu, however, the British and French pursued a policy, albeit haphazard, of land alienation in which respect for traditional culture played little part. For the people of Vanuatu, independence became associated with regaining their land as well as their cultural past. As Jolly puts it, "*kastom* was expressly the reclaiming of a place, against European occupation of the land and the reclaiming of a past which had been lost or expressly abandoned" (1990:17).

On Ambae, in the north of the archipelago, place has also been crucial to identity. Concentric circles of identity are expressed in place. This is similar to what Fernandez has called "envelopes of domestic space," in an African context (1982:106–110). *Vanue* is a word for place that implicates the site of one's dwelling, hamlet, district, island, and even the country, Vanua-tu. It is lived space in each of a succession of regional zones. Elsewhere I have explored dimensions of people's attachment to place, as well as ways to manipulate it (Rodman 1987). Later in this article, I will include an example of the multivocality that can be evident in such attachment — and detachment — at funerals.

William Rodman also has considered the importance of place-making in his analyses of legal autonomy on Ambae. He argues (1985, 1992) that people on Ambae felt effectively beyond the colonial and postcolonial horizon, that is, beyond the government's reach and/or interest. They formulated codes of law for local places, which they were able to enforce so long as the offense was not something as serious as murder. This suggests, as Philibert (personal communication, 1991; see also Philibert 1988) has commented, that "for an encapsulated social group, going outside group boundaries is a double-edged weapon not to be resorted to very often as it is an admission of helplessness and an invitation to even greater intervention by outsiders. The more porous the boundary, the greater the need for secrecy and self-reliance." Envelopes of lived space in this instance insulate regional zones of power, and it is to questions of power and place that I now turn.

Power

As the opening quote from Foucault (1980:70) suggests, it is time to stop devaluing space and begin "to trace the forms of implantation, delimitation, and demarcation of objects, the modes of tabulation, the organisation of domains [which means] the throwing into relief of processes — historical ones, needless to say — of power." Lamont Lindstrom applies a discursive model of knowledge and power to the analysis of Tannese society in southern Vanuatu. This is Foucault in the bush, a fine illustration of how Foucault's ideas play out incisively in a non-European context. And he adds a new dimension to Foucault, for on Tanna, in Lindstrom's view, power *is* localized (1990:22). He regards "geography," or place, as one of three Tannese "disciplines" that organize people's know-how. (The others are medicine and magic.) Power is crucial in the uneven distribution of all disciplinary knowledge. Inequality is such that men, especially older ones, are the most qualified to "talk seriously" and exercise power (1990:59). The verbal power so evident among adult men is, as Lindstrom recognizes, muted in women and in the young, who tend to be silenced where serious talk occurs and power is expressed.

Lindstrom's explanation of the intricacies of discursive power is impressively systematic and smart. It comes at a time in the history of anthropological thought when systematicity needs the kind of conceptual rehabilitation he provides. By this I mean that Lindstrom recognizes the complexity of social patterns while never assuming that culture is a bounded whole. He traces the links between dreams, land disputes, kava drinking, and quashing dissent in national politics. He persuasively shows how, in all these domains, "knowledge is made to be ordinary or ridiculous, truth or lies" (1990:173). His analytic framework would work as well for Ambae, where I conducted fieldwork, as it does for Tanna. In this sense it provides a framework for regional analysis of discursive practice. But to understand nondiscursive power one would have to go further, taking place more seriously than Lindstrom does.

Practical rather than discursive knowledge organizes much of social life in Vanuatu. Lindstrom recognizes this but sets aside serious consideration of it in order to focus on his topic. Nondiscursive knowledge is harder for anthropologists to get at, even though it is expressed right before our eyes. Lindstrom acknowledges that "[s]ignificant bases of power stand outside conversation per se: the physical structures of village house and forest clearing mutely organize island talk" (1990:175). Nevertheless, he privileges the verbal, which in Vanuatu means privileging the powerful, those who "know how" (and are allowed) to talk.

Multivocality

To hear the voices of those silenced in island conversations requires listening with all of one's senses. Multivocality often involves multilocality. Polysemic places bespeak people's practices, their history, their conflicts, their accomplishments. Narratives of places are not just told with words; they can be told and heard with senses other than speech and hearing.[10] Such narratives can be expressed through the sight of a rock that grew, through certain smells, in the way the wind blows, or the taste of a mango. The house in which my family and I lived in Vanuatu looked out on a large rock that had been brought to the village as a small stone. The village itself was named for a wind shift that touched the cheek of a culture hero who was passing through. On his journey, like many an explorer, he named the places he "discovered" and, by discovering, created. He transformed the physical landscape into a multilocal, social one.

In *Masters of Tradition* (1987), I discussed the grounding of identity in place evident in both a child's and an old man's tour of the area surrounding the village where we lived. The rootedness of identity is similar to processes Salmond describes for the Maori, for whom "specific knowledge is 'bound into' specific landmarks" (1982:84).[11] The narrative landmarks of the influential old man included black palms that had once been little stakes to which tusked pigs were tied when he first took rank in the graded society. He pointed out palisades surrounding his natal village, now abandoned, that had taken root and grown into trees that towered above the forest floor. Warfare and pig killing were reciprocally related; pig killing signaled and required peace. Both rank-taking ceremonies and raids were multilocal phenomena. A rank-taker could not kill primarily his own pigs but was dependent on the gifts of others, often people from distant villages and even other islands. Warfare, too, was a multilocal pattern of shifting alliances.

The landscapes of the ten-year-old boy described in my book identified places with names and owners. In part, I think this reflected the emphasis on food in a boy's landscape. A boy needed to know who owned which mango tree, for example, to know if he could eat freely of the fruit. Unlike girls, who stayed close to home, boys on Ambae ran freely through plantations, gardens, and forest. Except for those who had an opportunity to travel by plane or boat, a boy's sense of place was of one continuous territory with clearly defined centers, paths, and boundaries. Place, while regionally zoned, was not locally fragmented, as in our own lives. But it was multilocal in that there were many connected, named places within that territory, places that linked living people and dead ones with the child through landmarks.

The landmarks of women also speak. As I mapped the village, a grandmother told me about the birth sites of her children. One birth house had been over here, another time she had given birth in a menstruation hut over there, realizing she would not make it to the hospital eight miles away in time. Although I put an X on my map in the locations she pointed out, they were marked by nothing I could see in the landscape. Yet for the old woman these memories were etched as clearly in the landscape as if they bore commemorative plaques. Other memories had visible landmarks with special meanings for her. She thought of her daughters every time she harvested nuts or mandarins from trees they had planted. One of the mandarin trees shaded the smoothed ground where the first house she and her husband had shared once stood.

In the woman's, child's, and man's narratives of place that I have described, use values predominate. The exchange value of the land that means so much to them is negligible, except for the portion of the old man's land planted in coconuts. The child and the woman have no claims of ownership in any case, but only rights of use. These use rights, nevertheless, are a modicum of power.

The most powerless people have no place at all. Here, as elsewhere, the discursive and practical worlds intersect. A widowed woman from Santo island remained on Ambae island for eight years after her husband's death. She lived in a house on land set aside for the Anglican church. She was allowed to use a garden belonging to her husband's kin, but she felt she lived on the sufferance of others. As Lindstrom (1990) might have predicted, she expressed her insecurity about having no place that was really her own by saying how afraid she was of talk: "If I weren't careful people would talk about me. They would say, 'Where's her place?'" (Rodman 1987:40). On my last visit to Ambae, she was dead and her bamboo home was gone. The house site had reverted to communal use. It had become the village volleyball court.

Moving houses, including disappearing ones like the widow's, trace multilocal social patterns in Vanuatu (Rodman 1985b). Overlays of village maps I made in the course of several field trips revealed tremendous individual mobility in an area where the total number of residents remained constant. Houses, as well as people, were moving around. A close analysis of this place-based phenomenon revealed a good deal about kinship and residence patterns. In another study (Rodman 1985a), I considered why the design of men's houses remained the same while women's house forms changed considerably with missionization.

Social Landscapes

A focus on place, like Marcus's multi-locale ethnographies, can eliminate the micro-macro distinction, for region and village are points on a sliding scale. Both are "social landscapes," albeit seen in different degrees of detail. The concept of a lived space is phenomenological, emphasizing individuals' experience in the world. But a "social landscape" takes a broader view of time and space. The concept is not new in Melanesian ethnography (cf. Leenhardt 1979[1947]). As developed by Pacific archeologist Chris Gosden (1989), it links the archeological record to the ways that social groups interact with landscapes that are partly structured by previous social groups. The social landscape is both context and content, enacted and material. It is the lived world in physical form. It can be radically emic — the social landscape indigenous people (collectively or individually) define through particular experiences or interests. Or it can be an analyst's map, marking "differences that make a difference," in Bateson's (1972:453) sense, and depicting the archeologist's classification or understanding of the local people's categories.

Miriam Kahn (1990) provides recent examples of the "spatial anchoring of myth" in what might well be viewed as social landscapes in Papua New Guinea.[12] She observes that places in the landscape, notably stones, are linked to mythical stories, often about traveling culture heroes or ancestors. "Melanesian ideas about the passage of time are conceived of in a spatial framework" (1990:61). Consequently, she argues, anthropologists should be careful not to give too much weight to verbal (discursive) communication; they should be more aware of the ways "myths are recorded and recalled by other devices, such as physical forms in the landscape. Stones, while not the only type of physical marker, provide pertinent and interesting examples of the Melanesian attachment to place and the recording of myth and history in terms of space" (Kahn 1990:53).

Through greater awareness of the social construction of meaning in the landscape, we can begin to understand the experience of places that live in ways different from our own. Places in Vanuatu, for example, include rocks that grow, people turned to stone, spirits, ancestors, and memories piled upon memories with scarcely a visible mark on the landscape to show that people lived there. Even islands move around. Two islands at either end of the beach in Port Olry on Santo island, where I studied fisheries development (Rodman 1989), moved to their present location from somewhere else. Another island, Araki, used to be there, too, but one day it moved off to a new location about fifty kilometers to the south. The moving island took some people's wives and other people's husbands along, much to the anger of the partners who were left behind. This multilocal narrative explains why the kinship systems of Araki and Port Olry are so similar.

Kahn asserts that "each village uses local landscape to make the myth its own" (1990:59). Each village, in this sense, creates its own social landscape, as does each person. But each community, or each individual, is also part of a chain of attachment to places. "Geographic copyright" (Lindstrom 1990:78) is the authority to speak in public about names and places. It would seem to apply as well to the Papua New Guinean situation of which Kahn writes as to Tanna. Men can silence the less knowledgeable or those who might be said to be out of place in speaking about what is not theirs. So when Kahn comments that Melanesians discredited each other's versions of a myth or discovered kin connections to each other through the fact that they told her identical details of a myth, she is speaking implicitly of this kind of "copyright." Each teller and each mythically charged stone is part of a social landscape whose horizons overlap other social landscapes. Individuals are most strongly attached to particular named places, and can speak of those places (and their pasts) with the most authority. But the story and its larger landscape binds them to other experts and other places.

Conclusion

The themes of power, multivocality, multilocality, narrativity, and social landscape are intertwined in a final example. The dynamic, socially constructed qualities of place in Ambae are especially evident at the boundaries expressed in funerary feasts. These feasts are heterotopias in Foucault's (1986) sense. They mark and contest boundaries between the living and the dead, between places, and between the conflicting interests of different people.

When a person dies, he or she does not go far from the land of the living for one hundred days. The dead person's spirit hovers near the tops of fruit trees or coconut palms, waiting and watching as kinsmen exchange gifts below. The dead person is still strongly attached to his or her place. Gift exchanges and feasting occur after every death, but the scale of the activity varies. The biggest and most contested ceremonies are those following the death of a major landholder. Landholders are almost always male.

Multilocality comes into play in understanding funerals at several levels. First, it is important to realize that the stakes have changed during the past half-century as plantation land has become commoditized. Elsewhere (Rodman 1987), I have described the multilocal "chain of copra" that linked the beaches of the colonial New Hebrides with oil-processing mills in Marseilles. Second, the use value of land for subsistence gardening and housing competed with the exchange value of the same land for growing coconuts that could be dried and sold as copra. If a person had access to multiple locales, he or she could earn some money from copra while still keeping a garden. Third, the funerary ceremonials dislocate dead individuals from the places that were integral to their identities as persons and, in establishing new ownership, shape new identities. In this sense, multilocality is the goal of the exchanges and feasts.

When a landholder dies, funerary feasts held every five days are competitive arenas in which each gift can help build a claim to the dead person's land. Knowledge about the history of the land's connection to people, living and dead, is displayed in competing men's verbal power plays and assertions of what Lindstrom calls "geographic copyright." The social landscape is in flux during the transition between one person's control of a large parcel of land and the new order that follows the feast on the hundredth day after a death. Multivocality is evident in the flow of competing gifts as some relatives use a rhetoric of "helping" to undercut each other's claims or give huge gifts to shame those who cannot reciprocate. It is evident, too, in the silences, in the women and less powerful men who would say they "cannot speak" to oppose an influential man who tries to take control of their dead relative's land through funerary gifts.

At the end of a hundred days, members of a dead person's matriline give a final gift that detaches the deceased from his or her place. With this gift, the dead person leaves the treetops and departs from the world of humans. (In the past, the spirit would have jumped off a cliff into the sea and ended up in the crater lake at the top of the island. Now, many feel, the spirit goes to heaven.) As this detachment of the person's identity from his or her place occurs, a new social landscape is affirmed, for these gifts also ensure that fertility will return to the dead person's trees. Death is turned to life in a living place as life moves on, away from the trees, to the place of death.

In this article, I have suggested that place should be taken more seriously. Although the problem of voice has received considerable attention, related problems of place have too often been reduced to questions of setting. We must acknowledge and try to understand the complex reality of the places in which we do fieldwork. But in empowering place conceptually, it must not be exoticized or misconstrued as the essence or totality of other cultures. Place must not become, for example, a metonym for Melanesia. The socially contested, dynamic construction of places represent the temporary grounding of ideas. These are often overlapping narratives of place, as the examples drawn from a man, woman, and child's landscapes illustrate. They can be competing narratives, as in the example of funerary feasts. We need to consider how different actors construct, contest, and ground experience in place.

Rather than being "incarcerated" (Appadurai 1988b) in ethnographic places anthropologists define, the people we study are constructing their own places. These places are not simply settings for social action, nor are they mere reflections of society. I have tried to show that Melanesian places can be as rich and polyphonous an expression as their voices. By joining multilocality to multivocality, we can look "through" these places, explore their links with others, consider why they are constructed as they are, see how places represent people, and begin to understand how people embody places.

Notes

Acknowledgments. Portions of an earlier version of this paper were presented at a workshop called "Not in Isolation: Regional Studies in Melanesian Anthropology," organized by John Terrell and Rob Welsch. The workshop, held April 3–5, 1991, at Field Museum of Natural History, was sponsored by the museum and by the Wenner-Gren Foundation for Anthropological Research. I am grateful to the sponsoring institutions, as well as to the Social Sciences and Humanities Research Council of Canada, which supported my research in Vanuatu in 1978, 1982, and 1985. The ethnographic material on funerals was part of a paper I gave at the 1991 annual meeting of the American Anthropological Association in an American Ethnological Society invited session organized by Setha Low. I am especially grateful to her and to William Rodman for their detailed suggestions and sustained support. I also appreciate the helpful comments made by anonymous reviewers, by Matthew Cooper, James Fernandez, Michael Lambek, and Edward Relph, and by participants in the Wenner-Gren workshop.

1. Although place generally has played a passive role in ethnography, some have taken its interaction with social life seriously from the earliest days of anthropology. Durkheim, Mauss, and Morgan all addressed the interplay between the built environment and society. For a discussion of early theories of accommodation and adaptation of people and places to each other, see Lawrence and Low (1990:456–457).

2. A notable exception is Ferguson and Gupta's (1992) theme issue of *Cultural Anthropology*, entitled "Space, Identity, and the Politics of Difference," which appeared as this article was in preparation.

3. See, for example, the papers in Agnew and Duncan (1989a), and in Buttimer and Seamon (1980).

4. The problem social analysts face of being part of the phenomena they study is at issue here. See Giddens's (1990:45 and earlier publications) comments on the reflexivity of knowledge and the double hermeneutic of modern social life.

5. Harris (1991) also notes the increasing importance of cultural context as historical geography becomes more interdisciplinary. Relph (1991:102) makes a similar observation regarding postmodern geography.

6. This view is shared with Soja (1989:11), who calls for spatializing the narrative of historical explanations integral to Marxist geography.

7. The Place and Space group meets at each American Anthropological Association annual meeting and keeps members informed of planned place-related sessions and meetings via a newsletter.

8. Marilyn Strathern (1988, 1991) has contributed a great deal to rethinking comparison through her concern with polyphony; see also Holy (1987) for a defense of the comparative method.

9. This section in no way seeks to deal comprehensively with literature from Melanesia about place. Were I to do so, Malinowski's (1922) "mythic landscapes" and Leenhardt's (1979[1947]) observations about space, social landscape, and personhood would be cornerstones of such a review. Instead, this section deals with a few, selected recent examples, mostly from Vanuatu, to apply the theoretical points made so far.

Place has also figured prominently in the work of the French geographer Joel Bonnemaison (1986), in Vanuatu. Other anthropologists who have written about place in Vanuatu include Larcom (1982), Rubinstein (1978), and Tonkinson (1982).

10. For a recent example of anthropology that acknowledges the importance of senses other than the auditory and verbal see Howes (1991).

11. Salmond (1982) compares the Maori embeddedness of knowledge and place with Western "theoretical landscapes," in which knowledge is represented metaphorically as if it were a territory.

12. Myths of rootedness are common in Melanesia. For another recent example of the persisting power of such myths see Gewertz and Errington's (1991:33–38) discussion of the mythic charter for construction of a Chambri men's house as, literally, a tourist "attraction."

References Cited

Agnew, John A., and James S. Duncan, eds.

1989a   The Power of Place. London: Unwin Hyman.

1989b   Introduction. *In* The Power of Place. John A. Agnew and James S. Duncan, eds. Pp. 1–8. London: Unwin Hyman.

Appadurai, Arjun

1988a   Introduction: Place and Voice in Anthropological Theory. Cultural Anthropology 3:16–20.

1988b   Putting Hierarchy in Its Place. Cultural Anthropology 3:36–49.

Basso, Keith

1988   "Speaking with Names": Language and Landscape among the Western Apache. Cultural Anthropology 3:99–130.

Bateson, Gregory

1972   Steps to an Ecology of Mind. New York: Ballantine.

Berdoulay, Vincent

1989   Place, Meaning, and Discourse in French Language Geography. *In* The Power of Place. John A. Agnew and James S. Duncan, eds. Pp. 124–139. London: Unwin Hyman.

728 RODMAN

Bonnemaison, Joel

1986 La Dernière Ile. Paris: Arlea-ORSTOM.

Brookfield, Harold C., with Doreen Hart

1971 Melanesia: A Geographical Interpretation of an Island World. London: Methuen.

Buttimer, Anne

1971 Society and Milieu in the French Geographic Tradition. AAG Monographs, Vol. 6. Chicago: Rand McNally.

Buttimer, Anne, and David Seamon, eds.

1980 The Human Experience of Space and Place. London: Croom Helm.

Castells, M.

1977 The Urban Question. London: Edward Arnold.

Claval, P.

1984 The Concept of Social Space and the Nature of Social Geography. New Zealand Geographer 40:105–109.

Cooper, M., and M. Rodman

1990 Conflict over Use Values in a Toronto Housing Cooperative. City and Society 4:44–57.

1992 New Neighbours: A Case Study of Cooperative Housing in Toronto. Toronto: University of Toronto Press.

Cultural Anthropology

1988 Theme Issue: Place and Voice in Anthropological Theory. 3(1).

Entrikin, J. Nicholas

1989 Place, Religion and Modernity. In The Power of Place. John A. Agnew and James S. Duncan, eds. Pp. 30–43. Winchester, MA: Unwin Hyman.

1991 The Betweenness of Place: Toward a Geography of Modernity. Baltimore, MD: Johns Hopkins University Press.

Fabian, Johannes

1990 Presence and Representation: The Other in Anthropological Writing. Critical Inquiry 16: 753–772.

Fardon, Richard

1990 General Introduction. In Localizing Strategies: Regional Traditions of Ethnographic Writing. R. Fardon, ed. Pp. 1–35. Washington, DC: Smithsonian Institution Press.

Ferguson, James, and Akhil Gupta, eds.

1992 Theme Issue: Space, Identity, and the Politics of Difference. Cultural Anthropology 7(1).

Fernandez, James W.

1982 Bwiti. Princeton, NJ: Princeton University Press.

1988 Andalusia on Our Minds. Cultural Anthropology 3:21–35.

Foucault, Michel

1970 The Order of Things. New York: Random House.

1980 Power Knowledge. Brighton: Harvester.

1986   Of Other Spaces. Diacritics 16(1):22–27.

Geertz, Clifford

1973   The Interpretation of Cultures. New York: Basic Books.

Gewertz, Deborah, and Frederick Errington

1991   Twisted Histories: Representing the Chambri in a World System. Cambridge: Cambridge University Press.

Giddens, Anthony

1979   Central Problems in Social Theory: Action, Structure and Contradictions in Social Analysis. Berkeley: University of California Press.

1984   The Constitution of Society. Berkeley: University of California Press.

1990   The Consequences of Modernity. Stanford, CA: Stanford University Press.

Gosden, Chris

1989   Prehistoric Social Landscapes of the Arawe Islands, West New Britain Province, Papua New Guinea. Archaeology in Oceania 24:45–58.

Gottdiener, M.

1985   The Social Production of Urban Space. Austin: University of Texas Press.

Gupta, Akhil, and James Ferguson

1992   Beyond "Culture": Space, Identity, and the Politics of Difference. Cultural Anthropology 7:6–23.

Harris, Cole

1991   Power, Modernity and Historical Geography. Annals of the Association of American Geographers 81(4):671–683.

Harvey, David

1973   Social Justice and the City. London: Edward Arnold.

1989   The Urban Experience. Baltimore, MD: Johns Hopkins University Press.

Holy, Ladislav, ed.

1987   Comparative Anthropology. Oxford: Basil Blackwell.

Howes, David, ed.

1991   The Varieties of Sensory Experience. Toronto: University of Toronto Press.

Jolly, Margaret

1990   Custom and the Way of the Land: The Politics of Tradition in Vanuatu and Fiji. Paper presented at the annual meeting of the Association for Social Anthropology in Oceania, Kauai, and Hawaii.

Kahn, Miriam

1990   Stone-Faced Ancestors: The Spatial Anchoring of Myth in Wamira, Papua New Guinea. Ethnology 29:51–66.

Larcom, Joan

1982   The Invention of Convention. Mankind 13(4):330–337.

Lawrence, Denise, and Setha Low

1990   The Built Environment and Spatial Form. Annual Reviews in Anthropology 19:453–505.

Leenhardt, Maurice
1979 [1947] Do Kamo: Person and Myth in the Melanesian World. B. M. Gulati, trans. Chicago: University of Chicago Press.

Ley, David, and M. Samuels, eds.
1978 Humanistic Geography. Chicago: Maaroufa Press.

Lindstrom, Lamont
1990 Knowledge and Power in a South Pacific Society. Washington, DC: Smithsonian Institution Press.

Logan, J., and H. Molotch
1987 Urban Fortunes: The Political Economy of Place. Berkeley: University of California Press.

Malinowski, Bronislaw
1922 Argonauts of the Western Pacific. London: Routledge and Kegan Paul.

Marcus, George
1989 Imagining the Whole: Ethnography's Contemporary Efforts to Situate Itself. Critique of Anthropology 9(3):7–30.

Marcus, George, and Michael Fischer
1986 Anthropology as Cultural Critique. Chicago: University of Chicago Press.

Munn, Nancy
1990 Constructing Regional Worlds in Experience: Kula Exchange, Witchcraft and Gawan Local Events. Man (N.S.) 25:1–17.

Nir, Dov
1990 Region as a Socio-environmental System: An Introduction to a Systemic Regional Geography. GeoJournal Library Series, Vol. 16. Wolf Tietze, ed. Boston: Kluwer Academic Publishers.

Philibert, Jean-Marc
1988 Women's Work: A Case Study of Proletarianization of Peri-urban Villagers in Vanuatu. Oceania 58(3):161–175.

Rabinow, Paul
1988 Beyond Ethnography: Anthropology as Nominalism. Cultural Anthropology 3:255–364.

Relph, Edward
1976 Place and Placelessness. London: Pion.
1991 Post-Modern Geography. Canadian Geographer 35(1):98–105.

Rodman, Margaret C.
1985a Contemporary Custom: Redefining Domestic Space in Longana, Vanuatu. Ethnology 24(4):269–279.
1985b Moving Houses: Residential Mobility and the Mobility of Residences in Longana, Vanuatu. American Anthropologist 87:56–72.
1987 Masters of Tradition: Consequences of Customary Land Tenure in Longana, Vanuatu. Vancouver: University of British Columbia Press.
1989 Deep Water: Development and Change in Pacific Village Fisheries. Boulder, CO: Westview Press.

Rodman, M., and M. Cooper
  1989 The Sociocultural Production of Urban Space: Building a Fully Accessible Toronto Housing Cooperative. City and Society 3:9–22.
Rodman, William L.
  1985 A Law Unto Themselves: Legal Innovation in Ambae, Vanuatu. American Ethnologist 4:603–622.
  1992 The State of the Law and the Law of the State in Vanuatu. In Contemporary Pacific Societies: Studies in Development and Change. Victoria Lockwood, Tom Harding, and Ben Wallace, eds. Pp. 55–66. Englewood Cliffs, NJ: Prentice Hall.
Rosaldo, Renato
  1988 Ideology, Place and People without Culture. Cultural Anthropology 3:77–87.
Rubinstein, Robert
  1978 Placing the Self on Malo: An Account of the Culture of Malo Island, New Hebrides. Ph.D. dissertation, Department of Anthropology, Bryn Mawr.
Said, Edward W.
  1989 Representing the Colonized: Anthropology's Interlocutors. Critical Inquiry 15:205–225.
Salmond, Anne
  1982 Theoretical Landscapes: On a Cross-Cultural Conception of Knowledge. In Semantic Anthropology. David Parkin, ed. Pp. 65–87. London: Academic Press.

Smith, Carol A., ed.
  1976 Regional Analysis, Vol. 2: Social Systems. New York: Academic Press.
Soja, Edward
  1989 Postmodern Geographies: The Reassertion of Space in Critical Social Theory. London: Verso Press.
Strathern, Andrew
  1990 Review of The Evolution of Papua New Guinea Societies, by D. K. Feil. American Ethnologist 17:376–383.
Strathern, Marilyn
  1988 Commentary: Concrete Typographies. Cultural Anthropology 3:88–96.
  1991 Partial Connections. ASAO Special Publications, No. 3. Deborah Gewertz, ed. Lanham, MD: University Press of America.
Tonkinson, Robert
  1982 National Identity and the Problem of Kastom in Vanuatu. Mankind 13(4):306–315.
Tuan, Yi-Fu
  1991 Language and the Making of Place: A Narrative-Descriptive Approach. Annals of the Association of American Geographers 81(4):684–696.
Werbner, R. P., ed.
  1977 Regional Cults. New York: Academic Press.
Williams, Raymond
  1977 Marxism and Literature. Oxford: Oxford University Press.

"Our Ancestors the Gauls":

Archaeology, Ethnic Nationalism, and the

Manipulation of Celtic Identity in Modern Europe

Michael Dietler

VOL. 96, 1994, 584–605

A united Gaul forming a single nation
animated by the same spirit can defy the universe.
— Caesar, *De Bello Gallico*, VII.29

These words are taken from Julius Caesar's account of his war of conquest against the Celtic peoples of western Europe in the first century B.C. He attributed them to his enemy Vercingetorix, leader of the last great defense of Gaul against the Roman legions. More important in the context of the present discussion, they are inscribed at the base of a monumental bronze statue of Vercingetorix (Figure 1) that surmounts the hilltop fortress of Alésia in Burgundy, the site of the final stand against the Romans. The statue was commissioned in 1865 by the French Emperor Napoleon III, who also lavishly financed archaeological excavations at the site. Over a century later, in 1985, standing in the middle of the nearby ancient hilltop fortress of Bibracte (Mont Beuvray), where Vercingetorix had attempted to rally a united opposition against the Romans, French president François Mitterand launched an appeal for national unity. Stating that Bibracte was the place where the "first act of our history took place" (Mitterrand 1985:54), he officially declared it a "national site." A monument was also erected to commemorate his visit, and archaeological excavations were begun with financing on an unprecedented scale.

It is my contention that such appeals to an ancient Celtic past have played and continue to play a number of important and often paradoxical roles in the ideological naturalization of modern political communities at several contradictory levels, including: (1) pan-European unity in the context of the evolving European Community, (2) nationalism within member states of that community, and (3) regional resistance to nationalist hegemony. An understanding of this complex process requires exploration of the ways in which language, objects, places, and persons have been differentially emphasized to evoke antiquity and authenticity at each of these levels in the process of constructing and manipulating emotionally and symbolically charged traditions of Celtic identity. As an archaeologist specializing in the study of those societies of ancient Iron Age Europe that serve as a touchstone of authenticity in the invocation of Celtic identity, I have an interest in examining the ways that archaeology has been appropriated, or has collaborated, in these "invented traditions" (Hobsbawm 1983), and its potential role in sorting out the competing claims of what Benedict Anderson (1983) has called "imagined communities."

An exploration of the relationship between archaeology and the construction of identity in modern communities is of considerable importance in Europe today, where attempts to establish a new supranational community are matched by a resurgence of xenophobic nationalism; where tensions based in emotionally charged appeals to ethnic heritage are currently erupting in violence in many areas; where the bonds holding many national polities together are fragmenting and reforming around smaller ethnic identities; and where archaeology has been conscripted frequently to establish and validate cultural borders and ancestry, often in the service of dangerous racist and nationalist mythologies.[1] Given that ethnicity and nationalism are such powerful forces in modern Europe, it is crucial for anthropologists to understand the historical processes through which identities are constructed and transformed by competing groups and the ways in which the distant past is marshaled as a symbolic resource to establish authenticity and continuity (Hobsbawm 1992; MacDonald 1993). It is equally important for archaeologists, as the principal conduit to that distant past, to develop a critical awareness of their own situation in this process in order to understand how it informs their practice by conditioning research goals, interpretation, and evaluation of knowledge claims and in order to recognize their responsibilities in presenting the past in the midst of rival appeals to its use in authenticating modern collective identities.

While there are many political cases worthy of investigation, this article focuses on the Celtic situation, both because Celtic identity has been such a widespread, diverse, and important force in recent European

Fig. 1. Bronze statue of Vercingetorix by Millet (1865), erected at the site of Alésia. The statue was commissioned by Napoleon III, and the face is modeled after his.

history and because its complex relationship to Iron Age archaeology has yet to be adequately explored. While any of several regions could serve as a fruitful focus for this analysis — including Ireland, Scotland, Wales, Cornwall, and Galicia — the discussion here will center largely around the case of France.[2]

The Ancient Celts
It is perhaps wise to begin with a brief consideration of what archaeologists know of those ancient societies to which modern historical communities seek to establish links of identity. What, for example, does the word *Celtic* mean and where does it come from? Today the term is applied to everything from a basketball team in Boston to a soccer team in Scotland, to art and music styles, and to a literary genre. As with the Boston Celtics basketball team, the term is generally assumed by Americans to refer to an affiliation with an ethnic heartland in Ireland or Scotland. However, it is highly unlikely that the people of either of these regions ever called themselves Celts before the 19th century. This identification is a product of modern historical philology, which recognized the linguistic connections between modern Irish Goidelic, Scots Gaelic, Welsh, Breton, Cornish, Manx, and the ancient Celtic languages of the continent (Prichard 1857; Zeuss 1853).

The term *Celt* first appeared in the historical record during the late sixth century B.C. in the works of a Greek geographer named Hecataeus of Miletus, who mentioned that a "barbarian" people called *Keltoi* lived beyond the Ligurian peoples inhabiting the hinterland of Marseille in southern France (Tierney 1960:194). About a century later, Herodotus noted that the Danube River had its source in the territory of the Celts (*Historiai* 2.33). The Celts thus became, for the Mediterranean world, the first alien people on their northern border to emerge out of the mists of prehistory with a seemingly coherent identity. By the fourth century B.C., groups of these peoples crossed the Alps to wage war on the classical world. From this time until the first century B.C., when the Roman Empire expanded militarily to incorporate most of these peoples within its sphere of hegemony, Greek and Roman authors fleshed out the earlier sketchy references with descriptions of Celtic cultural practices and physical appearance. Celts also began to appear in classical statuary and vase painting (Andreae 1991).

Greeks generally called these peoples "Celts" (*Keltoi*), while Romans preferred to call them "Gauls" (*Galli, Galatae*), although usage was inconsistent and it is far from clear how these names related to native conceptualizations of identity (Chapman 1982; Renfrew 1987). Julius Caesar, for example, noted that Romans used the term "Gauls" to designate people who called themselves "Celts" (*De Bello Gallico* I.1). Strabo, on the other hand, wrote that the inhabitants of the hinterland of the Greek colony of Marseille in southern France were called "Celts" and that Greeks simply projected this name onto all the barbarian peoples of northwestern Europe (*The Geography* IV.I.14). The term *Celt* was never applied by classical authors to the inhabitants of Britain or Ireland, although we now know that these insular peoples spoke dialects similar to those of continental Gaul before the latter peoples gradually abandoned their mother tongue in favor of Latin. Scholars today usually reserve the term *Celtic* to designate a group of closely related languages of the Indo-European family that were spoken in the first millennium B.C. over large portions of central and western Europe and that are now spoken only in Ireland, Scotland, Wales, and Brittany.[3] This linguistic unity was recognized only in the 18th century and well documented only in the 19th century.[4] Ironically, if Strabo is correct in his etymology of the term *Celtic*, it is quite possible that the original Celts may have spoken Ligurian rather than the language that their name has subsequently come to signify (Greene 1964:14).

Speakers of these languages are portrayed in historical texts of the classical world and in the much later heroic and legal literature of early Christian Ireland. They are also represented in the archaeological record of the Iron Age by the remnants of their material culture, settlements, and burials (Collis 1984; Moscati 1991). Certain aspects of Iron Age material culture, such as the well-known La Tène art styles (Megaw and Megaw 1989), exhibit considerable similarity over wide regions. However, much of the material culture shows a great deal of local variation over both time and space, and it would be misleading to speak of anything as homogeneous as a unified "Celtic culture" that could be linked isomorphically to a linguistic community or population. For example, it is not possible to assume that all peoples represented in the archaeological record by La Tène material culture spoke Celtic languages or that all ancient Celtic speakers participated in the La Tène material culture complex; there is, at best, a rather general correlation. It is more appropriate to think of ancient Celtic speakers in terms of a fluid network of autonomous societies speaking a set of related languages, linked by exchange, and differentially sharing certain cultural elements, but exhibiting considerable variation in political organization and other sociocultural structures and practices resulting from local trajectories of historical development. It is doubtful that the peoples of these diverse societies ever had a cohesive collective identity or ethnonym, and they clearly never constituted a unified political community. The Gaul portrayed by Caesar on the eve of his conquest consists of a series of named tribal polities linked through patron-client relations into a shifting configuration of unstable alliances engaged in mutual hostilities (Crumley 1987).

The term *Celtic* is clearly a dubious candidate for an indigenous ethnonym for the peoples that constitute the raw material from which Celtic identity has been fashioned in modern Europe. It first entered the historical record as an alien classificatory concept used in ancient Mediterranean states, projecting an outsider's sense of uniformity upon diverse peoples. Gradually, as contact with these peoples increased, this sense of uniformity was bolstered by generalizations about character, customs, and physical appearance. These generalizations were based in part on observations made in a few limited areas, but also largely on prejudices born of the conceptualization of "barbarians" as a necessary source of contrast for self-definition as "civilized" Greeks and Romans.[5] In the course of modern European history, this classical conceptualization has been influential in the reinvention of two types of essentializing concepts of Celticity. Sometimes Celtic identity has been constructed as a means of classifying "others" and ascribing characteristics to them that serve as a means of self-defining contrast, as in the case of English prejudices concerning the Irish and Scots (Chapman 1978, 1982; Curtis 1968). However, as in the cases examined in this article, Celticism has also been adopted and developed indigenously as a concept of ethnic self-identity, often relying heavily on more positive readings of these same alien stereotypical images from the ancient classical world.

French Nationalism and Celtic Identity

Let us begin the analysis of Celticism with a consideration of the role of Celtic identity in French nationalism. Postrevolutionary France is a classic case of the state preceding the nation and then having to forge a sense of national identity for an invented community of people who had little in common except a political bond and who did not even speak the same language. Naturalization of this invented sense of popular unity required establishing sentiments of authenticity through appeals to the antiquity of a common ethnic heritage. Given the history of France, there are three major strands of ethnic identity that could have been drawn upon. Each of these was invoked in the struggle for power by which the French nation was formed and transformed, and it is revealing to examine which of these identities was emphasized at different periods by different social groups, factions, and classes in the construction of a French nationalist tradition.[6] One possibility was provided by the people after whom the country is named: the Franks. These were Germanic-speaking peoples who penetrated Gaul in the waning days of the Roman Empire and established the Merovingean dynasty in the fifth century A.D. (James 1988). The other two possibilities were the Iron Age Celts (or Gauls) and the Romans who conquered them in the first century B.C.

Frankish identity was jealously monopolized by the nobility and royalty until the Revolution of 1789. By tracing their roots and the birth of the nation back to the fifth-century reign of the Frankish king Clovis, the nobility were able to assert the legitimacy of their rule through its supposed origin in the right of conquerors over the mass of subject commoners. The fact that Clovis converted to Christianity provided the monarchy with convenient connections to the church and divine sanction of its rule. This naturalization of class distinction through appeals to differences of ethnic identity tended to take on a strongly racial character, as in the influential historical writings of the Comte de Boulainvilliers (1727). He repeatedly asserted that France was composed of two races of people: the nobility, who were the descendants of the Franks, and the Third Estate, who were descended from the Gallo-Romans. The former were, by virtue of conquest, "the only people recognized as lords and masters" (Boulainvilliers 1727, III:84). As Barzun (1932) and Poliakov (1971) have pointed out, this concept served to bolster the objections of Boulainvilliers and his peers to the creeping social mobility whereby bourgeois commoners ("Gauls") were being promoted by the king into positions among the nobility. Despite the rare objections of skeptics such as Voltaire, the historical and philosophical literature of the time reflects a general acceptance among intellectuals of the ethnic construction of class.

This invented ethnic/racial dichotomy, ideologically underpinning the class structure, formed an obvious focus of popular countermobilization with the outbreak of the Revolution of 1789. Celtic identity was used both to oppose the nobility in a revolution represented as a racial conflict and, subsequently, as a unifying theme in the new process of popular nationalism by which the nation was defined as a community. For example, the Abbé de Sieyès (1789) urged that those claiming to be a race of conquerors should be "sent back to the forests of Franconia" by the Third Estate in order to purge the nation, which would then be "constituted solely of the descendants of the Gauls and Romans."

The revolutionary leaders, having disposed of the Franks as a legitimate source of ethnic identity for the new republican nation, were faced with crafting a new popular tradition out of the heritage of the ambivalent relationship between the ancient Celts and their Roman conquerors. The dynamic tension of this relationship, which a later writer likened to the "two poles necessary for electricity" (Schrader 1898:85), offered myriad possibilities for symbolic manipulation that were exploited in complex ways throughout French history. The democratic institutions of the ancient Roman Republic constituted an attractive precedent, and much of the political vocabulary of the revolutionary government was inspired by Rome. The members of the *Directoire* even adorned themselves in crimson Roman togas while legislating (Séguy 1989). But while Rome provided a source for institutional models, the Celts provided a better potential foundation for an emotionally charged sense of ethnic community. Although there had been scattered scholarly interest in the Celts before the revolution, including some suggestions of national origins and the first use of the phrase "our ancestors the Gauls" (Pelloutier 1740; Pezron 1703), the Celts had not been a popular candidate for ancestry aside from fanciful speculations about their place in schemes of biblical genealogy devised for the nation by a few "Celtomaniacs" (Dubois 1972). The revolution, however, found the Celts undergoing an image transformation through the influence of the pan-European popularity of the Ossian epic forgeries (Trevor-Roper 1983) and the Romantic Celtophilia of writers such as Walter Scott and Chateaubriand. La Tour d'Auvergne (1792) went so far as to claim that Celtic was the original human language. Amid cries that "We are descended from the pure-blooded Gauls," it was even proposed that the name of France be abandoned (Poliakov 1971:29).

With the establishment of the French Empire under Napoleon, the ambiguous possibilities of the relationship between Celtic and Roman identities were further developed. On the one hand, Napoleon furthered the popular republican tradition of Gallic identity by founding the *Académie Celtique* in 1805, with the Empress Josephine as its patron. The task of this body of scholars was to exhaustively research Celtic antiquities and languages in order to "avenge our ancestors" for the neglect they had suffered as a result of the contempt of the Greeks and Romans and to restore to the Celts the glory they deserved (Johanneau 1807:62–63). A political goal may also be detected in the project of the academy: an ideological justification of the military expansion of the boundaries of the French Empire, "which, through a series of brilliant victories, has reclaimed all the ancient territory of the Gauls" (Mangourit 1807:65). Johanneau claimed in his opening address to the academy that "nearly all the peoples of Europe are descendants of the Celts, almost all are children of *la Celtique:* newly reunited, they nearly all form again today a single great family under one federative government," but he added the stipulation that, "as the eldest daughter of *la Celtique,*" France should have the best and largest part of the "glorious heritage" of the Celts (Johanneau 1807:42).

Napoleon was even more intrigued by the symbolic potential of the Roman imperial legacy as a naturalization of his aspirations for French military conquest and the legitimacy of his own rule as emperor. His invocation of Roman symbols is evident in such things as the construction of monumental triumphal arches, the portraits of himself in chariot and laurel crown by Ingres and David, and his status in Roman garb atop the monumental column of the Place Vendôme, which imitates Trajan's Column at Rome. According to Hautecoeur, Napoleon insisted that public monuments "ought always to be in the style of the Romans. His empire ought to be the continuation of that Empire which spread from Egypt to the British Isles" (quoted in Ridley 1992:1). Not coincidentally, after centuries of neglect, the first systematic archaeological excavations and restoration of ancient monuments in Rome were undertaken by the French under Napoleon's orders at precisely this time (Ridley 1992).

A brief resurgence of Frankish national ancestry during the Bourbon Restoration was cut short during the Revolution of 1830 by a forceful counterattack on the part of Celtophile Romantic historians such as Guizot, the Thierry brothers, and Henri Martin. This movement permanently established the Celts as a primary ethnic foundation for the modern French nation through the popularization of an essentialist racial vision of Celtic identity and French history. Here began the construction of a heroic nationalist myth founded in the Celtic past, focused on the character of Vercingetorix, that would develop dramatically later in the century.

With the return of the French Empire under Napoleon III in 1852, the dynamic tension between Celtic and Roman identities also returned. It was personalized through a focus on the two dominant characters in the historical drama of the Roman conquest: Vercingetorix and Caesar. Napoleon III (1865–66) wrote a two-volume study of the life of Caesar while at the same time founding the Museum of National Antiquities. He also financed excavations at three of the main Iron Age settlements that had witnessed major events during the revolt of Vercingetorix: Alésia (the site of the final Celtic defeat), Gergovia (the site of a victory of the Celts over Caesar), and Bibracte (where Vercingetorix attempted to rally united opposition against the Romans). From his personal treasury he commissioned the sculptor Millet to create at Alésia a monumental bronze statue of Vercingetorix with the face modeled after his own (see Figure 1).

Napoleon's choice of Alésia (rather than Gergovia or Bibracte) as the site for the statue reveals his conception of the identity of the French nation and of the utility of this ancient conflict as a national symbol. It was, as he saw it, the site both of heroic self-sacrifice by the Gauls in defense of their nation and of the ultimately beneficial, if temporarily painful, victory of Roman "civilization" over "barbarism." As he wrote,

> In honoring the memory of Vercingetorix, we must not lament his defeat. Let us admire the ardent and sincere love of this Gallic chief for the independence of his country, but let us not forget that it is to the triumph of the Roman armies that our civilization is due. [Napoleon III 1866:397]

While admitting that Roman domination was accomplished "across streams of blood, it is true," he concluded that it "led these peoples to a better future" (Napoleon III 1866:397). This notion of the ultimate transformative benefits of the Roman enrichment of a proud barbarian people served as a subtle and convenient rationalization for expanding French colonial hegemony in Indochina, North Africa, and other overseas locations, while at the same time emphasizing, on the model of the Gauls, the wisdom and benefits of native submission to this heir of the Roman Empire. As a secondary school text of the period succinctly put it, "The Gauls had sufficient intelligence to understand that civilization is better than barbarism" (quoted in Gerard 1982:361). An informal survey by Goudineau (1990) suggests that this perspective on the Roman conquest is still influential.

At the same time that Alésia was being transformed into a physical symbol of colonial legitimacy, Vercingetorix, the fulcrum of this historical moral lesson, was being promoted to the role of an increasingly popular embodiment of French patriotism and national character. Indeed, the period from 1850 to 1914 marked a virtual frenzy of Celtic identity and the rise of Vercingetorix from obscurity to the status of a preeminent national hero (Simon 1989). Street names in Paris and elsewhere were changed to Vercingetorix, Gergovie, and Place des Gaules,

Fig. 2. Bronze statue of Vercingetorix by Bartholdi (1870), erected in the Place
de Jaude, Clermont-Ferrand, in 1903

and Gauls became a common theme of artwork and popular and scholarly literature. Pingeot (1982) lists over 200 sculptures of Gallic themes
by over 130 artists during this period, of which a number were monumental bronze works erected in town squares around France. Many
of these, like Millet's at Alésia (Figure 1), Bartholdi's in the center of
Clermont-Ferrand (Figure 2), and Mouly's in Bordeaux, were heroic

depictions of Vercingetorix. One statue of 1872 by Chatrousse carries the patriotic historical symbolism to the extreme by depicting Vercingetorix and Joan of Arc advancing hand in hand (Viallaneix and Ehrard 1982:9). Another sculptor, Préault, proposed to construct for Napoleon III "an acropolis of Gallic civilization" out of a mountain in the center of France, bedecked with monumental statues of Celtic warriors and topped by a 40-meter statue of a mounted Vercingetorix resting on a pedestal composed of arms, tools, and symbolic objects of "our ancestors" (Pingeot 1982). The Gauls also became popular subjects for a stream of books, including novels, plays, historical treatises, and military analyses of the Celtic-Roman battles. For the period between 1882 and 1925 alone, the catalogue of the Bibliothèque Nationale registered over 210 works on the Gauls (Croisille 1982:329). Moreover, the mid–19th century marked the first production of a continuing series of entire works specifically about Vercingetorix (Simon 1989:147–153), a character who is known really from only a few passages in Caesar's *Gallic Wars* and stylized depictions on a few coins.

It was also during this period that Vercingetorix began appearing in French schoolbooks for the first time, along with the conceptualization of national identity encapsulated in the cliché "our ancestors the Gauls." History became a mandatory subject in French primary schools only in 1867, two years after the erection of the statue of Vercingetorix at Alésia. The philosophy of primary education, which had a profound influence on the mass of the French population, favored instruction of national history through a focus on heroes and dramatic events. Vercingetorix became the seminal French national hero (Amalvi 1982). In special popularized texts by Celtophile historians, this primary historical education was accompanied by heroic drawings of "our ancestors" (Guizot 1872; Martin 1865). All these artistic and educational media served to widely diffuse and fix firmly in the popular imagination this invented tradition of national identity. An ironic byproduct of the educational system under French colonial administration is that generations of Vietnamese and African children also grew up reciting the phrase "our ancestors the Gauls."[7]

Much of the most fervent French Celticism, with a new focus on Vercingetorix as a national martyr and symbol of revenge, occurred after the humiliating French defeat by the Prussians in 1870. One year after the establishment in 1876 of the first chair of Celtic studies in France at the École Pratique des Hautes-Etudes, Albert Réville attributed a surge of interest in Celtic studies to a national crisis of identity. His comforting conclusion was that, despite some superficial influence on the course of the historical development of the nation from Roman and Germanic invaders, the French still exhibit the same characteristics Caesar described for the Celts and they are profoundly Gallic "in terms of character and blood" (Réville 1877:839). Moreover,

> Vercingetorix is for us more than a brave warrior. . . . . He had already the French physiognomy. . . . He fought and died not for a canton, not for a petty realm, not for a dynasty, but *pro patria*, for the Gallic fatherland which is still ours. [Réville 1877:867]

Race remained a powerful theme throughout the 19th and into the 20th century. It was prominent in the widely influential writings of the Romantic historians Guizot (1820), Thierry (1866), and Martin (1852), and it was lent further legitimacy by the writing of early physical anthropologists such as Broca (1873) and Topinard (1878). The latter, for example, stated that "the impulses inherent in the cerebral matter are so tenacious, in spite of education and civilisation, that they still continue after crossing and mixture of races, and are of assistance in recognizing them," concluding that "the predominating character of the French race is still that of the Gauls described by Caesar" (Topinard 1878:409). Much effort was also expended in attempting to define the physical characteristics of "the Celtic type," which, in contrast to the tall, dolichocephalic "Germanic race," was identified as short, dark, and brachycephalic (Broca 1873:591). Bretons were conceded to be an approximation of this type, but the purest living representatives, with a high brachycephalic index and a cranial capacity "considerably greater than that of Parisians," and with a physical type that "may be looked on as that of the people of Celtica at the time of Caesar and Strabo" (Topinard 1878:460), were held to be the inhabitants of the Auvergne, in the center of France. These Auvergnats were considered direct descendants of "the people who held firmly aloft the banner of national independence on the heights of Gergovia and Alésia."

Camille Jullian (1913), on the other hand, explicitly eschewed the racial perspective, arguing instead for the continuity of the political concept of a Celtic nation, a *"patrie Gauloise,"* which had "motivated Vercingetorix" and which was the source of modern patriotic sentiment (Jullian 1913:68). He believed that Gauls and Gaul "were the names of a people, of a nation constituted in a fixed territory, corresponding more or less to that of France," and that the inhabitants of that nation, although racially mixed, "sang together memories of their past and hopes for their future" (Jullian 1913:68). These views of an eternal Celtic nation with Vercingetorix as an embodiment of its heroic values were a powerful influence in marshaling sentiments of revenge against the Germans and in legitimizing the drive to reestablish the "natural" borders of France. On a larger, pan-Celtic scale, there were even several proposals during the 1890s for the formation of a *Confédération des Gaules*, with France, Belgium, the Netherlands, and a new Republic of the Rhine united to counter German power (Carbonell 1982:394).

Although the period of the Second Empire and the Third Republic undoubtedly marks the apex of emotional popular engagement with the nationalist tradition of Celtic identity, the Celts have continued to serve an important — if more subtle — role in this domain up to the present. As in the past, there have been continuing shifts in the nuances of the symbolic meaning of the places, objects, and persons used to invoke this link to the past and continuing struggles between factions to appropriate these symbols. During World War II, for example, the occupation government of Marshall Pétain and the Resistance struggled for control of the Celtic heritage. In 1942, Pétain organized a ceremony of national unity on the site of Gergovia, with representatives bringing handfuls of soil from all over the French Empire to deposit at the monument erected on the plateau where Vercingetorix and the Gauls had inflicted a defeat on the Roman invaders. The speeches delivered at this event sought to explicitly identify Pétain with Vercingetorix, emphasizing the fact that each, in the wisdom of surrender to overwhelming force, had sacrificed himself to save the nation (Ehrard 1982:313–314). The Resistance, of course, had a rather different reading of the symbolism of Vercingetorix, emphasizing instead his campaign of insurrection against the Roman conqueror and his status as France's first resistance leader (Simon 1989: 117–118). The fact that many of the 19th-century monumental bronze statues of Vercingetorix were later melted down by the Vichy government, whereas those of Joan of Arc were not touched, suggests that Pétain eventually came to regard the symbol of Vercingetorix as a threat (Pingeot 1982).

This manipulation of Celtic heritage has continued to play a role in the factionalism of French political life. In the same year that Socialist

President François Mitterrand gave his address at Bibracte, a newspaper photograph taken at the annual festival of the extreme right-wing Front National party showed a young member sporting a badge with the characteristically xenophobic slogan "Gaul for the Gauls." He is standing in front of a poster with a short list of French national heroes that begins with Vercingetorix and ends with Jean-Marie Le Pen, the leader of the party (Brocard 1985:11). The archaeological sites at which Napoleon III first undertook excavations have also continued to anchor national ethnic mythology in a sense of place (Crumley 1991). In addition to the appeals for national unity launched by Pétain at Gergovia in 1942 and by Mitterrand at Bibracte in 1985, the opposition leaders Giscard d'Estaing and Jacques Chirac chose the site of Gergovia, where Vercingetorix accomplished "the first victory of France," to kick off their campaigns for European elections in 1989 with a speech stressing the "continuance of French identity" (Carton 1989:10).

The ideologically naturalizing sense of a national Celtic heritage continues to be subtly reinforced in childhood socialization through schoolbooks, comic books, and illustrated histories.[8] Perhaps the best-known example is the enormously popular Asterix the Gaul comic series, the first issue of which opened with a depiction of the surrender of Vercingetorix to Caesar. Asterix has even spawned a Disneyland-style theme park outside Paris called *Parc Astérix*, paralleled in Ireland by the newly constructed Celtworld theme park. Everyday images of the Celtic heritage in France are present in everything from the state-owned *Gauloises* cigarettes to the myriad bars and cafés named *Le Gaulois*. The Gauls continue to excite the imagination of intellectuals, as well, resulting in a stream of publications, both popular and scholarly, on subjects such as Vercingetorix, druids, and Celtic military matters (for example, Harmand 1984; Lance 1978). That this multimedia invocation of the Gauls has been effective in subtly inculcating and maintaining an axiomatic sense of Celtic national identity is shown by a recent survey on the heroes of schoolchildren of 8 to 11 years of age. In the category of "history, politics, and current affairs," Vercingetorix ranked third. He was bested only by two current French political figures (including the president) and finished three places ahead of Joan of Arc (*Le Monde* 1979:14). It is also evident that, even among well-educated French adults, the sense of a Gallic heritage is something other than a product of accurate historical knowledge (Goudineau 1990:17–19).

Brittany

It is ironic that republican enthusiasm for establishing a nation with claims to authenticity rooted in the ancient Celtic past should have nearly succeeded in wiping out the one surviving link to Celtic identity that had a reasonable claim to continuity: the language spoken by the people of Brittany. It is equally ironic that regional resistance by the people of Brittany to a French state claiming descent from "our ancestors the Gauls" has centered around their counterclaims to Celtic ethnicity. A final irony is that some of the earliest Celtophiles responsible for the invention of the French nationalist myth (such as Dom Pezron and La Tour d'Auvergne) were of Breton origin, and nationalist French Celticists once looked admiringly toward the Breton people, their language, and their folklore as primitive living relics of the ancient nation of the Gauls.[9]

Brittany is not the only French region to have constructed a local vision of Celtic identity: Burgundy, for example, has an invented folkloric tradition of Celtic fire festivals (Marquardt and Crumley 1987). However, no region has had such a pervasive identification with Celtic identity as Brittany, and nowhere else has this identity served as such a strong focus for regional resistance to state hegemony. The development of the essentialist vision of Celtic identity promoted by the Breton movement is, of course, every bit as complicated in its symbolic nuances and its historical relationship to French nationalist ideology as the development of the nationalist myth.[10]

The basic paradox of the Breton situation is rooted in the fact that French nationalists and Breton regionalists seized upon language and history to construct competing ideological traditions of common identity for their imagined communities of Celts (Nicolas 1986:18). The language paradox is a product of the determination of the newly formed postrevolutionary French state to establish linguistic uniformity throughout the nation and the pragmatically arbitrary nature of the choice of the language used for this purpose. Despite suggestions that the new nation should revive and adopt Celtic, a language that had not been spoken in France outside of Brittany for nearly two millennia, the more practical solution of promoting the Latin-derived language of the Parisian state center as a national language was adopted. At the time of the founding of the French revolutionary state, however, only about 20 percent of the population of the country could properly speak French, and at least 30 percent could not understand it at all (Certeau et al. 1975). The state thus set out on a quasi-religious crusade to instill national unity by bringing French civilization, including especially the French language, to what were viewed as backward rural provinces. Regional languages and dialects became prime targets in the strategy designed to eradicate local popular cultures. The Celtic language of the people of Brittany became a victim of this process and, consequently, it has more recently been promoted as a symbolic focus of regional resistance by militants of the Breton movement.

The history of the decline of the Breton language is a complicated one that involves more than active suppression.[11] Initially, the Breton language and people were viewed by the Jacobin state as a reactionary threat. The promotion of French over Breton in schools and in official discourse was seen as a way of bringing these provincial peasant folk out of dangerous ignorance, superstition, and isolation into political community with the enlightened, rational, progressive nation. As Barère, the sponsor of a law mandating French language instruction, put it: "superstition speaks *bas breton*" (quoted in Certeau et al. 1975:10).

By the 20th century, the combined effects of Francophone educational policies, the stigma of rural backwardness as Brittany (especially the urban areas) became more integrated into the French economy, and the demand of the national bureaucracy for competent French speakers were causing the number and territorial extent of Breton speakers to shrink rapidly, with the linguistic frontier moving steadily westward. Since 1968, support for the Breton language has shifted from the right to the left wing of the political scale, and active revival of Breton (through instructional programs and publications) has been pushed forcefully by regional activists, especially intellectuals. To militants, competence in Breton is a fundamental aspect of the essentialist vision of ethnic identity they have constructed, though many of them are young, urban, Francophone intellectuals who learned Breton as a second language (McDonald 1989).

Most current Breton speakers are confined to an ever smaller rural portion of the unofficial region of Lower Brittany (the western part of the peninsula), while Upper Brittany (including the provincial capital of Rennes) has been historically French-speaking. Estimates are difficult to verify, but surveys from several sources in the 1980s put the number of people able to speak Breton at around 650,000 to 685,000, or about 45 percent of the population of Lower Brittany, although less than half of these spoke it often (Abalain 1989:207). There are four major dialects of modern Breton, with differences dating back several centuries.[12]

Linguistic features have played an important role in the construction of a historical model of the origin of the Breton people, which is a central feature of the vision of Celtic identity promoted by Breton militants. This model stresses close historical links with insular Celtic peoples in Cornwall, Wales, Ireland, and Scotland and denies connections with the continental Gauls, thus allowing an ethnic opposition to the French nation claiming Gallic ancestry. Militants consider Brittany not as a province of France but as an independent Celtic nation allied by ethnic kinship to other "oppressed" insular Celtic nations. This ethnic interpretation rests on the idea that Brittany was repopulated on a massive scale by Celtic immigrants from ancient Briton from the fourth to the sixth century and that Old Breton is a derivative of the language spoken by insular Celtic immigrants rather than a revived form of the indigenous Gallic language that had persisted during the Roman occupation.

This model of Breton ethnic origins represents a radical reversal of concepts that held sway until the 1840s (Guiomar 1987; Tanguy 1977). Until that time, kinship between Bretons and Gauls was an accepted fact and Brittany was seen as a living relic of ancient Gaul. It was for precisely this reason that members of the Académie Celtique were so interested in studying Breton language and folklore. However, the new, revised version of Breton origins gradually became institutionalized orthodoxy during the 1840s and 1850s. This was due in large measure to the influence of Hersart de la Villemarqué and several of his archaeological colleagues. In 1839 he had published the *Barzaz Breiz*, the Breton equivalent of the Ossian folkloric-epic invented in late-18th-century Scotland.

During the 1840s Villemarqué was instrumental in the addition of an archaeology section to the newly formed *Association bretonne*. Soon afterwards, archaeological societies were formed in each of the Breton *départements*. Two prominent archaeologists, Courson and La Borderie, argued forcefully at congresses of the Association bretonne and in print that Celtic immigrants chased from Briton by the invading Anglo-Saxons had settled in a Breton peninsula that had been left vacant by the indigenous Romanized Gauls during the fourth century (Courson 1863). This historical scenario triumphed over counterarguments claiming an ethnic continuity of the indigenous Gauls (Guiomar 1987; Tanguy 1977). The only major significant remaining debate after the 1850s concerned whether the immigrants had settled in a completely vacant land — the view favored by Villemarqué, Courson, and La Borderie — or whether they had inundated and enslaved a remnant population of Gauls (Loth 1883).

The archaeological evidence for or against the idea of a massive migration of insular Celts to Brittany is rather meager and ambiguous, at best, and the historical evidence is equally problematic (Galliou and Jones 1991:128–134). The strongest support for the massive incursion model comes from the evidence of place names (Falc'hun 1981; Fleuriot 1980). Other linguistic evidence is more difficult to interpret because most Celtic dialects of ancient Gaul appear to have been of the same general "P-Celtic" (or Brittonic) variety as Breton, Welsh, and Cornish (Whatmough 1970). Some scholars have noted close connections between Breton, Cornish, and (more distantly) Welsh and have hypothesized a common root protolanguage for the three (Jackson 1967; Loth 1883). Others have returned to a view of Breton — especially the Vannetais dialect — as being derived from the Celtic of the Continental Gauls. For Falc'hun, as for the Académie Celtique of the 19th century, "Breton preserves the last living vestiges of the first national language of France, that of Vercingetorix" and it is "a key to a better understanding of the Celtic past of the whole of France" (Falc'hun 1981:10).

Whatever the historical validity of a model of exclusive ethnic kinship with insular Celts, it has been adopted as a fundamental tenet by the Breton movement and it has helped to spawn a pan-Celtic cultural movement. Breton, Welsh, Irish, Scottish, and Cornish activists attend Interceltic Congresses (an institution started by Villemarqué in 1867) and publish in each other's journals. Reinvented druidic rituals have been imported from Wales, and druids from both sides of the English Channel officiate at common ceremonies (Nicolas 1985:56; Piggott 1968:123–182). Activists share a common cause of resistance to a perceived "cultural genocide" inflicted by France and England as well as a sense of mission to re-Celticize their ethnic homelands through linguistic and cultural revival.[13]

The European Community

Perhaps the most ironic of the three cases examined here is the attempt to establish authenticity through links to Celtic antiquity for the newest and largest imagined community on the European scene, the European Community (EC). Over a dozen major exhibitions on Celtic archaeology have been mounted in Europe since 1980, most of them well financed, sponsored by more than one nation, and constructed with objects from a wide array of countries. The political theme of these exhibitions is rarely far from the surface, and it conforms perfectly to the strategy for the formation of an integrated European identity through emphasis on cultural heritage, as charted by the European Commission (Shore and Black 1992). An early exhibition, held in Steyr, Austria, was subtitled "An Early Form of European Unity," while the most recent, mounted in Venice in 1991, is entitled "The Celts: The First Europe."

The catalogues of these exhibits are peppered with allusions to the Celts as constituting "the ethnic and cultural foundation of most western peoples" (Otte 1987:11). According to the catalogue of a recent Franco-Belgian exhibition on Celtic archaeology,

> The history of Europe begins with the Celts. The Celtic peoples were able to develop an original culture of great richness, the reflection of a singular spirit which will remain henceforward an essential component of the intellectual evolution of our countries. The multiform heritage of this 'First Europe' remains no less today one of the principal factors of our cohesion. [Kruta 1990:8]

Perhaps most explicit of all is the Venice exhibit, the introduction to which states that

> it was conceived with a mind to the great impending process of the unification of western Europe, a process that pointed eloquently to the truly unique aspect of the Celtic civilization, namely its being the first historically documented civilization on a European scale. . . . We felt, and still feel, that linking the past to this present was in no way forced, but indeed essential, and could effectively call us back to our common roots. [Leclant and Moscati 1991:4]

It remains to be seen how effective such appeals to Celtic identity will be in constructing and popularizing a sense of pan-European unity. Despite the claim that "it is commonly agreed that all European cultures can trace their roots to Celtic origins" (Benvenuti 1991:11), a logical interpretation of the archaeological evidence assembled in these exhibits would seem to exclude regions such as northern Germany and Scandinavia, which were never Celtic speaking and did not share in the La Tène material culture complex on view in the display cases. At the same time, it would necessarily include large areas of eastern Europe that are currently excluded from the EC but that (although of uncertain ancient linguistic affiliation) are central to the definition of La Tène material culture.

Another problem with a Celtic vision of European identity is that it would seem to particularly favor certain nations that already have well-developed nationalist myths of Celtic identity. France, for example, with its claim to be the embodiment of ancient Gaul and the "eldest daughter of *la Celtique*" (Johanneau 1807:42), might feel itself well placed to exercise a certain cultural hegemony within the EC. Indeed, Mitterrand's speech at Bibracte emphasized that, for the French, it was the site "where the first act of our history took place." But he also subtly noted that it was "one of the grand sites of Celtic civilization," a civilization that was "not defined by political boundaries but by common culture" and that "extended over the better part of Europe" (Mitterrand 1985:54).[14] If "the history of Europe begins with the Celts" and the Celts are the "First Europe," then one can easily imagine how the nation that claims Vercingetorix as a personification of its national character might perceive itself as the heart of that new and old Europe. On the other hand, this vision would be difficult to square with that of Breton activists, who interpret the last 2,500 years of European history as a bloody process of the "assassination of *la Celtique*" by Franks, Saxons, and Romans and who see the authentic flame of Celtic identity burning only among a small band of oppressed minorities on the western periphery of Europe (McDonald 1989:117). France, like England, enters this conceptualization of Celtic identity only as an alien oppressor.

Archaeology and Ethnic Nationalism

The ancient Celts, as the first "people" to emerge from the mists of European prehistory as a discrete category of identity by virtue of having a name applied to them, offer a wealth of possibilities for forging the symbolic and emotional links that bond people together in imagined communities. Language, places, objects, and persons have all been used to evoke antiquity and authenticity in the construction of traditions of communal identity for regions, nations, and supranational entities. Because such identities tend to be defined by contrast, different communities — or factions within communities — selectively stress and appropriate those aspects that symbolically highlight their own distinctiveness. The apparent paradox in the manipulation of Celtic identity is explained by the symbolically fecund ambiguities of the Celtic past and the mobile historical trajectories produced in the *bricolage* process of the construction of traditions as they are continually redefined in response to political demands (Abélès 1988; Crumley 1991).

Clearly, archaeological research in the Celtic domain is politically charged, and an awareness of the ramifications and historical situation of one's work is crucial. By the nature of their endeavor, archaeologists find themselves in an ambiguous and delicate position as both the furnishers of the symbolic hardware of invented traditions and the potential agents of deconstruction for those traditions. Archaeology provides for the popular imagination tangible connections to an identity rooted in the awe-inspiring past. Places and objects can be made into powerfully evocative symbols that serve to authenticate constructed traditions (Anderson 1983; Lowenthal 1985). "The most effective expression of ethnicity requires an anchor to a particular geography" (Crumley 1991:3), and archaeology provides that anchor by tying sites to ancient events and people.

It is largely for this reason that nation-states take an interest in archaeology. "What makes a nation *is* the past, what justifies one nation against another is the past" (Hobsbawm 1992:3). Hence the state is concerned to finance excavations, designate and preserve "national sites," and sponsor museums and exhibits that display the "national heritage." Moreover, given that the state is the major owner of the means of production for archaeological research, it is hardly surprising that the pattern of support for archaeological excavation and museum displays has been conditioned by national mythologies of identity. This was most blatantly clear in the projects of Napoleon I and Napoleon III, but it is also subtly operative in the demands placed on archaeologists today as they seek to justify the significance of their sites in the competitive process of requesting grants for excavation or in attempting to protect the archaeological record. Because state functionaries must balance considerations of scientific importance with the potential of sites as national symbolic resources, archaeologists can ill afford to neglect emphasizing the latter. However, one cannot hope to understand the development of what Trigger (1984) has called "nationalist archaeology" by simple reference to a uniform national ideology or set of national interests. Nation-states are not monolithic entities but dynamic social phenomena born of and propelled by the struggle among competing factions. The subtle demands that condition a nationalist archaeology are likely to be shaped by complex, historically evolving, factional contests as much as by overarching state interests.

Fig. 3. Painting of a "Gallic chief near the Roche Salvée of Beuvray inspecting the horizon," by Jules Didier (1895). Reprinted with permission from the Musée Rolin at Autun, France.

Archaeologists attempting to critically examine and challenge the incorporation of the past into invented traditions face other difficulties aside from state control of research funds. In the first place, although impressed by professional expertise and intrigued with the objects and monuments archaeologists bring to light, the public often pays little heed to the caveats voiced by archaeologists about the interpretation of these items. This is particularly the case with artistic creations and popular folk traditions. For example, 19th-century Romantic statues and paintings of Gauls are replete with weapons and armor copied carefully from archaeological specimens on view in museums. However, the artists assembled anachronistic collections of items drawn from past eras ranging from the Bronze Age to the Merovingean period. The statue of Vercingetorix at Alésia is a prime example of this practice (Figure 1), as is a painting by Jules Didier showing a "Gallic chief" wearing a mix of items including Bronze Age armor and what appears to be a form of kilt complete with sporran (Figure 3).[15] Despite the chronological and cultural discrepancies involved in the association of this material, for the nonspecialist they lend an aura of authenticity that is impervious to the criticism of scholars. The reinvention of druidism and its association with Celtic fire festivals at Burgundian archaeological sites and with Stonehenge offer further examples of the inventive incorporation of archaeological monuments in traditions of Celticity (Crumley 1991; Piggott 1968).

Another difficulty facing archaeologists, in the wake of a growing critical awareness of the problematic nature of the archaeological endeavor, has been a loss of confidence in the authority of their interpretations. The problem is not only that the archaeological record is partial and inherently ambiguous but also that archaeologists themselves are products of a particular sociohistorical context and that their interpretations and evaluations of plausibility are not independent of that context, a fact of which they have become increasingly aware.

In the case of the Celts, reconstructions of Celtic history and customs prior to the 19th century had been based almost entirely on interpretations of the alien testimony of classical texts. Archaeology appears to offer the promise of restoring the indigenous voice of the Celts by allowing their material culture, their own creations, to speak directly to later generations. However, this apparent communication is an act of interpretation by modern scholars. As such it remains an alien perspective subject to caveats that include, most critically, a realization of the social situation in which interpretations are formed.

Clearly, archaeologists must continually strive to be self-critical in evaluating the social and political contexts of their interpretive perspectives and their epistemological tools.[16] Examples of the unwitting (or sometimes conscious) participation of historians and archaeologists in the manipulation of the past in the cause of ethnic, nationalist, and colonialist mythologies illustrate the risks of unreflective interpretation and the illusion of objectivity.[17] Moreover, the fact that archaeology came of age as a professional discipline precisely in the context of the development of modern nation-states, with their demands for the construction of popular traditions of identity, should give cause for serious examination of the social construction of the field. Sensitivity to alternative conceptions of the past—especially those of disenfranchised groups—is both necessary and desirable (Layton 1989; Murray 1993). But the dangerous abuses and distortions of the archaeological record promulgated in Nazi Germany to justify territorial expansion and genocide[18] are a warning of the potential consequences of a failure to refute certain interpretations as seriously wrong. Popular traditions of regional ethnicity may seem to be a more benign manipulation of the past, but the violent effects of ethnic conflict, fueled by visions of identity rooted in emotionally charged appeals to the distant past, are readily apparent in Europe today.

If many archaeologists no longer feel comfortable imposing authoritative interpretations, we at least have a duty to engage in critically reflective debate about the manipulation of the past and to expose the profoundly ahistorical nature of essentialist visions of identity to the archaeological record of constant change. The case of "our ancestors the Gauls" offers a compelling example of the delicate challenge that faces archaeologists in sorting out the relationship between how the past has produced the present and how the present invites and manipulates its past.

Notes

Acknowledgments. My thanks to various colleagues in the Yale Anthropology Department (especially Niko Besnier, Richard Burger, Bill Kelly, and Helen Siu) and to Ellen Badone, Timothy Champion, Leon Doyon, James Fernandez, Jocelyn Linnekin, Jacquie Solway, and especially Ingrid Herbich for helpful advice. Thanks also to Colin Renfrew, Carole Crumley, two other anonymous reviewers, and the editors for thoughtful suggestions.

1. See Arnold 1990, Härke 1991, McCann 1990, and Trigger 1984.

2. France richly illustrates all three of the levels. For other areas, see, for example, Chapman 1978, Omnès 1987, Piggott 1989, Sheehy 1980, and Trevor-Roper 1983. A comparative study encompassing these other traditions of Celtic identity is in progress.

3. For a discussion of Celtic linguistics, see Abalain 1969, Renfrew 1987, and Whatmough 1970.

4. See Jones 1807, 3:23–46, Lhuyd 1707, Prichard 1857, and Zeuss 1853.

5. For example, see Chapman 1982, Dauge 1981, and Tierney 1960.

6. See Barzun 1932, Dubois 1972, Poliakov 1971, Simon 1989, Viallaneix and Ehrard 1982, and Weber 1991 on this subject.

7. For illustration and further discussion, see Achebe 1987:35 and Ferro 1981:37–39, 139.

8. See, for example, Harmand 1985, Pageaux 1982, and Simon 1989.

9. See Broca 1873, Johanneau 1807, and La Tour d'Auvergne 1792.

10. For more on this relationship, see McDonald 1989, Nicolas 1986, Reece 1977, and Tanguy 1977.

11. See Abalain 1989, Certeau et al. 1975, McDonald 1989, Nicolas 1986, Reece 1977, and Tanguy 1977.

12. See Abalain 1989, Falc'hun 1981, and Fleuriot 1980.

13. See McDonald 1989; and compare Brékilien 1976 and Gwegen 1975.

14. The site has recently been upgraded from a "national site" to a "European Archaeological Center."

15. This is a symbolic reference to a contemporary, invented tradition of Celtic dress from the Scottish Highlands (see Trevor-Roper 1983).

16. See, for example, Trigger 1989 and Yoffee and Sherratt 1993.

17. Here see Trigger 1984, as well as Fowler 1987 and Gathercole and Lowenthal 1990.

18. See Arnold 1990, Härke 1991, and McCann 1990.

References Cited

Abalain, Hervé
  1989 Destin des langues celtiques. Paris: Ophrys.

Abélès, Marc
  1988 Modern Political Ritual: Ethnography of an Inauguration and a Pilgrimage by President Mitterrand. Current Anthropology 29:391–404.

Achebe, Chinua
  1987 Anthills of the Savannah. New York: Anchor.

Amalvi, Christian
  1982 Vercingétorix dans l'enseignement primaire: 1830–1940. In Nos ancêtres les Gaulois. P. Viallaneix and J. Ehrard, eds. Pp. 349–355. Clermont-Ferrand: Faculté des Lettres et Sciences Humaines de l'Université de Clermont-Ferrand II.

Anderson, Benedict
  1983 Imagined Communities: Reflections on the Origin and Spread of Nationalism. London: Verso.

Andreae, Bernard
  1991 The Image of the Celts in Etruscan, Greek, and Roman Art.

In The Celts. S. Moscati, ed. Pp. 61–69. Milan: Fabbri.

Arnold, Bettina
1990   The Past as Propaganda: Totalitarian Archaeology in Nazi Germany. Antiquity 64:464–478.

Barzun, Jacques
1932   The French Race: Theories of its Origins and Their Social and Political Implications. Port Washington, NY: Kennikat.

Benvenuti, Feliciano
1991   Untitled preface. *In* The Celts. S. Moscati, ed. P. 11. Milan: Fabbri.

Boulainvilliers, Comte Henri de
1727   Histoire de l'ancien gouvernement de la France. 3 vols. The Hague and Amsterdam: Aux dépends de la Compagnie.

Brékilien, Yann
1976   Le Breton, langue celtique. Quimper, France: Nature et Bretagne.

Broca, Paul
1873   La race celtique ancienne et moderne. Revue d'Anthropologie 2:577–628.

Brocard, Véronique
1985   Bleu-blanc-rouge: Une fête, une tête, une fureur. Libération, October 21, Pp. 10–11.

Carbonell, Charles-O.
1982   Après 1870: Régénérescence de la France et renaissance de la Gaule. *In* Nos ancêtres les Gaulois. P. Viallaneix and J. Ehrard, eds. Pp. 391–394. Clermont-Ferrand: Faculté des Lettres et Sciences Humaines de l'Université de Clermont-Ferrand II.

Carton, Daniel
1989   M. Giscard d'Estaing défait Lucius Fabius à Gergovie. Le Monde, June 7, p. 10.

Certeau, Michel de, Dominique Julia, and Jacques Revel
1975   Une politique de la langue. La Révolution française et les patois: L'enquête Grégoire. Paris: Gallimard.

Chapman, Malcolm
1978   The Gaelic Vision in Scottish Culture. London: Croom Helm.
1982   "Semantics" and the "Celt." *In* Semantic Anthropology. D. Parkin, ed. Pp. 123–144. New York: Academic Press.

Collis, John
1984   The European Iron Age. London: Batsford.

Courson, Aurelien de
1863   La Bretagne du Ve au XIIe siècle. Paris: Imprimerie Impériale.

Croisille, Christian
1982   Le discours républicain: Introduction. *In* Nos ancêtres les Gaulois. P. Viallaneix and J. Ehrard, eds. Pp. 329–330. Clermont-Ferrand: Faculté des Lettres et Sciences Humaines de l'Université de Clermont-Ferrand II.

Crumley, Carole
1987   Celtic Settlement before the

Conquest: The Dialectics of Landscape and Power. *In* Regional Dynamics: Burgundian Landscapes in Historical Perspective. C. Crumley and W. Marquardt, eds. Pp. 403–429. New York: Academic Press.

1991 Region, Nation, History. Excursus 4:3–8.

Curtis, Lewis P.

1968 Anglo-Saxons and Celts: A Study of Anti-Irish Prejudice in Victorian England. Bridgeport: University of Bridgeport.

Dauge, Yves-Albert

1981 Le barbare. Recherches sur la conception romaine de la barbarie et de la civilisation. Collection Latomus, 176. Bruxelles: Latomus.

Dubois, Claude-Gilbert

1972 Celtes et Gaulois au XVIe siècle. Le développement littéraire d'un mythe nationaliste. Paris: Librairie Philosophique J. Vrin.

Ehrard, Antoinette

1982 Vercingétorix contre Gergovie? *In* Nos ancêtres les Gaulois. P. Viallaneix and J. Ehrard, eds. Pp. 307–320. Clermont-Ferrand: Faculté des Lettres et Sciences Humaines de l'Université de Clermont-Ferrand II.

Falc'hun, François

1981 Perspectives nouvelles sur l'histoire de la langue bretonne. Paris: Union Générale d'Éditions.

Ferro, Marc

1981 Comment on raconte l'histoire aux enfants à travers le monde entier. Paris: Payot.

Fleuriot, Léon

1980 Les origines de la Bretagne. L'émigration. Paris: Payot.

Fowler, Don D.

1987 Uses of the Past: Archaeology in the Service of the State. American Antiquity 52:229–248.

Galliou, Patrick, and Michael Jones

1991 The Bretons. Oxford: Blackwell.

Gathercole, Peter, and David Lowenthal, eds.

1990 The Politics of the Past. London: Unwin Hyman.

Gerard, Alice

1982 La vision de la défaite gauloise dans l'enseignement secondaire (particulièrement entre 1870 et 1914). *In* Nos ancêtres les Gaulois. P. Viallaneix and J. Ehrard, eds. Pp. 357–365. Clermont-Ferrand: Faculté des Lettres et Sciences Humaines de l'Université de Clermont-Ferrand II.

Goudineau, Christian

1990 César et la Gaule. Paris: Editions Errance.

Greene, David

1964 The Celtic Languages. *In* The Celts. J. Raftery, ed. Pp. 9–22. Cork: Mercier Press.

Guiomar, Jean-Yves

1987 Le bretonisme. Les historiens breton au XIXe siècle. Mayenne: La Manutention.

Guizot, François

1820   Du gouvernement de la France depuis la restauration. Paris: Ladvocat.

1872   L'histoire de France depuis les temps les plus reculés jusqu'en 1789 racontée à mes petits enfants, vol. 1. Paris: Hachette.

Gwegen, Jorj

1975   La langue bretonne face à ses oppresseurs. Quimper: Nature et Bretagne.

Härke, Heinrich

1991   All Quiet on the Western Front? Paradigms, Methods and Approaches in West German Archaeology. In Archaeological Theory in Europe. I. Hodder, ed. Pp. 187–222. London: Routledge.

Harmand, Jacques

1984   Vercingétorix. Paris: Fayard.

1985   Vercingétorix devant César. Les Dossiers, Histoire et Archéologie 92:24–31.

Herodotus

1987   The History (Historiai). David Grene, trans. Chicago: University of Chicago Press.

Hobsbawm, Eric J.

1983   Introduction: Inventing Traditions. In The Invention of Tradition. E. Hobsbawm and T. Ranger, eds. Pp. 1–14. Cambridge: Canto.

1990   Nations and Nationalism since 1780. Cambridge: Canto.

1992   Ethnicity and Nationalism in Europe Today. Anthropology Today 8(1):3–8.

Jackson, Kenneth

1967   A Historical Phonology of Breton. Dublin: Dublin Institute for Advanced Studies.

James, Edward

1988   The Franks. Oxford: Blackwell.

Johanneau, Eloi

1807   Discours d'ouverture sur l'établissement de l'Académie Celtique, les objets de ses recherches et le plan de ses travaux. Mémoires de l'Académie Celtique 1:28–64.

Jones, William

1807   The Works of Sir William Jones. 13 vols. London: J. Stockdale and J. Walker.

Julius Caesar

1980   The Battle for Gaul (De Bello Gallico). Anne and Peter Wiseman, trans. Boston: David R. Godine.

Jullian, Camille

1913   L'ancienneté de l'idée de nation. Revue Politique et Littéraire, Revue Bleue 51(3):65–70.

Kruta, Venceslas

1990   Introduction. In Les Celtes en France du Nord et en Belgique VIe-Ier siècle avant J.-C. Exhibition Catalogue. Pp. 8–9. Valenciennes: Musée des Beaux Arts de Valenciennes.

Lance, Pierre

1978   La défaite d'Alésia. Ses causes dans la société celtique, ses consequences dans la société française. Paris: La Septième Aurore.

La Tour d'Auvergne, Théophile M. C. de

1792 Nouvelles recherches sur la langue, l'origine et les antiquités des Bretons. Bayonne: Fauchet.

Layton, Robert L., ed.

1989 Who Needs the Past? Indigenous Values and Archaeology. London: Unwin Hyman.

Leclant, Jean, and Sabatino Moscati

1991 Foreword. In The Celts. S. Moscati, ed. Pp. 3–4. Milan: Fabbri.

Le Monde

1979 Mesrine et Jeanne d'Arc. October 17, p. 14.

Lhuyd, Edward

1707 Archaeologia Britannica. Oxford: Oxford University Press.

Loth, Joseph

1883 L'émigration bretonne en Armorique due Ve au VIIe siècle de notre ère. Rennes: Baraise.

Lowenthal, David

1985 The Past Is a Foreign Country. Cambridge: Cambridge University Press.

MacDonald, Sharon, ed.

1993 Inside European Identities. Oxford: Berg.

Mangourit, Michel-Ange de

1807 Discours de M. Mangourit. Séance du 9 germinal an XIII (30 mars 1805). Mémoires de l'Académie Celtique 1:65–71.

Marquardt, W. H., and C. L. Crumley

1987 Feux Celtiques: Burgundian Festival as Performance and Process. In Regional Dynamics: Burgundian Landscapes in Historical Perspective. C. Crumley and W. Marquardt, eds. Pp. 361–385. New York: Academic Press.

Martin, Henri

1852 Histoire de la France depuis les temps les plus reculés jusqu'en 1789, vol. 1. New edition. Paris: Furne.

1865 Histoire de France populaire depuis les temps les plus reculés jusqu'à nos jours, vol. 1. Paris: Furne et Jouvet.

McCann, W. J.

1990 "Volk und Germanentum": The Presentation of the Past in Nazi Germany. In The Politics of the Past. P. Gathercole and D. Lowenthal, eds. Pp. 74–88. London: Unwin Hyman.

McDonald, Maryon

1989 "We Are Not French!" Language, Culture and Identity in Brittany. New York: Routledge.

Megaw, Ruth, and Vincent Megaw

1989 Celtic Art from Its Beginnings to the Book of Kells. London: Thames and Hudson.

Mitterrand, François

1985 Allocution prononcée par M. François Mitterand [sic], Président de la République, au Mont Beuvray, Mardi 17 Septembre 1985. Nouvelles de l'Archéologie 21:51–55.

Moscati, Sabatino, ed.

1991 The Celts. Milan: Fabbri.

Murray, Tim
    1993   Communication and the
    Importance of Disciplinary Com-
    munities: Who Owns the Past? *In*
    Archaeological Theory: Who
    Sets the Agenda? N. Yoffee and
    A. Sherratt, eds. Pp. 105–116.
    Cambridge: Cambridge Univer-
    sity Press.
Napoleon III
    1865–66   Histoire de Jules Césare.
    2 vols. and 1 vol. of plates. Paris:
    Imprimerie Impériale.
Nicolas, Michel
    1986   Le séparatisme en Bretagne.
    Brasparts: Beltan.
Omnès, Robert
    1987   La Galice: Une Bretagne
    ibérique? *In* Études sur la Bre-
    tagne et les pays celtiques. Mé-
    langes offerts à Yves Le Gallo.
    Pp. 395–406. Brest: Centre de
    Recherche Bretonne et Celtique.
Otte, Marcel
    1987   Préface. *In* Hallstatt (700–
    400 av. J.-C.). A l'aube de la mét-
    allurgie. P. 11. Exhibition cata-
    logue: Europalia 87 Österreich.
    Liège: Musée de l'Architecture.
Pageaux, Daniel
    1982   De l'imagerie culturelle au
    mythe politique: Astérix le Gau-
    lois. *In* Nos ancêtres les Gaulois.
    P. Viallaneix and J. Ehrard, eds.
    Pp. 437–444. Clermont-Ferrand:
    Faculté des Lettres et Sciences
    Humaines de l'Université de
    Clermont-Ferrand II.
Pelloutier, Simon
    1740   Histoire des Celtes et par-
    ticulierement des Gaulois et des
    Germains depuis les temps fabu-
    leux jusqu'à la prise de Rome par
    les Gaulois, vol. 1 (vol. 2:1750).
    The Hague: Isaac Beauregard.
Pezron, Paul
    1703   Antiquité de la nation et de
    la langue des Celtes, autrement
    appelés Gaulois. Paris: Marchand
    and Martin.
Piggott, Stuart
    1968   The   Druids.   London:
    Thames and Hudson.
    1989   Ancient Britons and the
    Antiquarian Imagination. Lon-
    don: Thames and Hudson.
Pingeot, Anne
    1982   Les Gaulois sculptés (1850–
    1914). *In* Nos ancêtres les Gau-
    lois. P. Viallaneix and J. Ehrard,
    eds. Pp. 255–282. Clermont-
    Ferrand: Faculté des Lettres et
    Sciences Humaines de l'Univer-
    sité de Clermont-Ferrand II.
Poliakov, Leon
    1971   The Aryan Myth. New
    York: Basic Books.
Prichard, James C.
    1857   The Eastern Origin of the
    Celtic Nations Proved by a Com-
    parison of their Dialects with the
    Sanskrit, Greek, Latin, and Teu-
    tonic Languages. London: Houl-
    ston and Wright.
Reece, Jack E.
    1977   The Bretons against France:
    Ethnic Minority Nationalism in
    Twentieth   Century   Brittany.

Chapel Hill: University of North Carolina Press.

Renfrew, Colin
1987   Archaeology and Language: The Puzzle of Indo-European Origins. Cambridge: Cambridge University Press.

Réville, Albert
1877   Vercingétorix et la Gaule au temps de la conquête romaine. Revue des Deux Mondes 22:838–869.

Ridley, Ronald
1992   The Eagle and the Spade: Archaeology in Rome during the Napoleonic Era. Cambridge: Cambridge University Press.

Schrader, F.
1898   Gaule et France. Revue Mensuelle de l'École d'Anthropologie de Paris 8:73–85.

Séguy, Philippe
1989   Costume in the Age of Napoleon. In The Age of Napoleon: Costume from Revolution to Empire, 1789–1815. K. le Bourhis, ed. Pp. 23–117. New York: Metropolitan Museum of Art.

Sheehy, Jeanne
1980   The Rediscovery of Ireland's Past: The Celtic Revival 1830–1930. London: Thames and Hudson.

Shore, Chris, and Annabel Black
1992   The European Communities and the Construction of Europe. Anthropology Today 8(3):10–11.

Sieyès, Emmanuel J.
1789   Qu'est-ce que le Tiers-Etats? Pamphlet. Paris.

Simon, André
1989   Vercingétorix et l'idéologie française. Paris: Imago.

Strabo
1923   The Geography. Horace L. Jones, trans. London: Heinemann.

Tanguy, Bernard
1977   Aux origines du nationalisme breton. 2 vols. Paris: Union Générale d'Éditions.

Thierry, Augustin
1866   Dix ans d'études historiques. Paris: Garnier Frères.

Tierney, J. J.
1960   The Celtic Ethnography of Posidonius. Proceedings of the Royal Irish Academy 60:189–275.

Topinard, Paul
1878   Anthropology. London: Chapman and Hall.

Trevor-Roper, Hugh
1983   The Invention of Tradition: The Highland Tradition of Scotland. In The Invention of Tradition. E. Hobsbawm and T. Ranger, eds. Pp. 15–42. Cambridge: Canto.

Trigger, Bruce G.
1984   Alternative Archaeologies: Nationalist, Colonialist, Imperialist. Man 19:355–370.
1989   A History of Archaeological Thought. Cambridge: Cambridge University Press.

Viallaneix, Paul, and Jean Ehrard, eds.
1982   Nos ancêtres les Gaulois.

Clermont-Ferrand: Faculté des Lettres et Sciences Humaines de l'Université de Clermont-Ferrand II.

Weber, Eugen

1991   My France: Politics, Culture, Myth. Cambridge, MA: Belknap.

Whatmough, Joshua

1970   The Dialects of Ancient Gaul. Cambridge, MA: Harvard University Press.

Yoffee, Norman, and Andrew Sherratt, eds.

1993   Archaeological Theory: Who Sets the Agenda? Cambridge: Cambridge University Press.

Zeuss, Johann K.

1853   Grammatica Celtica. Leipzig: Weidmannos.

How Native Is a "Native" Anthropologist?

Kirin Narayan

VOL. 95, 1993, 671–686

How "native" is a native anthropologist? How "foreign" is an anthropologist from abroad? The paradigm polarizing "regular" and "native" anthropologists is, after all, part of received disciplinary wisdom. Those who are anthropologists in the usual sense of the word are thought to study Others whose alien cultural worlds they must painstakingly come to know. Those who diverge as "native," "indigenous," or "insider" anthropologists are believed to write about their own cultures from a position of intimate affinity. Certainly, there have been scattered voices critiquing this dichotomy. Arguing that because a culture is not homogeneous, a society is differentiated, and a professional identity that involves problematizing lived reality inevitably creates a distance, scholars such as Aguilar (1981) and Messerschmidt (1981a:9) conclude that the extent to which anyone is an authentic insider is questionable. Yet such critiques have not yet been adequately integrated into the way "native" anthropologists are popularly viewed in the profession.

In this essay, I argue against the fixity of a distinction between "native" and "non-native" anthropologists. Instead of the paradigm emphasizing a dichotomy between outsider/insider or observer/observed, I propose that at this historical moment we might more profitably view each anthropologist in terms of shifting identifications amid a field of interpenetrating communities and power relations. The loci along which we are aligned with or set apart from those whom we study are multiple and in flux. Factors such as education, gender, sexual orientation, class, race, or sheer duration of contacts may at different times outweigh the cultural identity we associate with insider or outsider status. Instead, what we must focus our attention on is the quality of relations with the people we seek to represent in our texts: are they viewed as mere fodder for professionally self-serving statements about a generalized Other, or are they accepted as subjects with voices, views, and dilemmas — people to whom we are bonded through ties of reciprocity and who may even be critical of our professional enterprise?

I write as someone who bears the label of "native" anthropologist and yet squirms uncomfortably under this essentializing tag. To highlight the personal and intellectual dilemmas invoked by the assumption that a "native" anthropologist can represent an unproblematic and authentic insider's perspective, I incorporate personal narrative into a wider discussion of anthropological scholarship. Tacking between situated narrative and more sweeping analysis, I argue for the *enactment of hybridity* in our texts; that is, writing that depicts authors as minimally bicultural in terms of belonging simultaneously to the world of engaged scholarship and the world of everyday life.

The Problem in Historical Perspective

The paradigm that polarizes "native" anthropologists and "real" anthropologists stems from the colonial setting in which the discipline of anthropology was forged: the days in which natives were genuine natives (whether they liked it or not) and the observer's objectivity in the scientific study of Other societies posed no problem. To achieve access to *the native's* point of view (note the singular form), an anthropologist used the method of participant-observation among a variety of representative natives, often singling out one as a "chief informant" (Casagrande 1960). A chief informant might also be trained in anthropological modes of data collection so that the society could be revealed "from within." As Franz Boas argued, materials reported and inscribed by a trained native would have "the immeasurable advantage of trustworthiness, authentically revealing precisely the elusive thoughts and sentiments of the native" (Lowie 1937:133 cited in Jones 1970:252). Or better yet, a smart and adequately Westernized native might go so far as to receive the education of a bona fide anthropologist and reveal a particular society to the profession with an insider's eye. Ordinary people commenting on their society, chief informants friendly with a foreign anthropologist, or insiders trained to collect indigenous texts were all in some sense natives contributing to the enterprise of anthropology. Yet, it was only those who received the full professional initiation into a disciplinary fellowship of discourse who became the bearers of the title "native" anthropologist.

Even if such a "native" anthropologist went on to make pathbreaking professional contributions, his or her origins remained a perpetual qualifier. For example, writing the foreword to M. N. Srinivas's classic monograph on the Coorgs, Radcliffe-Brown emphasized that the writer was "a trained anthropologist, himself an Indian" and went on to add that he had "therefore an understanding of Indian ways of thought which it is difficult for a European to attain over many years" (Srinivas 1952:v). As Delmos Jones has charged, it is likely that "natives" who could get "the inside scoop" were first admitted into the charmed circle of professional discourse because they were potential tools of data collection for white anthropologists (Jones 1970:252). Admittedly, in an era prior to extensive decolonization and civil rights movements, that "natives" were allowed to participate at all in professional discourse was remarkable. In this context, calling attention to, rather than smoothing over, "native" identity perhaps helped to revise the ingrained power imbalances in who was authorized to represent whom.

Viewed from the vantage point of the 1990s, however, it is not clear that the term *native anthropologist* serves us well. Amid the contemporary global flows of trade, politics, migrations, ecology, and the mass media, the accepted nexus of authentic culture/demarcated field/exotic locale has unraveled (Appadurai 1990, 1991; Clifford 1992; Gupta and Ferguson 1992). Although many of the terms of anthropological discourse remain largely set by the West, anthropology is currently practiced by members (or partial members) of previously colonized societies that now constitute the so-called Third World (Altorki and El-Solh 1988; Fahim 1982; Kumar 1992; Nakhleh 1979; Srinivas, Shah, and Ramaswamy 1979). These scholars often have institutional bases in the Third World, but some have also migrated to Europe and the United States. Furthermore, in the First World, minority anthropologists also hold university positions and their contributions to ongoing discourse have helped to realign, if not overthrow, some of the discipline's ethnocentric assumptions (Gwaltney 1981; Jones 1970; Limon 1991). Feminist scholarship questioning the formulation of "woman as Other" has underscored the differences between women, and the multiple planes along which identity is constructed, thus destabilizing the category of "Other" as well as "Self" (Abu-Lughod 1990; Alarcon 1990; Lauretis 1986; Mani 1990; Mohanty and Russo 1991; Strathern 1987). It has also become acceptable to turn the anthropological gaze inward, toward communities in Western nations (Ginsburg 1989; Ginsburg and Tsing 1990;

Martin 1987; Messerschmidt 1981b, Ortner 1991). The "field" is increasingly a flexible concept: it can move with the travels of Hindu pilgrims (Gold 1988), span Greek villagers and New Age American healers (Danforth 1989), or even be found in automobile garages of South Philadelphia (Rose 1987). In this changed setting, a rethinking of "insider" and "outsider" anthropologists as stable categories seems long overdue.

Multiplex Identity

"If Margaret Mead can live in Samoa," my mother is reputed to have said when she moved to India, "I can live in a joint family." The daughter of a German father and American mother, she had just married my Indian father. Yet these terms — *German, American, Indian* — are broad labels deriving from modern nation-states. Should I instead say that my mother, the daughter of a Bavarian father and a WASP mother who lived in Taos, New Mexico, became involved with her fellow student at the University of Colorado: my Indian-from-India father? Yet, for anyone familiar with India shouldn't I add that my father's father was from the Kutch desert region, his mother from the dense Kathiawari forests, and that while he might loosely be called "Gujarati" his background was further complicated by growing up in the state of Maharashtra? Should I mention that Mayflower blood supposedly mingles with that of Irish potato famine immigrants on my maternal grandmother's side (I'm told I could qualify as a "D.A.R."), or that as temple builders, members of my paternal grandfather's caste vehemently claimed a contested status as Brahman rather than lower-ranking carpenter? Should I add that my father was the only Hindu boy in a Parsi school that would give him a strictly British education, inscribing the caste profession-based title "Mistri" (carpenter) onto the books as the surname "Contractor?" Or would it better locate my father to say that he remembers the days when signs outside colonial clubs read "No Dogs or Indians?" Also, is it useful to point out that my mother — American by passport — has now lived in India for over 40 years (more than two-thirds of her life) and is instructed by her bossy children on how to comport herself when she visits the United States?

I invoke these threads of a culturally tangled identity to demonstrate that a person may have many strands of identification available, strands that may be tugged into the open or stuffed out of sight. A mixed background such as mine perhaps marks one as inauthentic for the label "native" or "indigenous" anthropologist; perhaps those who are not clearly "native" or "non-native" should be termed "halfies" instead (cf. Abu-Lughod 1991). Yet, two halves cannot adequately account for the complexity of an identity in which multiple countries, regions, religions, and classes may come together. While my siblings and I have spent much of our lives quipping that we are "haylf" (pronounced with an American twang) and "hahlf" (with a British-educated accent), I increasingly wonder whether any person of mixed ancestry can be so neatly split down the middle, excluding all the other vectors that have shaped them. Then too, mixed ancestry is itself a cultural fact: the gender of the particular parents, the power dynamic between the groups that have mixed, and the prejudices of the time all contribute to the mark that mixed blood leaves on a person's identity (cf. Spickard 1989).

Growing up in Bombay with a strongly stressed patrilineage, a Hindu Indian identity has weighted more than half in my self-definition, pushing into the background Pilgrim fathers and Bavarian burghers who are also available in my genealogical repertoire. This would seem to mark me as Indian and, therefore, when I study India, a "native" anthropologist. After all, researching aspects of India, I often share an unspoken emotional understanding with the people with whom I work (cf. Ohnuki-Tierney 1984). Performing fieldwork in Nasik on storytelling by a Hindu holy man whom I called "Swamiji," I had the benefit of years of association with not just Swamiji himself, but also the language and wider culture. Since Nasik was the town where my father grew up, a preexisting identity defined by kinship subsumed my presence as ethnographer (cf. Nakhleh 1979). Similarly, researching women's songs and lives in the Himalayan foothills, I bore the advantage of visiting the place practically every year since I was 15, and of my mother having settled there. All too well aware of traditional expectations for proper behavior by an unmarried daughter, in both places I repressed aspects of my cosmopolitan Bombay persona and my American self to behave with appropriate decorum and deference (cf. Abu-Lughod 1988).

In both Nasik and in Kangra, different aspects of identity became highlighted at different times. In Nasik, when elderly gentlemen wearing white Congress caps arrived and Swamiji pointed me out as "Ramji Mistri's granddaughter," my local roots were highlighted, and I felt a diffuse pride for my association with the Nasik landmark of the Victorian bungalow that my grandfather had built in the 1920s. Visiting Nathu Maharaj, the barber with buckteeth and stained clothes, to discuss interpretations of Swamiji's stories, I felt uncomfortable, even ashamed, of the ways in which my class had allowed me opportunities that were out of reach for this bright and reflective man. My gender was important in the observance of menstrual taboos not to touch Swamiji or the altar—injunctions that left me so mortified that I would simply leave town for several days. Borrowing the latest Stevie Wonder tapes from one of "the foreigners"—a disciple from new Jersey—I savored a rowdy release, becoming again a woman who had lived independently in a California university town. When Swamiji advised that in written texts I keep his identity obscure ("What need do I have for publicity?"—yet his doctor took me aside to advise that I disregard such modesty and identify him by name, "so people abroad will know his greatness"), I felt my role as culture broker with the dubious power to extend First World prestige to Third World realities. Yet, when Swamiji challenged my motives for taking his words on tape "to do a business," I was set apart from all planes of locally available identification, thrown outside a circle of fellowship forged by spiritual concerns, and lumped instead with academics who made it their business to document and theorize about other people's lives (Narayan 1989:59–62).

For my second extended research project in the Himalayan foothill region of Kangra, I had no deep local roots. Unmoored from a certain base for identification, the extent to which *others* can manipulate an anthropologist's identity came into dizzying focus (Dumont 1978; Stoller 1989). Explaining my presence, some of the village women I worked with asserted that I was from such-and-such village (where my mother lives), hence local. At other times I was presented as being "from Bombay," that is, a city dweller from a distant part of the country although still recognizably Indian. A wrinkled old woman I once fell into step with on an outing between villages asked if I was a member of the pastoral Gaddi tribe (to her, the epitome of a close-by Other). At yet other times, and particularly at weddings where a splash of foreign prestige added to the festivities, I was incontrovertibly stated to be "from America . . . she came *all* the way from there for this function, yes, with her camera and her tape recorder!" In the same household at different times, I was forced to answer questions about whether all Americans were savages (*jangli log*) because television revealed that they didn't wear many clothes, and to listen as a member of a spellbound local audience when a dignified Rajput matron from another village came by to tell tales about how she had visited her emigrant son in New Jersey. In the local language, she held forth on how, in America, people just ate "round breads" of three sizes with vegetables and *masalas* smeared on top (pizza); how shops were enormous, with everything you could imagine in them, and plastic bags you could rip off like leaves from a tree; how you put food in a "trolley" and then a woman would press buttons, giving you a bill for hundreds and hundreds of rupees! Bonded with other entranced listeners, my own claims to authoritative experience in this faraway land of wonders seemed to have temporarily dropped out of sight.

Now it might be assumed that I had experienced these shifting identifications simply because of my peculiar background, and that someone who was "fully" Indian by birth and upbringing might have a more stable identity in the field. For a comparison, I could turn to Nita Kumar's lively and insightful *Friends, Brothers, Informants: A Memoir of Fieldwork in Banaras* (1992), which makes many of the same points. Instead, I look further back (to pre-postmodern times) and draw out some of the implications about identity from M. N. Srinivas's compelling ethnography, *The Remembered Village* (1976). Srinivas is one of India's most respected anthropologists, although given the division of labor between anthropologists as those who focus on the Other (tribal groups) and sociologists who research the Self (village and urban dwellers), in India he is known as a sociologist. Srinivas was educated in Oxford in the 1940s. On Radcliffe-Brown's advice, he planned to do fieldwork in a multi-caste village called Rampura in Mysore (Karnataka State). Srinivas's ancestors had moved several generations before from neighboring Tamil Nadu to rural Mysore; his father had left his village for the city so that his children could be educated. In returning from Oxford to live in a village, Srinivas stated his hope that "my study . . . would enable me better to understand my personal cultural and social roots" (1976:5).

But did the presence of these roots mean that he was regarded as a "native" returning home to blend smoothly with other "natives"? No, he was an educated urbanite and Brahman male, and the power of this narrative ethnography lies very much in Srinivas's sensitivity to the various ways in which he interacted with members of the community: sometimes aligned with particular groups, sometimes set apart. As he confesses, "It was only in the village that I realized how far I (and my family) had travelled away from tradition" (1976:18). From his account, one gets the impression that villagers found him a very entertaining oddity. He struggled regularly with villagers' expectations that he behave as a Brahman should (1976:33–40). Growing up in the city, he had not internalized rules of purity and pollution to the extent that they bound local Brahmans, and he found himself reprimanded by the headman for shaving himself *after* rather than before a ritual bath. On the other hand, a political activist criticized him for his involvement with the headman, rather than with all sections and factions of the village (1976:22). When he did move throughout the village, he found himself received with affection: "word must have gone round that I did not consider myself too high to mix with poor villagers" (1976:24). Yet, as he was a respected guest and outsider, villagers as a group also colluded in keeping details of unpleasant "incidents" regarding sex, money, and vendettas from him (1976:40–47). In a lighter vein, many villagers knew him by the exotic object he sported, a camera that fulfilled not just their ends (such as the use of photographs in arranging marriages) but also his anthropological responsibilities of recording for a foreign audience. He became "the camera man — only they transformed 'camera' into 'chamara' which in Kannada means the fly-whisk made from the long hair of yak tails" (1976:20). Villagers plied him with questions about the English, and the headman even planned a tour of England in which Srinivas was to be adopted as guide (1976:29). In short, his relationships were complex and shifting: in different settings, his caste, urban background, unintended affiliations with a local faction, class privilege, attempts to bridge all sectors of the community, or alliance with a faraway land could be highlighted.

Even as insiders or partial insiders, in some contexts we are drawn closer, in others we are thrust apart. Multiple planes of identification may be most painfully highlighted among anthropologists who have identities spanning racial or cultural groups (Abu-Lughod 1988, 1991; Kondo 1986, 1990; Lavie 1990). Yet, in that we all belong to several communities simultaneously (not least of all, the community we were born into and the community of professional academics), I would argue that *every* anthropologist exhibits what Rosaldo has termed a "multiplex subjectivity" with many crosscutting identifications (1989:168–195). Which facet of our subjectivity we choose or are forced to accept as a defining identity can change, depending on the context and the prevailing vectors of power. What Stuart Hall has written about cultural identity holds also for personal identity:

> Cultural identities come from somewhere, have histories. But like everything which is historical, they [identities] undergo constant trans-formation. Far from being eternally fixed in some essentialised past, they are subject to the continuous "play" of history, culture, and power. Far from being grounded in

a mere "recovery" of the past, which is waiting to be found, and which, when found, will secure our sense of ourselves into eternity, identities are the names we give to the different ways we are positioned by, and position ourselves within, the narratives of the past. [Hall 1989:70]

Rethinking Connections through Fieldwork

We are instructed as anthropologists to "grasp the native's point of view, his relation to life, to realize *his* vision of *his* world" (Malinowski 1961 [1922]:25). Yet who is this generic subject, "the native"? To use a clump term is to assume that all natives are the same native, mutually substitutable in presenting the same (male) point of view. Yet even received anthropological wisdom tells us that in the simplest societies, gender and age provide factors for social differentiation. To extend conceptual tools forged for the study of heuristically bounded, simple societies to a world in which many societies and subgroups interact amid shifting fields of power, these very tools must be reexamined. We would most certainly be better off looking for the natives' points of view to realize *their* visions of *their* worlds while at the same time acknowledging that "we" do not speak from a position outside "their" worlds, but are implicated in them too (cf. Mani 1990; Mohanty 1989; Said 1989): through fieldwork, political relations, and a variety of global flows.

Arjun Appadurai (1988) has persuasively teased out some of the underlying assumptions in anthropological use of the term *native* for groups who belong to parts of the world distant and distinct from the metropolitan West. As he argues, the concept is associated with an ideology of *authenticity:* "Proper natives are somehow assumed to represent their selves and their history, without distortion or residue" (1988:37). Those in the position to observe "natives," however, exempt themselves from being authentic and instead represent themselves in terms of complexity, diversity, and ambiguity. Furthermore, the term is linked to *place*. "Natives" are incarcerated in bounded geographical spaces, immobile and untouched yet paradoxically available to the mobile outsider. Appadurai goes on to show how in anthropological discourse, "natives" tied to particular places are also associated with particular *ideas:* one goes to India to study hierarchy, the circum-Mediterranean region for honor and shame, China for ancestor worship, and so on, forgetting that anthropological preoccupations represent "the temporary *localization* of ideas from *many* places" (1988:46, emphasis in original).

The critique that Appadurai levels at the term *native* can also be extended to *native anthropologist*. A "native" anthropologist is assumed to be an insider who will forward an authentic point of view to the anthropological community. The fact that the profession remains intrigued by the notion of the "native" anthropologist as carrying a stamp of authenticity is particularly obvious in the ways in which identities are doled out to non-Western, minority, or mixed anthropologists so that exotic difference overshadows commonalities or complexities. That my mother is German-American seems as irrelevant to others' portrayal of me as "Indian" as the American mothers of the "Tewa" Alphonso Ortiz, the "Chicano" Renato Rosaldo, or "Arab" Lila Abu-Lughod. For those of us who are mixed, the darker element in our ancestry serves to define us with or without our own complicity. The fact that we are often distanced — by factors as varied as education, class, or emigration — from the societies we are supposed to represent tends to be underplayed. Furthermore, it is only appropriate (and this may be the result of our own identity quests) that sooner or later we will study the exotic societies with which we are associated. Finally, while it is hoped that we will contribute to the existing anthropological pool of knowledge, we are not really expected to diverge from prevailing forms of discourse to frame what Delmos Jones has called a genuinely "native" anthropology as "a set of theories based on non-Western precepts and assumptions" (1970:251).

"Native" anthropologists, then, are perceived as insiders regardless of their complex backgrounds. The differences between kinds of "native" anthropologists are also obliviously passed over. Can a person from an impoverished American minority background who, despite all prejudices, manages to get an education and study her own community be equated with a member of a Third World elite group who, backed by excellent schooling and parental funds, studies anthropology abroad yet returns home for fieldwork among the less privileged? Is it not insensitive to suppress the issue of location, acknowledging that a scholar who chooses an institutional base in the Third World might have a different engagement with Western-based theories, books, political stances, and technologies of written production? Is a middle-class white professional researching aspects of her own society also a "native" anthropologist?

And what about non-"native" anthropologists who have dedicated themselves to long-term fieldwork, returning year after year to sustain ties in a particular community? Should we not grant them some recognition for the different texture this brings to their work? It is generally considered more savvy in terms of professional advancement to do fieldwork in several different cultures rather than returning to deepen understandings in one. Yet to use people one has lived with for articles and monographs, and not maintain ties through time, generates a sort of "hit-and-run" anthropology in which engagement with vibrant individuals is flattened by the demands of a scholarly career. Having a safe footing to return to outside the field situation promotes "a contemplative stance . . . [that] pervades anthropology, disguising the confrontation between Self and Other and rendering the discipline powerless to address the vulnerability of the Self" (Dwyer 1982:269). Regular returns to a field site, on the other hand, can nourish the growth of responsible human ties and the subsuming of cultural difference within the fellowship of a "We-relation" (Schutz 1973:16–17). As George Foster and the other editors of the book *Long-Term Field Research in Social Anthropology* point out in their concluding comments, an ongoing personal involvement with people in the communities studied often makes for an interest in "action" or "advocacy" work (Foster et al. 1979:344). Looking beyond the human rewards to the professional ones, long-term fieldwork leads to the stripping away of formal self-presentations and the granting of access to cultural domains generally reserved for insiders, thus making better scholarship. Returns to the field allow for a better understanding of how individuals creatively shape themselves and their societies through time. Finally, repeated returns to the field force an anthropologist to reconsider herself and her work not just from the perspective of the academy but also from that of the people she purports to represent. As Paul Stoller has written about his long-term fieldwork among the Songhay in Niger:

> Besides giving me the perspective to assess social change, long-term study of Songhay has plunged me into the Songhay worlds of sorcery and possession, worlds the wisdom of which are closed to outsiders — even Songhay outsiders. My insistence on long-term study forced me to confront the interpretive errors of earlier visits. Restudying Songhay also enabled me to get a bit closer to "getting it right." But I have just begun to walk my path. As Adamu Jenitongo once told me, "Today you are learning about us, but to understand us, you will have to grow old with us." [Stoller 1989:6]

While Stoller was not born Songhay, his ongoing engagement has given him a niche in the society, a place from which he is invited to "grow old" *with* his teacher. Like all long-term relationships, his encounters in the field have had exhilarating ups and cataclysmic downs, yet persevering has brought the reward of greater insight. Do not anthropologists who engage sensitively in long-term fieldwork also deserve respect from their professional colleagues as partial insiders who have through time become bicultural (cf. Tedlock 1991)? Need a "native" anthropologist be so very different?

It might be argued that the condescending colonial connotations of a generic identity that cling to the term *native* could be lessened by using alternative words: *indigenous* or *insider,* for example. Yet the same conceptual underpinnings apply to these terms too: they all imply that an authentic insider's perspective is possible, and that this can unproblematically represent the associated group. This leads us to underplay the ways in which people born within a society can be simultaneously both insiders and outsiders, just as those born elsewhere can be outsiders and, if they are lucky, insiders too. Also, as Elizabeth Colson has bluntly stated, " 'Indigenous' is a misnomer, for all of us are indigenous somewhere and the majority of anthropologists at some time deal with their own communities" (Fahim et al. 1980:650). We are *all* "native" or "indigenous" anthropologists in this scheme, even if we do not appear so in every fieldwork context. Rather than try to sort out who is authentically a "native" anthropologist and who is not, surely it is more rewarding to examine the ways in which each one of us is situated in relation to the people we study.

Situated Knowledges

Visiting Nasik as a child, I knew better than to touch Maharaj, the chubby Brahman cook, as he bent over to fill our shining steel *thalis* on the floor; yet, if asked, I would never have been able to explain this in terms of "purity and pollution." I knew that servants were frequently shouted at and that they wore ill-fitting, cast-off clothes, but I did not call this "social inequality." I observed that my girl cousins were fed after the boys and that although they excelled in school they were not expected to have careers, but I did not call it "gender hierarchy." I listened raptly when the Harveys, a British couple who had stayed on after 1947, told us stories about viceroys and collectors, but I did not know the words "colonization" or "decolonization." When, amid the volley of British authors who shaped our minds in school, we finally came across poems by Rabindranath Tagore, I noticed that these were different but could not call them "nationalist." Reflecting on India with the vocabulary of a social analyst, I find that new light is shed on many of the experiences that have shaped me into the person — and professional — I am today.

In some ways, the study of one's own society involves an inverse process from the study of an alien one. Instead of learning conceptual categories and then, through fieldwork, finding the contexts in which to apply them, those of us who study societies in which we have preexisting experience absorb analytic categories that rename and reframe what is already known. The reframing essentially involves locating vivid particulars within larger cultural patterns, sociological relations, and historical shifts. At one further remove, anthropological categories also rephrase these particulars as evidence of theoretical issues that cross cultures and are the special province of trained academics.

Yet, given the diversity within cultural domains and across groups, even the most experienced of "native" anthropologists cannot know everything about his or her own society (Aguilar 1981). In fact, by opening up access to hidden stores of research materials, the study of anthropology can also lead to the discovery of many strange and unfamiliar aspects of one's own society (cf. Stewart 1989:14). I have learned, for example, a good deal more about village life, regional differences, and tribal groups than what my urban upbringing supplied. Institutions and belief systems that I took for granted as immutable reality — such as caste or Hinduism — have been dismantled as historical and discursive constructions. Even for a purported insider, it is clearly impossible to be omniscient: one knows about a society from particular locations within it (cf. Srinivas 1966:154).

As anthropologists, we do fieldwork whether or not we were raised close to the people whom we study. Whatever the methodologies used, the process of doing fieldwork involves getting to know a range of people and listening closely to what they say. Even if one should already be acquainted with some of these people before one starts fieldwork, the intense and sustained engagements of fieldwork will inevitably transmute these relationships. Fieldwork is a common plane binding professional anthropologists, but the process and outcome vary so widely that it is difficult to make a clear-cut distinction between the experiences of those with prior exposure and those who arrive as novices. As Nita Kumar writes in her memoir of fieldwork in Banaras (which she had only visited before as the sheltered, Anglicized daughter of a highly placed Indian government official): "Fieldwork consists of experiences shared by all anthropologists; the personal and the peculiar are significant as qualities that *always* but *differently* characterize each individual experience" (1992:6, emphasis in original).

To acknowledge particular and personal locations is to admit the limits of one's purview from these positions. It is also to undermine the notion of objectivity, because from particular locations all understanding becomes subjectively based and forged through interactions within fields of power relations. Positioned knowledges and partial perspectives are part of the lingo that has risen to common usage in the 1980s (Clifford 1986, 1988; Haraway 1988; Kondo 1986; Rosaldo 1989). Yet, let us not forget the prescient words of Jacques Maquet from an article in which he argued that decolonization laid bare the "perspectivist" character of anthropology in Africa, showing anthropology's claim to objectivity as entwined with power relations in which one group could claim to represent another. Arguing against objectivity in a polemic at least 20 years ahead of its time, he writes:

> A perspectivist knowledge is not as such non-objective: it is partial. It reflects an external reality but only an aspect of it, the one visible from the particular spot, social and individual, where the anthropologist was placed. Non-objectivity creeps in when the partial aspect is considered as the global one. [Maquet 1964:54]

Enacting Hybridity

"Suppose you and I are walking on the road," said Swamiji, the holy man whose storytelling I was researching in 1985. "You've gone to University. I haven't studied anything. We're walking. Some child has shit on the road. We both step in it. 'That's shit!' I say. I scrape my foot; it's gone. But educated people have doubts about everything. You say, 'What's this?!' and you rub your foot against the other." Swamiji shot up from his prone position in the deck chair, and placing his feet on the linoleum, stared at them with intensity. He rubbed the right sole against the left ankle. "Then you reach down to feel what it could be," his fingers now explored the ankle. A grin was breaking over his face. "Something sticky! You lift some up and sniff it. Then you say, 'Oh! This is *shit.*'" The hand that had vigorously rubbed his nose was flung out in a gesture of disgust.

Swamiji turned back toward me, cheeks lifted under their white stubble in a toothless and delighted grin. Everyone present in the room was laughing uncontrollably. I managed an uncomfortable smile.

"See how many places it touched in the meantime," Swamiji continued. "Educated people always doubt everything. They lie awake at night thinking, 'What was that? Why did it happen? What is the meaning and the cause of it?' Uneducated people pass judgment and walk on. They get a good night's sleep."

I looked up at Swamiji from my position on the floor and tried to avoid the eyes of the others, who watched me with broad smiles on their faces. "What was that? Why did it happen? What is the meaning and the cause of it?" rang in my ears as a parody of my own relentless questioning as an anthropologist interviewing both Swamiji and his listeners. I had to agree that among the academics I represented analysis could often become obsessive. But I also felt awkward, even a little hurt. This parable seemed to dismiss all the years that education had dominated my life. It ridiculed my very presence in this room. In his peculiar mixture of sternness and empathy, Swamiji must have read the discomfort on my face. When he settled back into his deck chair, he turned to me again. "It's not that you shouldn't study," he said, voice low and kind. "You should gain wisdom. But you should realize that in the end this means nothing."

Once again, Swamiji was needling any possible self-importance that might be ballooning inside me as self-appointed documenter and analyst of what to others was everyday life. While others enjoyed his stories and learned from them, I brought the weightiness of perpetual enquiry to the enterprise. Every action was evaluated (at least partially) in terms of my project on folk narrative as a form of religious teaching. Now Swamiji had turned his technique of instruction through stories on me. Through a parable, he dramatized how we both coexisted in shared time and space, "walking the same road," yet each with a different awareness. The power relations of "structured inequality" (Dwyer 1982; Rabinow 1977) that allow anthropologists to subsume their subjects in representation had been turned upside down with such a critique.

This uncomfortable scene dramatizes how the issue of who is an insider and who is an outsider is secondary to the need for dismantling objective distance to acknowledge our shared presence in the cultural worlds that we describe. Pioneering works on "native" anthropology emphasized the need for such anthropologists to achieve distance. Yet, distance, as Dorinne Kondo (1986) has observed, is both a stance and a cognitive-emotional orientation that makes for cold, generalized, purportedly objective and yet inevitably prejudiced forms of representation. As Kondo argues, it can be replaced with the acceptance of "more experiential and affective modes of knowing" (1986:75) in which the ethnographer's identity and location are made explicit and informants are given a greater role in texts. This is what Michael Jackson (1989) more recently called "radical empiricism": a methodology and discursive style that emphasizes the subject's experience and involvement with others in the construction of knowledge (cf. Stoller 1992).

To question the discipline's canonical modes of objective distance is not, however, to forfeit subjective distance and pretend that all fieldwork is a celebration of communitas. Given the multiplex nature of identity, there will inevitably be certain facets of self that join us up with the people we study, other facets that emphasize our difference. In even the closest of relationships, disjunctures can swell into distance; ruptures in communication can occur that must be bridged. To acknowledge such shifts in relationships rather than present them as purely distant or purely close is to enrich the textures of our texts so they more closely approximate the complexities of lived interaction. At the same time, frankness about actual interactions means that an anthropologist cannot hide superficial understandings behind sweeping statements and is forced to present the grounds of understanding. Further, as Lila Abu-Lughod has argued in regard to what she calls "ethnographies of the particular," by writing in terms of "particular individuals and their changing relationships, one would necessarily subvert the most problematic connotations of culture: homogeneity, coherence, and timelessness" (1991:154).

These insights hold radical implications for anthropological modes of representation. As I see it, there are currently two poles to anthropological writing: at one end stand accessible ethnographies laden with stories, and at the other end stand refereed journal articles, dense with theoretical analyses. We routinely assign narrative ethnographies in "Intro to Anthro" classes (even if these are written not by professional anthropologists, but by their wives [Fernea 1965; Shostak 1981]) because it is through narratives lively with people, places, and events that we know recalcitrant undergraduates are likely to be seduced by the discipline. Reading these ethnographies, we ourselves may forget we are judgmental professionals, so swept along are we in the evocative flow of other people's experiences. Narrative ethnography is one arena in which the literary critic Mary Louise Pratt's blunt diagnosis that ethnographic writing is boring (1986:33) simply does not apply. Journal articles, on the other hand, tend to be exclusively of interest to academics initiated into the fellowship of professional discourse, and subscribing members of a particular, academically formed society. Journal articles are written according to formulas that include a thesis introduced in the beginning and returned to at the end, and the convention that theoretical frameworks and generalized statements should be emphasized, suppressing vivid particulars. We read these articles with our minds more than our hearts, extorting ideas and references from their pages.

Need the two categories, compelling narrative and rigorous analysis, be impermeable? Increasingly, they seep into each other, and here I want to argue for an emerging style in anthropological writing that I call the *enactment of hybridity* (cf. Abu-Lughod 1992; Behar 1993; Jackson 1989; Kondo 1990; Lavie 1990; Rose 1987; Stoller 1989; Rosaldo 1989, Tedlock 1992). In using the word "enactment," I am drawing on Dorinne Kondo's view that "the *specificity* of . . . experience . . . is not opposed to theory; it *enacts* and *embodies* theory" (1990, emphasis in original): any writing, then, represents an enactment of some sort of theory. By "hybridity," I do not mean only a condition of people who are mixed from birth, but also a state that all anthropologists partake of but may not consciously include in our texts. As Edward Bruner (1993) has elegantly phrased it, every anthropologist carries both a personal and an ethnographic self. In this scheme, we are all incipiently bi- (or multi-) cultural in that we belong to worlds both personal and professional, whether in the field or at home. While people with Third World allegiances, minorities, or women may experience the tensions of this dual identity the most strongly, it is a condition of everyone, even of that conglomerate category termed "white men." Whether we are disempowered or empowered by prevailing power relations, we must all take responsibility for how our personal locations feed not just into our fieldwork interactions but also our scholarly texts. When professional personas altogether efface situated and experiencing selves, this makes for misleading scholarship even as it does violence to the range of hybrid personal and professional identities that we negotiate in our daily lives.

Adopting a narrative voice involves an ethical stance that neither effaces ourselves as hybrid nor defaces the vivid humanity of the people with whom we work. Narrative transforms "informants" whose chief role is to spew cultural data for the anthropologist into subjects with complex lives and a range of opinions (that may even subsume the anthropological enterprise). At a moment in which scholarship has a "multinational reception" (cf. Mani 1990), it seems more urgent than ever that anthropologists acknowledge that it is *people* and not theoretical puppets who populate our texts, and that we allow these people to speak out from our writings. Also, narratives are not transparent representations of what actually happened, but are told for particular purposes, from particular points of view: they are thus incipiently analytical, enacting theory. Analysis itself is most effective when it builds directly from cases evoked through narrative, so providing a chance to step away, reflect on, and reframe the riveting particulars of the story at hand. In including the perspective of the social analyst along with narratives from or about people studied, a stereoscopic "double vision" can be achieved (Rosaldo 1989:127–143). Some skillfully constructed analyses are as gripping as good mystery stories, starting from a conundrum, then assembling clues that finally piece together. Narrative and analysis are categories we tend to set up as opposites, yet a second look reveals that they are contiguous, with a border open even to the most full-scale of crossovers.

Calling for a greater integration of narrative into written texts does not mean that analysis is to be abandoned, but rather that it moves over, giving vivid experience an honored place beside it. By translating professional jargon into "the language of everyday life" (cf. Abu-Lughod 1991:151), analysis can also be made intriguing to audiences who would otherwise be compelled only by narrative. Admittedly, writing cannot singlehandedly change the inequalities in today's world; yet, in bearing the potential to change the attitudes of readers, ethical and accessible writing unquestionably takes a step in the right direction. As companions clothed in nontechnical language, narrative and analysis join to push open the doors of anthropological understanding and welcome in outsiders.

Conclusions

I have argued for a reorientation in the ways that we perceive anthropologists as "outside" or "inside" a society. The traditional view has been to polarize "real" anthropologists from "native" anthropologists, with the underlying assumption that a "native" anthropologist would forward an authentic insider's view to the profession. This view sprang from a colonial era in which inegalitarian power relations were relatively well defined: there was little question about the "civilized" outsider's ability to represent "primitive" peoples, and so it was worthy of note when a person excluded from dominant white culture was allowed to describe his or her own society. With changing times, however, the scope of anthropology has shifted to include industrialized societies, even as it is also practiced in "Third World" countries and by minority and "Third World" scholars. Identity, always multiplex, has become even more culturally complex at this historical moment in which global flows in trade, politics, and the media stimulate greater interpenetration between cultures.

In this changed setting, it is more profitable to focus on shifting identities in relationship with the people and issues an anthropologist seeks to represent. Even if one can blend into a particular social group without the quest of fieldwork, the very nature of researching what to others is taken-for-granted reality creates an uneasy distance. However, even if one starts out as a stranger, sympathies and ties developed through engaged coexistence may subsume difference within relationships of reciprocity. "Objectivity" must be replaced by an involvement that is unabashedly subjective as it interacts with and invites other subjectivities to take a place in anthropological productions. Knowledge, in this scheme, is not transcendental, but situated, negotiated, and part of an ongoing process. This process spans personal, professional, and cultural domains.

As we rethink "insiders" and "outsiders" in anthropology, I have argued that we should also work to melt down other, related divides. One wall stands between ourselves as interested readers of stories and as theory-driven professionals; another wall stands between narrative (associated with subjective knowledge) and analysis (associated with objective truths). By situating ourselves as subjects simultaneously touched by life-experience and swayed by professional concerns, we can acknowledge the hybrid and positioned nature of our identities. Writing texts that mix lively narrative and rigorous analysis involves enacting hybridity, regardless of our origins.

Notes

Acknowledgments. This essay emerged from fieldwork in Nasik between June and September 1983, and July and October 1985, as well as an association with the place since birth. Formal fieldwork in Kangra took place between September 1991 and August 1992, although I have visited there since 1975. I am extremely grateful for an array of grants and fellowships through the years. In building on insights garnered collectively from research enabled by these different funding sources, I lump them together here: a National Science Foundation Graduate Fellowship, a University of California at Berkeley Graduate Humanities Research Grant, a Robert H. Lowie Fellowship, a Charlotte W. Newcombe Dissertation Writing Fellowship, support from the University of Wisconsin Graduate School, an American Institute of Indian Studies Senior Fellowship, and a National Endowment for the Humanities Fellowship. My deep thanks to Eytan Bercovitch, Ruth Behar, Ed Bruner, Janet Dixon-Keller, Ann Gold, Smadar Lavie, Maria Lepowsky, Renato Rosaldo, Janis Shough, Paul Stoller, Barbara Tedlock, Anna Tsing, and Kamala Visweswaran for conversations about and comments on issues raised in this essay.

References Cited

Abu-Lughod, Lila

1988 Fieldwork of a Dutiful Daughter. *In* Arab Women in the Field. S. Altorki and C. Fawzi El-Solh, eds. Pp. 139–161. Syracuse: Syracuse University Press.

1990 Can There Be a Feminist Ethnography? Women and Performance: A Journal of Feminist Theory 5:7–27.

1991 Writing against Culture. *In* Recapturing Anthropology. Richard Fox, ed. Pp. 137–162. Santa Fe, NM: School of American Research Press.

1992 Writing Women's Worlds: Bedouin Stories. Berkeley: University of California Press.

Aguilar, John

1981 Insider Research: An Ethnography of a Debate. *In* Anthropologists at Home in North America. Donald Messerschmidt, ed. Pp. 15–26. Cambridge: Cambridge University Press.

Alarcon, Norma

1990 The Theoretical Subject(s) of This Bridge Called My Back in Anglo-American Feminism. *In* Making Face/Making Soul: Creative and Critical Perspectives on Women of Color. G. Anzaldua, ed. Pp. 356–369. San Francisco: Aunt Lute Foundation.

Altorki, Soraya, and Camillia Fawzi El-Solh, eds.

1988 Arab Women in the Field: Studying Your Own Society. Syracuse: Syracuse University Press.

Appadurai, Arjun

1988 Putting Hierarchy in Its Place. Cultural Anthropology 3: 36–49.

1990 Disjuncture and Difference in the Global Cultural Economy. Public Culture 2:1–24.

1991 Global Ethnoscapes: Notes and Queries for a Transnational Anthropology. *In* Recapturing Anthropology. Richard Fox, ed. Pp. 191–210. Santa Fe, NM: School of American Research Press.

Behar, Ruth

1993 Translated Woman: Crossing the Border with Esperanza's Story. Boston: Beacon Press.

Bruner, Edward M.
1993 Introduction: The Ethnographic Self and the Personal Self. *In* Anthropology and Literature. Paul Benson, ed. Pp. 1–26. Urbana: University of Illinois Press.

Casagrande, Joseph, ed.
1960 In the Company of Man: Twenty Portraits by Anthropologists. New York: Harper and Row.

Clifford, James
1986 Introduction: Partial Truths. *In* Writing Culture: The Poetics and Politics of Ethnography. James Clifford and George Marcus, eds. Pp. 1–26. Berkeley: University of California Press.
1988 The Predicament of Culture. Cambridge, MA: Harvard University Press.
1992 Travelling Cultures. *In* Cultural Studies. L. Grossberg, C. Nelson, and Paula Treichler, eds. Pp. 96–116. New York: Routledge.

Danforth, Loring
1989 Firewalking and Religious Healing: The Anasteria of Greece and the American Firewalking Movement. Princeton: Princeton University Press.

Dumont, Jean Paul
1978 The Headman and I. Austin: University of Texas Press.

Dwyer, Kevin
1982 Moroccan Dialogues: Anthropology in Question. Prospect Heights, IL: Waveland Press.

Fahim, Hussein
1982 Indigenous Anthropology in Non-Western Countries. Durham, NC: Carolina Academic Press.

Fahim, Hussein, Katherine Helmer, Elizabeth Colson, T. N. Madan, Herbert C. Kelman, and Talal Asad
1980 Indigenous Anthropology in Non-Western Countries: A Further Elaboration. Current Anthropology 21:644–663.

Fernea, Elizabeth
1965 Guests of the Sheik: An Ethnography of an Iraqi Village. New York: Doubleday.

Foster, George M., T. Scudder, E. Colson, and R. V. Kemper, eds.
1979 Long-Term Field Research in Social Anthropology. New York: Academic Press.

Ginsburg, Faye
1989 Contested Lives: The Abortion Debate in an American Community. Berkeley: University of California Press.

Ginsburg, Faye, and Anna Lowenhaupt Tsing
1990 Uncertain Terms: Negotiating Gender in American Culture. Boston: Beacon Press.

Gold, Ann
1988 Fruitful Journeys: The Ways of Rajasthani Pilgrims. Berkeley: University of California Press.

Gupta, Akhil, and James Ferguson
1992 Beyond "Culture": Space, Identity, and the Politics of Dif-

ference. Cultural Anthropology 7:6–23.

Gwaltney, John L.
1981 Common Sense and Science: Urban Core Black Observations. *In* Anthropologists at Home in North America: Methods and Issues in the Study of One's Own Society. D. Messerschmidt, ed. Pp. 46–61. Cambridge: Cambridge University Press.

Hall, Stuart
1989 Cultural Identity and Cinematic Representation. Framework 36:68–81.

Haraway, Donna
1988 Situated Knowledges: The Science Question in Feminism and the Privilege of Partial Perspective. Feminist Studies 14: 575–599.

Jackson, Michael
1989 Paths towards a Clearing: Radical Empiricism and Ethnographic Enquiry. Bloomington: Indiana University Press.

Jones, Delmos J.
1970 Toward a Native Anthropology. Human Organization 29: 251–259.

Kondo, Dorinne
1986 Dissolution and Reconstitution of Self: Implications for Anthropological Epistemology. Cultural Anthropology 1:74–96.
1990 Crafting Selves: Power, Gender and Discourses of Identity in a Japanese Workplace. Chicago: University of Chicago Press.

Kumar, Nita
1992 Friends, Brothers, and Informants: Fieldwork Memoirs of Banaras. Berkeley: University of California Press.

Lauretis, Teresa de
1986 Feminist Studies/Critical Studies: Issues, Terms, and Contexts. *In* Feminist Studies/Critical Studies. T. de Lauretis, ed. Pp. 1–19. Bloomington: Indiana University Press.

Lavie, Smadar
1990 The Poetics of Military Occupation. Berkeley: University of California Press.

Limon, Jose
1991 Representation, Ethnicity, and the Precursory Ethnography: Notes of a Native Anthropologist. *In* Recapturing Anthropology. Richard Fox, ed. Pp. 115–136. Santa Fe, NM: School of American Research Press.

Lowie, Robert
1937 A History of Ethnological Theory. New York: Holt, Rinehart and Winston.

Malinowski, Bronislaw
1961 [1922] Argonauts of the Western Pacific. New York: E. P. Dutton.

Mani, Lata
1990 Multiple Mediations: Feminist Scholarship in the Age of Multinational Reception. Feminist Review 35:24–41.

Maquet, Jacques
1964 Objectivity in Anthropol-

ogy. Current Anthropology 5:47–55.

Martin, Emily
  1987 The Woman in the Body: A Cultural Analysis of Reproduction. Boston: Beacon Press.

Messerschmidt, Donald
  1981a On Anthropology "at Home." *In* Anthropologists at Home in North America: Methods and Issues in the Study of One's Own Society. D. Messerschmidt, ed. Pp. 1–14. Cambridge: Cambridge University Press.
  1981b [ed.] Anthropologists at Home in North America: Methods and Issues in the Study of One's Own Society. Cambridge: Cambridge University Press.

Mohanty, Chandra, and Ann Russo, eds.
  1991 Third World Women and the Politics of Feminism. Bloomington: Indiana University Press.

Mohanty, Satya
  1989 Us and Them. New Formations 8:55–80.

Nakhleh, Khalil
  1979 On Being a Native Anthropologist. *In* The Politics of Anthropology: From Colonialism and Sexism to the View from Below. G. Huizer and B. Mannheim, eds. Pp. 343–352. The Hague: Mouton.

Narayan, Kirin
  1989 Storytellers, Saints, and Scoundrels: Folk Narrative in Hindu Religious Teaching. Philadelphia: University of Pennsylvania Press.

Ohnuki-Tierney, Emiko
  1984 "Native" Anthropologists. American Ethnologist 11:584–586.

Ortner, Sherry
  1991 Reading America: Preliminary Notes on Class and Culture. *In* Recapturing Anthropology. Richard Fox, ed. Pp. 163–189. Santa Fe, NM: School of American Research Press.

Pratt, Mary Louise
  1986 Fieldwork in Common Places. *In* Writing Culture. James Clifford and George Marcus, eds. Pp. 27–50. Berkeley: University of California Press.

Rabinow, Paul
  1977 Reflections on Fieldwork in Morocco. Berkeley: University of California Press.

Rosaldo, Renato
  1989 Culture and Truth: The Remaking of Social Analysis. Boston: Beacon Press.

Rose, Dan
  1987 Black American Street Life: South Philadelphia, 1969–71. Philadelphia: University of Pennsylvania Press.

Said, Edward
  1989 Representing the Colonized: Anthropology's Interlocutors. Critical Inquiry 15:205–225.

Schutz, Alfred

 1973 Collected Papers, Volume 1: The Problem of Social Reality. The Hague: Mouton.

Shostak, Marjorie

 1981 Nisa: The Life and Words of a !Kung Woman. Cambridge, MA: Harvard University Press.

Spickard, Paul R.

 1989 Mixed Blood: Intermarriage and Ethnic Identity in Twentieth-Century America. Madison: University of Wisconsin Press.

Srinivas, M. N.

 1952 Religion and Society among the Coorgs of Southern India. New Delhi: Oxford University Press.

 1966 Some Thoughts on the Study of One's Own Society. In Social Change in Modern India. M. N. Srinivas, ed. Pp. 147–163. Berkeley: University of California Press.

 1976 The Remembered Village. Berkeley: University of California Press.

Srinivas, M. N., A. M. Shah, and E. A. Ramaswamy

 1979 The Fieldworker and the Field: Problems and Challenges in Sociological Investigation. Delhi: Oxford University Press.

Stewart, John D.

 1989 Drinkers, Drummers, and Decent Folk: Ethnographic Narratives in Village Trinidad. Albany: State University of New York Press.

Stoller, Paul

 1989 The Taste of Ethnographic Things. Philadelphia: University of Pennsylvania Press.

 1992 The Cinematic Griot: The Ethnography of Jean Rouch. Chicago: University of Chicago Press.

Strathern, Marilyn

 1987 An Awkward Relationship: The Case of Feminism and Anthropology. Signs 12:276–294.

Tedlock, Barbara

 1991 From Participant Observation to the Observation of Participation: The Emergence of Narrative Ethnography. Journal of Anthropological Research 47: 69–94.

 1992 The Beautiful and the Dangerous: Encounters with the Zuni Indians. New York: Viking.

Archaeology, Anthropology, and the Culture Concept

Patty Jo Watson

VOL. 97, 1995, 683–694

Although I have belonged to the American Anthropological Association since 1953, my first year in graduate school, I have been so deeply immersed in my own archaeological corner for the past 20 years that I hadn't noticed, until I began thinking about this talk, how *very* different the current anthropological landscape is from the one in which I came of age in the discipline. That fact makes the present assignment a considerable challenge: to say something that might hold the attention of an audience representing the diversity of 1990s anthropology. So I decided to structure much of my discussion around something central to anthropology and anthropologists since the formational period of the discipline: culture.

As a University of Chicago graduate student, I encountered the anthropological culture concept not long after my commitment to a particular form of Protestantism, as a matter of personal faith and belief, had faded away. So it is perhaps not surprising that during my pre-M.A. period I concluded culture was a crucial tenet of anthropological faith. It seemed to me absolutely necessary to commit myself to one of the many definitions of *culture* then under discussion (Kroeber and Kluckhohn 1952) before I could be confirmed as a real anthropologist (before I could pass the comps). After that, I would earn a Ph.D. and live my anthropological career in accord with my own personal understanding of culture, which might also be Kluckhohn's or Kroeber's or Linton's. As a matter of fact, it was Robert Redfield's version of E. B. Tylor's classic definition that I chose to cleave to. Tylor said, "Culture . . . is that complex whole which includes knowledge, belief, art, morals, law, customs, and any other capabilities and habits acquired . . . as a member of society" (Tylor 1871:1). In Redfield's rendering, "Culture is 'an organized body of conventional understandings manifest in art and artifacts which, persisting through tradition, characterizes a human group'" (Redfield 1940; see Kroeber and Kluckhohn 1952:61).

Redfield's definition is a little shorter and snappier than Tylor's, and hence easier to memorize for a person struggling — as I was then — not only with detailed culture-historical sequences in several parts of the Old and New Worlds but also with Murngin, Naskapi, and Nuer kinship systems; with how to tell a phoneme from a phon; and with how precisely the Australopithecine pelvis differs from ours and from a chimpanzee's. Also relevant was the fact that Redfield was a senior member of the Chicago anthropology faculty and someone my adviser (Robert J. Braidwood) respected. Moreover, Redfield's definition specifically mentions manifestations of culture ("art and artifacts") and explicitly invokes duration through time, two characteristics that appeal strongly to archaeologists.

Secure in my grip on the culture concept, I passed my comps, got an M.A., and went on to dissertation research in Near Eastern prehistory. Redfield, Eggan, Tax, Braidwood, Washburn, and McQuown taught us that anthropology was a unitary enterprise made up of four equal parts: social anthropology or ethnology, archaeology, physical anthropology, and linguistics. A prominent Harvard archaeologist, Philip Phillips, also formally emphasized the close ties between archaeology and the broader field of anthropology in an influential article published in 1955, concluding that "American archaeology is anthropology or it is nothing."

I wholeheartedly accepted all this and identified with anthropology as fervently as with archaeology. Sometime during the late 1950s when I was completing my Ph.D. dissertation, I received an initial reality check concerning the relation between archaeology and anthropology. Having attended a lecture and subsequent reception for Ruth Landes, whose Ojibwa ethnographies I had read and admired, I introduced myself to her as an anthropologist. She asked what my specialty was and I said Near Eastern prehistory, at which point she turned away abruptly saying, "Then you're *not* an anthropologist, you're an archaeologist." Her remark was my first inkling that the anthropological world was not as well integrated as my mentors had led me to believe.

I had ample opportunity to confirm the inkling while carrying out research in the Old World, and then later as I transferred my fieldwork locale to eastern North America. By the early 1980s I knew of at least two North American departments of archaeology completely separate from anthropology (Calgary and Simon Fraser) with another (Boston University) on the way. There were also separatist themes clearly voiced in the literature by several archaeologists.[1] A few years later a full-scale anti-"archaeology as anthropology" assault was launched from England and northwestern Europe.[2] "American archaeology as anthropology" was rejected along with other tokens of American imperialism. And, of course, during the 1960s and 1970s I had noticed that the subdisciplinary balance in my alma mater department at Chicago had become markedly asymmetric in favor of one kind of sociocultural anthropology and against archaeology and physical anthropology.

All this I knew, but until I heard Kent Flannery's distinguished lecture at the annual meeting of the American Anthropological Association in December 1981 (Flannery 1982), I had not noticed that the other foundation of my basic anthropological training — the culture concept, even culture itself — was under attack within American sociocultural anthropology. Flannery quotes Eric Wolf's 1980 assessment:

> An earlier anthropology had achieved unity under the aegis of the culture concept. It was culture, in the view of anthropologists, that distinguished humankind from all the rest of the universe, and it was the possession of varying cultures that differentiated one society from another. . . . The past quarter-century has undermined this intellectual sense of security. The relatively inchoate concept of "culture" was attacked from several theoretical directions. As the social sciences transformed themselves into "behavioral" sciences, explanations for behavior were no longer traced to culture: behavior was to be understood in terms of psychological encounters, strategies of economic choice, strivings for payoffs in games of power. Culture, once extended to all acts and ideas employed in social life, was now relegated to the margins as "world view" or "values" [Wolf 1980]

Flannery mourns the loss of an integrating concept of culture in ethnology, and fears the threat of such loss in archaeology. Now, somewhat more than ten years later, it appears that the culture situation in ethnology and sociocultural anthropology is even more problematic.

Back in 1952, Kroeber and Kluckhohn (1952:149) noted that after Tylor published his definition of *culture* in 1871, there were no other formal definitions offered for 32 years. Between 1900 and 1919, they found six; between 1920 and 1950 there were 157. The word *culture* had great currency throughout this whole time, including the three decades post-Tylor, but it was being used without explicit definition.

According to a recent summary volume (Borofsky 1994), research on or about the culture concept, or "the cultural," now ranges from linguistic, cognitive, and psychological approaches to a variety of postmodern and post-postmodern experimental efforts on the literary side to politically, historically, empirically, and/or methodologically oriented work, to that which focuses explicitly on the nexus of biology and culture, of natural science and human science, and to that which concentrates on intercultural encounters in premodern, modern, or postmodern world systems.[3] I return to this issue below, in the concluding section, but first take up something with which I am somewhat more familiar: recent travels of the culture concept in archaeology.

The culture concept in anthropological archaeology has followed a well-marked but nonlinear trajectory over the past several decades. After a freewheeling and primarily data-free speculative period in the 19th century (Willey and Sabloff 1993: ch. 2), North American archaeology developed around a culture-historical approach parallel to but separate from concurrent processes in European archaeology (Trigger 1989:187, 195). At the turn of the century, "the term culture was first applied to groups of sites containing distinctive artifact assemblages in the Ohio Valley. By 1902 William C. Mills had distinguished the Fort Ancient and Hopewell cultures" (Trigger 1989:187).

At this time in North American archaeological parlance, Trigger says a "culture" was mainly a geographical entity—a taxon for one of several synchronic units—because so little was known about chronology. The period between World War I and World War II was characterized by intense concern with temporal relations and by a great deal of historical particularism in North American archaeology. Trigger notes, as have other scholars, that Americanist archaeologists of the 1930s and 1940s paid no attention to human behavior, to function, ecology, or even quantification.[4] There was no interest in culture per se, although widely used classificatory units (foci, aspects, phases) were implicitly understood to be cultural units, possibly reflecting ancient tribes or groups of related tribes. Archaeological cultures in North America were believed to be conservative, changing slowly if at all in response to diffusion of objects and ideas, and/or to migration of large and small human groups. Walter Taylor's detailed critique of Americanist archaeology, published in 1948 and promoting a very different view of culture to and for archaeologists, was a radical departure from mainstream 1940s archaeological practice.

Taylor's argument (1948: ch. 4) included a view of culture as composed of two concepts, one holistic — Culture — and one partitive — cultures. Holistically speaking, Cultural phenomena are distinguished from natural phenomena, both organic (nonhuman biological) and inorganic (geological, chemical). Cultural phenomena are emergent, more than the sum of the partitive parts, they are in a realm of their own, a realm created and maintained solely by human cognitive activity.

Partitively, the culture concept also denotes a specific *piece* of the whole of human Culture, *a* culture. Either way, C/culture "is a mental phenomenon, consisting of the contents of minds, not of material objects or observable behavior" (Taylor 1948:96). Cultural content is cumulative: "The culture-whole existing today owes its form and at least the majority of its content to what is called the cultural heritage" (Taylor 1948:98). The (or a) cultural heritage consists of mental constructs. "Mere physical form is extraneous as far as culture is concerned, being a property of the world of physics and not of culture" (Taylor 1948:99). What was once called "material culture" (as distinct from "nonmaterial culture" or "social culture"), according to Taylor, is not culture and is in fact two removes from the real thing: the locus of culture is mental, ideas in people's minds.[5] Artifacts and architecture are the results of behavior, which itself derives from mental activity. "Culture [the first-order phenomenon for Taylor] is unobservable and non-material." Behavior (second-order phenomenon) is observable but nonmaterial, and only with third-order phenomena resulting from behavior do we come to artifacts, architecture, and other concrete materials making up the archaeological record: "this [third] order consists only of objectifications of culture and does not constitute culture itself" (Taylor 1948:100).

Taylor's handling of the culture concept is seemingly a departure from the position held more or less contemporaneously by Kroeber, who says that materials and objects are all part of culture equally with ideas and customs: "We may forget about this distinction" (Kroeber 1948:295–296). If one reads Kroeber's whole discussion, however, one realized that his view is probably the same as Taylor's (and Redfield's). He says,

> What counts is not the physical ax or coat or wheat but the idea of them, their place in life. It is this knowledge, concept, and function that get them-

selves handed down through the generations, or diffused into other cultures, while the objects themselves are quickly worn out or consumed. [Kroeber 1948:295]

So it is not difficult to see how Taylor, beginning with the traditional, then-current views on culture, and thinking about how to transform observations on the archaeological record into information about culture, came to the formulation outlined above. If only the ideas and knowledge in people's minds are culture and the ultimate source of culture, then archaeologists who want to contribute to cultural anthropology, the discipline that studies culture, must address their thrice-removed materials in ways calculated to delineate past cognitive patterning. The archaeological record can reveal ancient culture — the mental activities of long-dead people — if skillfully interrogated. The archaeologist as archaeologist is merely a technician digging up physical materials and their associations, in space and time, but the archaeologist as anthropologist is uniquely qualified to produce truly cultural information about ancient peoples and extinct societies throughout time and space.

One might think that to be an exciting and appealing prospect, but virtually no one heeded Taylor's call to reshape the practice of archaeology and make it more anthropological. Nothing happened even after two eminent, well-respected members of the archaeological establishment, Gordon Willey and Philip Phillips, repeated Phillips's earlier admonition that "American archaeology is anthropology or it is nothing" in a widely read and highly influential volume, *Method and Theory in American Archaeology* (Phillips 1955; Willey and Phillips 1958:2). Why not?

One very immediate and practical obstacle was the ad hominem, or straight-to-the-jugular, technique Taylor used to highlight the sins and errors committed by living, active, and highly influential senior archaeologists, who, he said, preached anthropology but practiced "mere chronicle" sterile time-space distributions of selected artifacts. Such personal assaults are almost never successful as a long-term strategy. In a published Ph.D. dissertation, they are suicidal.

Another a priori reason why Taylor's program was never implemented, not even by Taylor himself, is that the demands it placed upon field and laboratory recording and analysis were simply impossible to meet at the time *A Study of Archaeology* was published. Even now, with quite powerful computer hardware and software available to archaeologists, and with greater knowledge of site-formation processes as well as more widespread interest in ancient ideational patterns, Taylor's conjunctive archaeology is a rather tall order.

As Dunnell (1986:36) has pointed out, there is yet another possible explanation why Taylor's reform call was virtually totally ignored, and that is the concept of culture he provided as the source and center of his formulation. Taylor asserted, with most sociocultural anthropologists of his day, and indeed since Tylor, that the locus of culture is mental. Artifacts are not culture, they are only *objectifications* of culture at several removes from the real thing. Moreover, he insisted that the highest goal archaeologists could aspire to was eliciting cultural anthropology from archaeological remains, which meant the mental processes (the true, the real culture) of those past peoples. This argument easily led to a view of archaeology as being highly marginal within general anthropology.

As indicated earlier, Taylor's views also ran counter to the basic operating assumptions of most Americanist archaeologists at the time he was writing (Binford 1987:397), many of whom did not believe that the original meanings — to their creators — of the items they excavated could be retrieved, and most of whom were less immediately interested in this proposition than they were in basic time-space systematics. In 1943, Griffin matter-of-factly stated,

> The exact meaning of any particular object for the living group or individual is forever lost, and the real significance of any object in an ethnological sense has disappeared by the time it becomes a part of an archaeologist's catalogue of finds. [Griffin 1943:340]

Almost exactly 20 years after Taylor completed the dissertation published in 1948 as *A Study of Archaeology* — a closely reasoned, devastating critique that seemingly sank without a trace — another reformer published a much shorter and much more successful appeal, similar in some ways to that of Taylor but quite different in others: Lewis Binford's 1962 *American Antiquity* article, "Archaeology as Anthropology," initiated a period of dominance by processual archaeology, or "the New Archaeology," as it is often called.[6] Like Taylor, Binford and the New Archaeologists were intent upon expanding the goals of Americanist anthropological archaeology beyond those of typology and stratigraphy. Although Binford insisted that *all* aspects of past societies could be investigated archaeologically, in practice he focused almost exclusively upon subsistence and ecology. Processual or New Archaeology came to be a kind of neo-evolutionary "econothink" (Hall 1977) with heavy emphasis on hypothetico-deductive method, quantification, computers, and statistics. Binford's concept of culture, appropriate to the general tenor of New Archaeology and quite different from Taylor's, was that of his professor at the University of Michigan, Leslie White: "culture is man's extrasomatic means of adaptation" (Binford 1962; White 1959, 38–39).

Binford himself—like another of his Michigan professors, James Griffin—had little interest in the meanings archaeological materials might once have had for their makers and users, and he paid no serious attention to ideational issues, regarding them as epiphenomena at best. Thus, under his highly influential leadership, Americanist archaeology was materialist, functionalist, and evolutionist in orientation, overtly anthropological and scientific in its aspirations. This trajectory was very successful during the 1960s and 1970s. In fact, it still represents the mainstream of practicing archaeology in the United States (Willey and Sabloff 1993:317), partly because of the great initial success of the New Archaeology and partly because of the 1974 federal legislation (the Moss-Bennett Bill, or the Archeological Conservation Act) mandating the inclusion of archaeology in federally funded environmental impact assessments. This legislation formalized and routinized archaeological procedures in an early-1970s mode that persists throughout the United States today.

In the late 1960s, however, Binford's attempts to understand the morphological variation in Middle Paleolithic (Mousterian) assemblages in France resulted in his turning the full force of his research into ethnography in northern Alaska and elsewhere (Binford 1983:100–106). Largely, although not by any means entirely, owing to Binford's influence, ethnoarchaeology became a standard research focus during the 1970s and 1980s for Americanist and other prehistorians and is now an established, productive sub-subdiscipline.[7]

Meanwhile, in the late 1970s and the 1980s, the few anthropological archaeologists who were not entirely swept away by Binfordian, processualist New Archaeology with its heavy methodological emphasis received powerful reinforcement from British and European advocates of postmodernist (postprocessualist) directions in archaeology, wherein ontological issues were central. The most influential among these—at least in the anglophone world—is usually said to be Ian Hodder (1982a, 1985, 1991a, 1991b). Although Hodder strongly opposes nearly everything Binford advocates, and Binford wholeheartedly embraces their adversarial relations, both are deeply committed to ethnoarchaeology as an essential archaeological technique.[8] Obviously the foci of their ethnographic observations differ. Binford, to whom culture is humankind's extrasomatic means of sustaining themselves in a wide array of physical environments through space and time, documents the interplay of climatic, topographic, floral, faunal, geological, and other natural factors with human hunter-gatherer-forager subsistence and technology. Hodder, to whom culture is mental (symbolic), material, social behavioral, and the recursive relations among all three, takes note of the important roles played by artifacts in the complex, dynamic tensions characterizing human social and societal encounters. He insists on the primacy of archaeology as archaeology and archaeology as history, rather than archaeology as anthropology, and stresses an empathic, particularistic approach to understanding the past, much like that of R. G. Collingwood (1939, 1946).

Binford rejected the traditional anthropological culture concept (Tylor's, Kroeber's, Redfield's, Taylor's) because it was not appropriate to his goals and practice as an archaeologist, not even as an explicitly anthropological one. Hodder is committed to a fluid semiotic version of the traditional culture concept in which material items, artifacts, are full participants in the creation, deployment, alteration, and fading away of symbol complexes. Hodder advocates a contextualist archaeology — as did Walter Taylor — but one in which artifacts are not just objectifications of culture, they *are* culture.

Like Binford's earlier explicit rejection of an archaeologically unworkable, mentalist-idealist concept of culture in favor of Leslie White's functionalist, neo-evolutionist formulation, Hodder's move is clever and strong; but it is in the opposite direction of Binford's. Hodder begins with the mentalist concept of culture, then takes archaeology from a completely peripheral position with regard to that concept and places it squarely in the center of symbolic-structuralist inquiry. Artifacts — their creation, use, and discard — are "symbols [i.e., Culture] in [social] action" (Hodder 1982a). Hence, archaeology with its primary focus on material culture is very centrally and strategically located in the arena of social theory.

Binford does not deny that artifacts had intrinsic meaning, semiotic content, for their makers and users, but this does not interest him. He rejects the traditional archaeologist's narrow focus on artifacts solely as markers of time and space, and he also rejects Taylor's focus on artifacts as mere *clues* to — objectifications of — cultural patterns in minds long gone, as he rejects the further implication that, no matter how hard they try, archaeologists who accept Taylor's program can never be more than cultural anthropologists manqué. Binford views artifacts and associated non-artifactual/ecofactual information as the essential means to interpret the interactive dynamics of paleoenvironments and human paleo-economies in synchronic and diachronic detail, important work that only archaeologists can do. To make the artifacts and ecofacts comprising the archaeological record speak substantively to these issues, however, those artifacts and ecofacts must be approached via site formation processes and ethnoarchaeology, all of which Binford refers to as "middle range theory."

Hodder is not interested in matters of subsistence and brute livelihood. Rather, the intrinsic meanings with which the artifacts were imbued, the roles they once played in complex social actions and interactions, are central. He agrees with the symbolic anthropologists and other social theorists that symbol systems are what distinguish the human primate from all other beasts; those symbol systems include and are importantly shaped by material objects and architectural forms. Hodder approaches these issues of symbolic systems, past and present, via ethnoarchaeology (Hodder 1982a, 1982b).

So what is this thing called ethnoarchaeology, upon which the most influential representatives of contemporary Euro-American archaeology have converged? Ethnoarchaeology is one of the multitudinous ways in which archaeologists obtain information relevant to creating and expanding their inferences from archaeological data, and to making those inferences more plausible. Ethnoarchaeology can be as simple as collating descriptive and functional details about objects and processes archaeologists frequently encounter — stone scrapers, bone awls, sherds from wheel-made pots, metallic ore, and slag — from archival sources, such as old ethnographies, ancient histories, museum exhibits and collections; or from published and unpublished photos, drawings, paintings. But, classically, ethnoarchaeology means designing and carrying out ethnographic research in one or more contemporary locales, chosen for their relevance to some archaeological problem. Binford picked the Nunamiut of northern Alaska because he believed the caribou hunting techniques they practice in an arctic environment are relevant to his archaeological interpretation of Middle Paleolithic caribou hunters in arctic western Europe during the Late Pleistocene. The Nunamiut also instructed Binford about the dynamics of mobile, successful hunting-gathering groups in close touch with relevant natural resources in their landscapes. Binford's books and articles on lessons learned from the Nunamiut were, and are, highly influential among Americanist archaeologists, as is the other ethnoarchaeological or actualistic research he has done in the interests of middle-range theory: "the relationship between statics and dynamics, between behavior and material derivative."[9]

Hodder initially chose East Africa as a suitable place to investigate, for archaeological purposes, spatial patterning of artifacts in relation to ethnic boundaries (Hodder 1982a), but then he was distracted by other aspects of the contemporary scene in Baringo and turned to the study of material objects, symbol systems, and their intersection with archaeological interpretation. In examining ideas about spatial patterning of material culture, ideas that were widely held among archaeologists, Hodder found that his observations among several East African groups (the Njemps or Ilchamus, the Lonkewan Dorobo and Samburu, the Lozi, the Nuba) contradicted these ideas, or at any rate made them appear highly problematic. For example, most archaeologists would readily agree that material culture reflects the degree of interaction between groups: the more interaction, the greater the similarity of artifacts, and vice versa. Hodder noted that the nature of the interaction and the degree of competition between the groups play an important role in how basketry or styles of ear decoration are used "to constitute and reproduce ethnic group distinctions despite the long history and high degree of inter-ethnic flows" (Hodder 1982a:35). He also found that the symbolic status and functioning (the cultural meaning) of material items, such as the spears carried by young unmarried men and the calabashes decorated by young married women, determine the morphology and distribution of those items within and beyond a single society (Hodder 1982a: ch. 4, 1991a:109–119). Finally, he was strongly impressed with the fluidity and activity of symbolic loading on and in objects of material culture, which are continually created but also continually act back on their creators, users, and perceivers to maintain or to disrupt culturally defined boundaries within and between social groups (young men versus old men, men versus women, Samburu versus Dorobo):

> material culture transforms structurally rather than reflects behaviorally . . . refuse and burial patterns relate to social organization via such concepts as

purity and pollution. . . . So, how material culture relates to society depends on the ideological structures and symbolic codes.[10]

Hodder and other postprocessualists are also very concerned about the sociopolitical setting of contemporary archaeology. They urge archaeologists to be aware and self-critical about their biases and preconceptions, lest they unwittingly create a past in the image of their own present, a past that then helps legitimate contemporary social or political themes (Hodder 1991a: ch. 8; Shanks and Tilley 1988: ch. 7).

In sum, regarding the two men and their programs: one may, and should, quarrel with Binford's narrow "econothink" focus, as does Robert Hall (1977:499), who coined the word in reference to 1970s New Archaeology (see also Fritz 1978; Redman 1991). And one may object to the ahuman (no people in it) ecosystemic orientation (Brumfiel 1992), and the general theoretical underpinning of Binford's position (P. Watson 1986a, 1986b; Wylie 1985), but his influence has instigated and continues to impel a considerable amount of fruitful archaeological research. That is, Binford has been successful in defining goals and methods that many archaeologists find feasible and rewarding.

Much of the work of Hodder, his students, and his postprocessualist colleagues has been heavily dependent on ethnographic and historic information, and the method he advocates has yet to be comprehensively demonstrated for purely prehistoric data, although such a demonstration is perhaps forthcoming from the work he is currently directing at the famous site of Chatalhöyük in Turkey. Meanwhile, however, Hodder and other postprocessualists (by now a diverse group scattered through Europe, Australia, and North America) *have* certainly influenced contemporary archaeological practice in the heartland of the old Binfordian New Archaeology, and even in parts of the cultural resource management universe. There is much more interest now than even five years ago in semiotic approaches and in critical theory applied to the archaeological record and to the practice of archaeology. It is perhaps too soon to see a comprehensive synthesis emerging, but some manner of rapprochement is definitely underway (see Willey and Sabloff 1993:312–317).

Beginning in 1989, the Archaeology Division of the American Anthropological Association requested a prominent archaeologist to deliver a distinguished lecture at the yearly divisional get-together during the annual meeting of the association. Very conveniently for my purposes here, the four lectures published so far all address this very issue.[11] The four distinguished archaeological lecturers provide a series of authoritative opinions and examples concerning relations between archaeological theory — past and present — and the actual doing of archaeology (fieldwork, laboratory and library work, interpretation and publication). Each speaker focuses upon crucial themes in archaeological theory and practice, past and present, and provides suggestions about how to improve our present understanding of the past.

Redman (1991) begins the series by pointing out how much continuity there is between 1970s and 1980s archaeology. He also notes that although contextualist or post-processualist archaeology and New Archaeology (processual archaeology) are obviously complementary, it is unlikely that there will be significant integration. He thinks coexistence is the best we can expect because a major impetus for postprocessualist critiques comes from fundamental differences between archaeologists with humanistic goals and those committed to science. He advocates making the most of both approaches, and recommends that "we encourage serious scholars to do what they are best at doing and to coordinate diverse thinking to form a loose but lasting alliance for new knowledge of the past and present" (Redman 1991:304).

In spite of Redman's well-founded reservations about explicit integration between processual and postprocessual archaeology, Bruce Trigger (1991) sets himself the task of indicating what such a synthesis might look like. He characterizes processual archaeology as neo-evolutionism and ecological determinism, counterposing it to postprocessualist emphases on "the contingent, psychological, and mental aspects of human experience" (Trigger 1991:553). In other words, the confrontation is between "reason" and "culture" (Trigger 1991:551, 554). Trigger then discusses external and internal constraints on human behavior: ecological, technological, and economic factors and forces being the most familiar external constraints, whereas cultural traditions made up of mental constructions — some unique to specific societies, some much more widespread cross-culturally — are the internal constraints. Because cultures are "historical precipitates," the invention of new concepts is not random, but is strongly affected by earlier concepts and their history. The best means archaeologists have to get at the cultural meanings of historically related archaeological evidence is to develop the direct historic approach, Trigger says (1991:562), admitting that we will probably never know the specific meaning that Upper Paleolithic cave art, say, had for its creators. Nevertheless, he urges archaeologists to embrace whole-heartedly "the study of cultural traditions as well as of ecological and systemic constraints . . . to take account of the constraints imposed on human behavior by cultural traditions as well as by rational accommodations to external factors," thus synthesizing the ecological determinism of processual archaeology with the historical particularism of postprocessual archaeology (Trigger 1991:562–563).

Trigger's optimism about the possibility for synthesis is encouraging, but he fails to give any consideration to the very significant problems involved in deciding what is "cultural" ("internal") and what is "natural" ("external") in ethnographically or archaeologically documented societies. Hence, this part of his discussion misses the whole point of the anthropological enterprise, which is to obtain knowledge about that very conjunction: How is it that human individuals and human societies—past and present—intricately blend and intertwine nature and culture?

Brumfiel's distinguished lecture (1992) is a clear and eloquent argument about the importance of paying attention to social change in ways that the dominant ecosystemic orientation of New Archaeology discouraged or disallowed. She is especially concerned with gender, class, and faction, and argues three points:

> First, the ecosystem theorists' emphasis upon whole populations and whole adaptive behavioral systems obscures the visibility of gender, class, and faction in the prehistoric past. Second, an analysis that takes account of gender, class, and faction can explain many aspects of the prehistoric record that the ecosystem perspective cannot explain. Third, an appreciation for the importance of gender, class, and faction in prehistory compels us to reject the ecosystem-theory view that cultures are adaptive systems. Instead, we must recognize that culturally based behavioral "systems" are the composite outcomes of negotiation between positioned social agents pursuing their goals under both ecological and social constraints. [Brumfiel 1992:551]

In the body of the address, Brumfiel succeeds in showing how thoughtful archaeologists could actually begin to forge the synthesis Trigger speaks of, or at least the "loose but lasting alliance" Redman hopes for.

Cowgill's distinguished lecture to the Archeology Division (1993) is an even more explicit attempt to bring together and build upon the most successful aspects of processual archaeology and the most exciting promises of postprocessual archaeology. In describing the achievements and shortcomings of processual archaeology, Cowgill notes that one characteristic of most archaeologists is underconceptualization of the past at different levels: On the lowest level there are no people at all, just pots or potsherds, projectile points, or other artifacts. At the second level, people are present but they have no individuality; they are Ruth Tringham's "faceless blobs" (Tringham 1991). At the third level, people are "rational actors." Cowgill points out that we badly need a fourth level, where people not only find food, shelter, mates, allies, and enemies while creating, using, modifying, losing, breaking, and discarding material things, but also these people perceive, they think, they plan, they make decisions, and in general they are ideationally active. In the rest of his paper, Cowgill discusses how archaeologists might hope to approach the ideational realms of prehistoric peoples by trying harder to get at ancient ideation; by becoming more sophisticated about direct historical approaches (here he obviously agrees with one of Trigger's points); and by working imaginatively and responsibly to develop what he calls "Middle Range Theory of the Mind." By this he means, in part, seeking out widespread aspects or principles of symbolization, attempting to link design properties (in art styles or architecture) with social features and/or culturally specific cognitive maps, and in general taking seriously what he dubs "psychoarchaeology."

What is most interesting and heartening to me about this suite of distinguished lectures is that all four explicitly, creatively, and thoughtfully address the major schism in contemporary Americanist archaeology, and all four explicitly, creatively, and thoughtfully recommend ways to bridge the schism at various points, as well as ways to advance archaeological knowledge using methods from both sides of the fault line.

Another very promising development is the new generation of ethnoarchaeological fieldworkers who are undertaking and completing longer-lasting, finer-grained investigations than those of Binford and Hodder. Of many good examples I note just three here: the 30-year trajectory of ethnoarchaeology among the San of Botswana from the work of Yellen and Brooks to that of Hitchcock, Weissner, and Kent; Longacre's 20-year-long Kalinga ceramics project in northern Luzon; Herbich and Dietler's ten years of research on Luo pottery and on Luo settlement biographies in western Kenya.[12]

As regards the other focus of this paper, is there an edifying conclusion to be drawn from comparing the odysseys of the culture concept in Americanist sociocultural anthropology/ethnology and in archaeology?

Yes, there is. In each subdiscipline, certain practitioners took that concept very seriously, not just as a more or less meaningless piece of antiquated anthropological dogma. Because archaeologists of the 1930s did not attempt to operationalize the prevailing culture concept, but rather ignored it while absorbed in creating time-space frameworks essential to North American prehistory, Walter Taylor (1948) made a strenuous effort to align Americanist archaeology with Americanist sociocultural anthropology by taking the traditional, Tylorean culture concept as a central tenet in his argument. He had very little immediate influence on his archaeological colleagues, in large part because that culture concept could not be implemented or operationalized in ways congruent with archaeological concerns of the 1940s and 1950s. Binford enjoyed much greater success in the 1960s and 1970s by insisting with Taylor that archaeology must be anthropology, while highlighting a non-Tylorean, nontraditional concept of culture, that of Leslie White. Hodder has gone back to something like the traditional culture concept but modified it to place artifacts, architecture, and archaeology in the center of anthropology and social theory, while explicitly rejecting Phillips's conclusion that "archaeology is anthropology or it is nothing." "Archaeology is archaeology," he and the postprocessualists insist, even as portions of their program are being incorporated into both academic and cultural resource management Americanist anthropological archaeology, partly to reinforce certain minority themes present there before the postprocessualist movement, and partly to further syntheses between processual and postprocessual goals in archaeology.[13]

The revisionists in sociocultural anthropology and ethnology eventually found that the traditional culture concept was not very useful to them, so they modified it to suit their purposes. Many of them, past and present, are quite explicit about this, and many of them were quite successful at initiating productive research lines based upon their new formulations.[14] In sociocultural anthropology over the past 40 to 50 years, there has accordingly been a proliferation in approaches to culture from the earlier essentialist concept to cultures as configurations of a psychological sort, as a series of distinctive cognitive maps, as symbolic and/or adaptive systems, as infinitely varying surface phenomena that may reveal deep truths about universal human thought processes, as social knowledge networks, and as trait complexes defined and studied within neo-Darwinian frameworks.

Does this mean that the center of anthropology — belief by all anthropologists in some widely sanctioned variant of a unified culture concept — has been destroyed? If so, does the lack of unanimity about culture — what it is and where it is and whether it matters — mean that anthropology itself as a holistic discipline is, or is about to be, no more?

More than 20 years ago, that was Rodney Needham's prediction for the very near future about academic anthropology (Needham 1970). He thought that pieces of anthropology would be redistributed among neighboring disciplines. That was Wolf's conclusion 14 years ago (Wolf 1980), the theme picked up by Flannery in his 1981 American Anthropological Association Distinguished Lecture; and apparently James Clifford (1986:4) was of the same opinion eight years ago when he remarked that " 'Man' as *telos* for a whole discipline" has disintegrated. Clifford Geertz, in his *Current Anthropology* interview with Richard Handler (Handler 1991) says 50 to 75 years from now academic anthropology departments will no longer exist because anthropology will have evolved into several different disciplines.

Perhaps these conclusions are correct; perhaps general, integrated anthropology is already or soon will be gone. Although I care deeply about this issue, owing to my 1950s imprinting in holistic anthropology, I cannot get too worked up over the disintegration prediction. Anthropologists have been worrying about this for at least 40 years and recently went through another bout of explicit fretting in the pages of the *Anthropology Newsletter* (see Givens and Skomal 1992). Those who contributed to the discussion are pro-integration and pro-four fields. Givens and Skomal (1993) conclude that a four-field holistic anthropology is, at the present time, both myth and reality.

Another reason that I manage to remain calm in the face of savage attacks on the old-time culture concept, attacks supposed by some to mark or presage the disintegration of anthropology, is that the sociocultural subdiscipline, and, ultimately, all of anthropology benefits from the culture conceptual shifts briefly referred to above. In sociocultural anthropology, as in archaeology, each new research trajectory counterposed to some aspect of the traditional culture concept results in new data, new insights, and new knowledge. Moreover, the old-time culture concept still plays an integrating role as a central reference point even for the radically revisionist anthropologists, for whom it is variously a bête noire, a punching bag, or a springboard to alternative perspectives on the human condition, past and present.

Finally, the 1950s characterization of anthropology is true enough and strong enough to bear the weight of most contemporary, intra-disciplinary construction and reconstruction. Anthropology is still the only human science all about humankind, from four million years ago to the present: Who are we? Where did we come from? What happened to us between origin and now? What is the scope in all its compelling detail of past and contemporary human physical and cultural variation, and what does that variation mean in biological, social, and cultural terms?

No other discipline has ever asked these questions about the entire spatial and chronological sweep of the human past and present, as well as about the particulars concerning specific portions of that sweep. And certainly no other scholarly band ever set out to actually obtain answers to such questions. In spite of episodic skeptical crises within anthropology, and a chronic agoraphobia about where our center is and where our boundaries are, anthropology is still here — even Geertz gives it another half-century: an undisciplined discipline, an unruly semiaggregate, but one with research methods and research results of enormous global importance and great intrinsic interest.

Notes

Acknowledgments. I am grateful to Anna M. Watson for insights on culture in the partitive sense and on cultural diversity in the contemporary world, to Rubie S. Watson for providing some crucial bibliographic guidance, to James L. Watson for many lively discussions about contemporary developments in sociocultural anthropology, and to Richard A. Watson for commentaries on postmodernism in literature and elsewhere. David Browman and Richard Fox kindly supplied important reference material on short notice; a chance remark of Jean Ensminger's was the inspiration for the direction taken by this essay. My account of the culture concept in archaeology originated during a short course on archaeological theory that Don Fowler invited me to teach in the Cultural Resource Management program at the University of Nevada–Reno in January 1992, and was developed further during successive meetings of a seminar on archaeological theory at Washington University, St. Louis; I owe a special debt of gratitude to the students in those classes. Prepublication revisions to this paper were made at the Camargo Foundation, Cassis, France; I am grateful to Michael Pretina, director, and Anne-Marie Franco, administrative assistant, for their support.

1. Dunnell 1980; Gumerman and Phillips 1978; Meltzer 1979; Wiseman 1980.

2. Chippindale 1989:69; Clarke 1968:13; Hodder 1991a: ch. 9; Shanks and Tilley 1988:213, item 6.5; Shennen 1986; Tilley 1989: especially 110.

3. Barth 1994; Bernard 1994; Bloch 1994; Goodenough 1994; Harris 1994; Keesing 1994; Kottak and Colson 1994; Marcus 1994; Sahlins 1994; Salzman 1994; Scheper-Hughes 1994; Strauss and Quinn 1994; Tambiah 1994; Tishkov 1994; Wolf 1994; see also A. Watson 1992–94; J. Watson 1994; R. A. Watson 1964; R. R. Watson 1978; R. S. Watson 1994.

4. Bennett 1943; Binford 1962; Kluckhohn 1940; Taylor 1948.

5. See also Kroeber 1948:295–296; Kroeber and Waterman 1931:11.

6. Caldwell 1959; P. Watson, LeBlanc, and Redman 1971, 1984; R. A. Watson 1972.

7. Gould 1978; Kleindienst and P. Watson 1956; Kramer 1979, 1994; Longacre 1974; P. Watson 1979; Yellen 1977.

8. Binford 1987, 1988; Binford and Stone 1988; Hodder 1988, 1989, 1991a; P. Watson 1991.

9. Binford 1976, 1978a, 1978b, 1980, 1981, 1982. Quotation comes from Binford 1981:29; see also parts 3 and 4 in Binford 1989.

10. Hodder 1982a:210–211; see also pp. 155–170 for his detailed discussion of bone refuse disposal and burial customs among the Nuba.

11. Redman 1991; Trigger 1991; Brumfiel 1992; Cowgill 1993.

12. Kramer 1994 provides references and commentaries on the San work; see Longacre 1991 for overviews of the Kalinga research, and of other work in ceramic ethnoarchaeology, some of which long predates the era of New Archaeology; Herbich and Dietler's project is summarized in Herbich 1987 and Herbich and Dietler 1991.

13. See, for example, Fritz 1978; Hall 1976, 1977; Kehoe and Kehoe 1974; Marshack 1972.

14. For earlier and more recent examples, see Aunger 1992, in press; Benedict 1934, especially ch. 3; Geertz 1973:4–5; Fox 1989; Harris 1964; Kroeber 1952: part 1; Lévi-Strauss 1955, 1962; Tyler 1969.

References Cited

Aunger, Robert
  1992   An Ethnography of Variation: Food Avoidances among Horticulturalists and Foragers in the Ituri Forest, Zaire. Ph.D. dissertation, University of California, Los Angeles.
  In press   Are Food Avoidances Maladaptive in the Ituri Forest of Zaire? Journal of Anthropological Research.

Barth, Fredrik
  1994   A Personal View of Present Tasks and Priorities in Cultural and Social Anthropology. In Assessing Cultural Anthropology. R. Borofsky, ed. Pp. 349–360. New York: McGraw-Hill.

Benedict, Ruth

1934 Patterns of Culture. New York: Houghton Mifflin.

Bennett, John

1943 Recent Developments in the Functional Interpretation of Archaeological Data. American Antiquity 9:208–219.

Bernard, H. Russell

1994 Methods Belong to All of Us. *In* Assessing Cultural Anthropology. R. Borofsky, ed. Pp. 168–177. New York: McGraw-Hill.

Binford, Lewis R.

1962 Archaeology as Anthropology. American Antiquity 28:217–225.

1976 Forty-Seven Trips: A Case Study in the Character of Some Formation Processes of the Archaeological Record. *In* Contributions to Anthropology: The Interior People of Northern Alaska. Mercury Series 49. E. S. Hall, Jr., ed. Pp. 299–351. Ottawa: National Museum of Man.

1978a Nunamiut Ethnoarchaeology. New York: Academic Press.

1978b Dimensional Analysis of Behavior and Site Structure: Learning from an Eskimo Hunting Stand. American Antiquity 43:255–273.

1980 Willow Smoke and Dogs' Tails: Hunter-Gatherer Settlement Systems and Archaeological Site Formation. American Antiquity 45:4–10.

1981 Bones: Ancient Men and Modern Myths. New York: Academic Press.

1982 The Archaeology of Place. Journal of Anthropological Archaeology 1:5–31.

1983 In Pursuit of the Past. London: Thames and Hudson.

1987 Data, Relativism and Archaeological Science. Man 22: 391–404.

1988 *Review of* Reading the Past: Current Approaches to Interpretation in Archaeology, by Ian Hodder. American Antiquity 53: 875–876.

1989 Debating Archaeology. New York: Academic Press.

Binford, Lewis R., and Nancy Stone

1988 Reply to Hodder. Man 23: 374–376.

Bloch, Maurice

1994 Language, Anthropology, and Cognitive Science. *In* Assessing Cultural Anthropology. R. Borofsky, ed. Pp. 276–282. New York: McGraw-Hill.

Borofsky, Robert, ed.

1994 Assessing Cultural Anthropology. New York: McGraw-Hill.

Brumfiel, Elizabeth

1992 Distinguished Lecture in Archeology: Breaking and Entering the Ecosystem — Gender, Class, and Faction Steal the Show. American Anthropologist 94: 551–567.

Caldwell, Joseph

1959 The New American Archeology. Science 129:303–307.

6

Chippindale, Christopher
1989 Philosophical Lessons from the History of Stonehenge Studies. *In* Critical Traditions in Contemporary Archaeology. V. Pinsky and A. Wylie, eds. Pp. 68–79. Cambridge: Cambridge University Press.

Clarke, David L.
1968 Analytical Archaeology. London: Methuen and Company.

Clifford, James E.
1986 Introduction: Partial Truths. *In* Writing Culture: The Poetics and Politics of Ethnography. J. Clifford and G. Marcus, eds. Pp. 1–26. Berkeley: University of California Press.

Collingwood, R. G.
1939 An Autobiography. Oxford: Oxford University Press.
1946 The Idea of History. Oxford: Oxford University Press.

Cowgill, George
1993 Distinguished Lecture in Archeology: Beyond Criticizing New Archeology. American Anthropologist 95:551–573.

Dunnell, Robert
1980 Evolutionary Theory in Archaeology. *In* Advances in Archaeological Method and Theory, Vol. 3. M. Schiffer, ed. Pp. 35–99. New York: Academic Press.
1986 Five Decades of American Archaeology. *In* American Archaeology Past and Future: A Celebration of the Society for American Archaeology 1935–

1985. D. Meltzer, D. Fowler, and J. Sabloff, eds. Pp. 23–49. Washington, DC: Smithsonian Institution Press.

Flannery, Kent
1982 The Golden Marshalltown. American Anthropologist 84: 265–278.

Fox, Richard G.
1989 Gandhian Utopia: Experiments with Culture. Boston: Beacon Press.

Fritz, John
1978 Paleopsychology Today. *In* Social Archaeology: Beyond Subsistence and Dating. C. Redman, M. Berman, E. Curtin, W. Langhorne, Jr., N. Versaggi, and J. Wanser, eds. Pp. 37–59. New York: Academic Press.

Geertz, Clifford
1973 The Interpretation of Cultures: Selected Essays. New York: Basic Books.

Givens, David, and Susan Skomal
1992 The Four Fields: Myth or Reality? Anthropology Newsletter 33(7):1, 17.
1993 The Four Fields: Myth and Reality. Anthropology Newsletter 34(5):1, 19.

Goodenough, Ward
1994 Toward a Working Theory of Culture. *In* Assessing Cultural Anthropology. R. Borofsky, ed. Pp. 262–273. New York: McGraw-Hill.

Gould, Richard A., ed.
1978 Explorations in Ethno-

archaeology. Albuquerque: University of New Mexico Press.

Griffin, James B.

1943 The Fort Ancient Aspect: Its Cultural and Chronological Position in Mississippi Valley Archaeology. Ann Arbor: University of Michigan Press.

Gumerman, G., and D. Phillips, Jr.

1978 Archaeology beyond Anthropology. American Antiquity 43:184–191.

Hall, Robert L.

1976 Ghosts, Water Barriers, Corn and Sacred Enclosures in the Eastern Woodlands. American Antiquity 41:360–364.

1977 An Anthropocentric Perspective for Eastern United States Prehistory. American Antiquity 41:499–518.

Handler, Richard

1991 An Interview with Clifford Geertz. Current Anthropology 32:603–613.

Harris, Marvin

1964 The Nature of Cultural Things. New York: Random House.

1994 Cultural Materialism Is Alive and Well and Won't Go Away Until Something Better Comes Along. In Assessing Cultural Anthropology. R. Borofsky, ed. Pp. 62–75. New York: McGraw-Hill.

Herbich, Ingrid

1987 Learning Patterns, Potter Interaction and Ceramic Style among the Luo of Kenya. The African Archaeological Review 5:193–204.

Herbich, Ingrid, and Michael Dietler

1991 Space, Time and Symbolic Structure in the Luo Homestead: An Ethnoarchaeological Study of "Settlement Biography" in Africa. Paper presented at the 12th International Congress of the Union Internationale des Sciences Préhistoriques et Protohistoriques, Bratislava, Czechoslovakia.

Hodder, Ian

1982a Symbols in Action: Ethnoarchaeological Studies of Material Culture. Cambridge: Cambridge University Press.

1982b The Present Past: An Introduction to Anthropology for Archaeologists. New York: Pica Press.

1985 Postprocessual Archaeology. In Advances in Archaeological Method and Theory, Vol. 8. M. Schiffer, ed. Pp. 1–26. New York: Academic Press.

1988 Correspondence: Archaeology and Theory. Man 23:374–376.

1989 Comments made during the plenary session, "Advice and Dissent," organized by Nancy Stone for the annual meeting of the Society for American Archaeology, Atlanta, GA, April 5–9.

1991a Reading the Past: Current Approaches to Interpretation in Archaeology. 2nd edition. Cambridge: Cambridge University Press.

1991b Postprocessual Archaeology and the Current Debate. *In* Processual and Postprocessual Archaeologies: Multiple Ways of Knowing the Past. R. Preucel, ed. Pp. 30–41. Occasional Paper No. 10, Center for Archaeological Investigations, Southern Illinois University, Carbondale.

Keesing, Roger M.
1994 Theories of Culture Revisited. *In* Assessing Cultural Anthropology. R. Borofsky, ed. Pp. 301–310. New York: McGraw-Hill.

Kehoe, Alice B., and Thomas F. Kehoe
1974 Cognitive Models for Archaeological Interpretation. American Antiquity 38:150–154.

Kleindienst, Maxine R., and Patty Jo Watson
1956 Action Archeology: The Archeological Inventory of a Living Community. Anthropology Tomorrow (student journal, Department of Anthropology, University of Chicago) 5(1):75–78.

Kluckhohn, Clyde
1940 The Conceptual Structure in Middle American Studies. *In* The Maya and Their Neighbors. C. Hay, R. Linton, S. Lothrop, J. Shapiro, and G. Vaillant, eds.

Pp. 41–51. New York: Dover Publications.

Kottack, Conrad, and Elizabeth Colson
1994 Multilevel Linkages: Longitudinal and Comparative Studies. *In* Assessing Cultural Anthropology. R. Borofsky, ed. Pp. 396–411. New York: McGraw-Hill.

Kramer, Carol
1979 Ethnoarchaeology: Implications of Ethnography for Archaeology. New York: Columbia University Press.

1994 The Quick and the Dead: Ethnography in and for Archaeology. Distinguished lecture to the Archeology Division, Annual Meeting of the American Anthropological Association, Atlanta, GA, December 2.

Kroeber, A. L.
1948 Anthropology. Revised edition. New York: Harcourt, Brace, and Company.

1952 The Nature of Culture. Chicago: University of Chicago Press.

Kroeber, A. L., and Clyde Kluckhohn
1952 Culture: A Critical Review of Concepts and Definitions. Papers of the Peabody Museum of American Archaeology and Ethnology, Harvard University, vol. 47, no. 1. Cambridge, MA.

Kroeber, A. L., and T. T. Waterman.
1931 Source Book in Anthropology. New York: Harcourt, Brace, and Company.

Lévi-Strauss, Claude

1955 Tristes Tropiques. Paris: Plon.

1962 La Pensée Sauvage. Paris: Plon.

Longacre, William

1974 Kalinga Pottery-Making: The Evolution of a Research Design. In Frontiers of Anthropology: An Introduction to Anthropological Thinking. M. J. Lear, ed. Pp. 51–71. New York: Van Nostrand.

1991 Ceramic Ethnoarchaeology: An Introduction. In Ceramic Ethnoarchaeology. W. Longacre, ed. Pp. 1–10. Tucson: University of Arizona Press.

Marcus, George E.

1994 After the Critique of Ethnography: Faith, Hope, and Charity, but the Greatest of These is Charity. In Assessing Cultural Anthropology. R. Borofsky, ed. Pp. 40–52. New York: McGraw-Hill.

Marshack, Alexander

1972 The Roots of Civilization. New York: McGraw-Hill.

Meltzer, David

1979 Paradigms and the Nature of Change in American Archaeology. American Antiquity 44:644–655.

Needham, Rodney

1970 The Future of Anthropology: Disintegration or Metamorphosis? In Anniversary Con-

tributions to Anthropology. P. E. de Josselin de Jong, J. van Baal, G. W. Locher, and J. W. Schoorl, eds. Pp. 34–47. Leiden: Brill.

Phillips, Philip

1955 American Archaeology and General Anthropological Theory. Southwestern Journal of Anthropology 11:246–250.

Redfield, Robert

1940 Definition of Culture, as Quoted in W. F. Ogburn and M. F. Nimkoff. Sociology (1940): 25.

Redman, Charles L.

1991 Distinguished Lecture in Archeology: In Defense of the Seventies. American Anthropologist 93:295–307.

Sahlins, Marshall

1994 Good-bye to Tristes Tropes: Ethnography in the Context of Modern World History. In Assessing Cultural Anthropology. R. Borofsky, ed. Pp. 377–394. New York: McGraw-Hill.

Salzman, Philip Carl

1994 The Lone Stranger in the Heart of Darkness. In Assessing Cultural Anthropology. R. Borofsky, ed. Pp. 29–38. New York: McGraw-Hill.

Scheper-Hughes, Nancy

1994 Embodied Knowledge: Thinking with the Body in Critical Medical Anthropology. In Assessing Cultural Anthropology.

R. Borofsky, ed. Pp. 229–239. New York: McGraw-Hill.

Shanks, Michael, and Christopher Tilley
1988 Social Theory and Archaeology. Albuquerque: University of New Mexico Press.

Shennan, Stephen
1986 Towards a Critical Archaeology? Proceedings of the Prehistoric Society 52:327–338.

Struass, Claudia, and Naomi Quinn
1994 A Cognitive/Cultural Anthropology. In Assessing Cultural Anthropology. R. Borofsky, ed. Pp. 284–297. New York: McGraw-Hill.

Tambiah, Stanley J.
1994 The Politics of Ethnicity. In Assessing Cultural Anthropology. R. Borofsky, ed. Pp. 430–441. New York: McGraw-Hill.

Taylor, Walter W.
1948 A Study of Archeology. Memoir 69, American Anthropological Association. Reprinted, Carbondale, IL: Southern Illinois University Press, 1967.

Tilley, Christopher
1989 Archaeology as Socio-Political Action in the Present. In Critical Traditions in Contemporary Archaeology. V. Pinsky and A. Wylie, eds. Pp. 104–116. Cambridge: Cambridge University Press.

Tishkov, Valery A.
1994 Inventions and Manifestations of Ethno-Nationalism in Soviet Academic and Public Discourse. In Assessing Cultural Anthropology. R. Borofsky, ed. Pp. 443–452. New York: McGraw-Hill.

Trigger, Bruce
1989 A History of Archaeological Thought. Cambridge: Cambridge University Press.
1991 Distinguished Lecture in Archeology: Constraint and Freedom—A New Synthesis for Archeological Explanation. American Anthropologist 93:551–569.

Tringham, Ruth E.
1991 Households with Faces: The Challenge of Gender in Prehistoric Architectural Remains. In Engendering Archaeology: Women and Prehistory. Joan Gero and Margaret Conkey, eds. Pp. 93–131. Oxford: Basil Blackwell.

Tyler, Stephen
1969 Introduction. In Cognitive Anthropology. S. Tyler, ed. Pp. 1–23. New York: Holt, Rinehart, and Winston.

Tylor, E. B.
1871 Primitive Culture. London: John Murray.

Watson, Anna M.
1992–94 Mousie: The Racial Politics of Desire, Issues 1–5. Arlington, MA: A. M. Watson.

Watson, James L.
1994 McDonald's in Hongkong:

Reinventing Cantonese Public Culture. Paper presented at the 93rd Annual Meeting of the American Anthropological Association, Atlanta, GA, November 30–December 4.

Watson, Patty Jo

1979   Archaeological Ethnography in Western Iran. Viking Fund Publications in Anthropology, 57. Tucson: University of Arizona Press.

1986a   Archaeological Interpretation, 1985. *In* American Archaeology Past and Future. D. Meltzer, D. Fowler, and J. Sabloff, eds. Pp. 439–457. Washington, DC: Smithsonian Institution Press.

1986b   An Archaeological Odyssey: Lewis Binford's *Working at Archaeology*. Reviews in Anthropology 13:263–270.

1991   A Parochial Primer: The New Dissonance as Seen from the Midcontinental United States. *In* Processual and Post-processual Archaeologies: Multiple Ways of Knowing the Past. R. Preucel, ed. Pp. 265–274. Occasional Paper No. 10, Center for Archaeological Investigations, Southern Illinois University, Carbondale.

Watson, Patty Jo, Steven A. LeBlanc, and Charles L. Redman

1971   Explanation in Archaeology: An Explicitly Scientific Approach. New York: Columbia University Press.

1984   Archaeological Explanation: The Scientific Method in Archaeology. New York: Columbia University Press.

Watson, Richard A.

1964   The Snow Sellers of Mangalat, Iran. Anthropos 59:904–910.

1972   The "New Archaeology" of the 1960s. Antiquity 46:210–215.

Watson, Roscoe R.

1978   Boyhood Days on an Ozark Farm. New Market, IA: College Hill Press.

Watson, Rubie S., ed.

1994   Memory, History, and Opposition under State Socialism. Santa Fe: School of American Research Press.

White, Leslie

1959   The Evolution of Culture. New York: McGraw-Hill.

Willey, Gordon, and Philip Phillips

1958   Method and Theory in American Archaeology. Chicago: University of Chicago Press.

Willey, Gordon, and Jeremy Sabloff

1993   A History of American Archaeology. 3rd edition. London: Thames and Hudson.

Wiseman, James

1980   Archaeology in the Future: An Evolving Discipline. American Journal of Archaeology 84:279–285.

Wolf, Eric

1980   They Divide and Subdivide and Call It Anthropology. New York Times, November 30:E9.

1994   Facing Power: Old Insights,

New Questions. *In* Assessing Cultural Anthropology. R. Borofsky, ed. Pp. 218–227. New York: McGraw-Hill.

Wylie, M. Alison
1985 The Reaction against Analogy. *In* Advances in Archaeological Method and Theory, Vol. 8.

M. Schiffer, ed. Pp. 63–111. New York: Academic Press.

Yellen, John E.
1977 Archaeological Approaches to the Present: Models for Reconstructing the Past. New York: Academic Press.